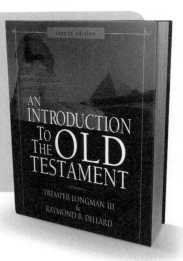
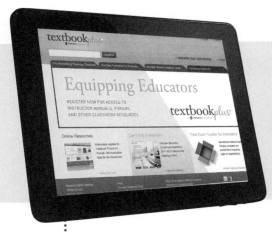

SECOND EDITION

AN INTRODUCTION TO THE OLD TESTAMENT

TREMPER LONGMAN III
&
RAYMOND B. DILLARD

ZONDERVAN®

ZONDERVAN.com/
AUTHORTRACKER
follow your favorite authors

We want to hear from you. Please send your comments about this book to us in care of zreview@zondervan.com. Thank you.

ZONDERVAN

An Introduction to the Old Testament
Copyright © 1994, 2006 by Tremper Longman III and Raymond B. Dillard

Requests for information should be addressed to:

Zondervan, *Grand Rapids, Michigan 49530*

Library of Congress Cataloging-in-Publication Data

Longman, Tremper.
    An introduction to the Old Testament / Tremper Longman and Raymond B. Dillard.—Rev. ed.
      p. cm.
    Rev. ed. of: An introduction to the Old Testament / Raymond B. Dillard and Tremper Longman. c1994.
    Includes bibliographical references and indexes.
    ISBN-13: 978-0-310-26341-8
    ISBN-10: 0-310-26341-7
    1. Bible. O.T.—Introductions. I. Dillard, Raymond B., d. 1993. II. Dillard, Raymond B., d. 1993. Introduction to the Old Testament. III. Title.
    BS1140.3.L66 2007
    221.6'1—dc22   2006005249

This edition printed on acid-free paper.

Interior design: Nancy Wilson

Printed in the United States of America

14 15 /DCI/ 36 35 34 33 32 31 30 29 28 27 26 25 24 23 22 21 20 19 18 17 16

CONTENTS

PREFACE TO THE SECOND EDITION

In one sense, it seems like only yesterday that Ray Dillard and I were laboring together to finish the first edition of this *Introduction to the Old Testament*. In another sense, many years have passed and a new edition is certainly necessary.

The preface to the first edition describes the great joy and sadness that I felt when the *Introduction* made its first appearance. The sadness was the result of the relatively recent death of my mentor, co-worker, and friend, Ray Dillard, who never saw the book in final form. Working on the revision over the past couple of years has reminded me afresh of Ray's able mind and wonderful communication skills. He is still deeply missed as a close friend. I also missed his help in revising the book!

Since writing the first edition of the book, I have made a move from Westminster Theological Seminary to Westmont College in Santa Barbara. Even so, I continue to get ample opportunity to teach classes at various seminaries in North America and occasionally abroad. I enjoy teaching at a college for a change of pace, but I am very glad to continue teaching on a graduate level, particularly since this textbook is directed primarily toward a seminary audience.

When Ray and I wrote the first edition, his three sons and my three sons were still at home. Now all six are grown and out of the house, pursuing their own dreams. I am very proud of my three sons—Tremper, Tim, and Andrew—as well as my daughter-in-law, Jill, Tremper's wife, and my first granddaughter, Gabrielle. And I know that Ray would be very proud of his children. This second edition, like the first, remains dedicated to my wife, Alice, and Ray's widow, Ann.

Tremper Longman III
Robert H. Gundry Professor of Biblical Studies
Westmont College

ABBREVIATIONS

AB	Anchor Bible
AJSL	*American Journal of Semitic Languages and Literature*
AnBiB	Analecta Biblica
ANET	*Ancient Near Eastern Texts*, 3rd ed., ed. J. B. Pritchard (Princeton, 1969)
ANETS	Ancient Near Eastern Texts and Studies
AS	Assyriological Studies (Oriental Institute of the University of Chicago)
ASTI	*Annual of the Swedish Theological Institute*
ATANT	*Abhandlungen zur Theologie des Alten and Neuen Testaments*
ATD	*Das Alte Testament Deutsch*
AUSS	*Andrews University Seminary Studies*
BA	*Biblical Archaeologist*
BAR	*Biblical Archaeological Review*
BASOR	*Bulletin of the American Schools of Oriental Research*
BBB	Bonner biblische Beiträge
BCOTWP	Baker Commentary on the Old Testament Wisdom and Psalms
BETL	Bibliotheca Ephemeridum Theologicarum Lovaniensium
BHS	Biblia Hebraica Stuttgartensia
Bib	*Biblica*
BibRes	*Biblical Research*
BibSac	*Bibliotheca Sacra*
BJRL	*Bulletin of the John Rylands Library*
BJS	Brown Judaic Studies
BKAT	Biblischer Kommentar: Altes Testament
BN	*Biblische Notizen*
BS	Bibliotheca Sacra

BSC	Bible Student's Commentary
BST	Basel Studies of Theology
BTB	*Biblical Theology Bulletin*
BWANT	Beiträge zur Wissenschaft vom Alten und Neuen Testament
BZ	Biblische Zeitschrift
BZAW	*Beihefte zur Zeitschrift für die alttestamentliche Wissenschaft*
CAT	Commentaire de l'Ancien Testament
CBC	Cambridge Bible Commentary
CBOTS	Coniectanea Biblica Old Testament Series
CBQ	*Catholic Biblical Quarterly*
CBQMS	Catholic Biblical Quarterly Monograph Series
CC	Continental Commentaries
CEB	Commentaire Evangélique de la Bible
CTM	*Concordia Theological Monthly*
CTR	*Criswell Theological Review*
CurrTM	*Currents in Theology and Missions*
DH	Deuteronomic (or Deuteronomistic) History
DOTHB	*Dictionary of the Old Testament: Historical Books,* IVP Bible Dictionary Series
DOTP	*Dictionary of the Old Testament: Pentateuch,* IVP Bible Dictionary Series
DSB	Daily Study Bible
EBC	Expositor's Bible Commentary
EphTL	*Ephemerides Theologicae Lovanienses*
ETRel	*Études Théologiques et Religieuses*
EvQ	*Evangelical Quarterly*
EvTh	*Evangelische Theologie*
ExpTim	*Expository Times*
FCI	Foundations of Contemporary Interpretation Series
FOTL	Forms of Old Testament Literature Series
FRLANT	Forschungen zur Religion und Literatur des Alten und Neuen Testaments
FTS	Frankfurter theologische Studien
GraceTJ	*Grace Theological Journal*
HAR	*Hebrew Annual Review*
HAT	Handbuch zum Alten Testament
HCOT	Historical Commentary on the Old Testament
HKAT	Handkommentar zum Alten Testament
HS	*Hebrew Studies*
HSM	Harvard Semitic Monograph Series
HTR	*Harvard Theological Review*

HUCA	*Hebrew Union College Annual*
IB	*Interpreter's Bible*
ICC	International Critical Commentary
IDBSup	*Interpreter's Dictionary of the Bible, Supplementary Volume*
IEJ	*Israel Exploration Journal*
Interp	*Interpretation* (journal)
Interp	Interpretation: A Bible Commentary for Teaching and Preaching
IOT	*Introduction to the Old Testament*
	R. K. Harrison (Eerdmans, 1969)
	E. J. Young (Eerdmans, 1958)
IOTS	*Introduction to the Old Testament as Scripture*, B. S. Childs
ITC	International Theological Commentary
JAOS	*Journal of the American Oriental Society*
JBL	*Journal of Biblical Literature*
JBR	*Journal of Bibles and Religion*
JETS	*Journal of the Evangelical Theological Society*
JJS	*Journal of Jewish Studies*
JNES	*Journal of Near Eastern Studies*
JNWSL	*Journal of North West Semitic Languages*
JPS	Jewish Publication Society
JR	*Journal of Religion*
JSOT	*Journal for the Study of the Old Testament*
JSOTS	Journal for the Study of the Old Testament Supplements
JSS	*Journal of Semitic Studies*
JTS	*Journal of Theological Studies*
KAT	*Kommentar zum Alten Testament*
LTQ	*Lexington Theological Quarterly*
LXX	The Septuagint
MGWJ	*Monatsschrift für Geschichte und Wissenschaft des Judentums*
MT	Masoretic Text
NAC	New American Commentary
NCB	New Century Bible
NIB	New Interpreter's Bible
NIBCOT	New International Bible Commentary, Old Testament
NICOT	New International Commentary on the Old Testament
NIVAC	The NIV Application Commentary
OSt	*Ostkirchliche Studien*
OTE	*Old Testament Essays* (Journal of the Old Testament Society of South Africa)
OTI	*The Old Testament: An Introduction*, R. Rendtorff
OTL	Old Testament Library Commentary Series

OTM	Old Testament Message Series
OTS	Oudtestamentische Studien
OTSWA	*Oud Testamentiase Werkgemeenschap in Suid-Afrika*
PEQ	*Palestine Exploration Quarterly*
PTR	*Princeton Theological Review*
RB	*Révue Biblique*
ResQ	*Restoration Quarterly*
RevQ	*Revue de Qumran*
RSciRel	*Recherches de Science Religieuse*
RTP	*Review of Theology and Philosophy*
RTR	*Reformed Theological Review*
RvExp	*Review and Expositor*
SBLDS	Society of Biblical Literature Dissertation Series
SBLMS	Society of Biblical Literature Monograph Series
SBT	Studies in Biblical Theology
SCM	Studies in the Christian Movement
SHBC	Smith and Helwys Bible Commentary
SJT	*Scottish Journal of Theology*
SOTI	*A Survey of Old Testament Introduction*, G. L. Archer
SPCK	Society for the Propagation of Christian Knowledge
SSN	Studia semitica Neerlandica
ST	*Studia Theologica*
SWJT	*Southwestern Journal of Theology*
TBC	Torch Bible Commentaries
TDOT	*Theological Dictionary of the Old Testament*
TJ	*Trinity Journal*
TOTC	Tyndale Old Testament Commentaries
TynBul	*Tyndale Bulletin*
TZ	*Theologische Zeitschrift*
USQR	*Union Seminary Quarterly Review*
VT	*Vetus Testamentum*
VTSup	*Vetus Testamentum* Supplements
WBC	Word Biblical Commentary
WEC	Wycliffe Exegetical Commentary
WMANT	Wissenschaftliche Monographien zum Alten und Neuen Testament
WTJ	*Westminster Theological Journal*
YNER	Yale Near Eastern Researches
ZAW	*Zeitschrift für die alttestamentliche Wissenschaft*
ZDMG	*Zeitschrift der Deutschen Morganländischen Gesellschaft*
ZNW	*Zeitschrift für die neutestamentliche Wissenschaft*
ZTK	*Zeitschrift für Theologie und Kirche*

CHAPTER ONE

INTRODUCTION

ORIENTATION

Bibliography

B. W. **Anderson,** *Understanding the Old Testament* (Prentice-Hall, 1975); G. L. **Archer,** *A Survey of Old Testament Introduction* (*SOTI*; Moody, 1964); W. **Brueggemann,** *An Introduction to the Old Testament: The Canon and Christian Imagination* (Westminster John Knox, 2003); B. S. **Childs,** *The Book of Exodus* (Westminster, 1974); idem, *Introduction to the Old Testament as Scripture* (*IOTS*; Fortress, 1979); P. C. **Craigie,** *The Old Testament: Its Background, Growth, and Content* (Abingdon, 1986); J. G. **Eichhorn,** *Einleitung in das Alte Testament,* 3 vols. (Leipzig, 1780–83); O. **Eissfeldt,** *The Old Testament: An Introduction* (*OTI*; Oxford, 1965); R. H. **Gundry,** *Jesus the Word according to John the Sectarian: A Paleofundamentalist Manifesto for Contemporary Evangelicalism, Especially Its Elites, in North America* (Eerdmans, 2001); R. K. **Harrison,** *Introduction to the Old Testament* (*IOT*; Eerdmans, 1969); O. **Kaiser,** *Introduction to the Old Testament* (Oxford, 1975); Y. **Kaufmann,** *The Religion of Israel* (University of Chicago Press, 1960); A. L. **Laffey,** *An Introduction to the Old Testament: A Feminist Perspective* (Fortress, 1988); W. S. **LaSor,** D. A. **Hubbard,** and F. W. **Bush,** *Old Testament Survey* (OTS; 2nd ed.; Eerdmans, 1996); R. **Rendtorff,** *The Old Testament: An Introduction* (*OTI*; Fortress, 1986); A. **Rivetus,** *Isagoge, seu introductio generalis, ad scripturam sacram veteris et novi testamenti* (Leiden, 1627); J. A. **Soggin,** *Introduction to the Old Testament* (*IOT*; Westminster, 1976); M. **Sternberg,** *The Poetics of Biblical Narrative* (Indiana University Press, 1985); E. J. **Young,** *An Introduction to the Old Testament* (*IOT*; Eerdmans, 1949).

The Genre

The genre of introduction has a well-established place in the field of Old Testament studies. It is one of the first volumes that serious students of the Bible encounter in their quest to understand the text. Its very title connotes the preliminary nature of its subject matter. As E. J. Young commented, the word derives from the Latin *introducere* that means "to lead in" or "to introduce" (1949, 15).

It is thus the purpose of this introduction, like all introductions, to acquaint the reader with information that is important to know in order to read the books of the Old Testament with understanding. In more contemporary terminology, our goal is to provide the student with resources needed to achieve reading competence.[1]

Many introductions have been written during the history of biblical studies. Since the history of the genre may be found elsewhere (see Young 1945, 15–37; Childs 1979, 27–47), it will not be repeated here. Nevertheless, a few of the major transitional points will give the reader a feel for the evolution of the genre and provide a framework for the present volume.

The church fathers did not write what we would recognize today as introductions to the Old Testament, but they did deal with topics that would later occupy volumes that go by that name. Thus Jerome, Augustine, Origen, and others wrote concerning authorship, literary style, canonics, text, and theological issues. Their comments, however, may be found in scattered locations and not in any single volume.

Childs and Young disagree over the date of the first truly modern Old Testament introduction. Young attributes it to Michael Walther (1636) because of his distinction between matters of general and special introduction (see below). Childs, on the other hand, dates it later with J. G. Eichhorn, whose three-volume *Einleitung* was first published between 1780 and 1783. The difference reflects the theological disagreement between Young, who as a conservative acknowledges the work of Walther, who held a high view of inspiration, and Childs, a critic (though moderate), who requires the advent of the critical method to find the first "truly modern, historical critical Introduction" (1979, 35).

In the twentieth century the introduction continued its evolution along the lines of the development of the discipline as a whole. Thus, after Julius Wellhausen introduced the documentary hypothesis, all succeeding introductions had to take his theory into account (see Historical Background below). The same is true with later developments, including form criticism, tradition criticism, and, more recently, the literary approach.

While mainstream introductions agree in their acceptance of critical methodology, there are differences among them. These differences may be observed in a sampling of the introductions that are still in use. The introduction by Eissfeldt represents classic German criticism. Much of his work is devoted to reconstructing the history of the composition of the individual sec-

---

[1]J. Culler, *Structuralist Poetics: Structuralism, Linguistics, and the Study of Literature* (Ithaca, NY: Cornell University Press, 1975), 113–30.

tions of the Bible. Although his work is idiosyncratic in detail, Eissfeldt devotes detailed attention to a source analysis of the Pentateuch. In the critical tradition, Rendtorff adopts a somewhat different approach in that he follows in the line of Noth and von Rad to present a more historical analysis of the Pentateuch. B. S. Childs, on the other hand, brackets many of these questions of the historical development of the individual books in order to delineate the canonical function of the books (Brueggemann 2003).

The preceding paragraphs describe the general contours of mainstream Old Testament studies. Specifically, they delineate the developments of critical Protestant Old Testament studies in Europe, Britain, and the United States. Protestant scholarship was mainstream because ever since the early part of the nineteenth century this approach to the text controlled most of the large churches and virtually every major academic post. The majority of Catholic and Jewish scholars who were writing and teaching at this time also accepted many of the tenets that were developed by these Protestant scholars.

Nonetheless, there was still a small but determined group of conservative Protestant scholars who were active in the field and produced Old Testament introductions. The four most significant works are by Young, Archer, Harrison, and LaSor-Hubbard-Bush. They differ in length, in areas of interest, and—though they are all conservative in their approach to the text—in theology. A characteristic of conservative scholarship as represented in most of these volumes is an apologetic interest. This concern is represented least in the LaSor-Hubbard-Bush volume, but conservative scholars have felt it necessary to direct much of their discussion toward combating the historical-critical method and in particular a source analysis of the Pentateuch.

The Purpose of the Present Volume

The above discussion provides a backdrop for a description of the purposes and aims of the present volume. The following comments provide a guide to the plan of this introduction and give a rationale for the approach adopted here. We highlight the direction of this introduction and also some of the ways in which it differs from typical introductions.

Theological Perspective

In the first place, this introduction represents a Protestant and evangelical approach to the text. This theological orientation will become immediately obvious in the discussion of various critical issues. An evangelical doctrine of Scripture, however, does not answer all hermeneutical and interpretive questions, nor does it prevent us from learning from the tradition of historical criticism. Indeed, our introduction will provide example after example of dependence on the previous labors of scholars in both the evangelical and critical camps. Many of the issues that have divided evangelical and critical scholars are as contested today as they were in the past, but we appear to be entering a new era of communication and mutual respect about which we can all be grateful. This introduction will depart from many of the well-entrenched conclusions of critical study, but it will do so with respect and not with rancor. We also concur with R. H. Gundry in his warning that evangelical scholarship sometimes simply uncritically follows in the steps of nonevangelical scholarship in order to find acceptance. We will do our best to avoid that temptation.

What does it mean to write an introduction from an evangelical perspective? Among other things, it means treating the text as the church has received it. While not denying the possibility of sources and the history of development of individual biblical books, the focus of this introduction will be squarely on the finished form of the canonical text. This approach dovetails with recent interests in canonical theology and literary study of the Bible. However, the similarities, though welcome, are in some sense superficial, since most critical scholars who take a synchronic approach to the text merely bracket diachronic issues for the moment. Childs is a good example. He is careful never to disown typical historical criticism, while in his introduction and elsewhere he downplays these concerns in order to highlight the canonical role that the Bible plays in theology and the church. His commentary on Exodus (1974) is a prime example of both his synchronic and diachronic concerns. They are both present but are not integrated with one another.

> *What does it mean to write an introduction from an evangelical perspective? Among other things, it means treating the text as the church has received it.*

Scope

Old Testament introduction is often subdivided into two areas: general and special introduction. General introduction treats topics that cover the whole testament: issues such as text and canon. Special introduction handles individual books. Our introduction will focus on special introduction and will proceed book by book. The order adopted will be that recognized by readers of the Bible in English. This differs from a number of introductions that follow the order of the Hebrew Bible in the Masoretic tradition (for instance, the introductions by Young and Childs).

Most of the introductions mentioned above concentrate on historical questions surrounding a biblical book. This diachronic impulse crosses the conservative-critical line. Issues such as who wrote the book and when, the history of the development of the text, and the historical background of its contents are typical. These are important problems that will be treated here when necessary. Nonetheless, there are other equally important topics that help introduce the reader to the books of the Old Testament. For instance, the literary genre, shape, and style of a book are essential keys to its proper interpretation. In addition, while a book of the Bible may have been produced separately from the rest of the canon, its meaning now resides in the context of the other books of the Old Testament and, for Christians, the New Testament. Accordingly, we will reflect at some length on the theological message of the books within their broader canonical context. Three general topics constitute the discussion in each chapter: historical background, literary analysis, and theological message.

By now our readers may be asking how we intend to cover all of these topics while keeping the introduction to a reasonable length. We feel that it is important, especially if the book is to be used effectively in the classroom, to limit its size. One area that will get less coverage than is found in some other introductions is the history of research. Except in some critical areas such as source analysis of the Pentateuch (and even here the discussion is brief), we will feature only the high points in research and mention representative scholars rather than attempt an exhaustive delineation of past scholarship. We will, of course, be careful to give credit to those whose research has enlightened us. Furthermore, the bibliographies at the beginning of each chapter refer to the works that can lead interested students to the history of research on any given book. In these bibliographies a premium is placed on books and articles written in English. In part, this signals the end of the period when German scholarship was considered the vanguard in the field. But more significantly, it is part of our attempt to tailor these bibliographies for the English-speaking seminary student. Foreign language references are added to the bibliographies only when they are crucial for the discussion.

The Major Topics

As we said above, each chapter deals with the historical background, literary analysis, and theological message of the book under discussion. The rest of this introductory chapter is devoted to explicating these three topics. What follows will allow readers to understand the orientation of the authors and will also allow the authors to refer back to these more general statements.

While these three topics are treated separately, it must be borne in mind that they function in a fully integrated manner in the biblical text (Sternberg 1985). The history has theological meaning; the theology is based on historical events. The texts that narrate this theological history or historicized theology are fittingly described as literary art.

HISTORICAL BACKGROUND

Bibliography

R. **Alter,** *The Art of Biblical Narrative* (Basic Books, 1981); M. Z. **Brettler,** *The Creation of History in Ancient Israel* (London: Routledge, 1995); D. **Damrosch,** *The Narrative Covenant: Transformation of Genre in the Growth of Biblical Literature* (Harper & Row, 1987); P. R. **Davies,** *In Search of "Ancient Israel"* (Sheffield: JSOT Press, 1992); B. **Halpern,** *The First Historians* (Harper & Row, 1988); D. M. **Howard** Jr. *An Introduction to the Old Testament Historical Books* (Moody,

1993); K. A. **Kitchen,** *On the Reliability of the Old Testament* (Eerdmans, 2003); N. P. **Lemche,** *Ancient Israel: A New History of Israelite Society* (Sheffield: JSOT Press, 1988); B. O. **Long,** *I Kings with an Introduction to Historical Literature* (FOTL 9; Eerdmans, 1984); V. P. **Long,** *The Art of Biblical History* (Zondervan, 1994); idem (ed.), *Israel's Past in Present Research: Essays on Ancient Israelite Historiography* (Eisenbrauns, 1999); A. R. **Millard,** J. K. **Hoffmeier,** and D. W. **Baker,** eds., *Faith, Tradition, and History* (Eisenbrauns, 1994); I. **Provan,** "Ideologies, Literary and Critical," *JBL* 114 (1995): 585–606; I. **Provan,** V. P. **Long,** and T. **Longman** III, *A Biblical History of Israel* (Westminster John Knox, 2003); G. W. **Ramsey,** *The Quest for the Historical Israel* (John Knox, 1981); T. L. **Thompson,** *Early History of the Israelite People from the Written and Archaeological Sources* (Leiden: Brill, 1992); J. **Van Seters,** *Prologue to History: The Yahwist as Historian in Genesis* (Westminster John Knox, 1992); idem, *The Life of Moses: The Yahwist as Historian in Exodus–Numbers* (Westminster John Knox, 1994); K. W. **Whitelam,** *The Invention of Ancient Israel: The Silencing of Palestinian History* (Routledge: London, 1996).

Cautions

Even new Bible readers hear the warning to read the Bible "in its context" and not to treat passages in an isolated fashion. However, many understand the context to be literary only and then forget to read the Bible in its historical context, that is, the time period in which it was written and about which it narrates.

One cause is the misunderstanding that describes the Bible as a timeless book. The Bible is a timeless book only in the sense that it has an impact on every generation. The books of the Bible are also culture-bound. They were written for people in antiquity in a language and culture and with literary conventions that they understood.

As modern readers, we are distanced from the events that motivated the writings of the book. So even though the authority of the Bible is focused on the text and not on the events it narrates, it is still of utmost importance to read the Bible in the light of the time period from which it comes.

As such, the books of the Bible are careful to signal their relative age. Not every book is able to be dated with precision, but with few exceptions, each book informs the reader of its time of composition and describes events of a historical character.

While ignorance of the historical context of the Bible threatens a correct understanding of the Bible, a second major danger confronts the reader. This danger is the imposition of contemporary Western values on the historical writings of the Old Testament.

It is thus of great importance that we not only describe the value of a historical approach to the Old Testament but also explore the nature of Old Testament historiography.

What Is History?

In the first place it is important to differentiate history and historiography. The first refers to the events that have taken place in the past, and the second, to writing about the events. To ask whether a book is historical or not is a complex question. It could refer to the intention of an author or to his success in achieving his intention.

In this book, when we identify a biblical book's genre as historical, we are asserting that the author's intention is antiquarian and that the narrative presents what the author supposes to have happened in space and time in the past. We must, however, go even further. A book may intend to be historical but not be a history textbook in the modern sense of the word. In other words, history is different from a videotaped representation of the past in that it involves a historian, one who must interpret these events for his contemporary audience. Indeed, as Howard has indicated, "Only that account is 'history' that attempts to impose some coherence on the past" and "all history writing is of necessity 'perspectival,' even 'subjective,' in the sense that it owes its shape to its author's activity in selecting and communicating material" (1993, 30, 35). The subjectivity involved in historical narration does not invalidate the historical intention, as some skeptics argue; rather, the interpreter of the biblical historian must take into account the latter's perspective on the past.

Biblical history does have an antiquarian interest. The author(s) of the Pentateuch believed that God actually created the universe in the past, Abraham migrated from Mesopotamia to Palestine, Moses parted the Red Sea, David ascended the throne of Israel, the kingdom was divided under Solomon's son, the Babylonians defeated the Israelites, and Ezra and Nehemiah led a reform in the postexilic community. However, the historicity of these acts is assumed in that they are stated and not proved. The concern of the text is not to prove the history, but rather to impress the reader with the theological significance of these acts. History and theology are closely connected in the biblical text.

Indeed, biblical history is not objective history—that is, uninterpreted history—but rather, history narrated with a divine purpose. For this reason, commentators have referred to biblical history as "theological history," "prophetic history," and "covenantal history." The last is especially appealing, because covenant is the primary divine-human relationship metaphor used in the Bible, and the Bible charts this relationship from the time of Adam and Eve (Genesis) through the time of consummation (Revelation).

Moreover, we must explore the relationship between history and fiction, especially in light of the work of scholars such as Alter (1981) who tend to confuse the two. Alter observes the literary artifice of the history books of the Bible and labels it "fictional history" or "historical fiction." As Long (1994, 66) points out, however, "fictionality is a possible but misleading category for biblical historiography since after all an account of something is not literally that something. But fiction is a genre that is not constrained by any 'something.'" He offers the adjective "artistic" in the place of "fictional" to describe the "creative, though constrained, attempt to depict and interpret significant events or sequences of events from the past."[2]

This issue leads to the question of historicity. Is it important that the events actually took place in space and time in the past? Ramsey pointedly asks the question, "If Jericho is not razed, is our faith in vain?" (1981; see discussion in Long 1994, 83ff.).

The phrasing of the question lures one to a simplistic answer. The destruction of Jericho has no direct bearing on our faith in Christ. Nonetheless, indirectly the question is crucial. It certainly raises the issue of the epistemological basis of our faith. Many people, even modern people, will agree with Paul when he states, "If Christ has not been raised, our preaching is useless and so is your faith" (1 Cor. 15:14, the verse in whose language Ramsey poses his question). Our knowledge of this resurrection comes from the Bible, which purports to be God's Word and thus claims to be trustworthy. The Gospels present themselves as historical, though theological and artistic, accounts of the resurrection. The book of Joshua, as an example of an Old Testament historical book, also presents itself as an account of the past acts of God to save his people. On what basis, besides arbitrary modern sensibilities and desires, would we accept the teaching of the Gospels and reject the teaching of Joshua? Thus, to suspect or reject the historical facticity of the razing of Jericho does indeed raise an obstacle to faith. The historicity of the historical books of the Old Testament is important because "the Bible makes numerous claims—explicitly and implicitly—concerning the factuality of the events it records. At the most fundamental level, at the central core of Christian beliefs, is the fact that Christ did indeed die for the sins of humanity and then rose from the grave in a great victory over death. This forms the ground and basis of our faith" (Howard 1993, 35).

History and the Supernatural

A major issue as one approaches the subject of history and the Bible is the occurrence of supernatural events. This immediately brings the role of the interpreter's presuppositions to the fore.

In the Old Testament one reads of a bush that burns but is not destroyed, a donkey that speaks, dead people who live again, seas that part, the sun's stopping in mid-sky, and more. If an interpreter approaches the Old Testament as he would any other book—that is, if he perceives it as written from a human vantage point, about human affairs—skepticism is warranted. However, a second

[2]See the introductory chapters to Provan, Long, and Longman (2003) for an extensive discussion of these issues, and the rest of the volume for an attempt to write a history of Israel with sensitivity to the literary and theological concerns of the text.

interpreter, who admits the reality of God and who believes that God is the ultimate and guiding voice of the Bible, will not have difficulty accepting the supernatural events of the Bible.

This, of course, is where the dialogue between conservative and critical scholars gets stalled. Nonetheless, conservatives must guard against the tendency to overhistoricize the Bible. Legitimate genre questions must be addressed in the interpretation of certain books. Why are there differences between the narration of the same events in Samuel–Kings over against Chronicles? What is the historical kernel of the Job story? Is Jonah history or parable? These issues will be addressed in later chapters.

The Challenge of Minimalism

The 1990s saw the rise of growing skepticism concerning the possibility that actual history could be reconstructed based on the Hebrew Bible. Such authors as Davies, Thompson, Whitelam, and Lemche, among others, have, despite their differences, come to be regarded as a school of thought that is commonly referred to as *minimalism,* after their conclusion that a minimum of historical memory may be found in the text. Indeed, Whitelam (1996, 69) has proclaimed the "death of 'biblical history.'"

Their argument in a nutshell is that since the biblical text is clearly not an objective work of history, it must be supported by extrabiblical evidence before its historical claims may be taken as true. Since direct and specific historical evidence is rare and not realistically to be expected in many cases, this drastically limits the biblical text's value as a historical source. The minimalists will even cast doubt on the scant direct evidence that we do have (the Merneptah Stela, the David inscription, and so forth). It appears that the minimalists are intent on undermining the text as reliable history. Instead, they propose what they think is a more objective way of reconstructing the history of Palestine, namely, archaeology, ignoring the obvious hermeneutical and ideological problems inherent in that discipline (see below).

The wholesale skepticism of the minimalist is hardly justified and has received significant critique (see Provan; Provan, Long, and Longman). Even so, their critique can lead to a more sophisticated view of the nature of biblical historiography, a subject to which we now turn our attention.

The Nature of Biblical Historiography

Biblical history is not an objective reporting of purely human events. It is an impassioned account of God's acts in history as he works in the world to save his people. Accordingly, it is "theological," "prophetic," "covenantal history." The following traits characterize this history:

Selectivity. No history can tell everything about its subject. It would take longer to write about an event than it does to experience it if the historian's goal were to be comprehensive. Thus all history writing involves selectivity. What will be included and what excluded?

A look at the synoptic accounts of the history of David's reign in Samuel-Kings and Chronicles illustrates the point. In the former, there is a long narrative about David's sin with Bathsheba and her later role in the transition of the kingship to Solomon (2 Sam. 11–12; 1 Kings 1–2), but no mention of Bathsheba by the Chronicler (except in the genealogy in 1 Chron. 3:5).

But selectivity is not only a necessity of space but also a part of the function and intention of the historiographer. The biblical historian is not interested in every aspect of the past but focuses on the community of Israel (often as represented by its king). And although the community interests often find expression in the political and military life of the people of God, the historical books of the Old Testament are not interested in politics for its own sake, but only in how politics and military action affect Israel's relationship with God.

One of the keys to a proper interpretation of biblical historical books is the discovery of the writers' intentions and how they affect their principle of selectivity. These issues will be addressed in the following chapters as we study specific books, but we can illustrate our point quickly, though not exhaustively, by comparing Samuel-Kings and Chronicles. Samuel-Kings emphasizes the sins of the kings of both Israel and Judah, particularly their rejection of the law of centralization. The role of the prophets is emphasized as is God's delayed retribution. Our later chapters on Samuel and Kings will argue that the evidence indicates an exilic date for this book and an intention to answer the question "Why are we, God's favored people, in exile?" So, for example, it fits into the purpose of this historian to include the Bathsheba account, which highlights David's sins. Chronicles, on the other hand, focuses on Judah alone, minimizes the sins of the kings, and asks questions of Judah's historical continuity with the past. There is also an emphasis in reporting on the temple. Once we discover that the time of composition of this historical work is the restoration period, we see that its principle of selectivity is driven by different questions: "What are we to do now that we are back in the land?" and "What is our connection with Israel in the past?"

Emphasis. This trait is closely connected to the previous one. Not all acts of God, not everything that occurred to Israel, was equally important to the biblical historians. Some events are emphasized over others. Thus emphasis often supports the intention of the book in a way similar to that of the principle of selectivity. For instance, the emphasis on the temple in Chronicles in contrast to Samuel-Kings arises, in part at least, because of the fact that the temple was being rebuilt at the time. Thus through the use of emphasis and by drawing analogies with the past, the Chronicler shows the continuity between the people of God at the end of the period of the Old Testament and the people of God at the time of Moses and David.

But sometimes emphasis serves other, more didactic purposes. Of the many cities that were overrun at the time of the conquest, two stand out in the narrative in terms of emphasis: Jericho and Ai. These are emphasized because they are first, but also because they are a paradigm for the proper waging of holy war. The lesson of Jericho (Josh. 6) is that obedience to the Lord results in military victory, while the lesson of Ai (Josh. 7) is that disobedience, even by a single individual, will grind the conquest to a halt.

Order. For the most part, biblical history follows a roughly chronological order. Much of it rehearses the history of Israel under the reigns of its various kings. However, chronology is not a straitjacket, as can be observed in a number of places in the narrative. Occasionally other, often thematic concerns take precedence.

For instance, 1 Samuel 16:14–23 recounts David's early service to Saul as the musician whose gift soothed Saul's tormented soul. The following chapter introduces David a second time as the one who defeats Goliath. The problem with the latter story is that when David is presented to Saul, the king does not recognize him (17:58); this would be strange if he had been serving in Saul's court for a period of time. A probable explanation of this anomaly is that the text is not focused on chronological reporting but intends rather a dual topical introduction of David, who as a young man already manifested the gifts that would gain him renown as the sweet psalm-singer of Israel as well as the mighty warrior of the Lord.

Application. We have already commented that the biblical historians make no attempt to be dispassionate. They were not modern historians seeking the brute facts of history. On the contrary, they were prophets who mediated God's Word to his people. They were the vehicles of God's interpretation of his own holy acts.

As a matter of fact, it is not misleading to envision the historians of Israel as preachers. Their texts are the events. They apply them with zeal to the congregation of Israel. These texts are a wonderful integration of history, literature, morality, and theology.

> *Biblical history follows a roughly chronological order, but chronology is not a straitjacket. Occasionally other, often thematic concerns take precedence.*

BIBLICAL HISTORY AND ARCHAEOLOGY

Bibliography

W. F. **Albright,** "The Impact of Archaeology on Biblical Research—1966," in *New Directions in Biblical Archaeology,* ed. D. N. Freedman and J. Greenfield (Doubleday, 1969): 1–14; W. G. **Dever,** "Archaeological Method in Israel: A Continuing Revolution," *BA* 43 (1980): 40–48; idem, "Retrospects and Prospects in Biblical and Syro-Palestinian Archaeology," *BA* 45 (1982): 103–8; I. **Finkelstein** and N. A. **Silberman,** *The Bible Unearthed: Archaeology's New Vision of Ancient Israel and the Origin of Its Sacred Texts* (Free Press, 2001); K. A. **Kitchen,** *On the*

Reliability of the Old Testament (Eerdmans, 2003); G. E. **Wright,** "Archaeological Method in Palestine—An American Interpretation," *Eretz Israel* 9 (1969): 125–29; idem, "The Phenomenon of American Archaeology in the Near East," in *Near Eastern Archaeology in the Twentieth Century: Essays in Honor of Nelson Glueck,* ed. J. A. Sanders (Doubleday, 1970), 3–40.

Since the Bible does have a historical intention, it makes claims about what happened in the past. Archaeology is the field of study that investigates the material remains of a culture to reconstruct its history. Thus two sources, the biblical text and the material remains recovered by archaeological study, make claims about the past.

The relationship between these two objects of study is highly disputed. Some would argue that archaeology is the handmaiden of biblical studies. The former is mute, so to give the remains voice, we must turn to texts such as the Bible. Others object strongly to such a subservient role for the discipline (Dever 1980), even rejecting the label of biblical archaeology in favor of the more neutral Syro-Palestinian archaeology (though recently Dever has reversed his position). Some today even argue that archaeology is the only true guide to reconstructing ancient history since textual sources like the Old Testament are ideologically invested (see above on minimalism as well as Finkelstein and Silberman, who argue that biblical history is largely a work of the imagination constructed during the seventh-century reign of King Josiah).

This volume is not a biblical history (for which see Provan, Long, and Longman 2003; and Kitchen 2003), but we must address for a moment the hermeneutical issues involved in archaeology in order to assess its value in connection with biblical historiography. The issue is actually very complex, and the interested student should turn elsewhere for further study (see bibliography). For our purposes we can point out that the use of archaeology involves more than simply digging up artifacts and holding them up against the biblical facts.

We have already considered some of the issues involved on the textual side. For example, we are not presented with simple bare facts in the Bible. On the other side, we must point out that archaeological remains also need interpretation. This involves the presuppositions of the interpreter just as the interpreter of texts begins with certain presuppositions. Indeed, the case can be made that archaeology is a more subjective discipline precisely because the objects are mute (except for extrabiblical textual material, which is subject to the same issues as the interpretation of biblical material) as opposed to the biblical text, which provides us with interpretation of events.

In the final analysis, it is much too simplistic to expect from archaeology either an independent verification of biblical claims or a certain scientific refutation of them. For a specific example, see the discussion on the date of the exodus.

LITERARY ANALYSIS

Bibliography

R. **Alter,** *The Art of Biblical Narrative* (Basic Books, 1981); idem, "A Response to Critics," *JSOT* 27 (1983): 113–17; idem, *The Art of Biblical Poetry* (Basic Books, 1985); A. **Berlin,** *Poetics and Interpretation of Biblical Narrative* (Sheffield: Almond, 1983); idem, *The Dynamics of Biblical Parallelism* (Indiana University Press, 1985); P. **Brooks,** *Reading for the Plot: Design and Intention in Narrative* (Vintage Books, 1984); G. B. **Caird,** *The Language and Imagery of the Bible* (Westminster, 1980); S. **Chatman,** *Story and Discourse* (Cornell University Press, 1978); N. **Frye,** *Anatomy of Criticism* (Princeton University Press, 1957); idem, *The Great Code* (London: Ark, 1982); S. A. **Geller,** *Parallelism in Early Biblical Poetry* (HSM 20; Missoula: Scholars, 1979); J. **Kugel,** *The Idea of Biblical Poetry* (Yale University Press, 1981); T. **Longman** III, "A Critique of Two Recent Metrical Systems," *Bib* 63 (1982): 230–54; idem, "Form Criticism, Recent Developments in Genre Theory and the Evangelical," *WTJ* 47 (1985): 46–67; idem, *Literary Approaches to Biblical Interpretation* (FCI 3; Zondervan, 1987); idem, *How to Read the Psalms* (InterVarsity, 1988); idem, "Storytellers and Poets in the Bible: Can Literary Artifice Be True?" in *Inerrancy and Hermeneutics,* ed. H. M. Conn (Baker, 1988), 137–49; idem, *Reading the Bible with Heart and Mind* (NavPress, 1997); idem, "Literary Approaches to Old Testament Studies," in *The Faces of Old Testament Studies* (Baker, 1999), 97–115; T. **Longman** III and L. **Ryken,** eds., *A Complete Literary Guide to the Bible* (Zondervan, 1993); R. **Lowth,** *Lectures on the Sacred Poetry of the Hebrews* (1778; repr. London: T. Tegg and Son, 1835); M. **Minor,** *Literary-Critical Approaches to the Bible: An Annotated Bibliography* (Locust Hill, 1992); M. **O'Connor,** *Hebrew Verse Structure* (Eisenbrauns, 1980); G. R. **Osborne,** *The Hermeneutical Spiral: A Comprehensive Introduction to Biblical Interpretation* (InterVarsity, 1991); M. H. **Pope,** *Song of Songs* (AB 7C; Doubleday, 1977); M. A. **Powell,** *What Is Narrative Criticism?* (Fortress, 1990); D. **Rhoads** and D. **Michie,** *Mark as Story: The Introduction to the Narrative as Gospel* (Fortress, 1982); L. **Ryken,** *How to Read the Bible as Literature* (Zondervan, 1984); L. **Ryken,** J. **Wilhoit,** and T. **Longman** III, eds., *The Dictionary of Biblical Imagery* (InterVarsity, 1998); M. **Sternberg,** *The Poetics of Biblical Narrative* (Indiana University Press, 1985); D. **Stuart,** *Studies in Early Hebrew Meter* (Missoula: Scholars, 1976); P. **Trible,** *Rhetorical Criticism: Context, Method, and the Book of Jonah* (Fortress, 1994); K. J. **Vanhoozer,** *Is There a Meaning in This Text? The Bible, the Reader, and the Morality of Literary Knowledge* (Zondervan, 1998); W. G. E. **Watson,** *Classical Hebrew Poetry* (JSOTS 26; Sheffield: JSOT, 1984).

Stories and Poems

The Old Testament contains very little technical material. For the most part, its contents may be described under two rubrics: stories and poems. Certainly, there are items like the list of tribal boundaries in the second half of Joshua or the description of the main sacrifices in the first chapter of Leviticus, the pentateuchal laws, and the seemingly endless genealogy that begins the book of Chronicles. Even these passages, however, are within the context of stories about Israel's past and God's great acts in their midst. We encounter nothing quite like our modern history or scientific textbooks and certainly nothing approaching a theological essay or confession. Surprisingly, we encounter stories and poems.

Stories and even poetry speak to a broader segment of the people of God than would a more technical and precise form of communication. Even the youngest and the uneducated can appreciate and understand the stories of Samson and Delilah, Esther, or Ruth. In addition, stories and poems do more than inform our intellect. They also arouse our emotions, appeal to our will, and stimulate our imagination in a way that a modern systematic theology cannot.

Since such a large amount of the Old Testament comes in the form of stories and poems, it is important to raise the question of interpretation before entering a survey of its various components. Cultures differ in their method of telling stories and writing poems, and as "foreign" interpreters, we need to discover the conventions that governed the writing of the biblical authors. Thus we offer an analysis of storytelling and poem writing in ancient Israel with the intention of developing a "reading strategy" for interpretation.

The Conventions of Old Testament Poetry

Poetry is highly stylized language that is usually easy to distinguish from prose stories. Poetry is an artificial language in the sense that it does not follow the normal rules for communication.

While there are characteristics of poetry, there is no single or even group of defining traits. In rare instances, particularly in some of the prophets, it is difficult to tell whether the passage is poetic or highly stylized prose.

Terseness. The leading characteristic of poetry is terseness or conciseness. While prose is composed of sentences and paragraphs, poets use short clauses, grouped together by varying levels of repetition, and stanzas. As a result, poetic lines are very short. This trait becomes obvious in many English translations of the Bible because the poetic material has wider margins.

Poetry says much in very few words. This economy of language comes about in various ways, the two most interesting being: (1) the suppression of conjunctions and other particles, and (2) a high frequency of imagery (discussed later). Conjunctions are short but important words that show the relationship between one clause and another. In poetry, however, they are used very sparingly, and intentionally so. They are often implied, as for instance in Psalm 23:1: "The LORD is my shepherd; I shall not want" (KJV). There are no conjunctions here in the original, but a cause-effect relationship is implied: *Because* the Lord is my shepherd, *therefore* I shall not be in want.

The relative absence of conjunctions in poetry lends to its terseness and necessitates a slower, more meditative reading.

Parallelism. Most Hebrew poetry contains a high proportion of repetition. The most frequent type of repetition is within a poetic verse or line, but parallelism may also occur over wide distances within the psalm (see Ps. 8:1, 9). The repetition, while sometimes nearly synonymous, is rarely verbatim.

Parallelism is almost always present in poetry, but it is also a linguistic ornament that is occasionally found in prose contexts. Thus parallelism alone is not a sufficient criterion to define poetry. Wherever there is a high proportion of parallel lines, however, we can be certain that we are dealing with a poetic passage.

Parallel lines are not strictly identical; they are similar, yet different. Parallelism is not "saying the same thing using different words." The different words of the second part of the parallelism advance the thought of the first part in some appreciable way. For example,

> I will praise you, LORD, with all my heart;
> I will tell of all your wonderful deeds. (Ps. 9:1)

In the second part (also called the second colon) of this rather typical bicolon, the psalmist specifies the nature of his praise. He answers the question, How will I praise God? He will praise the Lord by witnessing to God's great acts in history.

The proper way to interpret a parallel line, then, is to meditate on the relationship between its parts. Nothing can be assumed ahead of time except that the second and following cola will in some way elaborate or specify the thought of the first line (Kugel; Alter; Berlin; Longman 1988).

Parallelism is another reason to slow down and meditate on poetry. It takes some moments of reflection to determine the relationship between the cola and between the lines of a poem in the Old Testament.

Meter. Meter plays an important role in most poetry of the world. Greek and Latin poetry, for example, operate with definite metrical schemes. Thus it is not surprising that early exegetes, trained in classical rhetoric, sought to identify the metrical canons of Hebrew poems by using the categories of classical poetry (e.g., Josephus, Augustine, and Jerome).

The quest for the key to unlock the mysteries of biblical meter have continued unabated ever since. Bishop Lowth, in his magisterial work on Hebrew poetry in the eighteenth century, considered meter along with parallelism to be an essential trait of poetry. He could not discover, however, the particular type of meter that was at work in biblical poetry and attributed his failure to his distance from the time of composition.

Lowth's reticence did not hinder those who followed him. For over two hundred years various scholars have claimed that they have finally discovered metrical canons that allow us to scan and even to reconstruct poems. One has only to look at the text-critical apparatus to see how frequently an emendation is introduced *metri causa* ("for reasons of meter").

The attitude of more recent scholars toward meter has largely changed. An increasing number have come to the conclusion that meter does not exist in Hebrew poetry (O'Connor 1980; Kugel 1981). Although some have continued to argue for metrical schemes (Stuart 1976), that view has been unable to convince many scholars (Longman 1982).

Imagery. Although images are found throughout the Bible, they occur with more frequency and intensity in the poetic portions. Imagery contributes to the compactness of poetry because it allows the authors to communicate their message using fewer words.

Imagery is an indirect way of speaking or writing. Unlike direct statement, an image compares something or someone with another thing or with someone else. For instance, Song of Songs 1:9:

> I liken you, my darling, to a mare
> among Pharaoh's chariot horses.

In this verse the speaker draws a comparison between two things: his beloved and a mare harnessed to a chariot of Pharaoh. The difference between the two objects in the comparison draws our attention and sets us thinking. The next step is to identify the comparison. In this particular case, some historical background is necessary to understand the impact of the compliment. Research makes it clear that the chariots of Egypt used stallions, not mares. The presence of a mare would sexually excite the stallions. Pope points out in his commentary (1977, 336–41) that Israel knew of a battle tactic that called for the release of a mare among the enemy's chariot horses to divert their attention.

In brief, then, poetry is characterized by a high proportion of imagery (Caird). Imagery is a further reason to slow down and meditate on a passage. Imagery excites our imagination. It is a way of saying much in a few words. Images also contribute substantially to the emotional texture of a passage.[3]

Conclusion. Terseness, parallelism, and imagery are the most common characteristics of Hebrew poetry. It is necessary to become familiar with these conventions to interpret the Old Testament properly. Poetry, however, is not read by applying a rigid formula. Parallel lines take on many permutations, and while some images are common, others are unique and must be carefully studied in their context.

In addition, while these are the major poetic ornaments, there are many other devices used by the biblical poets. Handbooks on biblical poetry (Watson

---

[3]For a survey of the major images of the Bible, see Ryken, Wilhoit, and Longman 1998.

1984; Longman 1988) should be consulted for other devices that occur less frequently.

Hebrew poetry is not easy to read. This form requires one to slow down and reflect on the lines, their relationship, and their meaning. The effort is worth it. After all, so much of the Old Testament is poetic in form. Indeed, if all the poetry were gathered together into one location, the corpus would be longer than the New Testament.

The Conventions of Old Testament Stories

Although the Old Testament contains a considerable amount of poetry, it is written primarily in prose. Prose is closer to normal conversational language than is poetry. While cola and stanzas are the building blocks of a biblical poem, sentences and paragraphs are the stuff of prose. It is also true to say that prose, for the most part, is less "literary" than poetry. That is, there is less concern in prose for *how* something is said: the language is ordinarily not as "high" or formal, and fewer metaphors or other images are used.

It is a great mistake, however, to draw a sharp dichotomy between the prose and poetry of the Bible. Most of the narrative of the Old Testament is literarily shaped. Accordingly, the prose of the Old Testament resembles what we call the stories of literature and, not surprisingly, is amenable to a literary analysis.

A literary analysis applies the categories and methods of contemporary literary theory to discover the conventions of Hebrew literature. Alter (1983, 113–17) observed that

> every culture, even every era in a particular culture, develops distinctive and sometimes intricate codes for telling its stories, involving everything from narrative point of view, procedures of description and characterization, the management of dialogue, to the ordering of time and the organization of plot.

A literary approach explores and makes explicit the conventions of biblical literature in order to understand the message it intends to carry. In the following few pages, we will outline the rudiments of a literary approach to Hebrew prose. This study should be supplemented by some of the more complete studies listed in the bibliography.

Genre. The concept of genre relates to both prose and poetry, though we have reserved a discussion of it until now. Genre is of crucial importance, since the reader's identification of a text's genre directs his or her reading strategy (see Osborne 1991 and Longman 1997 for hermeneutical surveys that take seriously the issue of genre).

The study of genre recognizes that there are many different types of literature. Authors choose a vehicle through which to send a message to the reader, and the choice of genre signals to the reader how to take the message. For

If all the poetry of the Old Testament were gathered together into one location, the corpus would be longer than the New Testament.

example, if a text begins, "Once upon a time . . . ," the author has deliberately sent a signal to the reader through the use of a traditional formula. Educated readers and children know that they are to read or hear the story that follows not as a historically accurate tale but as a fairy tale.

The Bible, however, is an ancient text, distanced from us not only by time but also by culture. Genre is one of the conventions that, as Alter described in the quote above, is specific to culture. We must study each biblical book to discern its genre and the implications for its interpretation. In this introductory chapter, we trace the broad outlines of genre study for the interpretation of the Old Testament (see Longman 1987, 76–83; 1988, 19–36 for more detail). Each of the following chapters on the individual books of the Bible will include a discussion of the book's genre.

What Is a Genre? A genre is a group of texts that bear one or more traits in common with each other. These texts may be similar in content, structure, phraseology, function, style, and/or mood.

When writers produce their text, they write in a literary context. That is, they do not produce literary works that are totally new, unrelated to anything that has been done before. They write in a tradition, which they may indeed stretch, but never break. For instance, biographies vary considerably from one another, but by definition they are similar in subject matter—a person's life. Short stories may have different subject matter, but they are united by their relative length and fictionality.

When all is said and done, though, it must be admitted that genre is a fluid category (Longman 1985). This fluidity is seen on two levels. In the first place, one text may belong to different genres on the same level of abstraction. A psalm like Psalm 20 may be categorized with either the kingship songs or hymns. The Micaiah narrative (1 Kings 22; 2 Chron. 18) is simultaneously royal autobiography, battle report, and a story about prophetic efficacy.

In the second place, genres are fluid in that they exist at different levels of abstraction from the text. Since genres are defined by shared traits, there are different levels of genre, depending on the number of similarities with other texts. A broad genre will include many different texts that share a few traits in common. A narrow genre will contain a few texts with many traits in common.

Psalm 98 is a case in point. It is in the genre of "Hebrew poetry" by virtue of its parallelism, terseness, and imagery. On another level, it is in the narrower category of "hymn" because of its mood of unrestrained joy. On an even narrower level, it is a "divine warrior hymn" because it specifically extols God's power as savior in a military situation.

The Significance of Genre in Interpretation. The study of genre has many important implications for interpretation (Longman 1985). Nonetheless, two stand out as most significant: genre as a trigger to reading strategy, and genre as a second literary context.

Consciously or unconsciously, genre identification triggers expectations on the part of the reader. Indeed, it sets a whole reading strategy in motion. Consider the second stanza of Psalm 1:

> Not so the wicked!
> > They are like chaff
> > that the wind blows away.
> Therefore the wicked will not stand in the judgment,
> > nor sinners in the assembly of the righteous.

For various reasons, we immediately recognize these lines as poetry. We expect the use of images and repetitions.

In another passage we read, "In the twelfth year of Ahaz king of Judah, Hoshea son of Elah became king of Israel in Samaria, and he reigned nine years" (2 Kings 17:1). This time our immediate reaction is that the passage is historical narrative, and we recognize that the author intends to communicate historical or chronological information.

We might have the same initial reaction to the following words of Jesus: "Two men went up to the temple to pray, one a Pharisee and the other a tax collector" (Luke 18:10). These words, however, are preceded by "Jesus told this parable." Here we have an explicit genre signal that invokes a reading strategy significantly different from the one we adopted for the 2 Kings 17 passage. Jesus' story is fictional. More specifically, it is didactic fiction—that is, it intends to impart a moral to the hearer or reader.

A second major benefit of the study of genre is that it provides a secondary literary context. This is summed up by Frye (1957, 247–48):

> The purpose of criticism by genres is not so much to classify as to clarify
> ... traditions and affinities, thereby bringing out a large number of literary
> relationships that would not be noticed as long as there were no context
> established for them.

In other words, the very practice of examining a collection of generically related texts will result in the illumination of each individual text. This result is particularly helpful for individual texts that are themselves difficult to understand but that may be elucidated by comparing them with clearer examples in the same genre.

For different reasons, then, it is important to discover the genre of a text. By prompting a reading strategy and ruling out false expectations and standards of judgment of text, genre classification represents an entree to the meaning of the text.

The Dynamics of Narrative. Space prohibits an extensive discussion of the dynamics of biblical narrative, but this short introduction may be supplemented by a number of recent studies (Alter; Longman; Berlin; Sternberg;

Trible). We will here deal with only a handful of selected topics, chosen because they reveal distinctive cultural conventions that provide an insight into reading strategy.

Narrator and Point of View. A description of the role of the narrator in a story is closely related to the issue of point of view. The narrator plays a pivotal role in shaping the reaction of the reader to the passage he or she is reading. The narrator achieves this response in a variety of ways, from presenting and withholding information from the reader to explicit commentary.

Narratives may be divided into first- and third-person types. In the former, the narrator is usually a character in the story and, as a result, presents a limited point of view. Third-person narrative refers to all the characters impersonally, and in this mode the narrator may display omniscience and omnipresence. Most narrative in the Bible is third-person omniscient narrative (the exceptions include, for example, part of Ezra-Nehemiah, Qohelet's "autobiography" in Ecclesiastes, and the "we" passages in Acts). Rhoads and Michie (1982, 36) describe the narrator's point of view in the gospel of Mark:

> The narrator does not figure in the events of the story; speaks in the third person; is not bound by time or space in the telling of the story; is an implied invisible presence in every scene, capable of being anywhere to "recount" the action; displays full omniscience by narrating the thought, feelings, or sensory experiences of many characters; often turns from the story to give direct "asides" to the reader, explaining a custom or translating a word or commenting on the story; and narrates the story from one overarching ideological point of view.

This summary describes the bulk of biblical narrative. The voice of the narrator is often the authoritative guide in the story, providing the point of view. The narrator directs the reader in his or her analysis and response to the events and characters of the story.

It has been pointed out that readers react to a third-person omniscient narrator with unconscious submissiveness. Rhoads and Michie note, "When the narrator is omniscient and invisible, readers tend to be unaware of the narrator's biases, values, and conceptual view of the world" (1982, 39). The choice of such a powerfully persuasive literary device fits in with the Bible's concern to proclaim an authoritative message.

Plot and Character. Plot and character are closely related and may be separated only for purposes of analysis. Henry James (quoted in Chatman 1978, 112–13) related the two elements by asking, "What is character but the determination of incident? What is incident but the illustration of character?"

Descriptions of the dynamics of plot differ in detail among literary critics. The first and simplest is Aristotle's: he describes a plot as having a beginning, middle, and end. Brooks (1984, 5) defines plot in the following helpful way:

"Plot is the principle of interconnectedness and intention which we cannot do without in moving through the discrete elements—incidents, episodes, actions—of a narrative." Poythress (see Longman 1987, 92) provides a more sophisticated analysis of narrative, which may be represented graphically in the following way:

Figure 1
Analysis of Narrative

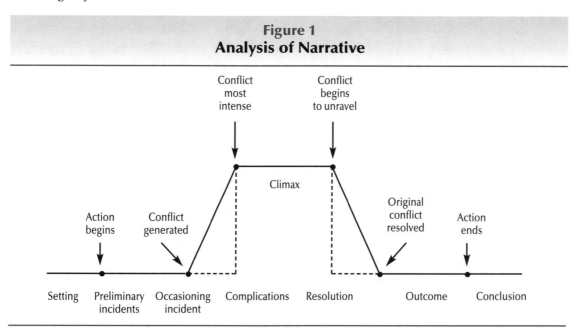

As a general rule, plot is thrust forward by conflict. The conflict generates interest in its resolution. The beginning of a story, with its introduction of conflict, thus pushes us through the middle toward the end, when conflict is resolved.

As one studies Old Testament stories, a helpful first step is to do a simple plot analysis. This study provides the frame for future analysis.

As mentioned above, characters form the gist of a plot. Some Bible readers will hesitate at this point. Should we treat David, Solomon, Ezra, Esther, Jonah—even Jesus—as characters? Such a move appears to equate biblical personages with King Arthur, Billy Budd, Felix Holt, or Captain Ahab and thus to reduce them to fictional beings.

To analyze David as a literary character in a text, however, is not to deny that he was a historical king or that the events reported in the books of Samuel and Kings are accurate. We must admit, however, that we have a selective account of the life of David and can agree that there is value in taking a close look at how the text portrays David and others. In other words, we must recognize that these accounts are shaped—that is, the Bible gives selective, emphasized, and interpreted accounts of historical events.

Conclusion. The prose narratives of the Old Testament are multifunctional. Most intend to impart historically accurate information while leading the reader to a deeper theological understanding of the nature of God and his relationship with his people. The stories, for the most part, are carefully crafted literary works. There are differences between, say, the Joseph narrative and Leviticus in terms of literary intent and sophistication, but in most places we can detect a self-consciousness not only in what is said but also in how it is said. A literary analysis, while only a partial analysis, is helpful toward getting at the author's meaning in a book or a passage of Scripture.

THEOLOGICAL MESSAGE

Bibliography

J. **Barr,** *The Concept of Biblical Theology: An Old Testament Perspective* (Fortress, 1999); R. **Beckwith,** *The Old Testament Canon of the New Testament Church* (SPCK, 1987); W. **Brueggemann,** *Theology of the Old Testament* (Fortress, 1997); W. J. **Dumbrell,** *Covenant and Creation: An Old Testament Covenantal Theology* (Paternoster, 1984); P. **Enns,** *Inspiration and Incarnation* (Baker, 2005); J. **Goldingay,** *Old Testament Theology: Israel's Gospel* (InterVarsity, 2003); G. F. **Hasel,** *Old Testament Theology: Basic Issues in the Current Debate* (Eerdmans, 1975); W. C. **Kaiser** Jr., *Toward an Old Testament Theology* (Zondervan, 1978); M. G. **Kline,** *Images of the Spirit* (Baker, 1980); T. **Longman** III, *Reading the Bible with Heart and Mind* (NavPress, 1997); E. **Martens,** *God's Design* (Baker, 1981); T. E. **McComiskey,** *The Covenants of Promise: A Theology of Old Testament Covenants* (Baker, 1985); J. **Murray,** "Systematic Theology: Second Article," *WTJ* 26 (1963): 33–46; C. M. **Pate** et al., *The Story of Israel: A Biblical Theology* (InterVarsity, 2004); V. S. **Poythress,** *Symphonic Theology* (Zondervan, 1987); O. P. **Robertson,** *The Christ of the Covenants* (Presbyterian and Reformed, 1980); S. L. **Terrien,** *The Elusive Presence: Toward a New Biblical Theology* (Harper & Row, 1978); W. **Van Gemeren,** *The Progress of Redemption: The Story of Salvation from Creation to the New Jerusalem* (Zondervan, 1988); G. **Vos,** *Biblical Theology* (Eerdmans, 1948).

Each of the following chapters concludes with a section devoted to the book's theological message. Since it is unusual for an introduction to include lengthy discussions of theology, allow us to explain. As stated above, we believe that the goal of Old Testament introduction is to prepare students to read its various books with understanding—that is, to provide the kind of preliminary background information that enables them to bridge the gap between the present time and the Old Testament's ancient context. In the study of the Old Testament there are three main areas where this bridging must take place: history, literature, and theology.

In the first place, each book was written in a specific historical context and refers to history in the past and present. Since modern readers are divorced from this ancient context, introductions provide this kind of information as a matter of course. Second, the various books have different literary forms, and these literary forms are difficult for the modern reader to appreciate because the literary conventions of an ancient culture differ from those of a modern one. Without implying a radical separation of the three categories, however, it is appropriate to remark that the purpose of the Bible is neither historical nor literary; it is theological. Thus we believe, third, that it is not only legitimate, but necessary, to introduce students to the theological function of the various Old Testament books in order to achieve reader competence.

It is true that the type of information we are providing in this third section may be found elsewhere: monographs, journal articles, and especially commentaries. But these are scattered resources, so there is value to collecting brief statements of the theological message of each book of the Old Testament in one volume.

Another approach at justifying the inclusion of theology in an Old Testament introduction is simply to point out that the historical, literary, and theological issues are intertwined and thus are most profitably treated together. In any case, the particular type of theological approach that is taken in this introduction needs description, and to that we now turn.

Theology in Its Old Testament Context

Theology here refers to discourse about God, his nature, and, even more important, his relationship with his creatures. It asks the question, What does a book tell its readers about God and their relationship with him?

The first step toward a proper approach to a book's theological purpose is to inquire about the message that is addressed to its ancient audience, the audience that first heard or read the book. What did they learn about God? Our discussion will be limited and will focus on what we have decided are the major themes of a book. This information is achieved when interpreters divorce themselves from their contemporary setting and imagine themselves to be part of the ancient setting of the book. This reading of the text obviously involves bracketing the illumination that the New Testament throws on the Old. Furthermore, as John Murray pointed out a number of years ago, biblical theology stands between exegesis and systematic theology. That is, the major themes of the biblical books are understood through careful exegesis of individual biblical texts. In addition, this study of biblical themes provides the data for the work of systematic theology.

A Center to Old Testament Theology?

Is there unity to the Old Testament message or is there irreconcilable diversity (see most recently the excellent work by Enns [2005])? This question has been at the center of recent theological inquiry into the Old Testament. Indeed, it is a question that has also been of critical importance to the wider discipline of biblical theology.

There have been many attempts, even in recent years, to present the theology of the Old Testament (Hasel). Among recent evangelical writers, this impulse has often taken the form of the study of one central motif under which, it is thought, the whole message of the Old Testament can be explained. God's promise (Kaiser), his design (Martens), covenant (Robertson; McComiskey; Dumbrell), and theophany (Kline) are among the most popular themes selected as a center to Old Testament theology.

Such attempts, however, have failed to persuade a majority of the scholarly community. It does not seem possible to subordinate all of biblical revelation under a single theme. Wisdom literature is the most recalcitrant. As a result, Old Testament theologians have questioned whether there is a center. The most productive response to this situation has come from those who argue that while there is an organic unity to biblical revelation, there is also a proper diversity. Poythress has labeled such an approach "multiperspectival." A multiperspectival approach to biblical theology is more in keeping with the rich and subtle nature of biblical revelation.

The question that biblical theology asks is, What is the message of the Bible? A multiperspectival approach responds that the Bible is about God. The Old Testament in particular is a message from the God of Israel about the God of Israel. However, it is not about Yahweh in the abstract. There is very little, if any, abstract theologizing in the Old Testament. No, the Old Testament is a revelation about Yahweh in relationship with humankind, specifically with his chosen people. Furthermore, this relationship is not so much described as it is narrated. There is a historical dimension to biblical revelation. Thus a proper biblical theology must take into account both the subject matter of the Bible, which is the divine-human relationship, and the fact that the Bible's message is told through time.

Terrien has written a theology with Yahweh as a key, but such a center is too general. To say that the Old Testament is about God, even to say that it is about God in relationship with people, is not really informative. A multiperspectival approach to biblical theology takes account of the many-faceted nature of God's relationship with his creatures. It notes, in particular, the variety of metaphors that emphasize different aspects of that relationship. No one metaphor is capable of capturing the richness of God's nature or the wonder of his relationship with his creatures. God's compassion and love for his creatures lies behind the image of the mother-child relationship (Ps. 131) as well as the marriage metaphor (Song of Songs). His ability to guide his people lovingly is suggested by the shepherd-sheep image (Ps. 23). The Lord's wisdom is displayed in the figure of Lady Wisdom (Prov. 8–9). God's power and authority over his people are communicated through a wide variety of images including that of king (the covenant-treaty image finds its place here) and also the pervasive divine warrior theme.

Thus the most fruitful biblical-theological studies are those that focus on one of these important metaphors of the relationship and follow it from the beginning of biblical revelation to its end, from Genesis to Revelation. Many years ago Vos, the father of modern biblical theology, showed how revelation was a reflex to the history of redemption. Thus as God's redemptive plan progressed through the ages, so the history of revelation unfolded.

The Old Testament from the Perspective of the New Testament

Each of the following chapters contains a section entitled "Approaching the New Testament." Here one or more of the main themes of an Old Testament book are followed into the New Testament. There are many questions surrounding the relationship between the Old and New Testaments that are assumed here but discussed by others elsewhere (e.g., Vos; VanGemeren; Longman 1997). A primary text encouraging such an approach is found in the gospel of Luke. In his post-resurrection appearance to two unnamed disciples, Jesus remarks, properly, "'How foolish you are, and how slow to believe all that the prophets have spoken! Did not the Messiah have to suffer these things and then enter his glory?' And beginning with Moses and all the Prophets, he explained to them what was said in all the Scriptures concerning himself" (Luke 24:25–27). Then again to the broader circle of disciples Jesus said, "This is what I told you while I was still with you: Everything must be fulfilled that is written about me in the Law of Moses, the Prophets and the Psalms" (v. 44).

Roger Beckwith (1987, 111–15) has persuasively shown that in both cases Christ is speaking of the entire Old Testament. In other words, the Old Testament does not simply provide proof texts for the coming Messiah. Its major themes point forward to Christ's coming suffering and glory. It is the hope of the authors that our readers learn to appreciate the christocentric nature of the Old Testament.

CHAPTER TWO

GENESIS

The opening book of the Bible appropriately begins with the phrase "In the beginning." This phrase (Heb. $b^e r \bar{e} \hat{i} t$) is also used as the title of the book in Jewish tradition. Indeed, it is a book of beginnings, or "origins" as its English title, Genesis (derived from the Septuagint [Gen. 2:4a is its likely source]), suggests. Although infrequently cited elsewhere, the book is foundational to the rest of the Torah (the first five books of the Bible), to the Old Testament, and even to the New Testament.

These five books of the Torah share a unity of history, plot, and theme that draws them together, as does their traditional ascription to a single author— Moses (see below). Thus it will be impossible to completely isolate Genesis from the other four books in the following discussion of authorship, style, and theological message.

Genesis covers an immensely long period of time, longer perhaps than the rest of the Bible put together. It begins in the distant past of creation, an event about whose absolute date we cannot even speculate, through millennia to reach Abraham at the end of chapter 11. At this point the story line slows down and focuses on four generations of the family of promise as they move from Mesopotamia to the land of promise, only to conclude the book in Egypt. Thus we have a book of foundations that spans a time period of unknown duration and follows the people of God as they travel from one end of the Near East to the other.

BIBLIOGRAPHY

Commentaries

G. C. **Aalders,** *Genesis* (BSC; Zondervan, 1981); W. **Brueggemann,** *Genesis* (Interp; John Knox; 1982); U. **Cassuto,** *Commentary on Genesis,* 2 vols., trans. I. Abrahams (Jerusalem: Magnes, 1964); G. W. **Coats,** *Genesis with an Introduction to*

Narrative Literature (FOTL 1; Eerdmans, 1983); V. **Hamilton,** *Genesis 1–17* (NICOT; Eerdmans, 1990); idem, *Genesis 18–50* (NICOT; Eerdmans, 1995); J. E. **Hartley,** *Genesis* (Hendrikson, 2000); D. **Kidner,** *Genesis* (TOTC; InterVarsity Press, 1967); K. A. **Matthews,** *Genesis 1:1–11:26* (NAC; Broadman, 1996); R. W. **Moberley,** *The Old Testament of the Old Testament: Patriarchal Narratives and Mosaic Yahwism* (Fortress, 1992); M. **Noth,** *Exodus* (Westminster, 1962); O. P. **Robertson,** *Christ of the Covenants* (Baker, 1980); J. H. **Sailhamer,** "Genesis" (EBC, Zondervan, 1990); N. M. **Sarna,** *Genesis* (JPS Torah Commentary; Jewish Publication Society, 1989); J. **Skinner,** *Genesis* (ICC; T. & T. Clark, 1910); E. A. **Speiser,** *Genesis* (AB 1; Doubleday, 1964); G. **von Rad,** *Genesis* (OTL; Westminster, 1961); B. K. **Waltke,** *Genesis* (Zondervan, 2001); J. H. **Walton,** *Genesis* (NIVAC; Zondervan, 2001); G. J. **Wenham,** *Genesis 1–15* (WBC 1; Word, 1987); idem, *Genesis 16–50* (WBC; Word, 1994); C. **Westermann,** *Genesis: A Commentary,* trans. J. J. Scullian (Augsburg, 1984–86).

Monographs and Articles

T. D. **Alexander,** *Abraham in the Negev: A Source-Critical Study of Genesis 20:1–22:19* (Paternoster, 1997); O. T. **Allis,** *The Five Books of Moses* (Presbyterian and Reformed, 1943); R. **Alter,** *The Art of Biblical Narrative* (Basic Books, 1981); idem, "Harold Bloom's 'J'," *Commentary* 90 (1990), 28–33; J. **Barton,** *Reading the Old Testament* (Westminster, 1984); H. **Blocher,** *In the Beginning: The Opening Chapters of Genesis* (InterVarsity Press, 1984); H. **Bloom,** (with D. Rosenberg), *The Book of J* (Grove Weidenfeld, 1990); P. **Borgman,** *Genesis: The Story We Haven't Heard* (InterVarsity Press, 2001); D. M. **Carr,** *Reading the Fractures of Genesis: Historical and Literary Approaches* (Westminster John Knox, 1996); U. **Cassuto,** *The Documentary Hypothesis,* trans. I. Abrahams (Jerusalem: Magnes, 1961 [Heb. ed., 1941]); B. S. **Childs,** *Introduction to the Old Testament as Scripture* (*IOTS*; Fortress, 1979); D. L. **Christiansen** and M. **Narucki,** "The Mosaic Authorship of the Pentateuch," *JETS* 32 (1989): 465–72; D. J. **Clines,** *The Theme of the Pentateuch* (Sheffield, 1978); T. B. **Dozeman,** *God on the Mountain* (SBLMS; Missoula: Scholars, 1989); B. **Eichler,** "Nuzi and the Bible: A Retrospective," in *DUMU-E-DUB-BA-A: Studies in Honor of Ake W. Sjoberg,* ed. H. Behrens et al. (Samuel Noah Kramer Fund, 1989), 107–19; J. A. **Emerton,** "An Examination of Some Attempts to Defend the Unity of the Flood Narrative, Part II," *VT* 38 (1988): 1–21; J. P. **Fokkelman,** *Narrative Art in Genesis* (Assen and Amsterdam, 1975); R. E. **Friedman,** *The Bible with Sources Revealed* (Harper SanFrancisco, 2003); W. R. **Garr,** *In His Own Image and Likeness* (E. J. Brill, 2003); D. **Garrett,** *Rethinking Genesis: The Sources and Authorship of the First Book of the Bible* (Mentor, 2003); J. **Goldingay,** *Old Testament Theology: Israel's Gospel* (InterVarsity Press, 2003); J. **Hoffmeier,** *Israel in Egypt* (Oxford, 1997); I. M. **Kikawada** and A. **Quinn,** *Before Abraham Was: The Unity of Genesis 1–11* (Abingdon, 1985); K. A. **Kitchen,** *Ancient Orient and Old Testament* (InterVarsity Press, 1967); idem, *The Bible in Its*

World (InterVarsity Press, 1978); H.-J. **Kraus,** *Geschichte der historisch-kritischen Erforschung des Alten Testaments* (Neukirchen-Vluyn, 1956); J. D. **Levenson,** *Creation and the Persistence of Evil* (Princeton University Press, 1988); T. **Longman** III, "Form Criticism, Recent Developments in Genre Theory, and the Evangelical," *WTJ* 48 (1985): 46–67; idem, *How to Read Genesis* (InterVarsity Press, 2005); A. A. **MacRae,** "Response" in *Hermeneutics, Inerrancy, and the Bible,* ed. E. D. Radmacher and R. D. Preus (Zondervan, 1984), 143–62; J. G. **McConville,** *Law and Theology in Deuteronomy* (JSOTS 33; Sheffield: JSOT, 1984); S. E. **McEvenue,** *The Narrative Style of the Priestly Writer* (Rome: Biblical Institute Press, 1971); A. R. **Millard** and D. J. **Wiseman,** eds. *Essays on the Patriarchal Narratives* (InterVarsity Press, 1980); I. **Provan,** V. P. **Long,** and T. **Longman** III, *A Biblical History of Israel* (Westminster John Knox, 2003); R. **Rendtorff,** *Die überlieferungsgeschichtliche Problem des Pentateuch* (1977); J. W. **Rogerson,** *Old Testament Criticism in the Nineteenth Century: England and Germany* (Fortress, 1985); A. P. **Ross,** *Creation and Blessing: A Guide to the Study and Exposition of Genesis* (Baker, 1988); W. H. **Schmidt,** "Playdoyer für die Quellenscheidung," BZ 32 (1988): 1–14; M. **Selman,** "Comparative Customs and the Patriarchal Age," in *Essays on the Patriarchal Narratives,* ed. A. Millard and D. J. Wiseman (InterVarsity Press, 1980), 91–140; J. A. Soggin, *Introduction to the Old Testament (IOT,* Westminster John Knox, 3rd ed., 1989); R. J. **Thompson,** *Moses and the Law in a Century of Criticism Since Graf* (Leiden: Brill, 1970); T. L. **Thompson,** *The Historicity of the Patriarch Narratives* (*BZAW* 133; 1974); J. H. **Tigay,** *The Evolution of the Gilgamesh Epic* (University of Pennsylvania Press, 1982); L. A. **Turner,** "Book of Genesis," DOTP (InterVarsity Press, 2003), 350–59; J. **Van Seters,** *Abraham in History and Tradition* (Yale University Press, 1975); idem, *Prologue to History: The Yahwist as Historian in Genesis* (Westminster John Knox, 1992); B. K. **Waltke,** "Historical Grammatical Problems," in *Hermeneutics, Inerrancy, and the Bible,* ed. E. D. Radmacher and R. D. Preus (Zondervan, 1984), 69–130; G. J. **Wenham,** "The Date of Deuteronomy: Linchpin of Old Testament Criticism: Part II," *Themelios* 11 (1985): 15–17; idem, "Genesis: An Authorship Study and Current Pentateuchal Criticism," *JSOT* 42 (1988): 3–18; idem, *Story as Torah: Reading the Old Testament Ethically* (Baker, 2004); R. N. **Whybray,** *The Making of the Pentateuch: A Methodological Study* (JSOTS 53; Sheffield: JSOT, 1987); M. J. **Williams,** *Deception in Genesis: An Investigation into the Morality of a Unique Biblical Phenomenon* (Peter Lang, 2001).

HISTORICAL BACKGROUND

Composition and Authorship

The issue of the authorship of Genesis is inescapably intertwined with the question of the composition and origin of the entire Pentateuch. Thus this section on authorship will be longer than those found in other chapters, but it will serve as the basis for the following chapters. Even so, this subject needs fuller treatment, and for this reason special attention will be given to secondary literature.

This issue is one that has severely divided conservative scholars from others. The focus of debate, to be defined below, is Mosaic authorship. Debate may be too strong a word, though, since nonconservative scholars quietly ignore those who still defend a traditional viewpoint on authorship (Eissfeldt, *OTI*, 166). In fairness, it must also be said that conservative Christians have been too quick to distance themselves from the possibility of sources and too closed to any evidence of significant post-Mosaic activity. The sharp division between conservatives and others has recently been softened by a stronger emphasis on the thematic unity of the Pentateuch by critics, while conservatives have been less hesitant to speak of sources (e.g., Ross; Wenham). Nonetheless, because of the nature and importance of the issue, we will describe both the traditional conservative and the critical positions, attempt to capture the present state of the discussion, and draw some final conclusions.

Text and Tradition

In a strict sense, the Torah is anonymous. Nowhere do these five books explicitly or implicitly claim that Moses is their exclusive author (Aalders 1981, 5). On the other hand, early Jewish and Christian tradition (see Harrison, *IOT*, 497, who cites Ecclesiasticus 24:23, Philo, Josephus, the Mishnah, and the Talmud) is virtually unanimous in ascribing Genesis through Deuteronomy to him. On what grounds?

Although a connection is never specifically made between Moses and the present Torah (in the Torah), there are a number of references to his writing activity (Allis 1943, 1–18). God commands him to record certain historical events (Ex. 17:14; Num. 33:2) and laws (Ex. 24:4; 34:27) as well as a song (Deut. 31:22; see Deut. 32). While Moses is not identified as the author of much of the Torah, the text does witness to the fact that he was the recipient of revelation and a witness to redemptive acts.

According to later biblical testimony, there was a book of the Law that was associated with Moses' name (Josh. 1:7, 8). Late in the history of Israel, the Israelites could refer to a "Book of Moses" (2 Chron. 25:4; Ezra 6:18; Neh. 13:1). These passages provide strong intrabiblical data for a Mosaic writing, while not being specific about its shape or scope. It is also clear that Jesus and the early church connected much, if not all, of the Torah with Moses (Matt. 19:7; 22:24; Mark 7:10; 12:26; John 1:17; 5:46; 7:23).

This evidence has led to the belief that Moses wrote the Torah. Nonetheless, this statement is always qualified by the admission that certain passages were added after Moses' death. The most obvious of these so-called post-Mosaica is Deuteronomy 34, the narrative of the death of Moses. Although even this chapter has been attributed to Moses by some, most conservatives argue that it was a later addition, possibly added by Joshua (Archer, *SOTI*, 83), though more probably at a later date. Other passages that show indication of post-Mosaic origins include Genesis 11:31, which associates Abraham's Ur with the Chaldeans (a tribe that dominated southern Mesopotamia in the first millennium), and Genesis 14:14, which mentions Dan, an ancient city known by this name only much later (see also Gen. 32:32; 36:31; 40:15; Deut. 3:14; 34:1, 6, 10). Besides these and other passages that were most likely written after the death of Moses, there are also passages that are awkward if they are ascribed to Moses (the so-called a-Mosaica). For instance, Numbers 12:3 refers to Moses as the most humble man who ever lived, scarcely a statement the world's most humble man would make about himself.

Thus the conservative view has always been qualified, however subtly, by admitting non-Mosaic elements to the Torah. While in the minds of most, these non-Mosaic parts are few and far between, it does indicate that to speak of Moses as author of the Pentateuch is not the same as saying that every word is the result of his work. Since there are what appear to be obvious later additions, many conservatives speak in terms of the "essential authorship" of Moses. This expression vigorously affirms Moses as the author of the Torah, while also leaving open the possibility of later canonical additions. Indeed, the post- and a-Mosaica could be just the tip of a large iceberg. There could be considerable later redactional activity that could extend to the latest period of Old Testament history.

Along with this, it must also be admitted that sources have been used in the composition of the Torah. The sources are rarely explicitly cited (see Num. 21:14, the "Book of the Wars of the LORD," which was likely a post-conquest document, and Exodus 24:7, "the Book of the Covenant"). In addition, the *Toledoth* formula may indicate widespread use of sources in the book of Genesis (see discussion under Structure). Neither the biblical text nor the traditional doctrine of Scripture are contradicted by a widespread use of sources on the part of the biblical author.

Historical-Critical Approaches

Space will permit only the most general description of the historical-critical approach to the question of the composition of the Pentateuch. Detailed treatments of the development of the method and its conclusions are available in Kraus, Rogerson, and R. J. Thompson.

Although there were isolated individuals who early on questioned the literary coherence of Genesis through Deuteronomy, the most notable was the philosopher Spinoza (1632–77). He was soon followed by J. Astruc (1684–1766), a physician who developed a simple criterion to differentiate two sources he believed were used in the composition of Genesis. By differentiating these sources on the basis of the use of the two names for God (Elohim and Yahweh), Astruc attempted to defend the Mosaic authorship of Genesis. His method, however, was soon divorced from his conclusions as scholars during the next century (most notably Eichhorn, professor at Göttingen from 1788 to 1827) and beyond continued to search for sources. In the period that ended in 1880, a number of criteria had been developed to isolate four basic sources (and at this period they followed this order): the Jehovist source (J), the Elohistic source (E), the Priestly source (P), and the Deuteronomic source (D). None of these was directly associated with Moses.

The 1880s were a pivotal decade in the development of the historical-critical approach to the Pentateuch because this decade saw the publication of J. H. Wellhausen's monumental *Prolegomena zur Geschichte Israels* (published in 1883, English in 1885). Wellhausen's work had a massive influence because, for the first time, he was able to associate the history of the development of the Pentateuch with the history of the development of Israelite religion in a way that convinced most of the leading scholars of Europe, England, and America, while pushing his critics (notably Hengstenberg and Delitzsch) to the margins of scholarship. Even today, with all of the basic criticisms of the documentary hypothesis (see below), to reject it is to be relegated to the realm of the "naive and arrogant" (Childs, *IOTS*, 127).

The classic expression of the documentary hypothesis may be associated with Wellhausen's viewpoint, though today very few scholars would consider themselves Wellhausian. Nonetheless, since it is his view against which everyone places his or her own opinion, it is helpful to describe it.

Wellhausen argued, in continuity with the scholarship that preceded him, that the Pentateuch was composed of four basic sources. These sources could be differentiated from one another on the basis of the following criteria:

1. The use of different divine names, especially Yahweh (J) and Elohim (E).

2. The existence of doublets, that is, the same basic story that is repeated more than once, though different characters may be involved. Doublets could be repeated accounts (e.g., the wife-sister stories, Gen. 12:10–20; 20; 26) or separate incidents serving the same purpose in the narrative context (e.g., Joseph's dreams of stars and sheaves, Gen. 37:5–11).

3. Differences of style, including the use of two different names to designate the same person, tribe, or place (Reuel/Jethro; Horeb/Sinai; Jacob/Israel; Ishmaelites/Midianites).

4. Different theologies. For instance, J is commonly characterized as portraying God anthropomorphically; D presents a form of retribution theology; P is replete with priestly concerns and tends to emphasize the transcendence of God. The differing viewpoints in the putative documents are often alleged to show progression in Israel's theology from animism, to henotheism, and finally to monotheism. Furthermore, traditional critical scholars see a chronological progression among the sources in terms of form of worship, for example, the issue of centralization of worship. According to traditional criticism, J is

unaware of centralization (Ex. 20:24–26); D calls for it (Deut. 12:1–26); and P assumes it (Ex. 25–40, Numbers, and Lev. 1–9).

On the basis of these criteria, Wellhausen differentiated the following sources (given with dates and descriptions):

J. By the time of Wellhausen, J was universally recognized as the earliest source. It had not been many years before his work, though, that E1, now called P, was considered the earliest. The characteristic that resulted in its name (Jehovist, Yahwist) is its use of the covenant name for God. Most critics assign J to the early monarchy, in the tenth or ninth century BC, and because of its positive references to Judah in texts like Genesis 49:8–12, believe it originated there. J's style is often characterized as "clear and direct, but its simplicity is that of consummate art" (Speiser 1964, xxvii). In its style and in its theology, J contrasts most sharply with P. While P focuses on God, J attends to man and earth. J uses anthropomorphisms to describe God; for instance, God molds man from the clay of the earth, and he walks with Adam in the Garden. J begins in Genesis 2 (the so-called second creation account) and continues through the book of Numbers, though it may include a few verses in Deuteronomy. (For a complete listing of passages associated with J, consult Eissfeldt, *OTI*, 199–201.) The literary critic Harold Bloom has presented a provocative analysis of J in a form that has received a wide readership. His view that J was a woman, perhaps even David's granddaughter, is pure speculation (Alter 1990).

E. While J is associated with God's name, Yahweh, E is identified by the use of the more generic name, Elohim. This source is dated about a century later than J (because it presumes the division of the kingdom, cf. Soggin, *IOT*, 107) and is given a northern setting (though Eissfeldt, *OTI*, 203, doubts it). This latter opinion is inferred from what looks like an emphasis on northern matters and northern personalities such as Joseph. In theology, E focuses more on "religious and moralistic" concerns (Harrison, *IOT*, 502). E is more fragmentary than J or P (and recent opinion is assigning more and more of E to J, see below). It opens with Genesis 15 and continues through Numbers 32, though a few passages in Deuteronomy are also assigned to E (see full list in Eissfeldt, *OTI*, 200–201).

D. One of Wellhausen's contributions was to reverse the order of D and P (Rogerson 1985, 266). Thus the third narrative strand isolated by classical source criticism is D (Deuteronomic), associated in the Torah predominantly with the book from which it derives its name (see extensive discussion there). The core of the book of Deuteronomy is often identified as the document that was found in the temple during the reign of Josiah (2 Kings 22–23, but see Wenham 1985). There are great debates over the form of the document found at this time, but in any case, almost all critics date D to the time of Josiah (late seventh century). While D rarely extends back to the first four books of the Torah, its influence is felt strongly through much of the canon. D's theology will be explained in the chapter on the book of Deuteronomy.

P. P is perhaps the most distinctive of the four strands of the Pentateuch. Its concerns include chronology, genealogy, ritual, worship, and law—areas easily associated with the priesthood, and thus its name, Priestly source.

This source has traditionally been given a late date in the fifth or the fourth century and is related to the exile and after. P reflects postexilic order of the priesthood and also that time period's concern with obedience to the law. This date is for the collection that now constitutes P, since much of the material is believed to have come from an earlier time. One argument used to support the late date of the source is the fact that P shows influence only on Chronicles, a book dated to the fifth century at the earliest (Eissfeldt, *OTI*, 208).

P is extensive throughout Genesis to Numbers. Great portions of these books are assigned to P, as are a few verses of Deuteronomy (see Eissfeldt, *OTI*, 188–89). They can stand side by side with other material from other sources (such as Gen. 1:1–2:4a=P and Gen. 2:4b–25=J) or interweave with other sources (see traditional analysis of the flood narrative into J and P).

McEvenue (1971) has studied P's style in the manner of New Criticism (close reading). He has argued against the typically negative assessments of P's literary quality and theological contribution.

Some scholars conclude that P was not itself a continuous narrative source, but rather that "P" was the final redactor of the Pentateuch (see Wenham, 1987, xxxii, with bibliography).

Redactors. So far we have described the four main narrative sources in the Torah. These are not simply brought together side by side, but are creatively integrated with one another. Those responsible for the editing of the sources are commonly referred to as redactors or editors. These redactors were responsible for the growth of the tradition, as first of all J and E were joined, then D with JE, and finally P with JED. The most important redactor would have been the last, since he put the distinctive cast on the final form of the Torah. For a recent presentation of one view of the documentary hypothesis, see the interesting work of Friedman (2003).

ALTERNATIVE CRITICAL VIEWS

The pages above have described the classical documentary hypothesis. As we will mention below, there are a number of variations on the theme, and indeed, there has been some fundamental questioning of the approach. Before evaluating the documentary hypothesis, however, three alternative critical views will be

> *P is perhaps the most distinctive of the four strands of the Pentateuch. Its concerns include areas easily associated with the priesthood, and thus its name, Priestly source.*

briefly described: (1) the fragmentary approach, (2) the supplementary approach, and (3) form criticism and tradition history.

Fragmentary Approach

The distinguishing characteristic of the documentary hypothesis (as a particular type of source analysis) is not that it postulates sources to explain the composition of the Pentateuch, but rather that these sources were originally four independent, continuous narratives. The fragmentary approach denies that the sources had an original independent unity. The first scholars to describe such an approach seriously were A. Geddes, J. S. Vater, and W. M. L. de Wette (late eighteenth and early nineteenth centuries, see Rogerson 1985, 35, 154–57). The documentary hypothesis has a far greater burden of proof—not only must it identify the sources for individual blocks of material (fragments), but it must also show that the fragments themselves originally belonged to the four continuous narratives the theory posits.

Supplementary Approach

Other scholars felt that there was a single basic document that was then supplemented either by a later author who used it or by a later redactor who used one document (*Grundschrift*) as the base and another to supplement it. As developed by the early H. G. A. Ewald (nineteenth century) and others (including the early Delitzsch), E was understood to be the basic document, and J was the text used to supplement it at a later date. Soon after that, however, E was divided into two separate documents (thereafter called E and P), thus resulting in more than one continuous document. Some recent studies (Wenham, see below), however, have returned to a form of supplementary hypothesis, based on the fact that E is rarely recognized as an independent source these days.

Form Criticism and Tradition History

Influenced by the folklore studies of his day, H. Gunkel significantly altered the course of the study of the origin of the Pentateuch at least for a number of important German scholars (Longman 1985). Instead of documentary sources (whose existence he never contested), Gunkel focused on form-critical units, primarily saga, in the Pentateuch. He posited their oral origin and their development through time. In the next generation, his thought particularly influenced Noth, von Rad, and Westermann, all of whom (like Gunkel) continued to support the traditional documentary hypothesis. Noth, though, concentrated on what he considered to be the six basic themes of the Pentateuch:

1. Primeval history
2. Patriarchal stories
3. Exodus
4. Sinai

5. Wilderness wanderings

6. Settlement

Noth argued that these six themes arose and developed independently, coming together only at a late stage. Von Rad agreed and drew attention to the absence of Sinai from the exodus tradition. He cited Deuteronomy 26:5–10 (an early statement of faith that does not mention Sinai) as strong evidence that these two traditions had an independent history of development.

It was Rendtorff in the German tradition (*OTI*, 160–63, and 1977[1]), who recognized the incompatibility of tradition history and documentary approaches. In his work he describes how independent traditions are brought together into individual complexes of tradition (such as the different patriarchal stories—Abraham, Isaac, Jacob, and Joseph). These were then combined into even larger complexes—the patriarchal narrative, with insertions uniting them. After this, the narratives were brought into even larger units by means of theological redaction and finally given a Deuteronomistic and Priestly revision.

Rendtorff is certainly correct to move away from a documentary approach that sees the present text as the awkward joining of different continuous documents. His approach takes into account the smoothness of the narrative in a way foreign to the older critical approach. But more recent literary approaches question the older approach, and indeed the tradition-critical approach, at an even deeper level.

EVALUATION OF THE CRITICAL APPROACH

The critical approach to the Pentateuch has always found conservative resistance from both Jewish and Christian circles. Incisive attacks on the method were rendered in the nineteenth century most notably by Hengstenberg and Delitzsch (who held a modified source approach himself), and in the twentieth century by Allis, Cassuto, Kitchen, Wenham, and even more recently by Alexander. All of these works may still be read today with great profit, though their most pointed criticisms are directed at Wellhausen, many of whose distinctive views are no longer live options. While the work of these scholars has often been unjustifiably ignored by the mainstream of biblical scholarship, it is gratifying to see their arguments reappearing (without acknowledgment) in recent criticism of traditional pentateuchal studies from within critical circles. Indeed, at the present time traditional source criticism is on the wane in all circles. The cutting edge of scholarship is devoting less and less energy (there are exceptions; see Emerton) to the question of sources and more and more to the final composition of the Pentateuch and the individual books within it. This

---

[1]See also the Scandinavian school represented by I. Engnell, *Critical Essays on the Old Testament*, ed. J. T. Willis and H. Ringgren (London, 1970).

trend away from documentary analysis is attributable to two causes: (1) problems with the method and (2) newer and more holistic approaches to the text. These two are closely related. The problems have encouraged interpreters toward a holistic reading of the text, and a holistic reading of the text accentuates the problems. Nonetheless, these two points will be described separately.

Problems

Recent years have witnessed a surge of skepticism about the documentary hypothesis (Kikawada and Quinn; Whybray; Alexander). In the first place, there is doubt concerning the criteria (listed above) used to separate the sources. For instance, the use of different divine names (particularly Elohim and Yahweh) may result from stylistic practice rather than the presence of sources. One alternative explanation is suggested by Kikawada and Quinn (1985, 19) who state:

> When discussing aspects of primeval history appropriate to wisdom literature, he would use Elohim; when dealing with those aspects emphasizing specific revelations, he would feel inclined to introduce Yahweh.

Although it would be impossible to prove that every case of Elohim and Yahweh have this kind of intentional usage, it does cast suspicion on its use as a criterion for separating sources (see Wenham in Millard and Wiseman 1980, 157–88, for a third alternative). Furthermore, the use of multiple names for a god in a single text is reasonably common in extrabiblical Near Eastern texts.

No one can deny the presence of doublets, similar or nearly similar stories, in the pentateuchal narratives. A quick reading of Genesis 12:10–20; 20; and 26 (actually a triplet!) is convincing enough. In each text, a patriarch protects himself in a foreign court by passing off his wife as his sister. Traditional criticism takes a source-critical approach and assigns the first and the last to J, the middle story to E (Speiser 1964, 91). Recent study on Semitic literary style suggests that such repetitions were consciously employed in the literature to achieve a certain effect. For example, Alter's studies show that these doublets are actually "a purposefully deployed literary convention" that he names "type scenes" (1981, 50). Alter defines a type scene as a commonly recurrent narrative pattern in which the author highlights similarities in order to draw the reader's attention to the connection between the two stories. Alter contrasts this literary solution to the presence of "couplets" over against the source hypothesis. He is content to highlight the literary connections between the stories. Those who believe that God acts purposefully in history can see his hand behind the text as he shapes the events himself (see full discussion in Alter 1981, 47–62; and in Moberly, 31–32).

One can easily discern the difference in style between the storylike J and the more list-oriented, formal P. However, is this a difference in authorship or a difference in subject matter? And if one granted a difference of authorship (or more precisely, the use of existing sources for, say, genealogies), on what grounds should P be dated later than J?

Concerning the presence of two names for some places, people, or things, the solution is much the same as for doublets. The phenomenon has been noted in extrabiblical texts whose single authorship is beyond doubt (Harrison, *IOT*, 521–22; Kitchen 1967), and in some cases a literary impulse may be at work (Alter 1981, 131–47).

The last criterion is that of theological differences. Virtually no one today accepts Wellhausen's idea that in the pages of the Old Testament one could trace a religious evolution from animism to henotheism to monotheism. His Hegelian presuppositions are all too well recognized and rejected by contemporary critics. Furthermore, Wellhausen was motivated by the Romantic desire to recover the ideal, primitive past, and he applied this concept to his study of the Bible.

Today's mind-set is different for the most part. Even in the critical circles that are directly descended from Wellhausen, the focus of attention has shifted away from source analysis and toward the final form of the text. In addition, many of the theological differences that have been used to delineate sources may be interpreted in a different fashion and point in a different direction. For instance, concerning the issue of the centralization of worship, there is no question but that the Pentateuch records different attitudes toward the central altar. It is true that Exodus 20 assumes more than one place of worship, while Deuteronomy 12 calls for centralization and the texts in Leviticus and Numbers assume it. A close examination of Deuteronomy 12, however, indicates that the call was not for an immediate centralization but for one that would take effect when God had given them "rest from all [their] enemies around [them]" (Deut. 12:10). This condition did not arise until late in David's reign (2 Sam. 7:1), and soon after that the temple was constructed. Until that time, the law in Exodus 20 was in effect, regulating the building of multiple altars. The laws in Leviticus and Numbers envision the time after the central sanctuary is built. (For an alternative harmonization, see McConville.)

Besides the criteria themselves, the critical approach has always foundered on the failure to achieve consensus in the delineation of the sources. Apparently a subjective element is involved that casts doubt on the scientific basis for the method. This failure to achieve consensus is represented by the occasional division of source strata into multiple layers (see Smend's J1 and J2) that often occasions the appearance of new sigla (for instance, Eissfeldt's *L[aienquelle]*, Noth's *G[rundschrift]*, Fohrer's N [for Nomadic], and Pfeiffer's S [for Seir]. A further indication of the collapse of the traditional documentary hypothesis is the widely expressed doubt that E was ever an independent source (Voz, Rudolph, Mowinckel; cf. Kaiser, *IOT*, 42 n.18). Similar disagreements are also found in the dating of the sources. J has been dated to the period of Solomon by von Rad, though Schmidt would argue for the seventh century, and Van Seters (1992, 34) has advocated an exilic date. While most scholars believe P is postexilic, Haran has argued that it is to be associated with Hezekiah's reforms in the eighth century BC.

Although disconcerting, these disagreements do not disprove the existence of sources. They cast doubt on the possibility of clearly distinguishing the sources within the final form of the text and encourage interpreters to concentrate on that level.

Recent Literary Approaches to the Pentateuch

In the 1970s, but particularly in the 1980s and 1990s, an interest in the literary approach to the Bible recaptured the attention of biblical scholars (see Literary Analysis in chap. 1). This interest has reemphasized the literary quality of much biblical narrative, and in particular the narratives of the book of Genesis (Fokkelman; Clines; Kikawada and Quinn; Wenham; Whybray; Borgman). The literary approach often brackets questions concerning origins and historical reference, and thus the issue of literary sources is put to the side by these researchers. Their results, however, demonstrate that the book of Genesis has a literary unity that displays artistic brilliance when judged according to the canons of its own Semitic culture.

The book of Genesis has a literary unity that displays artistic brilliance when judged according to the canons of its own Semitic culture.

These studies have had a debilitating effect on the practice of source criticism. While many feel that source analysis can go hand in hand with the literary approach, others recognize that it actually undercuts the possibility, or at least the necessity, to do source analysis. If the Joseph story, for instance, shows such a level of cohesiveness and literary excellence as it stands in the text, it is almost certainly not the result of a mechanical union of two diverse sources. A recent trend toward canonical criticism (Childs) also points to the importance of the text before us (not an earlier form of it) as the exegetically relevant object of study (see Barton 1984 for the close connection between the literary approach and canonical criticism).

Summary and Conclusions

Among critical approaches to the question of the composition of the Pentateuch, the documentary hypothesis has held dominance for over two hundred years (since Eichhorn). It has been viewed with tremendous confidence as one of the "assured results of criticism" for over a century (since the work of Wellhausen). Surprisingly, it is today only loosely held as problems are recognized, alternatives are given, and scholarly energy is expended in other directions. It is easy to predict that the next decade will witness some defense of the method, but these will likely be dying gasps of an approach whose relevance is no longer seen.

Dozeman (1989, 1) is correct when he characterizes the state of the question as a "creative period." By this he means in part that it is a period of transition away from the classic documentary hypothesis. It is difficult to say what the new consensus will be or even if a consensus will emerge, but it is certain that the alternative will not be a return to a precritical acceptance of Mosaic authorship with only minute exceptions (the so-called a- and post-Mosaica) or to anything like a classic documentary approach. In the period immediately preceding the first edition of this book, it appeared that critical scholarship was leaning in the direction of a tradition-historical approach along the lines represented by Rendtorff and by Dozeman. In any case, the concern was and still is increasingly on the final form of the text. Indeed, Dozeman's thesis accentuates a positive picture of the work of the final redactors of the tradition. However, one of the most recent attempts to shift the focus of Pentateuchal studies back on diachronic issues has come from Carr's *Reading the Fractures of Genesis* (1996). Here he argues for a type of diachronic analysis that takes into account the insights gained by synchronic narrative analysis and also considers the insights into literature of deconstruction. Still, he believes he can distinguish a non-P source from a P source.

On the other hand, the traditional evangelical position on the question of the composition of the Pentateuch is undergoing a subtle but important shift as well. Evangelical scholars recognize that the Pentateuch contains pre-Mosaic sources as well as post-Mosaic glosses. Indeed, some are willing to identify the sources along the lines of the older documentary hypothesis. Wenham (1987, xxxvii–xlv), for instance, believes that P is an ancient source and that J is the final editor-author (and he implicitly allows that J is Moses). Ross (1988, 35 n.12), nevertheless, reverses the sigla, arguing that J is the source and P is Moses.

It should be clear that the evidence is elusive. The best interpretation of the data admits the presence of sources and indications of development without dogmatically delineating their scope or date. The post- and a-Mosaica display the presence of glosses; the question remains their extent.

In the final analysis, it is possible to affirm the substantial Mosaic authorship of the Pentateuch in line with the occasional internal evidence and the strong external testimony, while allowing for earlier sources as well as later glosses and elaboration. It is in keeping with the evidence to remain open and nondogmatic concerning the particulars of the composition (for instance, what is pre-Moses, Moses, post-Moses—see Christensen and Narucki 1989, esp. 468, for some helpful analogies). In any case, our concern is the final form of the text, since that is what God has given the church as canon for its edification.

ANCIENT NEAR EASTERN BACKGROUND

While all Old Testament literature has an ancient Near Eastern background, the interpretation of Genesis is especially aided by an acquaintance with comparable literature from Mesopotamia, Canaan, and Egypt. While this is not the place to go into detail (see Longman 2005), it is appropriate to provide a partial survey to show its importance.

In the first place, the creation account should be studied in the context of ancient Near Eastern, particularly Babylonian and Ugaritic, texts. From Babylon, we have the creation text known as the *Enuma Elish,* which describes the god Marduk's victory over the sea monster Tiamat and his forming, from her dead body, the heavens and the earth. Afterwards, he executes her henchman-consort Qinqu, and from his blood and the clay of the earth, he forms humanity. The myth Atrahasis adds the purpose of the creation of humans. They are to take the place of the lesser gods in their work as irrigation diggers. The Ugaritic myth of Baal may well provide a west Semitic parallel to this story. Here the chief god Baal vanquishes the sea god Yam. Though the clay tablet breaks at this point, most scholars think that it went on to describe the creation of the heavens and earth. When Genesis 1–2 is read in the context of these myths, we clearly see the polemic. Creation in Babylon is the result of divine sexual activity and conflict, whereas in Genesis God is sovereign, self-sufficient, and supreme. In the Near East, the creation comes from preexistent stuff, while in the Bible creation is from nothing (contra Levenson).

Secondly, the flood story should be studied in the context of ancient flood myths, particularly that recorded in the eleventh tablet of the *Gilgamesh Epic* (see most recently, Mitchell 2004). The similarities between the two accounts are overwhelming. Divine anger leads to global destruction by means of a flood. However, one human being and his family escape by building an ark on which he brings the animals. When the flood waters recede, the ark comes to rest on a mountain. To check whether it is safe to disembark, the flood hero, Utnapishtim, releases three birds in succession. When he leaves the ark, he first offers a sacrifice. The contrasts are equally compelling, however, most notably in the conflict between the gods and also their own fear when the flood waters rise. Indeed, the whole idea of a flood turns out to be a bad idea for the gods since they depend on the sacrifices of human beings for food. When Utnapishtim offers his sacrifice, the text says they gather around "like flies." The relationship between these texts is debated, some believing that the biblical text is simply a rewrite of the Babylonian original. However, it may also be suggested that the Babylonian and the biblical versions descend from a common tradition. For those who accept a biblical worldview, it may be hypothesized that the Babylonian version got corrupted to conform to the polytheistic religions of its people.

Thirdly, the patriarchal narratives should be read in the light of nearly contemporary texts from Mari and Nuzi that contain similar social customs. Though these similarities have been overplayed in the past and used inappropriately at times to argue for an early date of these materials, they still provide helpful information that enriches our understanding of the time period (Selman). In the same way, studying the Joseph narrative in the light of what we know about Egyptian customs is also illuminating (Hoffmeier).

LITERARY ANALYSIS

Structure

The book of Genesis is a pie that may be cut in more than one way, depending on the perspective and interests of the reader. Perhaps the most fascinating structural device is the so-called *Toledoth* formula, which clearly displays the structure intended by the author of the final form of the text. The Hebrew phrase *'ellēh tôlᵉdôt* occurs eleven times (2:4; 5:1; 6:9; 10:1; 11:10, 27; 25:12, 19; 36:1, 9 [may be part of the same section signified by 36:1]; 37:2). The phrase has been translated a number of different ways, including "these are the generations," "this is the family history," and "this is the account." The phrase is followed by a personal name, with the exception of the first occurrence, which names instead the "heavens and the earth." Following this first occurrence, the narrative divides into the following sections: "these are the generations of" Adam, Noah, Noah's sons, Shem, Terah, Ishmael, Isaac, Esau (the formula is given twice in this section, 36:1 and 9), Jacob. Thus the book of Genesis has a prologue (1:1–2:3), followed by ten episodes. The person named is not necessarily the main character but is the beginning point of the section that also closes with his death. This device, accordingly, provides a sense of unity to the book of Genesis that cuts across the hypothetical sources discussed in the previous section. Critical scholars associate the formula with P.

A second approach to the structure of Genesis considers the book's transitions in terms of content and style. In the first place, it is possible to divide the book into two subsections: Genesis 1:1–11:32 and 12:1–50:26. The former is the Primeval History and covers the time between creation and the tower of Babel. These chapters cover an indeterminably long period of time in the far distant past. The second part of Genesis is characterized by a slowing down of the plot and a focus on one man, Abraham, and his family for four generations. These chapters, often called the patriarchal narratives, follow the movements of the people of promise from Abraham's call in Genesis 12:1 to the death of Joseph at the end of the book. Both of these divisions of Genesis begin with a creation initiated by the word of God. In Genesis 1:1 God calls the universe into existence by the power of his word; in Genesis 12:1 God calls a special people into existence by the power of his word (Brueggemann, 105).

A further subdivision can be made within the second part of Genesis between the patriarchal narratives and the Joseph story. The former are episodic, short accounts of the events in the lives of Abraham, Isaac, and Jacob. The Joseph story (Gen. 37; 39–50) is a connected plot, which recounts how Abraham's family came to Egypt in the first place. The story continues in the book of Exodus (see Theological Message). It provides the transition between a family of seventy to seventy-five people that went down into Egypt and a nation that, four hundred years later, is poised on the edge of the Exodus.

The Genre of the Book of Genesis

Our focus in this section is on the book as a whole in its present canonical form. This discussion does not deny the obvious variety within the book of Genesis, a variety observed as the reader moves from the broad temporal sweep and spatial scope of the first eleven chapters to the episodic patriarchal narratives and then finally to the storylike character of the Joseph account. Nor does it gainsay the variety of forms that compose the whole book: genealogy (chap. 5), battle report (chap. 14), poetic testament (chap. 49), and many others.

In spite of the obvious variety within the book, it is useful to reflect on the genre of the book as a whole. After all, it contains a unity of narrative plot that takes the reader from the creation of the world to the sojourn in Egypt. It recounts past events and does so with a chronological structure. This last sentence sounds like a definition of a work of history, and indeed, such a label makes sense of the generic signals that the reader encounters in the work.

Much of the book, for instance, is recounted using the so-called *waw* consecutive verbal form that is the basic characteristic of narrative in the Hebrew Bible (Aalders, 45). Furthermore, the frequent *tôlᵉdôt* formulae that structure the book also indicate a historical impulse. In addition, there are no dramatic genre shifts between the book of Genesis and the rest of the Pentateuch, and none between the Pentateuch and the so-called historical books that would lead us to read it in any other way than as history. Indeed, if we are speaking of the original intention of the biblical writer(s), the style of the book leaves little space to argue over the obvious conclusion that the author intended it to be read as a work of history that recounts what has taken place in the far-distant past.

We must emphasize that we are describing the intent of the book as far as it can be discerned from the text itself. It is possible that a book intends to be historical but fails to do so successfully. Nonetheless, a long tradition of scholarship in both Jewish and Christian circles supports the view that the narrative intends to impart information about events and characters of the past. Of course, Genesis, like all biblical history writing, may be described as "theological history," in the sense defined in chapter 1.

It has been only in the twentieth century and into the twenty-first that alternative genres have been seriously proposed. (For a detailed account of critical attitudes toward Genesis in the twentieth century, see Van Seters 1992, 10–23.) This is the case, for instance, with Gunkel's belief that Genesis is composed primarily of saga. Coats defines saga as "a long, prose, traditional narrative having an episodic structure developed around stereotyped themes or objects. . . . The episodes narrate deeds or virtues from the past insofar as they contribute to the composition of the present narrator's word" (1983, 319). While this definition is not inherently antagonistic toward a historical intention in the text, it is usually assumed that such sagas "tend to consist of largely unhistorical accretions upon a possibly historical nucleus" (Moberly, 36). Other proposed genre labels for all or part of Genesis include novella, legend, fable, etiology, and myth (Coats, 5–10). Such terms are obviously prejudicial to the historical intentionality of the book. They are, however, motivated more by modern interpreters' unwillingness and inability to accept the reality of the world of Genesis than by a clear insight into the intention of the text.

Van Seters (1992) is an example of a recent critic who affirms the historical intentionality of Genesis (or at least of the Yahwist) by means of comparison with Greek historiography. Of course, this does not mean he believes that the events that the Yahwist narrates actually took place in space and time.

The generic signals of the book require the reader to receive the book as an attempt to explain Israel's past, a work of history. (See chap. 1 for a fuller description of biblical historiography.) Debates have raged over the accuracy of the account. The opening chapters have brought the Bible into conflict with science (Blocher), and biblical scholars have locked horns over the extrabiblical evidence surrounding the patriarchal materials (most helpfully, see Selman; and more recently Provan, Long, and Longman, 112–17).

The function of the history contained in Genesis is to provide a prologue and foundation of the founding of the nation of Israel and the giving of the law in the book of Exodus. It recounts how God chose Abraham and guided his family as his special people.

Literary Artistry in Genesis

As a result of the new interest in literary artistry and close reading of the Scriptures (see Literary Analysis in chap. 1), Genesis has newfound respect. Scholars cite the stories of Genesis as prime examples of sophisticated literary prose in the Bible. Space does not permit a lengthy discussion of the style of Genesis, but interested readers may consult the helpful studies of Alter, Berlin, Fokkelman, and Borgman. Indeed, it is the recognition of the artistry of Genesis that has led commentators' attention away from source studies and has renewed interest in the overall theological message of the book.

One brief example must serve to illustrate the pervasive and profound literary artistry of the book of Genesis. Fokkelman's close reading of the Tower of Babel story (Gen. 11:1–9) has revealed its intricate design. He begins his study by noting word plays throughout this short episode. Certain word groups are bound together by their similar sound: "let's make bricks" (*nilbᵉ nâ lᵉ bēnîm*); "bake them thoroughly" (*niśrepâ śᵉrēpâ*); "tar" and "mortar" (*hēmār/hōmer*). There is also an alliteration between "brick" (*lᵉ benâ*) and "for stone" (*lᵉ'âben*). These nearly similar sounds give the story a rhythmic quality to it that draws

> It is the recognition of the artistry of Genesis that has led commentators' attention away from source studies and has renewed interest in the overall theological message of the book.

the reader's attention not only to the content of the words but to the words themselves. Other repeated words also sound alike: "name" (*šēm*), "there/that place" (*šām*), and "heaven" (*šāmayîm*) "The place" (*śām*) is what the rebels use as a base for storming "heaven" (*šāmayîm*) in order to get a "name" (*šēm*) for themselves. God, however, reverses the situation because it is "from there" (v. 8) that he disperses the rebels and foils their plans. The ironic reversal of the rebels' evil intentions is highlighted in more than one way by the artistic choice of words. Fokkelman lists the numerous words and phrases that appear in the story with the consonant cluster *lbn*, all referring to the human rebellion against God. When God comes in judgment, he confuses (*nbl*) their language. The reversal of the consonants shows the reversal that God's judgment effected in the plans of the rebels. This reversal is also reflected in Fokkelman's analysis of the chiastic structure of the story:

```
A    11:1
   B    11:2
      C    11:3a
         D    11:3b
            E    11:4a
               F    11:4b
                  X    11:5a    "But the Lord came down"
               F'    11:5b
            E'    11:5c
         D'    11:6
      C'    11:7
   B'    11:8
A'    11:9
```

Unity of language (A) and place (B) and intensive communication (C) induce the men to plans and inventions (D), especially to building (E) a city and a tower (F). God's intervention is the turning point (X). He watches the buildings (F') people make (E') and launches a counter plan (D') because of which communication becomes impossible (C') and the unity of place (B') and language (A') is broken.

Fokkelman's analysis of Genesis 11:1–9 shows on a small scale what is true on a larger scale: Genesis is an artfully constructed piece of literature.

THEOLOGICAL MESSAGE

As the first book of the Torah and indeed as the opening work of the canon, the book of Genesis is a book of foundations. It serves as an introduction to the Mosaic law, and it begins the history of redemption that occupies the rest of the Bible. While the plot imparts a unity to the book, it is best to survey its theological message by examining its three major sections.

Genesis 1–11: From Creation to the Tower of Babel

The Bible may be described as a four-part symphony, moving from creation to the fall, then on to redemption and finally re-creation. The book of Genesis lays the foundation for the rest of the Bible by narrating briefly the first two movements, while beginning the third. The fourth movement is the subject of the last two chapters of the Bible (Rev. 21–22), and it is interesting to note the pervasive creation imagery in those chapters (Rev. 21:1, 5; 22:1–6). The end of history is like the beginning in that a harmonious and wonderful relationship with God is reestablished.

Thus the book of Genesis begins with the creation. It is striking to observe, in the light of the discussions of the past century and a half, how little the text is concerned with the process of creation (see Walton, 82–92). Creation is described in such a way as to show God to be the sole cause behind the creation of the universe and of humankind. Genesis 1 and 2 reveal that God is the powerful Creator and also that men and women are his dependent creatures. The description of the creation in these chapters, however, does not allow us to be dogmatic over such questions as the length of time and order of God's creative process (cf. the debates between those who hold to a twenty-four-hour, day-age, or framework hypothesis approach to Genesis 1). On the one hand, the passage definitely guards against a mythological or parabolic interpretation (contra Goldingay, 42–130; see discussion of genre above). On the other hand, the theme of Genesis 1 and 2 is not how God created, but that God created the creation, and that he made it from no preexistent stuff (*creatio ex nihilo*) in contrast to the beliefs of the other Near Eastern religions (contra Levenson). There is a further emphasis on the fact that when God created creation he pronounced it good. The impact of this phrase may be seen when it is remembered that the book of Genesis was written at a time when the creation was anything but good; it was filled with sin and injustice. Thus the reader realizes that the present sinful world is not the result of God's activity but of the activity of his creatures.

Indeed, Genesis 3–11 presents story after story that emphasizes the sin and rebellion of God's creatures. Furthermore, these episodes narrate the rapid moral decline of humankind as time moves on. While sin spreads and increases, God reveals himself to be longsuffering and patient with his creation. Westermann (1948) has vividly shown this movement by noting the structure of the five principle stories of Genesis 3 through 11. He notes that there is a pattern of sin, followed by a judgment speech, and then the execution of God's judgment. Men and women deserved death; however, from the time of their first sin (Gen. 2:17), God always reached out to them in a gracious way to mitigate the punishment.

While Westermann's pattern may not hold up in detail under rigid scrutiny (note the double use of 6:8, 18ff., and 7:6–24), it nonetheless does reveal the important theological motifs of Genesis 3–11 (Clines, 63). In the first place, sin intensifies as time progresses. "From Eden to Babel . . . there is an ever growing

	Sin	Speech	Mitigation	Punishment
		Table 1		
	Literary Patterns in Genesis 1–11			
Fall	3:6	3:14–19	3:21	3:22–24
Cain	4:8	4:11–12	4:15	4:16
Sons of God	6:2	6:3	6:8, 18ff.	7:6–24
Flood	6:5, 11ff.	6:7, 13–21	6:8, 18ff.	7:6–24
Babel	11:4	11:6ff.	10:1–32	11:8

'avalanche' of sin . . . . a movement from disobedience to murder, to reckless killing, to titanic lust, to total corruption and violence, to the full disruption of humanity" (Clines, 65).

Second, the punishment for sin also increases. This intensification may be seen not only in the episodes themselves but also in the diminishing human life span as attested by the genealogies (Gen. 5). Perhaps the most striking message of Genesis 3–11, however, is the overwhelming patience and love of God, who pours out blessing upon blessing on this rebellious people.

As Clines points out, however, this schema does not do justice to the importance of the flood narrative in Genesis 1–11. The flood climaxes God's judgment against the rebellious people of the world. Indeed, by emphasizing the importance of the flood, it is possible to recognize the connections between the creation account and the flood narrative, thus establishing a three-part pattern that moves from Creation to Uncreation and then finally to Re-creation (Clines, 73–76). The flood in essence takes one giant step backward in the creation process. The waters return the world to a state that may be described as "formless and empty" (Gen. 1:2). In other words, there is a reversal of creation. Noah and his family provide a link with the old creation order, but the language of the Noetic covenant (9:1–7) echoes the language of Genesis 1–2 in such a way as to see that Noah is in effect a new start. The similarities with the creation texts include the command to multiply (9:1, 7), the talk about mankind made in the image of God (v. 6), as well as God's commands to reestablish the daily and seasonal cycles (8:22).

When such an emphasis is placed on the flood narrative, which after all is the longest episode in the first part of Genesis, then the Tower of Babel story seems anticlimactic. This short and artistically precise passage (Fokkelman) is, however, the precursor to the Abraham story as the focus of the narrative moves from the entire world to one person who will found a new nation.

Genesis 12–36, 38: The Patriarchal Narratives

In a sense, these divisions are artificial. Note how Genesis 38 links the patriarchal narratives with the Joseph story. For purposes of description, however, we will treat these two parts separately.

Genesis 11:27–32 (the conclusion to the genealogy of Gen. 11:10–26) provides the link between the primeval history and the patriarchal narrative in that it narrates the move of Abram (later called Abraham) from Ur to Haran along with his father. It was in Haran that the Lord called Abram in words whose importance reverberate through the canon:

Go from your country, your people and your father's household
    to the land I will show you.
I will make you into a great nation
    and I will bless you;
I will make your name great,
    and you will be a blessing.
I will bless those who bless you,
    and whoever curses you I will curse;
and all peoples on earth
    will be blessed through you. (Gen. 12:1–3)

God promised Abram that he would have numerous descendants who would form a mighty nation, thus implying that he was to receive a gift of land from the Lord. Also, God told him that he would be blessed and would also serve as a channel of God's blessing to others. On the basis of these promises, Abram left Haran and traveled to Palestine.

The stories that follow have the consistent theme of the fulfillment of these promises and the patriarchs' reaction to them. Abram's life in particular focuses on his wavering faith toward God's ability to fulfill his promises.

Each of the episodes of his life may be read as a reaction to God's promises. For instance, when he first arrives in Palestine, Abram encounters an obstacle to the fulfillment of the promise of the land when a famine forces him to flee to Egypt (Gen. 12:10–20). He obviously does not trust God to care for him, for he forces Sarah to lie about her relationship with him in order to save his own life. By way of contrast, in the next story (chap. 13), Abram responds with calm confidence that God is with him. The Lord has so prospered Abram that he and Lot, his nephew, must find separate pasturage. Abram could have grasped at the promise by claiming that God gave him the promise of the land, so he should have first choice. Instead, he allows Lot to choose. As he might have expected, Lot chooses the best land, the region around Sodom and Gomorrah (the attentive reader would immediately connect this reference to Gen. 18). Abram does not hesitate, but allows him to take this prime land.

This is not the end of the story, however. Later Abram betrays his growing lack of confidence in God's ability to fulfill the promises by trying to grasp at the promise of offspring by using means common in the ancient Near East for having a family in spite of barrenness (Gen. 15:3 [adopting a household slave]; chap. 16 [concubinage]). However, God in his grace comes to Abram/Abraham several times in order to confirm his intention to fulfill his promises (chaps. 15, 17, 18). By waiting until Abraham and Sarah's extreme old age to give them a child, God demonstrates that this child is truly a divine gift. Isaac is not the product of purely normal human means. After the birth of Isaac, Abraham demonstrates that at last he has come to a profound trust in God's willingness and ability to fulfill his promises. In Genesis 22, God commands Abraham to take this son of the promise to Mount Moriah in order to sacrifice him. Abraham shows that he now trusts God completely when the narrative informs the reader that he silently and without complaint carried out God's request. The reader is left to make the connection between the Mount Moriah of the sacrifice (Gen. 22:2) and the location of the future site of the temple (2 Chron. 3:1). In any case, the lives of Abraham and the other patriarchs illustrate for the reader the life of faith. They show how God works out his promises in spite of obstacles and threats to their fulfillment in order to show that they are divine gifts (Clines, 77–79).

Genesis 37, 39–50: The Joseph Story

The Joseph story, though different in style from that of the patriarchs, continues the theme of the patriarchal narratives—God overcomes obstacles to the fulfillment of the promise. In this case, the family of God is threatened by famine that could easily have brought all the promises to a rapid end. Nonetheless, God wonderfully preserved his people through near-miraculous means.

Joseph himself gives us a theological grid through which to view the events of his life. After his father's death, his brothers worry that Joseph will now take vengeance against them. They thus approach him, asking that he spare their lives. Joseph's response indicates his awareness of God's guiding hand in the course of his life: "Don't be afraid. Am I in the place of God? You intended to harm me, but God intended it for good to accomplish what is now being done, the saving of many lives" (Gen. 50:19–20).

God reveals himself in the life and story of Joseph to be a God in control of even the details of history. From a human perspective, it appears that Joseph falls prey to ill luck as he moves from Palestine to Egypt and from Potiphar's house to prison. Indeed, his life seems determined by those who seek to harm him, his brothers and Potiphar's wife. Joseph, however, is aware that God is the one behind the events of his life. Furthermore, he knows that God has overruled the evil intentions of his brothers and others and raised him to a position within the government in order to bring about the salvation of his family and the continuation of the covenant promise.

This theme, that God overrules the wicked intentions of men and women in order to save his people, runs throughout the Old Testament, but perhaps nowhere more explicitly than in the Joseph narrative.

APPROACHING THE NEW TESTAMENT

As might be expected from such a rich and varied book, it is impossible to exhaust its biblical-theological implications. At best, we can only be suggestive.

Genesis 1–11. Creation, as has often been stated, is the foundation of all that follows. The garden of Eden represents everything that men and women have lost due to their sin in the past and everything they yearn for in the present. The account of the fall (Gen. 3) triggers the whole history of redemption that concerns most of the rest of the Old and New Testament. The creation account, however, is particularly echoed in Revelation 21–22. The "new earth and new heavens" will reflect many of the features of the garden of Eden, thus expressing the belief that the end will involve a restoration of the beginning.

The account of the fall records not only God's judgment but also the mitigation of that punishment. Perhaps most notable of all is his curse upon the serpent:

> Cursed are you above all the livestock
>> and all wild animals!
> You will crawl on your belly
>> and you will eat dust
>> all the days of your life.
> And I will put enmity
>> between you and the woman,
>> and between your offspring and hers;
> he will crush your head,
>> and you will strike his heel. (Gen. 3:14–15)

This curse has come to be known as the Protoevangelium, the earliest statement of the gospel of salvation, though some dispute the appropriateness of this. That there is an ancient anticipation of Christ the deliverer here may be supported by the allusion to this curse in Romans 16:20 and by the fact that the entire New Testament witnesses to Christ's defeat of Satan on the cross (see Rev. 12:9 for the identification of the serpent with Satan). That defeat leads to the reversal of God's judgment on humankind. In the same way, it is striking to read the account of the gift of the knowledge of foreign languages at Pentecost in the light of the Babel story.

Genesis 12–36. Theologically speaking, the centerpiece of this middle section of Genesis is the Abrahamic covenant. Here God promises Abraham descendants and lands and finally assures him that he will be a blessing to the nations. The Old Testament acknowledges that these promises are fulfilled in part within its own time frame as Isaac is born and from him descends the Israelite nation, as Israel itself occupies Palestine, and as individuals from the nations (Rahab, Naaman, Nebuchadnezzar) turn to Israel's God. All of the promises of God, however, including those to Abraham, "are 'Yes' in Christ" (2 Cor. 1:20), and Christians are now considered "Abraham's offspring" (Rom. 9:8). For a more detailed discussion of the relationship between the Abrahamic covenant and the new covenant, consult Robertson.

Even further, however, the book of Hebrews (11:8–19) draws our attention to Abraham's life as a struggle of faith. As described above, Abraham received God's promise and then struggled in the face of obstacles to the fulfillment of that promise. So Hebrews draws an analogy with Christians. They too have received the promise of God but daily confront obstacles. Abraham is presented as an example in order to support the Christian reader in this struggle.

Genesis 37–50. Joseph recognized that he was not at the mercy of chance; he was deeply aware of God's hand in his life, positioning him to serve as a deliverer of his people (Gen. 50:20). In this regard, Joseph's life foreshadows Jesus Christ. In the same way as did Joseph, God overruled the intentions of wicked people in order to bring about deliverance. Jesus, after all, was crucified by people who only sought to destroy him. God, however, "intended it for good to accomplish what is now being done, the saving of many lives" (Gen. 50:20; see Acts 2:22–24). In the light of this truth that God overrules evil for good, the Christian may rest content in the well-known promise that "God works for the good of those who love him" (Rom. 8:28).

CHAPTER THREE

EXODUS

As the second part of the Pentateuch, the book of Exodus continues the story that began in Genesis (see Fokkelman, 59–62). The Hebrew title for the book is "And these are the names" (*we ellēh šemôt,* the opening words of the book) and demonstrates the connection with Genesis in two ways. In the first place, the book begins with the conjunction *and,* showing that it is a continuation of a preceding narrative. Second, the opening phrase repeats a phrase in Genesis 46:8, both passages naming those "sons of Israel" who went down to Egypt at the time of Joseph. The concluding episode in Genesis (50:22–26) also highlights the connection between Genesis and Exodus. At his death, Joseph requested that his bones be carried up from Egypt. When Israel finally left Egypt, the text mentions that Moses took the bones of Joseph (Ex. 13:19).

Thus, Exodus continues the story of Genesis. There is, however, a considerable time lapse between the two books. When the curtain closes in Genesis, the people of God are a moderate-sized extended family prospering in the land of Egypt. When the action begins in Exodus, they are a large group, nation-sized, living in bondage and cruel oppression.

BIBLIOGRAPHY

Commentaries

U. **Cassuto,** *Commentary on Exodus,* trans. I. Abrahams (Jerusalem: Magnes Press, 1967); B. S. **Childs,** *The Book of Exodus* (Westminster, 1974); G. W. **Coats,** *Exodus* (FOTL; Eerdmans, 1999); R. A. **Cole,** *Exodus* (TDOT; InterVarsity Press, 1973); J. I. **Durham,** *Exodus* (Word, 1987); P. **Enns,** *Exodus* (NIVAC; Zondervan, 2000); T. E. **Fretheim,** *Exodus* (Interp; Westminster John Knox, 1990); W. H. **Gispen,** *Exodus* (BSC; Zondervan, 1987); D. E. **Gowan,** *Theology in Exodus: Biblical Theology in the Form of a Commentary* (Westminster John Knox, 1994); J. B. **Hyatt,** *Exodus* (NCB; Eerdmans, 1971); W. **Kaiser,** "Exodus" (EBC, Zondervan, 1990);

M. G. **Kline,** *Treaty of the Great King: The Covenant Structure of Deuteronomy* (Eerdmans, 1963); M. **Noth,** *Exodus* (Westminster, 1962); W. H. C. **Propp,** *Exodus 1–18* (AB; Doubleday, 1998).

Articles and Monographs

G. L. **Bahnsen,** *Theonomy in Christian Ethics* (Craig Press, 1977); J. J. **Bimson,** *Redating the Exodus and Conquest* (JSOTS 5; Sheffield: JSOT, 1978); W. M. **Clark,** "Law," in *Old Testament Form Criticism* (Trinity University Press, 1974), 99–140; G. W. **Coats,** *Rebellion in the Wilderness: The Murmuring Motif in the Wilderness: Traditions of the Old Testament* (Abingdon, 1968); T. B. **Dozeman,** *God on the Mountain* (SBLMS; Scholars Press, 1989); J. P. **Fokkelman,** "Exodus," in *The Literary Guide to the Bible,* ed. R. Alter and F. Kermode (Harvard, 1987): 56–65; D. W. **Gooding,** *The Account of the Tabernacle* (Cambridge, 1959); B. **Halpern,** "Radical Exodus Redating Fatally Flawed," *BAR* 13 (1987): 56–61; M. **Haran,** *Temples and Temple-Service in Ancient Israel* (Oxford, 1978); J. K. **Hoffmeier,** *Israel in Egypt: The Evidence for the Authenticity of the Exodus Tradition* (Oxford University Press, 1997); C. J. **Humphreys,** "The Number of People in the Exodus from Egypt: Decoding Mathematically the Very Large Numbers in Numbers 1 and 26," *VT* 50 (2000): 196–213; P. **Kiene,** *The Tabernacle of God in the Wilderness of Sinai* (Zondervan, 1977); K. A. **Kitchen,** *Ancient Orient and the Old Testament* (London, 1966); idem, *On the Reliability of the Old Testament* (Eerdmans, 2003); D. **Livingston,** "The Location of Biblical Bethel and Ai Reconsidered," *WTJ* 33 (1970): 20–44; idem, "Traditional Site of Bethel Questioned," *WTJ* 34 (1971): 39–50; T. **Longman** III, "The Divine Warrior: The New Testament Use of an Old Testament Motif," *WTJ* 44 (1982): 290–307; idem, "God's Law and Mosaic Punishment Today," in *Theonomy: A Reformed Critique,* ed. W. S. Barker and W. R. Godfrey (Zondervan, 1990): 41–54; idem, *Literary Approaches to Biblical Interpretation* (FCI 3; Zondervan, 1987); idem, *Immanuel in Our Place* (P and R Publishing, 2001); idem, *Reading the Bible with Heart and Mind* (NavPress, 1997); T. **Longman** III and D. **Reid,** *God Is a Warrior: Studies in Old Testament Biblical Theology* (Zondervan, 1995); G. **Mendenhall,** "Covenant Forms in Israelite Tradition," *BA* 17 (1954): 50–76; P. D. **Miller** Jr., *The Divine Warrior in Early Israel* (Harvard University Press, 1973); R. **Moberly,** *At the Mountain of God: Story and Theology in Exodus 32–34* (Sheffield: JSOT, 1983); I. **Provan,** V. P. **Long,** and T. **Longman** III, *A Biblical History of Israel* (Westminster John Knox, 2003); J. R. **Rushdoony,** *The Institutes of Biblical Law* (Craig Press, 1973); H. W. **Soltau,** *The Holy Vessels and Furniture of the Tabernacle of Israel* (London, 1865); M. **Sternberg,** *The Poetics of Biblical Narrative* (Indiana University Press, 1985); A. **Stock,** *The Way in the Wilderness* (Liturgical Press, 1969); B. K. **Waltke,** "The Date of the Conquest," *WTJ* 52 (1990): 181–200; J. H. **Walton,** "Book of Exodus," DOTP (InterVarsity Press, 2003), 249–72; J. W. **Wenham,** "Large Numbers in the Old Testament," *TynBul* 18 (1967): 19–53.

HISTORICAL BACKGROUND

Authorship and Composition

The authorship and composition of Exodus as part of the Pentateuch was covered in general in the preceding chapter. It remains only to point out a few items that relate specifically to Exodus.

According to traditional critical scholarship, the book of Exodus continues the three main sources that characterize the first four books of the Pentateuch, namely J, E, and P. As Noth (1962, 13) remarked, though, "The literary relationships are rather more complicated than in Genesis." For one thing, it is very difficult to separate J and E. For another, though it is clear that P comes into its own particularly in the latter half of the book with its focus on cultic matters, it is difficult to tell whether it is a separate source or an extensive redaction. There is also the question of a possible Deuteronomic redaction.

One important issue that comes up for the first time with the book of Exodus is the relationship between narrative and the corpora of law. Within Exodus there are the Decalogue (Ex. 20:1–17) and the Book of the Covenant (Ex. 20:22–23:19). Whereas at one point the Decalogue was considered to come from E (and therefore contrasted with Deuteronomy 5=J), most now believe that law (with the exception of Exodus 34=J) is composed of independent compositions that were brought into the narrative at a later point.

On the other hand, scholars since Mendenhall have pointed to Hittite treaties with their integration of law and historical prologue in order to assert the integrity of the two parts. Recently, the Hittite treaty model has been criticized and even discounted due to the fluidity of the genre, among other things, but the basic point that law flows from history stands intact. Indeed, recently Kitchen (2003, 283–307) has given us the fullest discussion of all the relevant ancient treaties to date in support of the idea that the evidence argues for a traditional date of authorship.

In the light of our conclusion in the chapter on Genesis, it should be pointed out that Exodus witnesses to Mosaic writing activity explicitly in three chapters: Exodus 17:14; 24:4; 34:4, 27–29.

The Nature and Date of the Exodus

Read naturally and without an agenda, the biblical account gives a straightforward version of the exodus, at least in broad outline. The descendants of Abraham had grown into a mighty people in fulfillment of the divine promise (Gen. 12:1–3; 15:5). Indeed, we know that during the initial phase of the wilderness wanderings males over twenty years numbered 603,550, according to the book of Numbers (1:46). This implies that the total population numbered in the millions. These people were living in state slavery, serving the interests of the pharaoh. God raised up Moses as their leader and used him to bring Israel out of Egypt's grasp through miraculous wonders, plagues, and the Red Sea crossing. The book of Exodus also narrates the beginning of the wilderness wanderings, particularly the giving of the law at Sinai and the building of the tabernacle.

In light of the fact that the text does not name the pharaoh of Egypt at the time, the dating of the exodus event is difficult. Two biblical texts are relevant to the date of the exodus. The first and most direct statement is 1 Kings 6:1: "In the four hundred and eightieth year after the Israelites had come out of Egypt, in the fourth year of Solomon's reign over Israel, in the month of Ziv, the second month, he began to build the temple of the LORD." This passage places the exodus 480 years before Solomon's fourth regnal year, for which scholars are able to give an absolute date of 967 BC. The date of the exodus is then 1447 BC or thereabouts, allowing for the possibility of a rounded-off number (see Bimson, 81–86). The second relevant passage is Judges 11:26 (see Bimson, 86–111). The context is Jephthah's negotiations with the king of Ammon. The latter is attempting to take back the area of Moab that he claims is his because Moab had previously been under Ammonite control. In response, Jephthah claims that Israel had held this area since they entered the land three hundred years before, thus placing the end of the wanderings three hundred years before his time. As we work our way back from this text to the time of the exodus, we must admit that the evidence is not as compelling as the 1 Kings passage, since we are not as sure about Jephthah's date as we are about Solomon's. A close study of the chronological notices in the book of Judges allows the interpreter to arrive at an approximate date for Jephthah's time period. The end result is that the Judges passage collaborates the 1 Kings passage in placing the exodus in the fifteenth century BC.

In the modern period, this picture of the exodus and wilderness wanderings has been questioned and modified either slightly or radically, or it has been downright rejected (so the minimalists; see The Challenge of Minimalism in chap. 1). Among the questions that are raised against the biblical description of the exodus is, in the first place, the number of people who left Egypt. Some argue that the Hebrew word translated "thousand" is really a group measurement much smaller than one thousand (Mendenhall; Wenham; for the most recent discussion, see Humphreys). Others feel that the biblical account is hopelessly exaggerated and postulate that only a small group actually left Egypt. This small group, often associated with the Levites, joined a larger group in the land of Canaan, and the tradition of the exodus became the tradition of the whole group. A second question concerns Moses. Is the tradition surrounding Moses accurate? Scholars have gone as far as to question the existence of Moses. Third, the date of the exodus has frequently been challenged. Many date the exodus much later than the biblical passages alluded to above seem to date it. Some reject outright the date given by the Bible in favor of a later date in the thirteenth century (Hoffmeier 1997; Kitchen 2003) or, less frequently, the twelfth or eleventh centuries, as supported by some archaeological study. Others adopt this later date but find an alternative explanation for the biblical passages in question (Kitchen 1966; Harrison, *IOT*). The description of the tabernacle in the last part of the book has also been subject to question from a historical perspective. Many scholars argue that the tabernacle never existed and is simply a later projection of the temple back into the time of the wilderness ("desert," TNIV).

These and other similar questions have led to alternative reconstructions of the exodus and the conquest. The exodus and the conquest are closely related, with the wilderness wanderings serving as the middle part of the three-part redemptive action by God. A fuller discussion of the conquest and alternative models of the emergence of Israel may be found in the chapter on Joshua.

While there have been more radical approaches (see the description in Waltke), the most common solution to the questions raised about the exodus is to date it in the thirteenth century and to argue that a smaller group actually left Egypt than that apparently described by the Bible.

There are two main reasons why a fifteenth-century date is often rejected, though the most natural reading of the biblical text places it there. The first is Exodus 1:11, which describes the Israelites as slave laborers who "built Pithom and Rameses as store cities for Pharaoh." Archaeologists have identified these two cities with Tell el-Maskhouta and Tanis respectively (Bimson 1978, 37, citing Naville). These two sites show no occupation in the fifteenth century, and Naville has demonstrated that el-Maskhouta was built by Rameses II (c. 1290–1224 BC). Also, the name of the city of Rameses is most naturally associated with the pharaoh of that name.

The second reason for dating the exodus to the thirteenth century is the archaeological remains in Palestine that have been associated with the conquest by scholars like Albright, Wright, and Yadin. A whole series of sites shows destruction layers in the thirteenth century, and these have been identified with the incursion of Joshua and the Israelites into Palestine. The economically inferior dwellings that arose on top of these destruction layers are taken as further indications that the seminomadic Israelites were the ones who destroyed and then settled the sites.

Before going on to give arguments for an early date of the exodus, we will pause and deal with these two issues. Bimson (1978) has shown how uncertain it is to associate Rameses and Pithom with Tanis and Tell el-Maskhouta. He writes that "contemporary scholarship substantially favours Qantir as the site of Pi-Ra'messe" (42) and demonstrates that Qantir, unlike Tanis, evidences earlier (Middle Kingdom) occupation that allows for a fifteenth-century date for the site. The name of the city Rameses in Exodus 1:11 could, like that of Dan in Genesis 14:14, be the result of a later textual updating. Furthermore, Bimson shows the likelihood that the city of Pithom may be identified with either the site of Tell er-Retebah (so Kitchen 2003, 257–58) or Heliopolis, once again sites with a history earlier than the thirteenth century (Bimson, 47–48).

Bimson's interpretation of the archaeological evidence is even more provocative in answer to the second argument used to deny a fifteenth-century date for the exodus. He points out that there is no reason to believe that the thirteenth-century destruction layers mentioned above should be identified with Joshua's conquest. He rightly notes that there are many other candidates for the cause of the city burnings during the volatile period of Judges that identify earlier destruction layers with the supposed Egyptian attacks upon Hyksos fortifications in Palestine during the Middle Bronze period. He thus believes that a better harmonization between text and archaeology takes place when one associates the earlier destructions with the conquest by Joshua and brings their date down into the fifteenth century BC. Bimson realizes that he cannot argue dogmatically for his conclusions due to the difficulty of interpreting archaeological evidence, but his alternative approach demonstrates that the dogmatic conclusions of proponents of a thirteenth-century date should be looked at skeptically.

Perhaps the most significant secondary argument (see Bimson, 67–80) for the late date of the exodus is based on Nelson Glueck's survey of the Transjordan region. In a series of studies done in the 1930s, Glueck published the results of his surface survey of the area across the Jordan. It was in this area, according to the book of Numbers, that the wandering Israelites encountered groups such as the Moabites and the Edomites. Glueck, however, claimed that there was no evidence of permanent habitation in this region from 1900 BC until 1300 BC, thus adding fuel to the argument in favor of a late date. This survey has been used by many up until the present day to cast aspersions on the biblical account of the exodus and the conquest. Glueck's survey, however, was a primitive one by today's standards. He simply sent out his survey teams to map tells and to pick up a selection of sherd types from the top of the tell that he then used to date the periods of occupation. Today, it is recognized that some control must be placed on sherd selection—for instance, dividing the tell up into small squares and then selecting all the sherds of a certain percentage of the squares (randomly chosen by computer). Otherwise, the samplers are attracted only to certain types of sherds (colored or with certain types of rims) that seriously skew the dating. In addition, hard evidence against Glueck's survey has come forth with the discovery of Middle Bronze tombs and architectural structures in the area around Ammon (Bimson, 70–71). Glueck's survey should no longer be used as evidence against an early date of the exodus.

In conclusion, the archaeological arguments that some take to lead inexorably toward a late date of the exodus are questionable or wrong. If Bimson's critical work does anything (and he has his vociferous critics, e.g., see Halpern), it leads to a better perspective on archaeological results. They are not brute facts with which the biblical material must conform and that can prove or disprove the Bible. Rather, archaeology produces evidence that, like the Bible, must be interpreted.

The archaeological arguments that some take to lead inexorably toward a late date of the exodus are questionable or wrong.

It is with such an understanding that Bimson presents his own reconstruction of the archaeological evidence as he asks whether it is capable of harmonization with the biblical material. He notes that there are two clusters of destruction layers in the towns said to have been destroyed by Joshua during the conquest, those dated to the thirteenth century and associated with the conquest by scholars like Albright, Wright, and Yadin, and those traditionally dated to the sixteenth century (Middle Bronze Age) and identified as the work of Egyptian armies as they pursued the Hyksos into Palestine. We observed above how Bimson dissociates the conquest from the thirteenth-century evidence (and suggests the volatile period of the Judges). He goes further and critiques the flimsy evidence on which the earlier destruction layers are associated with the Hyksos and then argues that these layers should be dated in the fifteenth century and associated with Joshua's conquest. Thus, Bimson states, "I have tried to show that the Conquest and the end of the MBA cities can both be dated in such a way that they are seen to be the same event" (229). He further notes that there is almost unanimous agreement between the biblical account of city destructions and the cities that demonstrate destruction layers in the fifteenth century (230) as opposed to those cities that show destruction layers in the thirteenth. The only exception is Ai, which continues to vex any dating of the exodus and perhaps involves a faulty site identification (Livingston 1970; Bimson, 218–25).

Thus it appears that the archaeological evidence may be harmonized with the most natural reading of biblical texts that describe a fifteenth-century exodus and conquest. The text, however, does not permit certainty on the subject. There are arguments for a late date for the exodus (Harrison; Kitchen 1966; Bright) and in favor of a smaller number of Israelite participants (Wenham; Humphreys) that treat the text with integrity. Thus we agree with the statement of Waltke (1990, 200) on the date of the conquest (which, of course, is integrally connected with the date of the exodus) that "the verdict *non liquet* must be accepted until more data puts the date of the conquest beyond reasonable doubt. If that be true, either date is an acceptable working hypothesis, and neither date should be held dogmatically."[1]

LITERARY ANALYSIS

While the book of Exodus is a continuation of Genesis (and much of the discussion in that chapter applies here), it is still helpful to isolate it and to examine its own structure, genre, and style.

---

[1] See more recently the fuller discussion found in Provan, Long, and Longman 2003, and for more on alternative models of Israel's emergence in Palestine, see the chapter on Joshua.

Structure

Exodus may be divided in more than one way, depending on what the reader attends to in the book. For instance, Durham (1987) correctly notes a three-part structure based on location:

Part One: Israel in Egypt (1:1–13:16)
Part Two: Israel in the Wilderness (13:17–18:27)
Part Three: Israel at Sinai (19:1–40:38)

Another equally fruitful analysis on the structure of the book, however, highlights the contents:

I. God Saves Israel From Egyptian Bondage (1:1–18:27)
II. God Gives Israel His Law (19:1–24:18)
III. God Commands Israel to Build the Tabernacle (25:1–40:38)

With this structure, we can clearly see the book's concern with salvation, law, and worship.

God Saves Israel From Egyptian Bondage (1:1–18:27). The first section is the most action-filled part of the book. This is matched later only by chapters 32–34. Indeed, the exodus account is one of the foundational stories of the Old Testament, narrating the paradigmatic salvation event of ancient Israel (see Theological Message).

The first chapter states the problem and introduces the conflict that propels the plot. The people of God are forced to be slaves in Egypt. Not only that, but the pharaoh so fears the Israelites that he attempts a ruthless form of population control (Ex. 1:18–22). The situation is dire, and in the second chapter we are introduced to the main human character of the book, Moses, whose name is perhaps rivaled only by those of Abraham and David in terms of importance in the Old Testament period.

Miraculous events surround the occasion of Moses' birth and upbringing. God not only provides for his deliverance as an infant but causes him to be raised in the very household of Pharaoh. The narrative thus emphasizes that God is full of surprises as he works Israel's salvation.

Chapters 3 and 4 are transitional as providential events push Moses out of Egypt and into the desert where he will spend most of the rest of his life. In the pivotal third chapter, Moses learns more about the nature of God as well as the focus of his own mission: to be God's human agent of deliverance for Israel in Egypt.

Chapters 5 through 12 narrate Moses' struggle with Pharaoh that is also a fight between deities, since Moses represents Yahweh and Pharaoh is himself thought to be one of the Egyptian gods (see also the claim of 12:12). The reader observes God's double-edged work as he saves his people Israel by judging the Egyptians. As the plagues occur one after another, they increase in intensity of destruction; they also more clearly distinguish between the Israelites, who are unaffected by the plagues, and the Egyptians, who are struck hard. This culminates in the tenth plague with the death of the Egyptian firstborn, while the Israelites celebrate the Passover.

The first part of the book climaxes in 13:17–15:21, the account of the departure from Egypt and the crossing of the Red Sea (Heb. Reed Sea; for the argument that the sea is actually one of the freshwater lakes north of the western finger of the Red Sea, see Hoffmeier 1997). It is here that God releases Israel from bondage and brings death upon the Egyptians. The Red Sea crossing is the epitome of God's work of salvation, since in the same act God brings deliverance by splitting the sea and also judgment by causing the waters to close again. It is in this instance that God explicitly shows himself as the divine warrior for the first time (Ex. 15:3). His warring activity and his control over the sea have a background in ancient Near Eastern religion and speak polemically against paganism.

As Durham points out, the next chapters (15:22–18:27) show a change of location. Israel moves from Egypt to the wilderness. This location will remain stable in the narrative through the rest of the Pentateuch. The next move will be into the Promised Land with the conquest. From the start, a theme emerges that is characteristic of the wilderness narratives: the complaints and grumblings of the ungrateful people of Israel. They murmur against God, though they also see evidence of God's presence in great power again and again.

God Gives Israel His Law (19:1–24:18). Three months after leaving Egypt, Israel arrives at Mount Sinai, a location where they spend almost two years. Even more striking, the rest of the book of Exodus, all of Leviticus, and the first part of Numbers (through 10:11) take place at Sinai.

The first significant event at Sinai was the giving of the law. The account begins with an awesome display of God's presence. He appears on the mountain with smoke and fire (Ex. 19:16–19). The mountain becomes holy space because of his presence.

Moses ascends the mount and receives the Ten Commandments (Ex. 20:1–17) as well as the so-called Book of the Covenant (20:22–24:18). For the significance of these documents, see Theological Message.

God Commands Israel to Build the Tabernacle (25:1–40:38). Much attention is devoted to the tabernacle in the exodus narrative. Indeed, modern readers often find this section highly repetitive, especially since God's directions to build the tabernacle and the execution of those plans are narrated in detail, using the same language in a command-fulfillment pattern. This is one of the keys to the structure of this third part of the book. It also highlights the importance of the tabernacle to the wilderness generation. These details are lovingly dwelt on because the tabernacle was the primary symbol of God's presence with Israel.

The section opens with an appeal for materials with which the tabernacle would be built (25:1–9). The presence of these precious materials in the wilderness can be explained only as a result of the so-called plundering of the Egyptians (Ex. 12:33–35). In this way God provided the materials for his own house.

Most of the rest of the book is taken up with the instructions for the various parts of the tabernacle, the furnishings of the tabernacle, and the vestments of the priests (25:10–31:18) and also with the detailed narration of the execution of these commands (35:1–40:38).

Genre

In this section, we discuss the whole text and not the parts. Exodus is made up of a number of different types of literature, including narrative, law, and poetry. What is the best way to describe the whole book?

As with so much of the Old Testament, the primary generic label for the book of Exodus is prophetic or theological history. The intention of the book is to inform its readers about God's great acts in the past. This history is called theological or prophetic in recognition of the fact that it is history with the particular intention of revealing the nature of God in his acts. Biblical historical narrative has a theological and didactic function besides its historical intention (see Sternberg; Longman 1987; and Provan, Long, and Longman 2003; as well as chap. 1 on biblical historiography in this volume).

The three events — exodus, law, and tabernacle — emphasize one important truth: God is present with Israel as its savior and king.

Exodus is somewhat different from many other books of history in the Bible because of the important role that law plays in it. It is not within the scope of this book to discuss the important work that has been done on a formal analysis of law (for discussion and bibliography, see Clark), but we must point out the integration of narrative and legal materials in the book. The law is not just an appendage or separate part of the book but flows within the history of redemption (see Theological Message).

THEOLOGICAL MESSAGE

The book of Exodus, as we have seen, narrates the great events of the exodus, the deliverance from Egyptian bondage, as well as the beginnings of the wilderness wanderings. Two of the most significant occurrences of the wanderings are also reported in the book: the giving of the law, and the building of the tabernacle. All three events—exodus, law, and tabernacle—emphasize one important truth: God is present with Israel as its savior and king. We will examine each of these three moments in the redemptive history of Israel to explore this broader theme of the presence of God.

The Exodus from Egypt

Its Significance. From the significance of the event itself as well as its reverberations through the canon, it is clear that the exodus was God's greatest act of salvation in the Old Testament. After all, the Israelites, God's chosen people, were living in oppressive conditions in Egypt. They were treated as slaves and exploited as cheap labor. There are indications in the text that Israel had forgotten God during their sojourn in Egypt, but God had not forgotten them. Specifically, he remembered the Abrahamic covenant (Gen. 12:1–3; 15; 17), in which he promised the patriarch numerous descendants and a land of their own (12:1–3). The Israelites originally arrived in Egypt in fulfillment of that promise, since to stay in Palestine at the time of Jacob and Joseph would have resulted in death and famine. But at the time narrated by Exodus, a generation of Egyptians existed that did not know Joseph. In the midst of these conditions, God raised up a deliverer through incredible circumstances. As happens so often in the Old Testament, God preserved his future deliverer's life through great danger in his infancy (Ex. 1, 2). Not only did God preserve Moses' life, but he did so in such a way that Moses was raised under the nose of Pharaoh himself (Ex. 2:5–7). Later, God used Moses to bring Israel out of their Egyptian bondage.

That it is God who saves his people from bondage may be seen both from the plague accounts and from the miraculous delivery from Pharaoh's army at the sea. The ten plagues increase in intensity and scope as they climax in the final horrible scene of the death of the firstborn. Throughout the plagues (but explicitly beginning with the fourth), the Israelites are clearly differentiated from the Egyptians. While the territory of the Egyptians is plunged into darkness (the ninth plague, Ex. 10:21–29), "all the Israelites had light in the places where they lived" (v. 23). This differentiation takes place most significantly in the tenth plague, the death of the firstborn, an event commemorated in the Passover celebration (Ex. 12). Finally, Pharaoh reluctantly gave permission for Israel to leave. When Moses had first approached Pharaoh for permission to leave Egypt, Pharaoh responded by declaring, "I do not know the LORD and I will not let Israel go" (Ex. 5:2). After the ordeal of the plagues, Pharaoh knew that God was present with Israel and was sovereign over all that happened in Egypt.

Pharaoh's permission for Israel to leave was reluctantly given, however, and he soon reneged, leading his chariot troops to pursue them. It was at the sea that God manifested his powerful presence in a climactic way that was remembered in song both at the moment of deliverance (Ex. 15) and later (Ps. 77). It was then that God explicitly manifested himself as the divine warrior (Miller 1973; Longman 1982; Longman and Reid 1995) for the first time:

The LORD is a warrior;
    the LORD is his name.
Pharaoh's chariots and his army
    he has hurled into the sea.
The best of Pharaoh's officers
    are drowned in the Red Sea. (Ex. 15:3–4)

As mentioned above, the exodus deliverance helped mold Israel's self-understanding that they were God's people. The significance of the event is clearly seen in the way that the exodus theme is constantly reapplied throughout the Old Testament and into the New.

Indeed, this great act of salvation becomes in essence the paradigm for future deliverances. This is most noticeable as the prophets anticipate the Babylonian captivity and Israel's ultimate restoration. In the minds of the prophets, the Babylonian captivity was going to be a second Egyptian captivity that would ultimately be followed by a wilderness trek back into the Promised Land (e.g., Isa. 35:5–10; 40:3–5; 43:14–21; Hos. 2:14–16). In fact, such a restoration took place after the decree of Cyrus and under the leadership of such men as Ezra and Nehemiah.

Approaching the New Testament. That more is to come is signaled by the opening of the gospel of Mark, which quotes Isaiah 40:3 as well as Malachi 3:1:

> "I will send my messenger ahead of you,
>   who will prepare your way"—
> "a voice of one calling in the wilderness,
> "'Prepare the way for the Lord,
>   make straight paths for him.'" (Mark 1:2–3)

John the Baptist is then introduced as the one who came to prepare the way for Jesus. Christ began his earthly ministry in the wilderness, and the gospels clearly show that his life was a fulfillment of the exodus.

The act that initiates Jesus' ministry was his baptism. In analogy with the exodus experience, baptism is Jesus' Red Sea crossing (cf. 1 Cor. 10:1–6). Not surprisingly then, Jesus moved to the wilderness, where he experienced forty days (corresponding to the forty years of wilderness wandering) of temptation (Matt. 4:1–11). Strikingly, the three temptations all relate to the temptations that Israel confronted in the wilderness. While Christ resisted temptation, however, Israel gave in to it. Jesus' replies to Satan confirm the analogy since all are taken from Moses' speech recorded in Deuteronomy (8:3; 6:16; 6:13), in which he admonishes Israel not to behave as they did in the wilderness. Jesus thus demonstrates to his followers that he is obedient precisely where the Israelites were rebellious.

The next major episode that corresponds to the wilderness temptations in the gospel of Matthew is the Sermon on the Mount. That Matthew locates the sermon on a mountain draws the reader's attention because in Luke the sermon is given on a plain (Luke 6:17). While harmonization between the two accounts is possible, the mountain setting draws a close connection between Jesus' sermon with its focus on law and the giving of the law on Mount Sinai.

Many other parallels may be drawn between the Israelite's exodus experience and Christ's earthly ministry (Stock; Dennison), but it all climaxed during his passion. Jesus went to the cross during the time of Passover (Matt. 26:19; Mark 14:16; Luke 22:13). In essence, he became the Passover lamb who died for others (1 Cor. 5:7).

Thus in one sense Christ fulfilled the exodus during his earthly ministry. In another sense, Christians today experience life as a wilderness wandering, looking to the future for the rest that comes at the end of the exodus (Heb. 3:7–4:13), the entering of the Promised Land (heaven).

Mount Sinai—the Law of God (19–24)

The Significance of the Law. God made his presence as Savior known among the Israelites at the time of the exodus and in particular at the crossing of the Red Sea. As the Israelites left the land of their slavery and went toward the Promised Land, God continued to be present with them. Perhaps the single most important occurrence during the journey took place just three months after their departure when they arrived at Mount Sinai. Here God made his powerful presence known to them again as he revealed his will to Israel through the law.

The episode that precedes the giving of the law emphasizes God's holiness and the people's sin (Ex. 19). God revealed himself in cloud, fire, and smoke. The mountain became a sacred place because of his presence. The people were required to ceremonially prepare themselves for an encounter with God, and only Moses and Aaron were permitted to approach the mountain.

God met with Israel at Sinai in order to give them his law, the written expression of his will for their corporate and individual life. While it is easy to think of the law as an isolated entity, it is crucial to recognize that the law was given within the context of the covenant. Kline has observed that Exodus 19–24 is in the form of a covenant treaty document. The historical prologue (Ex. 20:2) identifies the author of the law as the one who has already saved them by his grace. Thus the law as found in Exodus 20–24 is not the basis of the divine-human relationship even during the Old Testament period, but rather it is the guide for its maintenance. It is not the key to the establishment of a relationship with God, but rather to its continuance and well-being. In fact, the giving of the law is historically and canonically surrounded by God's gracious acts as it looks back to the exodus (which took place on the basis of the Abrahamic covenant), and it looks forward to the conquest and settlement of the Promised Land.

The law itself may be divided into two parts: the Ten Commandments, and the Book of the Covenant. The Ten Commandments are given first (Ex. 20:3–17) and have the form of direct address to the hearer-reader. They cover the basics of the divine-human relationship (the first four) as well as human-human relationships (the last six). The various laws that compose the Book of the Covenant (the name is derived from Ex. 24:7) flow from the more basic principles enunciated in the Ten Commandments. They specify the Ten Commandments to the cultural and redemptive-historical moment of the people of God at the time of the exodus. For instance, the law of the goring ox (Ex. 21:28–36) is a specification of the sixth commandment to an agrarian society, and Exodus 23:10–13 spells out more fully the fourth commandment concerning the Sabbath.

Approaching the New Testament. Attempts like those of a movement called theonomy to impose the laws and penalties found in the Book of the Covenant to contemporary society (Bahnsen 1977; Rushdoony) are ill-founded and dangerous (Longman 1990 and 1997). They simply do not take into account the radically different cultural and, more importantly, redemptive-historical differences between Old Testament Israel and contemporary society. Theonomy used to be an attractive lens through which to read Scripture for many Christians, particularly in Reformed and Pentecostal circles in the 1970s and into the 1990s, among those who looked with horror at the secularization of society and longed for a more powerful Christian influence. Fortunately, as we begin the twenty-first century this movement has lost significant influence.

The law remains relevant for today, however, as the principles behind the various stipulations are summarized in a general way in the Ten Commandments. The Christian is not given a specification of the law in the New Testament along the lines of the Book of the Covenant or the other law codes of the Pentateuch. The Christian must think through contemporary ethical issues with the Ten Commandments as a guide. How does the commandment not to steal apply to computer theft? How does the commandment not to kill apply to the abortion pill? Nuclear arms?

The New Testament, of course, is not bereft of comments on law. Jesus shows that he is God himself as he deepens our understanding of the law in his Sermon on the Mount (Matt. 5–7). Certainly, the most startling news in the New Testament about the law is that Jesus Christ has freed his followers from the curse of the law (Rom. 7). Thus the law, which was never the means to a relationship with God, becomes for Christians a guide to God's will for their life.

The Tabernacle—God Dwells With His People (25–40)

The Significance of the Tabernacle. The last section (Ex. 25–40) is taken up mostly by a discussion about the tabernacle (for a fuller discussion of the tabernacle and the biblical theology of sacred place, see Longman 2001). The tabernacle was God's earthly dwelling during the period from Moses to David. As his dwelling, the tabernacle emphasizes God's presence with his people, continuing a theme that has run throughout the book of Exodus.

To understand the significance of the tabernacle, it is good to be reminded of what has led up to its construction. When Adam and Eve were first created, there was no need to meet with God in a special location. They met with God anywhere in the garden of Eden. The fall, however, resulted in a fundamental alienation between God and his human creatures, so that they could no longer easily enter into his presence. After the fall, people could come before the Lord, but only at specially designated locations. During the period of the patriarchs, altars were constructed so that worship could be conducted by the head of the family (Gen. 12:8; 13:18). At the time of the exodus, however, the people of God were no longer an extended family, but were now a mighty nation. Thus, due to the redemptive-historical moment and the sociological situation of the Israelites, God commanded Moses to build a tabernacle so that he might be approached in worship.

The tabernacle had the form of a nomad's tent. It was possible to take it down, pack it, and move it to the next location. This mobility was necessary because the people of God were wandering in the wilderness and unsettled in the land. The transition from the tabernacle to the temple, a more permanent dwelling for God, would take place only when the conquest of the land was completed at the time of Solomon (1 Kings 6–8).

During the period from Sinai to Solomon, the tabernacle served as the earthly dwelling of God. It was the place to which his people would go in order to meet with him. As the place of God's special presence, the tabernacle was holy ground. The location, architectural design, building materials, and accessibility of the tabernacle all highlight the fact that a holy God dwelt in the midst of the Israelite people.

When Israel was encamped during the wilderness wanderings, the tabernacle was set up in the middle of the camp. Each tribe had its location surrounding it. The center of the camp, according to ancient Near Eastern tradition, was the place for the king's tent. Since God was king of Israel, his tent rightly was in the center. When the tent was taken down and Israel was on the march, the ark, which was located in the Holy of Holies of the tabernacle, led the way, just as a Near Eastern king would lead his army into battle.

The design of the tabernacle also pointed to the presence of a holy God in Israel's midst. The tabernacle area was divided into different parts: a courtyard (Ex. 27:9–19), a Holy Place, and a Most Holy Place (26:31–35). There were gradations of holiness as one approached the tabernacle and then entered through these different parts. Outside of the camp of Israel was the realm of the Gentiles and the unclean. When an Israelite was ritually polluted, he or she had to go outside of the camp for a certain period of time. The camp itself was closer to the presence of God and was where all Israelites in covenant with the Lord dwelt. However, only the Levites were permitted to approach the area immediately surrounding the tabernacle. They were set apart for special service to the Lord. Crossing from the courtyard to the Holy Place and then finally to the Most Holy Place, one drew closer to the presence of God, and the ground became progressively more holy. This may be seen in the quality of the tabernacle materials as well as in the tabernacle's accessibility.

There was a correlation between proximity to the Most Holy Place where the ark was kept and the preciousness of the materials used in tabernacle

The transition from the tabernacle to the temple, a more permanent dwelling for God, would take place only when the conquest of the land was completed at the time of Solomon.

construction. This gradation may first of all be observed in the four coverings of the tabernacle. The outermost curtain was the most functional; it was a covering of the hides of sea cows (Ex. 26:14). Exposed to the elements, this water-repellent material was a perfect external covering for the tabernacle. In addition, layers of ram skins dyed red (v. 14) and goat hair (v. 7) also served to protect the contents of the building. The innermost curtain was a carefully and intricately crafted curtain of "finely twisted linen and blue, purple and scarlet yarn, with cherubim worked into them" (v. 1). This curtain was the one that could be seen from the inside of the tabernacle. Its sky-like color and the presence of the heavenly creatures on it demonstrate that the tabernacle was considered to be heaven on earth. Thus the closer the material was to the ark, the more precious it was.

This principle is borne out for the metallic materials as well (Haran 1978). Out in the courtyard, less precious materials like bronze and silver are found (Ex. 27:9–19). In the tabernacle itself, gold and the even more precious "pure gold" are used to construct the furniture of the tabernacle (the ark, Ex. 25:10–22; the table, 25:23–30; and the lampstand, 25:31–40).

Thus the very materials of the tabernacle symbolically represent the fact that a holy God dwells in the midst of his people. Recourse to more fanciful and allegorical approaches to understand the symbolic function of the tabernacle (Kiene 1977; Soltau 1865) are unnecessary and sound foolish.

Finally, the principle of accessibility to the tabernacle and its Most Holy Place also demonstrates the presence of God in the midst of Israel. There are circles of holiness surrounding the tabernacle: Outside of the camp was the realm of the Gentiles and the unclean. There were no special qualifications required for those in this space. However, only those who were in covenant with God and were ritually clean were permitted to move into the camp. Only Levites, who were specially consecrated to the service of the Lord, were permitted to set up their tents in the vicinity of the tabernacle, and they surrounded the site. The Levites, in other words, served to buffer the tabernacle from the rest of the camp. Even most Levites were not permitted to minister close to the tabernacle, however. This service was restricted to one family of Levites, the descendants of Aaron. Furthermore, the most holy place of all, the inner sanctum of the tabernacle where the ark was kept, was the most restricted space of all. Only the current high priest could enter, and he only once a year—on the Day of Atonement (Lev. 16).

The tabernacle, like any home, also had furniture, the most important of which were the ark of the covenant and the menorah, both potent symbols of the presence of God. The ark had a simple design; in essence it was a small box, three and three-quarters feet long, two and a quarter feet wide, and two and a quarter feet high. It also had rings attached to the sides, through which poles were slid for carrying it. Though simple, it was precious, being constructed of high-quality acacia wood and covered inside and out by gold. Much could be

Figure 2
Circle of Holiness in the Tabernacle

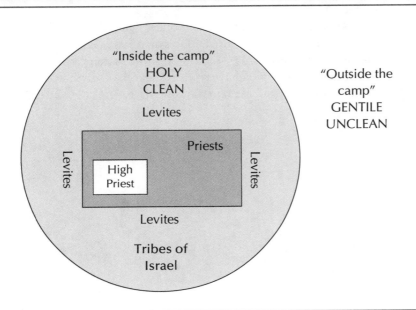

"Inside the camp"
HOLY
CLEAN
Levites

"Outside the camp"
GENTILE
UNCLEAN

Priests

Levites

High
Priest

Levites

Levites

Tribes of
Israel

said about the ark, but for now it is important to emphasize its role as an object representing God's presence. When Israel was stationary and the tabernacle was set up, it was protected by two cherubim represented by statues at each end with wings outstretched over the ark and heads down. The reason for their posture was that the ark was a most potent symbol of God's presence. It was seen as the footstool of his throne (1 Chron. 28:2), perhaps even occasionally as the throne itself (Jer. 3:16–17). God the King sat in his earthly house on his throne, and the cherubim, whose wings supported him, looked to the ground to shield their gaze from the radiance of his glory.

The menorah was a lampstand described in Exodus 25:31–40. Its description is debated in its details, but no question surrounds the fact that it is a tree symbol, described as having branches and almond blossoms. A treelike menorah reminds us of the garden of Eden and thus represents the presence of God on earth.

Thus a variety of indications show that the tabernacle was God's earthly home. It demonstrated to the Israelites that God was with them as they journeyed through the wilderness and as they settled in the Promised Land.

Approaching the New Testament. As a symbol of God's presence with Israel, the tabernacle served an important function in the life and religion of the people of God. However, it was a temporary institution. Under Solomon, the tabernacle was replaced by the temple. Now that the people of God were permanent dwellers in the land, God's dwelling took on the form of a house rather than a nomad's tent. All of the Old Testament symbols for God's dwelling on earth, however, were provisional and temporary. They all pointed forward and anticipated the coming of Jesus Christ, God's own Son, who "became flesh and tabernacled for a while among us" (John 1:14, author's translation). Ultimately, the tabernacle and temple, which represented heaven on earth, looked forward to the merging of heaven and earth in the New Jerusalem (Rev. 21–22).

CHAPTER FOUR

LEVITICUS

Leviticus is the third part of the Pentateuch. The concluding chapters of Exodus that focus on the construction of the tabernacle (chaps. 25–40) lead naturally to the opening of Leviticus, which describes the various sacrifices performed in the Holy Place (chaps. 1–7). The name Leviticus comes from the Septuagint via the Vulgate and highlights the main subject matter. The name means "pertaining to the Levites," and although that tribe as such is not emphasized throughout the book, the priestly subject matter renders the title appropriate. The Hebrew title, like those of the other books of the Pentateuch, derives from the initial words of the book. Leviticus is thus *wayyiqrâ'*, "And he called."

The book of Leviticus is often seen by the church as irrelevant to the present day. In those few cases where it is considered significant, an allegorical interpretation is used to "bridge the gap" between the time of the Old Testament and today. A close study of its contents, however, will reveal its rich contribution to our understanding of God and the history of redemption without recourse to allegory.

BIBLIOGRAPHY

Commentaries

W. H. **Bellinger** Jr., *Leviticus, Numbers* (NIBCOT; Hendrickson/Paternoster, 2001); R. **Gane,** *Leviticus, Numbers* (NIVAC; Zondervan, 2004); E. **Gerstenberger,** *Leviticus* (OTL; Westminster John Knox, 1996); R. K. **Harrison,** *Leviticus* (TOTC; InterVarsity Press, 1980); J. E. **Hartley,** *Leviticus* (WBC; Word, 1992); G. A. F. **Knight,** *Leviticus* (DSB; Westminster, 1981); B. A. **Levine,** *Leviticus* (JPS Commentary; Jewish Publication Society, 1989); J. **Milgrom,** *Leviticus 1–16* (AB; Doubleday, 1991); idem, *Leviticus 17–27* (AB; Doubleday, 2001); A. **Noordtzij,** *Leviticus* (BSC; Zondervan, 1982); M. F. **Rooker,** *Leviticus* (NAC; Nashville, 2000); N. H. **Snaith,** *Leviticus and Numbers* (NCB; Eerdmans, 1967); G. J. **Wenham,** *The Book of Leviticus* (NICOT; Eerdmans, 1979).

Monographs and Articles

A. A. **Cody,** *History of Old Testament Priesthood* (Rome: Pontifical Biblical Institute, 1969); D. **Damrosch,** "Leviticus," in *The Literary Guide to the Bible,* ed. R. Alter and F. Kermode (Harvard, 1987), 66–77; D. J. **Davies,** "An Interpretation of Sacrifice in Leviticus," *ZAW* 89 (1977): 387–99; M. **Douglas,** *Purity and Danger* (London, 1969); M. **Haran,** *Temples and Temple-Service in Ancient Israel* (Oxford, 1978); P. P. **Jenson,** "The Levitical Sacrificial System," in *Sacrifice in the Bible,* ed. R. T. Beckwith and M. J. Selman (Baker, 1995), 25–40; Y. **Kaufmann,** *The Religion of Israel* (University of Chicago Press, 1960); N. **Kiuchi,** *The Purification Offering in the Priestly Literature: Its Meaning and Function* (JSOTS 56; Sheffield Academic Press, 1987); idem, "Book of Leviticus," DOTP (InterVarsity Press, 2003), 522–32; M. G. **Kline,** *Images of the Spirit* (Baker, 1980); B. A. **Levine,** *In the Presence of the Lord* (Leiden: Brill, 1974); T. **Longman** III, *Immanuel in Our Place* (P and R Publishing, 2001); J. **Milgrom,** *Cult and Conscience: The "Asham" and the Priestly Doctrine of Repentance* (Leiden: Brill, 1976); J. **Neusner,** *The Idea of Purity in Ancient Judaism* (Leiden: Brill, 1973); G. J. **Wenham,** "The Theology of Unclean Food," *EvQ* 53 (1981): 6–15; idem, "The Theology of Old Testament Sacrifice," in *Sacrifice in the Bible,* ed. R. T. Beckwith and M. J. Selman (Baker, 1995), 75–87.

HISTORICAL BACKGROUND

The composition of Leviticus is integrally related to the composition of the entire Pentateuch. The following comments must be situated in the broader discussion found in Historical-Critical Approaches in chapter 2.

In the midst of the uncertainty about a source analysis of the Pentateuch, most critical scholars agree on the character and scope of P. It is not surprising that virtually the whole of Leviticus is assigned to P. After all, its contents revolve around priestly matters of cult and law; even the sparse narrative sections (8–10, 16) concern priestly matters.

Critical scholars, nevertheless, still have questions concerning the extent to which P, a late document, used earlier sources. The so-called Holiness Code, chapters 17–27, is a good example of an earlier source absorbed into the Priestly document. These chapters cohere by their structure and subject matter, and because of this many scholars think they were originally an independent composition. Indeed, many think the only original contributions by P are the infrequent narrative sections (8–10, 16; described by Wenham 1981, 7). However, the critical consensus, going back to Wellhausen, is that P is post-Deuteronomic (Levine 1974, xxviii-xxix) and most likely exilic or postexilic. A less radical but still nontraditional approach is represented by Kaufmann, who argues that Leviticus is P but that P is neither postexilic nor post-Deuteronomy, though he would not go so far as to say that P is Mosaic.

For a defense of the traditional position on the composition of Leviticus, refer to the discussion above (see Evaluation of the Critical Approach in chap. 2). While Leviticus never claims to be authored by Moses, the internal testimony is quite strong that its contents were mediated through him to the people. The book opens with the phrase "The LORD called to Moses" (1:1), and the expression "The LORD said to Moses" (occasionally adding "and to Aaron") recurs at many transition points in the text (e.g., 4:1; 5:14; 6:1, 8, 19, 24; 11:1; 12:1; 13:1; 14:1, 33; 15:1; 16:1; 19:1; 20:1; 21:1; 24:1; 27:1). There are no clear indications that Leviticus contains late preexilic or postexilic materials (however, see Levine 1974, xxix–xxx, for an opposing view).

LITERARY ANALYSIS

Genre

The high proportion of law in Leviticus should not obscure the narrative flow of the book. The initial episode sets the scene at the Tent of Meeting, where Moses hears God's voice as he instructs him in how the Israelites should act. All the laws of the book have this narrative setting.

There is also nonlegal narrative in the book, though it is brief (chaps. 8–10, 16). All of this indicates that Leviticus continues the genre of the Pentateuch as a whole—that is, primarily instructional history. It intends to inform the reader about what went on in the past, in this case providing a historical background to the law. Indeed, as Damrosch has pointed out, "the story exists for the sake of the laws which it frames" (66).

Structure

Leviticus may be outlined as follows:
I. Sacrificial laws (1:1–7:38)
  A. Instruction for the laity (1:1–6:7)
    1. Burnt offering (1)
    2. Grain offering (2)
    3. Fellowship offering (3)
    4. Sin offering (4:1–5:13)
    5. Guilt offering (5:14–6:7)
  B. Instructions for the priests (6:8–7:38)
II. Priestly narrative (8:1–10:20)
  A. The formal beginnings of the priesthood (8:1–9:24)
  B. The limits on the priesthood—Nadab and Abihu (10)
III. Laws to protect ritual cleanness (11:1–16:34)
  A. Dietary prescriptions (11)
  B. Birth laws (12)
  C. The discernment and cleansing of skin diseases (13–14)

      1. Discerning the disease (13)

      2. Cleansing the disease (14)

    D. Laws about bodily discharges (15)

    E. The Day of Atonement (16)

  IV. Holiness code (17–27)

    A. The laws (17:1–25:55)

      1. Handling blood (17)

      2. Incest laws (18)

      3. Miscellaneous laws (19–20)

      4. Laws concerning priests and sacrifices (21–22)

      5. Sabbath and festivals (23)

      6. Tabernacle law (24:1–9)

      7. The story of the punishment of a blasphemer (24:10–23)

      8. The Jubilee (25)

    B. Blessings and curses (26)

      1. Blessings for obedience (26:1–13)

      2. Curses for disobedience (26:14–46)

    C. Gifts to the Lord (27)

Style

The single most obvious characteristic of the book is its clear and simple structure. The high incidence of law and ritual necessitates a straightforward presentation. The purpose of the book is to provide guidelines to priests and laypeople concerning appropriate behavior in the presence of a holy God, thus the emphasis is on communicating information, not on subtle or artificial literary plays.

Accordingly, Leviticus is among the least literary of the Old Testament books (contra Damrosch). This judgment is not a slight on the book, because the book does not intend to stimulate the reader's aesthetic imagination to the same level as do other biblical books. Its interest to the original audience as well as to the contemporary reader is found elsewhere, for instance, in its theological ramifications.

THEOLOGICAL MESSAGE

Old Testament Context

The Holiness of God. The bulk of the book of Leviticus contains laws and rituals surrounding the formal worship of Israel (see Longman 2001). Among other topics, there is a description of sacrificial ritual and laws concerning dietary and sexual purity. Before getting lost in the details, it is important for us to discern, behind all these laws and the central concepts of purity and cleanness, the central teaching of the book—that God is holy. Standing as motivation behind the various commands is the divine statement "I am the LORD your God" (18:2,

4; 19:3–4, 10; 20:7). Furthermore, God is not only present, he is holy: "Therefore be holy, because I am holy" (11:45; see also 19:2; 20:26).

The book of Leviticus thus teaches that God is separate from the present world and that only those who are also freed from the taint of sin are permitted into his presence. In the following pages, we will observe how this works out in three important areas in Leviticus: the sacrificial system, the priesthood, and purity. Although this is not an exhaustive analysis of all the contents of Leviticus, it will give an indication of the overall theological message of the book.

The Sacrificial System. The book of Leviticus opens with a long consideration of sacrifice (chaps. 1–7, see Wenham 1995). This emphasis on sacrifice is not at all surprising since it is the most important activity of formal worship during the Old Testament period. What is striking from our contemporary perspective is the little interest in explicating the meaning or significance of the ritual; the focus is on description. Apparently, the meaning of the rite was understood by the original audience, both lay and priestly, and all that was necessary was a reminder of proper procedure. Fortunately for us, we are able, at least in general, to infer the meaning of sacrifice as a whole and the individual sacrifices by the symbolism of the acts and by their use in worship.

The examination of individual sacrifices that follows leads to a covenantal interpretation of sacrifice in Israel. Covenant refers to the relationship that exists between God and his people Israel. This covenant relationship is related to sacrifice in three ways. First, sacrifice is a *gift* on the part of the worshiper to his covenant Lord. Second, a number of sacrifices include a notion of *communion* or fellowship between covenant partners. Last, and perhaps most important, sacrifice plays a major role in healing rifts in the covenant relationship. This function is frequently described by the technical theological term *expiation*. Wenham (1979, 26) graphically illustrates this last function with the following diagram:

Table 2
Sacrifice and Expiation

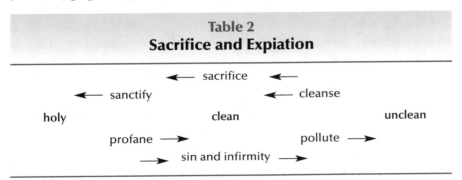

When the covenant relationship was broken through certain types of offenses, repentant Israelites could seek God's forgiveness by offering a substitute to take the penalty of their sin. In this way, sacrifice served as the divinely sanctioned means for restoring covenant relationship. Sacrifice thus fits in very closely with the overarching theological concept of God's holiness. God is holy and cannot tolerate the presence of sin and uncleanness. Sacrifice is a way of making the unholy pure again and restoring fellowship in the presence of God. It allows the unclean, who have been forced from the presence of God, to return once again to the camp that is the realm of the holy.

As we will observe, sacrifice often, but not always, focuses on the blood of the victim. Some critical scholars speak of this as a magical understanding of sacrifice, and some evangelical readers of the Old Testament seem to have this idea also when they insist on the translation "blood" rather than its symbolical referent, death. It is the death of the sacrificial victim that renders the rite effective, and the manipulation of the blood highlights the death that stands in the place of the sinner who offers it.

Burnt offering (chap. 1). The common English name for this sacrifice comes directly from the Greek translation; the Hebrew term means "ascending" (*'ôlâ*) and derives from the fact that the fragrant aroma of the sacrifice rises up to heaven in the form of smoke.

The worshiper was to bring an unblemished animal to the priests and prepare it for sacrifice. There may have been more than one reason for the requirement of an unblemished animal, but it certainly disallowed anyone from bringing in a deformed animal and thus going through the form of the sacrifice without paying any real price.

The purpose of the sacrifice, however, was not to impoverish anyone. Indeed, the law allowed for the substitution of less expensive forms of sacrifice, most likely dependent on the economic status of the worshiper:

Cattle (1:3–9)
Sheep and goats (vv. 10–13)
Birds (vv. 14–17)

The burnt offering was a sacrifice that was concerned with expiation of sins. Here the technical term "to make atonement for" (*kippēr*) is used (1:4). There is a debate over the etymology of this term that is applicable to more than one form of sacrifice. While some relate the term to the verb "to ransom" (*kôper*), others associate it with Akkadian "to cleanse" (*kuppuru*; see discussion in Wenham 1979, 28). While Levine leans toward the latter, he is correct to argue that the meaning and significance of the term have taken on a technical force in the context of Leviticus. (For a full technical discussion, see Kiuchi 1987, 87–109.) In further support of the expiatory function of this sacrifice, the rite of laying a hand on the head of the sacrificial victim is rightly interpreted as an act of identification between the worshiper and the victim before it is slaughtered.

The sacrifice, however, was also a gift to God. With the exception of the skin, which went to the priests (7:8), the whole sacrifice was burned and dedicated to the Lord.

The burnt offering was probably the most frequently occurring sacrifice, though it was often made in association with the next two (Ex. 29:38–41; Num. 6:11–12; 28:2–8; 2 Chron. 29:20–24).

Grain offering (2; 6:14–23). The grain offering gets its name from its main ingredient, fine flour. Two other components are oil and incense. Only a small portion of the flour and the oil were combined with all of the incense and burned as a gift to the Lord. The incense provided a pleasant smell to the sacrifice, but it was withheld from the rest of the flour and oil that was given to the priests for their sustenance.

This sacrifice emphasizes the gift function mentioned above. Indeed, as is often pointed out, the term "grain offering" (*minḥâ*) may be and often is translated "tribute" (e.g., Judg. 3:15, 17–18; 2 Sam. 8:6; 1 Kings 4:21). The offering was a gift made to the sovereign Lord of the covenant.

It was most often performed in accompaniment with the whole burnt offering that preceded it (Ex. 29:40–41; Num. 15:1–10; 28:5–8). The description of the sacrifice is divided into three subcategories:

Uncooked grain offering (2:1–3)
Cooked grain offering (vv. 4–10)
Other types of grain offering (vv. 11–16)

Fellowship offering (Lev. 3; 7:11–38). The Hebrew term for this sacrifice (*šᵉlâmîm*) comes from the common Hebrew word that means "peace" (*âlôm*), thus many English translations refer to this as the "peace offering." The alternate rendering, "fellowship offering," is based on the fact that this sacrifice is predominately for fellowship between both the worshiper and God and among the worshipers.

The term "peace" has a definite covenant significance in the Scriptures, denoting the "whole" relationship that exists between covenant partners. The corporate meal that is the outcome of this sacrifice is a celebration of that relationship. Everyone gets a piece of this offering—the Lord (3:3–4), the priest (7:31–36), and the worshipers.

While the gift function of this sacrifice is accentuated, we should not miss the fact that the sacrifice is a gift *and* an act of expiation. The latter may be seen in the ritual of placing the hands on the head of the sacrificial animal (3:2).

Like the previous two chapters, this chapter may also be subdivided into three parts, describing different forms the sacrifice can take. The worshiper may offer any of the following animals:

Cattle (3:1–5)
Sheep (vv. 6–11)
Goats (vv. 12–17)

Purification offering (4:1–5:13; 6:24–30). The purification offering, sometimes known as the sin offering (*ḥaṭṭā 'at*; see Kiuchi 1987, and Jenson 1995, 29), obviously has to do with the removal of sin. As we have already seen, however, it is not the only sacrifice that has an expiatory function. The distinction here has to do with the fact that it is effective for those who have sinned unintentionally. Some instances of unintentional sins may be found in 5:1–6, and a distinction between unintentional and "high-handed" sins may be found in Numbers 15:22–31.

The type of sacrifice here is dependent on the status of the offender. From greater to lesser, this sacrifice is for:

The priest (4:3–12)
The Israelite community (vv. 13–21)
The Israelite community leader (vv. 22–26)
The Israelite layperson (vv. 27–35)

Guilt offering (5:14–6:7; 7:1–10). The guilt offering has much in common with the sin offering. The examples given for the former, however, are restricted to offenses against the "things of the Lord"—that is, the *sancta* (Milgrom 1976). This sacrifice requires an additional payment of 20 percent, which makes up for the offense. This characteristic leads Milgrom and Wenham to dub this sacrifice the reparation offering.

Priesthood. In addition to sacrifice, priesthood is a major concern of this book. Indeed, it appears that the name Leviticus points to its heavy emphasis on the priesthood. Much of the book is instruction to priests or to laypeople as they interact with priests. The brief narrative sections focus on the ordination of the priesthood and present a story of the dangers inherent in the responsibilities of the priesthood (Lev. 8–10).

While it is true that a full understanding of the theology of priesthood must take into account much of the Old Testament, Leviticus provides a core of information for our understanding of the priesthood.

In the first place, the teaching on priesthood in the book of Leviticus accentuates the overall theme of God's holiness. After all, the priests spend much of their time in the presence of the Holy One. As a result, much of their behavior is regulated by the fact that they too must be holy. We can see this in their ordination (Lev. 8). The ordination service set Aaron and his children apart for special service to the Lord. Their investiture in priestly clothing as well as their being sprinkled with oil identifies them with the tabernacle that is a place set apart for the presence of God's holiness (Kline 1980). They also offer sacrifices to atone for their sins. In this way, they themselves become holy.

After their ordination, the priests begin their service of protecting the holiness of the camp through sacrifice (Lev. 1–7; 9). The book of Leviticus also warns the priests that they must be very strict in their behavior while in the presence of a holy God. When two sons of Aaron, Nadab and Abihu, offered "strange fire" before the Lord (chap. 10), they were immediately consumed, and God proclaimed:

> Among those who approach me
>   I will be proved holy;
> in the sight of all the people
>   I will be honored. (10:3)

Many of the laws in Leviticus were directed toward the priests so that they might preserve their holiness (Lev. 21–22). It was also a part of their duty to teach the Israelites the law (2 Chron. 17:7–9) so that they could protect God's holiness in the camp. As God says to Aaron in Leviticus 10:11, "You [must] teach the Israelites all the decrees the LORD has given them through Moses."

Thus we may briefly summarize the main function of the priesthood according to the book of Leviticus: they were to protect the holiness of God in the camp.

Purity. A major concern of the laws of Leviticus has to do with cultic purity, also called cleanness. Food (chap. 11), childbirth (chap. 12), skin diseases and mildew (chaps. 13–14), and discharges (chap. 15) are a few among the many topics that are treated in the book in connection with cleanness. God was present with Israel; therefore, the purity of the camp had to be maintained. These laws guided Israel and the guardians of God's holiness, the priests, as to how to keep the camp pure.

At the center of the camp stood the tabernacle in which the ark, the primary symbol of God's presence, resided. From this spot different levels of holiness were represented, among other things, by exclusion of certain classes of people (see Figure 2 on page 79). Everyone and anyone might dwell outside the camp; it was the realm of the unclean and Gentiles. Only Israelites were permitted to dwell in the camp. Levites functioned as a buffer between the camp at large and the tabernacle, while only the priests were permitted to go into the tabernacle itself (for the role of priests as the bodyguards of God's holiness, see Longman 2001, 139–50). Leviticus 16 tells about the one time a year in which the high priest alone was to go into the Holy of Holies to perform a rite of expiation.

The point at issue in this section, however, concerns the distinction between the clean and the unclean. The priest was responsible to distinguish the two and to know who could dwell in the camp and who was required to go outside of the camp so as not to offend God.

Many explanations have been offered as to the rationale behind the purity laws of Leviticus. One favorite interpretation is that God was protecting the health of Israel through these laws. For instance, he was protecting them from birth defects due to incest by the laws in Leviticus 18 and 20, and he was protecting them from illness in the *kosher* laws of Leviticus 11. While there may be some truth to this approach, it does not provide a holistic rationale for interpreting these laws. Some of the foods are not unhealthful. Among other reasons, the fact that Jesus Christ declared these foods clean indicates that it is more than hygiene at issue here (Wenham 1979, 166–67).

A second common interpretation of these laws fits them into the effort to keep Israel separate from idolatry. Not much of the law, however, can be explained in this way. Perhaps the most potent animal symbol in Canaan at this time was the bull, which, for Baal worshipers, was a symbol of Baal. Because of this cultic interpretation it is difficult to understand why the bull was not proscribed in Israel.

Wenham is most helpful in his discussion of these laws (1979, 18–25 and 166–77). He bases his insights on the work of the anthropologist Mary Douglas who insists that "holy means more than separation to divine service. It means wholeness and completeness." Thus those animals that are in conformity with the natural order of creation are clean, whereas those animals that seem to confuse kinds are considered unclean. In Douglas's words, "Holiness requires that individuals shall conform to the class to which they belong" (Douglas 1969, 53). Accordingly, the laws of Leviticus 11 may be understood in this way:

> Those creatures which in some way transgress the boundaries are unclean. Thus fish without fins and scales are unclean (Lev. 11:10; Deut. 14:10). Insects which fly but which have many legs are unclean, whereas locusts which have wings and only two hopping legs are clean (Lev. 11:20–23). Animals with an indeterminate form of motion, i.e., which "swarm," are unclean (Lev. 11:41–44).

That "wholeness" is a fundamental principle in determining what is clean is confirmed by the fact that the law states that it is only those who are partially covered with skin disease who are unclean. Both those whose skin is unaffected as well as those whose skin is completely covered with disease (as long as the surface of the skin is unbroken) are considered clean (see Lev. 13, particularly vv. 12–17).

What is the enduring value of the book of Leviticus? This question has plagued Jewish and Christian readers for centuries.

APPROACHING THE NEW TESTAMENT

What is the enduring value of the book of Leviticus? This question has plagued Jewish and Christian readers for centuries. For the former, the loss of the temple raises the issue, but the continuation of dietary laws (*kashrut*) and the hope that some day temple worship will start again provide at least a partial answer (Levine). For Christians, the book of Hebrews provides guidance in that it presents Jesus Christ as the perfect High Priest who offers himself as the perfect sacrifice. As it says in Hebrews 9:26: "But he has appeared once for all at the culmination of the ages to do away with sin by the sacrifice of himself."

Jesus is the ultimate High Priest. By contrasting the regular Old Testament priesthood with the mysterious figure of Melchizedek, the author of Hebrews also solves the problem of Jesus' non-Levitical background (7:14). In any case, the Aaronic priesthood and the Old Testament sacrificial system all anticipated a greater reality, namely, Jesus Christ as final priest and sufficient sacrifice (Heb. 4:14–5:10; 7–10; see also Rom. 8:3; Eph. 5:2).

CHAPTER FIVE

NUMBERS

The descriptive, yet prosaic title Numbers (derived from the Septuagint *Arithmoi*) has contributed to a general lack of interest in the book by the Christian community at large. The title conjures up thoughts of censuses and other lists. Indeed, there are many such in the book (Num. 1; 3:15–31; 7:10–83; 26:5–51; 28–29; 31:32–52), but even these are not devoid of theological interest (see below). Furthermore, there is much of immediate interest in the narratives (e.g., Balaam, Num. 22–24) and laws of Numbers.

In Jewish circles the book goes by the name "In the wilderness" (*be midbar*, the fifth word in the text). This title names the setting of the entire book as the Israelites move from Sinai (1:19) to the wilderness of Paran (10:12) and finally to the plains of Moab (22:1; 36:13). Like Exodus and Leviticus, Numbers begins with the conjunction *and,* showing the continuity that exists between the books of the Pentateuch.

Numbers serves an important role as it narrates the transition from the old generation that left Egypt and sinned in the desert to the new generation that stands on the brink of the Promised Land. The book thus presents the reader with a vision of new beginnings and hope.

BIBLIOGRAPHY

Commentaries

R. **Allen,** "Numbers," in EBC, vol. 2 (Zondervan, 1990), 655–1008; T. R. **Ashley,** *The Book of Numbers* (NICOT; Eerdmans, 1993); W. H. **Bellinger** Jr., *Leviticus, Numbers* (NIBCOT; Hendrickson, 2001); P. J. **Budd,** *Numbers* (WBC; Word, 1984); R. D. **Cole,** *Numbers* (NAC; Broadman, 2000); E. W. **Davies,** *Numbers* (NCB; Eerdmans, 1995); T. **Dozeman,** "The Book of Numbers," in NIB, vol. 2 (Abingdon, 1994), 149–53; R. **Gane,** *Leviticus, Numbers* (NIVAC; Zondervan, 2004); G. B. **Gray,** *Numbers* (ICC; T. & T. Clark, 1903); H. **Gressmann,** *Mose und* *seine Zeit. Kommentar zu den Mose-Sagen* (Vandenhoek & Rubrecht, 1913); R. K. **Harrison,** *Numbers* (WEC; Moody, 1990); B. **Levine,** *Numbers 1–20* (AB; Doubleday, 1993); idem, *Numbers 21–36* (AB; Doubleday, 2000); J. **Milgrom,** *Numbers* (JPS Torah Commentary; Jewish Publication Society, 1990); A. **Noordtzij,** *Numbers* (BSC; Zondervan, 1983); M. **Noth,** *Numbers: A Commentary* (OTL; Westminster John Knox, 1966); D. T. **Olson,** *Numbers* (Interp; John Knox Press, 1996); P. **Philip,** *Numbers* (CC; Word, 1987); W. **Riggans,** *Numbers* (DSB; Westminster, 1983); N. H. **Snaith,** *Leviticus and Numbers* (NCB; Eerdmans, 1967); G. J. **Wenham,** *Numbers* (TOTC; InterVarsity Press, 1981).

Monographs and Articles

W. **Baroody,** "Exodus, Leviticus, Numbers, and Deuteronomy," in *A Complete Literary Guide to the Bible* (Zondervan, 1993), 121–36; D. J. A. **Clines,** *The Theme of the Pentateuch* (JSOTS; Sheffield: JSOT, 1978); G. W. **Coats,** *Rebellion in the Wilderness* (Abingdon, 1968); G. I. **Davies,** *The Way of the Wilderness* (Cambridge University Press, 1979); M. **Douglas,** *In the Wilderness: The Doctrine of Defilement in the Book of Numbers* (Sheffield Academic Press, 1993); J. **Hackett,** *The Balaam Text from Deir'Alla* (Chico: Scholars, 1984); Won W. **Lee,** *Punishment and Forgiveness in Israel's Migratory Campaign* (Eerdmans, 2003); D. T. **Olson,** *The Death of the Old and the Birth of the New: The Framework of the Book of Numbers and the Pentateuch* (BJS 71; Chico: Scholars, 1985); idem, "Book of Numbers," in DOTP (InterVarsity Press, 2003), 611–18.

HISTORICAL BACKGROUND

Authorship and Composition

Numbers is a continuation of the preceding three books, thus falling into the same general pattern of composition for the rest of the Pentateuch (see pp. 42–51). Within Numbers itself, there is only a single reference to Mosaic writing activity (33:1–2). Throughout the book, however, it is noted that Moses is the recipient of the divine revelation that forms the substance of the book (e.g., 1:1; 2:1; 4:1). The fact that the book refers to Moses in the third person rather than the first person does not invalidate Mosaic authorship (contra Gray 1903, xxix-xxx) since this reflects customary writing style in ancient times (so Harrison 1990, 23–24).

Numbers also contains some material that is most naturally understood as post-Mosaic additions. These include the short poem that is taken from the "Book of the Wars of the Lord" (21:14–15) as well as Numbers 32:34–42, which describes the building activity of the two and a half tribes that settled in the Transjordan after the conquest. This section is best taken as a post-Mosaic expansion of the chapter. The notorious passage in which Moses is described as the most humble man ever to live (Num. 12:3), while capable of a rather strained argument in favor of a Mosaic origin, is also most naturally read as a non-Mosaic gloss.

Furthermore, it must be said that Moses likely used source material in his composition of the book. The census accounts in Numbers 1 and 26, while contemporary, surely had a life prior to and independent of the book of Numbers. It is also possible that the Balaam story was an independent narrative incorporated into Moses' work.

This analysis of Numbers is in keeping with our characterization of the Pentateuch as a whole. That is, it is essentially Mosaic but includes source material and glosses. Its final redaction, however, may well be exilic. After all this is said, we must remember that we cannot be precise or certain about our reconstruction of the composition of pentateuchal books. It is fruitless to speculate about it more carefully in the manner of most source criticism.

Before surveying the history of critical opinion on Numbers, we may briefly mention a new, intriguing line of argumentation presented by Harrison (1990, 15–21). He elucidates evidence for the existence of a class of annalists or scribes (*ûôt̤ᵉ rîm*) by citing Numbers 1:16–18 and Joshua 1:10. He believes that these scribes were charged with the responsibility not only of recording the census lists but also of keeping account of events. While this theory is interesting and possible, the evidence is capable of more than one interpretation and must remain hypothetical. That such record keeping was likely is, however, beyond doubt. At a minimum it indicates the probability of ancient traditions that are part of the final Pentateuch.

The critical study of Numbers has a long history. Olson (1985, 9–30) has provided a masterful synthesis of the main movements of that study over the past one hundred years. He describes three main phases. The first began with August Dillmann's commentary written in 1886 in which he applied Wellhausen's documentary hypothesis to the book (see Historical-Critical Approaches in chap. 2). Ever since and up to the present day, Numbers has been characterized as a work in which P predominates. Budd (1984, xviii), for instance, summarizes contemporary opinion in this way:

> In the book of Numbers there is very general acceptance of a total priestly contribution in the following chapters—1–9, 15, 17–19, 26–31, 33–36— and of a substantial influence in 10, 13–14, 16, 20, 25, 32. The only chapters lacking such influence would appear to be 11–12, 21–24.

Those sections that are not identified with P are associated with JE. While some earlier researchers tried to differentiate J from E in Numbers, it is now seen as difficult to do so. According to critical reconstructions, D plays only a minor role in the book of Numbers.

The second stage of modern study of Numbers began with Gressmann's form-critical study (1913). Gressmann was applying the method of his mentor,

H. Gunkel. Subsequent applications of form criticism to Numbers have been associated with a source critical approach, but as Olson (1985, 19) has pointed out, by concentrating on the individual episodes' preliterary structure, there was an increasing openness to the antiquity of the material, even that embedded in the late P source.

The third stage builds on the previous two and is associated with the influence of M. Noth, whose commentary on Numbers first appeared in 1966. He advocated a tradition-historical study of the five major themes of the Pentateuch and thought that there was a lengthy oral stage where these five themes developed independently before they were brought together in a literary form. Thus his analysis is extremely complex and led him to the conclusion that "the book lacks unity, and it is difficult to see any pattern in its construction" (quoted in Olson 1985, 21).[1]

LITERARY ANALYSIS

Genre

What impresses one about Numbers is its generic variability. That is, the reader encounters many different types of literature from beginning to end. Milgrom (1990, xiii) lists a number of genres with examples: "narrative (4:1–3), poetry (21:17–18), prophecy (24:3–9), victory song (21:27–30), prayer (12:13), blessing (6:24–26), lampoon (22:22–35), diplomatic letter (21:14–19), civil law (27:1–11), cultic law (15:7–21), oracular decision (15:32–36), census list (26:1–51), temple archive (7:10–88), itinerary (33:1–49)." The sheer diversity of materials can confuse modern readers and render understanding difficult. Most of these genres, however, exist within the broader context of the instructional history writing that characterizes the Pentateuch as a whole. Indeed, due to its integral connection with the rest of the Pentateuch (especially Leviticus) the genre of the book as a whole can be discussed only in relationship to its broader literary context.

All of the above categories describe the genre of isolated episodes of the text. Upon closer examination we may say that they occur within the broader contexts of narrative and law. For instance, the poem that Milgrom cites in chapter 21 is part of a narrative, as are the oracular decision, the prophecy, the victory song, the prayer, the blessing, the diplomatic letter, the census list, the temple archive, and the itinerary. The civil and cultic laws are, of course, both part of the broader genre category of "law." Indeed, as Baroody (1993, 126) has pointed out, "the dozen major shifts back and forth (from narrative to law), not counting the short passages of narrative implementation within the legal sections are

What impresses one about Numbers is its generic variability. That is, the reader encounters many different types of literature from beginning to end.

---

[1]For an application of Noth's approach to a specific tradition, see Coats 1968.

almost dizzying." Moreover, as in Leviticus, the law finds its setting in the narrative. In this way, it is best to identify the genre of Numbers as instructional history writing.

Structure

Numbers' generic variability and its associated episodic nature make delineating the structure extremely difficult. Olson (1985, 31) surveys forty-six commentaries and uncovers twenty-four proposed outlines for the book. The different structures arise as scholars take their cues from different elements within the text. Perhaps the two most common suggestions are based on chronology and geography.

Milgrom (1990, xi) divides Numbers into three parts based on chronology:

1:1–10:11:	From the first day of the second month of the wilderness wandering to the nineteenth.
21:10–36:13:	Five months during the fortieth year in the wilderness
10:12–21:9:	Undated but falls within the forty years

Thus, Numbers brings the reader from the beginning to the end of the forty years of wilderness wandering.

In another attempt, Milgrom (xiii) illustrates the topographical structure to the book once again in three parts. He notes that there are forty stations of the journey mentioned in three main phases:

1:1–10:10:	The wilderness of Sinai
10:11–20:13:	The area around Kadesh
20:14–36:13:	From Kadesh to Moab

Budd (1984, xvii), on the other hand, gives a topical outline:

1:1–9:14:	Constituting the community at Sinai
9:15–25:18:	The journey—its setbacks and success
26:1–35:34:	Final preparations for settlement

While none of these schemes are persuasive in the final analysis as the intended structure of the book, they all give insightful perspectives on its contents. They throw light on the time and setting of the book. The study by Olson more significantly reveals an outline of Numbers that highlights its theological message. In this section we will describe the structure, while in the next we will present its theological implications.

Olson's first step is to show that Numbers is both a part of the Pentateuch and a distinct unit within it (43–53). He points to the tradition of the text in Hebrew and Greek transmission as well as to rabbinic quotations to demonstrate the antiquity of Numbers as a separate book. This external evidence is supported by Olson's demonstration that each book within the Pentateuch, including Numbers, has a clear introduction and conclusion that marks them off from each other.

Next, Olson studies the importance of the two census lists in the book (Num. 1 and 26). He concludes that these are the structural pillars of the book, marking off the two wilderness generations. Numbers 1–25 tells the story of the first generation—the generation that sinned by doubting the Lord's power to help them against the inhabitants of Palestine. This generation died in the wilderness and was replaced by their descendants, those represented by the census in Numbers 26. The book concludes with a narration of their rise. Indeed, the title of Olson's book captures the theological significance of Numbers that is revealed by paying attention to this important structural marker: *The Death of the Old and the Rise of the New.* The outline that follows is taken from Olson (1985, 118–20):

I. The End of the Old: The First Generation of God's People Out of Egypt on the March in the Wilderness (1:1–25:18)
  A. The Preparation and Inauguration of the March of the Holy People of Israel (1:1–10:36)
    1. Preparation and ritual organization of the march (1:1–10:10)
    2. The inauguration of the march (10:11–10:36)
  B. The Cycle of Rebellion, Death, and Deliverance of the Holy People of Israel with Elements of Hope but Ultimate Failure and Death (11:1–25:18)
    1. Repeated incidents of rebellion and atonement, each involving the death and/or the threat of death of a portion of the first generation (11:1–20:29)
    2. The end of the first generation: signs of hope coupled with ultimate failure (21:1–25:18)
II. The Birth of the New: The Second Generation of God's People Out of Egypt as They Prepare to Enter the Promised Land (Num. 26:1–36:13)
  A. The Preparation and Organization of the New Holy People of God as They Prepare to Enter the Promised Land (26:1–36:13)
  B. Will This Second Generation Be Faithful and Enter the Promised Land (Promise) or Rebel and Fail as the First Generation (Warning)?

In the most recent contribution to the study of the structure of Numbers, Lee (2003) argues that previous attempts to delineate a structure have not been persuasive because they have only focused on the surface elements of the story. Lee then gives a detailed argument for an under-the-surface conceptual analysis that leads him to first differentiate 1:1–10:10 from 10:11–36:13. The first part is preparation for, and the second part the execution of, what he calls

"Israel's migratory-sanctuary campaign." At the heart of the second part of Numbers is the failure of this campaign because of the Israelites' fear generated by the spy report narrated in 13:1–14:45. When all is said and done, however, Lee's analysis, while occasionally insightful, is not an improvement on Olson's. Indeed, one can question just how important it is to get the outline just right in order to understand the plot and message of a book like Numbers.

Style

The book of Numbers is not among the literary high points of the Old Testament. This assessment is certainly true from the perspective of modern literary tastes, and nothing we know would lead us to expect that ancient tastes were any different. For this reason, Numbers has not been the subject of much aesthetic analysis.

While this must be admitted for fear of overextending our literary appreciation of the Bible, it must also be recognized that parts of the book are interesting from a literary point of view. Readers should note that the narrative sections of the book (especially the story of Balaam in chaps. 22–24) are as artistically pleasing as the stories found in such well-studied books as Genesis and Samuel. These narratives are amenable to the same kind of analysis as other prose stories of the Old Testament (see The Conventions of Old Testament Stories in chap. 1)

The above analysis of the book is not to be taken negatively. Just because a book is in the Bible does not mean that it has to be a literary masterpiece. The Bible is more than a collection of good stories, and Numbers has a crucial message to communicate. Furthermore, even those parts of the book that are not as appealing to our literary sense utilize recognizable literary conventions. Milgrom is very sensitive to these in his commentary:

> The individual pericopes of Numbers manifest design. Their main structural device is chiasm and introversion. Also evidenced are such artifices as parallel panels, subscripts and repetitive resumptions, prolepses, and septenary enumerations. The pericopes are linked to each other by associative terms and themes and to similar narratives in Exodus by the same itinerary formula. (1990, xxxi)

Milgrom backs up these observations with numerous examples throughout the commentary. He highlights chiasm and introversion as the most prevalent structuring device in the book. He cites 14:2; 30:15; 30:17; and 33:52–56 as examples of chiasm on a microlevel, while mentioning 5:11–31; 31; and 32 as three examples of longer chiasms. A second structural device is "parallel patterns." Instead of a crossing pattern like chiasm (ABCDC'B'A', this method gives two lists side by side (ABCDABCD). Examples include chapters 11 and 12, each chapter paralleling the other in structure. Among the remaining devices he mentions, the most interesting is the septenary repetition, where "a word or phrase is repeated seven times" (xxxi). He notes that in chapter 32 five words are each used seven times, obviously not a coincidence (see also his discussion in 492–94).

THEOLOGICAL MESSAGE

Olson's structural analysis of Numbers is a prelude to his understanding of its theology. Numbers narrates an important transition in the history of redemption as it records the death of the first wilderness generation (the subject of the first twenty-five chapters) and its replacement by the second generation (Num. 26–36).

The story of the first part of the book is therefore a story of sin and judgment. Lay and priestly leaders rebel against Moses, God's appointed leader (Num. 12, 16–17). The people are constantly grumbling against God's provision in the wilderness (e.g., Num. 11). It is the spy story recorded in Numbers 13–14 that triggers God's judgment, however, with the result that the first generation was doomed to die in the wilderness and not see the Promised Land. Only two spies, Caleb and Joshua, who believed that God was able to bring them into the land, were exempted from this judgment (Num. 26:26–35). Nonetheless, God continued to provide for the Israelites in the wilderness, though they continued to rebel and complain. Even Moses, according to an enigmatic passage (Num. 20:1–13), displeased the Lord and was not permitted to enter the land of promise.

That God continued to treat the Israelites as his special people is highlighted in the Balaam narrative (Num. 22–24). Balaam, a non-Israelite prophet (now known from extrabiblical texts; see Hackett 1984), is called in by Balak the king of Moab to curse the Israelites as they come near his land. Balaam, though, blesses Israel because of the intervention of God. Even with all of this divine care and concern, Israel continues to turn against their God, and the section ends with God's people turning against the Lord by worshiping a local manifestation of the god Baal.

While the first section of the book concentrates on the judgment of the first generation, Olson argues that the second part (chaps. 26–36) "is basically positive and hopeful" (1985, 151). No one who was an adult at the time of the spies' report was still alive. A new generation now stood before the Lord, and the time was right for entering the Promised Land. Thus, as Olson points out, the contents of these chapters is definitely positive:

> After all the deaths of the first generation, not one death of a member of the second generation is recorded. Military engagements are successful (Numbers 28), potential crises are resolved (Numbers 32), and laws which look forward to the future life in the land of Canaan are promulgated (Numbers 34). The threat remains, but the promise of the future is the dominant note which is sounded at the end of the book. (151)

Numbers narrates an important transition in the history of redemption as it records the death of the first wilderness generation and its replacement by the second generation.

It is on this note of expectant hope that the book ends. Note that the hope never turns into certainty. That is, the hope of the second generation is an untried hope. This generation too will face severe threats to its faith (see Joshua), and it remains to be seen how they will respond.

Olson suggests that the abiding significance of the book of Numbers is that it "functions as a paradigm for every succeeding generation of God's people. . . . [It] invites every generation to put itself in the place of the new generation" (183).

APPROACHING THE NEW TESTAMENT

God Stays Involved

Numbers illustrates one of the main themes of the whole Bible. The sin of the first generation could have led to the end of the story of redemption and the destruction of the people of God. But God does not abandon his people even in their rebellion and sin. As Milgrom nicely puts it: "The principal actor in Numbers is Yahweh. Even under extreme provocation, he keeps his covenant with Israel, guides them through the wilderness and provides for their needs" (1990, xxxvii). God stays involved with his people because of his covenant love for them.

The New Testament continues this theme. Indeed, the New Testament is its climax. The Old Testament is simply a prelude to what happens on the cross. God's people continued to turn against him, but still he sent his Son, Jesus Christ, whom they treated brutally (Mark 12:1–12). Nonetheless, God did not abandon his people but provided hope for them in the salvation offered by Jesus Christ.

Each generation of Christians should place themselves in the position of the new generation of the book of Numbers. God has acted redemptively in our midst, and by so doing, he has given our lives meaning and hope. Just like the Numbers generation, we are called upon to respond to God's grace with obedience.

The Wilderness Theme

The wilderness provides the background for most of Exodus, Leviticus, Numbers, and Deuteronomy. As explained in chapter 3, the exodus–wilderness wanderings–conquest theme is an important one that reverberates throughout the Bible. (For more information about this important theological perspective on the book of Numbers, see The Exodus from Egypt in chapter 3.)

God's Holiness

Numbers also continues the important theme of God's presence and his holiness. This may be observed in the care with which the text deals with the place of the Levites as guardians of God's holiness (Num. 3), especially in their responsibility to transport the tabernacle and its furniture (Num. 4). Many of the laws presented throughout Numbers are there to assure the purity of the camp. The biblical-theological theme of God's presence and his holiness has already been explored in chapter 4, "Leviticus," and the interested reader may turn there (see The Holiness of God).

CHAPTER SIX

DEUTERONOMY

The name of this book of the Bible comes from a Greek compound that means "second law" or "repetition of the law." Ironically, it derives from a misunderstanding in the Septuagint of a Hebrew phrase in Deuteronomy 17:18, where the king is instructed to make a "copy of this law." Although the title of the book rests on a mistranslation in the Septuagint, it is nevertheless a fortuitous error, since Deuteronomy contains a second version of the law delivered on Mount Sinai as recorded in Exodus, Leviticus, and Numbers.

The book consists largely of a series of addresses delivered on the plains of Moab by Moses. Moses led the people in a covenant renewal before they undertook the wars of conquest for the land promised to the fathers; he prepared the people for his imminent death.

Deuteronomy is arguably one of the most significant books of the Old Testament. It is the culmination of the Pentateuch, and it throws the shadow of its distinctive theological perspective on the rest of the Old Testament—history (particularly Samuel-Kings) and prophets (e.g., Jeremiah) alike. For good reason, Wenham (1985) has called Deuteronomy the linchpin of the Old Testament.

BIBLIOGRAPHY

Commentaries

D. L. **Christensen,** *Deuteronomy 1:1–21:9* (WBC; Word, 2001); idem, *Deuteronomy 21:10–34:14* (WBC; Word, 2002); R. **Clifford,** *Deuteronomy with Excursus on Covenant and Law* (OTM; Wilmington: M. Glazier, 1982); P. C. **Craigie,** *The Book of Deuteronomy* (NICOT; Eerdmans, 1976); G. **Cunliffe-Jones,** *Deuteronomy* (TBC; SCM, 1951); S. R. **Driver,** *A Critical and Exegetical Commentary on Deuteronomy* (ICC; Scribner, 1895); A. D. H. **Mayes,** *Deuteronomy* (NCB; Eerdmans, 1979); J. **McConville,** *Deuteronomy* (Apollos, 2002); E. H. **Merrill,** *Deuteronomy* (NAC; Broadman, 1994); P. D. **Miller** Jr., *Deuteronomy* (Interp; John Knox,

1990); D. F. **Payne,** *Deuteronomy* (DSB; Westminster, 1985); J. **Ridderbos,** *Deuteronomy* (BSC; Zondervan, 1984); J. A. **Thompson,** *Deuteronomy* (TOTC; London: InterVarsity Press, 1974); J. H. **Tigay,** *Deuteronomy* (JPS Torah Commentary; Jewish Publication Society, 1996); G. **von Rad,** *Deuteronomy* (OTL; Westminster, 1966); C. K. **Wright,** *Deuteronomy* (NIBCOT; Hendrickson/Paternoster, 1996).

Monographs and Articles

E. **Achtemeier,** "Plumbing the Riches: Deuteronomy for the Preacher," *Interp* 3 (1987): 269–81; J. A. **Baker,** "Deuteronomy and World Problems," *JSOT* 29 (1984): 3–17; C. M. **Carmichael,** *The Laws of Deuteronomy* (Cornell University Press, 1974); R. E. **Clements,** *Deuteronomy* (OT Guides; Sheffield: JSOT, 1989); idem, *God's Chosen People* (Allenson, 1968); G. D. **Collier,** "The Problem of Deuteronomy: In Search of a Perspective," *ResQ* 26 (1983): 215–33; F. M. **Cross,** *Canaanite Myth and Hebrew Epic* (Harvard University Press, 1972); R. **de Vaux,** "La lieu que Yahve a choisi pour y etablir son nom," in *Das ferne und nahe Wort,* ed. L. Rost (*BZAW* 105; 1967): 219–28; J. **Gold,** "Deuteronomy and the World: the Beginning and the End," in *The Biblical Mosaic,* ed. R. Polzin and E. Rothman (Fortress, 1982): 45–59; R. P. **Gordon,** "Deuteronomy and the Deuteronomic School," *TynBul* 25 (1974): 113–20; B. **Halpern,** "The Centralization Formula in Deuteronomy," *VT* 31 (1981): 20–38; L. J. **Hoppe,** "The Meaning of Deuteronomy," *BTB* 10 (1980): 111–17; idem, "The Levitical Origins of Deuteronomy Reconsidered," *BibRes* 28 (1983): 27–36; W. **Kaiser,** *Toward an Old Testament Ethics* (Zondervan, 1983); S. A. **Kaufman,** "The Structure of the Deuteronomic Law," *Maarav* 1/2 (1978–79): 105–58; K. A. **Kitchen,** *Ancient Orient and Old Testament* (Leicester: InterVarsity Press, 1966); idem, "The Fall and Rise of Covenant, Law and Treaty," *TynBul* 40 (1989): 118–35; idem, *On the Reliability of the Old Testament* (Eerdmans, 2003); M. G. **Kline,** *Treaty of the Great King* (Eerdmans, 1963); L. **Kuyper,** "The Book of Deuteronomy," *Interp* 6 (1952): 321–40; N. **Lohfink,** ed., *Das Deuteronomium: Entstehung, Gestalt und Botschaft* (Leuven University Press, 1985); idem, *Das Hauptgebot: Eine Untersuchung literarischer Einleitungsfragen zu Dtn 5–11* (AnBib; Rome: Pontifical Biblical Institute, 1963); R. **MacKenzie,** "The Messianism of Deuteronomy," *CBQ* 19 (1957): 299–305; G. T. **Manley,** *The Book of the Law: Studies in the Date of Deuteronomy* (London: Tyndale, 1957); S. D. **McBride,** "Polity of the Covenant People: the Book of Deuteronomy," *Interp* 3 (1987): 229–44; D. J. **McCarthy,** *Old Testament Covenant: A Survey of Current Opinions,* 2nd ed. (Rome: Pontifical Biblical Institute, 1978); J. G. **McConville,** "God's 'Name' and God's 'Glory,'" *TynBul* 30 (1979): 149–63; idem, *Law and Theology in Deuteronomy* (JSOTS 33; Sheffield: JSOT, 1984); idem, *Grace in the End* (Zondervan, 1994); idem, "Book of Deuteronomy," DOTP (InterVarsity Press, 2003), 182–93; J. G. **McConville** and J. G. **Millar,** *Time and Place in Deuteronomy* (JSOTS 179; Sheffield Academic Press, 1994);

E. W. **Nicholson,** *Deuteronomy and Tradition* (Fortress, 1967); D. **Olson,** *Deuteronomy and the Death of Moses* (Fortress, 1994); R. H. **Polzin,** "Deuteronomy," in *The Literary Guide to the Bible,* ed. R. Alter and F. Kermode (Harvard University Press, 1987): 92–101; idem, *Moses and the Deuteronomist* (Seabury, 1980); idem, "Reporting Speech in the Book of Deuteronomy: Toward a Compositional Analysis of the Deuteronomic History," in *Traditions in Transformation,* ed. B. Halpern and J. Levenson (Eisenbrauns, 1981): 193–211; G. **von Rad,** *Studies in Deuteronomy* (Westminster, 1953); J. H. **Walton,** "Deuteronomy: An Exposition of the Spirit of the Law," *GraceTJ* 8 (1987): 213–25; M. **Weinfeld,** *Deuteronomy and the Deuteronomic School* (Oxford: Clarendon, 1972); G. **Wenham,** "The Date of Deuteronomy: Linchpin of Old Testament Criticism" (in two parts) *Themelios* 10 (1985): 15–20; 11 (1985): 15–18.

HISTORICAL BACKGROUND

This section deals with the authorship of Deuteronomy, its historical background, and issues in the history of interpretation.

The book of Deuteronomy is largely a record of the speeches of Moses delivered shortly before his death east of the Jordan. In form it is the record of a covenant renewal ceremony on the plains of Moab where Israel once again affirmed its allegiance to God and its national commitment to keep his law (Deut. 29:1–31:29). In some respects Deuteronomy is also "the last will and testament of Moses." In addition to reiterating the covenant made earlier at Sinai (29:1), the book prepared Israel for two major issues that the nation would soon face: (1) life without Moses, and (2) the wars for the conquest of the land. Substantial portions of the book provide for the orderly governance of Israel after Moses' death through a system of judges and courts, the priests and Levites, kings, and prophets (Deut. 16:18–18:22). More than any other book of the Pentateuch, Deuteronomy prepares the nation for the wars of conquest by stipulating laws governing holy war (chaps. 7, 20).

Jewish and Christian tradition alike assigned the authorship of the book to Moses in precritical periods. Scattered comments among Jewish and Christian commentators showed awareness of a series of passages that were often described as "post-" or "a-Mosaica," but these were viewed as isolated insertions into the text by later editors who added a comment here and there to update or clarify geographical (2:10–11, 20–23; 3:9, 11, 13b–14) or historical (10:6–9) information. The superscription to the book says that it contains the words Moses spoke to all Israel "on the other side of the Jordan" (1:1 various translations). This requires, then, that the superscription was written by someone on the western side of the Jordan at a later point after Moses' death east of the Jordan. Obviously, Moses was not responsible for the account of his own death (chap. 34). Apart from these sorts of questions, the book was accepted as the work of Moses' hands. Toward the end of the book, frequent reference is made to the written character of the covenant document that Moses had produced (27:3, 8; 28:58; 29:21, 29; 30:10, 19; 31:24).

With the rise of the Enlightenment and the development of historical-critical approaches to the Bible, Deuteronomy was quickly severed from historical contact with Moses. Although many continued to defend the essentially Mosaic origin of the book, critical scholarship assigned to Deuteronomy a crucial role in its efforts to recover a history of Israel's religion that was in fact quite different from what the text itself presented. The amount of literature on Deuteronomy is enormous,[1] and a bewildering array of opinions and options has been suggested for the historical setting and development of the book. Any effort to collate and summarize will unavoidably oversimplify. We will sketch some of the highlights of the history of critical research roughly in chronological order, though describing particular positions may take us beyond the chronological bounds in the outline below.

In the Nineteenth Century

The identification of Deuteronomy with the book of the law found in the temple during Josiah's reign had been suggested as early as Jerome (AD 342–420). However, with the rise of rationalism, in 1805 W. M. L. de Wette laid the cornerstone for later developments in pentateuchal criticism by identifying Deuteronomy as Josiah's law book. Subsequent efforts to date the putative sources of the Pentateuch (J, E, D, P) would array these sources before or after D (Deuteronomy), depending on whether or not the individual source presumed a knowledge of the law as propounded in D. Assigning Deuteronomy to the late seventh century BC would become a linchpin for critical scholarship in the heyday of source criticism (Wenham 1985). Deuteronomy's link with Moses was all but completely severed.

There was good reason to suggest that Josiah's law book was either Deuteronomy itself or some earlier alternate edition of material that eventually became the book. The book of Kings was widely recognized to have been influenced by the laws of Deuteronomy in general. Features of Josiah's response to the law book suggest his acting under the influence of laws largely unique to Deuteronomy: (1) Deuteronomy 12 required the destruction of Canaanite high places and conducting worship at a centralized sanctuary, and Josiah follows these provisions (2 Kings 23:4–20). (2) Whereas Exodus 12 provided for observing Passover in the confines of the family, Deuteronomy 16 set the observance at the central sanctuary. Passover under Josiah was observed in accord with the specifications of Deuteronomy 16 instead of those in Exodus 12 (2 Kings 23:21–22).

---

[1]Christensen's commentary (2001, 2002) contains the most exhaustive bibliography published to date on research in Deuteronomy.

(3) Deuteronomy also enjoined the elimination of mediums, spiritists, and diviners from Israel; Israel was not to hear the will of God through these means, but rather through the prophets (Deut. 18:14–22). Josiah removed the mediums and spiritists in order to fulfill the requirements of the law book (2 Kings 23:24) and sought direction from a prophetess (22:14). (4) The book presented to Josiah contained a series of curses (2 Kings 22:13, 19), probably those in Deuteronomy 28. (5) Deuteronomy requires of kings in Israel that they rule in accordance with a copy of the law (Deut. 17:18–19), precisely the action attributed to Josiah (2 Kings 22:11; 23:2–3). (6) The law book was identified as a "Book of the Covenant" (23:2), confirmed when later critical studies demonstrated the structural affinities between Deuteronomy and covenants written in the ancient Near East. (7) The Kings account also reflects the "name theology" of Deuteronomy (Deut. 12:5, 11; 2 Kings 23:27) and reiterates the inevitability of divine judgment as already announced in Deuteronomy (Deut. 31:24–29; 2 Kings 22:16–20; 23:26–27).

By insisting that the date of the book's discovery in the temple was also its approximate date of composition and then for this reason assigning a seventh-century date either to the book of Deuteronomy or to an initial phase of its composition, critical scholarship was forced, by and large, to regard the book as a pious fraud, possibly developed by Josiah and his partisans to legitimate his bid for authority and the extension of Jerusalem's sway over the outlying areas.

In the Late Nineteenth and Early Twentieth Centuries

Largely satisfied that they had successfully identified the major sources underlying the Pentateuch, critical scholars turned to investigating the underlying strata within Deuteronomy itself. C. Steuernagel (1923) and W. Staerck (1924) both sought to isolate redactional layers in the book on the basis of changes in the form of address between second person singular and plural forms. The earlier stratum of material was thought to have used the singular forms. G. A. Smith (1918) in his commentary had also examined this variation between singular and plural and had concluded that it may reflect different hands but was not sufficiently clear to isolate distinct documents. This distinction between singular and plural second person forms of address has continued to play a role in research into the redactional history of the book to this day. Nicholson (1967, 22–36) uses the change from second person singular to plural as his main criterion for isolating Ur-Deuteronomy from later Deuteronomistic additions; Mayes (1979, 35–37) is more cautious in using this same approach.

S. R. Driver (1895) provided a thorough investigation of issues concerning Mosaic authorship. He identified apparent contradictions between Deuteronomy and Genesis–Numbers, contrasted the differences in particular laws, described the style of Deuteronomy in contrast to the other books, concluded that Deuteronomy must be from a period subsequent to Moses, and associated it with Josiah's reform. In addition to Deuteronomy's unique laws regarding centralized worship or provision for different requirements for observing Passover, proponents of the classical documentary hypothesis isolated pentateuchal sources, depending in part on their respective views of the relationship between priests and Levites. The role of the priesthood came to be associated with the tribe of Levi sometime during the monarchy, so that in Deuteronomy (from the seventh century) all Levites were priests (Deut. 18:1–8; 21:5; 33:8–11), whereas in the Priestly stratum of the Pentateuch (a later stratum), there was a sharp distinction between the roles of the priests (descended from Aaron) and their subordinate assistants, the Levites.

Specific enactments differ in Deuteronomy from the other legal texts; for critical scholarship, these differences required a different author and setting from the other law codes. For example, in the law regarding the seduction of a virgin who is not engaged to be married, Exodus allows the father to refuse the marriage of the two parties (Ex. 22:17), whereas Deuteronomy requires the marriage and prohibits any future divorce (Deut. 22:28–29). The reason for observing the Sabbath in Exodus (20:11) is God's own rest after creation; in Deuteronomy (5:15), it is to remember Israel's enslavement in Egypt. In Leviticus (17:3–5) all slaughter of animals, even for purposes of domestic consumption, is clearly sacrificial; in Deuteronomy (12:15–17), as a consequence of centralizing worship in one location, provision is made for profane slaughter away from the sanctuary. The tithe is reserved for the Levites in the other law codes (Num. 18:21–24; Lev. 27:30–33), whereas in Deuteronomy (14:22–29) a portion is consumed by the offerer and his family. On the whole, the laws in Deuteronomy were regarded as reflecting a more "humanitarian" approach than is found in other legal corpora (Weinfeld 1972, 282–97).

G. von Rad supplemented the traditional critical criteria for source analysis with an interest in theological themes and issues (tradition history).[2] Von Rad argued that the exodus and Sinai traditions were originally independent of one another. He concluded that the Sinai materials originally had a cultic setting in a covenant renewal ceremony at Shechem. For von Rad, both the Book of the Covenant (Ex. 19–24) and Deuteronomy reflected the same cultic occasion. Because Deuteronomy was largely hortatory (addresses, homilies, and admonitions to a group of people) and consisted in the main of preached law, he suggested that the book originated among the Levites. Because it was addressed to all Israel, emphasized the role of Shechem (Deut. 27), and opposed Baalism, he suggested an origin in the northern kingdom. Some portion of the book was

---

[2]See his 1938 essay published in *Beiträge zur Wissenschaft vom Alten und Neuen Testament,* 4th series, 26 (1938), and translated into English as "The Form Critical Problem of the Hexateuch," *The Problem of the Hexateuch and Other Essays* (McGraw-Hill, 1966), 1–78.

taken to Judah and revised to serve as the basis for Josiah's reform. It received further elaboration during the exile. Although the polished book as we have it is fairly late, it contains many ancient materials.

Because the Levites and priests were presented as "preachers" or "teachers" of the law (Deut. 33:10; Lev. 10:11; 2 Chron. 15:3; 17:7–9; Jer. 18:18; Mal. 2:7; Hos. 4:6), the hortatory character of Deuteronomy would naturally suggest an origin among Levites. Others, however, suggested that Deuteronomy developed among Israel's prophets. The book presents Moses as the ideal prophet (Deut. 18:14–22); other prophetic books (Hosea, Jeremiah) show marked connections with Deuteronomy. Ur-Deuteronomy allegedly developed in the North and had an antimonarchical tone, reflecting the preaching of the prophets. A prophetic origin for the book was suggested by, among others, Wellhausen, Driver, Alt, and most recently Nicholson (1967, 76). Weinfeld (1972, 55) argued against the Levitical origin of the book: for the Levites to argue for centralization of worship would have been to undercut their jobs at the local sanctuaries; instead, Weinfeld called attention to the affinities of Deuteronomy with wisdom literature and argued for a setting in the wisdom traditions of Israel. Hoppe (1983) rejected the earlier efforts to determine the circle from which Deuteronomy emerged and argued instead that it should be assigned to the elders of Israel. Ultimately, all of the major authority centers in Israel (Levites, prophets, elders, sages at the royal court) have been suggested as possible sources for the book.

Ultimately, all of the major authority centers in Israel (Levites, prophets, elders, sages at the royal court) have been suggested as possible sources for the book.

From Mid-twentieth Century to the Present

In 1943 Noth first published his thesis that Deuteronomy through Kings constituted in the main a single history largely the product of a single author.[3] Noth contended that this exilic Deuteronomistic historian (Dtr) took over the Deuteronomic code in roughly the form we now have it in Deuteronomy 4:44–30:20 (1981, 16). Scholars had long noted that the book appears to have two historical introductions (chaps. 1–3 or 4 and 5–11). Noth argued that Deuteronomy 1–3 (or 4) did not contain the introduction to the book of Deuteronomy itself, but rather the introduction to the entirety of the Deuteronomistic History (DH). Noth contended that the core of the book could be found in the you-

---

[3]The first edition appeared as *Schriften der Königsberger Gelehrten Gesellschaft* in 1943, though it is generally known by the title of the second edition, *Überlieferungsgeschichtliche Studien* (Tübingen: Max Niemeyer Verlag, 1957; 3rd unaltered edition, 1967). The first half of the volume, dealing with Noth's approach to the Deuteronomistic History, was translated into English and appeared as *The Deuteronomistic History* (JSOTS 15; Sheffield: JSOT, 1981). The second half was devoted to Noth's approach to the Chronicler's work; it was translated into English by H. G. M. Williamson and appeared as *The Chronicler's History* (JSOTS 50; Sheffield: JSOT, 1987).

singular and you-plural passages, which were then supplemented through a process of gradual growth and elaboration that resulted primarily from the oral reading and exposition of the law (31:9–13). Noth's thesis had a monumental impact on all research to follow, and his views commonly serve as a starting point for subsequent writers. According to Noth, although Deuteronomy in its present form dates from the exilic period, it contains many ancient materials.

During this period researchers also began to notice that the literary structure found in ancient Near Eastern treaties between nations also resembled the structure of Deuteronomy. Kline (1963) argued that the book of Deuteronomy was specifically constructed along the lines of a second-millennium international treaty as distinct from the treaty pattern during the Assyrian period in the first millennium. As a consequence, Kline provided a strong argument for the antiquity of Deuteronomy. Although not all have followed Kline's argument, the relationship of Deuteronomy to ancient Near Eastern covenants and treaties has continued to play a large role in scholarship. Kline's view has recently been supported and expanded upon by Kitchen (2003, 283–94). See the discussion under Literary Analysis.

Biblical scholarship in the past two decades has turned increasingly to synchronic readings of biblical books. In synchronic approaches scholars are more interested in the books as they now exist than in reconstructing the underlying sources or the history of composition. Literary approaches assume that the book is a unity and attempt to explain the author's rhetorical strategy and compositional techniques (see Polzin 1980; McConville 1984 and 1994; Lohfink 1963). Items that traditional criticism regarded as clues to the redactional layers of a composite work often become, in literary analysis, evidence for sophisticated handling of complex theological issues in a unified manner. For example, McConville (1984) has explained the peculiarities of the cultic laws in Deuteronomy in terms of the theology of the book; that is, within the context of Deuteronomy as a whole rather than as evidence of composite composition. Polzin's (1983) analysis cuts across the presumed distinctions between Deuteronomic (Ur-Deuteronomy) and Deuteronomistic (later additions to the DH) material.

There is no clear consensus on most issues surrounding Deuteronomy. Issues of date and authorship are tightly bound up with questions of the relationship of the book to the remainder of the Deuteronomistic History (Joshua–Kings), the relevance of the treaty parallels for genre and setting, questions of provenance (from the North? from Levites, prophets, sages?), and the issue of the relationship of the book to Josiah's reforms.

LITERARY ANALYSIS

The literary features of Deuteronomy have been explored from a number of different vantage points, not all of which are equally important or helpful.

Deuteronomy as Treaty

Following the preliminary explorations of others, Kline (1963) proposed that the book of Deuteronomy had the same outline and structure as the international treaties known from the Hittite culture of the second millennium BC. Kitchen (2003) has recently bolstered Kline's perspective.

Table 3
The Treaties and Deuteronomy

I. Preamble (1:1–5)
II. Historical Prologue (1:6–3:29)
III. Stipulations (chaps. 4–26)
  A. Basic (4:1–11:32)
  B. Detailed (12:1–26:19)
IV. Curses and Blessings, Ratification (chaps. 27–30)
V. Succession Arrangements (chaps. 31–34)
  A. Invocation of Witnesses
  B. Provision of Public Reading

Kline argued that the treaty relationship between a conquering king and a subject people was the paradigm used to define the relationship between God as suzerain lord and his vassal people Israel. The parties were identified in the treaty preamble. In the second millennium treaties, this was followed by a historical prologue in which the past relationship between the suzerain and the vassal was recounted, emphasizing the beneficence of the king to his servant. The stipulations contained the detailed laws agreed to by the vassal in his submission to the suzerain. The most prominent demand was for the exclusive allegiance of the vassal to his covenant lord. The stipulations ordinarily included provisions for the tribute the vassal was to bring to his lord. In the context of Israel's relationship with Yahweh, this tribute consisted in part of the required offerings and sacrifices specified in the cultic laws. The second-millennium treaties then included a lengthy list of blessings and cursings that would follow obedience or disobedience to the covenant stipulations. These blessings and cursings were invoked in the names of the gods of both suzerain and vassal; the gods were invoked as witnesses to the oaths accompanying ratification.

In God's covenant with Israel there could be no thought of invoking third-party deities to witness the ratification of the covenant; instead, "the heavens and the earth" are called to fulfill this function (Deut. 4:26; 30:19; 31:28). The treaties included provisions for future public readings of the covenant document in order to remind both suzerain and vassal of their duties under its provisions (31:9–22). The treaties contained provisions for the vassal's sons to succeed their father (vv. 1–8). Duplicate copies of the treaty document were made ("two tables of the law"—Ex. 34:1, 28; Deut. 10:1–5; 17:18–19; 31:24–26), one each to be deposited in the respective sanctuaries of the suzerain and vassal. Since this sanctuary was one and the same in the covenant between God and Israel, the tablets were placed in the ark.

Because of its strong affinities with the structure of second-millennium treaties as opposed to the structure of treaties known from the first millennium, Kline's argument provided a prima facie case for a date for Deuteronomy close to the period of Moses instead of at a later time such as the seventh century. Treaties from the Assyrian period did not contain the historical prologue. Instead of listing both curses and blessings, the Assyrian treaties mentioned only the maledictions to be inflicted on the disobedient vassal. The requirement that a copy of the treaty be deposited in the sanctuary of both suzerain and vassal is not found in the first-millennium documents. In the Hittite treaties the demand that the vassal love (be faithful to) the suzerain is accompanied by assurances of the suzerain's affection (fidelity), but this is not found in the Assyrian treaties. To be sure, these items could be gaps in the documentary evidence—a future archaeological excavation could unearth Assyrian treaty texts in which these elements were present. Of the five major Assyrian treaties, three are damaged at that point in the tablets where a historical prologue could have occurred (see Weinfeld 1972, 63–65, 67–69). However, on the whole, Deuteronomy does show clear affinities with extrabiblical treaty documents, and more specifically with those of the second millennium; it is fairly clear that Deuteronomy was well described as a "covenant" (29:9, 12, 14, 21) document.

A number of scholars have taken similar approaches to that advocated by Kline (Craigie 1976). Kitchen (1989, 2003) and Wenham (1969) concur in the pervasive influence of the treaty forms on Deuteronomy but also regard it as a fusion of treaty forms with the structure of ancient Near Eastern law codes. Weinfeld (1972, 146–57) finds a similar convergence of law code and treaty forms.

Others have disputed the identification of distinctive and different treaty forms in the first and second millennia (McCarthy 1978). Weinfeld acknowledges the treaty structure of Deuteronomy but argues that the book is following the structure of first-millennium treaties, particularly as known from the vassal treaties of Esarhaddon. Weinfeld's primary argument (1972, 121–22) is that the curses at the end of the Assyrian treaties are invoked in the order of the Assyrian pantheon. In one of these treaties, the order of subjects in the curses resembles the sequence of subject matter in the curses of Deuteronomy 28, a fact that Weinfeld regards as strong evidence for a first-millennium date for Deuteronomy. However, these parallels are far from exact and pertain only to a general level of subject matter. As McConville has stated, "it is best to think of Deuteronomy as drawing on the treaty traditions of the ANE rather freely" (2002, 24).

This debate about the structure of Deuteronomy and its relationship to extrabiblical documents is far from over. Future study of the book must give renewed attention to this issue.

Deuteronomy as Polity

If Deuteronomy was in fact a treaty-covenant document as well as having features of a law code, it in effect became the "constitution" of ancient Israel. It was the written deposit that defined her social order, the codification of her legal principles and juridical procedures, and her self-understanding under the rule of God. As a document, it administered the covenant life of God's people. Although not himself concerned to define Deuteronomy as a treaty text, McBride (1987) called attention to many features of this "deuteronomic constitutionalism." He highlighted the way in which Deuteronomy sought to empower and protect segments of the population most vulnerable to abuse. McBride argued that Deuteronomy should be understood as the archetype and forerunner of modern Western constitutionalism.

Deuteronomy as Speech

Deuteronomy has long been understood as a series of three addresses by Moses to Israel on the plains of Moab. Each address begins by specifying the location and setting in which it was given—"east of the Jordan in the territory of Moab" (1:5), "in the valley near Beth Peor east of the Jordan" (4:44–49),[4] and "in Moab" (29:1)—but all three may well refer to the same locale. Moses' first address (chaps. 1–4) is oriented toward the past and recounts Israel's journey to the border of the land. The second address (chaps. 5–28) is oriented to the future and concerns Israel's life under the law in the land. In the third address (chaps. 29–32), the nation is led in covenant renewal. These addresses are then supplemented with an account of Moses' death (chaps. 33–34).

Polzin (1981, 1983, 1987) has pioneered a literary approach to Deuteronomy that concentrates on speech analysis. There are two dominant voices in the book of Deuteronomy, those of Moses and God. For most of the book Moses speaks alone, himself the hearer and reporter of God's words. Whereas earlier traditional readings of the book had identified a series of post- and a-Mosaica as the result of largely random editorial activity, Polzin finds instead a third voice in the book: it is not that scribes occasionally glossed the book from historical points later than Moses, but rather that a narrator (in the exile, according to Polzin) has provided a framework for the book and occasionally breaks into the narration in his own voice. This third voice, the narrator's voice, is heard in only sixty-two verses (1:1–5; 2:10–12, 20–23; 3:9, 11, 13b–14;

---

[4]It is possible to understand 4:44–49 as summarizing and concluding the first address rather than as introducing the second.

4:41–5:1a; 10:6–7, 9; 27:1a, 9a, 11; 28:68; 29:1; 31:1, 7a, 9–10a, 14a, 14c–16a, 22–23a, 24–25, 30; 32:44–45, 48; 33:1; 34:1–4a, 5–12). However, the effect of these "frame breaks" in which the narrator's presence is felt is to make the narrator himself a voice as reliable and authoritative as Moses. In this way the narrator in effect prepares the reader to accept his authoritative reporting of the history of Israel in the remainder of the DH from Joshua through Kings. Thus the narrator becomes as important and necessary to his contemporaries as Moses was to the wilderness generation. In Deuteronomy, reported speech predominates and narration is at a minimum; in the remainder of the DH, this proportion is reversed, but only after the reader has already been prepared for this authoritative narrator in the book of Deuteronomy. Just as Moses alone knew God face to face (34:10), so it is the narrator who alone really knows Moses. Both Moses and the narrator become the conveyers of an authoritative word of God to Israel.

Deuteronomy as Exposition of the Decalogue

Kaufman (1978–79) suggested that the book of Deuteronomy was structured to elucidate the underlying moral principles set forth in the Ten Commandments; Walton (1987; see also Kaiser) has sought to establish the validity of this suggestion. Walton groups the Ten Commandments around four major issues, each of which is expounded and clarified in the further legal portions of Deuteronomy. For example, the third commandment's prohibition against misuse of God's name is explicated in other ways that reflect on the necessity to take God seriously (13:1–14:21) by not tolerating false prophets (13:1–5) or wickedness, even among family and friends or whole towns (13:6–18). Taking God seriously, respecting his name, includes observing Israel's special dietary laws (14:1–21). The commandment not to profane God's name has its analog in the ninth commandment, which forbids bearing false witness against others. The ninth commandment is in turn expounded through examples of false accusation and other issues of relationships among neighbors (24:8–16).

This sort of approach to Deuteronomy is fertile ground for reflection on ethical questions. It shows how all parts of the law are to varying degrees mutually implicit and interpenetrating in any of the commandments. Yet it is not clear that this structure was actually intended by the author-compiler of the book; Walton (1987, 219), for example, struggles with the thematic connections needed for this system of classification, particularly in reference to the seventh commandment. The book does not provide explicit signals that this was the author's intention, and it would naturally be the case that individual laws would be particular legal enactments of the more general commandments.

Even so, this approach does help one to understand some of the differences between Deuteronomy and the other pentateuchal law codes. The concern in Deuteronomy is more hortatory—it is exhortation more than legislation—so that its provisions tend to be less technical or specific than other codes. Deuteronomy is more interested in the "spirit" than in the "letter" of the law.

Table 4
Deuteronomy as Exposition of the Decalogue
Adapted from Walton (1987)

ISSUES	RE: GOD	RE: MAN
Authority	Commandment 1 5:7 (chaps. 6–11)	Commandment 5 5:16 (16:18–17:13)
Dignity (19:1–24:7)	Commandment 2 5:8–10 (12:1–32)	Commandments 6–8 5:17–19 6th: 19:1–21:23 7th: 22:1–23:14 8th: 23:15–24:7
Commitment	Commandment 3 5:11 (13:1–14:21)	Commandment 9 5:20 (24:8–16)
Rights and Privileges	Commandment 4 5:12–15 (14:22–16:17)	Commandment 10 5:21 (24:17–26:15)

THEOLOGICAL MESSAGE

In some respects Deuteronomy portrays what an ideal Israel would be. It presents an Israel with "one God, one people, one land, one sanctuary, and one law." Its theological contributions are intimately bound up with some of the distinctive concerns that set it apart from the remainder of the Pentateuch.

Israel in Deuteronomy

The covenant between God and Israel made at Sinai and renewed on the plains of Moab before Moses' death presumes an Israel that is a united, unified people. Deuteronomy does not urge or exhort unity among the people, rather it assumes it. The nation exists—it receives its national identity—as a people in covenant with Yahweh. It is a nation set apart and defined by its adherence to this covenant (Deut. 5:1–3; 6:1–25). It was to be an enduring relationship, regularly renewed in successive generations. The covenant into which Israel had entered was not simply the legal acquiescence to a detailed contract, but rather a living relationship that required the loving commitment of both parties (6:5; 7:9, 12–13; 11:1, 13, 22; 13:3; 33:3).

Israel's unified existence is reflected also in the book's practice of referring to members of the people as "brothers" (NIV; Hebrew *'ahîm;* for example, 1:16;

3:18, 20; 10:9; 15:3, 7, 9, 11; 17:20; 18:15, 18).[5] This designation intentionally disregards the tribal and other divisions that characterized the nation in favor of treating it as an undifferentiated unity.

Deuteronomy also understands Israel as an elect nation, chosen by God (4:37; 7:6–7; 10:15; 14:2). God not only chose Israel, but he also chose the king (17:15), the priests (18:5; 21:5), and the place where he was to be worshiped (sixteen out of twenty times the verb *choose* is used in chaps. 12–26; McConville 1984, 30). The book emphasizes the sovereign initiative of Israel's covenant Lord, one who chose them out of his own mysterious love (7:7–8). The nation owes its very existence to that gracious sovereign initiative; this grace calls for a response of loving obedience on the part of the nation. Israel is a unique nation, a nation in covenant with the Creator and their redeemer. This covenant permeates the entirety of the book, even its literary structure (see above).

God's Name in Deuteronomy

Deuteronomy refers to the name of God twenty-one times. Although God's name as a means of his revealing himself is not unique to Deuteronomy, critical scholarship (e.g., von Rad 1953, 37–38) has commonly found in this characteristic emphasis of the book a theological corrective to earlier and cruder concepts that God himself was somehow actually present in Israel's shrines. Deuteronomy is presented as in some way "demythologizing" the divine presence—what is present is not God himself (for he dwells in heaven), but his "name." This theology is commonly said to have developed in Israel after either the loss of the ark or the division of the kingdom when the northern tribes no longer had access to this important object.

McConville (1979) has shown, however, that the contexts in which the "name" is invoked are ordinarily ones of personal devotion and relationship, where covenant is the overarching theological theme in contrast to God's presence in his "glory," a more universal and dramatic denotation. To proclaim God's name is to make open declaration of his character as revealed in his actions toward his people (32:3).

A similar expression is found twice in the Amarna letters from the second half of the second millennium BC (de Vaux 1967; Mayes 1979, 224). King Abdu-Heba "set his name in the land of Jerusalem." This expression suggests

---

[5]The Koran records Muhammad's belief that the Hebrew scriptures prophesied his appearance. When asked where this is so, most often knowledgeable Muslims will appeal to Deuteronomy 18:15, 18 where it is prophesied that a prophet like Moses would arise "among your brothers." Who are the brothers of Israel? Esau and Ishmael, it is claimed, the ancestors of Arabic-speaking, Islamic peoples among whom Muhammad appeared. The answer to this claim is to review the use of the word "brothers" in Deuteronomy, where in every other passage it means simply "fellow Israelites."

both ownership and conquest. For God to place his name on a place or nation is also to imply his ownership—of the world, of Israel, and of her land. In Deuteronomy, where the emphasis is on possessing the land and on Israel's covenant with God, expressing God's presence through his "name" reminds the nation of his ownership and dominion. Rather than diminish or correct the notion of God's presence, God's name in Deuteronomy affirms the very real presence of God in the fullness of his character and covenantal commitment to those on whom he had set that name.

God's Word in Deuteronomy

In Deuteronomy the word of God is authoritative and it is written. As a covenant document, the words of the "book of the law" that Moses wrote governed, structured, and defined the nation's relationship with her suzerain Lord and with one another. The book reaffirms in Israel the idea of a "canon," a collection of written materials by which the life of the nation would be administered.

Originally, the nation had heard the actual voice of God at Sinai, but the terror of this event prompted the people to plead that they not repeat the experience. So God committed the declaration of his word to human beings—first to Moses (5:22–33) and then to a succession of prophets who would follow his model (18:14–22). These prophets would be distinguished from false prophets by their adherence to the covenant (13:1–5) and by the fulfillment of their utterances (18:21–22). As the word of the all-powerful sovereign of the universe, God's word in the mouth of Moses and the prophets would not fail—what he revealed would come to pass. It was Moses, the great prophet, who also foresaw that Israel would not heed the demands of her covenant with God but would turn away (31:27–29). In this sense, Deuteronomy itself becomes a prophecy for which the remainder of the Deuteronomistic History is the fulfillment. God's word in the book is not only the written documents that govern life under the covenant; it is also the authoritative preaching and teaching of Moses and those who would come after him.

Centralization of Worship

Deuteronomy repeatedly describes Israel's worship at "the place the LORD your God will choose" (12:5, 11, 14, 18, 21, 26; 14:23–25; 15:20; 16:2, 6, 11, 15; 17:8, 10; 18:6; 26:2). In critical scholarship this choice of a single place for Israel's worship has traditionally been associated with Josiah's effort to centralize worship in Jerusalem. Some regard the insistence on centralization at one locality as a later insertion into earlier Deuteronomic materials; for example, Halpern (1981) distinguishes between an earlier stratum that was ambiguous about centralization and a later one that eliminated this ambiguity. There is no serious question that in the record from the time of David onward, both the books of Samuel and Kings would identify Jerusalem as the chosen site for this exclusive sanctuary.

Is the centralization of worship at one site a sufficient criterion to insist on a late date for the book, or are there other explanations that would be compatible with an earlier date for the material? Some have argued that Deuteronomy 12 could have a distributive sense that would allow for a number of "central sanctuaries" to exist at the same time among the various tribes, none of which was to be the "sole sanctuary" (McConville 1984, 36).

It is difficult to escape the fact that the language of Deuteronomy 12:5 envisages a single site among the tribes. Centralization of worship reflects Deuteronomy's ideal picture of "one God, one people, one sanctuary." "Centralization," however, is somewhat a misnomer. Israel's worship was to some degree always centralized at those shrines where the ark was kept (e.g., Bethel and Shiloh; cf. McConville 1984, 23–29; Thompson 1974, 36–37). The ark was the preeminent representation of God's presence; wherever the ark was, God's "name" was also there. If Deuteronomy were limiting worship to Jerusalem alone, then the altar at Shechem (chap. 27) would make little sense. The primary contrast in Deuteronomy 12 is between the multiplicity of "places" where the Canaanites worshiped as they chose (12:1–3), and "the place" that God would choose (12:5—McConville 1984, 29–38). Just as God had chosen the nation, so also he would choose the place and the character of worship there. What is new in the later choice of Jerusalem is not the idea of centralization itself, but rather that Israel would now have a permanent sanctuary instead of a portable one. Worshiping God at the place he had chosen and in the way he had prescribed was but one part of Israel's covenant allegiance; it reflected at a national level the status of Israel as a treasured people (7:6; 14:2; 26:18), set apart as holy to the Lord. But this law did not eliminate the possibility that the chosen place might change at various times.

Retribution and the Land in Deuteronomy

The land is repeatedly described as "the land that the God of your fathers is giving to you." Once again, the book emphasizes the prior action and initiative of the Lord in his gracious provision for Israel in accord with his promises to the fathers. In 131 of the 167 times the verb *give* occurs in the book, the subject of the action is Yahweh (McConville 1984, 12). The gracious and multiple gifts of God to his people are a sustained theme.

But God's giving also requires a response from Israel. Possessing the land in the first place and keeping it in the second are both tied to Israel's obedience to God's commands (4:25–26; 6:18; 8:1; 11:8–9, 18–21; 16:20). This theme of conditionality is commonly linked to the Deuteronomic theology of retribution (4:25–31; 11:26–28; 28:1–2; 30:15–20). Obedience to the righteous commands of God will not only result in possessing and keeping the land, but it will also bring prosperity and well-being; whereas disobedience issues in disaster, disease, death, and the loss of the land.

This unresolved tension between God's gracious promise-gift to Israel and the conditionality of her inheritance prompted F. M. Cross to propose his solution of a double redaction of the Deuteronomistic History: one a preexilic edition at the time of Josiah emphasizing God's grace and faithfulness, and the other emphasizing conditionality, updated later in light of the disastrous events that had led to the exile. This approach, however, eviscerates Deuteronomy and the DH. It turns the putative first edition of the DH into a "failed sermon, one whose basic ideology was shown to be deficient by subsequent events of history" (Polzin 1989, 12). It makes the present text of the DH a seriously flawed product, since the editor of the second edition ideologically undercut his sources but could not identify and remove the underlying tensions introduced by his own work. It seems premised on the notion that the theological reflection of ancient Israel was insufficiently sophisticated to handle a complex and multifaceted issue.

However, this is to misunderstand Deuteronomy. Here law and grace are held in an unrelieved tension, the very tension that energizes the remainder of the Deuteronomic History. What was to become of Israel? Which would prevail—threat or promise? Deuteronomy is far more capable of a depth and subtlety in its theological reasoning than modern scholars have been prone to recognize, far more than the flat and pat ideology behind either of Cross's proposed editions. The tension between law and grace is an essential ingredient in Deuteronomy and the DH rather than the end product of secondary editorial tampering.

Few books of the Old Testament have had as great an impact on the authors of the New Testament as Deuteronomy.

APPROACHING THE NEW TESTAMENT

Few books of the Old Testament have had as great an impact on the authors of the New Testament as Deuteronomy. It is one of the four Old Testament books cited most frequently in the New Testament.

Deuteronomy had spoken of a day when God would raise up a prophet like Moses (18:14–22). Although the context suggests that a succession of numerous prophets was also in view, the language in the passage in reference to this prophet is all in the singular. When the book ends by saying that there had never been a prophet like Moses (34:10), a simple syllogism influenced Jewish interpreters:

1. God will raise up a prophet like Moses (chap. 18).
2. There has not been a prophet like Moses (chap. 34).
   Therefore, we must keep looking for such a prophet.

This syllogism formed the background for much of the speculation among the Jews as they encountered John the Baptist (John 1:21) and Jesus. Jesus had fed them with bread and meat, just as Moses had done in the wilderness; he must be the prophet who would do the signs and wonders that Moses had done (Deut. 34:11–12; John 6:14). When Jesus promised an unfailing stream of life-giving water, the crowd remembered the miracles of Moses in the wilderness and the promise of a prophet who would perform such deeds (John 7:40). Peter and Stephen would leave no doubt in anyone's mind that Jesus was the prophet like Moses (Acts 3:22; 7:37).

Jesus' own insistence that he and the Father are one (John 10:30; 17:21–23) should be understood against the backdrop of the great central confession of Israel's faith in the *Shema*: "Hear, O Israel: The LORD our God, the LORD is one" (Deut. 6:4). The Old Testament does not often use the title Father in reference to God, but this pervasive practice in the New Testament, especially in John's gospel, is probably to be traced to Deuteronomy (1:31; 8:5; 32:6). Jesus also made direct appeal to Deuteronomy as he repulsed Satan during his temptation in the wilderness (Deut. 6:13, 16; 8:3; Matt. 4:1–10). As the embodiment of faithful Israel, Jesus would live by every word out of the mouth of God; he would succeed in Israel's mission, whereas the nation itself had failed. As a righteous king he would not amass great wealth or think of himself more highly than his brothers, but rather he would rule in accord with the commandments of God (Deut. 17:14–20). As God's Spirit had hovered over the creation (Gen. 1:2) and over Israel in the wilderness (Deut. 32:10–11), so Jesus sought to gather his people beneath his wings (Matt. 23:37; Luke 13:34). The pervasive concern of Deuteronomy (e.g., 15:1, 9) with the classes of society vulnerable to abuse and exploitation is reflected in the ministry of Jesus to the widows and the poor. Jesus reiterates the greatest commandment (Deut. 6:5; Matt. 22:37–40).

Just as Israel had been chosen as the least among the nations (Deut. 7:6–7), so the church is chosen among the weak, the foolish, and the lowly (1 Cor. 1:26–30). Just as Israel had been the treasured possession of God (Deut. 7:6; 14:2; 26:18; cf. Ex. 19:5), so the new Israel would be his treasure (Eph. 1:14; Titus 2:14; 1 Peter 2:9).

This new Israel has its central sanctuary in the heavenly Zion (Heb. 12:18–24). Just as God had committed his word to human agents in Deuteronomy—to Moses (5:22–33) and to the prophets (18:14–22)—so also the church assembles to hear God speaking from heaven as it hears the preaching of his Word (Heb. 12:25–28). God is a consuming fire, both for Israel and for the church (Deut. 4:24; Heb. 12:29). Just as Israel needed a mediator in the divine presence (Deut. 5:27), so the church has a righteous mediator in Jesus (Heb. 4:14–16).

The early church saw in itself the recreation of an ideal Israel. Just as Israel was portrayed in Deuteronomy as a unity having one God, one people, one land, one sanctuary, and one law, so the church is exhorted to a similar unity, for there is one body, one Spirit, one hope, one Lord, one faith, one baptism, one God and Father of all (Eph. 4:4–5). Jesus prayed that his people might be one (John 17:11).

CHAPTER SEVEN

JOSHUA

The greatest act of salvation history in the Old Testament was not the exodus alone. The exodus was just half of a great redemptive complex. God had not promised his people only that he would redeem them from bondage but also that he would give them the land he promised to the fathers as their inheritance (Gen. 12:2–3; 15:18–21). The great work of redemption from bondage in Egypt cannot be separated from the inheritance of land that God had promised. The book of Joshua takes us into that inheritance: it describes the conquest and distribution of the land. Thus we can observe how Joshua is a natural continuation of the story of the Pentateuch that ended with the Israelites poised to enter the Promised Land. It also begins the story of Israel's presence in the land that will continue with the books that follow it.

BIBLIOGRAPHY

Commentaries

A. G. **Auld,** *Joshua, Judges, and Ruth* (DSB; Westminster, 1984); R. G. **Boling** and G. E. **Wright,** *Joshua* (AB; Doubleday, 1982); T. **Butler,** *Joshua* (WBC 7; Word, 1983); C. J. **Goslinga,** *Joshua, Judges, Ruth* (BSC; Zondervan, 1986); E. J. **Hamlin,** *Joshua: Inheriting the Land* (ITC; Eerdmans, 1983); L. D. **Hawk,** *Joshua* (Berit Olam; Liturgical Press, 2000); R. S. **Hess,** *Joshua* (TOTC; InterVarsity Press, 1996); D. M. **Howard** Jr., *Joshua* (NAC; Broadman and Holman, 1998); J. M. **Miller** and G. M. **Tucker,** *The Book of Joshua* (CBC; Cambridge University Press, 1974); R. D. **Nelson,** *Joshua* (OTL; Westminster John Knox, 1997); M. **Noth,** *Das Buch Josua* (HAT 7; Tübingen: Mohr, 1953); J. **Soggin,** *Joshua* (OTL; Westminster, 1972); M. **Woudstra,** *The Book of Joshua* (NICOT; Eerdmans, 1981).

Monographs and Articles

A. **Alt,** idem, *Essays on Old Testament History and Religion* (Oxford: Blackwell, 1966); "Die Landnahme der Israeliten in Palästina," *Kleine Schriften,* 2 vols. (Munich: C. H.

Beck'sche, 1959): 1:89–125; A. G. **Auld,** *Joshua, Moses, and the Land: Tetrateuch-Pentateuch-Hexateuch in a Generation Since 1938* (T. & T. Clark, 1980); P. **Bienkowski,** "Jericho Was Destroyed in the Middle Bronze Age, Not the Late Bronze Age," *BAR* 16 (1990): 45–46, 69; J. J. **Bimson,** *Redating the Exodus and the Conquest* (JSOTS 5; Sheffield: JSOT, 1978); W. **Brueggemann,** *The Land* (Fortress, 1977); idem, *Introduction to the Old Testament* (*IOT*; Westminster John Knox, 2003); J. A. **Callaway,** "Was My Excavation of Ai Worthwhile?" *BAR* 11 (1985): 68–69; B. **Childs,** "A Study of the Formula 'Unto This Day,'" *JBL* 82 (1963): 279–92; G. W. **Coats,** "The Ark of the Covenant in Joshua," *HebAnnRev* 9 (1985): 137–57; idem, "The Book of Joshua: Heroic Saga or Conquest Theme," *JSOT* 38 (1987): 15–32; idem, "An Exposition for the Conquest Theme," *CBQ* 47 (1985): 47–54; R. C. **Culley,** "Stories of the Conquest," *HAR* 8 (1984): 25–44; P. R. **Davies,** *In Search of "Ancient Israel"* (JSOT Press, 1992); W. G. **Dever,** *Who Were the Israelites and Where Did They Come From?* (Eerdmans, 2003); I. **Finkelstein** and N. **Silberman,** *The Bible Unearthed: Archaeology's New Vision of Ancient Israel and the Origin of Its Sacred Texts* (Free Press, 2001); L. J. **Greenspoon,** *Textual Studies in the Book of Joshua* (HSM 28; Chico: Scholars, 1983); D. M. **Gunn,** "Joshua and Judges," in *The Literary Guide to the Bible,* ed. R. Alter and F. Kermode (Harvard University Press, 1987); B. **Halpern,** "Gibeon: Israelite Diplomacy in the Conquest Era," *CBQ* 37 (1975): 303–16; L. D. **Hawk,** *Every Promise Fulfilled: Contesting Plots in Joshua* (Westminster John Knox, 1991); idem, "Book of Joshua," in DOTHB (InterVarsity Press, 2005); R. S. **Hess,** "Asking Historical Questions of Joshua 13–19: Recent Discussion Concerning the Date of the Boundary Lists," in *Faith, Tradition, and History: Old Testament Historiography in Its Near Eastern Context,* ed. A. R. Millard et al. (Eisenbrauns, 1994): 191–205; Y. **Kaufmann,** *The Biblical Account of the Conquest of Palestine,* 2nd ed. (Jerusalem: Magnes, 1985); K. A. **Kitchen,** *On the Reliability of the Old Testament* (Eerdmans, 2003); 242–74; H. J. **Koorevaar,** *De Opbouw van het Boek Jozua* (Heverlee: Centrum voor Bijbelse Vorming Belgie, 1990); N. P. **Lemke,** *Early Israel: Anthropological and Historical Studies on the Israelite Society before the Monarchy* (VTSup 37; Leiden: E. J. Brill, 1985); D. **Livingston,** "The Location of Biblical Bethel and Ai Reconsidered," *WTJ* 33 (1970): 20–44; idem, "Traditional Site of Bethel Questioned," *WTJ* 34 (1971): 39–50; T. **Longman** III and D. **Reid,** *God Is a Warrior: Studies in Old Testament Biblical Theology* (Zondervan, 1995); G. E. **Mendenhall,** "The Hebrew Conquest of Palestine," *BA* 25 (1962): 66–87; idem, *The Tenth Generation* (Johns Hopkins University Press, 1973); E. H. **Merrill,** "Palestinian Archaeology and the Date of the Conquest: Do Tells Tell Tales?" *GraceTJ* 3 (1982): 107–21; J. M. **Miller,** "Archaeology and the Israelite Conquest of Canaan: Some Methodological Observations," *PEQ* 109 (1977): 87–93; J. J. **Niehaus,** "Joshua and Ancient Near Eastern Warfare," *JETS* 31 (1988): 37–50; M. **Noth,** *Überlieferungsgeschichtliche Studien* (1st ed., 1943; 2nd ed.; Tübingen: Max Niemeyer Verlag, 1967; first half trans. as *The Deuteronomistic History* [JSOTS 15; Sheffield: JSOT, 1981]); R. **Polzin,** *Moses and the Deuteronomist* (Seabury, 1980); I. **Provan,** V. P.

Long, and T. **Longman** III, *A Biblical History of Israel* (Westminster John Knox, 2003); G. W. **Ramsey,** *The Quest for the Historical Israel* (John Knox, 1981); G. **von Rad,** "The Promised Land and Yahweh's Land in the Hexateuch," *Problems of the Hexateuch and Other Essays* (McGraw-Hill, 1966), 79–93; B. **Waltke,** "The Date of the Conquest," *WTJ* 52 (1990): 181–200; M. **Weinfeld,** "Divine Intervention in War in Ancient Israel and in the Ancient Near East," in *History, Historiography, and Interpretation,* ed. H. Tadmor and M. Weinfeld (Jerusalem: Magnes, 1983), 121–47; M. **Weippert,** *The Settlement of the Israelite Tribes in Palestine* (Allenson, 1971); G. J. **Wenham,** "The Deuteronomic Theology of the Book of Joshua," *JBL* 90 (1971): 140–48; B. G. **Wood,** "Did the Israelites Conquer Jericho? A New Look at the Archaeological Evidence," *BAR* 16 (1990): 44–58; idem, "Dating Jericho's Destruction: Bienkowski Is Wrong on All Counts," *BAR* 6 (1990): 45–49, 69; Y. **Yadin,** "Is the Biblical Account of the Israelite Conquest of Canaan Historically Reliable?" *BAR* 8 (1982): 16–23; E. J. **Young,** "The Alleged Secondary Deuteronomic Passages in the Book of Joshua," *EvQ* 25 (1953): 142–57; K. L. **Younger** Jr., *Ancient Conquest Accounts: A Study in Ancient Near Eastern and Biblical History Writing* (JSOTS 98; Sheffield: JSOT, 1990); idem, "Early Israel in Recent Biblical Scholarship," in *The Face of Old Testament Studies: A Survey of Contemporary Approaches* (Baker, 1999), 176–206; Z. **Zevit,** "Problems of Ai," *BAR* 11 (1985): 56–69.

HISTORICAL BACKGROUND

Authorship and Historical Period

In this section we will consider authorship and the historical period together. As with all of the historical books of the Old Testament, the author of Joshua remains anonymous. Decisions about the authorship and date at which the book was written are thoroughly bound up with larger historical and theological questions.

Although the Talmud said that "Joshua wrote his own book" apart from the account of his death,[1] the internal evidence of the book itself makes this improbable. The recurring phrase "to this day" (4:9; 5:9; 6:25; 7:26; 8:28–29; 9:27; 10:27; 13:13; 15:63; 16:10—see Childs 1963) suggests that some time had passed between the events narrated and the writing of the record. Furthermore, during at least one stage of the book's composition, the author was using previously written sources describing the earlier events (10:13), placing the author at a time later than this earlier writing. Two different approaches to the question of authorship have dominated the discussion.

---

[1]*Baba' Bathra* 15a. The Talmud assigned the account of Joshua's death (24:29–30) to Eleazar the son of Aaron, and the account of Eleazar's death to his son Phinehas (24:33).

A Literary Critical Approach

In the heyday of traditional pentateuchal criticism, some scholars believed they could trace vestiges of the original pentateuchal sources (J, E, D, and P) into the book of Joshua. Instead of speaking of a "pentateuch" of five books, these scholars posited a "hexateuch" of six books: the Law plus Joshua. Since the patriarchal promises of possessing the land were so important in the Pentateuch, how could this body of literature end without reporting the realization of this promise? Judges 1 contains an account of the conquest at some tension with Joshua 1–12; since Judges 1 was assigned by many to J, the Yahwist source, then Joshua 1–12 must have contained an alternative record of the conquest, identified in part as the work of E, the Elohist. The lists of towns and cities (Josh. 13–22), especially those concerned with Levitical cities and the cities of refuge, were largely assigned to P, the priestly writer. The extensive language and theology of the book of Deuteronomy found throughout Joshua also meant that the book had at least one redaction by that school. This debate and its various permutations dominated the scholarly discussion of the book during the nineteenth and early twentieth centuries. By and large, however, scholars have now abandoned the attempt to find the pentateuchal source documents in Joshua. The E (Elohist) source has become extremely elusive (even illusory) in the Pentateuch itself, much less in materials beyond the Pentateuch.

A Tradition-Historical Approach

Rather than trace individual literary sources, scholars taking a tradition-historical approach sought to identify smaller units underlying the larger narrative complexes. Scholars in this school were influenced by the notion that stories were tied to particular localities (Ortsgebundenkeit) where they were transmitted, elaborated, and gathered. These stories were largely etiological stories: stories that provided the rationale for a current state of affairs. Examples of the sorts of questions that produced etiological stories would be "Daddy, why does our family/tribe live here?" (a question prompting a report of conquest or migration), or "Daddy, why do the Gibeonites serve Israel at the tabernacle?" (a question prompting the narrative in Joshua 9). Noth considered chapters 1–9 as largely etiological stories from Benjamite sources in and around Gilgal; chapter 10 from Ephraim; chapter 11 from Galilean traditions; and chapter 12 as an independent narrative. These stories and scattered information from the various tribes and regions were united around the man Joshua. Noth attributed chapters 13–19 to two documentary sources: a list of tribal boundaries from the time of the judges, and a later list from the time of Josiah. Both Noth and Alt assigned a higher degree of antiquity to the city and boundary lists than had any earlier scholars. Traditions from the area of Shechem (Josh. 24) and Shiloh (Josh. 18–22) also were included in the book.

Noth's greatest contribution, however, was his argument that the "former prophets" of the Hebrew canon had more in common with Deuteronomy than with any other putative pentateuchal sources. Noth identified these books as the Deuteronomistic History, a single composition embracing Joshua through Kings (see below under Theological Message).

Research into the composition of Joshua is complicated by two larger questions: (1) the date of the exodus and conquest; (2) the nature of the conquest.

Date of the Exodus and Conquest. There is little doubt from the evidence of the biblical text itself that the exodus and conquest should be set in the second half of the fifteenth century and the early fourteenth. Solomon began construction of the temple 480 years after the exodus (1 Kings 6:1), making the date for the exodus approximately 1446 BC. Unless one dodges the demands of this date by making it a stylized figure (perhaps for twelve generations) or a total that represents sums including concurrent years, this chronological note requires a fifteenth-century date for the exodus. If the judge Jephthah is assigned a date (c. 1100 BC) a century or so before the appearance of the monarchy in Israel, his boast to the Ammonites that Israel had been in the land for 300 years (Judg. 11:26) would mean the conquest began around 1400 BC, after the 40 years in the wilderness. According to 1 Chronicles 6:33–37, there were at least eighteen generations between Korah at the time of the exodus and Heman, the musician in David's court. Allowing for approximately 25 years to each generation, the figure is close to 480 years between the exodus and Solomon.

However, many scholars argue that this "early date" cannot be reconciled with the archaeological record, and instead they assign the exodus to the mid-thirteenth century (c. 1250 BC, the "late date"). At issue is the position of many archaeologists that Jericho, Ai, and Hazor do not show evidence of a destruction level from the early fourteenth century, whereas destruction layers from burning are evident in other Palestinian sites (Lachish, Bethel, Eglon, Debir, Hazor, etc.) from the thirteenth century. Assuming that the Israelite arrival was a military conquest, archaeologists look for evidence of extensive destruction and therefore commonly associate these destruction levels with an Israelite invasion and insist on a thirteenth-century date for the conquest.

The main difficulty in identifying these destruction levels with the Israelite invasion, however, is the biblical text itself (Merrill 1982). The military practice of Israel and the accounts of her conquests support a very different picture, that of driving out the inhabitants in order to preserve their cities for Israelite use (Deut. 6:10–11; 19:1–2). The nations were to be driven out and their shrines destroyed (Ex. 23:23–30; Num. 33:50–56), but there is no mention of the destruction of cities (Deut. 20:10–20) apart from Jericho, Ai, and Hazor (Josh. 6:24; 8:28; 10:1; 11:13). Israel "took" many cities and repopulated them, but did not burn them (Josh. 11:10–13). Burn levels at a large number of excavations in Israel cannot then be used to establish the date of the conquest.

Nevertheless, Jericho, Ai, and Hazor were burned, and the evidence from these excavations remains difficult. For generations Kathleen Kenyon's conclusions have dominated the interpretation of the ruins at Jericho. She argued that Jericho was destroyed at the end of the Middle Bronze period (c. 1550 BC) and remained unoccupied in the Late Bronze period (1550–1200 BC), the time traditionally associated with the Israelite conquest. Kenyon found no evidence of an Israelite invasion. However, recent reassessments of the data have spawned a vigorous debate (cf. Wood 1990, and Bienkowski 1990). Wood finds the ruins of toppled walls, which he dates to around 1400 BC, a fact that would comport remarkably well with the biblical data. The excavations at Hazor revealed an extensive destruction of that city in stratum 1a, and the excavator (Y. Yadin) identified this destruction with the Israelite conquest c. 1230 BC. There as yet is no clear evidence of a destruction that could be associated with an earlier date for Israel's burning of the city. At Ai the excavators found a gap in the settlement of the site between Early Bronze III (c. 2300 BC) and Iron I (c. 1200 BC); this gap left no trace of the Late Bronze town presupposed in the biblical account (Josh. 7). Other scholars have disputed the identification of biblical Ai with the site at et-Tell (Livingston 1970, 1971). The development of hundreds of new settlements in Israel around 1200 BC favors a late date for the conquest. On the whole the archaeological data will not settle the question of the date of the conquest (Waltke 1990). Today's archaeology too often becomes tomorrow's footnote about earlier mistaken efforts. One can only hope that further excavation will eventually put the question of date beyond reasonable doubt.[2]

Archaeological data will not settle the question of the date of the conquest. Today's archaeology too often becomes tomorrow's footnote about earlier mistaken efforts.

The Nature of the Conquest. The book of Joshua presents the account of a unified effort by the tribes of Israel under Joshua's leadership to conquer the land in accord with a prearranged plan of conquest. After his commissioning, the book proceeds to recount the conquest of Jericho and Ai (Josh. 2–8), the southern campaign (chaps. 9–10), the northern campaign (chap. 11), a summary of conquered cities (chap. 12), the distribution of the land among the tribes (chaps. 13–22), and Joshua's death (chaps. 23–24). The whole gives the impression of a fairly straightforward narrative of historical events.

Scholars have found this record difficult to accept as actual history, however, in large measure due to the tension within the biblical narrative between the claims of total victory from a unified assault (11:23; 18:1; 21:43–44) and evidence that territory was instead conquered by individual tribes over a period of time without their being able to eradicate the indigenous population (15:13–19, 63; 16:10; 17:11–13; 19:47; Judg. 1). This difficulty has spawned a number of alter-

---

[2]For the fullest discussion of the issue in favor of an early date of the exodus and conquest, see Bimson 1978 and Provan, Long, and Longman 2003, 131–32. For a recent expression of a late date for the exodus, see Kitchen. Minimalists deny that the exodus and conquest ever took place (see chap. 1).

natives to viewing the conquest as a mass invasion: (1) *Total rejection.* Those scholars described as minimalist (see The Challenge of Minimalism in chap. 1) conclude that Israel did not even exist until the Persian period or later. The exodus
and conquest and the history of Israel up to the so-called postexilic period is a literary and theological creation unsupported by archeology (Davies; Lemke). (2)
An immigration model. Alt (1959, 1966) noted a strong Egyptian presence and
influence in Canaan during the Middle Kingdom (c. 2000–1800 BC), but after
the Hyksos period, the data from New Kingdom (c. 1580–1350 BC) inscriptions
showed the emergence of powerful ethnic city states in the region. In his view,
Israel entered the land through a peaceful infiltration into the hill country where
the sparse population could not withstand the eventual development of an
Israelite state. Noth, Weippert, and others largely followed Alt's observations.
Noth concluded that the various legends and records of individual regions were
only later integrated into an account of common origins and a joint conquest. This
approach is characterized by great skepticism regarding the historical validity of
the biblical account and basically eliminates any notion of a "conquest," even
though the conquest of the land is deeply embedded in a variety of biblical materials. It remains an unsubstantiated, somewhat ad hoc construal of the data. (3) *A
peasant revolt model.* Where Alt had appealed primarily to extrabiblical texts, the
revolt model appeals primarily to the social sciences. Mendenhall (1962, 1973)
and Gottwald (1979) proposed instead a sociopolitical model in which the great
feudal city-states ruled by a foreign military aristocracy were overthrown by a
peasants' revolt triggered in part by a small number of slave-labor captives (Israel)
who escaped Egypt in the thirteenth century. These agrarian serfs allied with other
oppressed groups to overthrow their oppressors; they adopted the Yahwistic faith
as a religious expression of egalitarian hopes for freedom. Most recently, this
model has been affirmed by Brueggemann (*IOT* [2004], 112). This model is
highly speculative and has little direct support from biblical or extrabiblical materials. One has the impression that a preconceived model is controlling the reading of the texts rather than developing from them. (4) *A collapse model.* This view
is most closely associated with the work of the eminent archaeologist W. Dever
(2003), and like the peasant revolt model argues that Israel emerged from within
Canaan. He points to evidence that the highlands of central Palestine at the beginning of the Iron Age have evidence of numerous (about 300) new small settlements. They had advanced agricultural technology, including stone-lined silos,
plastered cisterns, and terracing on hillsides. In the light of the fact that the large
Canaanite coastal cities show signs of collapse at the end of the Late Bronze Age,
Dever sees the origins of Israel in this move from coast to hill country. He remarks
that it is noteworthy that these sites show no evidence of pig bones. (5) *A cyclic
view.* Another archaeologist, Israel Finkelstein (2001), places a different nuance
on the same evidence, though he also has considerably less confidence in the Bible
as a historical source than does Dever. He does not believe that the central hill

country sites resulted from a collapse of the Late Bronze coastal cities. Rather, he believes they are part of a cycle where nomadic peoples will eventually settle down. Thus, he associates these cities with settled nomads.

Others have viewed the tension between a total conquest and an incomplete conquest as evidence of redactional layers or vestiges of contradictory sources, one redactor more oriented to grace and promise, and another to law and condition. Yet this tension is deeply embedded in Deuteronomy: God will give the land, but Israel will not keep the covenant (Deut. 31:15–18, 27–29). The intimations of Israel's failure to remove the indigenous peoples set the stage for the growing influence of idolatry that will eventually consume the nation (Deut. 31:20–21). Literary-critical suggestions of contradictory sources or redactions underestimate the profundity of the theological questions raised in the Deuteronomic History and in Joshua in particular. Younger's study (1990, 197–240) of Joshua 9–12 in comparison with other ancient Near Eastern conquest accounts has shown that the various elements in the biblical narrative are also found in the extrabiblical accounts, including hyperbolic statements of absolute total conquest (1990, 241–43, 248; McConville 1993). See also the work of Hess (1996, 26–31), where he argues that some of the material of Joshua is connected to the late second millennium.

The result of these debates has been a wide range of assessments about the historicity and date of the book of Joshua. In some reconstructions of the history of the book's development, independently circulating oral narratives ("traditions") were only tied to the man Joshua as a way of uniting these diverse materials, and one can have little confidence in the factuality of the material. Dates assigned to the book have been as late as the postexilic period, when the issue of possessing the land was again before Israel. Conservative scholars have commonly assigned a time not long after the events (Woudstra 1981) or early in the monarchy (Harrison 1969, 673). Making such determinations is very difficult. While one may reject the negative skepticism of the more critical approaches, a distinction is still necessary between the date of sources and the later editor(s) who produced the book in its present form. The book does share the viewpoint of the Deuteronomistic History (Joshua–Kings) and could reflect some compositional or editorial work as late as the exilic editor of Kings (2 Kings 25:27–30).

Literary Analysis

The book of Joshua should be read firmly as a part of its narrative context. Just as Deuteronomy ended with the death of Moses, so the book of Joshua culminates in the death of Joshua. It began "after the death of Moses," and the book of Judges will begin "after the death of Joshua" (Josh. 1:1; Judg. 1:1; cf. 2 Sam. 1:1; cf. Gunn 1987, 102). Joshua is the literary bridge between Israel's wilderness experience and the narrative of struggles in the early years of occupying the land (Judges).

Chapters 1–12 are narrative accounts of Israel's military conquest of the land; they are filled with vivid details of battles, success and failure, victory and defeat. The army of Israel spreads through the land almost as fast as the news of their victories (9:3; 10:1; 11:1). It is a narrative that revels in God's power exercised in behalf of the nation. God would fight for Israel and bring her to possess the land that he had sworn to the fathers.

In chapters 13–22 we move from achieving what was promised to enjoying it. Here the writer's strategy shifts from dramatic accounts of warfare to the rhetoric of listing and ordering; narrative progress is slowed for a more static, administrative prose (Gunn 1987, 103). The stability and unity of "the people," the new reality of an Israel in its inheritance, is portrayed through lists of the tribes and clans and their territorial allotments.

Chapters 23–24 round out the narrative with the renewal of Israel's ancient covenant with God, Joshua's dismissing the people to enjoy their inheritance, and the death of Joshua. The parallels with Moses are not to be missed: at his life's end, Israel's ancient covenant was renewed (Deut. 26:16–19; 29:1–32:47) and the people were sent to possess their inheritance. But there is a new note at the end of Joshua, a gap that prepares the way for the narrative in Judges: at the death of Moses, preparations had been made for the transfer of leadership to Joshua (Deut. 31:1–8; 34:9), but at the death of Joshua, no provisions are made for a succession to leadership. We are left with the people in the land, but without a leader to guide them so that they will serve the Lord. What will become of this situation? That is the story of Judges.

Deeply embedded in almost every part of the Bible is a tension between the holiness of God and his graciousness. As a holy God he demands compliance with his law and sets before human beings choices of obedience or disobedience on which are conditioned blessing or judgment. As a merciful, gracious, and compassionate God, he makes unconditional promises reflecting the grace and favor he has set on his people. But what of the land? Is it the inheritance that accompanies redemption from Egypt, the unconditional promise of God to the fathers? Or is it possessed only on condition of obedience? Is it a unilateral grant because of God's own oath, fulfilled in his fighting for Israel so that not one word of all God's promises has failed (11:23; 21:43–45; 23:14–15)? Or is it an incomplete inheritance, an incomplete conquest in which the nations remain in the land (13:13; 15:63; 16:10; 17:12–13) and Israel's continued possession there is tied to faithfulness (23:6–8; cf. Deut. 20:17–18)? In the gap between the language of fulfillment and the language of incompletion, these basic questions arise (Gunn 1987, 109): Is the gift of the land unconditional? Or will the punishment consequent on the nation's failure to keep God's commands override the promises? Moses in Deuteronomy had already described the national penchant for backsliding and the disaster that would eventually befall them (Deut. 31:27–29). The Lord who is abundant in mercy, forgiving, and slow to anger, will not let sin go unpunished (Deut. 5:8–10; Num. 14:18). Israel would begin to emulate the Canaanites who remained in the land, and she would be driven from the land for the same reasons they were (Deut. 18:9–12; 2 Kings 17:8–18; 21:3–15). The dynamics that would eventually lead to exile are already in place in Joshua; the book cannot be understood apart from this larger context. Rather than a tension introduced through contradictory editors, this issue drives the narrative forward in ways already intimated in Deuteronomy.

Koorevaar (1990) analyzes the book of Joshua in four main sections, each dominated by a particular Hebrew word and concept: (1) going over (ʻâbar—1:1–5:12), (2) taking (lâqah—5:13–12:24); (3) dividing (hâlaq—13:1–21:45); (4) worshiping (ʻâbad—22:1–33). Those who read Hebrew will recognize the play on Hebrew word pairs, which are formed from similar consonants. Koorevaar (1990, 290) sees 18:1 as a crucial point in the book: setting up the tent of meeting at Shiloh signals bringing the whole land under Israel's control and the establishment of a place where Yahweh had chosen to dwell.[3]

THEOLOGICAL MESSAGE

The major influence on the theology of the book of Joshua is Deuteronomy. In addition to the important tension between law and grace already present in that book, Wenham (1971) identifies five major theological motifs that bind Deuteronomy and Joshua together. Beyond these five motifs, the influence of the language and perspective of Deuteronomy is everywhere present in the book.

Holy War

Deuteronomy spelled out the principles of holy war under which Israel was to engage in battle (7:1–26; 20:1–20; 21:10–14; 25:17–19). The book of Joshua illustrates these principles of holy war in the accounts of the conquest of Jericho and Ai (chaps. 2, 6, 8, 10, 11) and in failure to follow these principles in the initial attack on Ai and in the treaty with the Gibeonites (chaps. 7, 9). These accounts include battlefield speeches (Josh. 1:6, 9; 6:2; 8:1; 10:8; 11:6), Yahweh's fighting for Israel and striking terror into the hearts of the enemy (Josh. 2:9, 24; 5:1; 9:24; 10:21), and reports of national obedience to divine command. Failure to keep the command of God results in defeat and in divine judgment on Achan and his family (Deut. 7:25–26; Josh. 7). Yahweh was present for Israel's warfare when Joshua met the commander of the heavenly armies (5:13–15). Apart from the Gibeonites and a few other peoples that remained, the Canaanite peoples were placed under the ban and eradicated from the land (Deut. 7:1–5; Josh. 6:21; 8:24–25; 10:10, 28–40; 11:11, 14, 21; cf. 9:16–18).

The major influence on the theology of the book of Joshua is Deuteronomy.

---

[3]See the discussion of Koorevaar's work in J. G. McConville, *Grace in the End: A Study of Deuteronomic Theology* (Zondervan, 1993).

The Land

Deuteronomy is set on the edge of the Promised Land; it was in effect the last will and testament of Moses and prepared the nation to take possession of what was promised (Deut. 1:8; 6:10, 18; 7:8). The book of Joshua records the conquest of the land (chaps. 1–12) and its distribution among the tribes (chaps. 13–23). For the writer of the book, the chapters devoted to the distribution of the land (chaps. 13–22) are tantamount to a hymn of praise to God for giving to Israel that which he had promised. After all, the conquest and settlement represent the beginning of the fulfillment of the Abrahamic promise of land. To truly understand chapters 13–22 we must imagine the excitement that must have been generated by the mention of every city or other border marking. The fulfillment had finally come.

The Unity of Israel

Deuteronomy regularly addresses itself to "all Israel" (e.g., 5:1, 3; 11:6; 29:10), and a similar view of Israel pervades the book of Joshua (e.g., 3:7, 17; 4:14; 7:23–24; 24:1). All the tribes participate in punishing transgression (Deut. 13:9; Josh. 7:25) and in the nation's war of conquest. The nation was a union of twelve tribes acting in concert (18:2), each receiving a part of the inheritance (chaps. 13–21), each commemorated in the pile of stones near Gilgal (chap. 4). The Transjordan tribes erect an altar as a visible symbol of their unity with the other tribes (chap. 22).

The Role of Joshua

Deuteronomy presents Joshua as the divinely chosen successor to Moses and as the one who was to lead Israel into the land (e.g., Deut. 1:38; 3:21, 28; 31:3; 34:9). The book of Joshua portrays him in this role. Joshua assumes the military leadership that had once belonged to Moses and rules in accordance with the book of the law that Moses had written (Josh. 1:8–9). Joshua in effect completes the work of Moses by bringing the people into their inheritance. The people recognize Joshua as Moses' successor (1:17; 4:14). Aspects of the crossing of the Red Sea are reenacted under Joshua's leadership (Josh. 3–4). Like Moses, Joshua removes his shoes in the presence of God (5:15; cf. Ex. 3:5) and intercedes for the nation when they have sinned (7:7–9; cf. Deut. 9:25–29). Joshua leads the nation in the observance of the Passover, just as Moses did (Josh. 5:10–11). Both men are paired in their military roles: Joshua 12:1–6 lists the victories of Moses; 12:7–24, the victories under Joshua. Both make provisions for the allotment of the land: Joshua 13:8–32 lists the allotment of the land specified by Moses; 14:1 begins the report of allotments under Joshua.

The Covenant

Scholarship in recent decades has come to recognize that Deuteronomy resembles in many respects the treaties between kings and nations of the ancient

Near East. Many elements of this treaty (or covenant) form are found in the book. The book of Deuteronomy presents itself as "the Book of the Law" (31:26), the document containing the pledges and stipulations of Israel's covenant with her God. This covenant would be administered in accord with the terms of this written document. The book of Joshua is concerned to show life under this "Book of the Law" (1:8–9). It stresses the authority of the law of Moses in the national history by reporting ways in which the commandments of Moses served as a standard for conduct (e.g., Josh. 1:13; 4:10; 8:30–35; 9:24). Joshua leads the nation in covenant renewal at Mount Gerizim and Mount Ebal (Josh. 8) in accordance with the specific command of Moses (Deut. 27:1–8).

Even where the commands of Moses are not specifically mentioned, detailed obedience to the provisions of Deuteronomy undergird the various reports. Since Israel has been tricked by the Gibeonites, the provisions of Deuteronomy 20:10–11 serve to define the relationship between Israel and that nation (Josh. 9:23–27). The bodies of five slain kings are removed from the trees where they had been hung before sunset (Josh. 10:27), in accordance with the provisions of Deuteronomy 21:23. Achan is punished (Josh. 7:25) in accordance with provisions of Deuteronomy (Deut. 13). Both curses and blessings are set before Israel at the time of Joshua's death, just as they had summed up the stipulations of the law in Israel's covenant at the time of Moses' death (Josh. 23:14–16; Deut. 28). At the time of his death, Joshua, like Moses, was certain that the nation would not keep the covenant (24:19–20; Deut. 31:15–29).

The influence of Deuteronomy is felt in many other ways as well. The Anakim are wiped out as promised (11:21; Deut. 9:2). No one can withstand Israel (1:5; Deut. 11:25). The "hornet" expels the enemy (24:12; Deut. 7:20).

APPROACHING THE NEW TESTAMENT

The name "Jesus" is but a Greek writing of the Hebrew name "Joshua," so it is not surprising to see the New Testament drawing many parallels between Israel under Joshua's leadership and the formation of a new Israel under Jesus. In particular, the writer of the book of Hebrews makes frequent use of these connections (Heb. 4:8).

The Promised Rest

Joshua was leading Israel into their inheritance, into their rest (Deut. 3:20; 12:10; 25:19; Josh. 1:13, 15; 14:15; 21:44; 22:4; 23:1). But at best, it was a temporary rest from enemies, for Israel would have many more foes in the centuries ahead. Although Yahweh had secured an inheritance for his people, it could still be taken away from them, and eventually would be when both northern and southern kingdoms were carried into exile. There is an open-endedness to the book of Joshua (Woudstra 1981, 33): the people have an inheritance, but there is land still as yet unpossessed (Josh. 13:1–7; 15:63; 17:12). From the vantage point of the New Testament, Joshua's successes were only partial at best, and therefore they pointed beyond themselves to a time when Joshua's greater namesake, Jesus, would bring God's people into an inheritance that could not be taken away from them (1 Peter 1:3–5). Jesus would provide the rest Joshua had not attained (Heb. 3:11, 18; 4:1–11).

Models of Faith

The people of Israel at the battle of Jericho and Rahab the prostitute are presented as models of faith, examples of those who were looking for a country (Heb. 11:30–31; 11:14–16) but who did not attain what was promised (11:39–40) because God had planned something better.

God's Warrior

According to the New Testament, Jesus is not only Joshua's greater namesake, but he is also the Divine Warrior (Longman 1982; Longman and Reid 1995), the captain of the Lord's army who fights in behalf of his people and achieves victory for them (Josh. 5:13–15; Rev. 19:11–16). The inheritance he gives is not a stretch of rocky land in the eastern Mediterranean, but rather renewed heavens and earth and a heavenly city (Rev. 21:1–2).

The Conquest

Many have also drawn a comparison between Joshua and the book of Acts. After redemption from Egypt in the exodus, Israel began the conquest of her inheritance; after the redemptive work of Jesus at the cross, his people move forward to conquer the world in his name. Israel enjoyed an earthly inheritance and an earthly kingdom, but the kingdom of which the church is a part is spiritual and heavenly.

CHAPTER EIGHT

JUDGES

The book of Judges traces the period between the death of Joshua and the rise of the monarchy in Israel. In some respects the title of the book is a bit misleading to English readers. The "judges" were not primarily judicial officials; rather, they were military leaders and clan chieftains who appeared periodically in different areas among the tribes to effect deliverance from enemies threatening parts of Israel. The book is in many respects a dialogue about a relationship: the relationship between God and Israel. A loving heavenly Father would not rescind his election of Israel—he had pledged himself to the descendants of Abraham irrevocably. Yet how can a holy God who demands the allegiance and submission of his people tolerate their continuing sin and rebellion? Several of the judges are portrayed as deeply flawed human beings chosen to deliver a deeply flawed nation. Every reader of the book learns that God is long-suffering and compassionate; every reader cannot but see aspects of his or her own life refracted in the characters of the narrative.

BIBLIOGRAPHY

Commentaries

A. G. **Auld,** *Joshua, Judges, and Ruth* (DSB; Westminster, 1984); D. I. **Block,** *Judges, Ruth* (NAC; Broadman and Holman, 2002); R. G. **Boling,** *Judges* (AB; Doubleday, 1975); C. F. **Burney,** *The Book of Judges* (London: Rivingtons, 1918); A. E. **Cundall** and L. **Morris,** *Judges and Ruth* (TOTC; InterVarsity Press, 1968); C. J. **Goslinga,** *Joshua, Judges, Ruth* (BSC; Zondervan, 1986); J. **Gray,** *Joshua, Judges, and Ruth* (NCB; Eerdmans, 1967); E. J. **Hamlin,** *Judges: At Risk in the Promised Land* (ITC; Eerdmans, 1990); A. H. **Lewis,** *Judges/Ruth* (EBC; Moody, 1979); J. D. **Martin,** *The Book of Judges* (CBC; Cambridge University Press, 1975); G. F. **Moore,** *A Critical and Exegetical Commentary on Judges* (ICC; T. & T. Clark,

1895); T. J. **Schneider,** *Judges* (Berit Olam; Liturgical Press, 2000); J. A. **Soggin,** *Judges* (OTL; Westminster, 1981); L. **Younger,** *Judges/Ruth* (NIVAC; Zondervan, 2002).

Monographs and articles

Y. **Amit,** *The Book of Judges: The Art of Editing* (Brill, 1998); M. **Bal,** *Death and Dissymmetry* (University of Chicago Press, 1988); idem, *Murder and Difference,* trans. M. Gumpert (Indiana University Press, 1988); W. R. **Bodine,** *The Greek Text of Judges: Recensional Developments* (HSM 23; Chico: Scholars, 1980); M. Z. **Brettler,** "The Book of Judges: Literature as Politics," *JBL* 108 (1989): 395–418; M. **Buber,** *Kingship of God,* trans. R. Scheimann (3rd ed.; Harper & Row, 1967); F. M. **Cross,** *Canaanite Myth and Hebrew Epic* (Harvard University Press, 1973); A. E. **Cundall,** "Judges—An Apology for the Monarchy?" *ExpTim* 81 (1970): 178–81; D. R. **Davis,** "A Proposed Life-Setting for the Book of Judges" (Ph.D. diss., Southern Baptist Theological Seminary, Louisville, Ky., 1978); idem, *Such a Great Salvation* (Baker, 1990); W. **Dietrich,** *Prophetie und Geschichte: eine redaktionsgeschichtliche Untersuchung zum deuteronomistischen Geschichtswerk* (FRLANT 108; Göttingen: Vandenhoeck und Ruprecht, 1977); C. **Exum,** "The Center Cannot Hold: Thematic and Textual Instabilities in Judges," *CBQ* 52 (1990): 410–29; F. E. **Greenspan,** "The Theology of the Framework of Judges," *VT* 36 (1986): 385–96; K. R. R. **Gros Louis,** "The Book of Judges," in *Literary Interpretations of Biblical Narratives,* ed. K. Gros Louis, J. Ackerman, T. Warshaw (Abingdon, 1974): 141–62; B. **Halpern,** *The First Historians* (Harper & Row, 1988); A. J. **Hauser,** "The Minor Judges: A Re-evaluation," *JBL* 94 (1975): 190–200; idem, "Unity and Diversity in Early Israel Before Samuel," *JETS* 22 (1979): 289–303; L. R. **Klein,** *The Triumph of Irony in the Book of Judges* (Sheffield: Almond, 1988); W. S. **LaSor,** D. A. **Hubbard,** and F. W. **Bush,** *Old Testament Survey* (Eerdmans, 1982); J. P. U. **Lilley,** "A Literary Appreciation of the Book of Judges," *TynBul* 18 (1967): 94–102; A. D. H. **Mayes,** *Israel in the Period of the Judges* (SBT 29; Allenson, 1974); E. T. **Mullen** Jr., "The 'Minor Judges': Some Literary and Historical Considerations," *CBQ* 44 (1982): 185–201; M. **Noth,** *Überlieferungsgeschichtliche Studien* (1st ed., 1943; 2nd ed.; Tübingen: Max Niemeyer Verlag, 1967; first half trans. as *The Deuteronomistic History* [JSOTS 15; Sheffield: JSOT, 1981]); R. H. **O'Connell,** *The Rhetoric of the Book of Judges* (VTSup 63; Brill, 1996); R. **Polzin,** *Moses and the Deuteronomist* (Seabury, 1980); W. **Richter,** *Die Bearbeitungen des "Retterbuches" in der Deuteronomischen Epoche* (BBB 18; Bonn: Peter Hanstein, 1964); R. **Smend,** "Das Gesetz und die Volker: ein Beitrag zur deuteronomistischen Redaktionsgeschichte," Probleme biblischer Theologie: Gerhard von Rad zum 70 Geburtstag, ed. H. W. Wolff (Munich: Chr. Kaiser Verlag, 1971), 494–509; L. **Stone,** "Book of Judges," in DOTHB (InterVarsity Press, 2005); T. **Viejola,** *Das Königtum in der Beurteilung der deuteronomistischen Historiographie: ein redaktionsgeschichtliche Untersuchung* (Annales Academiae Scientiarum Fennicae, Ser. B.,

Tom. 198; Helsinki: Suomalainen Tiedeakatemia, 1977); B. G. **Webb**, *The Book of the Judges: An Integrated Reading* (JSOTS 46; Sheffield: JSOT, 1987).

HISTORICAL BACKGROUND

The book of Judges is set against the period between the death of Joshua and the rise of the monarchy. This was the period of large ethnic migrations throughout the Near East in the second half of the second millennium BC. It was a period that saw the demise of some great cultures (e.g., the Hittites in Asia Minor, the Minoans, and the Myceneans), the onset of the Iron Age in the Near East, and the arrival of the Philistines in the coastal plain.

As with all of the Old Testament historical books, the author of Judges remains anonymous. The author clearly lived at some point after the monarchy had begun in Israel (17:6; 18:1; 19:1; 21:25). The only other overt clue to the date of composition is found in Judges 18:30–31, where the writer states that the priests who descended from Jonathan son of Moses continued to serve until the captivity of the land and that Micah's idol continued in use for as long as the ark was in Shiloh. But these verses are themselves somewhat ambiguous. There are several views regarding the "captivity of the land": (1) Many scholars view the entirety of Deuteronomy–2 Kings as from the hand of an exilic author-compiler, so that the captivity of the land would be understood as a reference to the Babylonian captivity and thus suggests a date as late as the sixth century. (2) The captivity of the land could refer to the captivity of the region around Dan, the time when this part of Israel basically ceased to exist as part of the nation. The Israelite sanctuary at Dan would have survived until the Assyrian invasion under Tiglath-Pileser III (c. 733 BC, 2 Kings 15:29–30) or the deportation of the population by Sargon after the fall of Samaria (722 BC). This argues for a date in the eighth century BC. (3) It is also possible that the captivity of the land refers either to (a) the Philistine incursions during the time the ark was at Shiloh (1 Sam. 4:1–11), or (b) a time shortly after the death of Saul when David was ruling over Judah, and descendants of Saul held a truncated kingdom in Transjordan, the remainder falling to Philistine domination. The destruction of Shiloh is remembered in Jeremiah 7:12, 14; 26:6 and Psalm 78:60. This last approach favors a fairly early date for the book.

The closing chapters of the book are written with a distinctive political viewpoint that is also relevant for dating. The account of Micah's idol and the migration of the tribe of Dan (Judg. 17–18) suggests that the author was making a point about idolatry in the northern tribes. Micah's shrine and idol were initially located in the hill country of Ephraim (presumably near Bethel—17:1; 18:2) and were then purloined and installed in Dan. The author may be making the point that the northern tribes were always involved in idolatry: from a point in time after the schism and after the erection of golden calves in Dan and Bethel by Jeroboam, the author could in effect be saying, "Look, this is no surprise—those tribes were always prone to false worship and idolatry." The date of the book would then be after the schism.

The account of the Levite and his concubine (chap. 19) and the subsequent war against Benjamin (chaps. 20–21) also makes a few political points that broadly bear on the date of the book. In the earlier story, a Levite left Bethlehem to live in the hill country of Ephraim. Here a Levite from the hill country of Ephraim travels to Bethlehem to retrieve his concubine from her father's house. In Bethlehem he is treated royally and shown every courtesy. As he sets out with his concubine and servant for the return trip, the Levite is unwilling to stop in a city Israel had not conquered (Jebus or Jerusalem) and travels on to Gibeah in Benjamin before turning aside for the night. In Gibeah (the hometown of Saul), his party is not shown any hospitality by the native citizens of the town; however, a man from Ephraim finally comes to his aid. The Levite and his party are then confronted by great evil—evil reminiscent of Sodom and Gomorrah (Judg. 19:22–26; cf. Gen. 19:1–11). After the death of the concubine, the Levite rallies the tribes to war against Benjamin.

Underlying the details of the story is somewhat of a political allegory addressed to those from Ephraim and the northern tribes: Who will treat you well? (Someone from Bethlehem.) Who will treat you poorly? (Someone from Gibeah.) Who will remove the aliens from Jebus and make it safe? Everyone reading the story knows that David and his lineage were from Bethlehem and that David had made Jebus/Jerusalem a safe city. The story appears to advocate loyalty from the northern tribes to a family from Bethlehem, rather than to a family from the corrupt Gibeah (Saul and his descendants). This historical account is strongly pro-David and anti-Saul, suggesting a setting fairly early in the monarchic period. The internal evidence of the book therefore suggests a setting sometime shortly after the schism and possibly as late as the sixth century BC. Traditional scholarship commonly advocated a date as early as the end of the reign of Saul or early in the Davidic period (see Davis 1978, 24, 80–82, 130–31).

Much of critical scholarship has been characteristically preoccupied with the history of the book's composition. Some advocates of the documentary hypothesis in the Pentateuch sought to trace the putative pentateuchal sources into both Joshua and Judges (Moore 1895; Burney 1918). This approach has now been all but abandoned, largely due to the influence of Noth's monumental thesis in 1943 regarding the "Deuteronomistic History" (DH).

Noth argued that the books of Deuteronomy through 2 Kings formed a single distinct theological and literary work reporting the history of Israel from the exodus to the exile, and he rejected the effort to trace pentateuchal sources into this material. Although Noth's argument is more complex than we can detail here, he essentially held that a single author-compiler of the DH had combined two bodies of earlier literature to fashion his account of the judges: (1) a series of narratives about tribal heroes was integrated with (2) a list of judges (the "minor judges"). For Noth, these "minor judges" (10:1–5; 12:7–15) were established leaders of a tribal confederacy (an "amphictyony") and had primarily sacral duties at a central shrine. When this putative list of minor judges was combined with the narratives of tribal heroes, these heroes then also became known as "judges." The author then provided this material with a theological and chronological framework as part of the larger DH. Noth also identified a number of passages as accretions to the narrative added by later editors. Noth tried to isolate the language and ideology of his Deuteronomist (Dtr) from the post-Dtr additions. For example, he regarded the promonarchical outlook of Judges 17–21 as a later addition to Dtr's work, in contrast to a purportedly antimonarchical tone in the cyclical stories of the judges.

Subsequent scholarship has raised serious questions about the existence of an amphictyony in Israel. Furthermore, what little is known about the minor judges suggests that they were instead military leaders and clan chieftains quite like the major judges (Hauser 1975; Mullen 1982). The period of the judges was characterized by the kind of regional independence and autonomy that was found also among the contemporary Canaanite city-states (Hauser 1979); no single religious or political office provided cohesiveness, and affiliation among the tribes appears to have been rather loose.

Commentaries since the time of Noth have largely accepted his thesis of the existence of a DH and the place of Judges within it. Various scholars have modified Noth's theory to some degree. Richter (1964) argued for three separate redactions of material in the book, starting with a northern Israelite "book of deliverers" (*Retterbuch*), which was expanded by at least two later redactions before its incorporation into the DH. Dietrich (1977) and Smend (1971) identified a basic Deuteronomist (DtrG) revised by prophetic (DtrP) and monistic (DtrN) editors. Viejola (1977) examined the attitudes to the monarchy in these three alleged redactions and concluded that Judges 17–21 is part of DtrG and not later accretions; this would integrate these final chapters into the central concerns of the book. Another approach to the DH is associated with Cross and his students. Cross (1973) identified two primary redactional layers in the DH, a Dtr_1 from the time of Josiah, and a Dtr_2 from the time of the exile. The primary criterion for isolating the respective editions was attitudes toward the monarchy: unconditional promises belonged to the preexilic period and the optimistic climate at the time of Josiah, whereas passages emphasizing conditionality belonged to the exilic edition after the monarchy had ended in disaster. All of these approaches have the common understanding that the book is composed of a variety of sources/editions that have different ideologies and vocabulary whereby the history of composition can be reconstructed.

More recent scholarship has shown less interest in recovering the compositional history of the DH and has instead turned to synchronic methods (literary

The period of the judges was characterized by the kind of regional independence and autonomy that was found also among the contemporary Canaanite city-states.

criticism, narrative analysis, rhetorical criticism) that read the text as a coherent literary unit that is ideologically and theologically unified. Authors taking this approach are more interested in questions of organization, imagery and themes, characterization, plot development, ideology, and point of view. Instead of fragmenting the text as it stands into earlier and later materials, these approaches emphasize the overall design, coherence, and authorial skill of the text read as a unity (see Lilley 1967; Gros Louis 1974; Webb 1987; Klein 1988). The number of strong female characters in the book (Deborah, Jael, Sisera's mother, Jephthah's daughter, Samson's wives) and the frequent occurrence of incidents reflecting relationships between the genders have prompted a number of feminist readings as well (Bal 1988a, 1988b). See the discussion under Literary Structure below.

The chronological notices in the book have also been a subject of considerable debate since they bear on the question of the date of the exodus. When these notices are added together, they total a period of 410 years between the invasion of the land and the death of Samson (LaSor, Hubbard, and Bush, 220). This figure is reasonably close to the figure of 480 years between the exodus and the start of temple construction; for this reason it may be thought to favor an early date for the exodus, as does Jephthah's statement in Judges 11:26. However, the narrator of Judges has not provided information about the length of the various periods of Israel's apostasy between the judges, and unless one assumes that these periods of apostasy overlapped the number of years during which a judge was said to have been active, the total length of time in the book probably exceeds the time between the conquest and the death of Samson, regardless of whether one opts for an early or late date for the exodus. For this reason, several of the judgeships probably overlapped in different regions of Israel, but there is insufficient data to reconstruct this arrangement.

The ancient Greek translations of Judges preserve two distinct text types for the book, and research has concentrated on (1) whether they are two distinct translations or whether one is a revision of the other, (2) the classification and identification of the manuscript groups, and (3) which represents the earliest recoverable Greek translation. Bodine (1980) offers a good look at this investigation.

LITERARY STRUCTURE

Most scholars are agreed that the book contains three distinct sections: a prologue (1:1–2:5), a center (2:6–16:31), and an epilogue or appendix (17:1–21:25) consisting of two main stories.

The Prologue

The book begins by recapitulating the death of Joshua recorded in Joshua 24:29–31 and reporting how the conquest continued after his death (1:1–36);

the legacy of Joshua has already begun to break down (Childs, *IOTS*, 261). The angel of the Lord announces that, because of God's displeasure about Israel's having entered into alliances with the indigenous peoples, Israel would be unable to drive them out of the land; these nations would remain as "traps" for them (2:1–5; NIV "thorns in [their] sides"). However, the function of this introductory material is not simply to tie the ongoing history to the earlier account in Joshua. It sets the stage for the narratives to follow, in which Israel will be repeatedly oppressed by the surrounding and remaining peoples (3:1–5). A book that begins with the tribes cooperating in conquest (1:1) will end with the tribes united against one of their own (chaps. 20–21). The failure to conquer Jerusalem (1:19–21) will have ominous consequences at the end of the story (19:10–13).

As the title of her book implies, Klein (1988, 11–21), sees Judges as a tour de force of irony resulting from two different perspectives on events: that of Yahweh, and that of the people. This difference in perspective is set up in the prologue to the book, where two accounts present respectively the people's perspective on the conquest (1:1–36), and Yahweh's perspective on it (2:1–3:6). Webb (1987, 81–122) also sees 1:1–3:6 as the introduction to the book; it establishes the theme of the whole composition, the question of why the Canaanites were not completely driven from the land.

The Center

Any reader who has even a cursory acquaintance with the book of Judges is familiar with the series of stories that make up the core of the book (2:6–16:31). The accounts of the major judges (Othniel, Ehud, Deborah, Gideon, Jephthah, and Samson) are among the most familiar stories in the Bible. This section of the book is often described as having a "cyclical" view of history due to the predominant framework that unites the various accounts. This framework is introduced in the preface to the accounts of the judges (2:6–3:6), which summarizes the pattern of the accounts that follow. A number of recurring phrases or motifs make up this framework (Greenspan 1986), though it is not found in full form for all the judges:

1. The children of Israel do evil in the eyes of the Lord (2:11; 3:7, 12; 4:1; 6:1; 10:6; 13:1).
2. Although the nature of this evil is rarely spelled out, their sin prompts the anger of God and results in oppression at the hands of some foreign nation (2:14; 3:8; 4:2; 10:9). The nature of the evil Israel commits is summarized in 2:10–3:5 as idolatry and intermarriage. Because of their sin, the Israelites are not only unable to expel the Canaanites, but they themselves fall before foreign powers.
3. During their oppression, the Israelites cry out to the Lord (3:9, 15; 6:6–7; 10:10).

4. The Lord hears their cry and raises up a deliverer, one of the judges (2:16; 3:9, 15; 10:1, 12). The deliverer is chosen and empowered by the Spirit of the Lord (3:10; 6:34; 11:29; 13:25; 14:6, 19).

5. This deliverance is often followed by the submission of the enemy and a period of peace during which the deliverer judged Israel, followed in turn by the death and burial of the judge (3:10–11; 8:28–32; 10:2–5; 12:9–15).

This recurring sequence of sin-oppression-deliverance is often called "cyclical." But this designation is somewhat misleading if it is understood to imply that each "cycle" is more or less aimless or equal to all the others. A better way to describe it would be as a "downward spiral": it is not that each cycle is more or less a repeat of the earlier ones; rather, there is a deterioration in the quality of the judges and the effect of their leadership. A quick survey of the major judges will demonstrate this.

Othniel (3:7–11) appears first as the model of what a judge should be. He is raised up by God and invested with his Spirit; he was an able warrior when Joshua lived (Josh. 15:13–19), and he leads Israel in successful warfare as Joshua did.

In the case of *Ehud* (3:12–30), however, several important items are missing. The author does not tell us that God raised him up as he had done with Othniel; nor does Ehud enjoy investiture with the Spirit of God, and he does not "judge" Israel. We know only that he is "left-handed," a trait found among many in Benjamin (20:16; 1 Chron. 12:2), even though "Benjamin" in Hebrew means "son of my right hand." Ehud delivers Israel by deceit and treachery, and the text is silent about Yahweh's will and relationship to him.

Deborah (4:1–5:31) was a prophetess as she judged Israel. But in spite of her accomplishments and those of Jael, her judgeship raises questions about the failure of male leadership in Israel. Both Barak and Sisera lose the glory that should have been theirs to a woman (4:9). Is Israel unable to produce worthy male champions to lead in her wars for the land? Victory once again is less a feat of arms than a product of treachery. Jael, who finally destroys Sisera, is neither a judge nor a prophetess and only half Israelite (vv. 11, 17; 5:24). Rather than extolling a nation acting in concert and in faith, Deborah's song includes curses against other tribes that did not join the battle (5:15b–18, 23). The account anticipates the factionalism and intertribal disunity that was ultimately to culminate in the final episodes of the book (chaps. 20–21).

Gideon the farmer (6:1–9:56) is slow to recognize and respond to God's call for him to lead Israel; three miracles are required to convince the reluctant Gideon. And his obedience, when it does come, is not exactly courageous: he does tear down the Baal altar and the Asherah pole in his community as God commanded—he is still a bit of a coward and skeptic—and he does it at night (6:25–27; Klein 1988, 54). Although Gideon earns the sobriquet Jerub-baal

The recurring sequence of sin-oppression-deliverance is often called "cyclical." A better way to describe it would be as a "downward spiral."

("Let Baal contend with him"—6:32), he himself eventually succumbs to false worship that leads Israel astray (8:22–27). After the great battle when Gideon's three hundred prevail over a far greater number through faithful obedience, Gideon seems to forget the whole point of the exercise (7:2) and calls up his reserves, an army of thirty-two thousand (vv. 3, 24). A great victory once again erupts in factional rivalry and quarreling among the tribes and clans (8:1–9). Beyond the victory God had promised and given, Gideon pursues a personal vendetta (vv. 10–21). The story had begun with concern about the seed Israel had sown for her crops (6:3); Gideon had sown his own seed widely and had seventy sons, including one by a concubine from Shechem (8:31).

After Gideon's death, Israel again does wrong (8:33–35), and one anticipates the appearance of another judge/deliverer. But not so! Instead, *Abimelek*, Gideon's son by a concubine, attempts to seize power. God does not raise him up or call him to office. A story that began with concern about plant life (6:2–6) turns to Jotham's fable about the trees and bushes (9:7–15). The intertribal rivalry (8:1–9) during Gideon's time becomes now intrafamily strife and murder. In spite of the good that Gideon did for Israel, his son becomes not a deliverer but an oppressor, not a servant to the nation but a murderer of Israelites and of his own family.

Jephthah is the next major figure in the book. The account portrays something of the conflict within God himself about his relationship with Israel (Webb 1987, 48). They sin and provoke him to anger (10:6–16), so much so that he swears he will deliver them no more (v. 13). And yet he has committed himself to Israel so completely that he becomes vexed and indignant about their suffering (v. 16). When Jephthah appears on the scene, Yahweh has retired from the scene. Full of self-interest, Jephthah negotiates his way to power from his position as an outcast (11:1–11). Although God's Spirit had already come upon him for the battle with Ammon (v. 29), Jephthah makes a rash and redundant vow (v. 30), as if more were needed to secure the victory. The one who had been so calculating in his self-interest ends up destroying that which he counted most dear, his only child (11:34–40). Once again a victory erupts into intertribal squabbling and regional rivalry (12:1–6).

Samson is the last of the major judges. But he is a shadow of what a judge was supposed to be. He is self-indulgent and refuses to control his sexual appetite. Samson's proclivity for foreign women has become metaphorical for Israel itself, unwilling to resist going whoring after the enticement of foreign gods (2:17; 8:27, 33). Although, like Israel, he had been set apart to God from his birth (13:5), Samson would not fulfill his potential. Intermarriage with the Canaanites violated the command to drive them from the land (3:5–6). How could Samson succeed as the leader of Israel? He was more successful in death than in life (16:30).

The Epilogue

Leadership like that of these judges would not secure the land for Israel. Self-interest, self-indulgence, and all the sins that provoked God's anger with Israel also characterized her leaders. The legacy of a unified Israel left by Joshua has disintegrated into factional and regional rivalries. Conditions promoting religious and political chaos call for a different kind of leadership if Israel is to secure the land. Will having kings make the difference (17:6; 18:1; 19:1; 21:25)? Will kingship be a solution for both the religious (chaps. 17–18) and social (chaps. 19–21) ills of the nation? The last two stories (Micah's idol, and the Levite with a concubine—see Historical Background above) prepare the way for a turn to the monarchy in Israel's ongoing relationship with her God; the story continues in Samuel and Kings.

THEOLOGICAL MESSAGE

The themes and subject matter of Judges provide narrative exploration of two major theological questions.

1. *Grace and law, conditionality and unconditionality.* Throughout the Deuteronomic History (Joshua–Kings), the narrator explores and probes the nature of God's relationship with Israel. Will God's holiness and his demand for obedience to his commands override his promises to Israel? Or will his irrevocable commitment to the nation, his gracious promises to the patriarchs, mean that he will somehow overlook their sin? As much as theologians may seek to establish the priority of law over grace or grace over law, the book of Judges will not settle this question. What Judges gives the reader is not a systematic theology, but rather the history of a relationship. Judges leaves us with a paradox: God's relationship with Israel is at once both conditional and unconditional. He will not remove his favor, but Israel must live in obedience and faith to inherit the promise. It is this very tension that more than anything else propels the entire narrative.

2. *The administration of God's rule over his people.* God was to be Israel's king and lord (8:23). But how would his rule over his chosen people be expressed in history? The book of Judges shows clearly that decentralized rule, even blessed with periodic divine intervention in the nation's leadership and wars, would not produce a holy nation. Moses knew that Israel would someday have a king (Deut. 17:14–20), and Judges prepares for the transition to monarchy. Would kingship, already laden with the possibilities for abuse (Judg. 9), make a difference? The book prepares us for kingship as the next and inevitable step. Israel is enmeshed in regional and tribal factionalism—will kingship make the difference? The great national experiment with the judges had not worked. How else is Israel to secure the land and remain in it? Will a monarchy finally manage to drive out the Canaanites? End the anarchy? Keep the purity of national allegiance to Yahweh?

APPROACHING THE NEW TESTAMENT

What a collection of human beings in the book of Judges! Strange heroes they are—a reluctant farmer, a prophetess, a left-handed assassin, a bastard bandit, a sex-addicted Nazirite, among others. It is easy at a distance to point out the foibles and failures of the leading characters in this downwardly spiraling story. But lest we get too proud, Paul reminds us, "That is what some of you were" (1 Cor. 6:11). With similar mixtures of ignorance, frail obedience, and tangled motives, we, like them, were "washed, sanctified, and justified" by the grace of God. For all of their flaws, we are to learn from their faith. For it was in faith that Gideon, Barak, Jephthah, and Samson "conquered kingdoms, administered justice, and gained what was promised" (Heb. 11:32–33).

In spite of their failures, their faith was not misplaced. They become a part of that great cloud of witnesses calling for us to persevere and to fix our eyes on Jesus (Heb. 12:1–2). We too need a champion to fight our battles for us, one raised up by God and invested with his Spirit in full measure; we too need a leader to secure for us the inheritance that God has promised, one who will perfect our faith.

CHAPTER NINE

RUTH

The book of Ruth is a brief lull in the midst of a storm (Fewell and Gunn 1990, 11). In modern English versions it occurs right after the book of Judges, the time period in which the story is set, and right before 1 and 2 Samuel, for which it serves as an introduction. In contrast to Judges, however, Ruth narrates the account of the moral strength of its characters, and its plot resolves peacefully. Over against Samuel, with its familial and national politics and strife, Ruth's sexual intrigue has a blissful rather than a destructive ending.

The English order of books, which places Ruth after Judges, derives from the Septuagint and Vulgate order, which is more or less a chronological order. In most Hebrew Bibles, Ruth occurs immediately after Proverbs and before Song of Songs in the Writings, the third section of the Tanak. This placement associates Ruth with Proverbs 31, the poem of the virtuous woman, and the Song of Songs, in which the woman takes the lead in the relationship. It also places Ruth at the head of a subgroup of books (including the Song of Songs, Ecclesiastes, Lamentations, and Esther) that traditionally goes by the name Megillot or "Scrolls." These books are each associated with a different Jewish festival; Ruth is connected with Pentecost.

On first reading, the book's plot is simple, clear, short yet engaging—once again in contrast with the surrounding narratives. Although not all the characters are courageous, they are admirable, even noble. No one can be called evil in the book of Ruth. Nonetheless, behind the simplicity and clarity of the book stand a number of difficult issues that must be addressed in order to read it with understanding.

BIBLIOGRAPHY

Commentaries

D. Atkinson, *The Message of Ruth* (BST; InterVarsity Press, 1983); A. G. **Auld,** *Joshua, Judges, and Ruth* (DSB; Westminster, 1984); D. I. **Block,** *Judges, Ruth*

(NAC; Broadman and Holman, 1999); F. **Bush,** *Ruth/Esther* (WBC; Nelson, 1996); E. F. **Campbell** Jr., *Ruth* (AB; Doubleday, 1975); A. E. **Cundall** and L. **Morris,** *Judges and Ruth* (TOTC; InterVarsity Press, 1968); J. **Goslinga,** *Joshua, Judges and Ruth* (NCB; Eerdmans, 1967); R. L. **Hubbard** Jr., *The Book of Ruth* (NICOT; Eerdmans, 1988); K. **Nielson,** *Ruth* (OTL; Westminster John Knox, 1997); K. **Sakenfeld,** *Ruth* (Interp; Westminster John Knox, 1999); J. M. **Sasson,** *Ruth: A New Translation with Philological Commentary and a Formalist-Folklorist Interpretation* (2nd ed.; JSOT, 1989); L. **Younger,** *Judges, Ruth* (NIVAC; Zondervan, 2002).

Articles and Monographs

R. **Beckwith,** *The Old Testament Canon of the New Testament Church* (Eerdmans, 1985); M. **Bernstein,** "Two Multivalent Readings in the Ruth Narrative," *JSOT* 50 (1991): 15–26; J. L. **Berquist,** "Role Differentiation in the Book of Ruth," *JSOT* 57 (1993): 23–37; S. **Bertman,** "Symmetrical Design in the Book of Ruth," *JBL* 84 (1965): 165–68; D. N. **Fewell** and D. M. **Gunn,** *Compromising Redemption: Relating Characters in the Book of Ruth* (Westminster John Knox, 1990); B. **Green,** "The Plot of the Biblical Story of Ruth," *JSOT* 23 (1982): 55–68; R. M. **Hals,** *The Theology of the Book of Ruth* (Fortress, 1969); D. M. **Howard** Jr., *An Introduction to the Old Testament Historical Books* (Moody, 1993): 126–39; D. A. **Leggett,** *The Levirate and Goel Institutions in the Old Testament with Special Attention to the Book of Ruth* (Mack, 1974); W. S. **Prinsloo,** "The Theology of the Book of Ruth," *VT* 30 (1980): 330–41; D. F. **Rauber,** "Literary Values in the Bible: The Book of Ruth," *JBL* 89 (1970): 27–37; F. C. **Rossow,** "Literary Artistry in the Book of Ruth and Its Theological Significance," *Concordia Journal* 17 (1991): 12–19; L. **Ryken,** "Ruth," in *A Dictionary of Biblical Tradition in English Literature,* ed. D. L. Jeffrey (Eerdmans, 1992): 669–70; N. M. **Tischler,** "Ruth," in *A Complete Literary Guide to the Bible,* ed. L. Ryken and T. Longman III (Zondervan, 1993): 151–64.

HISTORICAL BACKGROUND

Date, Authorship, and Purpose

The superscription to the book of Ruth (1:1) places it in the period of the Judges (see below). The book says nothing, however, about its date of composition or about who wrote it. Nonetheless, scholars attempt to date the book by internal considerations, although these lead to no clear conclusion. While recent work tends to prefer a preexilic date (contra the analysis of Berquist 1993, 23), scholars of a previous generation have argued in favor of a postexilic one. The issue of dating the book is closely connected to the purpose of the book, so we must treat these topics together.

Arguments in favor of a late date include the following:

1. The book is said to contain Aramaisms. But this argument, which at one time was considered powerful and was applied to a number of different biblical

books, is no longer held in high esteem. The more we learn about the currency of Aramaic as early as the late second millennium, the less the appearance of similar words and phrases influence our dating of the book.

2. Scholars point to a clash between Ruth's presentation of certain legal customs (the levirate and the shoe-removal ceremony) and their mention in Deuteronomy. In Ruth, the shoe removal ceremony is considered obsolete, so it must be considerably after Deuteronomy (25:9), dated by such critics to Josiah's reform (late seventh century BC); and the levirate as it is described in Ruth seems a misapplication of the law, implying a long enough period of time for misunderstanding to set in. With Hubbard (26–27, 48–63; see also Leggett 1974), we reject the collocation of the Deuteronomic laws with the situation in Ruth on the following grounds: In the first place, although similar, the two shoe-removal ceremonies apply to different situations; and, second, it is the kinsman-redeemer law and not the levirate at play in Ruth.

3. Links between the superscription and Deuteronomic theology and between the genealogy (4:18–22) and priestly language lead those who date the Deuteronomic theology to the exile and the priestly theology to the postexilic period to consider Ruth to be a late book. Over against these views, many critical scholars argue that P and D, while finalized late in history, preserve early traditions.

4. Some argue that Ruth's appearance in the third part of the Hebrew canon, the Writings (*Ketubim*), indicates a postexilic origin. However, Beckwith has effectively demonstrated that inclusion in the Writings does not necessarily mean that a book is late, since there are other reasons than date for the grouping (see Beckwith, 138–53).

But perhaps the main reason why many want to date Ruth to a late period of Israel's history arises from an analysis of the book's purpose. Ruth presents the picture of a devoted Moabite woman whose sacrificial love rescues an Israelite family from oblivion and leads to the glory of the kingship of David. In the eyes of many, the message of this book contrasts sharply with the harsh postexilic policies of Ezra (10) and Nehemiah (13:23–27). Thus, as an alternative vision, the book of Ruth must be dated to the same period of time: the postexilic period.

However, there are a number of weaknesses with this hypothesis. For one, the book of Ruth does not have a polemical tone. Even when the opportunity clearly presents itself, there is no explicit condemnation of the type of policy mandated by Ezra and Nehemiah. For instance, when the unnamed kinsman-redeemer refuses to marry Ruth, the book implicitly shames him (4:6), an embarrassment easily avoided and turned to pride if he had insisted that a marriage with a Moabite were somehow improper.

The weaknesses with this approach to the book have become apparent to most scholars, and it is not a widely held position. On the contrary, a reexamination of the book's purpose reveals its probable preexilic setting.

Hubbard (1988) writes of two related purposes to the book. The first is pervasive throughout: the theme of God's providential salvation of Elimelech's family (see Theological Message below). Second, according to Hubbard, "the book has a political purpose: to win popular acceptance of David's rule by appeal to the continuity of Yahweh's guidance in the lives of Israel's ancestors and David" (42). God's providence results in the birth of Obed, who was the grandfather of David. The genealogy that charts this connection begins with Perez (Gen. 38:27–30), the son of Judah by Tamar (who also had to overcome obstacles in order to continue the family line).

When would such a political purpose have most utility? Hubbard reviews the possibilities and observes that David's time is fitting. However, he notes that the only obstacle to this setting is found in 4:7, which indicates that the book was written at a time when written legal documents were the norm and when the shoe-removal custom was forgotten. Hubbard suggests that 4:7 is a literary device (see below under Legal Traditions) but still favors Solomonic authorship because of this verse. However, he allows for a time of composition at the time of David and points out that the need was certainly there for the following reasons: First, supporters of the house of Saul likely viewed David as a royal interloper and so his kingship needed "legitimation." Second, foreigners were a large part of David's power base. Ruth, a paradigm of a foreigner's commitment to Israel and Yahweh, would serve such a situation well: "Foreigners who adopt Yahweh and outdo the Israelites in *hesed* merit acceptance as full-fledged Israelites" (45).

We may not be dogmatic about this conclusion. It is based on circumstantial evidence, but the best solution to the purpose of the book of Ruth leads us to favor a preexilic date for its composition.

The Talmud identifies Samuel as the author, but he lived too early. Tischler (1993) proposes that the author was a woman, because the book shows signs of being written with a woman's concerns in mind. She admits, however, that men are capable of writing empathetically, so her hypothesis may not be proved, though it is attractive.

Legal Traditions

The plot of the book turns on a number of legal traditions that, while rooted in the Old Testament, provide some problems for interpretation, since they are not applied as we might think from their parallels in the Pentateuch.

However, Ruth is not a legal document; it is a narrative. Although rooted in history, the actual application of laws and customs may be ignored in real-life situations. Furthermore, ancient law codes were not exhaustive or comprehensive. They gave general principles with flexibility as they are applied to specific situations (Hubbard 1988, 48–51).

Such issues are important to keep in mind as we look at the application of legal principles in the book. To illustrate the issue we will examine one of the

The plot of the book turns on a number of legal traditions rooted in the Old Testament. However, Ruth is not a legal document; it is a narrative.

disputed laws. Ruth proposed marriage to Boaz in chapter 3 based on his role as "kinsman-redeemer," or *gô 'ēl* (see Lev. 25:25–30, 47–55; cf. Jer. 32:1–15). But quick reference to the relevant laws indicates that marriage to a deceased relative's wife is not among the obligations of such a redeemer. This should not lead us to a negative conclusion regarding the historicity of the book of Ruth, however. The story's credibility to its original audience requires that the law have this application. It is most likely that the obligations of the *gô 'ēl* extend beyond that specified in the pentateuchal laws and "encompassed a variety of duties in support of weakened relatives, particularly the dead" (Hubbard 1988, 52).

LITERARY ANALYSIS

Genre

Gunkel's study was pivotal in the course of the literary analysis of the book. He saw the book as it stood as a novella, deriving from earlier saga and implying fictionality. Others (Campbell 1975, 3–4, 9–10; Hubbard 1988, 47–48; Howard 1993, 126–27) prefer "short story" (see also Bush 1996, 30–47; Block 1999, 599–603) and often add the adjective "historical." We remain unpersuaded that the highly artistic narration signals a nonhistorical text (see Historical Background in chap. 1).[1]

Structure

Tischler (1993, 151–53) has helpfully outlined the book as consisting of an introduction followed by five acts and a postlude:

Introduction (1:1–5)
Act 1: The Exodus (1:6–18)
Act 2: Bethlehem (1:19–22)
Act 3: Boaz Introduced (2:1–23)
Act 4: The Plan (3:1–18)
Act 5: The Public Pronouncement (4:1–12)
Postlude (4:13–22)

Literary Style

Ruth has always attracted attention for the clarity and simplicity of its style. The plot engages the reader by virtue of its balance and drama. But as Rauber (1970, 35) aptly stated, Ruth is "not a charming trifle; rather, we are impressed by its great resonances. It is indeed a gem, but gem in the sense of a gathered

---

[1]For an extensive argument in favor of a folkloristic interpretation along structuralist lines, see Sasson 1989.

and concentrated power, a bright clarity beneath a somewhat deceptive setting of lyric grace and simplicity."

The plot's setting and its major concerns heighten its charming simplicity. Ryken (1992, 669) notes that its interest in "home, family, religious devotion, earth, harvest, love, and nation" associate the book with pastoral literature.

Rauber (1970) further identifies the theme of "emptiness and fullness" as the heart of the narrative that seeks resolution in home and security. Green (1982, 56) observes that the field and its crops symbolize the woman and her needs. Naomi and Ruth's emptiness corresponds to the famine that drives Naomi's family away from Israel in the first place, though the latter precedes the former. The resolution of the plot, a happy ending that probably lends support to the prejudice that the book is rather lightweight, associates Ruth's new fullness (marriage and fertility) with the harvest. Rauber insightfully points out that this conclusion is artfully anticipated at the end of two previous episodes (see 2:18 and 3:17) as Boaz gives an earnest of the harvest to Ruth to take home to Naomi. The connection between the episodes in chapters 2 and 3 are heightened by the narrative balance observed by Bertman (1965).

THEOLOGICAL MESSAGE

Ruth appears to be an engaging story with little depth. At first glimpse its message appears to be ethical and not theological. The book promotes by example the virtues of loyalty, kindness, and generosity. Ruth demonstrates intense loyalty, and Orpah appears as a foil. Boaz incarnates kindness and generosity in contrast with the unnamed kinsman-redeemer. The message of the book could be characterized in this way: "Be loyal like Ruth and kind like Boaz, and God will reward you." Good overcomes evil for nice people.

Such an inane reading distorts the book and misses its profound theological teaching. Hals (1969) and Prinsloo (1980) (contra Sasson 1989, see 221 and elsewhere) explore the subtle theology of the book and locate its core teaching in the hidden and continuous providence of God. The narrative is subtle in its teaching about God and his ways in the world. As Hals and others have pointed out, while God's name occurs twenty-three times in this brief book, the narrator uses it only twice. It is through this subtlety that the book instructs its readers concerning God's ongoing work in the life of ordinary people.

Most striking and indicative of the book's theology is 2:3b. There we read that "as it turned out," Ruth "found herself working in a field belonging to Boaz." As Hals points out, the verse means the exact opposite of what it seems to say: "The labeling of Ruth's meeting with Boaz as 'chance' is nothing more than that no human intent was involved" (1969, 12).

No supernatural events or miracles punctuate the book of Ruth, but the attentive reader finishes the book knowing that God's hand guided the events of this story as directly as the story of the exodus from Egypt. In Prinsloo's words, "Human action sometimes even replaces divine action. Nevertheless . . . there is a limit to human initiative, and human initiative is futile without the divine blessing or action" (1980, 339). In this way, the book of Ruth functions similarly to the Joseph narrative and the book of Esther.

Furthermore, God's hidden and continuous providence does more than highlight the wonderful rescue of Elimelech's family. Although ordinary, the family produces one of the most important figures in Old Testament history: David. Thus the author says that David was a divine gift to Israel. In this way, the book of Ruth is analogous but not similar to the many stories in the Old Testament that narrate the births of other leaders of Israel. In each case, God provides the leader by overcoming tremendous obstacles (usually barrenness) to the birth (Isaac, Jacob, Samson, Samuel).

APPROACHING THE NEW TESTAMENT

Matthew's genealogy reminds the reader that Ruth was the grandmother of David but then continues by showing that the line of descent leads to Jesus. Only a handful of women are included in this genealogy: Tamar, Rahab, Ruth, and Mary. All of them had aspersions cast on them: whore, foreigner, unwed mother. But God used each of them to further the line that led to the Messiah.

Hals (1969, 17) provocatively calls the book of Ruth a "messianic history." Tischler (1993) notes the parallels between Ruth and Mary, most notably their common setting: Bethlehem. Rossow (1991, 17) further calls our attention to the parallel between Boaz as redeemer and Jesus Christ. Both voluntarily sacrificed themselves to redeem those in need.

But, in addition, we must note a continuity in God's hidden and marvelous providence as he redeems his people. It may be observed in the circumstances that led to the crucifixion of Christ. While to many in Jerusalem the crucifixion was just another execution, and to those who nailed him to the cross it was an expression of their desire to kill him, God's hidden hand was behind it. "This man was handed over to you by God's deliberate plan and foreknowledge; and you, with the help of wicked men, put him to death by nailing him to the cross. But God raised him from the dead, freeing him from the agony of death, because it was impossible for death to keep its hold on him" (Acts 2:23–24).

CHAPTER TEN

SAMUEL

The book of Samuel tells the story primarily of three individuals: Samuel, Israel's last judge; Saul, her first king; and David, the founder of a dynasty that would endure for more than three centuries. It is a book about transition—transition from theocracy to monarchy. Under the theocracy, God had provided the periodic leadership needed by the people (judges); now leadership would be institutionalized and hereditary.

BIBLIOGRAPHY

Commentaries

P. R. **Ackroyd,** *The First Book of Samuel* and *The Second Book of Samuel* (CBC; Cambridge University Press, 1971); A. A. **Anderson,** *2 Samuel* (WBC 11; Dallas: Word, 1989); B. T. **Arnold,** *1 and 2 Samuel* (NIVAC; Zondervan, 2003); J. **Baldwin,** *1 and 2 Samuel* (TOTC; Leicester: Inter-Varsity, 1988); W. **Brueggemann,** *First and Second Samuel* (Interp; John Knox, 1990); R. P. **Gordon,** *1 and 2 Samuel* (Zondervan, 1988); H. W. **Hertzberg,** *I and II Samuel* (OTL; Westminster, 1964); R. W. **Klein,** *I Samuel* (WBC 10; Word, 1983); P. K. **McCarter** Jr., *I Samuel and II Samuel* (AB; Doubleday, 1980 and 1984); D. F. **Payne,** *I and II Samuel* (DSB; Westminster, 1982); H. P. **Smith,** *Samuel* (ICC; T. & T. Clark, 1899); R. **Youngblood,** "1, 2 Samuel," in EBC (Zondervan, 1992), 551–1104.

Monographs and Articles

R. **Alter,** *The David Story: A Translation with Commentary of 1 and 2 Samuel* (W. W. North, 1999); B. **Arnold,** "Book of Samuel," in DOTHB (InterVarsity Press, 2005); B. C. **Birch,** *The Rise of the Israelite Monarchy: The Growth and Development of 1 Samuel 7–15* (SBLDS 27; Missoula: Scholars, 1976); A. F. **Campbell,** *The Ark Narrative* (SBLDS 16; Missoula: Scholars, 1975); R. A. **Carlson,** *David the Chosen King* (Stockholm: Almqvist and Wiksell, 1964); F. M. **Cross,** *Canaanite Myth and*

Hebrew Epic (Harvard University Press, 1973); W. **Dietrich,** *David, Saul, und die Propheten: Die Verhältnis von Religion und Politik nach den prophetischen Überlieferungen vom frühesten Königtum in Israel* (BWANT 122; Stuttgart: W. Kohlhammer, 1987); L. **Eslinger,** *Kingship of God in Crisis: A Close Reading of 1 Samuel 1–12* (Sheffield: Almond, 1985); J. **Flanagan,** "Court History or Succession Document? A Study of II Samuel 9–20 and I Kings 2," *JBL* 91 (1972): 172–81; idem, *David's Social Drama: A Hologram of Israel's Early Iron Age* (Sheffield: JSOT, 1985); J. P. **Fokkelman,** *Narrative Art and Poetry in the Books of Samuel,* 3 vols. (Assen: VanGorcum, 1981, 1986, 1990); M. **Garsiel,** *The First Book of Samuel: A Literary Study of Comparative Structures, Analogies and Parallels,* trans. P. Hackett (Ramat Gan: Revivim, 1985); K. R. R. **Gros Louis,** "The Difficulty of Ruling Well: King David of Israel," *Semeia* 8 (1977): 15–33; D. M. **Gunn,** *The Fate of King Saul* (JSOTS 14; Sheffield: JSOT, 1980); idem, *The Story of King David* (JSOTS 6; Sheffield: JSOT, 1978); B. **Halpern,** *The Constitution of the Monarchy in Israel* (HSM 24; Chico: Scholars, 1981); idem, *David's Secret Demons: Messiah, Murderer, Traitor, King* (Eerdmans, 2001); W. L. **Humphreys,** "From Tragic Hero to Villain: A Study of the Figure of Saul and the Development of 1 Samuel," *JSOT* 22 (1982): 95–117; idem, "The Tragedy of King Saul: A Study of the Structure of 1 Samuel 9–31," *JSOT* 6 (1978): 18–27; T. **Ishida,** *The Royal Dynasties in Ancient Israel* (*BZAW* 142; Berlin: de Gruyter, 1977); W. C. **Kaiser** Jr., *The Messiah in the Old Testament* (Zondervan, 1995); G. N. **Knoppers,** "The Historical Study of the Monarchy: Developments and Detours," in *The Face of Old Testament Studies: A Survey of Contemporary Approaches,* ed. D. W. Baker and B. T. Arnold (Baker, 1999), 207–35; V. P. **Long,** "First and Second Samuel: A Literary Introduction," in *A Complete Literary Guide to the Bible* (Zondervan, 1993); idem, "How Did Saul Become King? Literary Reading and Historical Reconstruction," in *Faith, Tradition, and History,* ed. D. W. Baker, J. Hoffmeier, and A. R. Millard (Eisenbrauns, 1994); idem, *The Reign and Rejection of King Saul: A Case for Literary and Theological Coherence* (SBLDS 118; Atlanta: Scholars, 1989); D. J. **McCarthy,** "The Inauguration of Monarchy in Israel," *Interp* 27 (1973): 401–12; S. L. **McKenzie,** *King David: An Autobiography* (Oxford University Press, 2000); P. D. **Miller** Jr. and J. J. M. **Roberts,** *The Hand of the Lord: A Reassessment of the "Ark Narrative" of I Samuel* (Johns Hopkins University Press, 1977); P. **Miscall,** *1 Samuel: A Literary Reading* (Indiana University Press, 1986); M. **Noth,** *Überlieferungsgeschichtliche Studien* (1st ed., 1943; 2nd ed.; Tübingen: Max Niemeyer Verlag, 1967; first half trans. as *The Deuteronomistic History* [JSOTS 15; Sheffield: JSOT, 1981]); R. **Polzin,** *Samuel and the Deuteronomist* (Harper & Row, 1989); I. **Provan,** V. P. **Long,** T. **Longman** III, *A Biblical History of Israel* (Westminster, 2003); L. **Rost,** *The Succession to the Throne of David,* trans. M. Rutter and D. Gunn (1926, Eng. trans. Sheffield: Almond, 1982); W. M. **Schniedewind,** *Society and the Promise to David: The Reception History of 2 Samuel 7:1–17* (Oxford University Press, 1999); M. **Tsevat,** "The Biblical Account of the Foundation of the

Monarchy in Israel," in *The Meaning of the Book of Job and Other Biblical Studies: Essays on the Literature and Religion of the Hebrew Bible* (Jersey City: KTAV, 1980): 77–99; E. **Ulrich,** *The Qumran Text of Samuel and Josephus* (HSM 19; Missoula: Scholars, 1978); A. **Weiser,** *Samuel: Seine geschichtliche Aufgabe und religiöse Bedeutung* (FRLANT 81; Göttingen: Vandenhoeck und Ruprecht, 1962); R. N. **Whybray,** *The Succession Narrative: A Study of II Sam. 9–20 and I Kings 1 and 2* (SBT 9, 2nd ser.; Allenson, 1968); E. **Würthwein,** *Die Erzählungen von der Thronfolge Davids—theologische oder politische Geschichtsschreibung?* (Zürich: Theologischer Verlag, 1974).

HISTORICAL BACKGROUND

Authorship

Like all other biblical historians, the author of the book of Samuel remains anonymous. Samuel was originally one book; however, probably due to the great length of the material, the book was divided in the Septuagint into two parts (called 1 and 2 Kingdoms). The first part ends with the death of Saul, and the second is largely devoted to the reign of David. The book is named after the first major character in the narrative; Samuel's birth is recorded in the first chapter, and his death in 1 Samuel 25 precludes the possibility that he wrote the entirety of the book (cf. 1 Chron. 29:29–30). The Talmud attributes 1 Samuel 1–24 to Samuel, while the rest has been connected with Nathan and Gad (b. Bat. 14b; 15a).

Since Samuel is part of the Deuteronomic History, most scholars view the final stages of its composition as the work of editors-authors during the period of the exile. However, it is all but impossible to recover the compositional history of the book, and it may well have been produced in essentially its present form at a much earlier date.

History of Composition

Critical scholarship during the last century and a half devoted itself to unraveling the compositional history of the book. The approaches can be summarized under the various critical methods employed.

Source-critical Approaches. Some scholars searched for underlying sources in ways similar to the model provided by pentateuchal criticism. The usual criteria involving perceived repetitions, doublets, tensions, and contradictions were used to isolate earlier narrative strands. When did Saul first meet David—prior to the battle with Goliath (1 Sam. 17:31, 55–58) or when Saul was needing the comfort of music (16:14–23)? Who killed Goliath—David (17:50) or Elhanan (2 Sam. 21:19)? What was God's attitude to instituting a monarchy in Israel—was it positive and approving (1 Sam. 9:15–16; 10:23–25) or negative and disapproving (8:4–22; 12:16–19)?

From these and similar tensions, analysts sought to isolate and identify earlier narrative strands. Wellhausen, for example, identified two sources, primarily depending on their respective attitudes to the monarchy. The earlier source was promonarchical in outlook and had a higher historical value; it reflected conditions during the monarchy when Israel still viewed kingship as the high point of national history. The later source reflected the experiences of Israel during and after the exile, when the end results of Israel's experience with kingship were felt. It reflected the attitudes of the Deuteronomist and was therefore antimonarchical in tone and, since it was a late source, not of much historical value. For example, the account of Saul's rise to power contains seemingly contradictory attitudes toward the monarchy: a favorable outlook (1 Sam. 9:1–10:19; 11:1–11) and an unfavorable outlook (7:1–8:22; 10:17–27; 11:14–12:25).

The dating proposed in Wellhausen's approach has been challenged. A number of scholars have argued that antimonarchical attitudes in Israel are probably set in the premonarchic period and reflect the actual debate within Israel about the transition to a monarchy (Weiser 1962; Tsevat 1980; Ishida 1977). Since Israel had formed her fundamental national institutions in the premonarchic period, resistance to the monarchy is what one should expect; reports of the tension between pro- and antimonarchical elements accurately reflect the social conditions of the period. Antimonarchic feeling could reflect a debate as far back as the days of Gideon (Judg. 8:22–9:57).

McCarthy (1973; cf. Long 1989, 174–75) pointed out that the sequence of pro- versus antimonarchical passages follows an alternating pattern in the text:

Table 5
Pro- Versus Antimonarchical Passages

B (–):	8:4–22	Report of an assembly: people request a king
A (+):	9:1–10:16	Story: secret anointing of Saul
B (–):	10:17–27	Report of an assembly: public presentation
A (+):	11:1–13	Story: Saul's first exploit
B (–):	11:14–12:25	Report of an assembly: Samuel's speech

The more negative elements consistently occur in public assemblies, where opinion and counter opinion would be expected.

Although a source-critical approach to this question has largely fallen into disrepute, Halpern (1981) attempted to revive it by assigning all passages in 1 Samuel 8–31 to either of two sources largely congruent with those identified in earlier scholarship.

Tradition-historical Approaches. Instead of two parallel and continuous sources, scholars taking a tradition-historical approach thought they could isolate previous collections of stories devoted to particular themes. Rost (1926 [1982]) identified a precanonical ark narrative (1 Sam. 4:1–7:1), a history of David's rise to power (1 Sam. 16:14–2 Sam. 5:10), and a succession narrative (2 Sam. 9–20; 1 Kings 1–2) as the major subunits of Samuel. Although individual analyses have varied, the following source collections have been suggested by many:

1. Stories from the boyhood of Samuel (1 Sam. 1–3).

2. The ark narrative (1 Sam. 4:1–7:2—cf. Campbell 1975; Miller and Roberts 1977). It is often suggested that this narrative continued in the account of the ark's transfer to Jerusalem (2 Sam. 6:1–15).

3. Stories about Samuel and Saul at Mizpah and Ramah (1 Sam. 7:3–12; 8:1–22; 10:17–27; 12:1–25; 15:1–35). These stories developed in particular locales and were largely anti-Saul or antimonarchy; prophetic oracles are prominent.

4. Stories of Samuel and Saul associated with Gilgal (1 Sam. 9:1–10:16; 13:1–14:46). Some assign portions of 1 Samuel 11, 15, 28, and 31 to this block of material. This putative source is generally more sympathetic to the monarchy and to Saul in particular.

5. A court history or succession narrative (2 Sam. 9–20; 1 Kings 1–2). It is rare to find as much unanimity among critical scholars as has attended the isolation and identification of the so-called court history or succession narrative. It has generally been viewed as a very early, almost eye-witness record of events during the reign of David. Rost's thesis (1926 [1982]) paved the way for succeeding generations of scholars to think in terms of relatively complete literary units covering segments of Israel's history more or less laid end to end to compose the larger work, instead of the ongoing search for parallel narratives on the model of older pentateuchal criticism. In the succession narrative, a series of skillfully woven human interest stories concentrates on the relationship between David and his sons, specifically revolving around the issue of which son would succeed him to the throne. Efforts to assess this earlier material have included identification as history writing, political propaganda (Rost 1926 [1982]; Whybray 1968; Würthwein 1974), and wisdom literature (Whybray 1968). There has been much debate about the beginning of this source: although 2 Samuel 9 is widely accepted, the narrative includes numerous references to events recorded in 1 Samuel 16–2 Samuel 8.

6. An "appendix" (2 Sam. 21–24). The materials in 2 Samuel 21–24 are widely viewed as an intrusion to the succession narrative, separating the accession of Solomon (1 Kings 1–2) from the earlier narratives leading to that event. The materials in this appendix consist of two narratives, two lists, and two

poems; they are chronologically dislocated and have their own internal chiastic structure as follows:

> A Narrative: three years of famine and death, averted by sacrifice (2 Sam. 21:1–14)
>> B David's valiant troops (21:15–22)
>>> C David's song when delivered from Saul (chap. 22)
>>> C' David's last song (23:1–7)
>> B' David's valiant troops (23:8–39)
> A' Narrative: three days of plague and death, averted by sacrifice (chap. 24)

Beyond these larger narrative units commonly suggested by scholars, the authors-compilers of Samuel and the earlier narrative collections appear to have had access to other individual narratives, poetic compositions (1 Sam. 2:1–10; 15:22–23; 2 Sam. 1:17–27; 3:33–34; 22:1–5; 23:1–7), archival material such as lists and annals (1 Sam. 7:13–17; 14:47–52; 2 Sam. 3:2–5; 5:13–16; 8:15–18; 20:23–26; 23:8–19; 24:5–9), and material about prophetic oracles (1 Sam. 2:27–36; 3:11–14; 6:3–9; 8:7–18; 9:15–16; 10:17–19; 12:6–17, 20–25; 15:10–11; 17:45–47; 2 Sam. 7:3–17; 12:7–14; 24:11–13).

Redaction-critical Approaches. Building on the results of tradition-historical analysis, redaction criticism sought to identify distinct editions or editorial layers. Noth in effect carried through the methodological shift represented by Rost's approach to the succession narrative. Noth (1943) detached Deuteronomy from the Pentateuch and identified it as the ideological foundation and literary beginning of a unified history of Israel extending from the beginning of Deuteronomy through Joshua, Judges, Samuel, and Kings. For Noth this "Deuteronomistic History" (DH) was the product of a single author writing during the exile to explain why God had rejected Israel. This exilic author had indeed used earlier collections of materials, and some passages in the text of these books as they now stand were, for Noth, insertions made after the work of his Deuteronomist (Dtr)—for example, the entire "appendix" (2 Sam. 21–24). Noth also identified some passages as the free compositions of the author himself; in Samuel the blocks of material from 1 Samuel 7:2–8:22 (the request for a king), 10:17–27a (the anointing of Saul at Mispah), and 12:1–25 (the summary speech of Samuel) were identified as compositions of Dtr. Noth's emphasis was on the unified character of the DH, a sharp contrast to earlier source-critical approaches. For Noth, Dtr's contribution was entirely negative: he sought to explain the exile and offered no hope for the future.

Although Noth's thesis was widely adopted and became the starting point for subsequent discussions, many scholars pointed out weaknesses in Noth's approach. Most particularly, Noth had not taken sufficient account of the importance of God's promises to David throughout the DH. The eternality of the Davidic covenant suggested a note of optimism contrary to Noth's negative reading. Noth had dismissed discordant material that suggested other than a negative thrust as material already found in Dtr's sources and simply incorporated without revision or elimination.

In light of the unresolved tensions in Noth's approach, other scholars sought to modify or refine the analysis. The efforts to perfect Noth's thesis have taken many different directions. Two in particular served as models: the double-redaction approach of F. M. Cross and many of his students, and the approach taken by Göttingen scholars Dietrich, Smend, and Viejola. Cross (1973) identified an initial edition of DH at the time of Josiah; it was written by a partisan of that king in order to support and legitimate Josiah's reforms, and it was promonarchic and optimistic in tone. This initial edition was then supplemented by an exilic redactor who added the accounts of the remaining kings up to the exile and edited earlier material; this second edition emphasized the conditionality of the Davidic promises and was more negative in outlook. Cross sought by this means to ease the tension between the conditionality and unconditionality of God's promises to David.[1]

Cross's approach has been influential primarily in America. On the Continent, Göttingen scholars Dietrich, Smend, and Viejola identified three redactional layers, all after the fall of Jerusalem in 586 BC.[2] A first edition (DtrG) provided the basic history; it was optimistic in tone and assumed that the conquest had been completed. A second redactor (DtrP) inserted the prophetic stories. A third redactor (DtrN) inserted the "nomistic" or legal materials; this level views the conquest as incomplete and the hold on the land as tenuous. Once again theological tensions are "resolved" by supposed editorial layering. The fundamental question of why the sources could be ideologically consistent when the later editors were not is left unanswered. With redactional explanations the final edition ends up as an ideologically confused document, lacking the theological consistency and skill of its sources.

In recent decades, sociological approaches have taken an increasingly important role in biblical studies. A number of scholars (e.g., Birch 1976; Flanagan 1988) have concentrated on the way in which the narrative betrays underlying sociological tensions. In particular, narratives such as the rise of the monarchy (1 Sam. 7–10), the plans for a temple (2 Sam. 7), and a census for purposes of taxation and conscription (2 Sam. 24) show the pressure toward centralization of political and religious power. These stories are juxtaposed with others that show resistance to centralization (1 Sam. 8; 2 Sam. 8, 24). The economic consequences of the centralization of religious and political power are also

---

[1]Some of this discussion unavoidably duplicates material covered in somewhat greater detail in the chapter on Kings.

[2]See the bibliography in the chapter on Judges for their respective works.

important: a monarchy meant taxation, corvée labor, and a standing military; the temple establishment had its own bureaucracy and the demand for offerings and contributions. Both monarchy and temple would drain resources from a subsistence agricultural economy like that of Iron Age Israel and could also encourage a class-stratified society. Centralization also meant reduced influence for traditional clan hierarchies in the face of a developing administrative bureaucracy. The quest for resources to maintain a centralized state also produced pressure for the military conquest of other states in order to provide additional wealth and affluence.

LITERARY STRUCTURE

Scholarly debate has for decades been preoccupied with questions of the ideology, date, extent, and secondary editing of the suggested sources, collections, or redactional layers. It has often seemed in scholarly debate that the purposes and ideology of these conjectured sources and layers have taken precedence over the ideology of the book as a whole. In some respects this is the inevitable consequence of a method that isolates earlier levels of material that were supposedly ideologically more consistent than the purportedly unharmonizable final work that betrays the competing and even opposing ideological tendencies of the various sources. More recent study has concentrated on the literary and aesthetic qualities of the text as it stands.

No book of the Bible has been the object of such intense interest to literary analysts as has Samuel. Studies of the narrative art and strategy abound (Fokkelman; Garsiel; Gros Louis; Gunn; Humphreys; Long; Miscall; Polzin; Alter). These have in common their devotion to questions about the ideology and literary excellence of Samuel as it now stands without recourse to hypothetical reconstruction of its literary history.

Although Samuel is made up almost exclusively of prose, a number of poetic sections are interspersed in the narrative. Two of these in particular provide a frame around the entire composition: Hannah's prayer in 1 Samuel 2:1–10, and David's songs in 2 Samuel 22:1–23:7. Polzin (1989, 33–34) shows how the sentiments of the triumphant king merge with those of an exultant mother. Both compositions rejoice in deliverance from enemies (2:1; 22:3–4); celebrate God as a rock (2:2; 22:32); speak of Sheol (2:6; 22:6); and describe God's thundering in the darkness (2:10; 22:14, 29), his protection of the faithful (2:9; 22:26), and his steadfast love for the Lord's anointed (2:10; 22:51; 23:1). Hannah's magnificat becomes a proleptic summary of the themes that fill the book as a whole: Hannah's prophetic song looks forward to the emergence of kingship in Israel, a victory David will live to celebrate as historical reality. The sanctity and protection of the Lord's anointed is among the unifying themes in the book (1 Sam. 16:3, 6, 12–13; 24:6; 26:9, 11, 16, 23; 2 Sam. 1:14, 16; 3:39; 19:21).

Two of the poetic sections provide a frame around the entire composition: Hannah's prayer and David's songs.

Hannah's request for a son also anticipates the remainder of the book in other ways (Polzin 1989, 24–25). In 1 Samuel 1:17, 20, 27; 2:20, Hannah and Eli refer to her son as the one "asked" or "requested" from the Lord, the same Hebrew verbal root (šâ'al) common in the people's request for a king (1 Sam. 8:10; 12:13, 17, 19). It is the same verbal root that underlies the name of Saul (ša'ûl—the one requested). Ironically, Hannah explains Samuel's name (1 Sam. 1:20) in a way that anticipates the appearance of Saul. When God grants Hannah's request for a son, the narrator finds in it an artistic prefiguring of the larger story about how and why God grants a king to Israel.

Another important theme in these narratives is the reversal of fortune. The rejection of Eli provides a rationale also for the rejection of Saul. Gunn (1980), Humphreys (1978), and Brueggemann (1990) find in Saul a star-crossed monarch whose rule began to end almost as soon as it began. Brueggemann regards Samuel as peevish and harsh in his dealings with Saul, who is submissive and deferential to the prophet. Gunn (1980, 131) concludes that Saul is experiencing the "dark side" of God, whereas David experiences only the other side. These are readings that view Saul more as victim than as villain. Long (1989), on the other hand, argues that the text presents a coherent rationale for the prophet's rebuke of Israel's first king (1 Sam. 13:13); the narrator presents Saul from the beginning as a hesitant and faltering monarch, hiding behind the baggage (1 Sam. 10:22, 27), failing to engage the Philistines (as done by Jonathan instead—1 Sam. 13:1–10), and paralyzed before Goliath (1 Sam. 17). For Long, God's rejection of Israel's first king was not an arbitrary dismissal for minor infractions, but rather it was consistent with the goodness, holiness, and justice of God. The writer emphasizes the similarities between Saul and Jonathan, the king and his heir (cf. 1 Sam. 13:22), as a means of emphasizing the sharp differences in their characters. Saul's inexorable decline is the countertheme to David's rise.

Gunn's analysis (1978, 87–111) of the narratives about David focuses on two primary themes: David as king, and David as a man. In his role as king, David acquires the kingdom and assures his tenure in office (the accounts about David and Saul, the rebellions of Absalom and Sheba) and founds a dynasty (the birth of Solomon, the rebellion of Adonijah, the elimination of other contenders and factions). These narratives are intertwined with the theme of David as a man: a husband (of Michal, Bathsheba) and father (of Amnon, Absalom, Solomon, Adonijah). The accounts are overlaid with themes of sexuality and political intrigue. Sexuality is a motif in the accounts of the sin with Bathsheba, the death of the child from an adulterous union, one son's rape of a half-sister, the competition for the father's bedmate Abishag, Uriah's refusal to visit his wife, the seizure of David's concubines, and the childlessness of Saul's daughter Michal. Violence and political intrigue are interspersed in the accounts of David's wars, Saul's attempts on David's life, the violence of Joab and his brothers, the murder of Uriah, fratricide among David's sons, the slaughter of the helpless Absalom, and David's plans for the deaths of his enemies soon after his own death.

The account of David's relationship with Bathsheba not only prepares for the eventual accession of Solomon, but it also sets in motion a curse that will dog the remainder of David's life: death and sexual outrage will follow, and "the sword will never depart from [his] house" (2 Sam. 12:10). The word *sword* becomes a key term unifying aspects of the narrative from Samuel through Kings. The entire account of David is presented as the interplay of his public (kingship) and private (father, husband) roles as they impinge on the question of who will succeed him to the throne. Gunn (1978, 94–108) also accents the themes of giving and grasping: whereas some accounts present David or other characters as somewhat passive in their roles, in others they seize or grasp at favor and power. For example, the king who will not seize the kingdom from Saul (2 Sam. 2–5) is nevertheless willing to seize a woman who is the object of his desire (Bathsheba); she who is seemingly passive in her seduction will later seize the kingdom for Solomon. Overall, it is the story of how David gains the throne, loses it temporarily in the face of rebellions, only to regain it again, and then lose it in death. It is an intricate picture of human greatness and folly, of wisdom and sin, of faith and faithlessness, of contrasting perspectives and conflicting desires.

For more recent attempts to read the story of David, see Halpern 2001 and McKenzie 2000. They agree in their rather unflattering portrait of the king since, while they affirm the basic facts of the story, they believe the Bible "spins" David's life to provide an apologetic for the king. For a powerful rebuttal of these reconstructionist approaches to David, see Long (in Provan, Long, and Longman, 217–27).

The aesthetic excellence of the overall work extends not just from its larger narrative structures but also to the smaller scale episodes and paragraphs. Fokkelman's analysis is the most detailed, about thirteen pages of interpretive text for each page of his translation (Polzin 1989, 301). Only some short examples are possible here.

One of the more frequent compositional techniques used by the writer is the repetition of key words. For example, in 1 Samuel 15 the terms "hear, listen" (*šm ʿ*) and "noise, voice" (*qôl*) alternate: will Saul *listen* to the *voice* of God (15:1)? Saul claims that he did so (15:13), but Samuel *hears* the *noise* of the livestock (15:14) and judges that Saul has *listened* to the *voice* of the people rather than the *voice* of God (15:19–24). For another example, a single Hebrew root (*kbd*) conveys the related ideas of "be heavy" and "consider weighty, honor" and "glory." In the narratives about Eli, the priest is described as "giving *honor*" to his sons instead of to God (1 Sam. 2:29) by allowing them to fatten themselves on the choice parts of the offerings. God says, "Those who *honor* [ascribe weight to] me I will *honor*, but those who despise me will be disdained [considered light]" (2:30). Eli's broken neck and death result from a fall because he was *heavy*

(4:18), and the loss of the ark prompts the naming of his grandson Ichabod ("*glory, honor* is no more"; 4:21).

The accounts also abound in irony. Neither Samuel's nor Eli's sons "know the Lord" (1 Sam. 2:12; 3:13). The faithful Uriah unknowingly honors an unfaithful king who has been unfaithful to him; he retains his ritual purity during warfare by refraining from sexual intercourse during time of war, only to be sent to his death in battle by a king who enjoyed sexual congress with his wife instead of going to the battle (2 Sam. 11).

Repetition marks many passages. For example (Gunn 1980, 77), in 2 Samuel 2, Abner and the sons of Ishbosheth *went out* (2:12) and met at the pool of Gibeon *together* (2:13), and Joab and the servants of David *went out* (2:13) and fell *together* in combat (2:16)—here the repetition forms an inclusio around the entire story. Extended repetitions of vocabulary or themes in inverse order often form chiasms in the accounts; Fokkelman has identified many in the narratives of Samuel, similar to that long recognized in the so-called appendix (see above).

The stories of Samuel, Saul, and David have held a fascination in the history of literature, art, and homiletics perhaps beyond that of any other body of texts.

TEXT-CRITICAL ISSUES

Scholars have long suspected that the Masoretic Text of Samuel, though comparatively intact, is nevertheless among the least well transmitted books of the Bible. At many places there are significant divergences from the Hebrew text that was used by the translators of the Septuagint, and when the writer of Chronicles quotes Samuel, he also often appears to follow a text of Samuel different from the Masoretic Text (MT). For generations scholars debated the merits of these variant readings. Was the Chronicler theologically editing the earlier text or following some independent source? Were the Septuagint translators incorporating their own theology, embellishing, or being careless—or were they carefully following a Hebrew text that differed from the MT?

With the discovery of the Qumran manuscripts and fragments, this debate was largely settled. Among three different fragmentary manuscripts of Samuel found in cave 4 at Qumran, two appeared in large measure to agree with the MT, whereas the bits and scraps of the third manuscript (what the worms had left) contained a text resembling the exemplar that was used by both the Chronicler and the Septuagint translators. The existence of an alternative Hebrew manuscript type (or types) was now no longer a question.

A few illustrations will suffice to provide the reader with an idea of the kinds of questions posed by the MT of Samuel. Consider an example from the text of 1 Samuel 14:41 as it is found in the MT and Septuagint. The two translations are provided in English but with several indications of the underlying Hebrew highlighted in order to see how the differences developed.

Septuagint	Masoretic Text
Table 6	
Scribes and the Hebrew Bible I	
Then Saul said, <u>"O Lord God of Israel,</u> why have you not answered your servant today? If this guilt is in me or in my son Jonathan, <u>O Lord God of Israel, give</u> Urim, but if this guilt is in your people Israel, give Thummim, (*tmyt*)." And Jonathan and Saul were indicated by the lot, but the people were cleared.	Then Saul said, <u>"O Lord God of Israel.</u> Give me *the right answer"* *tmyt*

The eye of the Hebrew scribe at some point appears to have jumped from the first occurrence of the phrase "O Lord God of Israel" to the second, and then from the first occurrence to the command "give" to the second, resulting in substantial omissions in the Hebrew text. The Hebrew word *tmym* underlies both the translation "Thummim" and "the right answer," although translating "the right answer" is otherwise unattested as the meaning for this word; that is to say, the translation "right answer" is a somewhat artificial adjustment because the word Urim was missing from the Masoretic Text.

A similar example can be seen from 2 Samuel 5:21 and the parallel text at 1 Chronicles 14:12.

2 Samuel 5:21	1 Chronicles 14:12
Table 7	
Scribes and the Hebrew Bible II	
The Philistines abandoned their idols there, and David and his men carried them off.	The Philistines had abandoned their gods there, and David gave orders to burn them in the fire.

Scholars had often argued that the Chronicler edited his source in order to bring David's actions into conformity with God's commands about burning the foreign idols (Deut. 12:2–3). However, the Lucianic recension of the Septuagint for 2 Samuel 5:21 preserves a reading that agrees with the text of Chronicles. It is at least possible that the Chronicler here was following a text of Samuel that differed from the MT.

One more example will have to suffice for our purposes. In the account of David's disastrous census, the Chronicler reports that David looked up and saw the angel of the Lord standing between heaven and earth and extended over Jerusalem (1 Chron. 21:16). This note is missing in the parallel text in 2 Samuel 24, where it would have occurred in verse 16. Many have thought that the more developed angelology of the postexilic period was the reason for the Chronicler's inclusion of this verse. However, the fragments of 4QSamb do contain this verse, once again suggesting that the Chronicler had at his disposal a version of Samuel somewhat different from the MT.

On the whole, the results of the Qumran discoveries for Samuel have been to increase interest in the text of Samuel that was presumably used by the Septuagint translators and the Chronicler. Ulrich (1978) discusses these issues at length.

THEOLOGICAL MESSAGE

Samuel is ordinarily described as part of the Deuteronomic History, that series of books from Joshua through Kings that applies the laws and worldview of Deuteronomy to the history of the nation. The influence of Deuteronomy can be felt in Samuel quite often at the level of phraseology and vocabulary. Three important theological concerns of Deuteronomy play a particular role in the book.

1. Deuteronomy envisaged a day when Israel would have a king (17:14–20) and set forth the principles under which a king should rule. Israel did eventually ask for a king "like all the nations around [them]" (Deut. 17:14; 1 Sam. 8:5, 20), and the book of Samuel records Israel's initial experiments with monarchy. Both Deuteronomy and Samuel had warned about kings who amassed too much wealth and power (Deut. 17:16–17; 1 Sam. 8:10–18) and had proclaimed the responsibility of kings to obey the written commands of God (Deut. 17:18–19; 1 Sam. 10:25). What would kingship in Israel be like? Would these kings keep God's commands and not think more highly of themselves than of their fellow countrymen? The book of Judges had ended in anarchy—would things be better under a monarch?

2. Deuteronomy also spoke of a day when Israel would have rest from the enemies that surrounded her (12:10); then God would choose one place to which his people would bring their offerings in worship (12:1–14, 20–25). The book of Samuel records the transition from the itinerating tabernacle to the first inklings that a temple would be built (2 Sam. 7:1–2). The choice of Jerusalem as the place for God's house is inseparably tied to God's choice of David. The house

of David and the house of God are the ingredients for the remainder of the story in Kings.

3. Deuteronomy also presented a God who responded to his people: with blessing when they obeyed, but in judgment when they did not (chap. 28). Although he was a God sovereign in all his ways, yet Israel would have many choices to make as individuals and as a nation. God would respond in accord with their choices. Throughout the narratives of Samuel the reader sees divine blessing and judgment in action. God rules over the affairs of history; he elects and foreordains the course of persons and nations (2 Sam. 7:7–9). But he is also a God who gives to human beings meaningful moral choices with far-reaching consequences for themselves and others. God requires the obedience of all people and that they worship him alone (1 Sam. 7:3–4). Human beings do not escape the consequences of the moral order of the universe as established by its Creator; people suffer for their sins in accordance with divine retribution. But above and beyond the ebb and flow of human excess and folly, a sovereign God continues to work his gracious purpose toward his chosen people and chosen king.

Deuteronomy and the other books of the Deuteronomic History all contain unresolved tensions. In Joshua and Judges the primary tension between divine election, grace, and promises on the one hand and divine holiness, justice, and law on the other focuses on the conquest and possession of the land. Will all the land be Israel's? Forever? In these earlier books, this tension revolves around the complete versus the partial conquest of the land, its status as gift from divine promises versus its loss through disobedience.

In Samuel this tension between the grace and law of God is extended by its application to the question of monarchy. Possession of the land is now tied to kingship (2 Sam. 7:10–11). Will kingship help Israel to hold the land? God authorizes and selects Israel's first two kings (Saul and David), but the request for a king is also simultaneously in some sense rejection of God's own rule. What will kingship mean for the nation? God makes an irrevocable promise to David that he will never lack a descendant sitting on his throne (2 Sam. 7:16, 29), but by the end of the story in Kings, both land and kingship have been lost through disobedience. This very paradox, the tension between God's promises and his justice, remains unrelieved throughout the Deuteronomic History. It is in fact the tension that drives the entire narrative forward.

APPROACHING THE NEW TESTAMENT

Saul's sins do not seem that much greater than David's. How is it that David can be described by the narrator as "a man after his [God's] own heart" (1 Sam. 13:14)? Israel had looked at Saul's height and musculature—there was no one like him among all the people (1 Sam. 10:24); although God had chosen Saul, he knew what was in his heart. Human beings might look at appearance and height, but God saw David's heart. David's heart was such that he would face Goliath virtually unarmed and would triumph through his faith, while Saul cowered in his tent (1 Sam. 17). The central demand of life in covenant with God, both from the mouth of Moses and from Jesus, was to love him with the whole heart (Deut. 6:5; Mark 12:30).

Yet something happened to David along the way. When we first meet him in the text of Samuel, he has taken a club to kill a bear and a lion for the sake of sheep (1 Sam. 17:34–35), but by the end of the book, he has decided that the sheep should die for him, though this time the sheep were people (2 Sam. 24:14, 17). David will not be the good shepherd that will give his life for the sheep— we must keep reading to find another (John 10:11).

One of the recurring themes in the book of Samuel is reference to the "Lord's anointed" (1 Sam. 16:3, 6, 12–13; 24:6; 26:9, 11, 16, 23; 2 Sam. 1:14, 16; 3:39; 19:21). The Hebrew term *messiah* means "anointed one," and the idea of a Messiah for Israel grows out of her ideology about a righteous king, one who would be like David. The Messiah as a figure is integrally involved in Israel's unique understanding of her place in history: their awareness from the beginning that God had made them a chosen people to bring blessing to the nations. God had raised up great leaders and deliverers for Israel during her history, and he would do so again in the person of a Messiah. The failures of the kings that followed David set him in an increasingly favorable light, so that Israel's hopes crystallized around the coming of a future David (Ezek. 34:23). Two groups of passages show this particular expectation most clearly—the royal psalms and Isaiah 7–12. The royal psalms center on a king who meets universal opposition, is victorious, and establishes righteous rule from Zion over the nations. His kingdom is peaceful, prosperous, everlasting, and faithful to the Lord. He is the friend of the poor and the enemy of the oppressor. He is the heir of the promises to David. He is himself divine (Ps. 45:6): like the angel of the Lord, he is both God and distinct from God. In the book of Immanuel (Isa. 7–12), the prophet speaks about the appearance of a wonder child who will be deliverer, world ruler, and righteous king. The writers of the New Testament see in Jesus the embodiment of a righteous king for Israel. They take pains to point to his descent from David (Matt. 1:1, 6, 17). The crowds and even the demons recognize him as the Son of David, the Messiah of Israel (Matt. 12:23; 20:30–31; 21:9, 15).[3]

This tension between God's electing love and his holy justice is resolved at the cross: there one who embodied faithful Israel—one who had himself been all that God had intended for Israel to be, God's chosen one, his own Son—bears the penalty of divine judgment for sin.

---

[3]For a recent study of the messianic theme in the Old Testament, see Kaiser 1995.

The longing for a child and for a righteous king and anointed one (1 Sam. 2:10) in Hannah's song is heard again in Mary's own magnificat as she anticipates the birth of Israel's king and Messiah (Luke 1:32–33, 46–55, 69). David had become the heir of God's promise to Abraham that he would give him a great name (Gen. 12:2; 2 Sam. 7:9); David's greater son receives a name above all others (Phil. 2:9–10). In the same way that David had once gone into single-handed combat with the great enemy of Israel (1 Sam. 17), so too Jesus would single-handedly triumph over the enemy of our souls.

CHAPTER ELEVEN

KINGS

Most modern translations follow the practice in the Septuagint and in Christian tradition of including Kings as part of a larger group of historical books beginning with Joshua and ending with Ezra-Nehemiah and Esther. The Hebrew Bible followed a different system of classification. It was divided into three sections: the Law, the Prophets, and the Writings. The Prophets were further subdivided into the "former" and "latter" prophets. The Former Prophets consisted of Joshua, Judges, Samuel, and Kings. These were followed in turn by the Latter Prophets, a division that included all the books ordinarily associated with the prophets (except for Daniel and Lamentations, both of which were in the third division, the Writings).

For those accustomed to the way the books are grouped in modern translations, at first glance it is something of a surprise to find Joshua–Kings classified among the Prophets. These books of historical narration are literarily quite different from what typifies the other prophetic books. Yet on further reflection, it is not difficult to understand why Kings was classified this way in the Hebrew Bible. (1) The deeds and exploits of a large number of prophets are recorded in Kings. We read there about Nathan, Ahijah, Jehu, Micaiah, Isaiah, Huldah, and several unnamed prophets, not to mention the extensive coverage of the ministries of Elijah and Elisha (1 Kings 17–2 Kings 6, 13). (2) The prophetic books also made use of the history recorded in Kings, citing it or some common source often at length almost verbatim (Jer. 52; 2 Kings 24:18–25:21; Isa. 36–39; 2 Kings 18:13–20:19). (3) The books of Chronicles may have influenced this classification. Some of the sources cited by the Chronicler suggest that the prophets also wrote historical narrative about the reigns of kings (1 Chron. 29:29; 2 Chron. 9:29; 12:15; 20:34; 26:22; 32:32). (4) The books of Joshua–Kings are often called the "Deuteronomic History" since they are written from a perspective strongly influenced by the book of Deuteronomy. The prophets, as Moses' successors (Deut. 18), continued to record the history of Israel from the point where

Deuteronomy ended (Deut. 1–4; 34); they demonstrated the historical realization of Moses' prophetic curses on a disobedient nation (Deut. 28).

It is probably for these reasons that Jewish tradition identified Jeremiah as the author of Kings. The Talmud (*Baba' Bathra* 15a) reports that "Jeremiah wrote his own book, the Book of Kings, and Lamentations." Jeremiah was active at the time of the destruction of Jerusalem, and the book bearing his name quotes extensively from the final chapters of Kings (see above) or from some other source that both books used in common. Nevertheless, Jeremiah probably was not the actual author of Kings. Jeremiah went into Egypt after the destruction of Jerusalem (Jer. 43:1–8). Although we do not know what became of the prophet after his departure, the last few verses of Kings were most probably written by an anonymous writer in exile in Babylon (2 Kings 25:27–30). There is no way to substantiate the predictable conclusions of Jewish tradition regarding the authorship of the book. The actual compositional history of the book may have been rather complex, as may be seen below.

The English name of the book, Kings, comes from its title in the Hebrew Bible. The Septuagint identified the book as "3–4 Reigns" following on 1–2 Reigns (the Septuagint title for 1–2 Samuel). It is clear that the two books of Kings were originally one book. The break between the books in the middle of the account of Ahaziah appears artificial.

BIBLIOGRAPHY

Commentaries

A. G. **Auld**, *I and II Kings* (DSB; Westminster, 1986); W. **Brueggemann**, *1 and 2 Kings* (SHBC; Smyth and Helwys, 2000); M. **Cogan**, *I Kings* (AB 10; Doubleday, 2001); M. **Cogan** and H. **Tadmor**, *II Kings* (AB 11; Doubleday, 1988); S. **DeVries**, *1 Kings* (WBC 12; Word, 1985); R. H. **Dilday**, *1, 2 Kings* (CC; Word, 1987); J. **Gray**, *I and II Kings, a Commentary* (OTL, 3rd ed.; Westminster, 1977); T. R. **Hobbs**, *2 Kings* (WBC 13; Word, 1985); P. R. **House**, *1, 2 Kings* (NAC; Holman, 1995); G. H. **Jones**, *1 and 2 Kings,* 2 vols. (NCB; Eerdmans, 1984); B. O. **Long**, *1 Kings* (FOTL 9; Eerdmans, 1984); R. D. **Nelson**, *First and Second Kings* (Interp; John Knox, 1987); M. **Noth**, *Könige* (BKAT; Neukirchen: Neukirchener Verlag, 1968); I. **Provan**, *1 and 2 Kings* (NIBCOT; Hendrickson, 1995); H. F. **Vos**, *1, 2 Kings* (BSC; Zondervan, 1989); D. **Wiseman**, *1 and 2 Kings* (TOTC; Inter-Varsity Press, 1993); E. **Würthwein**, *Das erste Buch der Könige* (ATD; Göttingen: Vandenhoeck und Ruprecht, 1977–84).

Monographs and Articles

S. **Bin-Nun**, "Formulas from Royal Records of Israel and of Judah," *VT* 18 (1968): 414–32; J. **Bright**, *A History of Israel,* 3rd ed. (Westminster, 1981); L. **Bronner**, *The Stories of Elijah and Elisha* (Leiden: Brill, 1968); W. **Brueggemann**, "The

Kerygma of the Deuteronomistic Historian," *Interp* 22 (1968): 387–402; A. F. **Campbell** and M. A. **O'Brien,** *Unfolding the Deuteronomistic History: Origins, Upgrades, Present Text* (Fortress, 2000); B. S. **Childs,** *Introduction to the Old Testament as Scripture* (*IOTS*; Fortress, 1979); idem, "On Reading the Elijah Narratives," *Interp* 34 (1980): 128–37; M. **Cogan,** *Imperialism and Religion: Assyria, Judah, and Israel in the Eighth and Seventh Centuries B.C.* (SBLMS 19; Missoula: Scholars, 1974); R. **Cohn,** "Convention and Creativity in the Book of Kings: The Case of the Dying Monarch," *CBQ* 47 (1985): 603–16; idem, "The Literary Logic of 1 Kings 17–19," *JBL* 101 (1982): 333–50; A. **Cook,** "Fiction and History in Samuel and Kings," *JSOT* 36 (1986): 27–48; F. M. **Cross,** *Canaanite Myth and Hebrew Epic* (Cambridge: Harvard University Press, 1973); H. **Donner,** "The Separate States of Israel and Judah," in *Israelite and Judean History,* ed. J. Hayes and J. Miller (OTL; Westminster, 1977): 381–434; J. **Ellul,** *The Politics of God and the Politics of Man* (Eerdmans, 1972); D. **Fewell,** "Sennacherib's Defeat: Words at War in 2 Kings 18:13–19:37," *JSOT* 34 (1986): 79–90; G. **Gerbrandt,** *Kingship According to the Deuteronomistic History* (SBLDS 87; Atlanta: Scholars, 1986); F. **Gonçalves,** *L'expédition de Sennachérib en Palestine dans la littérature hebraïque ancienne* (Études biblique, NS, 7; Paris: Librairie Lecoffre, 1986); D. **Gooding,** "Jeroboam's Rise to Power: A Rejoinder," *JBL* 91 (1972): 529–33; idem, "Problems of Text and Midrash in the Third Book of Reigns," *Textus* 7 (1969): 1–29; idem, "The Septuagint's Rival Versions of Jeroboam's Rise to Power," *VT* 17 (1967): 173–89; W. **Hallo,** "From Qarqar to Carchemish," *BA* 23 (1960): 34–61; R. **Klein,** "Jeroboam's Rise to Power," *JBL* 92 (1973): 217–18; idem, "Once More: Jeroboam's Rise to Power," *JBL* 92 (1973): 582–84; G. N. **Knoppers,** *Two Nations under God: The Deuteronomistic History of Solomon and the Dual Monarchies,* 2 vols. (Scholars Press, 1993–1994); G. N. **Knoppers** and J. G. **McConville,** eds., *Reconsidering Israel and Judah: Recent Studies on the Deuteronomistic History* (Eisenbrauns, 2000); A. **Lemaire,** "Vers l'histoire de la redaction des livres des Rois," *ZAW* 98 (1986): 222–36; A. **Malamat,** "Aspects of the Foreign Policies of David and Solomon," *JNES* 22 (1963): 1–22; idem, "Organs of Statecraft in the Israelite Monarchy," *BA* 28 (1965): 34–65; J. G. **McConville,** "Narrative and Meaning in the Books of Kings," *Bib* 70 (1989): 31–49; idem, "Book of Kings," in DOTHB (InterVarsity Press, 2005); J. **McKay,** *Religion in Judah under the Assyrians* (SBT, 2nd series; Allenson, 1973); S. L. **McKenzie,** *The Trouble with Kings* (Leiden: Brill, 1991); J. **Mejia,** "The Aim of the Deuteronomistic Historian: A Reappraisal," *Proceedings of the Sixth World Congress of Jewish Studies* (Jerusalem: 1977): I: 291–98; G. **Mendenhall,** "The Monarchy," *Interp* 29 (1975): 155–70; A. **Millard,** "Sennacherib's Attack on Hezekiah," *TynBul* 36 (1985): 61–77; R. **Nelson,** "The Anatomy of the Book of Kings," *JSOT* 40 (1988): 39–48; idem, *The Double Redaction of the Deuteronomistic History* (JSOTS 18; Sheffield: JSOT, 1981); M. **Noth,** *Überlieferungsgeschichtliche Studien,* 2nd ed.; Darmstadt: Wissenschaftliche Buchgesellschaft, 1967), the first half of this volume appeared in English as *The*

Deuteronomistic History (JSOTS 15; Sheffield: JSOT, 1981); B. **Peckham,** *The Composition of the Deuteronomistic History* (HSM 35; Atlanta: Scholars, 1985); B. **Porten,** "The Structure and Theme of the Solomon Narrative (1 Kgs 3–11)," *HUCA* 38 (1967): 93–128; I. **Provan,** *Hezekiah and the Books of Kings* (*BZAW* 172; Berlin: de Gruyter, 1988); A. **Rainey,** "Compulsory Labor Gangs in Ancient Israel," *IEJ* 20 (1970): 191–202; H. **Reviv,** "The History of Judah from Hezekiah to Josiah," *World History of the Jewish People* IV:1:193–204; H.-C. **Schmitt,** *Elisa: traditionsgeschichtliche Untersuchungen zur vorklassischennordisraelitischen Prophetie* (Gütersloh: Gütersloher Verlagshaus, 1972); H. **Spieckermann,** *Juda unter Assur in der Sargonidenzeit* (Göttingen: Vandenhoeck und Ruprecht, 1982); M. A. **Sweeney,** *King Josiah of Judah: The Lost Messiah of Israel* (Oxford University Press, 2001); M. W. **Thompson,** *Situation and Theology: Old Testament Interpretations of the Syro-Ephraimite War* (Sheffield: Almond, 1982); J. **Trebolle,** "Le texte de 2 Rois 7:20–8:5 a la lumiere des decouvertes de Qumran (6Q4 15)," *RevQ* 13 (1988): 561–68; idem, "Redaction, Recension, and Midrash in the Books of Kings," *Bulletin of Septuagint Studies* 15 (1982): 12–35; G. **von Rad,** "The Deuteronomic Theology of History in I and II Kings," *The Problem of the Hexateuch and Other Essays* (London: Oliver and Boyd, 1966), 205–21; R. S. **Wallace,** *Elijah and Elisha* (Eerdmans, 1957); M. **Weinfeld,** *Deuteronomy and the Deuteronomic School* (Oxford: Oxford University Press, 1972); J. **Wevers,** "Exegetical Principles Underlying the Septuagint Text of I Kings ii.12–xxi.42," *OSt* 8 (1950): 300–322; C. **Whitley,** "The Deuteronomic Presentation of the House of Omri," *VT* 2 (1952): 137–52; J. **Whitney,** "'Bamoth' in the Old Testament," *TynBul* 30 (1979): 125–47; H. W. **Wolff,** "The Kerygma of the Deuteronomic Historical Work," *ZAW* 73 (1961): 171–86; S. **Yeivin,** "The Divided Kingdom: Rehoboam-Ahaz/Jeroboam-Pekah," *World History of the Jewish People* IV:1:126–79; Z. **Zevit,** "Deuteronomistic Historiography in 1 Kings 12–2 Kings 17 and the Reinvestiture of the Israelian Cult," *JSOT* 32 (1985): 57–73.

Select Bibliography With Reference to the Chronology of the Kingdoms

W. F. **Albright,** "The Chronology of the Divided Monarchy of Israel," *BASOR* 100 (1945): 16–22; K. T. **Andersen,** "Die Chronologie der Könige von Israel und Judah," *ST* 23 (1969): 69–114; J. **Barr,** *Biblical Chronology, Legend or Science?* (London: University of London, 1987); D. J. A. **Clines,** "Regnal Year Reckoning in the Last Year of the Kingdom of Judah," *Australian Journal of Biblical Archaeology* 2 (1972): 9–34; S. **DeVries,** "Chronology, OT," *IDBSup*, 161–66; J. **Hayes,** *A New Chronology for the Kings of Israel and Judah and Its Implications for Biblical History and Literature* (John Knox, 1988); E. **Kutsch,** "Das Jahr des Katastrophe: 587 v. Chr: kritische Erwägungen zu neueren chronologischen Versuchen," *Bib* 55 (1974): 520–45; J. D. **Shenkel,** *Chronology and Recensional Development in the Greek Text of Kings* (HSM 1; Cambridge: Harvard University Press, 1968); H. **Tadmor,**

"The Chronology of the First Temple Period: A Presentation and Evaluation of the Sources," *World History of the Jewish People* IV:1:44–60; E. **Thiele**, *The Mysterious Numbers of the Hebrew Kings*, rev. ed. (Eerdmans, 1983); W. **Wifall**, "The Chronology of the Divided Monarchy of Israel," *ZAW* 80 (1968): 319–37.

HISTORICAL BACKGROUND

The book of Kings reports the history of Israel beginning with the transition of power from David to Solomon (c. 931 BC; 1 Kings 1:1–2:12) and ending with the release of Jehoiachin from prison during the Babylonian captivity (562–561 BC; 2 Kings 25:27–30).[1] The book of Kings is marked by the same theological themes and vocabulary that characterized Joshua–Samuel, and these books together with Kings should be thought of as a single literary work. The report of the transition in power from David to Solomon continues the narrative of Samuel from 2 Samuel 20.[2]

At least three major questions have dominated scholarly discussion of the book: (1) Who produced the book? How did it come into existence? And what was its purpose? (2) The ancient Greek translations differ significantly from the MT to varying degrees. What is the reliable text? (3) The author or compilers of this history obviously had particular interest in chronology. Yet on closer scrutiny, many of the chronological notices in the book appear mutually contradictory. How are we to understand or evaluate the chronological notices?

The History of Composition[3]

Extending the Pentateuchal Sources. For a time during the development and prominence of traditional source-critical analysis of the Pentateuch (largely the latter half of the nineteenth century), many interpreters of Kings thought they could identify the putative pentateuchal sources also in the historical books. Scholars thought that they could identify traces of J (the Yahwist) and E (the Elohist) sources through Judges and well into Kings. However, the fact that scholars taking this approach reached such widely divergent conclusions regarding the extent and nature of the sources proved to be the undoing of the theory. The pervasive influence of Deuteronomy in Joshua–Kings was not

---

[1] In the Lucianic recension (the Greek version ascribed to the martyr Lucian), the division between the books occurs at 1 Kings 2:11 after the record of David's death, so that the material in 1 Kings 1:1–2:10 is attached at the end of Samuel, and 3 Reigns (the LXX title for 1 Kings) begins with Solomon's sole rule.

[2] 2 Samuel 21–24 is a collection of miscellaneous material from earlier stages during the reign of David. See the chapter on the book of Samuel.

[3] Two of the most recent and detailed treatments of the history of research into the composition of Kings are Provan (1988, 1–32) and Jones (1984, 1:2–82).

easily reconciled with the concept of a more mechanical union of sources that characterized the older source criticism. Attempts to trace the putative sources of the Pentateuch through the historical books have now been abandoned. Instead of the small number of continuous narrative sources identified by traditional source criticism, more recent scholarship explains the wide variety of material found in Kings by suggesting that the compilers-authors used a larger number of independent sources in writing their accounts, approaches resembling more the "fragmentary" or "supplemental" approaches to pentateuchal composition.

A Double Redaction. Scholars identify the books from Joshua through Kings as the "Deuteronomic History" or "Deuteronomistic History" (DH). These books carry the imprint of the influence of Deuteronomy on their theology, themes, and vocabulary.[4] Critical scholarship had assigned the date of Deuteronomy to the time of Josiah. The law book Josiah discovered in the temple (621 BC) required the centralization of Israel's worship (Deut. 12), so it was argued that Deuteronomy was in reality composed as a way to legitimate Josiah's centralization of both political and religious power in Jerusalem. If this was the case, it was then argued that a partisan of Josiah's reforms, a person possibly involved in the production of Deuteronomy itself, composed a history showing how Josiah had been the ideal king (Deut. 17:14–20), ruling in accord with the book of the law and following the example of David. The schism had disrupted a unified kingdom including both North and South. The historian began his history of Israel after the schism with the prophecy that a man named Josiah would rectify the evils perpetrated by Jeroboam (1 Kings 13:2), and he ended his account by showing how Josiah had accomplished this (2 Kings 23:15–20) and had restored the unity of the kingdom through his exercise of authority in the North. These mentions of Josiah are bookends around the period of the divided kingdom; they form an inclusio focusing on him. This focus on Josiah and his Deuteronomic reforms provided the occasion for producing the initial edition of the book.

A later historian who lived during the period of the exile updated this earlier edition of the book by (1) providing the history following Josiah's reform through Jehoiachin's release from prison, and (2) adding his interpretive concerns to the earlier edition. This second editor-compiler was concerned to provide a theological explanation for why the exile had taken place. A number of passages presuppose the exile and the destruction of Jerusalem, and these are ordinarily attributed to the redactor of this second edition of the book (1 Kings 9:1–9; 11:9–13; 2 Kings 17:19–20; 20:17–18; 21:11–15; 22:15–20; 23:26–27;

---

[4]For an analysis of the phraseology and terminology that is characteristic of the DH, see Weinfeld (1972, 320–65). The theology and themes of the DH are described below, under Literary Analysis and Theological Message.

24:2–4; 24:18–25:30). Although a number of scholars had earlier anticipated this "double redaction" hypothesis, it has been modified and given its classic expression in the work of Cross (1973, 274–89) and his student R. Nelson (1981). More recently Provan has also argued for a double redaction of the book (see even more recently Sweeney and Knoppers). Provan agrees that the first edition was written during the reign of Josiah and that the later edition was written during the exile; however, he argues that the first edition included only the narrative through the reign of Hezekiah (1988, 171–73). Scholars arguing for two editions or redactions of the book ordinarily concentrate on linguistic and thematic-theological differences. DH1 (the Josianic edition) emphasized the eternality and unconditionality of the Davidic covenant (1 Kings 2:4, 24; 3:6–7; 6:12; 8:15–26; 9:5; 11:12–13, 32–39; 15:4–5; 2 Kings 8:19; 19:34; 20:6; 21:7–8) and therefore its ultimate fruition in the reign of Josiah. DH2 (the exilic edition), on the other hand, was written in light of the exile and emphasized both the vulnerability of the nation due to the sin of the people and the conditionality of the covenant (Deut. 17:20; 1 Kings 2:4; 2 Kings 17:7–23; 21:8b, 10–16). Proponents of a double redaction also note shifts in the formulaic accession and death notices.

A Single Historian. Noth (Engl. trans., 1981) rejected both the idea that the pentateuchal sources could be traced into the DH and the idea that there were two different stages in the composition of Kings. Noth was sufficiently impressed with the linguistic and thematic uniformity of the DH as to suggest that the DH was the unified product of a single author who also contributed Deuteronomy 1:1–4:43. Noth allowed that this single continuous narrative may have attracted subsequent fragmentary additions, but these were not continuous narratives such as posited by pentateuchal criticism, nor were they redactional layers. Instead, a single author selected from a wide variety of sources, which he accepted and modified to various degrees. This author introduced speeches at key points in his narrative (Josh. 12, 23; 1 Sam. 12; 1 Kings 8) in which important characters recapitulate the national history and offer advice concerning the actions of the people in the future. His purpose in writing was to account for divine retribution in the exile. The author was showing how God had been at work in the life of the nation but also warning the people against disobedience and apostasy. Noth argued that the history had an essentially negative thrust, accounting for the exile, and offered no hope or expectation of a return. Other scholars have agreed with Noth that the DH is a unified history from Joshua through Kings, but they have argued that the history does show hope for a return to the land and to divine favor (Wolff 1961; von Rad 1966).

McKenzie (1991) recognized the tendency of theories of redactional analysis to degenerate into increasingly complex redactional layers. Following Cross, he argued for an edition of the DH at the time of Josiah that was supplemented by extensive post-Dtr additions (e.g., 1 Kings 13; 17–19; 20; 22; 2 Kings 2; 3:4–8:15;

13:14–25). However, these additions, in McKenzie's opinion (135–45), do not exhibit the stylistic and thematic coherence that would allow them to be assigned to a single redactor—they are instead ad hoc miscellaneous insertions by an indeterminate number of later scribes. Although in a sense McKenzie could be viewed as following Noth in affirming the essential unity of the DH, he has done so by in effect exploding DH2 into uncounted smaller and disconnected fragments.

McConville (1989) argues that Kings is a unified composition. He warns against using the theological-thematic tensions in Kings as a key to redactional layers. Instead, he argues that the DH shows an increasing gulf between the promise of land and its actual fulfillment in Israel's experience (33). Through its ongoing disobedience, the nation forfeits its right to the land and is subject to judgment. According to McConville, the book of Kings traces the increasing failure of flawed kingship. As the book develops, less and less appeal is made to the divine promise to David, and conversely, more attention is paid to the conditionality of the divine promise. McConville traces an increasing discrepancy between expectation and performance, so that rather than expect salvation for Judah through her Davidic king, the book leads the reader to expect the opposite. The piety of the reforming kings was at best temporary and ineffectual in turning the nation from its course. The same steady downward spiral that characterizes the book of Judges also characterizes the book of Kings; alongside this downward spiral, there is the continual offering of divine grace to the repentant.

A Deuteronomic Circle. Other scholars envisaged a compositional history more complex than either a double redaction or a single author. They believe that the book of Kings grew within a Deuteronomic "school" or "circle." First, these tradents (bearers of tradition) produced a basic historical document. A later generation with the same philosophy of history added the stories about the prophets, and a yet later generation added material oriented to issues of keeping the law (Jones 1984, 1:42–43). Who were these anonymous tradents? Scholars have not agreed. Some have identified them as Levites or factions of the Jerusalem priesthood; others consider them to have been prophets; still others suggest that they were the counselors and wise men of the Jerusalem royal court (Jones 1984, 1:44–46). Others argue that they were not from a single social or career group, but rather from all segments of Israelite society, each preserving its distinctive interests while united as a movement through a common philosophy of history. Those scholars advocating this approach argue that it accounts for both the unity and diversity within Kings. The main weakness with the approach is that the stages and compilers remain highly amorphous and shadowy; it is an effort to explain one unknown (the compositional history of Kings) by another unknown (a "school" or "circle"). It is tacitly an admission that the riddle of the compositional history of Kings cannot be easily answered. Perhaps the greatest salutary result of the approach is to recognize the presence of a Deuteronomic influence in Israel over a long period prior to the time of Josiah.

The same steady downward spiral that characterizes the book of Judges characterizes the book of Kings; alongside it there is the continual offering of divine grace to the repentant.

It is clear that the author(s)-compiler(s) of Kings used a wide variety of sources. The "annals of the kings of Judah" (e.g., 1 Kings 14:29; 15:7; 2 Kings 8:23; 12:19; 14:18; 24:5), "the annals of the kings of Israel" (e.g., 1 Kings 14:19; 15:31; 2 Kings 1:18; 10:34; 13:8, 12), and "the book of the annals of Solomon" (1 Kings 11:41) appear to have been the major sources. The fact that the writer refers his reader to these other materials is an indication that he was consciously selective about his material and was not attempting to be comprehensive (Jones 1984, 1:47). These source citations are genre signals that the writer of Kings intends that his work be understood to be as historical as his sources. It is probable that yet more source material was also used, though not cited. For example, the extensive stories from the lives of Elijah and Elisha (1 Kings 17–2 Kings 6; 13:10–21) were probably not part of the apparently official "annals" used by the historian. The Elijah-Elisha stories may have come from some otherwise unknown prophetic work. Alternatively, the emphasis on the Baalism that flourished under the Omrides could suggest that the Elijah-Elisha stories were first written as part of a work legitimating the coup of Jehu and his suppression of Baalism (2 Kings 9–10). Such speculation is interesting, but we can have little confidence in the results. Approaches to Kings that view it as the product of a single author at least have the fortuitous result of focusing attention on the final form of the text rather than on the quagmire of insoluble problems involved in its compositional history.

The Variant Texts

The variations between the Masoretic Text, the Greek translations and revisions, and the manuscript finds at Qumran suggest that there was some fluidity in the text of Kings prior to the emergence of the Masoretic Text as the received textual tradition for the Old Testament. Rather than view the differences as exclusively secondary variations on the tradition represented by the MT, scholars have identified some variants as part of a textual tradition that antedates the tradition represented by the MT. It is particularly the discovery of fragmentary texts of Samuel at Qumran that takes pride of place in this discussion. At Qumran at least one fragmentary Hebrew text of Samuel (4QSamb) appears to represent a textual tradition used by translators and revisers of the Septuagint. This would mean that the Septuagint translators were not necessarily freely editing their sources, but rather were following an alternative text to that represented by the MT. This fact has resulted in general in a more positive evaluation of other Greek variants from the MT, especially those preserved in the Lucianic recension. Shenkel (1968) argues that variations in the chronological notices in Kings may reflect a textual tradition older than the MT. The chronological notices in the Old Greek and the Lucianic recension largely agree against the MT in 1 Kings. However, in 2 Kings the Old Greek reflects the proto-Theodotion (*kaige*) recension, which largely agrees with the MT, whereas the Lucianic recension appears to retain the chronology of the Old Greek translation, based on a text of Kings at variance from the MT.

In other cases the Septuagint translators and subsequent revisers were providing secondary exegesis of the Hebrew text that led to reordering and reinterpretation of some material (see Jones 1984, 1:7; Gooding 1967, 1969, 1972; Klein 1973a, 1973b). Extensive additions in the Septuagint account of the reigns of Solomon and Jeroboam (the so-called miscellanies, 3 Reigns 2:35a–o; 2:46a–l; 12:24a–z) represent midrashic embellishments on Solomon's wisdom and efforts to further discredit Jeroboam.

The order of the chapters at 1 Kings 20–21 is also reversed in the Septuagint, possibly representing a secondary change in order to consolidate the accounts of the wars with Aram (1 Kings 20, 22).

In summary, it is clear that generalizations regarding the textual variants of Kings are risky. Some variants may reflect textual evidence older than the MT, whereas others are the secondary editing of translators and revisers. Each variant must be weighed in its own right.

The Chronological Notices

Chronology is the backbone of historical writing; indeed, without a sound chronology, history becomes decidedly invertebrate. The writers-compilers of the book of Kings had a marked interest in chronology. Chronological information comes in at least three distinct forms in the book. (1) The accession notices of a king in one kingdom are ordinarily synchronized with the regnal year of his contemporary in the other kingdom. For example, we read that Zimri became king for his week-long reign in the twenty-seventh year of Asa (1 Kings 16:15), or that Jehoram son of Jehoshaphat began his reign in the fifth year of Joram son of Ahab (2 Kings 8:16). (2) The accession notices also ordinarily state the length of the reign of the king. For example, Jehoram ruled eight years (2 Kings 8:17), and his father Jehoshaphat ruled twenty-five (1 Kings 22:42). (3) Periodically events in either kingdom are synchronized with events involving other nations. For example, Pharaoh Shishak's campaign into Judah and Israel took place in Rehoboam's fifth year (1 Kings 14:25), and Assyria sent the northern kingdom into exile in Hoshea's ninth year (2 Kings 17:6).

In working with the abundance of chronological notices in Kings, it is often helpful to distinguish between relative and absolute chronology. A relative chronology seeks to make sense of the chronological data as we have it in the book; events are synchronized in terms of events in the other kingdom or other lands. An absolute chronology attempts to tie this relative data to fixed points in the Gregorian calendar or some other calendar at use in the world today. For extrabiblical chronological data, two primary sources provide a fairly secure absolute chronology for the first millennium BC. (1) The Greek astronomer Ptolemy, who lived in Alexandria in the second century AD, in his *Almagest* provided the length of reign for ancient Near Eastern kings from his own time back to 747 BC. He included solar, lunar, and planetary observations that make it possible to correlate his dates with an absolute calendar. (2) The Assyrian kings named years during their reigns by the names of individuals they wished to honor; the person whose name was assigned to the year was the *limmu,* or eponym of that year. These eponym lists also contain references to important events and some eclipses and therefore can also be tied to an absolute chronology through astronomical calculations. The *limmu* lists, when combined, provide the lengths of reigns for Assyrian kings from 649 BC back into the tenth century BC. Happily, these lists overlap the Ptolemaic canon by a century and serve mutually to corroborate the integrity of these records from opposite ends of the Fertile Crescent.

Yet in spite of the abundance of chronological data both from within and without the Bible, a coherent scheme for the chronology of the book of Kings has remained elusive. Many of the chronological notices seem overtly self-contradictory. For example, Ahaziah of Judah is said to have come to the throne both in the eleventh year of Joram of Israel (2 Kings 9:29) and in the twelfth (8:25). Joram of Israel began to reign in the eighteenth year of Jehoshaphat, according to 2 Kings 3:1; but according to 1:17, he began to rule in the second year of Jehoram of Judah. This latter note would require that Jehoram of Judah had begun his rule before Joram of Israel, but according to 2 Kings 8:16, Jehoram of Judah came to the throne in the fifth year of Joram of Israel (Thiele 1983, 36). If one adds up the total of the lengths of reign assigned to kings in Judah and Israel, other problems emerge. For example, Ahaziah of Judah and Joram of Israel both died at about the same time during the coup of Jehu. But if one adds the total of the reigns for the kings from the schism to this point, in the south the total is 95 years, whereas in the north, it is a bit over 98 years. Similarly, the fall of the northern kingdom in the ninth year of Hoshea is synchronized with the sixth year of Hezekiah (2 Kings 18:10). Adding the totals for reigns from Jehu in Israel and Athaliah in Judah to the fall of the northern kingdom yields 143 years and 7 months in Israel, but 166 years in Judah (Thiele 1983, 36–37).

A large number of questions must be answered in order to untangle the riddle of the chronology for the period of the kingdoms. Was the system used for counting regnal years the same in both kingdoms, or did the kingdoms follow different systems? Did the approach to recording chronological data remain the same throughout the history of either kingdom, or did it change at some point? If different systems were used, how would the scribes in one kingdom have recorded the years of a king in the other kingdom? What system may have been in use by the later compilers-editors of the book? Were there any interregna (periods without a king) in either kingdom, or were there co-regencies? When did the new year begin? Were years rounded off? If so, which way—up or down?

What about the evidence of divergent textual traditions for the chronological notices in the Masoretic Text and in the Septuagint and its revisions (see The Variant Texts above)?

Space does not permit a full discussion of these questions. Numerous books and articles have been devoted to the topic. A few observations will have to suffice for our purposes.

The great empires (in Mesopotamia and Egypt) that surrounded Israel did follow different practices in reckoning lengths of reign. In Egypt, *antedating* meant that a king's first year of rule was counted from the month of his accession to the new year. On this basis, if a pharaoh came to the throne in the eleventh month of the year, year one of his rule consisted of only one month, and the second year of his rule began with the new year. In theory, he may have been on the throne only two months, but would already be in the second year of his reign. In Mesopotamia, *postdating* was the practice. On this system, the period between the king's accession and the new year was "the year of the beginning of kingship," and year one of the rule only began with the new year. On this system, if a king came to the throne shortly after the new year, in theory he could have been on the throne twenty-three months and still be in the first year of his rule. It appears certain that at points in their respective histories, the kingdoms of Israel and Judah differed on which practice they followed. Israel appears to have followed the practice of Egypt, a fact not surprising, since Jeroboam I had taken refuge there during Solomon's rule (1 Kings 11:40; 12:2). The antedating system is known in Kings (2 Kings 25:27) and may have been used in Judah. Thiele argues that the kingdoms switched back and forth in their dating systems; this alternation enables him to account for some discrepancies.

There is also some uncertainty regarding the beginning of the new year in Judah and Israel. The Mishnah (*Rosh ha-shanah* 1:1) distinguishes between a royal New Year ("new year for kings") that began in the spring in the month Nisan, and a calendrical New Year ("new year for years") that began in the fall in the month of Tishri. Scholars suspect that two different New Years were known in ancient Israel as well, but they differ widely on the impact this may have had on the chronological records of the kingdoms (Jones 1984, 1:16–17). Thiele argued that at least during some periods, Israel began its regnal year with Tishri, and Judah with Nisan.

Many of the discrepancies in the chronological notices of the MT can be solved by positing a number of co-regencies in the kingdoms. By overlapping the number of years assigned to two kings, the total number of elapsed years can be reduced. Thiele argues that three co-regencies are specifically mentioned: (1) Omri and Tibni were both kings at the same time (1 Kings 16:21), (2) as were Jehoram and Jehoshaphat, and (3) Jotham and Azariah/Uzziah, due to the latter's leprosy (2 Kings 15:5). Thiele goes on to suggest five other co-regencies with the accompanying double dating and overlapping reigns, though without corroboration from the biblical text itself. Using this device as needed, Thiele is able to make sense of the figures in the MT without recourse to the evidence of alternate texts in the Greek translations. One is left with the impression that Thiele has multiplied the cases of co-regencies in order to reconcile his system with the data of the MT rather than to follow the evidence within the text itself.[5]

On the whole, the chronological notices in Kings remain something of an enigma. However, the Egyptian and Mesopotamian records do provide a rather firm absolute chronology for many events in the period of the kingdoms. These sources fix the following dates: (1) Ahab participated in the Battle of Qarqar in 853. (2) Jehu paid tribute to Shalmaneser III in 841. (3) Jehoash of Israel paid tribute to Adad-nirari III in 796. (4) Three kings are known to have paid tribute to Tiglath-Pileser: Menahem in 738, Ahaz in 733/32, and Hoshea in 731. (5) Samaria fell to Shalmaneser V in 722. (6) Pharaoh Neco clashed with Josiah at Megiddo in 609. (7) The Babylonian Chronicles provides dates for the activity of Nebuchadnezzar's army in Syria-Palestine. (8) The fall of Jerusalem occurred in 587/86. (9) Amel-Marduk (Evil Merodach) came to the throne in 562.

In spite of the problems and perplexities the chronological notes represent, it is important not to forget the literary and canonical function of these notices in the book of Kings. Childs (1979, 297–300) makes three observations on this issue: (1) The chronological notices establish a sequence in the historical experience of Israel. They provide a schema of continuity between the author's own day and the past of the nation. (2) By including the chronological data from both kingdoms, the story of Israel is given a comprehensive character that establishes the interrelatedness of the kingdoms and embraces the whole of the people of God. (3) By synchronizing with events outside the two kingdoms, these notices also relate Israel's experience to the history of the larger world. Although many problems regarding the chronology of Kings remain unresolved, it is clear that the chronological notices are a major device for structuring the history the book reports.

> On the whole, the chronological notices in Kings remain something of an enigma, though the Egyptian and Mesopotamian records serve to date many events.

LITERARY ANALYSIS

After his account of the reign of Solomon (1 Kings 2:12–11:43), the writer reports events surrounding the schism (1 Kings 12–14). The bulk of the narrative is then devoted to a history of the two kingdoms in which the writer shuttles back and forth between accounts of the overlapping reigns of the kings in

---

[5]Dillard has also raised objections to Thiele's system from another angle. Thiele stakes his case on a harmonization proposed for the reign of Asa, and it is a harmonization that can work only at the expense of the biblical author's intention. See Dillard, "The Reign of Asa (2 Chr 14–16): An Example of the Chronicler's Theological Method," *JETS* 23 (1980): 207–18.

each kingdom (1 Kings 15–2 Kings 17). The account of the reign of a king in one kingdom is followed each time by the accounts of the reign of the king or kings in the other kingdom who came to the throne during his reign. For example, the account of Asa's reign in Judah (1 Kings 15:9–24) is followed by the reigns in the North of Nadab, Baasha, Elah, Zimri, Omri, and Ahab (15:25–16:34), all of whom came to the throne during Asa's reign. The reign of Jehoshaphat (1 Kings 22:41–50), the king who followed Asa in Judah, is taken up only after the report of Ahab's death. The narrative fluctuates between reigns in the North and South until the northern kingdom is carried into exile by the Assyrians. Judah remains alone in the South as the spiritual successor of the kingdoms of Israel (2 Kings 18–25), and her history is reported until the Babylonian conquest, the destruction of Jerusalem, and Jehoiachin's release from prison during captivity.

The accounts for the reigns of individual kings are presented with a framework that gives the book much of its distinctive literary character. The framework for each reign consists of an introductory and a concluding notice. These notices vary slightly from reign to reign and differ between Judah and Israel, but a standard repertoire of elements is fairly consistent.

Introductory notices. (1) Accession notice: as long as the two kingdoms coexist, the accession of a king in one kingdom is synchronized with the regnal year of his contemporary in the other kingdom. (2) Age: for the kings of Judah, there is a statement of their age at the time of accession. (3) Length of the reign: this total includes the years of any possible co-regency. For kings in Israel, the location of the royal capital is ordinarily also specified. (4) Ancestry: for the kings of Judah the name of the king's mother is given, a fact reflecting the continuity of the Davidic succession in Judah. In Israel, on the other hand, the name of the king's father is ordinarily given. (5) Theological or moral evaluation: these evaluations of the king's piety are regularly formulaic (see below under Theological Message). This basic theological evaluation is often followed by narrative elaboration to demonstrate its validity (e.g., 1 Kings 15:12–15; 22:53).

Concluding notices. (1) Source citation: other sources available for fuller information (see History of Composition above). The writer often makes short references to other interesting events or accomplishments during the reign; though not elaborated at this point in Kings, the writer of Chronicles commonly provides more comment on these items. (2) Death notice: the king's death is reported. For kings of Judah this is ordinarily followed by reference to their burial, information not included for the kings of Israel. (3) Succession notice: the name of the royal son who succeeded his father is given for kings of Judah and Israel, unless, as often in Israel, there was a usurper.

The writer of Kings is concerned about demonstrating the continuity of the Davidic dynasty in Judah as a demonstration of God's faithfulness to his promises (2 Sam. 7). For this reason the entire characteristic framework is lacking for Athaliah—she was not counted among the rulers of Judah, but rather was viewed as a usurper and interloper.

Between these introductory and concluding notices, the writer-compiler of Kings has incorporated a wide variety of materials. The kings are remembered for at least one important incident that took place during their reigns, most often in connection with some military action (e.g., 1 Kings 14:25–28; 15:16–22; 2 Kings 13:4–7), though not always (e.g., 1 Kings 16:24).

THEOLOGICAL MESSAGE

While browsing in a used bookstore, one might pick up a volume of world history. If the title page and publication information were missing, how would you determine when the book was written? Perhaps the best procedure would be to turn to the final pages of the book. If the book ended speaking of "the Great War" and "the war to end all wars" and did not go on to describe the events of World War II, it would probably be a safe assumption that this volume of world history was written sometime after 1917 and before 1940. A person would scarcely write a world history without including some discussion of the Second World War.

Kings is an anonymous work. But the procedure described above helps to determine the time it was written. The book ends (2 Kings 25:27–30) by describing Jehoiachin's release from prison in the accession year of Awel-Marduk (562 BC). It does not show any awareness of the edict of Cyrus that sent the deported Judeans back to Jerusalem to rebuild their city and temple (2 Chron. 36:22–23; Ezra 1:2–4). This fact, alongside the concern of the book with the exile (see History of Composition: A Double Redaction above), establishes the fact that the author-compiler of the book in essentially its present form lived during the period of the exile itself (586–539 BC).

Any historian selects his data in terms of both his own philosophy of history and the perceived needs of his target audience. What issues would have been particularly pressing for the exiles?

Much of the faith of Israel in the preexilic period was built around two promises of God: (1) his choice of Jerusalem as his dwelling place, and (2) his promises to David of an enduring dynasty. History had ratified the national confidence in these promises. The dynasty of David had endured for over three centuries. A century earlier God had confirmed his choice of Zion by intervening to disperse the armies of Assyria that had come against Hezekiah in Jerusalem (2 Kings 18:13–19:37). For the exiles, however, these promises now had a hollow ring. There was no king ruling in Jerusalem; the rightful successor to the throne had been taken into captivity (2 Kings 24:8–17). The temple in Jerusalem had been reduced to a smoking ruin. Had God failed? Was he not able to keep his promises? Was Marduk, the god of the Babylonians, more powerful than Yahweh of Israel?

The writer of Kings sets out to explain the exile and the destruction of Judah in a way that would rescue the faith of the people in the face of such questions. A quick reading of the book gives the impression that Kings is overall not an upbeat history, but rather it records a downward spiral. Why should this be so? In part at least, it is because the writer is telling Israel that the exile was not the result of a failure on God's part, but that God had acted to confirm his holiness by judging the nation for its transgressions. The exile did not show that Yahweh lacked power—just the opposite: it was the proof that he was ruling over history and that the armies of Babylon were simply doing his bidding. The Deuteronomic History is largely a history of the nation's failure to keep its covenant with God. "From the day their ancestors came out of Egypt until this day" (2 Kings 21:15) the people had provoked God through disobedience until he decreed disaster for them.

In this sense we might call the book of Kings another example of theodicy. Theodicy is literature that seeks to justify the way God has dealt with people; it vindicates divine nature in the face of evil. We ordinarily think of Job in this connection. Job had certain expectations about the nature of God, particularly the way he would reward a righteous individual. But what Job expected of God and what he experienced in his family and his own body were in tension with the expectation. Similarly, Judah in the late preexilic period had certain expectations of God based on those two promises, but their experience belied their expectations. Just as Job was written to justify the way God had dealt with an individual, so Kings vindicates God's actions toward a nation.

In order to show that the exile was the product of the nation's disobedience, the writer of Kings adopts a precise literary program. He takes laws that are unique to the book of Deuteronomy as the spectacles through which he assesses the history of the nation. In this respect, Kings is transparently "Deuteronomic history." Following are some of the laws from Deuteronomy that function so prominently in Kings.

Centralization of Worship (Deut. 12)

The book of Deuteronomy is set on the edge of the Promised Land, just before the conquest of the land was to commence. It prepared the nation for life without Moses and for the changes that would attend the nation's entering the inheritance God had provided. During the wilderness period, Israel had worshiped at a portable shrine; they packed up and moved the tabernacle when the nation moved. However, once they entered the land, God would choose one place to dwell (Deut. 12:5), and Israel was to bring her sacrifices, offerings, and gifts to that place (vv. 5–7). No longer would they do as they saw fit in any place they happened to be (vv. 8–14), but they would make offerings only at the place God chose. All other places of worship used by the previous inhabitants of the land were to be destroyed (vv. 1–4).

The writer of Kings uses this particular law to form the core of his theological evaluation of the kings of Israel and Judah. Once the kingdom had broken into north and south, almost the first act of Jeroboam in the North is to erect rival sanctuaries at Dan and Bethel in order to divert the religious affections of the northern tribes away from Jerusalem, the place that God had chosen (1 Kings 12:25–30). This transgression at the inception of the northern kingdom is used to measure almost all the subsequent kings of Israel (see table 8). Almost all are condemned for following in "the same sin Jeroboam had caused Israel to commit." Even Zimri, who ruled for only one week, is condemned for "following the ways of Jeroboam" (1 Kings 16:19). Conversely, Omri, who represented perhaps the most able king the northern kingdom ever knew, is dismissed in a scant six verses, two of which concern his transgressions following the practice of Jeroboam (vv. 25–26). It is clear that the writer of Kings was not overly concerned with the kings' military or political successes, but rather with the individual king's faithfulness to the command of God.

Table 8
The Sins of Jeroboam and the Kings of Israel

Jeroboam:	1 Kings	11:26, 28, 29, 31; 12:26, 31; 13:1, 4, 33, 34; 14:16
Nadab:	1 Kings	15:29–30
Baasha:	1 Kings	15:34; 16:2–3, 7
Zimri:	1 Kings	16:19
Omri:	1 Kings	16:26
Ahab:	1 Kings	16:31; 21:22; 22:52
Joram:	2 Kings	3:3; 9:9
Jehu:	2 Kings	10:29, 31
Jehoahaz:	2 Kings	13:2, 6
Jehoash:	2 Kings	13:11, 13; 14:16
Jeroboam II:	2 Kings	14:24
Zechariah:	2 Kings	15:9
Menahem:	2 Kings	15:9
Pekahiah:	2 Kings	15:24
Pekah:	2 Kings	15:28
Summary Statement:	2 Kings	17:21
Josiah:	2 Kings	13:15

One would think that obedience to the command about centralized worship would be easy in the southern kingdom, for after all, the Jerusalem temple was located in the capital of the southern kingdom. What could rival the temple in the religious affection of Judah? But alas, there were many rivals. Although Deuteronomy 12 commanded the destruction of all the high places and other sites of Canaanite worship, the high places continued to flourish and to compete with the Jerusalem temple. Although Solomon would be given wisdom from God at Gibeon, the writer of Kings is only being consistent with himself when he introduces the trip to that great high place with some reservations (1 Kings 3:3–4). The high places stole the heart of Solomon himself (11:7–13) and eventually cost him his kingdom. Those who followed Solomon were similarly seduced, until ultimately the kingdom of Judah was itself destroyed. Just as the rival altars of Jeroboam were used by the author to measure the kings of Israel, so the high places became the yardstick to measure the kings of Judah. Two of the kings (Hezekiah and Josiah) did it right: they were not only faithful to the Jerusalem temple but also suppressed the high places. Another half dozen personally did what was right in the eyes of the Lord, but the high places continued to flourish during their reigns. Most of the remainder themselves participated in the cults that flourished at the high places (see table 9).

This single command to worship God at the place of his choosing was used to measure the reign of almost all the kings of Israel and Judah. The results were disappointing, and eventually God would take his temple away from his people.

Table 9
The High Places in Kings

Solomon:	1 Kings	3:2–4; 11:7
Jeroboam (first king in North):	1 Kings	12:31–32; 13:2, 32–33
Rehoboam:	1 Kings	14:23
Asa:	1 Kings	15:14
Jehoshaphat:	1 Kings	22:43
Joash:	2 Kings	12:3
Amaziah:	2 Kings	14:4
Azariah/Uzziah:	2 Kings	15:4
Jotham:	2 Kings	15:35
Ahaz:	2 Kings	16:4
Hoshea (last king in North):	2 Kings	17:9, 11, 29, 32
Hezekiah:	2 Kings	18:4, 22
Manasseh:	2 Kings	21:3; 23:5
Josiah:	2 Kings	23:8–9, 13, 15, 19–20

The Monarchy

A day would come when Israel would ask for a king, and there across the Jordan, Moses gives instruction and legislation about how kingship should function in Israel (Deut. 17:14–20). It was a good choice to name the book "Kings," for it is a history of this institution in Israel and Judah. At least two important features of the provisions in Deuteronomy 17 are important to the book of Kings. First, the king is charged with the decision about the basic religious orientation of the nation (vv. 18–19). The book of Kings traces out what the kings of Israel and Judah did with this responsibility. Most particularly it was Josiah who ruled in accordance with a scroll that contained a copy of the law (2 Kings 22:8–23:25). Second, the continuation of kingship and dynastic succession in Israel are tied to the fidelity of the kings. Only through a life of obedience would they reign a long time over the kingdom of Israel (Deut. 17:20). Eventually, the infidelity of the kings of both Israel and Judah would bring disaster to both kingdoms.

The influence of Deuteronomy on Kings is also seen in the virtual citation of Deuteronomy 17:16–17 as a description of conditions during Solomon's rule (1 Kings 4:26; 9:19; 10:14–28; 11:3). Concern with the monarchy is a theme in the earlier books of the DH as well: the reigns of Saul and David are described in Samuel, and other passages raise the question of whether having a king is desirable (Judg. 9; 18:1; 19:1; 21:25; 1 Sam. 8; 12:13–15).

The Efficacy of the Prophetic Word (Deut. 18:9–22)

A number of passages in the Pentateuch mention prophets (Gen. 20:7; Ex. 4:15–17; 6:28–7:2; Num. 12:1–8; Deut. 13:1–5 [MT 2–6]), but it is only in Deuteronomy 18:21–22 that the test of a true prophet is defined as whether or not his prophesies come to pass. The power and fulfillment of the prophetic word is a frequent theme in Kings (e.g., 1 Kings 13:1–2, 5, 21, 26, 32; 15:29; 2 Kings 1:17; 7:1; 9:26, 36; 10:17). For an audience that had witnessed what appeared to be the failure of God's promises, the writer was concerned to reassure them that the Lord's word remained powerful and true. For that matter, the exile itself showed, not that God had failed to keep his word, but that he had done what he had warned the nation he would do. He had brought against them the armies of Babylon, Aram, Moab, and Ammon "to destroy Judah, in accordance with the word of the LORD proclaimed by his servants the prophets" (2 Kings 24:2). Rather than undermine confidence in God's promises, the exile should establish that confidence. God had always been active in Israel's history to confirm his word and promises, and this was no less true in the events that led to the destruction of Jerusalem.

The Fulfillment of the Curses for Covenant Breaking (Deut. 28)

Moses was the model prophet and the founder of the prophetic institution in Israel (Deut. 18:15, 18). If the words of the prophets came to pass, how much more so the words of Moses! Toward the end of Deuteronomy, there is a chapter cataloging the blessings that would attend Israel's life if she kept covenant with God (28:1–14) and the curses that would come as a consequence of disobedience (Deut. 28:15–68). It appears that the writer of the Deuteronomic History deliberately sought to demonstrate the historical realization of these curses in the life of the nation: disease (28:21–22; 2 Sam. 24); drought (28:23–24; 1 Kings 17–18); cannibalism (28:53–57; 2 Kings 6:24–30); and perhaps most important, exile and defeat (28:36–37, 49–52; 2 Kings 17:24–32; 25:18–24). Josiah was concerned that all of the curses written in the book of the law would come to pass; Huldah assured him that they would not occur during his lifetime, but only after his death (2 Kings 22:11–20). The exile should not have come as a surprise to Israel—the writer of Kings is reminding his readers that Moses had long ago foretold that it would be so if the nation broke its covenant with God.

Other Examples

The influence of Deuteronomy in Kings is pervasive and appears at many other points. For example, a text in Deuteronomy is quoted in connection with events during the reign of Amaziah (Deut. 24:16; 2 Kings 14:6). The laws regarding Passover in Exodus 12:1–30 treat it as a celebration centered in the family; in Deuteronomy 16:1–7, however, it is a pilgrimage festival observed at the central sanctuary. When Kings describes the observance of Passover, it is in terms of the provisions in Deuteronomy (2 Kings 23:21–23).

It is important too to remember how the book ends. In a book that has so emphasized the power of God's rule over history and his fulfilling both the threats and the promises he made through the prophets, what about the divine promise to David? The writer of Kings wants his readers to know that this promise too has not fallen. Although the stream of divine favor that had attended the Davidic line may now be down to a trickle, even in exile God has not forgotten David's descendants (2 Kings 25:27–30). The God who had brought the Babylonians against Jerusalem could also cause them to show favor to a son of David. God has not forgotten his promise, even in a distant land and difficult circumstances. The book ends in the exile but with a muted note of hope—that God would continue to remember his promises to David.

APPROACHING THE NEW TESTAMENT

In a book as large as Kings and touching so many themes and motifs of redemptive history, space does not permit an exhaustive description of how subsequent biblical authors in the New Testament have reflected on and developed themes of interest in the book. A couple of examples will have to suffice.

The writer of Kings was concerned to demonstrate the historical reality of God's faithfulness to his promises to David. He presents an unbroken dynasty maintained in Judah through about three and a half centuries. The book ends on this note of hope, that even during the exile and under foreign domination, divine favor still attended David's descendants. The New Testament shows that this same hope was alive in Israel during the days of Roman rule. The gospel writers are concerned to trace the Davidic ancestry of Jesus and his rightful claim to the title "son of David," heir to the kingdom that God would erect as a consequence of his promises to David (Matt. 1:1, 6, 17, 20; 9:27; 12:23; 15:22; 20:31; 21:9, 15; Mark 10:47–48; 11:10; Luke 1:27, 32, 69; 2:4; 3:31; 18:39; John 7:42).

It is striking that the Old Testament itself ends remembering Elijah and proclaiming that he would come again (Mal. 4:5–6). The New Testament writers also make extensive use of the Elijah and Elisha narratives. Matthew provides a good example of how New Testament authors developed these materials.

Matthew draws literary parallels between the lives of Elijah and Elisha and the lives of John the Baptist and Jesus. He presents John as the fulfillment of Malachi's prophecy that Elijah would come again (Mal. 4:5), and he presents Jesus as the new Elisha. The Jews of Jesus' day apparently expected that Elijah would appear literally and physically from the grave, so when John the Baptist was asked if he was Elijah, he replied, "I am not" (John 1:21). At least early in his ministry, John the Baptist does not appear to have been aware that he was fulfilling the role of the expected Elijah. On the other hand, Jesus described John as "the Elijah who was to come" (Matt. 11:14; 17:12), and Matthew goes out of his way to demonstrate how this was so.

The New Testament writers — especially Matthew — make extensive use of the Elijah and Elisha narratives.

1. Elijah was known for his distinctive style of dress. When Ahaziah sent messengers to inquire of Baal-Zebub, the god of Ekron, his messengers encountered a mysterious figure who sent them back to the king. When the king asked the messengers, "What kind of a man was it who came to meet you?" the messengers answered, "He had a garment of hair and had a leather belt around his waist" (2 Kings 1:7–8). The king knew immediately from this rather minimal description that his messengers had encountered Elijah. When John the Baptist began his preaching, Matthew introduces him by saying, "John's clothes were made of camel's hair, and he had a leather belt around his waist" (Matt. 3:4). This sartorial singularity recalled the memory of Elijah.

2. Both Elijah and John the Baptist faced a hostile political power throughout their lives. In particular, the main antagonist for both was a woman who was seeking their lives. For Elijah, it was Jezebel (1 Kings 19:2, 10, 14); for John, it was Herodias (Matt. 14:3–12).

3. Both Elijah and John the Baptist anointed their successors at the Jordan River. Elisha had accompanied Elijah to the Jordan, and he asked that a double portion of the spirit of Elijah also rest on him (2 Kings 2:9–14). When John baptized Jesus at the Jordan, he saw the heavens opened and the Spirit of God descending upon God's Son (Matt. 3:13–17). Elijah was the forerunner of

Elisha, just as John the Baptist was for Jesus. Luke notes this theme as well: when the birth of John the Baptist was foretold to his father Zechariah, the angel Gabriel said that John would "go on before the Lord, in the spirit and power of Elijah" and that John would fulfill the mission assigned to Elijah by Malachi, to "turn the hearts of the parents to their children" (Luke 1:17; Mal. 4:6).

4. There is perhaps no section of the Old Testament that abounds in miracles as much as the Elisha narrative. Having given Elisha the double portion of the Spirit that he sought, God demonstrated his empowerment of the prophet and testified to the message he proclaimed through the miracles that accompanied Elisha's ministry. Similarly, miracles abound when God himself testifies to the ministry of his own Son (Heb. 2:3–4). The appearance of Elijah was supposed to inaugurate "that great and dreadful day of the Lord," the day when God would judge evil while protecting and preserving his people. While John was in prison, he heard that Jesus was preaching and teaching in Galilee. So John sent messengers to ask Jesus, "Are you the one who was to come, or should we expect someone else?" Matthew reports that Jesus told John's disciples, "Go back and report to John what you hear and see: The blind receive sight, the lame walk, those who have leprosy are cleansed, the deaf hear, the dead are raised, and the good news is proclaimed to the poor" (Matt. 11:4–5). This list is largely a list of the miracles of Elisha: Elisha had restored sight to the blind (2 Kings 6:18–20), cured leprosy (chap. 5), restored the dead to life (4:32–37; 8:4–5; 13:21), and brought good news to the destitute (6:1–7; 7:1–2; 8:6). This list conflates the miracles of Elisha with those of the promised Servant of the Lord (Isa. 61:1–3). Jesus was in effect telling John, "Elijah's successor has come. I am the one you are looking for."

Matthew drew these parallels between Elijah and John, Elisha and Jesus. In doing this, Matthew provides one of a number of interpretive grids with which Christians can read this portion of the Old Testament. Other gospel writers used the Elijah-Elisha account in equally creative and helpful ways. For example, Kings itself presents a number of parallels between Elijah and Moses. Moses had also experienced the power of God on a mountain, only to find idolatry underway when he came down (Ex. 32; 1 Kings 18). Through Moses, God had provided food and water for Israel during her forty years in the wilderness (Ex. 17; Num. 11, 20), just as he provided Elijah with food and beverage that sustained him for forty days (1 Kings 19:8). Moses had encountered God at Sinai, and now God leads the prophet to that same place (1 Kings 19). There, like Moses, Elijah would experience the presence of God in the wind, earthquake, and fire (cf. Ex. 19:16–19). The cave where Elijah took refuge (1 Kings 19:9) reminds us of the cleft in the rock that concealed Moses (Ex. 33:22). On that same mountain God would "pass by" both (vv. 19, 22; 1 Kings 19:11), and both would avoid looking at God (Ex. 33:22; 34:33; 1 Kings 19:13). Both would be sent back to their tasks, their commissions to serve God renewed (Ex. 33:12;

1 Kings 19:15–16). Both Moses and Elijah would complain that they had had enough and ask God to take their lives (Num. 11:15; 1 Kings 19:4; cf. Ex. 32:32), and God would appoint prophets as help for each (Num. 11:16–17, 25; 1 Kings 19:16–17).

Both Moses and Elijah would yet behold the glory of God and hear his voice another time on another mountain (Matt. 17:1–13). There the splendor of the godhead enveloped Jesus, the Son of God, the one who was "the radiance of God's glory and the exact representation of his being" (Heb. 1:3). Like Elijah, Jesus had spent forty days in the wilderness (Matt. 4:2), but unlike Elijah, he did not succumb to despair.

Biblical authors also pair Elijah and Moses in reference to the day of the Lord (Mal. 4:4–5), on the Mount of Transfiguration (Matt. 17:3–4; Mark 9:4–5; Luke 9:30–33), and in Revelation (Rev. 11:3–6). Moses represented the law, and Elijah, the prophets; in Jesus one greater than Moses and Elijah had come, and all the law and the prophets spoke of him (Luke 24:27).

CHAPTER TWELVE

CHRONICLES

In the Hebrew canon the two books of Chronicles are counted as one; they stand at the end of the Writings and are the last books in the Hebrew Bible. Their division into two and placement after the books of Kings in the English Bible are due to the influence of the LXX. The Hebrew name of the books is "events of the days" (*dibrê yâmîm*). This same phrase is often used in the Bible to designate what appear to be official histories cited by the biblical historians (e.g., 1 Kings 14:19; 15:31; 16:5, 14, 20, 27). Chronicles is one of two books in the Bible to cover all of human history from creation to the author's day; both Matthew and Chronicles use genealogies to accomplish this. In the introduction to his translation of Samuel and Kings, Jerome said the books contained "the chronicle of the whole of sacred history"; the practice of calling the books Chronicles derives from that statement.

In the LXX the Chronicles were called "the things omitted, left over" (*Paralipomenon*). This title was symptomatic. The Chronicles have long been among the most neglected books in the Hebrew Bible for a variety of reasons: (1) Already in antiquity they were relegated to being merely a supplement to the information in Samuel and Kings. (2) Modern readers also find it difficult to get past the first nine chapters of what one writer called "Scriptural Sominex," the genealogies of the tribes. (3) Because the books are among the latest books in the Old Testament and the author-compiler lived at a time some distance from the events he narrated, critical scholarship has been quite skeptical about their historical worth.

In recent decades there has been a renewed interest in these books. Chronicles has a fascinating literary program and theological agenda in its own right.

BIBLIOGRAPHY

Commentaries

P. **Ackroyd,** *I and II Chronicles, Ezra, Nehemiah* (TBC; SCM, 1973); L. **Allen,** *1, 2 Chronicles* (CC; Word, 1987); R. **Braun,** *1 Chronicles* (WBC 14; Word, 1986); R. J. **Coggins,** *The First and Second Books of the Chronicles* (CBC; London: Cambridge University Press, 1976); E. L. **Curtis** and A. **Madsen,** *A Critical and Exegetical Commentary on the Books of Chronicles* (ICC; T. & T. Clark, 1910); R. B. **Dillard,** *2 Chronicles* (WBC 15; Word, 1987); A. E. **Hill,** *1 and 2 Chronicles* (NIVAC; Zondervan, 2003); G. N. **Knoppers,** *1 Chronicles* (AB; Doubleday, 2002); idem, *2 Chronicles* (AB; Doubleday, 2004); J. G. **McConville,** *I and II Chronicles* (DSB; Westminster, 1984); F. **Michaeli,** *Les livres de Chroniques, d'Esdras et de Nehemie* (CAT 16; Neuchâtel: Delachaux et Niestlé, 1967); J. M. **Myers,** *I and II Chronicles* (AB 12, 13; Doubleday, 1965); W. **Rudolph,** *Chronikbucher* (HAT 1/21; Tübingen: J. C. B. Mohr, 1955); M. **Wilcock,** *The Message of Chronicles* (BST; InterVarsity Press, 1987); H. G. M. **Williamson,** *1 and 2 Chronicles* (NCB; London: Marshall, Morgan, and Scott, 1982).

Monographs and Articles

P. **Ackroyd,** "History and Theology in the Writings of the Chronicler," *CTM* 38 (1967): 501–15; idem, "The Theology of the Chronicler," *LTQ* 8 (1973): 101–16; L. **Allen,** *The Greek Chronicles,* 2 vols. (VTSup 25, 27; Leiden: Brill, 1974); R. **Braun,** "The Message of Chronicles: Rally 'Round the Temple," *CTM* 42 (1971): 502–14; idem, "A Reconsideration of the Chronicler's Attitude to the North," *JBL* 96 (1977): 59–62; idem, "Solomon the Chosen Temple Builder: The Significance of 1 Chronicles 22, 28, and 29 for the Theology of Chronicles," *JBL* 95 (1976): 581–90; idem, "Solomonic Apologetic in Chronicles," *JBL* 95 (1976): 581–90; A. **Caquot,** "Peut-on parler de messianisme dans l'oeuvre du Chroniste?" *RTP,* 3rd ser. 16 (1966): 110–20; W. M. L. **de Wette,** *Beitrage zur Einleitung ini das Alte Testament* (2 vols.; Schimmelpfennig, 1806); R. B. **Dillard,** "The Chronicler's Solomon," *WTJ* 43 (1980): 289–300; idem, "The Literary Structure of the Chronicler's Solomon Narrative," *JSOT* 30 (1984): 85–93; idem, "Reward and Punishment in Chronicles: The Theology of Immediate Retribution," *WTJ* 46 (1984): 164–72; idem, "The Reign of Asa (2 Chr 14–16): An Example of the Chronicler's Theological Method," *JETS* 23 (1980): 207–18; R. **Duke,** "Book of Chronicles," in DOTHB (InterVarsity Press, 2005); T. **Eskenazi,** "The Chronicler and the Composition of 1 Esdras," *CBQ* 48 (1986): 39–61; D. N. **Freedman,** "The Chronicler's Purpose," *CBQ* 23 (1961): 436–42; J. **Goldingay,** "The Chronicler as Theologian," *BTB* 5 (1975): 99–126; M. P. **Graham,** K. G. **Hoglund,** and S. L. **McKenzie,** eds., *The Chronicler as Historian* (Sheffield Academic Press, 1997); idem, *The Chronicler as Author: Studies in Text and Texture* (Sheffield Academic

Press, 1999); M. P. **Graham,** K. G. **Hoglund,** S. L. **McKenzie,** and G. N. **Knoppers,** eds. *The Chronicler as Theologian: Essays in Honor of R. W. Klein* (T. & T. International, 2003); S. **Japhet,** "Conquest and Settlement in Chronicles," *JBL* 98 (1979): 205–18; idem, "The Historical Reliability of Chronicles," *JSOT* 33 (1985): 83–107; idem, "The Supposed Common Authorship of Chronicles and Ezra-Nehemiah Investigated Anew," *VT* 18 (1968): 330–71; W. **Lemke,** "The Synoptic Problem in the Chronicler's History," *HTR* 58 (1965): 349–63; J. G. **McConville,** "Book of Kings," in DOTHB (InterVarsity Press, 2005); R. **Mosis,** *Untersuchungen zur Theologie des Chronistischen Geschichtswerkes* (FTS; Freiberg: Herder, 1973); J. D. **Newsome,** "Toward a New Understanding of the Chronicler and His Purposes," *JBL* 94 (1975): 204–17; R. **North,** "The Theology of the Chronicler," *JBL* 82 (1963): 369–81; K. **Peltonen,** *History Debated: The Historical Reliability of Chronicles in Pre-Critical and Critical Research,* 2 vols. (Helsinki: Finnish Exegetical Society, 1996); D. L. **Petersen,** *Late Israelite Prophecy* (SBLMS 23; Missoula: Scholars, 1977); W. **Rudolph,** "Problems of the Books of Chronicles," *VT* 4 (1954): 401–9; M. **Throntveit,** "Hezekiah in the Books of Chronicles," *SBL Seminar Papers,* 1988 (Atlanta: Scholars, 1988): 302–11; T. **Willi,** *Die Chronik als Auslegung* (FRLANT 106; Göttingen: Vandenhoeck und Ruprecht, 1972); H. G. M. **Williamson,** "The Accession of Solomon in the Books of Chronicles," *VT* 26 (1976): 351–61; idem, "Eschatology in Chronicles," *TynBul* 28 (1977): 115–54; idem, *Israel in the Books of Chronicles* (London: Cambridge University Press, 1977).

HISTORICAL BACKGROUND

The author-compiler of Chronicles did not choose to identify himself, so we are left to drawing inferences about him from what he wrote. He clearly lived in the postexilic period since he reports the decree of Cyrus (2 Chron. 36:22–23). Two other passages help to establish the earliest date at which he could have written. Although there are some difficulties surrounding the passage, the genealogy of the Davidic royal family after the return runs at least two generations beyond Zerubbabel, who was active in the last quarter of the sixth century (1 Chron. 3:17–24). In 1 Chronicles 29:7 part of the people's giving for the construction of the temple is reported in *darics.* The daric is a Persian coin named after Darius; it was not minted before 515 BC, and sufficient time must be allowed for it to gain wide circulation as a monetary standard also in Judah (though of course it could represent a late editorial updating). These two passages, then, suggest that the final form of Chronicles could not have been written before the mid-fifth century. It is more difficult to establish the latest date by which the Chronicler would have written, though it is improbable that he wrote later than the beginning of the fourth century. Although not all would agree with this assessment, the book appears most naturally to be the product of a single author; nevertheless, there is also the possibility of a further slight redaction or elaboration by a later reviser. Whether early or late in the period, it is certain that Chronicles was written sometime during the Persian, or Second Temple period (539–333 BC). As Duke reminds us, this is a "time in which the ancient Yahwistic religious core of the community of Israel was reconstituted in the form that became the foundation for modern Judaism and Christianity" (2005, 162).

While the book does show the imprint of a single author's vocabulary and theological perspective, the writer directs his readers to a wide variety of other sources; we know that he frequently quoted from Samuel-Kings at length and that he makes use of a number of other biblical books. Scholars are not agreed on the amount of his individual contribution versus the degree to which he simply quoted from other sources or the degree to which his own work was supplemented by later revisers. The book of Chronicles shows so much interest in the temple and particularly its Levitical personnel (1 Chron. 6; 9:2–34; 15:2–27; 23:2–6, 26–32; 24:30–31; 26:17–20; 28:13–21; 2 Chron. 5:4–12; 11:13–16; 13:9–10; 17:8; 19:8–11; 20:14, 19; 23:2–8, 18; 24:5–6, 11; 29:4–34; 30:15–27; 31:2–19; 34:9–13, 20; 35:3–18) that many have suggested that the author was himself a Levite, possibly a Levitical musician.

Since the mid-nineteenth century there has been a strong scholarly consensus that the books of Chronicles and Ezra-Nehemiah originally formed a single work. There were four major reasons for associating Chronicles with Ezra-Nehemiah: (1) Chronicles ends with the decree of Cyrus, and Ezra begins with it (2 Chron. 36:23; Ezra 1:1–4); this overlap was commonly viewed as evidence that the two histories were originally joined and that the text of Cyrus's decree was repeated to show that connection at a time that the books were divided, perhaps to fit within the confines of different scrolls. (2) The apocryphal book 1 Esdras quotes from 2 Chronicles 35 through much of Ezra-Nehemiah; the fact that this book joined Chronicles with Ezra-Nehemiah is understood as evidence of the original situation before the books were divided. (3) Chronicles and Ezra-Nehemiah share numerous features of vocabulary and syntax. (4) The books share a common ideology and theology, especially their concerns with the cult and the use of extensive lists.

Yet on closer scrutiny, these arguments are not compelling for several reasons. (1) The overlap due to the repetition of the decree of Cyrus could equally well represent an effort to join two works that were originally separate. (2) Scholars are not agreed that 1 Esdras represents the state of Chronicles-Ezra-Nehemiah before they were subsequently further developed and divided in the Hebrew Bible; many consider 1 Esdras to represent a secondary development rather than evidence for the unity of Chronicles and Ezra-Nehemiah. (3) It is not sufficient to show simply that Chronicles and Ezra-Nehemiah share much in linguistic data. These commonalities may show no more than the common linguistic substratum of fourth-century Jews living in Judah. Japhet (1968, 330–71) has argued that there are a number of differences between Chronicles and Ezra-Nehemiah in terms of their distinctive choices of vocabulary and syntax for items that would otherwise ordinarily be considered synonymous. (4) There are also some important perspectival differences between Chronicles and Ezra-Nehemiah. For example, the weekly Sabbath, which is so important in Ezra-Nehemiah (Neh. 9:14; 10:31; 13:15–22) plays no role in Chronicles. Conversely, the Chronicler shows great interest in the prophets and reports many instances of their preaching, whereas Ezra-Nehemiah does not show a similar interest. The Davidic succession, an important theme in Chronicles, plays virtually no role in Ezra-Nehemiah. Whereas Ezra-Nehemiah shows some hostility toward those occupying the regions of the former northern kingdom Israel (Ezra 4–6; Neh. 2:19–20; 4:1–15; 6:1–14; 13:4–29), the Chronicler is much concerned to secure their participation in the life of the nation (1 Chron. 11:1–3; 12:23–40; 2 Chron. 19:4; 30:1–2; 34:6–7). "All Israel" acting together in concert is a prominent theme in Chronicles (see The Genealogies below). The Chronicler does not report Solomon's sins involving his many wives, whereas Solomon is used as an example about the evil of mixed marriage in Nehemiah 13:26. In recent decades in the study of Chronicles the tide has been running against treating Chronicles and Ezra-Nehemiah as a unity; Williamson, Japhet, and Braun are prominent voices in the effort to sever that relationship. The ideology and theology of Chronicles emerge in a different light when it is read on its own rather than as a part of Ezra-Nehemiah.

The Chronicler made use of a wide range of sources both biblical and extra-biblical. He quotes at length from Samuel and Kings and uses material from a number of other biblical books. The form in which the Chronicler cites these other books is occasionally at variance with the Masoretic Text, particularly in the case of Samuel, where the Chronicler appears to have used a text similar to that used by translators and revisers of the LXX (Lemke 1965, 345–63). Whereas in Kings the sources to which the writer refers the reader appear to be primarily official records or histories (e.g., "the book of the annals of the kings of Judah" or "the book of the annals of the kings of Israel"), the Chronicler sends his readers largely to a variety of prophetic writings (e.g., "the records of Samuel the seer, the records of Nathan the prophet and the records of Gad the seer" [1 Chron. 29:29], "the records of Shemaiah the prophet and of Iddo the seer that deal with genealogies" [2 Chron. 12:15], "the annotations of the prophet Iddo" [13:22]). Two passages suggest that these were not independent works but were already integrated into a larger corpus (20:34; 32:32) and that the Chronicler may have cited this other source under the name of a prophet who ministered during the king's reign. Since the Chronicler's source citations (with the exception of Josiah, 2 Chron. 35:27) always occur in the same position as the source citation in the parallel account in Samuel-Kings, some consider the Chronicler to be directing his readers to Samuel-Kings itself.

As a Historical Source

Ever since the time of de Wette (1806), Chronicles has been viewed with suspicion as a source of true history. Comparison of the account in Samuel-Kings and Chronicles certainly does show a different perspective on that history, even though it is clear that the latter incorporates much of the former. A modernist view of history allowed for only one true presentation of that history, but as Provan, Long, and Longman (2003, 3–104) point out, such a view is extremely naïve, assuming the possibility of brute fact history. In actual fact, through his use of genealogies and sources, the Chronicler shows interest in presenting the past in a way that answers modern questions (Japhet 1993, 14–23; Peltonen 1996). Rather than demeaning Chronicles as a source for history, it is better to recognize it as a highly interpretive presentation of the events of the past. Thus, modern readers have two biblical presentations of the history of Israel, a synoptic history analogous to the three Synoptic Gospels. In the words of Duke (2005, 162), "there has grown an increasing appreciation of the process of history telling through which different people, or even the same person at different times, can look back at the same historical field of the past and draw out different but equally valid story lines. An analogy to this process would be how two skilled painters could paint two different but 'accurate' portraits of the same person."

> *Modern readers have in Samuel-Kings and Chronicles two biblical presentations of the history of Israel, a synoptic history analogous to the three Synoptic Gospels.*

LITERARY STRUCTURE AND THEOLOGICAL MESSAGE

The biblical historians were not only writing an account of their national history as it actually occurred, but they were also writing to address the theological issues of their contemporary audience. There is considerable interplay between the needs of the author's generation and his selection and presentation of data. The author of Kings lived during the exile or very early in the postexilic period. His readers had in recent times experienced the destruction of Jerusalem and the end of the Davidic succession. For them the burning theological issues that had to be addressed if faith was to survive were "Has God failed?" "How could this have happened to us?" and "Is Marduk of Babylon really more powerful than Yahweh?" The writer of Kings sets himself to address these questions by showing that God has not failed but has fulfilled his warnings to the nation by bringing upon them the consequences of failing to obey the covenant. The exile confirms the power of Yahweh rather than calling it into question.

The Chronicler lives at a later time than the writer of Kings. The needs of his audience are different. The restoration community is not asking, "How could this have happened?" Rather, it is asking questions about its relationship to its past: "In the judgment of the exile, had God ended his covenant with Israel?" "Are we still the people of God?" "Is God still interested in us?" "What do God's promises to Israel, Jerusalem, and David before the exile have to do with us who live after?" So the Chronicler prepares yet another history of the nation, one that addresses a different set of questions than those that influenced Kings.

The book of Chronicles naturally divides into three larger sections: the genealogies (1 Chron. 1–9), the united monarchy under David and Solomon (1 Chron. 10–2 Chron. 9), and the post-schism kingdom (2 Chron. 10–36). In each of these sections the Chronicler varies his compositional technique; though there is, of course, a unitary theological thrust to the book, these larger units also reflect different theological emphases.

The Genealogies (1 Chron. 1–9)

Today's Western readers are quite often discouraged from studying or even reading Chronicles because of what we consider its rather inauspicious beginning; the Chronicler and his audience would have looked at these nine chapters of genealogies through quite different eyes. For a generation asking about its relationship to Israel in the past, the genealogies directly address the question of the continuity of the restoration community with Israel of old. Using genealogies, the Chronicler relates his own generation to Adam (1 Chron. 1:1); for those wondering "Is God still interested in us?" the Chronicler gives a resounding "Yes! He always has been." The genealogies speak of Israel's continuity and her election as God's people.

One of the most prominent themes in Chronicles is the writer's concern with "all Israel" (e.g., 1 Chron. 9:1; 11:1, 10; 12:38; 14:8; 15:3, 28; 18:14; 2 Chron. 1:2; 7:8; 9:30; 10:3, 16; 12:1; 13:4, 15; 18:16; 24:5). At a time when the northern tribes had long been in exile, the Chronicler provides a genealogical listing for all the tribes (except Zebulun and Dan); in giving such a list, the Chronicler is (1) expressing his awareness of continuity with the larger number, (2) showing his concern to include the northern tribes rather than to exclude them, (3) suggesting that he regarded the schism as neither permanent nor desirable, and (4) possibly giving some expression to an eschatological hope for a revival of the nation in its largest extent.

The genealogies also had some very practical functions for the restoration community. They not only address the question of continuity with the past but also the question of legitimacy and legality in the present. Who was eligible for kingship or priesthood (Neh. 7:61–65)? Issues of social status, military obligation, land distribution, and hereditary rights are also in part addressed by genealogies.

Although these ancient genealogies may be somewhat of a "turn-off" to modern readers, the genealogies of the individual tribes contain many interesting features that repay the effort invested in studying them.

The United Monarchy (1 Chron. 10–2 Chron. 9)

When comparing the Chronicler's account of David and Solomon with that in Samuel-Kings, perhaps the most striking difference is the material that the Chronicler has chosen to omit. With the exception of the account of David's census (1 Chron. 21; cf. 2 Sam. 24), the Chronicler has not recorded incidents that would in any way tarnish the image of David or Solomon. The Chronicler does not report the rival kingdom in the hands of a descendant of Saul during David's seven years at Hebron or David's negotiations for rule over the northern tribes. He omits any account of the rebellion of Absalom and Adonijah and the actions of Amnon and Shimei; he makes no mention of David's sins in connection with Bathsheba and Uriah. The Chronicler deletes the narrative of Solomon's taking vengeance on David's enemies (1 Kings 2) and does not report the sins of Solomon, which according to Kings were ultimately the reason for the breakup of the kingdom (1 Kings 11). Even the blame for the schism is shifted from Solomon to Jeroboam (2 Chron. 13:6–7).

In Chronicles, David and Solomon are portrayed as glorious, obedient, all-conquering figures who enjoy not only divine blessing but also the support of all the nation. Instead of an aged, bedridden David, who only saves the kingdom for Solomon at the last minute due to the promptings of Bathsheba and Nathan (1 Kings 1), the Chronicler shows a smooth transition of power without a ripple of dissent. David himself publicly announces Solomon's appointment as his successor, an announcement greeted with enthusiastic and total support on the part of the people (1 Chron. 28:1–29:25), including the other sons of David, the officers of the army, and others who had supported Adonijah's attempted coup (1 Chron. 29:24; cf. 1 Kings 1:7–10). Whereas in Kings, Solomon's sins are a reason for the schism and Solomon is contrasted to his father David (1 Kings 11; cf. 11:11–13, 32–36), in Chronicles Rehoboam is commended for "following the ways of David and Solomon" (2 Chron. 11:17).

This idealization of the reigns of David and Solomon could be dismissed as a kind of glorification of the "good old days." Yet when coupled with the Chronicler's emphasis on God's promise to David of an enduring dynasty (1 Chron. 17:11–14; 2 Chron. 13:5, 8; 21:7; 23:3), the Chronicler's treatment of David and Solomon reflects a "messianic historiography." David and Solomon in Chronicles are not just the David and Solomon who were, but the David and Solomon of the Chronicler's eschatological hope. At a time when Israel was subject to the

Persians, the Chronicler still cherished hopes of a restoration of Davidic rule, and he describes the glorious rule of David and Solomon in the past in terms of his hope for the future.

Another feature of the Chronicler's account of David and Solomon is that their reigns are presented primarily in terms of their involvement in the building of the temple. As soon as he was inaugurated, David was immediately concerned to move the ark to Jerusalem (1 Chron. 13–16). The Chronicler adds an extensive section concerning David's preparations for the work he would leave to Solomon (chaps. 22–27); even the public ceremonies surrounding the transfer of royal power concern primarily the construction of the temple (chaps. 28–29). Whereas in Kings Solomon's wisdom is wisdom for ruling (1 Kings 3:7–15; cf. 3:16–4:34), in Chronicles it is wisdom for building (cf. 2 Chron. 2:12 and its parallel at 1 Kings 5:7). Solomon receives wisdom at the altar built by Bezalel (2 Chron. 1:5), who had earlier built the tabernacle.

Another of the Chronicler's most characteristic compositional techniques could be described as "recapitulative historiography." The Chronicler seems to delight in taking an earlier incident from Israel's history or from his own writings and using it as a paradigm or model to describe a subsequent situation. The Chronicler takes the relationship between Moses and Joshua as a model for his presentation of the succession of David and Solomon (Williamson 1976, 351–61). He also presents Solomon and the Tyrian craftsman Huram-Abi as a second Bezalel and Oholiab. Bezalel is mentioned in only two books of the Bible: Chronicles and Exodus. Just as Bezalel was endowed with the spirit of wisdom for building the tabernacle, so also Solomon was endowed with the same spirit at the altar built by Bezalel (1 Chron. 2:20; 2 Chron. 1:5; cf. Ex. 35:30–31). Both Bezalel and Solomon were from the tribe of Judah (Ex. 35:30).

> The Chronicler seems to delight in taking an earlier incident from Israel's history or from his own writings and using it as a paradigm or model to describe a subsequent situation.

The Chronicler modifies the account in Kings in order to draw parallels between Huram-Abi and Oholiab in four ways: (1) *Arrival time*. In the account in Kings, Huram appears in the narrative at a point when the construction of the temple itself has already been completed (1 Kings 7:13); the Chronicler brings him on the scene from the beginning, just as Oholiab was associated with Bezalel from the outset (2 Chron. 2:7, 13). (2) *Skill list*. In Kings Huram is a specialist in bronze (1 Kings 7:14) and he appears to make a large number of bronze castings (vv. 15–47). In Chronicles Huram-Abi's skill list is much longer, all but identical to the skill list of Bezalel and Oholiab (2 Chron. 2:7, 14; cf. Ex. 35:31–36:1). (3) *Name*. In Kings this Tyrian craftsman is called Hiram or Huram, but in Chronicles his name is given as Huram-Abi. This additional element on the end of his name makes his name end the same way as did the name of Oholiab. (4) *Ancestry*. Where Kings reports that Huram was the child of a widow from Naphtali (1 Kings 7:14), the Chronicler identifies her as a widow of Dan; this gives Huram-Abi the same ancestry as Oholiab (2 Chron.

2:14; cf. Ex. 35:34). While all of these differences can be reconciled fairly easily, it is important to see what the Chronicler is doing: by drawing parallels between the building of the tabernacle and the building of Solomon's temple, he is enhancing the continuity between Israel of old and the generations that witnessed the building of the second temple. Similar examples of patterned narratives can be found in the Chronicler's treatment of the last four kings of Judah, his likening Hezekiah to a second Solomon, his drawing parallels between events at the time of Abijah and Ahaz (2 Chron. 13, 28), and his modeling Jehoshaphat after his father Asa.

The Post-Schism Kingdom (2 Chron. 10–36)

One of the major concerns in the book of Kings is to show the accumulating history of wrongdoing that led to the exile: "They have done evil in my eyes and have aroused my anger from the day their ancestors came out of Egypt until this day" (2 Kings 21:15). The exiles themselves were not altogether appreciative of this explanation; they complained that they were being punished for sins they had not committed: "The parents have eaten sour grapes, and the children's teeth are set on edge" (Jer. 31:29; Ezek. 18:2). When the Chronicler retells the history of Judah, he is concerned to show that punishment for sin is not always deferred, but rather each generation will experience blessing or judgment in terms of its own actions. This characteristic of the Chronicler is commonly known as his "theology of immediate retribution." Although it is by no means confined to his account of the post-schism kings, it is more frequently used there.

In a number of passages unique to Chronicles (i.e., not found in the parallel text of Samuel-Kings) the author specifically articulates the theme of an immediate divine response to precipitating events (1 Chron. 28:8–9; 2 Chron. 12:5; 15:2; 20:20). Although it is not the first such notice, 2 Chronicles 7:14 (the most widely known verse from Chronicles) is a programmatic statement of great importance: "If my people, who are called by my name, will humble themselves and pray and seek my face and turn from their wicked ways, then I will hear from heaven, and I will forgive their sin and will heal their land."

Solomon's prayer at the dedication of the temple and God's response to that prayer (2 Chron. 6:1–7:22) constitute a kind of "charter" for the subsequent history of the nation. The divine response to Solomon's prayer is drawn almost verbatim from its parallel in 1 Kings 9:1–9, except that the Chronicler has added the material in 2 Chronicles 7:13–15. Here some vocabulary is used that will recur again and again as the Chronicler seeks to demonstrate the validity of his theology of immediate retribution. "Seeking God" (*drš, bqš*) becomes a touchstone for weal or woe (1 Chron. 10:13–14; 22:19; 28:9; 2 Chron. 11:16; 12:14; 14:4, 7; 15:2, 4, 12–13, 15; 16:12; 17:4; 18:4; 19:3; 20:4; 22:9; 25:20; 26:5; 30:19;

31:21; 33:12; 34:3); similarly "humbling oneself" (*kn* ') or the failure to do so determines the divine response (2 Chron. 12:6–7, 12; 28:19; 30:11; 33:12, 19, 23; 34:27; 36:12). Prayer (1 Chron. 4:10; 5:20; 21:26; 2 Chron. 13:12–15; 14:11; 18:31; 20:9; 30:18, 27; 32:20, 24; 33:13, 18–19) and "turning" (2 Chron. 15:4; 30:6, 9; 36:13) occur at critical junctures in the narrative.

Not only these terms, but also their antonyms are common vehicles for the Chronicler's convictions. The opposite responses to seeking God and humbling oneself are introduced through the use of "abandon, forsake" (*'zb*: 1 Chron. 28:9, 20; 2 Chron. 7:19, 22; 12:1, 5; 13:10–11; 15:2; 21:10; 24:18, 20, 24; 28:6; 29:6; 34:25) or "be unfaithful, rebellious" (*m 'l*: 1 Chron. 2:7; 5:25; 10:13; 2 Chron. 12:2; 26:16, 18; 28:19, 22; 29:6; 30:7; 36:14).

When one compares the account of the reign of a king of Judah in Kings with that in Chronicles, most of the differences are related to the Chronicler's theology of immediate retribution. Most of the material unique to Chronicles is providing a theological rationale for the events he narrates or showing how God does indeed bless or judge each generation in terms of its own response to his commands. The Chronicler uses a fairly stable set of motifs for showing divine disapproval or approbation. Acts of piety and obedience are rewarded with success and prosperity (1 Chron. 22:11, 13; 29:23; 2 Chron. 14:7; 26:5; 31:21; 32:27–30—contrast 13:12); building programs (2 Chron. 11:5; 14:6–7; 16:6; 17:12; 24:13; 26:2, 6, 9–10; 27:3–4; 32:3–5, 29–30; 33:14; 34:10–13—contrast 16:5); victory in warfare (13:13–18; 14:8–15; 20:2–30; 25:12; 26:11–15; 27:5–7; 32:20–22); progeny (1 Chron. 3:1–9; 14:2–7; 25:5; 26:4–5; 2 Chron. 11:18–22; 13:21; 21:1–3); popular support (2 Chron. 11:13–17; 15:10–15; 17:5; 19:4–11; 20:27–30; 23:1–17; 30:1–26; 34:29–32; 35:24–25); and large armies (2 Chron. 11:1; 14:8; 17:12–19; 25:5; 26:12–13). Conversely, disobedience and infidelity bring military defeat (2 Chron. 12:1–9; 16:1–9; 21:8–11, 16–17; 24:23–24; 25:15–24; 28:4–8, 16–25; 33:11; 35:20–24; 36:15–20), the disaffection of the population (2 Chron. 16:10; 21:19; 24:25–26; 25:27–28; 28:27; 33:24–25), and illness (16:12; 21:16–20; 26:16–23; cf. 32:24). Alongside cultic offenses and the failure to seek God and to humble oneself, foreign alliances represented failure to trust God and always resulted in judgment (16:2–9; 19:1–3; 20:35–37; 22:3–9; 25:7–13; 28:16–21; 32:31). In Chronicles, wicked kings do not engage in building programs; they have no great number of wives and progeny, no great wealth, and command no great armies; these tokens of divine blessing are reserved to the pious.

In his emphasis on immediate retribution, the Chronicler is warning the restoration community against any complacency or presumption that punishment might be deferred as it had been in the past. For a nation once again "serving the kings of other lands" (2 Chron. 12:8), survival and blessing were found through seeking God and humbling oneself before him.

It is a shame that the Chronicles have been so generally neglected in the history of the church. The Chronicler was an able historian and theologian whose work deserves more earnest attention. Christian readers will find the books instructive in innumerable ways. At a macrolevel the genealogies speak eloquently of the desire of believers to have their own names enrolled in the roster of God's people (Dan. 12:1; Phil. 4:3; Rev. 3:5; 13:8). They will see in the glorious David and Solomon described in Chronicles an anticipation of the glory of David's greater Son.

CHAPTER THIRTEEN

EZRA-NEHEMIAH

Although modern readers of the Bible are accustomed to treating the books of Ezra and Nehemiah separately, ancient tradition regards them as one. The titles of the individual books reflect the two main characters of the book. Although they were strong and important men, in the final analysis the book actually focuses on the community as a whole.

These books record the last events of the Old Testament period. They encompass the time from the immediate postexilic times (the decree of Cyrus, 539 BC) through the work of Nehemiah (end of the fifth century BC). Later tradition marks Ezra as the culmination of the Old Testament era and describes him as the one who completes the canon.

The books describe a time of transition. As Eskenazi indicates, it is a time when the community supersedes the elite leadership of the individual, a time when not just the temple but the whole city becomes holy ground, and a time when written documents supersede oral speeches in authority.

BIBLIOGRAPHY

Commentaries

J. **Blenkinsopp,** *Ezra-Nehemiah* (OTL; Westminster, 1988); L. H. **Brockington,** *Ezra, Nehemiah and Esther* (NCB; Eerdmans, 1969); D. J. A. **Clines,** *Ezra, Nehemiah, Esther* (NCB; Eerdmans, 1984); R. J. **Coggins,** *The Books of Ezra and Nehemiah* (CBC; Cambridge, 1976); F. C. **Fensham,** *The Books of Ezra and Nehemiah* (NICOT; Eerdmans, 1982); D. **Kidner,** *Ezra and Nehemiah* (TOTC; InterVarsity Press, 1979); J. G. **McConville,** *Ezra, Nehemiah and Esther* (DSB; Westminster, 1985); J. M. **Myers,** *Ezra, Nehemiah* (AB; Doubleday, 1965); M. A. **Throntveit,** *Ezra-Nehemiah* (Interp; Westminster John Knox, 1992); H. G. M. **Williamson,** *Ezra-Nehemiah* (WBC; Word 1985).

Monographs and Articles

P. R. **Ackroyd,** "The Historical Literature," in *The Hebrew Bible and Its Modern Interpreters,* ed. D. A. Knight and G. M. Tucker (Fortress/Scholars, 1985), 297–323; idem, "The Temple Vessels—A Continuity Theme," in *Studies in the Religion of Ancient Israel* (VTSup 23 [1972]): 166–81; J. **Berquist,** *Judaism in Persia's Shadow: A Social and Historical Approach* (Minneapolis: Fortress Press, 1995); M. J. **Boda,** *Praying the Tradition: The Origin and Use of Tradition in Nehemiah 9* (*BZAW* 277; Walter de Gruyter, 1999); R. L. **Braun,** "Chronicles, Ezra, and Nehemiah," in *Studies in the Historical Books of the Old Testament* (VTSup 30 [1979]): 52–64; P. **Briant,** *From Cyrus to Alexander: A History of the Persian Empire* (Winona Lake: Eisenbrauns, 2002); J. A. **Emerton,** "Did Ezra Go to Jerusalem in 428 BC?" *JTS* 17 (1966): 1–19; T. C. **Eskenazi,** "The Chronicler and the Composition of 1 Esdras," *CBQ* 48 (1986): 39–61; idem, *In an Age of Prose: A Literary Approach to Ezra-Nehemiah* (Atlanta: Scholars, 1988); L. L. **Grabbe,** *Judaism from Cyrus to Hadrian,* 2 vols. (Minneapolis: Fortress, 1992); D. **Green,** "Ezra-Nehemiah," in *A Complete Literary Guide to the Bible,* ed. L. Ryken and T. Longman (Zondervan, 1993), 206–15; K. G. **Hoglund,** *Achaemenid Imperial Administration in Syria-Palestine and the Missions of Ezra and Nehemiah* (Atlanta: Scholars, 1992); D. M. **Howard** Jr., "Ezra-Nehmiah" in his *An Introduction to the Old Testament Historical Books* (Moody, 1993), 273–313; S. **Japhet,** "Sheshbazzar and Zerubbabel—Against the Background of the Historical and Religious Tendencies of Ezra-Nehemiah," *ZAW* 94 (1982): 66–98; idem, "The Supposed Common Authorship of Chronicles and Ezra-Nehemiah Investigated Anew," *VT* 18 (1968): 330–71; R. W. **Klein,** "Ezra and Nehemiah in Recent Studies," in *Magnalia Dei: The Mighty Acts of God,* ed. F. M. Cross, W. E. Lemke, and P. D. Miller (Doubleday, 1976), 361–76; K. **Koch,** "Ezra and the Origins of Judaism," *JSS* 19 (1974): 173–97; T. **Longman** III, *Fictional Akkadian Autobiography* (Winona Lake: Eisenbrauns, 1991); D. J. **McCarthy,** "Covenant and Law in Chronicles-Nehemiah," *CBQ* 41 (1982): 25–44; J. G. **McConville,** "Ezra-Nehemiah and the Fulfillment of Prophecy," *VT* 36 (1986): 205–24; P. M. **McNutt,** *Reconstructing the Society of Ancient Israel* (London/Louisville: SPCK/Westminster John Knox, 1999); K. **Min,** *The Levitical Authorship of Ezra-Nehemiah* (JSOTS 409; London: T. & T. Clark, 2004); S. **Mowinckel,** "'Ich' und 'Er' in der Ezrageschichte," in *Verbannung und Heimkehr: Beitrage zur Geschichte und Theologie Israels im 6. und 5. Jahrhundert v. Chr.,* ed. A. Kuschke (Tübingen, 1961), 211–33; I. **Provan,** V. P. **Long,** and T. **Longman** III, *A Biblical History of Israel* (Westminster John Knox, 2003); Z. **Talshir,** "Ezra-Nehemiah and First Esdras: Diagnosis of a Relationship between Two Recensions," *Bib* 81 (2000): 566–73; M. A. **Throntveit,** "Linguistic Analysis and the Question of Authorship in Chronicles, Ezra and Nehemiah," *VT* 32 (1978): 9–26; J. C. **VanderKam,** "Ezra-Nehemiah or Ezra and Nehemiah?" in *Priests, Prophets and*

Scribes: Essays . . . in Honour of Joseph Blenkinsopp, ed. E. Ulrich et al. (JSOTS 149; Sheffield: Sheffield Academic Press, 1992), 55–75; G. **von Rad,** "Die Nehemia Denkschrift," *ZAW* 76 (1964): 176–87; J. P. **Weinberg,** *The Citizen-Temple Community* (JSOTS 151; Sheffield: Sheffield Academic Press, 1992); H. G. M. **Williamson,** "The Composition of Ezra i–vi," *JTS* 34 (1983): 1–30; idem, *Israel in the Books of Chronicles* (Cambridge University Press, 1977); idem, "Exile and After: Historical Study," in *The Face of Old Testament Studies*, ed. D. W. Baker and B. T. Arnold (Grand Rapids: Baker, 1999), 236–65; E. **Yamauchi,** *Persia and the Bible* (Grand Rapids: Baker, 1990); idem, "Books of Ezra-Nehemiah," in DOTHB (InterVarsity Press, 2005).

HISTORICAL BACKGROUND

Authorship, Composition, and Date

Tradition cites Ezra as the author of the book (*Baba' Bathra* 15a), but although this is not impossible, concrete internal evidence is lacking. Archer (*SOTI,* 419–20), an exception to the modern consensus, argues that since Ezra speaks in the first person in Ezra 8–10, he must have written the entire work (incorporating the Nehemiah Memoir).

In actuality, the issues of authorship, composition, and date are intertwined and quite complex. We begin with the issue of the composition of the book.

Unity of Ezra-Nehemiah. First, due to the common practice of printing the two books separately, we need to examine the evidence for their unity. Modern Hebrew Bibles and English versions print the books separately, obscuring the ancient unity of the books. Actually, it was not until the Middle Ages that the books were separated in Hebrew Bibles. Before that time, they were printed together, and when the Masoretes tallied the number of verses of the book, they did it for the combined Ezra-Nehemiah. They also identified Nehemiah 3:32 as the center of the book.

Origen is the first attested scholar to differentiate the two books, and Jerome's Vulgate represents this position for the first time in an edition of the Bible (see Howard 1993, 275; Williamson 1985, xxi).

We thus treat the books of Ezra and Nehemiah as a literary unity in the analysis to follow.

Connection With Chronicles. The next major issue is the connection of Ezra-Nehemiah with Chronicles. Since the time of L. Zunz in 1832 until recently, most scholars believed that Ezra-Nehemiah was written by the Chronicler. The most obvious key to the theory is the overlap between the end of Chronicles and the beginning of Ezra, but advocates of this position also point to linguistic and theological similarities between the two. Furthermore, they also invoke the noncanonical 1 Esdras, which retells the same story as the end of 2 Chronicles and Ezra, and does so without showing a break between the two.

In spite of the overwhelming consensus in favor of this view among scholars today, VanderKam has recently argued for separate origins of these two books.

The arguments for and against the unity of Chronicles and Ezra-Nehemiah are too involved to repeat in detail here. For the position in favor of a close connection between the two, consult Ackroyd, Talshir, and the summary in Eskenazi (1988, 14–32; 1986), though it is not her position. However, it is fair to say that Japhet, Williamson, and others have forged a new consensus that divorces Ezra-Nehemiah from Chronicles. Min (2004) represents a recent statement of this position. Upon evaluation of the evidence, we agree that Ezra-Nehemiah is a separate composition and will be treated as such in what follows.

Sources. It is obvious that the final redactor-author of Ezra-Nehemiah utilized sources in his composition. The shift in both parts of the book between first-person and third-person speech is a major indication of this. Later we will see that the shift to and from first-person narration has significant literary functions, but for now we concentrate on the phenomenon as an indication of sources. The two are not mutually exclusive. Howard (1993, 278–79) gives a helpful list of the major and minor sources found in the book:

Major Sources
  1. A historical review (Ezra 1–6)
  2. Ezra's Memoirs (Ezra 7–10 and Neh. 8–10)
  3. Nehemiah's Memoirs (Neh. 1–7 and 11–13)

Minor Sources
  1. Lists (Ezra 1:9–11; 2; 7; 8:1–14; Neh. 3; 10:18–43; 11:3–36; 12:1–26)
  2. Letters (Ezra 1:2–4; 4:11–16; 4:17–22; 5:7–17; 6:2–5; 6:6–22; 7:12–26)

Williamson (1985) persuasively argues that the composition of the books of Ezra-Nehemiah proceeded along the following lines: (1) the above sources were written close to the events about which they speak; (2) the Ezra Memoir and the Nehemiah Memoir are brought together; and then (3) Ezra 1–6 is added as an introduction to the whole work. The latter was composed of a variety of sources and indicates what happened from the time of Cyrus's decree until the advent of Ezra and Nehemiah.

Min has recently advanced the argument that, though we cannot identify the specific author of Ezra-Nehemiah, the contents indicate that it derived from Levitical circles around 400 BC.

Date. Since we cannot identify a specific author, we may not be precise about the date. Of course, a major factor in giving even a proximate time period for the final composition of the book relies on our ability to fix a date for the events which are narrated in the book. While there is scholarly disagreement, we side with a traditional date for Ezra's mission (458 BC), thus allowing us to fix a date as early as the turn of the century (400). However, it is possible that this marks the time when the Ezra and Nehemiah Memoirs were brought together, and it may not have been until a century later (300) that Ezra 1–6 was prefaced to the book (see Williamson 1983 and 1985, xxxvi; Japhet 1982, 88).

The Dates of the Missions of Ezra and Nehemiah

Scholars agree about the date of Nehemiah's mission to Jerusalem (see Klein 1976, 370–72, for the information to follow). Nehemiah 1:1 reads, "In the month of Kislev in the twentieth year, while I was in the citadel of Susa. . . ." Although no king's name is given, it has been assumed that Nehemiah went to Jerusalem in the twentieth year of Artaxerxes I (465–425 BC). This intuition is now confirmed by a letter found among the Elephantine papyri. This letter is dated to 408 BC (the seventeenth year of Darius II). It was sent to Bagoas, who may have been the one to follow Nehemiah as governor of Yehud, and reference is made to Johanan the high priest (Neh. 12:10, 22), who was the second person to succeed Eliashib, a contemporary of Nehemiah (Neh. 3:1; 13:28). It was also sent to Sanballat's sons. Since these individuals represent the generation after Nehemiah, it is reasonable to place Nehemiah's work during the reign of Artaxerxes I. Thus, the description of his work begins in 445 BC. His first term of office was twelve years (Neh. 5:14).

> *Ezra and Nehemiah were two different individuals with a common goal, to be sure, but also with different emphases.*

While Nehemiah's mission is firmly dated, Ezra's is not. The textual notice is as extensive as Nehemiah's: "during the reign of Artaxerxes king of Persia, Ezra . . . came up from Babylon. . . . Ezra arrived in Jerusalem in the fifth month of the seventh year of the king" (Ezra 7:1–8).

The traditional order, Ezra preceding Nehemiah, lends itself to identifying the king as Artaxerxes I, leading to a date of 458 BC for the beginning of his ministry. Of course, this would mean that Ezra would have been waiting for Nehemiah when the latter arrived in Jerusalem in 445. However, the fact that the books do not confirm any overlap between the two leaders has presented an obstacle to many scholars.

This problem led to two alternative constructions of the chronology: (1) dating Ezra to the seventh year of Artaxerxes II, which would place him in 398 BC, or (2) emending the text to read "thirty-seventh" (thirty and seven begin with the same Hebrew consonant [*shin*]), thus dating Ezra to 428 BC. Since most scholars object to such free emendation, the date 398 BC has been the most widely accepted alternative (see Emerton).

However, too much may be read into the lack of overlap between Ezra and Nehemiah (and see Neh. 8:9) in the biblical text. Ezra and Nehemiah were two different individuals with a common goal, to be sure, but also with different emphases. So it is not surprising to see a move back toward a traditional order and dating BC for the work of Ezra and Nehemiah in recent scholarship (Hoglund 1992).

Historical Period

While the book focuses on the missions of Ezra and Nehemiah, it opens with the edict of Cyrus of Persia, who allows the exiles to return home. The authenticity of this decree is supported by the fact that Cyrus had a policy of allowing nations that were subjugated by the Babylonians to return to their homelands and rebuild (see the Cyrus Decree, ANET, 316). Then follows an account of the events that took place between 539 and c. 515 BC.

Of course, only a few people decide to make the journey back to the decimated homeland to rebuild city and temple. Those who choose to go follow the leadership of Zerubbabel, a descendant of David (although this information comes, not from Ezra, but from 1 Chronicles 3:19 and elsewhere), and Shesh-bazzar (for the issue of the identity of the latter, see Japhet 1982).

Some evidence exists to indicate that this edict was part of an imperial strategy for many who were exiled under the rule of the Babylonians and, before that, the Assyrians. This policy led many to think of Persia as a liberator.

The Persian (Achaemenid) Empire organized itself into satrapies, Palestine falling into one large satrapy called Beyond the River. Zerubbabel was governor of one of the districts within this satrapy, called Yehud.

The stated purpose of the return to Palestine was to rebuild the temple. The priests started by rebuilding the altar in order to initiate sacrificial worship (Ezra 3:1–6). The foundation was laid (vv. 10–13), but before the temple itself could be built, opposition arose. The opposition came in the form of those, perhaps from the north, who were already in the area when the Judeans arrived. They offered to assist in the rebuilding, but Zerubbabel and the other leaders refused their offers (Ezra 4:1–3). Hoglund (1992, 26–27) distinguishes this opposition from the Jewish-Samaritan rift that occurred some time later. Their response was to appeal to the Persian authorities to bring the rebuilding activity to a close.

The efforts to foil the rebuilding of the temple succeeded when Artaxerxes ordered that temple construction be halted (4:18–22). It would not be completed until the reign of Darius, sometime around 515 BC.

Ezra 7–Nehemiah 13 recounts the events of 458–433 BC (Howard 1993, 284–85). During this time, Ezra and Nehemiah return to Judah and lead the people in a spiritual and nationalist revival. The focus of the revitalization of Jerusalem is on the rebuilding of the walls.

Hoglund's study illuminates the broader political-military context in which the missions of Ezra and Nehemiah need to be understood. Why would the Persian authorities encourage the rebuilding of the walls of a vassal city? This might well encourage later rebellion and thus come back to haunt them. Hoglund connects the revitalization of Jerusalem with events in Egypt in the middle of the fifth century BC. Most of our information for this revolt comes from the Greek historians Herodotus, Thucydides, Ctesias, Diodorus Siculus, and others. There is some disharmony in their accounts, and care must be taken in reconstructing the events, but in general the following picture emerges.

Xerxes died in 464 BC, encouraging revolt in Egypt, a vassal state at the time. The revolutionary leaders were Inaros, the "Great Chief of Libu," and Amyrtaeus, the "Great Chief of Meshwesh." They encountered Achaemenes, the satrap of Egypt and uncle of the new Persian king Artaxerxes I, in a battle at Papremis. The battle resulted in a great victory for the Egyptians. Achaemenes was killed, and the survivors fled to Memphis, where they dug in, expecting an onslaught.

The Greek Delian League, headed by Athens, saw this revolt as a golden opportunity to push its interests in the western Mediterranean. They thus entered the fray. Nonetheless, the combined Egyptian and Greek forces could not penetrate and destroy the Persian stronghold in Memphis, giving the empire time to launch a counterattack.

This counterattack came in the form of an army led by Megabyzos who quashed the revolt and avenged the death of the king's uncle. Some scholars go on to speak of a revolt of Megabyzos, who was enraged at what he considered to be the dishonorable treatment of the revolutionaries. But Hoglund (1992, 119–27) does not value this account, which is found only in Ctesias.

In spite of this, the picture that emerges from the data is that of an empire that has problems on its western flank. The Egyptians had revolted, and the Greeks were looking for opportunities to weaken the Persians in this part of the world. The empire could use a strong friend to safeguard its interests, and the Palestine of Ezra and Nehemiah might have provided it. In answer to the question why the empire encouraged what amounted to a military strengthening of Jerusalem (by rebuilding the walls), Hoglund's reply that the city could serve as a garrison against Egypt and Greek interests makes good sense. It also explains the shift from the earlier negative attitude of Artaxerxes I at the beginning of his reign toward the rebuilding of the city (Ezra 4:17–22; see Hoglund 1992, 223). Persian use of local leaders to serve their cause is supported by the analogous case of Udjahorresnet, an Egyptian admiral, who served the interests of two Persian kings, Cambyses and Darius I. It is also likely that since the latter king supported Udjahorresnet to codify Egyptian law, the same motive may have been behind Artaxerxes' support for Ezra, whose main task was the elevation of Torah observance (see Provan, Long, and Longman 2003, 290).

LITERARY ANALYSIS

Genre

The books contain a number of earlier sources, most notably the memoirs of Ezra and Nehemiah (see below). But before taking a closer look at the parts, we will address the issue of the identification of the book as a whole.

With Eskenazi (1988, 7) and many others, we agree that Ezra-Nehemiah is history writing. This genre identification is to be read in the light of the description of biblical historiography found in this book's chapter 1 (Orientation; Historical Background). Eskenazi is correct when she goes on to emphasize the literary shaping of the book, but in our opinion this does not lessen the accuracy of the historical account.

This historical work is composed of a number of different sources that have their own generic shape. Letters, royal edicts, and lists, for instance, appear throughout the book. Most notable and attracting the most discussion are the first-person narrations of Ezra (Ezra 7–10; Neh. 8 [some add Neh. 9–10]) and Nehemiah (Neh. 1–7; sections of 12:27–43 and 13:4–31).

Both of these writings are called "Memoirs" in the literature, and they do bear a resemblance to this genre. A memoir is a first-person writing that is distinguished from autobiography in that "the memoirist writes of great events that he or she has observed or in which he or she has participated, whereas the autobiographer writes of the self who has observed and participated in the events" (Longman 1991, 42). Scholars have attempted an identification of the Nehemiah Memoir by comparing it to ancient Near Eastern royal inscriptions (so Mowinckel 1961) or Egyptian tomb inscriptions (von Rad 1964). Williamson offers the suggestion that both the Nehemiah and Ezra Memoirs were reports to the Persian court concerning activities in Jerusalem. Thus they are actually a "mixture of literary genres" (Williamson 1985, xxviii).

Structure

Howard (1993, 278) provides a rough outline based on the shift between first- and third-person narration in the book. It glosses over some of the fine points of the text but still is a helpful guide:

A Historical Review (Ezra 1–6)
Ezra's Memoirs, Part 1 (Ezra 7–10)
Nehemiah's Memoirs, Part 1 (Neh. 1–7)
Ezra's Memoirs, Part 2 (Neh. 8–10)
Nehemiah's Memoirs, Part 2 (Neh. 11–13)

But it is Eskenazi (1988, 38) who follows the story line of the book most carefully. She finds the terminology of the structuralist scholar Bremond useful for her purposes. What follows is a translation of her outline into a more accessible form:

I. The goal initiated: Cyrus's decree to build the house of God (Ezra 1:1–4)
II. The community builds the house of God (Ezra 1:5–Nehemiah 7:72)
   A. Introduction: The people prepare to return to the land (Ezra 1:5–6)

B. The community returns and rebuilds altar and temple in the midst of opposition (1:7–6:22)

C. Ezra and the people of God return to the land to build a community in the midst of the conflict surrounding intermarriage (Ezra 7:1–10:44)

D. Nehemiah returns to the land in order to rebuild the city wall in spite of opposition (Neh. 1:1–7:5)

E. Closure: The list of returnees (Nehemiah 7:6–72, which reiterates Ezra 2 and binds the whole together)

III. The goal reached: "The community celebrates the completion of the house of God according to Torah" (Neh. 7:73–13:31).

Style

At first blush, Ezra-Nehemiah appears rather uninteresting from a literary perspective. The abrupt changes from first person to third person, the innumerable lists, and the frequent letters seem tedious. At times these seem to obscure the plot and characterization.

But a deeper analysis of the book's subtle use of plot, characterization, and changing point of view reveals a depth and richness that grasps the reader's attention. (Eskenazi and Green are particularly helpful in literary matters.)

Space will permit only a brief description of two of these subtleties. The first is the easily noted shifts between third- and first-person narration. This may be described on a source-critical level; that is, the book incorporates two earlier written memoirs. But a more attentive study uncovers the effect of the combination of the two perspectives. The first-person speech gives a personal or subjective viewpoint; the omniscient third-person narration is objective and authoritative (Eskenazi 1988, 129–30). This insight permits comparison between the two viewpoints. Does the objective narrator affirm the perspective of the first-person speakers?

This study leads to the second literary subtlety, the contrastive characterization of Ezra and Nehemiah. In short, the omniscient narrator consistently affirms the viewpoint of Ezra while slightly distancing himself from that of Nehemiah. Not that Nehemiah is disdained by the narrator (some scholars overplay the contrast), but Nehemiah's bold, self-aggrandizing statements are often subdued by the narrator's assessment. This is important to observe because one of the purposes of the book is to downplay individual leaders in the interests of the entire community (see below).

The interplay of point of view, characterization, and plot contribute to the message of the book of Ezra-Nehemiah, and it is to that subject that we now turn.

A deeper analysis of the book's subtle use of plot, characterization, and changing point of view reveals a depth and richness that grasps the reader's attention.

THEOLOGICAL MESSAGE

Eskenazi does a masterful job of delineating three major themes in the book and then shows how they reverberate through the whole. These themes indicate that the time period of Ezra and Nehemiah witnessed a transformation from a time of elite leaders, narrow holiness, and oral authority to a time of community, spreading holiness, and the authority of written documents. Adopting the language of Hegel, she notes a move from a poetic age to a prosaic one. Admirably, she does not denigrate this transition but rather speaks of the sanctification of the prosaic (1988, 1).

First, we see a shift from leaders to community. The Old Testament specializes in charismatic individuals: Abraham, Moses, Samuel, David, and Daniel are just a handful of examples. Indeed, Ezra and Nehemiah are striking characters, but Eskenazi charts how these men are absorbed, Ezra willingly and Nehemiah reluctantly, into the community. It is the community that accomplishes the task of rebuilding the temple and wall of Jerusalem. It is the people who turn to the Lord in corporate allegiance at the end.

Second, holiness is no longer restricted to certain special places. This theme is especially clear when the temple is rebuilt. This is the goal of the return, and when the structure is finished and consecrated, we almost expect the book to end. However, the house of God is not built once the temple is finished (Ezra 6:15); it continues, and more of Jerusalem is built. When the walls are finished, they too are consecrated (not "dedicated," so TNIV, see Neh. 3:1) indicating that they were considered a part of a rebuilt "holy city" (Neh. 11:1). Once temple, city, and walls are rebuilt, then come the "grand opening" ceremonies (Neh. 8–13; see Eskenazi 1988, 57).

The third major theme of the book, according to Eskenazi's analysis, is the shift from oral to written authority. It is amazing to see the role of written documents in the book. Letters from kings initiate and stop action on both the level of actual events and the story. The most important written document, however, does not have human origin but is the Torah of Yahweh. The people rededicate themselves to this divinely given book at a great covenant renewal ceremony at the end of the book (Neh. 8–10).

While Eskenazi's analysis is compelling and rich, it does not exhaust the theological message of this profound book. Green (1993) notes that Ezra-Nehemiah is a book about the building of "two walls." Most obviously, we recognize "Nehemiah's wall," a wall that physically separates the people of God from their enemies, the unclean "Gentiles." On the other hand, "Ezra's wall," the law of God that it was his mission to teach, erected a spiritual boundary between Israel and all other people. In essence, Ezra's law, which included a strong emphasis on the prohibition of intermarriage, constituted a people fit to live within Nehemiah's walls. At the end of the book of Ezra, we have a holy people dwelling in a holy city.

APPROACHING THE NEW TESTAMENT

Ezra-Nehemiah has a surprising and, at first sight, awkward conclusion. It is almost as if Nehemiah 13 is a careless addition to the end of the book. After all, the climax of a holy people in a holy city has been reached and celebrated. The last chapter narrates a number of problems that Nehemiah had to handle.

One case involved the high priest Eliashib, who lent rooms in the temple to the non-Israelite Tobiah. Nehemiah had to throw him out in order to preserve the sanctity of the building (13:4–9). Also the city officials failed to provide for the Levites, who then left the temple for the fields. Once again Nehemiah had to intervene (vv. 10–13). In addition, the men of Judah were breaking the Sabbath (vv. 14–22). But perhaps most frightening was the recurrence of intermarriage. Green (1993, 214) points to the significant mention of Solomon in this unit (vv. 26–27). The question is, Will Israel survive just to repeat the sins of the past? Intermarriage dragged Solomon and the entire nation into a vortex of doom that led to the exile. Will the postexilic generation go the same way?

Thus the book of Ezra-Nehemiah concludes with an open question and a look to the future. Perfection, in a word, has not been reached (Eskenazi 1988, 126).

The New Testament takes us well beyond the world of Ezra-Nehemiah. In the words of Koch (1974, 197), "Ezra was realizing certain prophetic predictions in pre-eschatological steps which were different from eschatological perfections, and . . . he was using the Torah also as a book of promise." For instance, Ezra-Nehemiah attests to the expansion of holiness beyond the confines of the temple to include the whole city of Jerusalem. Nonetheless, there remained a strong demarcation of the holy and the secular, the clean and the unclean. It is Jesus Christ who tears down the "wall of separation." First of all, he tears apart the veil that separated the Holy of Holies from the rest of creation. Second, he demolishes the division of humanity that separated Jew from Gentile (Eph. 2:14–18).

CHAPTER FOURTEEN

ESTHER

In some respects the book of Esther may well be the most unusual book in the Old Testament. We ordinarily think of the Bible as preeminently a book revealing to us the nature of God, both through his attributes and through his deeds. Yet in the book of Esther God is not mentioned, nor is there reference to worshiping him through prayer or sacrifice. On its surface the book appears to be a thoroughly secular story of Jews who continue to live on in the Diaspora rather than identify with the restoration community back in Jerusalem. The account describes one more chapter in the recurring threats to the existence of the Jews and how that threat was met. Yet on closer inspection, as described below, the book is deeply involved with other chapters of biblical revelation.

The book has provoked a wide range of responses in the history of interpretation. On the one hand, the famous Jewish scholar Maimonides (AD 1135–1204) considered Esther second only to the Torah in importance. The opposite extreme is illustrated by Luther's famous statement that he was so hostile to Esther (and 2 Maccabees) "that I could wish they did not exist at all; for they judaize too greatly and have much pagan impropriety." Esther is not listed among the books in the Old Testament in the oldest canonical catalog (Bishop Melito). It is the only book of the Old Testament not found in the documents from Qumran, though this may reflect no more than an accident of discovery rather than rejection of its canonical status. The rabbis at Jamnia (c. AD 100) did discuss the canonical standing of the book, but more in an effort to justify the status quo, which received the book, than to decide the question of canonicity. Other sources, both Christian and Jewish, have questioned the canonical status of the book.

The history of the book's composition, its purpose, historicity, and theology have all been vigorously debated. Often those pericopes where the Bible is curiously silent become the impetus for apocryphal stories. Such is certainly the case with Esther: apocryphal additions (which are included in the Roman Catholic canon) remove the book's difficulties that arise from its failure to mention God or religious worship.

BIBLIOGRAPHY

Commentaries

J. G. **Baldwin,** *Esther: An Introduction and Commentary* (TOTC; InterVarsity Press, 1984); H. **Bardtke,** *Das Buch Esther* (*KAT*; Gütersloh: G. Mohn, 1963); A. **Berlin,** *Esther* (Philadelphia: JPS Publishing Company, 2001); R. W. **Bush,** *Ruth/Esther* (WBC; Dallas: Word, 1996); G. **Gerleman,** *Esther* (BKAT 21; Neukirchen-Vluyn: Neukirchener Verlag, 1970–73); K. **Jobes,** *Esther* (NIVAC; Zondervan, 1999); J. D. **Levenson,** *Esther* (OTL; Westminster John Knox, 1997); C. A. **Moore,** *Esther* (AB 7B; Doubleday, 1971); L. B. **Paton,** *A Critical and Exegetical Commentary on the Book of Esther* (ICC; T&T Clark, 1908); W. **Vischer,** *Esther* (Munich: Chr. Kaiser Verlag, 1937).

Monographs and Articles

B. W. **Anderson,** "The Place of the Book of Esther in the Christian Bible," *JR* 30 (1950): 32–43; S. B. **Berg,** *The Book of Esther: Motifs, Themes, and Structure* (SBLDS 44; Missoula: Scholars, 1979); E. **Bickerman,** *Four Strange Books of the Bible* (Shocken, 1967); D. J. A. **Clines,** *The Esther Scroll* (JSOTS 30; Sheffield: JSOT, 1984); W. **Dommerhausen,** *Die Estherrolle* (Stuttgart: Verlag Katholisches Bibelwerk, 1968); M. V. **Fox,** "The Structure of the Book of Esther," *Isaac Leo Seeligmann Volume* (Jerusalem: E. Rubinstein, 1983), 3:291–303; idem, *Character and Ideology in the Book of Esther* (Columbia: University of South Carolina Press, 1991); G. **Gerleman,** "Studien zu Esther," *Biblische Studien* 48; Neukirchener-Vluyn: Neukirchener Verlag, 1966); R. **Gordis,** "Religion, Wisdom and History in the Book of Esther," *JBL* 100 (1981): 359–88; idem, "Studies in the Esther Narrative," *JBL* 95 (1976): 43–58; W. W. **Hallo,** "The First Purim," *BA* 46 (1983): 19–26; B. W. **Jones,** "Two Misconceptions about the Book of Esther," *CBQ* 39 (1977): 171–81; idem, "The So-Called Appendix to the Book of Esther," *Semitics* 6 (1978): 36–43; J. A. **Loader,** "Esther as a Novel with Different Levels of Meaning," *ZAW* 90 (1978): 417–21; W. **McClarty,** "Esther," in *A Complete Literary Guide to the Bible,* ed. L. Ryken and T. Longman (Zondervan, 1993); A. R. **Millard,** "Persian Names in Esther and the Reliability of the Hebrew Text," *JBL* 96 (1977): 481–88; C. A. **Moore,** "Archaeology and the Book of Esther," *BA* 38 (1975): 62–79; W. H. **Shea,** "Esther and History," *AUSS* 14 (1976): 227–46; S. **Talmon,** "'Wisdom' in the Book of Esther," *VT* 13 (1963): 419–55; T. C. G. **Thornton,** "The Crucifixion of Haman and the Scandal of the Cross," *JTS* 37 (1986): 419–26; J. S. **Wright,** "The Historicity of the Book of Esther," in *New Perspectives on the Old Testament,* ed. J. B. Payne (Word, 1970), 37–47; E. **Yamauchi,** "The Archaeological Background of Esther," *BibSac* 137 (1980): 99–117; R. **Zadok,** "On the Historical Background of the Book of Esther," *BN* 24 (1984): 18–23.

OUTLINE

HISTORICAL BACKGROUND

The author of Esther has chosen to remain anonymous. The events the book records are set in the reign of Xerxes (486–465 BC), and the initial version of the story was probably written not long after that; the author's knowledge of Persian court life and the absence of Greek vocabulary favor a time before Alexander's conquests. Some scholars have argued for a later date, suggesting, for example, that the confrontation between Jew and Gentile in the book reflects the intense clash between Judaism and Hellenism in the Hasmonean period; the first historical reference to the book is from this period (2 Macc. 15:36, "Mordecai's day").

The purpose of the book in its present form is clearly to account for the origin of the Jewish festival of Purim (9:18–10:3). The name of the festival derives from the Akkadian word *pur*, "lot" (3:7), and refers to the lots cast by Haman.

As is typical in so much biblical scholarship, scholars have not been content with the book's explanation of its own origin, but have rather sought to read between the lines in order to recover some other inciting setting that produced a prototype of the book in a form later adapted by Jewish writers to their own purposes. A wide range of other etymologies have been suggested to explain the word *Purim*. Some scholars have suggested that the book represents Jewish historicizing of a Babylonian or Persian religious rite or festival; the names of Esther and Mordecai on this approach are associated with the Babylonian gods Ishtar and Marduk. Others regard the inciting occasion for the story as the conflict between the traditional religion of Babylon and the inauguration of the Persian cult of Mithra: Esther and Mordecai portray the religious struggle of the cults of Ishtar and Marduk with the religion of their Persian masters represented by Haman and Xerxes. Bickerman (1967, 171–240) called attention to many parallels between Esther and the *Arabian Nights* and considered Esther pure folklore.

Research into other explanations for the origin of the basic story is also tied to discussions of its compositional history. Numerous scholars have considered 9:20–10:3 a secondary expansion of the story and regard 9:18–19 as providing a more satisfactory conclusion. Jones (1978) argues, to the contrary, that 9:20–10:3 is not an appendix, but an integral part of the story, necessary to its symmetrical balance. Clines (1984) distinguishes five different stories: (1) a pre-Masoretic story; (2) a proto-Masoretic account without the appendix in 9:20–10:3; (3) the Masoretic account itself; (4) the later elaborations, which led to the LXX; and (5) the so-called alpha-text, which developed collateral to these in its own history stemming from the pre-Masoretic story. This alpha-text has often in the past been associated with the Lucianic recension. The LXX contains six major additions to the narrative: (1) the dream of Mordecai, (2) the edict of Artaxerxes, (3) the prayer of Mordecai, (4) the prayer of Esther, (5) another edict from Artaxerxes, and (6) an interpretation of Mordecai's dream with reference to Purim. While the Hebrew version of the story contains 163 verses, the LXX contains 270, though it is clear that the additions were never part of the original story.

Classical and cuneiform sources by and large demonstrate the author's familiarity with Persian mores and court life. Herodotus, a Greek historian (490–425 BC) portrays Xerxes as an ill-tempered, impatient monarch with a wandering eye for women (Yamauchi 1980, 104). Herodotus also confirms that the Persian monarch was advised by seven counselors (1:13–14; cf. Ezra 7:14). A cuneiform tablet from Borsippa near Babylon identifies one Marduka as a civil servant or minister at the court of Susa in the early years of Xerxes; some have identified this individual with Mordecai. Herodotus (3:125, 159; 4:43; cf. Est. 2:23; 6:4; 7:9; 8:7; 9:14, 25) describes hanging (impalement) as a means of execution under the Persians, and he confirms (1:136) the degree to which a large number of sons was prized (Est. 5:11; 9:7–10). Under the Persians, the property of a traitor reverted to the crown (Herodotus 3:128–29; Josephus, *Ant* 11:17; Est. 8:1). Excavations also confirm the lavish extent of the Persian palace.

On the other hand, the classical sources also present a number of problems with details in Esther. Esther was queen in the seventh to twelfth years of Xerxes' reign (see Levenson 1997, 23–7, though he does acknowledge that the author does have an extensive knowledge of the Persian empire). According to the Greek historians, Xerxes' wife was named Amestris; though various efforts have been made to identify her with either Vashti or Esther (see, for example, Wright 1970, and Shea 1976), this problem cannot be considered resolved. Persian queens, according to Herodotus (3:84), had to be chosen from one of seven

Persian families, a fact that would rule out the king's choice of a Jew; however, this objection overlooks the fact that Amestris herself was the daughter of Otanes, not from one of the seven families, and that Darius too had married outside those families (Wright 1970, 38). There are a number of other difficulties in reconciling details of the book with extrabiblical sources; however, these are all comparatively minor and even border on pettifogging.

Table 10
Chronological Notes in Esther

Reference	Year/Month/Day	Day of Xerxes Event
1:3	3/–/–	Xerxes holds his banquets
2:16	7/10/–	Esther goes to Xerxes
3:7	12/1/–	Haman casts the lots
3:12	13/1/13	Haman's decree issued
3:13	13/12/13	Effective date of decree
8:9	13/3/23	Mordecai's decree issued
8:12	13/12/13	Effective date of new decree

LITERARY STRUCTURE

Genre

In recent decades the genre of Esther has been a focal point of study. Esther has traditionally been read as a straightforward historical narrative; this understanding is reflected in Esther's position among the historical books in the LXX and Christian Bibles. Many scholars have identified the book instead as a novella, a piece of short prose historical fiction. Recent research has also concentrated on the relation of the narrative to Wisdom Literature. Talmon (1963) notes a number of its features that are more characteristic of Wisdom Literature: (1) the anthropocentric concerns of the book and the lack of much attention paid to God, covenant, or cult; (2) the orientation to practical issues here and now as opposed to recitations of the past or eschatological expectation more characteristic of other biblical literature; and (3) the lack of specific concern with distinctively national motifs such as the land and the particularities of Jewish law. Some motifs in the story (such as the danger of alcohol abuse by kings, proper conduct in the presence of kings, or the danger of pride) also reflect themes dear to Proverbs (Prov. 14:35; 16:14–15, 18; 19:12; 20:2; 24:21; 25:6; 29:4; 31:4). In the Hebrew Bible Esther is found in the Writings, the third and final part of the Old Testament, which contains primarily the poetic and wisdom books; Esther's place in this group could reflect an awareness in antiquity of its proximity to Wisdom Literature.

A number of false dichotomies often seem to cloud discussion at this point. The evidence from the author's considerable literary skill and his use of wisdom motifs is often viewed as in tension with the historicity of the story. Yet anyone recognizes that a historian or author always chooses data in terms of the perspective from which he writes; the fact that Esther as a narrative is carefully crafted does not unavoidably entail that the detail of the narrative is false or created from whole cloth. Nor does the presence of wisdom themes invalidate historical foundation; it is a truism that "we learn from history." Yet on the other hand, one must recognize that biblical writers may of necessity have engaged in a certain amount of literary mimesis to lend color and interest to a story like Esther. This narrator clearly presents himself as chronicling actual events (2:23; 10:2–3). Thus, while appreciating the wisdom motifs within the narrative, it would probably be wrong to view Esther as a kind of extended parable or as a "historicized wisdom tale."

Two recent studies of the Esther story have concluded that the author was modeling his narrative on earlier events in Israel's history. Gerleman (1966) noted a number of parallels between Esther and the Exodus account: both stories take place in foreign courts, involve threats against the Jews, include accounts of deliverance and vengeance against enemies, and are followed by the institution of an annual festival. The parallels at a macrolevel are joined with parallels in details: both Esther and Moses were adopted (2:7; Ex. 2:10); both concealed their identity as Jews (2:10, 20; Ex. 2:6–10); and in both narratives the Amalekites are foes of Israel (3:1; Ex. 17:8–16). While these parallels are striking, there are numerous ways in which Esther and the Exodus narrative do not provide good parallels. Berg (1979, 6–7) argues that the following considerations undercut Gerleman's thesis: the two books manifest a quite different attitude taken to the foreign monarchs: Moses does not work through the administration, but against it; whereas the goal of the exodus narrative is escape from foreign dominion, no such desire to escape Susa surfaces in Esther. In Esther the Jews save the life of the king, whereas in the Exodus account they are involved in the death of the pharaoh's son. The fact that Moses' identity was concealed is far less central to the story than the same fact in the Esther narrative.

Berg (1979, 123–42) proposes instead that the author of Esther was deliberately drawing parallels with the Joseph story (Gen. 37–48). She calls attention to the verbal parallels between 6:11 and Genesis 41:42–43; 3:4 and Genesis 39:10; 8:6 and Genesis 44:34; 2:3–4 and Genesis 41:34–37. The stories have similar structures: both concern Jewish heroes who rise to prominence in a foreign court and become the means by which the Jews are saved; both put the Jewish heroes in contact with royal officials; in both stories the disturbed sleep of the monarch results in the promotion of the hero (6:1–3; Gen. 41); the reward of both Joseph and Mordecai includes a gift of garments and a ride through the city accompanied by a herald proclaiming royal favor (6:7–11; Gen. 41:42–43); both Joseph and Esther reveal their Jewish identities in a banquet scene (7:1–6;

Gen. 45). Yet as with her own criticisms of Gerleman's proposal, various of the parallels Berg suggests are not compelling: there is no personal enemy corresponding to Haman threatening the Jews in the Joseph story; Joseph reveals his identity to his brothers, not to a king or in the presence of an enemy as Esther does. One would expect scenes of royal reward and investiture to have elements in common, so that the parallels between 6:7–11 and Genesis 41:42–43 may not be the product of conscious imitation. As in the case with Gerleman, the parallels Berg suggests are striking and informative, but probably insufficient to establish conscious imitation by the author of Esther.

Literary Technique

The writer of Esther took considerable delight in using irony, satire, and recurring motifs in writing his account. The resulting blend is a gem of a little story.

The author's delight in *irony* is shown by his frequent reports of reversals of fortune (Jobes's commentary does an outstanding job pointing out the use of irony in the book). Particular actions or states of affairs often result in the opposite of the expected result, a theme specifically stated in 9:1, 22, 25. This literary device is called *peripety* (cf. Berg 1979, 104–6). Haman, who intends to destroy Mordecai and the Jews, ultimately destroys himself along with his own family. The gallows Haman erects for Mordecai becomes the instrument of his own demise. Haman's edict would have plundered the wealth of the Jews, but the story ends with Haman's wealth in Jewish hands. Haman, who writes the script for what he perceives would be his own glorification, becomes the royal agent to effect the glorification of Mordecai (6:1–11). Haman for a time possessed the royal signet, but it eventually would be Mordecai's to do with as he saw fit (3:10; 8:8).

Alongside these items are numerous smaller ironies within the story. Ahasuerus intends to show his power, but shows instead that he cannot control his wife (Est. 1); he intends to punish her by not allowing her to appear in his presence and so officially sanctions her refusal to appear. The unrewarded merit of Mordecai contrasts with the unmerited reward of Haman (2:21–3:2). Haman conceals the identity of his intended victims, unaware that the identity of one victim has also been concealed (2:10, 20; 3:8–9). Haman's rage is provoked when Mordecai does not rise in his presence (5:9), an ironic contrast to his earlier refusal to bow (3:2–6). The drinking of Haman and the king forms an ironic contrast to the fasting of the Jews (3:15; 4:1–3, 15–16). A decree initially celebrated with drinking (3:15) will ultimately bear fruit when Haman and the king drink together again (7:1–2).

Along with the frequent use of irony, the author appears to take particular delight in *satire* directed toward the Persians, and Persian men in particular (Clines 1984, 31–22). The king issues a decree that men should rule in their houses when he himself is unable to master his own wife (1:12, 21–22). The ruler of a vast empire is bested in the battle of the sexes by both of his wives. Xerxes himself seems befuddled by Vashti's refusal (1:15), and the royal advisors likewise fear the emergence of a new feminism in the Persian empire (1:17–18). An entire bureaucracy surrounds the choice of a royal bedmate (2:1–14), while shrewd and strong women effectively control the actions of their husbands. Esther effects decisions of state single-handedly; Zeresh both instructs her husband and speaks with insight and authority to the wounded male vanity of Haman (5:14; 6:13). The king who wanted to make a spectacle of his wife (1:11) ends up making a spectacle of himself (1:12; 2:1–2). The vaunted monarch whose law could not be changed (1:19; 8:8) is finessed and manipulated, the law notwithstanding.

> *The story of Esther derives much of its literary beauty from the recurring motifs of which it is woven.*

The story of Esther derives much of its literary beauty from the *recurring motifs* of which it is woven. Drinking and banqueting constitute one of the important themes in the book; important turns in the plot are ordinarily associated with banqueting (1:3, 5, 8, 9; 2:18; 5:4–5, 8, 12; 6:14; 7:8; 8:17; 9:17–19, 22), and in one case its opposite, fasting (4:3, 15–17). Items of apparel are likewise an important motif (1:11; 2:17; 3:10; 4:1–4; 5:1; 6:8–11; 8:8, 15). The book shows a pervasive concern with law and legality (1:13, 15, 19; 2:1; 3:8–9, 14; 4:11, 16; 8:8, 13; 9:31–32; cf. Clines 1984, 16–22). Conflicts explicit and implicit are found throughout: between Xerxes and Vashti, between Xerxes' power and his inability to control, between women competing for his attention, between the king and those seeking his death (2:21–23), between Haman and Mordecai, between the Jews and their enemies (Clines 1984, 10–11).

The writer also appears to delight in items that come in pairs. Esther is twice reported to have concealed her identity (2:10, 20); three groups of banquets in the beginning, middle, and end of the story come in pairs (two given by Xerxes, two by Esther, and the double celebration of Purim). There are two lists of the king's servants (1:10–14), two gatherings of the women (2:8, 19), two houses for the women (2:12–14), two fasts (4:3, 16), two consultations by Haman with his wife and friends (5:14; 6:13), two unscheduled appearances by Esther before the king (5:2; 8:3), two investitures of Mordecai (6:7–11; 8:15), two times that Haman's face is covered (6:12; 7:8), two references to Haman's sons (5:11; 9:6–14), two appearances of Harbona (1:10; 7:9), two references to the subsiding of the king's anger (2:1; 7:10), two references to the irrevocability of the Persian laws (1:19; 8:8), two days for the Jews to take vengeance (9:5–15), two letters instituting the commemoration of Purim (9:20–32). Reporting such "duplications" appears to be a favorite compositional technique for the writer.

THEOLOGICAL MESSAGE

The purpose of the canonical Esther is clearly related to its desire to account for the origin of Purim. But what does the book tell us about God? How does the book relate to the rest of the Bible?

Divine Sovereignty

These may seem like strange questions in reference to a book that does not so much as mention God. Yet here we encounter an aspect of the genius of the author of Esther. His story is built on an accumulating series of seeming coincidences, all of which are indispensable when the story reaches its moment of peak dramatic tension at the beginning of chapter 6. How "lucky" the Jews were that Esther was so attractive, that she was chosen over other possible candidates, that Mordecai overheard that assassination plot, that a record of Mordecai's report of the assassination plans was written in the royal chronicles, that Esther had concealed her identity, that the king would have seen her without having called for her, that the king could not sleep that night, that he asked to have the annals read, that the scribe read from that incident several years earlier concerning Mordecai, that the king was wide awake enough to inquire as to whether he had rewarded Mordecai. . . . Luck indeed! What the writer of Esther has done is to give us a story in which the main actor is not so much as mentioned—the presence of God is implied and understood throughout the story, so that these mounting coincidences are but the by-product of his rule over history and his providential care for his people. It is an extraordinary piece of literary genius that this author wrote a book that is about the actions and rule of God from beginning to end, and yet that God is not named on a single page of the story. For Jews at the author's own time, and for all readers of the story in the centuries and millennia since, this story of divine providence and election has provided a message of comfort and assurance. God's actions in history may be hidden; they are certainly not transparent to all. Yet in spite of our inability to understand divine purpose in all that transpires, none of it is beyond the reach of his hand.

This doctrine of divine sovereignty is fundamental to the book of Esther, but it is not a kind of fatalism. For where God's actions and purposes are not transparent, the importance of human obedience and faithfulness becomes the more apparent. In this respect, Esther 4:13–14 joins a number of other biblical texts that wonderfully integrate human responsibility and divine providence (e.g., Joel 2:32 [MT 3:5]; Matt. 26:24; Acts 2:23; 3:18–19).

Unfinished Business

The book of Esther is not a curious island in the midst of the biblical text, isolated from any contact with other events in the history of redemption recorded there. Quite to the contrary, the story of Esther is deeply involved with other events of redemptive history, most particularly with the ongoing conflict between Israel and the Amalekites. The genealogies of Haman and Mordecai introduce this conflict: Mordecai is identified as a Benjamite from the clan of Kish (2:5), the father of Saul; Haman is a descendant of Agag (3:1), the Amalekite king against whom Saul had fought (1 Sam. 15). From the time of the exodus there had been a history of conflict between Israel and the Amalekites;

Moses had said, "The LORD will be at war with the Amalekites from generation to generation" (Ex. 17:16). Israel was charged with "blotting out the memory of Amalek from under heaven" (Deut. 25:17–19; Ex. 17:14; 1 Sam. 15:2–3).
Intermittent conflict with the Amalekites dots the biblical record (Judg. 3:13;
5:14; 6:3, 33; 7:12; 10:12; 1 Sam. 27:8; 30:13–18; cf. Num 24:20). Saul had been
instructed by God to destroy the Amalekites (1 Sam. 15), but he disobeyed God;
this incident between Saul, Agag, and the Amalekites would ultimately become
the reason for Saul's own defeat and the loss of his dynasty (1 Sam. 28:18). An
Amalekite would later claim that he had killed Saul (2 Sam. 1:8). Israel was still
found fighting Amalekites in the days of Hezekiah (1 Chron. 4:43).

This conflict between the descendants of Saul and Agag is a continuation of
the age-old antipathy between Israel and the Amalekites. Numerous details of
the story of Esther can be understood on this background. It is this longstand-
ing enmity between Israel and the Amalekites that accounts for Mordecai's
unwillingness to bow before Haman. This same enmity also explains why
Haman, whose anger was originally directed only at Mordecai, would broaden
the object of his wrath and seek to destroy all the Jews, once he had learned that
Mordecai was a Jew (3:5–6). Haman's decree for the total destruction of all Jews
(3:13) is in effect his effort to do to Israel what Saul had failed to do to Amalek
(1 Sam. 15:3). When the tables are turned in Esther and the Jews are authorized
to take vengeance on their enemies, the Jews do not plunder the wealth of their
victims (9:10, 15); the Jews at the time of Mordecai would not make the same
mistake as Saul (1 Sam. 15:9–19). Israel's having rest from her enemies is tied to
the destruction of the Amalekites (Deut. 25:19); with this task completed, the
Jews enjoy "relief from their enemies" (Est. 9:22).

Much of the book of Esther is taken up with the issue of the relationship of
Jew and Gentile. This author wrote to a postexilic audience at a time when Israel
had long known subservience to a variety of world powers: Assyria, Babylon,
and Persia had held dominion, and others were yet to follow. Our author affirms
that Jews need not be servile in a world dominated by Gentile powers and that
it remained possible to live rich lives while remaining loyal to Judaism. One
readily appreciates why the book of Esther has remained so important in
Judaism: in the face of a history of anti-Semitic pogroms, persecution, and the
Holocaust, the book of Esther voices the confidence that "deliverance for the
Jews will arise" (4:14) and that the nation will endure because the electing purpose of God will not fail.

APPROACHING THE NEW TESTAMENT

Events in Susa threatened the continuity of God's purposes in redemptive history. For Christian readers what is at stake in the book of Esther is not only the
continued existence of the Jewish people but also the appearance of the redeemer

Messiah. Here in a distant city hundreds of miles and several centuries removed from events in Bethlehem, God still providentially ruled the course of history and brought it steadily to the appearance of his own Son, who would break down that barrier between Jew and Gentile (Gal. 3:28).

CHAPTER FIFTEEN

JOB

Suffering is at the heart of the book of Job. Since all men and women know the experience of suffering, the book has universal appeal. Its message cuts across time and culture. More specifically, the main character of the book suffers though he apparently is not the cause of his suffering. His physical ailments, accordingly, are compounded by mental anguish: "Why me? What have I done to deserve this fate?"

The book thus raises one of the most perplexing questions facing men and women: Are God's ways just? This is the question of theodicy. However, although the book raises the issue, does it really answer it with anything more than a simple and implied affirmative?

Job is both deeply moving and incredibly complex. It is one of the most difficult books of the Old Testament to translate and thus also to interpret.

BIBLIOGRAPHY

Commentaries

F. I. **Andersen,** *Job* (TOTC; InterVarsity Press, 1976); D. J. A. **Clines,** *Job 1–20* (WBC 17; Word, 1989); F. **Delitzsch,** *Job* (repr. Eerdmans, 1975); E. **Dhorme,** *A Commentary on the Book of Job* (Thomas Nelson, 1984 [orig. 1926]); S. R. **Driver** and G. B. **Gray,** *The Book of Job* (ICC; T. & T. Clark, 1921); R. **Gordis,** *The Book of Job: Commentary, New Translation, Special Studies* (New York: Jewish Theological Seminary, 1978); N. C. **Habel,** *The Book of Job* (OTL; Westminster, 1985); J. E. **Hartley,** *The Book of Job* (NICOT; Eerdmans, 1988); J. G. **Janzen,** *Job* (Interp; John Knox, 1990); R. E. **Murphy,** *Wisdom Literature: Job, Proverbs, Ruth, Canticles, Ecclesiastes, Esther* (FOTL 13; Eerdmans, 1981); M. H. **Pope,** *Job* (AB 15; Doubleday, 1965); H. H. **Rowley,** *Job* (NCB; Eerdmans, 1970).

Monographs and Articles

J. **Barr,** "The Book of Job and Its Modern Interpreters," *BJRL* 54 (1971–72): 28–46; D. J. A. **Clines,** "The Arguments of Job's Three Friends," in *Art and Meaning:*

Rhetoric in Biblical Literature, ed. D. J. A. Clines et al. (JSOTS 19; Sheffield: JSOT, 1982): 215–29; J. **Curtis,** "On Job's Response to Yahweh," *JBL* 98 (1979): 497–511; W. W. **Hallo** and K. L. **Younger,** *Context of Scripture* (Leiden: Brill Academic, 2003); W. G. **Lambert,** *Babylonian Wisdom Literature* (Oxford, 1960); L. **Newell,** "Job, Repentant or Rebellious?" (Th.M. thesis: Westminster Theological Seminary, 1983); C. A. **Newsom,** *The Book of Job: A Contest of Moral Imaginations* (Oxford, 2003); D. A. **Robertson,** *Linguistic Evidence in Dating Early Hebrew Poetry* (SBLDS 3; Missoula: Society of Biblical Literature, 1972); C. **Westermann,** *The Structure of the Book of Job,* trans. C. Muenchow (Fortress, 1981); P. **Zerafa,** *The Wisdom of God in the Book of Job* (Rome: Herder, 1978); B. **Zuckerman,** *Job the Silent* (Oxford, 1991).

HISTORICAL BACKGROUND

Date and Authorship

The book itself names no author and claims no definite date for its composition. It is therefore an anonymous work; any assertion about the author or date can only be inferred from the external evidence of the book.

The predominant scholarly opinion is that the book of Job is the result of a long process (for different views, see Zerafa 1978, 29–54). Most scholars believe that the dialogues (Job 3–31) form the basis of the book. At a later point an older prose folktale was divided and used as a frame. Some of these scholars also argue that the speeches of Elihu and Yahweh and the poem to wisdom (chap. 28) were even later additions. There is actually very little agreement among the scholarly community as to what is original to the book and what was added and when (see Analysis of Structure below).

Conservative biblical scholars have a tendency to treat the book as an original literary whole, and some (Archer, *SOTI,* 464) are ready to cite the early Jewish tradition that the book was either authored or rewritten by Moses. This early date accords with the belief that a historical book is more likely to be reliable when it was written close to the event it describes. Since the book of Job is set in an early period, it is easier for some to believe it was also written early.

Other equally conservative scholars, however, have dated the book to the Solomonic period (Young, *IOT*) or the eighth century (Hartley 1988) or have simply left the date open. The latter seems the wisest course in the light of the lack of evidence.

Historical Period

While the date of composition is shrouded in mystery, there are some indications that guide us in setting the events of the book. Nevertheless, the historical background provides no firm clues for the date of composition. Driver and Gray (1921, lxvi) state it well: "Since the author's imagination extends to the setting of the poem, it is a mistake to infer the age of the *writer* from the circumstances of the *hero* of the book."

The plot is definitely set in or before the patriarchal period. Job is a Gentile patriarch much like Abraham. Job's great wealth is measured in terms of the number of cattle in his possession and servants in his employ (Job 1:3; 42:12). He is also the head of a large family for whom he serves as priest much as Abraham did for his family. For instance, Job offers sacrifices (1:5), an act unthinkable after the formal priesthood was established at Sinai. Furthermore, Job's age exceeds those of the patriarchs. He lived 140 years after his restoration (42:16).

Most telling is that Job is a non-Israelite. Uz, while not definitely located, is clearly not within the boundaries of Israel (Gen. 10:23; Lam. 4:21; Clines 1989, 10–11). In terms of the progress of redemption, Job is best understood as having lived before the Abrahamic covenant, which narrows the covenant community to a particular family.

The evidence, as mentioned above, situates the plot but not the time of composition of the book. There are some indications, none of them certain, that the book was written rather late in the history of Israel. Many want to argue from the lateness of the language of Job that the book was late. This line of argumentation, though, is quite precarious. There is no reason to doubt that, on occasion at least, the book may have been periodically updated. In any case, the evidence is so ambiguous that a formidable case has been put forward that the language is actually quite early, though not as early as Moses (Robertson 1972).

Some of the religious ideas of the book are more likely to have appeared late in Israel's history. While it is wrong, on the one hand, to subscribe to a rigid evolutionary view of the development of religious ideas in the Old Testament (à la Wellhausen), it is also true that the Bible does slowly unfold truth as the history of redemption progresses. The developed angelology of the book is more likely to have come from a later period of Israel's history.

In conclusion, while the setting of the book is without a doubt early, the date of composition is unknown. Fortunately, nothing significant is at stake in our lack of knowledge of an author or a date of composition for the book. (For the historicity of Job, see Genre below.)

LITERARY ANALYSIS

The type of literature of the book of Job does have precursors in the ancient Near East, but it is nonetheless unique in many ways. It is a book that has deeply influenced Western literature through the ages and has itself captured the attention of literary critics.

An analysis of the book's structure will lead to a look at its Near Eastern literary background and its genre.

Structure

The structure of the book as it now stands provides a clear outline:

Job 1–2	Prose prologue that introduces the characters and plot
Job 3–31	Job's dialogues with his three "friends"
Job 3	Job's lament
Job 4–27	Three cycles of dialogues
Job 28	The poem on divine wisdom
Job 29–31	Job's last speech
Job 32–37	Elihu's monologue
Job 38–42:6	Yahweh speaks from the whirlwind
Job 42:7–17	The prose epilogue that draws the action to a close

Analysis of Structure

It is important to elaborate a bit regarding this structure for two reasons. In the first place, the literary integrity of the book has been questioned throughout the modern period of biblical criticism. Some of the more serious of these objections need to be addressed. More importantly, however, it is in the dynamic of the structure of the book that its genre and message may be readily seen.

The Prologue (1–2). The book of Job has a sandwich structure. It begins with a prose preamble, continues with poetic dialogue, and ends with a prose conclusion. The beginning and end are here called the prose frame. We will return to the epilogue later, but the critical issues associated with both will be dealt with in this section since they are so closely intertwined.

Some scholars have argued that the prose frame is the oldest of the various parts of the book of Job. Originally it was a simple folk tale that told the story of a man who was tested by God but remained faithful to him and as a result was rewarded with material blessings. Out of this story grew the present book.

Conservative scholars such as F. I. Andersen have shown that the present form of the prose sections presuppose the dialogues and Yahweh's response. After all, the epilogue begins "after the LORD had said these things to Job" and mentions the three friends. By contrast, those who believe that the prose story was originally independent respond that such verses are the result of "late redaction." By having the redactor handy, however, it is impossible to disprove or to prove the hypothesis that the prose section was originally independent of the poetic.

It is equally impossible to prove their original unity by means of the logical coherence of the story. It is possible that the smooth narrative flow from prologue through body to epilogue is the result of a long literary history or the result of single authorship. What is important is the function of the prologue and epilogue in the canonical shape of the book. Throughout the book there is a coherent theological message that runs from its prologue to the epilogue.

The prologue opens the narrative by introducing the main characters and the setting. It initiates the plot by raising the problem that needs a resolution: Job's suffering despite his apparent innocence. The prologue also takes the reader behind the scenes into the very council chamber of God. We know what the characters do not; we know that Job is suffering as a test of his faithfulness to God.

Job's Dialogue with His Three "Friends" (Job 3–31). *Job's lament (Job 3).* The prologue introduces Job's three friends at the end. However, before they speak, Job begins with the monologue in the form of a lament. He here bemoans his fate, even wondering why he was born. The form of this chapter is a lament similar in mood and structure to the individual laments found in the Psalter (Westermann).

The three cycles of dialogue (Job 4–27). The poetic nature of the dialogues is a signal that we are not reading transcripts of the conversation that took place between Job and his three friends. People in ancient times did not speak in poetic form to one another any more than we do today.

The highly literary nature of the dialogues is revealed by their structure. There are three cycles, in each of which one of the friends addresses Job and then Job responds to each one in turn. The order is always Eliphaz, Bildad, then Zophar.

Table 11
Speech Cycles in Job

First Cycle	Second Cycle	Third Cycle*
Eliphaz (4–5)	Eliphaz (15)	Eliphaz (22)
Job (6–7)	Job (16–17)	Job (23–24)
Bildad (8)	Bildad (18)	Bildad (25)
Job (9–10)	Job (19)	Job (26:1–27:12)
Zophar (11)	Zophar (20)	Zophar (27:13–23)**
Job (12–14)	Job (21)	Job (28–31)

*The friends' speeches get much shorter in the last cycle, reflecting the fact that the three are, we might say, running out of steam.

**For Zophar's place in the third cycle, see Zerafa (1–28).

Note that at the end of the third cycle Bildad's speech seems truncated; Zophar lacks a speech, and Job says things that simply contradict everything else he says (27:13–23). The third cycle probably suffers from an error in textual transmission (see extended discussion in Zerafa 1978) in that Job's words in 27:13–23 are either a part of the Bildad speech or the missing Zophar speech. Even with this minor textual correction, however, the short speeches of the third cycle complete the process that was begun in the second—that is, a rapid short-ening of the speeches. In this way, the dialogue communicates that the three friends ran out of arguments against Job. This literary device leads nicely to the speech of the frustrated Elihu (chaps. 32–37).

The three friends represent the age-old wisdom of retribution theology. In their case, however, it has become quite rigid and mechanical. God blesses the righteous; he curses the wicked. If so, then if Job suffers, he must be a sinner in need of repentance (4:7–11; 11:13–20).

Job reacts strongly against this line of reasoning. He is suffering, but not because of his sin. Job nowhere argues that he is totally without sin. He agrees with Bildad that no one can be righteous before God (9:2), but he questions whether he can get justice from God. He directly counters the wisdom of his friends in 9:21–24, and in this context he utters the bold words "He destroys both the blameless and the wicked."

At the heart of the debate between Job and his three friends is the question, Who is wise? Who has the correct insight into Job's suffering? Both Job and the friends set themselves up as sources of wisdom and ridicule the wisdom of the other (11:12; 12:1–3, 12; 13:12; 15:1–13). As we will see, this question, "Who is wise?" dominates the whole book.

The poem on divine wisdom (Job 28). In chapter 28 Job has a moment of insight as he responds to Zophar's speech (reconstructed from 27:13–23). In one of the most moving poems in the Old Testament, Job anticipates the con-clusion of the book by ascribing all wisdom to God.

While the beauty and power of the poem are universally recognized, its place in the book has been debated vigorously. The poem appears intrusive to those who demand a strict logical order to Job's thought. That is, he here bows before God's superior wisdom but then complains again in the following three chapters. The final resolution requires God to speak from the whirlwind.

Nevertheless, even those who deny the originality of the chapter often ascribe its authorship to the same person who wrote the dialogues, but they sug-gest that it was written later in his life and added later.

The problem is not with the book of Job but with the insistence on a logical flow of thought. Job suffers. In chapter 28 he has a moment of insight, but under the burden of his suffering, this soon passes and gives way to depression once again.

Job's last speech (Job 27–31). In Job's last words before the momentous con-clusion he broods on how things were in the past when he enjoyed God's bless-ings (29). He bemoans his present suffering and complains that God has turned a deaf ear toward him (30:20). He appeals to God once again, declaring that he is blameless and does not deserve the suffering that has come upon him.

Elihu's Monologue (Job 32–37). At this point, Elihu steps in. Whereas the three friends represented the wisdom of the elders of the time, Elihu is instead the brash young man who thinks he has all the answers. He has waited patiently out of respect for age, expecting the three friends to resolve the issue with Job; but they have failed, and he can no longer remain silent (32:6–9). He cannot stand to see Job complacent in his pride (v. 2). In essence, he sets himself up as still another wise man (33:33).

But in spite of his claim that he has something new to say (32:14), he comes back to the same old theology of retribution: Job suffers because he has sinned (34:11, 25–27, 37).

Two factors contribute to the common critical contention that the Elihu monologue is not original to the story. The first is that, while the three friends are addressed by God in the conclusion, Elihu is absent. As Barr has insightfully commented, however, God may be ignoring Elihu as insignificant, in effect putting the brash young man in his place. The other objection to the theory that the monologue is a later addition is the fact that he says nothing new. But that is precisely the point. Human wisdom has run out; it is time for God to take the stage.

Yahweh's Speech and Job's Response (Job 38–42:6). Throughout the dialogues, Job has hoped for an interview with God (Job 23:2–7). He finally gets his wish as God appears to him in the form of a storm. The stormlike form of God's appearance is an indication that he is coming in judgment (Pss. 18, 29; Nahum 1).

Job had hoped for a divine interview in order to learn why he was suffering. Significantly, God never directly answers that question except to rebuke Job for casting aspersions on his divine reputation (Job 40:8): "Would you discredit my justice? Would you condemn me to justify yourself?"

Instead of directly justifying himself, God answers another question, that of the source of wisdom. As we have seen, this issue has been smoldering under the surface throughout the book. Now God provides the definitive answer: He alone is wise.

His first words from the storm set Job's wisdom in its place and introduce the next few chapters as God asks Job a series of questions that only the Creator could possibly answer:

> Who is this that obscures my plans
>   with words without knowledge?
> Prepare to defend yourself;
>   I will question you,
>   and you shall answer me. (38:2–3)

The questions that follow demonstrate God's full knowledge and control of the natural order that he created and contrast this with Job's ignorance. The implication is that the same is true for the moral order as well. God knows, but Job is ignorant.

This conclusion to the questions of the source of wisdom is punctuated by a series of rhetorical questions that run through the divine speeches and ask about the source of wisdom more explicitly. Job 38:36–37 is illustrative (see also 39:13–18, 26):

> Who gives the ibis wisdom about the flooding of the Nile,
>   or gives the rooster understanding of when to crow?
> Who has the wisdom to count the clouds?

Job recognizes the power of God's speech and responds humbly and repentantly. He submits himself to the Almighty God of the universe and his will.

Epilogue (Job 42:7–17). The epilogue brings the story to a happy close. Job is reconciled with God and his fortune is restored to him. God blesses him and allows him to live a long life.

Job found favor in God's eyes because, though he grew impatient with God, he did not "curse God and die" nor did he give in to the facile arguments of the friends. When confronted by God, Job appropriately responded with repentance and submission. As a result, he became an intercessor for his friends, who had advocated a false wisdom of mechanical retribution.

LITERARY BACKGROUND

For two reasons it is not surprising to find other Near Eastern writings that bear some similarities to the book of Job. In the first place, Job is Wisdom Literature, and wisdom has an international flavor (Murphy 1981, 9–12). In the second place, suffering, and particularly suffering in relationship to one's piety, is an important and difficult question to all religious systems, not just that of the Bible.

It is possible to cite analogous texts from Sumer, Egypt, Babylonia, Ugarit, and India (Andersen 1976, 23–32). Rather than taking an exhaustive look at a large number of these, we will concentrate on the Babylonian texts as illustrative of the similarities and differences between Job and the literature of other Near Eastern cultures.

The oldest of the comparable Babylonian texts is called *Ludlul bēl nēmeqi* ("I will praise the Lord of wisdom" found in COS, 1:486–92) and is often referred to as the "Babylonian Job." The main character of the story, Šubši-mešre-Sakkan, is a sufferer who complains about his plight because he has been blameless in his devotion to god and king. The form of the book is a monologue, and the focus is on his restoration by Marduk. He never really questions the gods about his adversity. According to Lambert (1960, 21–62), who provides an excellent English translation, the text was written during the Kassite period in the middle of the second millennium BC.

The second Babylonian text is later, probably written about 1000 BC. It is commonly called the "Babylonian Theodicy" (COS, 1:492–5; Lambert 1960,

63–91). In form, it is a dialogue between a sufferer and a friend who represents the orthodox piety of Babylon. The sufferer questions the justice of the gods. The friend cautions him against blasphemy, but in the end comes around to the view that the gods made humanity perverse and

> . . . they harm a poor man like a thief,
> They lavish slander upon him and plot his murder,
> Making him suffer every evil like a criminal, because he has no
>   protection.
> Terrifyingly they bring him to his end, and extinguish him like a flame.
>   (lines 284–86)

In the light of these and similar texts, Job is not the first book written that addresses the question, Why do the righteous suffer? That question, however, is so pervasive that there is no need to posit any kind of actual connection between the Israelite and ancient Near Eastern exemplars. The author of Job may have known about the Babylonian texts, but we cannot be certain. In any case, Job is unique in so many ways.

Andersen (1976, 32) stated it well:

> Job stands far above its nearest competitors, in the coherence of its sustained treatment of the theme of human misery, in the scope of its many-sided examination of the problem, in the strength and clarity of its defiant moral monotheism, in the characterization of the protagonists, in the heights of its lyrical poetry, in its dramatic impact, and in the intellectual integrity with which it faces the "unintelligible burden" of human existence. In all this Job stands alone. Nothing we know before it provided a model, and nothing since, including its numerous imitations, has risen to the same heights. Comparison only serves to enhance the solitary greatness of the book of Job.

Genre

The Book of Job Is Unique. The above discussion of the structure and literary background of the book helps toward a genre identification. What kind of book is Job? This question is difficult because, as we have seen, there is nothing precisely like it.

In terms of content, the book could be called a theodicy, a justification of God's way in the world. How can God be great and loving and allow an innocent man to suffer? But if it is a theodicy, it raises the question without providing the expected answer. God's response is that the answer is beyond the ken of men and women.

Perhaps a better designation of the genre of the book is "wisdom debate." This describes both its form and the content (Zerafa). At the heart of the book is the question of the source of wisdom (see Theological Message), and the various parties represented in the book both claim it for themselves and dispute the wisdom of the others.

Is Job a Historical Book? This question of whether Job is a historical or a fictional book appropriately belongs under a discussion of genre. However, the issue is not cut and dried, because a book may have a historical core without an intense concern for historical precision. We call such books historical fiction. It is important to bear in mind here that we are asking the question of generic intention, not historical accuracy. That is, does the book of Job intend to be a historical record of an actual event in the past, and if so, how precise does it intend to be?

A number of factors may indicate that Job is not pure fiction but is based on a historical event. The first lines of a text are often important for genre identification, since they set the tone for what follows. The first verse of Job is similar to the opening verses of Judges 17 and 1 Samuel 1, two passages with an indubitable intention to communicate historical events. Second, the man Job is mentioned three times outside of the book, two times (Ezek. 14:14, 20) along with two other historical figures from the Old Testament, Noah and Daniel (though for issues concerning the latter name, see the chapter on Daniel).

Thus, there may well be a historical intention in the book. Job may well be a real person who lived in the past and who suffered. Obviously, however, there is no way to prove or disprove Job's existence outside of the book that bears his name—for instance, through archaeological attestation.

Although Job likely has a historical background, other signals from the book indicate that precision is not a high priority. For instance, the dialogues are all cast in poetic form. Clearly, then, since people did not normally speak to one another in poetic form (especially when in extreme distress), we have nothing like transcripts of the conversations that took place between the characters of the book. They may be accurate without being precise.

Poetry elevates the book from a specific historical event to a story with universal application. The book of Job is not simply a historical chronicle; it is wisdom that is to be applied to all who hear it. Indeed, whether one understands this book to be historical or not has little impact on the meaning of the book.

Does the book of Job intend to be a historical record of an actual event in the past, and if so, how precise does it intend to be?

THEOLOGICAL MESSAGE

Divine Wisdom

As our literary analysis uncovered, the question of wisdom is at the center of the book. The issue of the suffering of the innocent propels the story and is theologically important, but the question "Who is wise?" takes precedence in the unfolding of the plot.

While virtually all the characters of the book claim wisdom, it is only at the end that God speaks out of the whirlwind to settle the issue once and for all.

There is no contest; no human has a legitimate claim. God alone is the source of wisdom, and he distributes wisdom as he sees fit.

The proper human response, then, is repentance and submission. As Job himself says:

> My ears had heard of you
>> but now my eyes have seen you.
> Therefore I despise myself
>> and repent in dust and ashes. (42:5–6)

Such an approach to the book of Job is not popular among some modern interpreters. For instance, Curtis argues that Job's statements and gestures are actually an insult toward God (see his 1979 article for his eccentric translation and interpretation of Job's words). Karl Plank's comment in a Jewish Study Bible that "out of the whirlwind comes only the belching of divine power that overwhelms the exhausted Job" also illustrates this interpretive tendency.

These scholars, however, fall into the trap of unabashedly reading a biblical book in the light of the contemporary "spirit of the age" (*Zeitgeist*). Gordis noted this as a particular danger with the book of Job: it is common for an interpreter to "create a Job in his own image and find in the book a voice for his own vision of life and its meaning" (1978, xxxii). The view that Job comes to a heartfelt repentance of his own impatience toward God, no matter how right his defense against the three friends, is without doubt the correct interpretation of the original intention of the book, and it certainly fits in more appropriately with a canonical attitude of reverence toward God. That this flies in the face of contemporary impulses toward human autonomy is not important (see Newell for a defense of the traditional approach to Job's response). I would even suggest that God's comment that Job has spoken "what is right" (42:8) refers specifically to the repentance that he expresses in his response to the Yahweh speeches.

Human Suffering

God answers Job's question "Why do I suffer?" indirectly by answering the even more important question of the source of wisdom. However, the book does address the significant problem of suffering. After all, no one escapes the pain of life. We are all anxious for an insight into the reason for our plight and perhaps some easing of the anguish.

While God chooses not to reveal the answer to this question to his human creatures, we still learn much from this book about suffering. For instance, if we do not learn why we suffer, the book does disabuse one common belief, the so-called doctrine of retribution.

The basic premise of retribution as represented in the book by Eliphaz, Bildad, and Zophar is:

If you sin, then you will suffer.

Now, it must be admitted that there is some truth in this premise and that the Bible does teach that both obedience and sin have appropriate consequences. The covenant provides the framework for this by setting forth laws that if obeyed are met by blessings, but if disobeyed, by curses (Deut. 28). The Deuteronomistic History books also subtly instruct that the sins of the kings led to the exile. Proverbs teaches that those who follow God's way, the way of wisdom, will "live in safety and be at ease, without fear of harm" (1:33).

The three friends, however, went far beyond the generally true proposition that sin leads to suffering. They actually reversed the cause and effect to reach the belief that:

If you suffer, then you have sinned.

By reversing the cause and effect, they were saying that all suffering is explained by sin. Suffering becomes a telltale sign of sin. Job suffers; therefore he has sinned.

The book of Job is a canonical corrective against this type of faulty reasoning. It guards against an overreading and mechanical application of a proper biblical retribution theology. It does so by showing us a man who is suffering for a reason other than his sin. The reader has known since the prologue that Job's suffering is not caused by sin. He rather suffers for the same reason as the man who was born blind as recorded in John 9. Here the disciples see a blind man and their question reflects the same kind of retribution doctrine as that of the three friends: "Rabbi, who sinned, this man or his parents, that he was born blind?" Jesus' response could also be applied to Job: "Neither this man nor his parents sinned, but this happened so that the works of God might be displayed in him." The difficult truth of Job and John 9 and 10 is that God is glorified through the suffering of his faithful servants.

The book of Job does not begin to explain all the reasons for suffering in the world. It rejects the retribution theory of the three friends as the only explanation of the origin of suffering. Job establishes once and for all that personal sin is not the only reason for suffering in this world.

APPROACHING THE NEW TESTAMENT

The story of the relationship between God and human suffering does not end with the book of Job. Job teaches that God is in control; he reprimands the innocent sufferer for questioning his wisdom and power. Job appropriately responded with repentance.

The New Testament brings us to a deeper understanding of God's dealings with suffering. In Jesus Christ he reveals his love toward his sinful creatures by sending his Son to die on the cross. Jesus Christ is the true innocent sufferer, the only one completely without sin. He voluntarily (as opposed to Job) submits himself to suffering for the benefit of sinful men and women. As Andersen (1976, 73) states it, "That the Lord himself has embraced and absorbed the undeserved consequences of evil is the final answer to Job and all the Jobs of humanity." In Jesus, God enters into the world of human suffering in order to redeem humanity. Jesus experienced the height of human suffering on the cross, and he did so without complaining. The early Christian community saw the connection between Job and Jesus, so it was a common practice to read the book of Job during Passion week (Delitzsch 1975, 32).

Jesus' death on the cross did not bring suffering to an end. Indeed, Christians are characterized by their sharing in the sufferings of the Lord. To say that Christians are removed from the evil and pain of the present world on the basis of their conversion is a perversion of the gospel. In 2 Corinthians 1:3–11 Paul likens the suffering of Christians to that of Christ in order to communicate the comfort that is also available from Christ. It is interesting that he goes on to describe the Christian community as a fellowship of suffering and comfort.

Thus the book of Job retains its power for contemporary Christians. It can now, however, be properly read only in the light of the suffering of the totally innocent sufferer, Jesus Christ.

CHAPTER SIXTEEN

PSALMS

The book of Psalms has attracted more attention from Christians than any other Old Testament book. Its popularity dates back to the New Testament itself, where one finds frequent quotes and allusions to it. Christians today consider it the heart of the Old Testament. It is intellectually and emotionally stimulating. The piety and devotional mood that permeate the psalms and that find their origin in an intense personal relationship with God strike a responsive chord among modern men and women. Certain phrases of the Psalter (e.g., "the LORD is my shepherd" [Ps. 23:1]) are familiar and reassuring. One feels at home in the Psalter.

When examined closely, however, the Psalter surprises us, and we have difficulty understanding its message. For one thing, the individual psalms seem to be without a context, either historical or literary, in a way that is virtually unique to the Old Testament (though see below for another opinion offered by Wilson). In the second place, the attitude of the psalmist is occasionally hard to comprehend for Christians who have been taught to recognize their own sin and also to love their enemies. For example:

> Vindicate me, LORD,
> for I have led a blameless life;
> I have trusted in the LORD
> and have not faltered. (26:1)

> Daughter Babylon, doomed to destruction,
> happy are those who repay you
> according to what you have done to us.
> Happy are those who seize your infants
> and dash them against the rocks. (137:8–9)

The English name of the book comes to us from the Septuagint (*Psalmos*), via the Vulgate. The Greek word was used to translate the Hebrew word *mizmôr* that comes from the verbal root *zâmar* ("to sing" or possibly "to pluck"), which connects the book with music. The Hebrew title *Tehillim* means "praises" and highlights what is the dominant note (see below for qualification) of the book.

BIBLIOGRAPHY

Commentaries

L. C. **Allen,** *Psalms 100–150* (WBC; Word, 1983); A. A. **Anderson,** *Psalms* (NCB; Eerdmans, 1972); C. A. and E. G. **Briggs,** *A Critical and Exegetical Commentary on the Book of Psalms* (ICC; T. & T. Clark, 1906); C. **Broyles,** *Psalms* (NIBCOT; Hendrickson/Paternoster, 1999); P. C. **Craigie,** *Psalms 1–50* (WBC; Word, 1983); M. J. **Dahood,** *Psalms* (AB; Doubleday, 1965–70); F. **Delitzsch,** *Biblical Commentary on the Psalms* (Hodder and Stoughton, 1887); E. S. **Gerstenberger,** *Psalms* (FOTL; Eerdmans, 1989); idem, *Psalms, Part 2, and Lamentations* (FOTL; Eerdmans, 2001); H. **Gunkel,** *Die Psalmen ubersetzt und erklart* (HKAT; Vandenhoeck und Ruprecht, 1926); D. **Kidner,** *Psalms* (TOTC; InterVarsity Press, 1973–76); G. A. F. **Knight,** *Psalms* (DSB; Westminster, 1982); H.-J. **Kraus,** *Psalmen* (BKAT; Neukirchener Verlag, 1978; English trans., Augsburg, 1985); J. L. **Mays,** *Psalms* (Interp; Westminster John Knox, 1994); M. E. **Tate,** *Psalms 51–100* (WBC; Word, 1990); W. **VanGemeren,** "Psalms" (EBC, Zondervan, 1991); A. **Weiser,** *The Psalms* (OTL; Westminster, 1962); G. H. **Wilson,** *Psalms,* Vol. 1 (NIVAC; Zondervan, 2002).

Monographs and Articles

R. B. **Allen,** *When the Song Is New: Understanding the Kingdom in the Psalms* (Thomas Nelson, 1983); B. W. **Anderson,** *Out of the Depths: The Psalms Speak to Us Today* (Westminster, 1983); R. **Beckwith,** *The Old Testament Canon of the New Testament Church* (London: SPCK, 1985); W. **Beyerlin,** *Wir sind wie Träumende* (Stuttgart: Verlag Katholische Bibelwerk, 1977); W. **Brueggemann,** *The Message of the Psalms* (Augsburg, 1984); B. S. **Childs,** "Psalm Titles and Midrashic Exegesis," *JSS* 16 (1971): 137–50; E. P. **Clowney,** *Preaching and Biblical Theology* (Presbyterian and Reformed, 1973); idem, "The Singing Savior," *Moody Monthly* 79 (1978): 40–43; J. **Creach,** *Yahweh as Refuge and Editing of the Hebrew Psalter* (Sheffield, 1996); F. M. **Cross,** *Canaanite Myth and Hebrew Epic* (Harvard University Press, 1972); J. H. **Eaton,** *Kingship and the Psalms* (Allenson, 1976); E. **Gerstenberger,** "Psalms," in *Old Testament Form Criticism,* ed. J. H. Hayes (San Antonio: Trinity University Press, 1974), 179–224; J. **Goldingay,** "The Dynamic Cycle of Praise and Prayer in the Psalms," *JSOT* 20 (1981): 85–90; A. **Guilding,** "Some Obscured Rubrics and Lectionary Allusions in the Psalter," *JTS* (NS) 3 (1952): 41–55; A. **Harman,** "Paul's Use of the Psalms" (Th.D. dissertation, Westminster Theological Seminary, 1968); O. **Keel,** *The Symbolism of the Biblical World: Ancient Near Eastern Iconography and the Book of Psalms* (Seabury Press, 1978); S. **Kistemaker,** *The Psalms Citations in the Epistle of the Hebrews* (Amsterdam, 1961, repr. 1985); H.-J. **Kraus,** *Theology of the Psalms*, trans. K. Crim (Augsburg, 1986); C. S. **Lewis,** *Reflections on the Psalms* (London: Collins, 1961); T. **Longman** III, "The Divine Warrior: The Old Testament Use of a New Testament Motif," *WTJ* 44 (1982): 290–307; idem, "Form Criticism, Recent Developments in Genre Theory, and the Evangelical," *WTJ* 48 (1985): 46–67; idem, "Psalm 98: A Divine Warrior Victory Song," *JETS* 27 (1984): 267–74; idem, *How to Read the Psalms* (InterVarsity Press, 1988); P. D. **Miller** Jr., *Interpreting the Psalms* (Fortress, 1986); idem, *They Cried to the Lord: The Form and Theology of Biblical Prayer* (Fortress Press, 1994); S. **Mowinckel,** *The Psalms in Israel's Worship*, 2 vols. (Abingdon, 1962); E. **Slomovik,** "Toward an Understanding of the Formation of Historical Titles in the Book of the Psalms," *ZAW* 91 (1979): 350–81; M. S. **Smith,** *Psalms: The Divine Journey* (Paulist, 1987); J. R. **Vannoy,** *Covenant Renewal at Gilgal* (Mack, 1978); B. W. **Waltke,** "A Canonical Process Approach to the Psalms," in *Tradition and Testament*, ed. J. S. and P. D. Feinberg (Moody, 1981), 3–18; C. **Westermann,** *The Psalms: Structure, Content, and Message* (Augsburg, 1980); G. H. **Wilson,** "Evidence of Editorial Divisions in the Hebrew Psalter," *VT* 34 (1984): 337–52; idem, "The Use of 'Untitled' Psalms in the Hebrew Psalter," *ZAW* 97 (1985): 404–13; idem, *The Editing of the Hebrew Psalter* (SBLDS 76; Chico: Scholars, 1985).

HISTORICAL BACKGROUND

Introduction

A description of the historical background of the Psalms is difficult to provide for two reasons: first, the book is a collection rather than a unified composition; and second, the individual psalms themselves are historically nonspecific.

The canonical book of Psalms comprises 150 separate compositions. These poems were not written at one time, but over a long period. Indeed, if one takes the titles as serious indications of setting (see below), then at least one psalm (Ps. 90) dates as early as the time of Moses, while internal indications point to a postexilic date for others (for instance, Ps. 126). This is a time spread of close to one thousand years. From this perspective, the historical background of the Psalms is the history of the nation of Israel.

The historical background of the book is further complicated by strong evidence that the book as a whole and the individual psalms that are a part of it were open to adaptation during the whole Old Testament period. In regard to the book as a whole, it is clear that as individual psalms were added to the collection, they were not simply appended to the end. Psalm 72:20 concludes the second book of the Psalter in this way: "This concludes the prayers of David son of Jesse." We are to assume that at one point in the history of the transmission of the Psalter only Davidic psalms preceded this statement and no Davidic psalms appeared after it. As a matter of fact, in the present state of the Psalter, there are a number of non-Davidic psalms (even Psalm 72 itself!) before this verse and a number of Davidic psalms that follow it. This verse provides solid evidence that psalms were interwoven into the book and not simply added at the end.

Close study of individual psalms demonstrates that they too were subject to "updating" during the canonical period. If one takes seriously the authorship title of Psalm 69, dating that psalm to the time of David, and then reads the last three verses (34–36) that are most at home in an exilic time period, we observe that even individual psalms were open-ended, or dynamic, during the canonical period.

Nonetheless, some scholars have not recognized the dynamic character of the Psalter and have directed their attention toward the historical background of individual psalms. As a matter of fact, many commentaries on the Psalms attempt to recover the historical situation out of which a psalm originated by the analysis of the content of the psalm. Such attempts rarely persuade the rest of the scholarly community, so it is not unusual to find vast disagreements concerning the historical background of individual psalms. As one example, some scholars date Psalm 98 to the time of the Exodus on the basis of certain terms that are used elsewhere to describe God's victory over the Egyptians at the Red Sea ("marvelous things" and "his right hand and his holy arm"). On the other hand, Beyerlin (1977, 49) argues strenuously that Psalm 98 should be dated to the time of the restoration because, in his opinion, the psalm shows literary dependence on Isaiah.

Upon closer analysis, we must admit that such attempts to root individual psalms in one historical event work against the intention of the psalms themselves, which are nonspecific in terms of historical reference. This situation may be demonstrated by comparing a psalm of deliverance from the Psalms (Ps. 24) with a deliverance song from the historical books (Judg. 5). Judges 5 is deeply rooted in the events that took place in the Israelite defeat of the Canaanites toward the end of the second millennium BC. Psalm 24 also celebrates a military victory as the army approached the gates of the city and praised its Lord who is "mighty in battle" (v. 8). One would, however, be hard pressed to identify the particular battle that was the cause for the writing of this psalm.

The historically nonspecific nature of the psalms is a function of their continued use in the worship of Israel. Before describing the relationship between the psalms and Israel's worship, however, we must consider the titles of the Psalms.

Psalm Titles

The titles of the psalms are appropriately considered at this point because they are frequently used to give the psalms a more specific date. The nature and origin of the titles are tricky issues that must be handled with care and scholarly humility.

Description. Psalm titles are found at the beginning of individual psalms and give information about them. Titles can provide information concerning a variety of matters, including the psalm's author, its historical background, its melody, its use in the worship of Israel, and occasionally other items. Much debate surrounds the titles. Most important, are they original to the psalm, and, if not, are they reliable guides to its origin and background?

Authenticity of the Titles. The question of the authenticity of the titles is perhaps one of the most difficult questions facing the interpreter of the psalms. Many commentators and even more preachers have constructed their ideas about a psalm around the historical situation presented in the title. Psalm 51 is perhaps the best and most well-known example. The title to Psalm 51 introduces the situation of the psalm in the following way:

> When the prophet Nathan came to him after David had committed adultery with Bathsheba.

This title colors the way the rest of the psalm is read. The "I" of the psalm is David, and the transgression is his adultery with Bathsheba.

The historical titles also influence the interpretation of psalms that lack them. Scholars attempt to find the situation in the life of David or the history of Israel that best explains the psalm, and then they interpret the psalm in the light of that event.

Due to its difficulty and importance, it is not surprising that this issue has resulted in heated disagreement. Some scholars assert that the titles are authentic and infallible (Kidner), while others say they are neither (Mowinckel; Childs, *IOTS*). E. J. Young (*IOT*, 297–305) represents a mediating position when he argues that the psalm titles are not authentic but rather reflect early reliable tradition.

The question of the authenticity of the titles is, in the first place, the question of whether the titles were written by the inspired author of the psalm at approximately the same time that the psalm itself was written. It is impossible to be dogmatic in answer to this question. On the one side, there is no textual evidence that the psalms ever lacked titles. Of course, this fact proves only that the titles were present by very late Old Testament times, not that they were composed at the time the psalms were written. In support of the contrary position, however, there is considerable circumstantial evidence that the psalm titles were later additions.

In the first place, while it is true that no early manuscript lacks all the titles, the evidence shows a rapid increase in the number of titles in the early history of transmission. The Syriac tradition even witnesses the rejection of Masoretic titles and the creation of new ones (Slomovic 1979).

Second, the titles are written in the third person, even when the psalms themselves are first-person compositions (e.g., Pss. 3, 18, 51). Moreover, the historical titles, with only minor exceptions, share the same basic form (note particularly the use of the infinitive construct with the prefixed temporal preposition). The titles thus have the appearance of being later additions, though it is not inconceivable that David himself could have later added the titles.

More seriously, however, the titles occasionally appear at odds with the psalms with which they are associated. Psalm 30 is a case in point. The title places the setting of the psalm at the time of the "dedication," presumably of the temple, but the psalm itself has no apparent connection with the temple or any other "house." Rather, it is the prayer of a man who has recovered from a near-fatal illness.

The best solution is to regard the titles as early reliable tradition concerning the authorship and setting of the psalms. The titles, however, should not be taken as original or canonical. This conclusion leads to a discussion of the authorship and setting of the Psalter.

Authorship. Many psalm titles contain the names of specific individuals: Asaph (12 times), the sons of Korah (11 times), Solomon (2 times), Jeduthun (4 times), and Heman, Etan, and Moses (1 time each). David's name occurs some seventy-three times in the superscriptions. Traditionally, these names have been understood as designating authorship. Recent scholarship, however, has cast doubt on the validity of this assumption.

In the first place, the authorship titles, like the historical titles, are suspected of being late additions. Both multiply in the history of transmission of the Psalter. While the Hebrew textual tradition identifies seventy-three psalms as Davidic, this number rapidly increases in the Greek and Latin versions.

Second, some scholars register uncertainty over the function of the names found in the titles. The key to their function is located in the meaning of the preposition l^e that introduces the names. Semitic prepositions have a wide semantic field and depend heavily on their immediate context in order to generate their meaning. Unfortunately, there is no context to speak of in the title of a psalm. The preposition l^e with the personal name David can theoretically be translated "by David," "of David," "about David," and "for David." In the Old Testament period, the meaning of the preposition would have been understood because there was clearly a set form to the titles.

A third reason why some scholars (at least in the past) have rejected Davidic authorship of the psalms is their rigid conception of the development of Hebrew religion. Such scholars deny that Israel could produce such an elevated expression of piety as early as the reign of David. This view is hardly ever held today because we know more about ancient poetry from other Semitic cultures.

These are the fundamental reasons why some reject Davidic authorship of the psalms that are ascribed to him. These fundamental reasons are buttressed by a number of subsidiary arguments, such as the presence of Aramaisms in the psalms, references to the temple in Davidic psalms, and the use of the l^e preposition in the Ugaritic Baal epic.

It is of course impossible to prove that each and every psalm attributed to David was written by him. But at the same time it is inconceivable, considering the strength of the biblical tradition surrounding David's interest in and involvement with music in worship, that David did not write any of the psalms.

While it is possible to read the preposition l^e as denoting subject ("about David") or style ("according to Davidic style"), the evidence strongly supports taking it as denoting authorship ("of David" or "by David"). Habakkuk 3 presents a psalm of the prophet Habakkuk that also begins with a title. Included in the title is the phrase "a prayer of Habakkuk." In context, this can only be understood as an attribution of origin or authorship. It is not a prayer "about Habakkuk." Closer to the point, Psalm 18:1 presents an expanded title that indicates that authorship is meant by the l^e david: "For the director of music. Of David the servant of the LORD. He sang to the LORD the words of this song when the LORD delivered him from the hand of all his enemies and from the hand of Saul." This psalm title provides the expanded literary context that is lacking in the other titles and that enables us to see the function of the preposition in the titles.

The historical books strongly support a picture of David as vitally interested in singing in the setting of formal worship. David has a double introduction into public life, highlighting the two major contributions that he would make during his adult life. In 1 Samuel 17 David is introduced as a bold warrior of the Lord as he defeats Goliath. Immediately before (16:14–23), he appears in the narrative as a musician, hired to play soothing music before a mad Saul. David was the man who organized the musicians for the temple that would be built after his death (1 Chron. 25) and turned over songs to this chief musician (1 Chron. 16:7). Here indeed is the one who was named "Israel's singer of songs" (2 Sam. 23:1 NIV; cf. also Amos 6:5).

Doubt concerning the possibility of Davidic authorship of any of the psalms is a carryover from the beginning of the century when it was felt that the type of piety that finds expression in the psalms could come about only in the postexilic period. Such rigid evolutionist approaches to the development of Israel's religion have been discarded, and increasing numbers of scholars are recognizing that many of the psalms are considerably earlier than previously thought.

Therefore, while the titles are not canonical, they may be reliable. Nonetheless, they are not important to the interpretation of individual psalms. Although the psalms arose out of a historically specific situation, they are purposely devoid of direct reference to it. Thus it is to work against the intention of the psalmist to interpret a psalm in the light of a reconstructed original event.

The psalms are historically nonspecific so that they may be continually used in Israel's corporate and individual worship of God. The psalms are always relevant to the needs of the nations as well as to individual Israelites. Thus the suffering and persecuted Israelite may quickly identify with the "I" of Psalm 69,

> *It is impossible to prove that each and every psalm attributed to David was written by him. But at the same time it is inconceivable that David did not write any of the psalms.*

and the man who was just healed from a life-threatening illness has a model prayer in Psalm 30.

Social Setting

It is futile to reconstruct the elusive historical background of individual psalms. In place of it, the psalm interpreter must rather ask, How did this psalm function in the worship of Old Testament Israel? From the time of Sigmund Mowinckel, it has been generally recognized that the Psalter functioned as the "hymnbook of ancient Israel."

The most persuasive evidence of the use of the psalms in the context of worship comes from direct statements within the psalms themselves. For instance, some psalms provide their own setting by alluding to their use during a religious pilgrimage to the holy city of Jerusalem (or perhaps more specifically to the temple). In Psalm 24:3, the psalmist asks the question, "Who may ascend the mountain of the LORD?" The assumption is that the worshiper intends to go to the temple mount. The last four verses of the psalm are composed of a dialogue between those approaching the city and the gatekeeper, the former requesting entrance into the city.

Other psalms witness to the worship setting of the psalms by direct statement. Psalm 5:7 states:

> But I, by your great love,
> can come into your house;
> in reverence I bow down
> toward your holy temple.

Psalm 66 is a thanksgiving psalm. It is, accordingly, a psalm sung in response to God's answering an earlier lament. In verses 13–15 the psalmist says that he will follow through on a promise he had made in the context of the lament:

> I will come to your temple with burnt offerings
> and fulfill my vows to you—
> vows my lips promised and my mouth spoke
> when I was in trouble.
> I will sacrifice fat animals to you
> and an offering of rams;
> I will offer bulls and goats.

These are just two examples of psalms that show an explicit connection with worship acts. They could be multiplied easily (Mowinckel 1962, 2–22).

An analogy between the Psalter and a contemporary hymnbook is instructive. Many modern hymns arose as a result of a specific event in the life of a hymn writer, but the event remains hidden (at least without historical research) from the person who sings the song today. The hymn was written in such a way that it allows all who sing it to identify with it.

The psalms reflect many different reactions to life: joy, sadness, thanks, and calm meditation, to name but a few. The Israelite worshiper had a ready-made prayer for all of life's vicissitudes.

The historical books give us occasional glimpses into the use of psalms. The two most notable instances are the psalms of Hannah and Jonah. In 1 Samuel 2, Hannah comes before the Lord with a joyful heart. God has answered her prayers, and she has given birth to a son, Samuel. She sings an exuberant song of praise to God. Upon close analysis, the psalm she sings bears many similarities with a specific song found in the Psalter, Psalm 113. Jonah, on the other hand, sings a song to the Lord in much different circumstances. After he is thrown overboard, he is swallowed by a "great fish" and thus is saved from drowning. As a result, he offers a thanksgiving psalm (Jonah 2) to the Lord. The content of his prayer is made up of a pastiche of quotations from the Psalter.

Some scholars are unsatisfied with a general setting for the psalms in the formal worship of Israel and seek a more specific occasion for their use. The best-known attempt to connect the majority of the psalms with a specific festival is that of Mowinckel (1962). Mowinckel was a student of Gunkel and accepted his teacher's form-critical approach to the Psalms. However, he did not share Gunkel's lack of appreciation for the Psalter's role in the formal worship of Israel. Under the influence of contemporary anthropological theory (particularly that of Grønbeck), he sought to place the Psalter in the context of the worship of Israel. He believed that he had evidence to connect the book with the New Year's celebration.

Not much is said in the Old Testament about a celebration of the New Year, but Mowinckel has noted that many of the themes of the Mesopotamian New Year (*akîtu*) festival shared similarities with the Psalms. At the heart of the New Year's festival is the ritual of the reenthronement of the king and also of the chief deity. In Mesopotamia Marduk was proclaimed head of the pantheon, and the human king, who had been symbolically divested of his royal power, again assumes the throne.

Accordingly, at the core of Mowinckel's reconstruction of an Israelite New Year's festival are the so-called enthronement psalms (Pss. 47, 93, 95–98). These are psalms that sing hymns to Yahweh, who is proclaimed king anew. Most of the remaining psalms would also find a home in this reconstructed festival. For instance, the laments would fit in with the part of the ritual where the king is divested of his royal prerogatives.

While Mowinckel provided the first and classic attempt to place the psalms in the context of a single festival, few people would follow Mowinckel today. The lack of evidence for such a festival in biblical tradition, combined with the tenuous nature of the evidence from within the Psalter, lead most to reject his approach. It appears to be an imposition of Mesopotamian religious thought on the biblical world.

Other attempts have been made to associate the Psalter as a whole with a particular festival. Notable is Kraus's attempt to locate its use in a Zion festival whose intention is to celebrate the choice of Jerusalem as the place of God's dwelling. More persuasive, because of the close connection between the psalms and the covenant concept, is Weiser's reconstruction of a Covenant Festival. In the final analysis, however, it is best to simply say that the psalms were a vital part of the everyday public worship of God in ancient Israel.

Summary and Conclusion

The historical background of the Psalter as a whole and the individual psalms that constitute it is elusive. Psalms was a dynamic, growing, and changing book during the canonical period. The individual psalms were historically nonspecific in order to be always relevant for use in the formal worship of Israel. The titles are not original, but early; not canonical, but reliable.

LITERARY ANALYSIS

The literary structure of the book of Psalms is almost unique to the Hebrew Bible. With the exception of the Song of Songs, the Psalter is the only poetic anthology in the Scriptures. Also, the Psalms provide the classic examples of Hebrew poetry. A description and analysis of Hebrew poetic style is given in chapter 1 (see Stories and Poems; The Conventions of Old Testament Poetry).

Genre

Since the book is an anthology, it is best to begin with an analysis of its parts. The canonical shape of the book contains 150 separate poetic compositions. These poems may be helpfully differentiated into seven basic genres (Longman 1988, 19–36). Exemplars of these seven genres are not systematically or chronologically arranged within the book as a whole. Indeed, upon first reading, the arrangement appears totally arbitrary.

The three most commonly occurring genres are characterized by the emotion that they express. They are hymns of joy, laments, and thanksgivings. These three genres relate very closely to the life of the worshiper. When the Israelite was in harmonious relationship with God and his or her circumstances, he or she would sing hymns of praise to God. When God seemed distant and the worshiper experienced distress, a lament was in order. When the lament was answered, the Israelite responded with a song of thanksgiving. W. Brueggemann (1984, 25–167) has helpfully categorized these three genres as songs of orientation, disorientation, and reorientation.

Our study will begin with an analysis of these three major genres found in the Psalter:

The Hymn. The characteristic genre of the Psalter is the hymn. The lament is more frequent, but the hymn dominates the tone of the book. The book's Hebrew title witnesses to this statement, for *Tehillim* is translated "praises." While hymns are relatively infrequent at the beginning of the Psalter, they are in the majority at the end. Indeed, the Psalter concludes in a crescendo of praise with the five psalms (146–50) known as the Great Doxology.

The hymn is defined, and consequently most easily recognized, by its tone of exuberant praise to the Lord. It is evangelistic praise in that the psalmist calls others to join him:

> Shout for joy to the LORD, all the earth.
>> Worship the LORD with gladness;
>> come before him with joyful songs.
> Know that the LORD is God.
>> It is he who made us, and we are his;
>> we are his people, the sheep of his pasture. (Ps. 100:1–3)

The psalmist most often gives reasons for praise. As in the example found in Psalm 100, these reasons are not historically specific. Rather, they are general and even vague. The generality is intentional and allows the psalm to speak to later generations and in new situations.

> For the LORD is good and his love endures forever;
>> his faithfulness continues through all generations. (v. 5)

Although the reasons are nonspecific in relationship to historical events, it is possible to further divide the hymns into subgenres on the basis of the reason for praise. For instance, Psalm 29 sings praise to God because he is king (cf. Pss. 47, 93, 95, 96); Psalm 24 praises God because he won a victory over Israel's enemies; Psalm 45 praises God in the context of a royal wedding; and Psalm 48 extols Zion as the place of God's special presence (Pss. 46, 76, 87).

The Lament.

> Hasten, O God, to save me;
>> come quickly, LORD, to help me. (Ps. 70:1)

As we move from hymn to lament, we trade joy for sorrow. The psalmist experiences trouble in his or her life and turns to the Lord for aid. The trouble comes from three sources (Westermann 1980, 181–94), and laments may be differentiated on the basis of the source of the trouble, though it is not unusual that all three are present in a single psalm.

The trouble may come from the "enemy." The enemy is human and seeks to harm, even to kill the psalmist:

> I am in the midst of lions;
>> I am forced to dwell among man-eating beasts—
> whose teeth are spears and arrows,
>> whose tongues are sharp swords. (Ps. 57:4)

The enemy is not specified in the psalms. Names are not given; concrete charges are not lodged. The psalms are forever relevant to new situations.

Again, the trouble may come from the psalmist himself. He reacts poorly to the pain that he is experiencing:

> I am poured out like water,
>> and all my bones are out of joint.
> My heart has turned to wax;
>> it has melted within me.
> My mouth is dried up like a potsherd,
>> and my tongue sticks to the roof of my mouth;
>> you lay me in the dust of death. (Ps. 22:14–15)

Psalm 13:2 graphically pictures this internal struggle:

> How long must I wrestle with my thoughts
>> and day after day have sorrow in my heart?

However, most frightening to the psalmist is the struggle with God himself. He feels abandoned by God in the midst of his persecution, doubt, or pain:

> For I eat ashes as my food
>> and mingle my drink with tears
> because of your great wrath,
>> for you have taken me up and thrown me aside. (Ps. 102:9–10)

The lament is, accordingly, easily recognized by the mood of the psalm. It is a song of disorientation, of abandonment, distress, pain, and suffering.

Laments also have a distinctive structure composed of seven basic elements:

1. Invocation
2. Plea to God for help
3. Complaints
4. Confession of sin or an assertion of innocence
5. Curse of enemies (imprecation)
6. Confidence in God's response
7. Hymn or blessing

Very few psalms evidence all seven elements (and even fewer in this precise order), but any lament will contain more than one.

Psalm 28 provides a good short illustration. The psalm begins with an invocation and plea to God for help:

To you, LORD, I call;
> you are my Rock,
> do not turn a deaf ear to me. (v. 1a)

Afterward, he complains that he is treated like the wicked:

Do not drag me away with the wicked,
> with those who do evil. . . . (v. 3a)

He curses his enemies:

Repay them for their deeds
> and for their evil work. . . . (v. 4)

At the end, the psalmist asserts confidence in God and sings his praise:

Praise be to the LORD,
> for he has heard my cry for mercy. . . .
The LORD is the strength of his people,
> a fortress of salvation for his anointed one. (vv. 6, 8)

A common characteristic of the lament is that it turns to praise at the end. Gunkel and his followers believed that this mixing of sorrow and joy was evidence that a psalm was late (his *Mischgattung*). This view emanates from a rigid conception of genre (Longman 1985). One alternative interpretation is that the lament was brought to the priest, who then spoke a word of assurance to the psalmist. The assurance was not recorded in the psalm, but it allowed the worshiper to respond in trust and praise.

In any case, the turning from sorrow to joy at the end of many laments is an indication that the psalmist knew that God is a God who answers prayer. Thanksgiving psalms are also a witness to that truth.

Thanksgiving Psalms. After the prayer of lament was answered by God, the psalmist returned to offer his thanks. The thanksgiving psalm is closely related to the hymn and often sounds like a hymn at the beginning. The difference may be seen in the specific focus of the praise: the psalmist praises the Lord for delivering him from distress. Because of this, Brueggemann would rightly call these psalms songs of reorientation.

Psalm 18 begins like a hymn:

I love you, LORD, my strength.
The LORD is my rock, my fortress and my deliverer;
> my God is my rock, in whom I take refuge. (vv. 1–2)

In verses 4–6, however, the psalmist flashes back to the time of his distress when he called to the Lord for help:

The cords of death entangled me;
> the torrents of destruction overwhelmed me.

> *The turning from sorrow to joy at the end of many laments is an indication that the psalmist knew that God is a God who answers prayer.*

> The cords of the grave coiled around me;
> > the snares of death confronted me.
> In my distress I called to the LORD;
> > I cried to my God for help. (vv. 5–6)

Psalm 18 is similar to other thanksgiving psalms in that the bulk of the song is devoted to recounting God's deliverance and praising the Lord for that deliverance:

> He reached down from on high and took hold of me;
> > he drew me out of deep waters.
> He rescued me from my powerful enemy,
> > from my foes, who were too strong for me. (vv. 16–17)

The thanksgiving psalm is a witness to the Lord's goodness and power. It praises the Lord's name in front of the congregation and leads the rest of the congregation to praise his name:

> The LORD lives! Praise be to my Rock!
> > Exalted be God my Savior!
> . . .
> Therefore I will praise you, LORD, among the nations;
> > I will sing praises to your name. (vv. 46, 49)

Praise, lament, and thanks: these are the three major genres of the Psalter. It is helpful to go on now and recognize some of the lesser attested genres. We will examine four: psalms of confidence, psalms of remembrance, wisdom psalms, and kingship psalms.

Psalms of Confidence. As the name implies, psalms of confidence are recognized by the trust that the worshiper expresses in God as protector. Hymns and laments contain assertions of confidence in God, but this attitude takes a dominant role in approximately nine psalms (11, 16, 23, 27, 62, 91, 121, 125, 131).

While not having a distinctive structure, this genre is noted for its use of striking metaphors of God as a compassionate refuge: God is a shepherd (Ps. 23), a mother bird who covers her children with her wings (Ps. 91), and a stronghold and a light (Ps. 27).

Psalms of Remembrance. Memory plays a key role in the Psalter. The thanksgiving psalms recount to the congregation prayers that have been answered in the past. Many hymns and laments call to mind God's past acts of deliverance. Such reminders build confidence in God. He has shown himself in the past to be a reliable savior; he will do so in the present.

Not surprisingly, a few psalms may be grouped into a separate genre on the basis of their preoccupation with God's great redemptive acts in the past. These redemptive acts are recalled to build confidence in the present. Examples of this genre are Psalms 78, 105, 106, 135, 136.

Wisdom Psalms. Some psalms share themes and concerns with the part of the Old Testament canon that we classify as Wisdom Literature (particularly Job, Proverbs, Song of Songs, and Ecclesiastes). For instance, Proverbs is noted for its sharp antitheses between the wise and the foolish and the righteous and the wicked. The righteous wise are blessed, while the wicked fools are cursed. Psalm 1 functions as the entrance into the worship of God that is the Psalms by making this fundamental distinction and has been correctly categorized as a wisdom psalm:

> Blessed are those
>> who do not walk in step with the wicked
> or stand in the way that sinners take
>> or sit in the company of mockers,
>
> . . .
>
> For the LORD watches over the way of the righteous,
>> but the way of the wicked will be destroyed. (vv. 1, 6)

Scholars have also noted the close relationship between wisdom and law. Both concern right behavior within the community of God. Psalm 119 features lengthy praise of the law of God. Accordingly, it too is rightly classified as a wisdom psalm.

Other wisdom psalms include such diverse poems as Psalms 45 and 73. Psalm 45 is a royal marriage psalm and bears a number of similarities to the love poems of the Song of Songs. Psalm 73 deals with doubt and skepticism and, accordingly, may be profitably compared with the book of Ecclesiastes.

Kingship Psalms. No one doubts a close connection between the Psalms and the Israelite king. Scholars do debate, however, such issues as the theology and ideology of kingship implicit in the Psalter as well as the number of psalms to associate with the institution of kingship (Eaton 1976).

The difficulty lies in the identity of the unnamed "I" in a number of the psalms. The first-person speaker in Psalm 3 never explicitly identifies himself as the king of Israel. Nevertheless, a close reading provides evidence that Psalm 3 is a kingship psalm. For instance, the conflict between the first-person speaker and the "enemy" is more than a personal struggle:

> LORD, how many are my foes!
>> How many rise up against me!
> Many are saying of me,
>> "God will not deliver him."
>
> . . .
>
> I lie down and sleep;
>> I wake again, because the LORD sustains me.
> I will not fear though tens of thousands
>> assail me on every side. (vv. 1–2, 5–6)

The royal character of these psalms is heightened by the titles, many of which designate David as the author.

Without attempting to delineate each and every psalm that emanates from the royal court, we must recognize two basic types of kingship psalms in the Psalter: (1) psalms that extol God as king, and (2) psalms that extol the ruler of Israel as king.

Divine kingship psalms received much attention in the wake of Mowinckel's assertion that they provided the key to the function of the Psalter. Mowinckel used these psalms to reconstruct an annual divine reenthronement ceremony in Israel similar to the Babylonian New Year's Festival. Such a reconstruction has been severely criticized (Kraus; Weiser) and the hypothesis rejected. Nonetheless, the divine kingship psalms are still some of the most studied poems in the Psalter.

God is proclaimed king, not only of Israel but also of the cosmos (Ps. 24:1–2; 95:1–5). A close connection may be observed between the proclamation of God as king and military victory. God wins the victory for his people in battle, and they respond by praising him as their king:

> Sing to the LORD a new song,
>   for he has done marvelous things;
> his right hand and his holy arm
>   have worked salvation for him. (Ps. 98:1)

In Israel the human king was God's son, his servant. When the people requested a king, it was out of the lack of trust in God as deliverer (1 Sam. 8:7). In spite of the people's sin, God provided a king. Samuel made certain that the people understood that the human king was a pale reflection of the divine king; he did so through the celebration of a covenant renewal ceremony (1 Sam. 12; see Vannoy 1978). The monarchy does not replace theocracy, but furthers it.

A number of psalms, therefore, focus attention on the human king. Psalm 21 provides a good example, particularly in the first few verses:

> The king rejoices in your strength, LORD.
>   How great is his joy in the victories you give!
> You have granted him his heart's desire
>   and have not withheld the request of his lips.
> You came to greet him with rich blessings
>   and placed a crown of pure gold on his head. (vv. 1–3)

The Structure of the Psalter

The book of Psalms as we know it is composed of 150 separate poetic compositions. There is evidence that some psalms that are now separated were actually written as a single poem. For instance, Psalms 9 and 10 together constitute a single alphabetic acrostic, and in the Septuagint they appear as one psalm. In addition, a recurring refrain unites Psalms 42 and 43, and thus these should also be considered a single poem. Despite our inability to determine with absolute certainty the exact number of psalms, it is clearly true that the uniqueness of the Psalter is in part its nonnarrative structure.

Scholars have proposed various schemes to justify the present order of the psalms in the book, but none have been persuasive. Franz Delitzsch proposed a "catch word" structure. That is, each psalm picked up a key word or phrase from the preceding psalm. Other scholars have suggested a liturgical structure. In other words, the Psalter would have been read in the synagogue in a one- or three-year cycle, according to the structure of the book as a whole.

More recently, we may cite the work of G. Wilson, who has been very persuasive on a number of other Psalm scholars (including Creach). Wilson picked up on a suggestion of his teacher B. S. Childs that there may be some rationale to the arrangement of the final redaction of the Psalms. Wilson studies the arrangement of the psalms on the background of ancient Near Eastern collections that arguably show intentional placement of individual poems. After study, he concludes that it is possible to see a purposeful arrangement of the book of Psalms. He looks at what he calls the "seam psalms" (psalms that begin and end one of the five books of the Psalter, see below) as indicative of this structure. He is struck by the fact that most, though tellingly not all, have some possible connection to the Davidic covenant, where God promises David that he will have a descendant on the throne forever. Thus Psalm 2, the first psalm of Book 1, alludes to 2 Samuel 7 where this covenant is narrated, and Wilson treats the psalm as an announcement of the covenant. Then he reads Psalm 41, the last psalm of Book 1, as a statement of confidence in the Davidic covenant (though that covenant is not explicitly mentioned in the psalm). In Book 2 it is the ending psalm, Psalm 72, that is relevant. It is a psalm of Solomon, but he treats it as a psalm of David and a prayer for Solomon. So in this psalm the covenant promises are passed on to the son. Psalm 89 at the end of Book 3 is definitely connected to the Davidic covenant and is treated as a statement of the failure of that covenant. Book 4 is then taken by Wilson as an answer to the dilemma of the failed covenant. It asserts Yahweh as king and particularly the refuge of his people (a theme developed by Creach 1996). So it is a call to trust Yahweh now that the monarchy is gone. As for Book 5, Wilson does not believe that this section could be as ingeniously edited, since there are a number of psalms that came into the collection via pre-existent groups. In conclusion, he states that this fifth book is an answer to the "plea for help from exiles to return" (Wilson 1985, 227). The answer is to trust and depend on Yahweh.

Thus, Wilson sees a development within the structure of the Psalter from a confident assertion of Davidic covenant, to its failure, and then to a reassertion of hope in Yahweh's kingship in the absence of the monarchy. In his most recent writings (Wilson 2002), this hope is given Messianic significance.

While this reading is extremely ingenious and attractive, it is ultimately not convincing. The psalms used to create the narrative are selective. Not all the psalms that are at the seams are discussed, only those that are amenable to his theory. Moreover, in the case of Psalms 41 and 89 (is it really talking about the failure of the covenant?) Wilson interprets in a way that is debatable at best.

On the contrary, the evidence supports a picture of the Psalter as an open, dynamic book during the canonical period. Individual psalms were composed and added over a thousand-year period. It appears that occasionally groups of psalms were added to the Psalter at one time. The most common grouping within the Psalter is based on authorship. Psalms 42–49 are psalms of the "sons of Korah." Most scholars believe, rightly, that this reference is not to the biological descendants of Korah, but rather to his occupational descendants, that is the line of apprentices who follow one another in musical service in the temple. A second such group of psalms are those attributed to Asaph (Pss. 50, 73–83). Asaph is mentioned in 1 Chronicles 15:17 as one who made music before the ark as it was moved from Obed-Edom's house to Jerusalem. His family is mentioned as one of three who served the Lord with their musical abilities (1 Chron. 25:1–9).

David's songs constitute the most well-known group of psalms based on authorship. At one time David's psalms constituted a single group (Ps. 72:20), but in the course of the formation of the canonical book, non-Davidic psalms were inserted into this collection; and other Davidic psalms, which for some reason were not included with the initial group, were added later and so appear after Psalm 72. Such evidence clearly witnesses to the open, dynamic character of the Psalter.

A second type of grouping found in the book of Psalms is that based on cultic function. Psalms 120 to 134 are each classified as "a song of ascent." Much debate surrounds the significance of the title. Most probably, these psalms were used primarily during a religious pilgrimage to Jerusalem and more specifically to the temple.

It is even possible to discern psalms that are grouped together, united not by a common title but by a common content. Psalms 93 and 95–99 each proclaim God as King of the universe. Clearly, these psalms were either brought into the Psalter at the same time or, as they were individually added over time, were placed together in this section because of their similarities.

Before moving on from our identification of occasional structures within the Psalter, mention should be made of the division of the Psalter as a whole into five "books" (Pss. 1–41, 42–72, 73–89, 90–106, 107–50). The five books each conclude with a doxology, and they vary in preference of divine name. That is, Book 1 has a clear preference for the divine name Yahweh (it occurs 272 times, while Elohim occurs a mere 15 times), while in Book 2 the preference is reversed (Yahweh occurs 74 times; Elohim 207 times). The fivefold division is an attempt to mirror the fivefold Pentateuch.

It is impossible to determine why the books were divided where they were. Certain psalms are grouped together on the basis of similarity in authorship, content, or function. Nonetheless, these groups are occasional, and no overall organizational structure to the book may be observed. The last word has not yet been said. While an overall, formal structure may not be discovered in the Psalter, there are what appear to be intentional movements and placements within the book as a whole.

The most interesting movement is that from a predominance of laments to a predominance of hymns. Reading through the book of Psalms, one comes away with the impression that joy is the predominant mood. This overall impression explains why the Hebrew title of the book is *Tehillim,* "Songs of Joy." It is disconcerting, therefore, to discover that laments far outnumber hymns in the Psalter. However, the hymns are proportionally greater at the conclusion of the book. Thus the overall impression of joy comes both from the movements within the Psalter and from the intentional placement of the last five psalms. Psalms 146–50, placed at the end of the book, provide a Great Doxology (as these psalms have been traditionally known).

Noting that the final form of the Psalter shows evidence of an intentional placement of psalms at the end leads us back to the opening of the book. It has long been noticed that the first psalm provides an appropriate introduction to the whole book. Psalm 1 is fairly unusual in that it is a wisdom psalm that makes a sharp distinction between the wicked and the righteous. As one enters the sanctuary of the Psalter (see Theological Message), the worshiper is confronted with the basic choice of wickedness and righteousness.

The peculiar structure of the Psalter has some basic implications for the exegesis of the book. The most obvious is that most psalms do not have a normal literary context. Except under rare circumstances, it is inappropriate to exegete a psalm in the literary context of the psalms that precede and follow it. On the positive side, the structure of the Psalter shows the need for genre analysis. The primary literary context for the study of a psalm, therefore, is not the psalms that border it, but the psalms that are generically similar to it.

Reading through the book of Psalms, one comes away with the impression that joy is the predominant mood.

THEOLOGICAL MESSAGE

Introduction

A discussion of the theological message of the Psalter is difficult for two reasons. First, the book is composed of 150 individual compositions and, accordingly, does not present a systematically developed argument. Second, as will be more fully explored below, the psalms are prayers sung to God; thus, they present us with the words of the congregation addressed to God, rather than the word of God addressed to the people of Israel. How, then, is it possible to speak of the theological concerns of the Psalter?

It is true that the Psalter does not present us with a neatly developed systematic theology. The psalms do not progressively unfold the character of God or the nature of his relationship with human beings from its beginning to its end. However, the psalms are a rich source for theological teaching and reflection. While it is correct to say that the Psalter's theology is not systematic, we must be quick, on the other side, to affirm that it is extensive—so extensive, in fact, that the Psalter is a "microcosm" of the teaching of the whole Old Testament. In the well-known words of Martin Luther, the book of Psalms is "a little Bible, and the summary of the Old Testament." Therefore, the real difficulty in a discussion of the theology of the Psalter is not lack of subject matter, but the realization that the theology of the Psalter is coextensive with the theology of the Old Testament.

The other potential stumbling block to a theology of the Psalter is that it is a book composed primarily of prayers. Men and women cry out to God. In this regard, the Psalms may be contrasted with the bulk of the Old Testament. In the prophets, for instance, we clearly hear the voice of God as he addressed the community through his chosen mediator (cf. the familiar phrase "thus says the Lord"). Many conclude from this contrast that the book of Psalms presents us with the human response to the divine encounter. Thus, while instructive, the teaching is not normative theology. Many people support such a view of the Psalter with an appeal to the curses of the psalms (Pss. 69:22–29; 109:6–21). God is not teaching his people to hate his enemies, is he? After all, elsewhere God teaches that his people should love their enemies.

It is incontestably true that the psalms are prayers, not oracles. However, their inclusion in the canon attests to their nature as the word of God. After all, though the divine presence is much clearer in the prophets and even the historical books, these words also were delivered through the mediation of human beings. Furthermore, not every prayer of Israel is found in the Psalter. The prayers of the Psalter are the prayers accepted by the priests into the formal worship of Israel (1 Chron. 16:4–38).

Thus, it is meaningful to discuss the theology of the Psalter. However, we must bear in mind that the book's theology is extensive but not systematic, that it is confessional and doxological, not abstract.

Covenantal Prayerbook

Since a theology of the Psalter is coextensive with a theology of the Old Testament, a discussion of the former will be more suggestive than exhaustive. At the heart of the Psalms, as well as of the Old Testament, is the divine-human encounter. To put it another way, relationship between God and human beings is the focus of both the Old Testament and the book of Psalms. This relationship is described by means of a variety of images of God: shepherd, warrior, father, mother, king, husband, to name a few. Each emphasizes a particular aspect of God's relationship with his people.

Without demeaning the variety of images and perspectives with which the Old Testament provides the reader, a good case can be made that covenant is the most extensively used metaphor of relationship. There is no doubt that the people of God understood themselves to be in a covenant relationship with God from the time of their founding father Abraham (Gen. 15 and 17), through Moses (Ex. 19–24) and David (2 Sam. 7).

Thus, while the psalmist pours out his heart before the Lord in prayers of joy and sorrow, he understands himself to be in an intimate relationship with God. He knows that he is in covenant with the God of the universe.

The nature of the covenant and its literary and conceptual relationship with ancient Near Eastern treaties are discussed elsewhere (pp. 110–12). It must further be admitted that the term covenant ($b^e er\hat{i}t$) is explicitly used in only twelve psalms (it is a major theme only in Psalms 89 and 132). Nonetheless, we cannot ignore the fact that the psalmists speak out in the context of the covenant. These are people who speak to God and about God on the basis of being in a covenant relationship with him. Thus covenant is a concept that ties together many strands of the theology of the Psalms. We cannot hope to cover the topic exhaustively, but five selected topics will be treated for illustrative purposes.

Zion. God made his presence known in a special way on Mount Zion. It was on this mountain on the northern boundary of David's Jerusalem that Solomon constructed the temple. As the repository of the ark of the covenant as well as of other objects that symbolized God's presence, the temple represented God's intimate relationship with Israel.

As such, Zion itself is a frequent object of praise in the Psalms. Psalm 48 is a moving example of a "Zion" psalm that praises God by lovingly describing his holy dwelling place:

> Great is the LORD, and most worthy of praise,
>> in the city of our God, his holy mountain.
> Beautiful in its loftiness,
>> the joy of the whole earth,
> like the heights of Zaphon is Mount Zion,
>> the city of the Great King.
> God is in her citadels;
>> he has shown himself to be her fortress. (vv. 1–3)

The holiness that pertains to Zion is frequently widened to include the whole city of Jerusalem, with the result that that city is often extolled in the Psalms as well:

> Jerusalem is built like a city
>> that is closely compacted together.
> That is where the tribes go up—
>> the tribes of the LORD—

to praise the name of the LORD
   according to the statute given to Israel. (Ps. 122:3–4)

In all of this, it is important to remember that Zion and Jerusalem are not holy in and of themselves. Rather, they are holy because God has chosen to make his presence known there in a special way. It is from Zion that his blessings go forth.

History. History plays a key role in biblical covenants. The relationship between God and his people has a background that is recited at times of covenant formation and renewal (Ex. 20:2; Deut. 1:6–4:49; Josh. 24:2–13; 1 Sam. 12:8–15).

Historical memory is significant in the Psalms as well. God's past acts of deliverance and love toward his people are constantly called to mind by the psalmist. The people of God find occasion in them for joy (Ps. 98:1–3). They also call his merciful acts to mind as they are in the midst of trouble and distress (Ps. 77). While many psalms have a historical component, a select number of psalms (described above as psalms of remembrance) have as their principle aim the recounting of God's historical works (Pss. 78, 105, 106, 136).

Thus God's covenantal presence is not abstract, mystical, or individual. God enters into the realm of history and acts on Israel's behalf. The psalmist finds frequent occasions to extol God's work in space and time.

Law. God imposes on his people certain obligations that take the form of law. God gave the law to Israel after he had entered into a covenantal relationship with that nation and with the history of salvation as the background. This pattern may be clearly seen in the book of Exodus. Before the Ten Commandments and the rest of the Mosaic laws are given to the people, God delivered the people from Egyptian bondage. Law comes within and not before God enters into relationship with his people.

It is within this covenantal relationship that the psalmist extols the law and presses upon the people their obligation to keep it. Certain psalms take up the law as their main concern. Psalm 1 advises close adherence to the law, not by command but by the description of the blessings that flow to the one who keeps the law. Psalm 19 follows in the same vein but also evokes powerful images to describe the benefits of the law:

They are more precious than gold,
   than much pure gold;
they are sweeter than honey,
   than honey from the honeycomb. (v. 10)

Perhaps the most well-known psalm that extols the law of God is 119. This "Giant Psalm" of twenty-two stanzas (176 verses) expresses the most intense love for the law found in the Bible:

Oh, how I love your law!
I meditate on it all day long.
Your commands are always with me
and make me wiser than my enemies. (vv. 97–98)

But it is not just in these few psalms that covenantal obligation is brought to the fore. The psalmist continually exhorts the congregation to an obedient response to God, frequently turning to the congregation and addressing it in an imperative mood. The exhortation is often to worship God, to praise him for all that he has done (Ps. 30:4–5).

Kingship. The king stands behind the covenant. The covenant, like a treaty, is agreed upon by two kings representing their people. The vassal treaty, which is the model for the divine-human covenant in the Old Testament, is a political relationship between a king who represents a politically superior state and a less powerful king who subordinates himself and his people to the great king. In Old Testament covenants, God is the Great King, and Israel, represented by the Davidic king, is the servant nation.

It is not unexpected, therefore, that kingship is a major theme in the Psalter. On the one hand, a number of psalms extol God as king (Pss. 47, 93, 95–99). He is the King not only of Israel but of the entire universe, and the whole universe owes him praise (96:1). After all, he created all that exists (95:3–5).

On the other hand, the human king also plays a highly important role in the Psalter. He is the one whom God has chosen to lead his people and to mediate his kingship to them (Ps. 2). A number of psalms are explicitly connected with the royal theme, since the king is the subject (e.g., 20, 21). A number of other psalms are clearly connected with the human king by virtue of their title and the language that is used to describe the speaker. For instance, in Psalm 3 the number of foes and their ferocity suggests that the king is in view here (Eaton 1976). This assertion is supported by the title that claims Davidic authorship.

Psalm 2, most likely a coronation psalm (Craigie 1983, 62–69), reveals the relationship between God as king enthroned in heaven (v. 4) and the anointed king who rules and prospers with his blessing (vv. 6–9). The latter reflects the glory of the former. God protects and blesses his anointed human king in the face of hostile opposition.

The relationship between the king and God has been a topic of intense research in recent years. Prominent interpreters of the Psalms (Mowinckel and the Scandinavian school) argued that there was a close relationship between the human king and God, some even claiming that the Psalms presented a divine king. The primary argument used to support this position was from the ideology of kingship supposedly current in the broader ancient Near East. Such extreme views are no longer current in Psalms research. In the words of H.-J. Kraus (1986, 111), "It is beyond doubt that in Israel's worship the king was not the object of veneration. Not even rudiments can be found of any veneration offered to him." The king, while playing an important function in the religion of Israel and the Psalms, is nonetheless a human servant of God.

Warfare. The language of battle permeates the Psalter. It is possible to recognize various psalms that are prayers sung before, during, and after a battle (Longman 1982 and 1985). Behind these psalms is the biblical concept of holy war with its connection to the covenant between God and Israel.

In an ancient Near Eastern treaty, the Great King would make two promises to the vassal: first, he would attack the vassal if he rebelled against him; and second, he would come to the defense of any loyal vassal who was set upon. We see the same dynamic operative between God and Israel throughout the Old Testament. He comes as a warrior to fight on behalf of his obedient people (Ex. 15; Judg. 5; Josh. 6), and he fights against them when they rebel (Josh. 7–8; 1 Sam. 4–5; Lamentations). Israel's warfare in the Old Testament is holy because it is Yahweh who leads them into battle. He is the one who lays down the ground rules for Israel's warfare (Deut. 7, 20).

Psalm 7 is representative of a prayer before Israel enters into warfare. The psalmist calls on God to deliver him from his enemies (vv. 1–2). It is typical in the prebattle psalms for the psalmist to directly address God and call for his aid:

> Arise, LORD, in your anger;
>> rise up against the rage of my enemies.
> Awake, my God; decree justice. (v. 6)

God is frequently named with martial images (e.g., shield, v. 10) and is pictured as a soldier preparing for battle (vv. 12–13).

When the psalmist is in the midst of warfare, he turns to the Lord to express his trust in him as he faces great dangers. Psalm 91 finds its most appropriate setting in the war camp at night between battles. The psalmist faces the danger of battle (vv. 5, 7) and pestilence (v. 6). Yet he feels perfectly secure in God, his shelter and shadow (v. 1).

Finally, when the warfare is over, Israel recognized that God was the one who provided the victory. Psalm 98 contains three stanzas. The first celebrates the victory that God has accomplished for his people in the presence of the nations (vv. 1–3). As a result of the victory, God is proclaimed a king (vv. 4–6) and coming judge (vv. 7–9).

Many psalms find their primary setting in warfare. These psalms are motivated by the ideology of holy war and frequently present an awesome picture of God as the Divine Warrior:

> The LORD thundered from heaven;
>> the voice of the Most High resounded.
> He shot his arrows and scattered the enemy,
>> with great bolts of lightning he routed them. (Ps. 18:13–14)

Israel's warfare in the Old Testament is holy because it is Yahweh who leads them into battle. He is the one who lays down the ground rules.

Polemical Function of the Psalms

A modern-day pitfall is to think of the book of Psalms as a collection of timeless poetry. On the contrary, the psalms are well entrenched in their contemporary milieu. Their relevance to the time period of their composition may be clearly seen in their polemical edge.

One of the major dangers facing Israel during the period covered by the Old Testament was apostasy. Many Israelites were attracted to the gods and goddesses of the ancient Near East, particularly the Canaanite deities. The biblical historical accounts themselves indicate that Baal worship was particularly tempting to them.

The psalms speak to this danger in many subtle ways. Psalm 29 is a particularly rich example of a psalm that extols Yahweh at the implicit expense of Baal (Cross; Craigie). The modern reader is apt to miss the theological polemics of the psalm unless the psalm is read very carefully and with some knowledge of Canaanite religion.

Many of the details of Psalm 29 remind us of a Canaanite poem. It shares many traits with the type of poetry discovered at Ugarit. In the first place, the psalm is unusually heavy with tricola, and its parallelism is very repetitive. These are characteristics of Ugaritic as contrasted with Hebrew poetry. The psalm opens with an exhortation to the "mighty ones" (NIV). In Hebrew this phrase is $b^e n \hat{e}$ '$\bar{e}l\hat{i}m,$ more strictly translated as "sons of God" and resembling the Ugaritic expression bn 'ilm (also "sons of god"), which in that context refers to the divine assembly. The geographical references (vv. 6, 8) all reflect a northern orientation, the region toward Ugarit and other Canaanite enclaves.

Besides the details of the psalm, the imagery associated with Yahweh bears a striking resemblance to the descriptions of Baal in the Ugaritic texts. Yahweh is imaged in the psalm as a powerful storm cloud. His lightning and thunder ("voice") shake the landscape. Baal's specialty among the gods of Canaan was rain and fertility. The point of Psalm 29 appears to be that it is Yahweh, not Baal, who is behind the power of the rains. That a connection between Yahweh and Baal is being consciously and polemically drawn by the psalmist is confirmed by the concluding image of God sitting on a throne that is situated above a flood. This reminds us of the well-known episode in the Baal epic in which Baal defeats the Sea (Yam) and then occupies himself with the building of his royal palace.

Psalm 29 is illustrative of a fairly common phenomenon of allusions to Near Eastern mythological images that are found in the psalms. This is not to be interpreted as a kind of crass borrowing from Near Eastern religion. Rather, we are to understand the occurrence of these images as intentional and polemic. Far from showing that the psalmists are the intentional promulgators of a broad Near Eastern religion, it shows their concern to promote the exclusive worship of Yahweh over the other nonexistent gods and goddesses of the ancient Near East.

APPROACHING THE NEW TESTAMENT

Luke 24 recounts the postresurrection appearances of Jesus. In the latter half of the chapter when Jesus met with his frightened disciples, they were surprised at his appearance. In response to their doubts, he appealed to the Scripture: "This is what I told you while I was still with you: Everything must be fulfilled that is written about me in the Law of Moses, the Prophets and the Psalms" (v. 44). What is important for our present study is the mention of the Psalms. From the context it is clear that Jesus is referring not only to the book we call Psalms but more generally to the third part of the canon of the Hebrew Bible (Beckwith 1985, 111–12). Nonetheless, the reference also obviously includes the book of Psalms. Jesus is saying in no uncertain terms that the book of Psalms anticipated him, and that his coming in some sense fulfilled that book.

The New Testament writers recognized this connection between Jesus and the Psalms. The book of Psalms vies only with Isaiah for frequency of citation in the pages of the New Testament (Harman 1968; Kistemaker 1985). Of course, the New Testament cites the Psalms to support many different teachings, not just christological ones. In Romans 3 Paul alludes to a number of passages from the Psalter to establish his arguments. He asserts, for instance, that God is completely faithful (v. 4, citing Ps. 51:4) and that man is totally sinful (vv. 10b–18, citing a number of psalms and including a short passage from Isaiah).

However, of present interest to us is the large number of times the New Testament authors cite the Psalms to establish the identity of Jesus as Messiah and Son of God. For more extensive discussion, the work of Harman and Kistemaker may be consulted, but a brief example is found in Acts 4. Here Peter speaks to the Jewish leaders who are questioning them and describes the rejection and then the glorification of Jesus. He bolsters his argument by citing Psalm 118:22, saying that "Jesus is 'the stone you builders rejected, which has become the cornerstone'" (Acts 4:11). Jesus is the stone rejected and then placed in the most significant position in the building.

It is important to realize that psalms are not prophetic in the narrow sense. In some circles it is believed that a small number of very significant psalms have no Old Testament referent but apply only to the coming Messiah. Examples include Psalms 2, 16, 22, 69, and 110. Indeed, these psalms are particularly important if for no other reason than that the New Testament writers quote them more than any other psalms. However, they too have an Old Testament context. Psalm 2, for instance, is clearly a coronation psalm (Craigie 1983, 64–69); and Psalm 69 admits guilt on the part of the psalmist that would make it inappropriate as a prophetic statement of the sinless Christ (v. 5).

How then are the psalms fulfilled in Christ? There are two premises on which the connection between the psalms and Jesus is built. The first is the relationship between the psalmist and Jesus. The speaker in many of the psalms is the Davidic king. Furthermore, the Davidic king is often the focus of a psalm. We must remember at this point some facts about the theology of kingship in Israel. The Israelite king is the human reflection of the kingship of God. He rules because God established him as ruler. This is particularly the case with David, with whom God made a special covenant (2 Sam. 7), establishing his kingship and his dynasty. Accordingly, it is significant that so much of the Psalter is connected with the institution of kingship in Israel and more specifically with David and his dynasty.

As we turn to the New Testament, we see the fulfillment of the promise of the Davidic covenant that a son of David will sit forever on the throne. That promise is fulfilled in the person of Jesus Christ, who, according to Paul, "as to his earthly life was a descendant of David" (Rom. 1:3).

Thus Luke 1:31–33 (cf. Ps. 89:3–4) records the following blessing upon Mary:

> You will conceive and give birth to a son, and you are to call him Jesus. He will be great and will be called the Son of the Most High. The Lord God will give him the throne of his father David, and he will reign over the house of Jacob forever; his kingdom will never end.

In addition, Jesus is anticipated in the Psalter because he is the Son of God. The psalms are offered to God, and, as the second person of the Trinity, Jesus is the appropriate object of our praise and lament.

The author of Hebrews sets the pattern. In the first chapter, where he cites a number of Old Testament passages to show Christ's superiority to the angels, he includes Psalm 102:25–27 in reference to Jesus (see Heb. 1:8):

> In the beginning, Lord, you laid the foundations of the earth,
>   and the heavens are the work of your hands.
> They will perish, but you remain;
>   they will all wear out like a garment.
> You will roll them up like a robe;
>   like a garment they will be changed.
> But you remain the same,
>   and your years will never end. (Heb. 1:10–12)

In its Old Testament context, this psalm was sung to Yahweh. From a New Testament perspective, it is correctly sung to Jesus on the grounds that Jesus, while fully human, is fully God and worthy of divine praise.

On these grounds and following the New Testament examples, it is legitimate to read the Psalms from a christological perspective. Clowney (1973 and 1978) has written briefly, but suggestively, on a generic approach to a Christian reading of the Psalms. From that perspective, he states that the Psalms are properly thought of as the prayers of Jesus (Heb. 2:12) and prayers to Jesus. Thus, for example, the hymns as the songs of Jesus indicate his glorification and may be sung to him to glorify him. The laments indicate his humiliation (and are so applied by the New Testament authors), and they may be prayed to him as expressions of the sufferings of modern Christians.

CHAPTER SEVENTEEN

PROVERBS

Proverbs is the focus of attention in a number of Christian circles at the present time. Our age has become increasingly absorbed with interest in ourselves and how we relate to others, and many feel that this book provides divinely given help in understanding human personality and behavior.

Proverbs, though, is in another sense out of the mainstream of the Old Testament. There are no references to the great acts of redemption or to the covenant, and there is very little explicit talk about God. This absence of explicit religious language has led some to speak of the content of the book as "secular" wisdom.

However, as we explore the book more deeply, we come to see just how deeply theological the book is. It is a book of practical advice, but it is advice given in the context of the "fear of the LORD."

BIBLIOGRAPHY

Commentaries

R. J. **Clifford,** *Proverbs* (OTL; Westminster John Knox, 1999); M. V. **Fox,** *Proverbs 1–9* (AB; Doubleday, 2000); D. A. **Garrett,** *Proverbs. Ecclesiastes. Song of Songs* (NAC; Broadman, 1993); D. **Kidner,** *Proverbs* (TOTC; InterVarsity Press, 1964); T. **Longman** III, *Proverbs* (Baker, 2005); W. **McKane,** *Proverbs: A New Approach* (OTL; Westminster, 1970); R. E. **Murphy,** *Proverbs* (WBC; Thomas Nelson, 1998); L. G. **Perdue,** *Proverbs* (Interp: John Knox Press, 2000); R. B. Y. **Scott,** *Proverbs, Ecclesiastes* (AB; Doubleday, 1965); C. H. **Toy,** *The Book of Proverbs* (ICC; Scribner, 1916); R. **van Leeuwen,** "Proverbs," in *The New Interpreter's Bible* (Abingdon, 1997); B. **Waltke,** *Proverbs 1–15* (NICOT; Eerdmans, 2004); idem, *Proverbs 16–31* (Eerdmans, 2005); R. N. **Whybray,** *Proverbs* (NCB; Eerdmans, 1994).

Articles and Monographs

L. **Bostrom,** *The God of the Sages: The Portrayal of God in the Book of Proverbs* (CBOTS 29; Almqvist and Wiksell International, 1990); G. E. **Bryce,** *A Legacy of*

Wisdom: The Egyptian Contribution to the Wisdom of Israel (Lewisburg: Bucknell University Press, 1979); C. H. **Bullock,** *An Introduction to the Old Testament Poetic Books* (Moody, 1979); E. **Drioton,** "Le Livre des Proverbes et la sagesse d'Amen-emope," in *Sacra Pagina: Miscellenea Biblica Congressus internationalis Catholici de Re Biblica,* ed. J. Coppens, A. Desamps, E. Massux, col. 1; Bibliotheca ephemeridum theologicarum Lovaniensium, cols. 12–13 (Gembloux: J. Duculot, 1959); A. **Erman,** "Eine ägyptische Quelle der 'Sprüche Salomos,'" *Sitzungsberichte der Preussischen Akademie der Wissenschaften zu Berlin: Phi.-his. Klasse* 15 (1924): 86–93; H. **Gressmann,** "Die neugefundene Lehre des Amen-em-ope und die vorexilishche Sprochdichtung Israels," *ZAW* 42 (1924): 272–96; K. M. **Heim,** *Like Grapes of Gold Set in Silver: An Interpretation of Proverbial Clusters in Proverbs 10:1–22:16* (Walter de Gruyter, 2001); T. **Hildebrandt,** "Compositional Units in Proverbs 10–29," *JBL* 107 (1988): 207–24; P. **Humbert,** *Recherches sur les sources egyptiennes de la littérature sapientiale d'Israel* (Memoires de l'Universite de Neuchâtel, vol. 7; Neuchatel: Secretariat de'l Universite, 1919); C. **Kayatz,** *Studien zue israelitischen Spruchweischeit* (WMANT 28; Neukirchen-Vluyn, 1968); R. O. **Kevin,** *The Wisdom of Amen-em-ope and Its Possible Dependence upon the Book of Proverbs* (Austria: Adolf Mozhausen's Successors, 1931); K. A. **Kitchen,** "Proverbs and Wisdom Books of the Ancient Near East: The Factual History of a Literary Form," *TynBul* 28 (1977): 69–114; B. **Lang,** *Wisdom and the Book of Proverbs: An Israelite Goddess Redefined* (Pilgrim, 1986); T. **Longman** III, *How to Read Proverbs* (InterVarsity Press, 2002); W. O. E. **Oesterley,** *The Wisdom of Egypt and the Old Testament in the Light of the Newly Discovered 'Teaching of Amenem-ope'* (SPCK, 1927); J. **Ruffle,** "The Teaching of Amenemope and its Connection with the Book of Proverbs," *TynBul* 28 (1977): 29–68; E. **Sellin,** "Die neugefundene Lehre des 'Amen-em-ope' in ihrer Bedeutung für judische Literatur und Religionsgeschiechte," *Deutsche Literaturzeitung fur Kritik der internationalen Wissenschaft* 45 (1924): 1873–84; P. W. **Skehan,** *Studies in Israelite Poetry and Wisdom* (CBQMS 1; Washington, D.C.: Catholic Biblical Association of America, 1971); J. A. Soggin, *Introduction to the Old Testament (IOT,* Westminster John Knox, 3rd ed., 1989); R. C. **van Leeuwen,** Context *and Meaning in Proverbs 25–27* (SBLDS 96; Atlanta: Scholars, 1988); G. **von Rad,** *Wisdom in Israel* (Abingdon, 1972); R. N. **Whybray,** *Wisdom in Proverbs: The Concept of Wisdom in Proverbs 1–9* (Allenson, 1968); idem, *The Book of Proverbs: A Survey of Modern Study* (E. J. Brill, 1995); J. G. **Williams,** *Those Who Ponder Proverbs: Aphoristic Thinking and Biblical Literature* (Sheffield: Almond, 1981).

HISTORICAL BACKGROUND

Authorship

As our literary analysis will demonstrate, the book of Proverbs is an anthology composed of a number of texts from different authors and various time periods. Frequently, the sections are marked by captions that indicate authorship. They cite a group called "the wise" (22:17; 24:23), Agur (30:1), King Lemuel (31:1), and Solomon (1:1; 10:1; 25:1) as sources of the wisdom of the book. Only Proverbs 1:8–9:18 and 31:10–31 are without an explicit authorship attribution. Proverbs 1:1–7 serves as an extended superscription and introduction to the book that connects authorship to Solomon but does not claim it for the section itself.

It is Solomon's role in the book that has attracted the most attention, not only because so much of the book is connected with his name (10:1–22:16; 25:1–29:27), but also because the book opens with what looks at first blush like a superscription that attributes the entire book to him. From the conservative side, there has always been the tendency to argue that Solomon was responsible for more of the book than it explicitly gives him credit for. G. Archer, for instance, believed that 1:1, while covering the whole book, also ascribed Solomonic authorship to 1:8–9:18, arguing that the king assembled the "sayings of the wise," which Archer accordingly insisted (without evidence) came from a time period before Solomon (Archer, *SOTI*, 476–77). On the other hand, on the far left, some critical scholars assert that nothing in Proverbs may be directly attributed to Solomon (Toy 1916, xix–xx) and that his role in the book is the result of his legendary wisdom.

As usual, the hard evidence of the book leads to something between the two extremes, and this is the position of the majority of conservative and some present-day critical scholars. Following the information given by the captions, it is best to limit Solomon's contribution to 10:1–22:16 and 25:1–29:27. However, these sections still constitute the single major contribution of the book, and perhaps the earliest portion. Thus it is certainly appropriate for the first verse to identify Solomon as the main contributor and initiator of the anthology. After all, Solomon's connections with biblical wisdom is a major theme of the historical narrative concerning his reign as found in the book of Kings. He prays for and receives wisdom from God (1 Kings 3:1–15); he then demonstrates that wisdom in a practical case (vv. 16–28). His wisdom far surpasses that of those in the rest of the world (1 Kings 4:29–31), amazing even the Queen of Sheba, who travels a long distance to confirm what she has heard about him (1 Kings 10:1–13). His wisdom led to a prodigious production of proverbs; 1 Kings 4:32 declares that three thousand are attributed to him.

Nothing much is known about the other authors named in the book. Agur and Lemuel are names that occur only once and with very little additional information. The "wise" are anonymous, though their designation may indicate that they were professional scholars perhaps serving the court.

The only other group named in the book are the "men of Hezekiah." While early Jewish tradition may have ascribed authorship of the book to them ("Hezekiah and his company wrote the Proverbs," *Baba, Bathra* 15a), Proverbs 25:1 clearly gives them a scribal and perhaps redactional role.

Date

As an anthology, Proverbs was written over a long period of time. How long is not clear, since there are anonymous sections as well as a mention of authors about whom we know nothing outside of the book. Indeed, we are on firm ground only with those sections ascribed to Solomon (tenth century BC) and with the redactional activity of Hezekiah's men (c. 700 BC). Since the work of the latter is limited to one small portion of the book, it is reasonable to infer that there was a later redactional stage that arranged the entire book and provided the short introduction (1:1–7). The exact date of this final editing is not known.

It is virtually impossible to date, even relatively, the writing of the other parts of the book. It is often argued that 1:8–9:18 is the latest part of the book. Scholars cite the more complex and longer style (Prov. 2 is a single sentence, according to some), the more explicitly religious perspective (and specifically the personification of wisdom) as well as the supposed lateness of some words (particularly 'ēṭûn, "linens," in Prov. 7:16 [see McKane; Scott; Soggin, *IOT*, 384]). The first two arguments (presented most forcefully by McKane) have been resisted by von Rad (1972, 24–50), who believes they are a figment of the form critic's imagination, while the last runs into the difficulties of any linguistic argument for dating—the evidence is not abundant enough to give any certainty. Kayatz (1968) has suggested that the differences between 1:8–9:18 and the rest of the book have more to do with style than chronology.

> *Proverbs was written over a long period of time. How long is not clear, since there are anonymous sections and authors we know nothing about outside of the book.*

LITERARY ANALYSIS

Literary Structure

Proverbs is a book with a clear-cut general outline. In the first place, we can observe a distinction between Proverbs 1–9 and 10–31. As a general characterization, the first part contains extended wisdom discourses, while most of the latter part is composed of the short, pithy sayings we usually associate with the name of the book. We are able to go further and distinguish sections within these two parts of the book. Indeed, the final editor has provided the reader with captions or other signals at the head of each section. We thus recognize that the book of Proverbs is in actuality a collection or anthology.

Outline

Preamble (1:1–7)
Extended Discourses on Wisdom (1:8–9:18)
Solomonic Proverbs (10:1–22:16; 25:1–29:27)
Sayings of the Wise (22:17–24:34)
Sayings of Agur (30)
Sayings of King Lemuel (31:1–9)
Poem to the Virtuous Woman (31:10–31)

ANALYSIS OF THE CONTENTS

Preamble (1:1–7)

The preamble performs three functions. First, it presents the reader with the superscription for the whole book (1:1). In the first verse, Solomon is named as the source of wisdom found in the book. While this statement cannot be construed to imply that Solomon wrote the whole book (see Authorship above), it nonetheless indicates that he played a major role in its formation. Second, the preamble clearly states the purpose of the book (vv. 2–6). Proverbs functions to impart wisdom to both the simple and the wise. Young men were the particular audience of the book when it was first composed. The aim of the book, then, is to lay a foundation and offer some specific guidance to young men as they seek their way in the real world. However, 1:5 expands the audience to include the wise as well. Last, and perhaps more significant, the preamble offers the basis on which the rest of the book depends (v. 7). The presupposition of all wisdom is the fear of God. In other words, according to the author of the preamble, relationship precedes ethics.

Extended Discourses on Wisdom (1:8–9:18)

The opening chapters are radically different from the later ones in terms of form. While the last part of the book is dominated by the characteristic proverb form of short (predominantly bicola) aphorisms, the first nine chapters contain longer wisdom sayings. The discourses have two forms: either a teacher addresses his son, as for instance in 1:8–19, or personified wisdom speaks for herself (1:20–33).

There has been much disagreement about the exact division and structure of this section. In one of the most complete studies of the subject, Whybray (1968) identifies ten discourses, while more traditional interpreters find fifteen (Bullock, 174–75). In perhaps one of the most original analyses of the subject, Skehan (1971, 9–14) argues that some of the discourses are a frame (chaps. 1, 8, and 9) to seven others (chaps. 2–7), and these he identifies as the "seven pillars" of Lady Wisdom's house (9:1).

The most serious difficulty with Skehan's interpretation is that there is no reason for taking what appears to be two separate discourses in the first chapter (1:8–19; 1:20–33) as part of a frame. Indeed, it is difficult to make hard-and-fast decisions concerning divisions between some sections. Fortunately, it is not important to separate the discourses to understand the section. However, after careful study, the following division seems most appropriate:

1:8–19: Avoid evil associations
1:20–33: Don't resist woman wisdom
2:1–22: The benefits of the Way of Wisdom
3:1–12: Trust in Yahweh

3:13–20: Praising Wisdom
3:21–35: The integrity of Wisdom
4:1–9: Embrace Wisdom!
4:10–19: Stay on the right path
4:20–27: Guard your heart
5:1–23: Avoid promiscuous women; love your wife
6:1–19: Wisdom admonitions: loans, laziness, lying, and other topics
6:20–35: The danger of adultery
7:1–27: Avoid promiscuous women: Part II
8:1–36: Wisdom's autobiography
9:1–6, 13–18: The ultimate encounter: Wisdom or folly
9:7–12: Miscellaneous wisdom sayings

The discourses serve as the hermeneutical guide to the interpretation of the rest of the book. They provide the religious underpinnings for the proverbs that follow in chapter 10 and following (see Theological Message below).

Since the discourses serve in this way and since they are a more complex literary form than the *mᵉšālîm* to follow, these chapters are often taken as one of the latest additions to the book. However, it is not necessarily true that literary forms move from simple to complex (von Rad 1972, 27–28), and, while it is equally dangerous to insist on Solomonic dating, one must be careful about being dogmatic about a late date.

Solomonic Proverbs (10:1–22:16; 25:1–29:27)

Two captions (10:1; 25:1) identify Solomon as the author of the proverbs found in these sections. In the second, the men of Hezekiah have a role in the transmission of the text (see Authorship above).

In terms of form, these sections are composed almost totally of short, two-phrased parallel lines (bicola), though occasionally there is an expanded wisdom meditation (27:20–27). It is interesting that there is a concentration of antithetical parallelism (perhaps as much as 90 percent in the first collection, cf. von Rad 1972, 28), in which the same truth is examined from opposite perspectives:

> The heart of the righteous weighs its answers,
>   but the mouth of the wicked gushes evil. (15:28)

The use of the antithetical form fits in nicely with one of the main themes of these proverbs: the contrast between the righteous wise and the wicked fool.

It is difficult to read and absorb large numbers of these proverbs because of their compactness. In short compass, they express observations about human experience, imparting an intensity that calls for prolonged reflection. This intensity is heightened by the extensive use of metaphor and simile, which also requires unpacking by the reader.

Although intense, proverbs do not always express a profound truth. Indeed, sometimes the proverbial form creates a new perspective and interest on a rather mundane point. For instance, common observation concludes that a lazy person likes to stay put and not go outside where he or she might encounter work, but Proverbs 22:13 captures our attention with an aphorism containing a compact narrative:

> The sluggard says, "There's a lion outside!
> I'll be killed in the public square!"

The structure of the individual proverbs also complicates reading large numbers of them at one sitting. At least on a surface reading, the proverbs appear to have a random order. A saying about drunkards (20:1) is followed by proverbs about the king's wrath (v. 2), avoiding quarrels (v. 3), and sloth (v. 4). While there are some signs of grouping (sayings about the king [25:2–7] and about a fool and his folly [26:1–12]), it is more common that proverbs about a particular subject are scattered throughout the collection (for instance, on sloth 10:4, 5, 26; 12:24, etc.).

Recently, attempts have been made to uncover a structure to the proverbs found in these chapters, which traditionally have been considered relatively random. These studies often are quite sophisticated as they describe supposed connections between proverbs that have not been noticed before in the recorded history of interpretation (e.g., Heim 2001, who cites other studies including Hildebrandt [1988] and van Leeuwen [1988]). We should hesitate to sign on to this project, however. The criteria used to link proverbs together are often too broad and/or inconsistently applied. It is all too easy to suggest narrative connections between what are probably isolated proverbs, as is witnessed by the fact that there are as many suggestions for such connections as there are scholars who believe that they are there. It seems best to continue in our understanding of the proverbs in chapters 10–31 as essentially a randomly ordered collection (see Longman 2006).

Sayings of the Wise (22:17–24:34)

This section is clearly demarcated by the caption in 22:17 in which the speaker addresses the readers and exhorts them to listen to the "sayings of the wise." The section is brought to an end by the caption that introduces the next division of the book (25:1). There are two separate parts to the sayings of the wise, divided by an explanatory note: "These also are sayings of the wise" (24:23). The sayings of the wise cover many of the same topics as the Solomonic proverbs: sensitivity toward the poor (22:22–23); the transitory nature of riches (23:4–5); avoiding the wayward woman (23:26–28); ridicule of the lazy person (24:30–34). However, this short section contains a greater variety of literary forms than the Solomonic section. There are a few bicola (22:28; 23:9), but many of the discourses are longer.

Much has been written about the relationship between this section, especially the first part, with the Egyptian instruction genre, particularly the Instruction of Amenemopet (ANET, 421–25). The latter was first introduced to the scholarly world by E. A. W. Budge in 1924 (though it came to light in 1888). While Budge recognized some similarities between Proverbs and Amenemopet, it was A. Erman (1924) who first argued at some length that there was a definite connection between the two texts. He believed that the Hebrew text was dependent on the Egyptian on the basis of connections between words and phrases. He used this connection to emend the text of Proverbs to bring it into closer connection with the Egyptian text. He was followed by many other biblical scholars (e.g., Gressmann, Sellin, and Humbert). On the other hand, some scholars were of a mind to reverse the relationships and were willing to argue that the Egyptian text is dependent on the book of Proverbs (Oesterley, Kevin, Drioton). In support of their thesis, they pointed to alleged Semitisms in the Egyptian text and made much of the "higher" level of morality in Amenemopet as compared to other Egyptian texts.

That there is some kind of relationship between the two texts is hard to deny. This connection may be illustrated with a couple of examples. The first example:

> Do not move an ancient boundary stone
>   set up by your ancestors. (Prov. 22:28)

> Do not carry off the landmark at the boundaries of the arable land, Nor
>   disturb the position of the measuring-cord. (excerpted from chap. 6
>   of Amenemopet)

Another example:

> Do not wear yourself out to get rich;
>   do not trust your own cleverness.
> Cast but a glance at riches, and they are gone,
>   for they will surely sprout wings
>   and fly off to the sky like an eagle. (Prov. 23:4–5)

> Cast not thy heart in pursuit of riches.
> Place not thy heart upon externals . . .
> they [riches] have made themselves wings like geese
> And are flown away to the heavens. (excerpted from chap. 8 of Amenemopet)

These and many other connections show a relationship of some sort between the two texts (see ANET, 424–46 for a list of connections). There are even similarities in their structure. Amenemopet is divided into thirty brief chapters, while the introduction to the first part of the sayings of the wise mentions "thirty sayings" (22:20, assuming a commonly accepted emendation). However, although there is a close relationship, the two texts are not simply copies of one another. G. Bryce (1979) has moved the discussion away from an issue of "borrowing," noting that the Proverbs text "adapts, assimilates, and/or integrates" the Egyptian material to its own worldview.

The similarities between the texts may be at least in part explained by the international character of wisdom that is recognized even within the Bible itself (1 Kings 4:29–34). The wise men of Israel knew the writings of Egypt and vice versa. Indeed, recent writing on the subject has emphasized that the similarities shared by Amenemopet and this section of Proverbs may be found in other ancient wisdom texts (Ruffle; Kitchen). However, there are two reasons why it is more likely that the Egyptian text influenced the Israelite: (1) a dominant culture (like the Egyptian) is less likely to be influenced by a subdominant culture (like that of Israel); and (2) though the date of the Amenemopet text is uncertain, the evidence leans toward one that is earlier than Solomon.

Sayings of Agur (30); Sayings of Lemuel (31:1–9); Poem to the Virtuous Woman (31:10–31)

The book of Proverbs concludes with three relatively brief, independent sections. The second section, and probably also the first, come directly from non-Israelite sources.

The sayings of Agur are very difficult to translate and interpret. Agur opens on a skeptical note, questioning the possibility of knowing God. His skepticism is answered by an appeal to divine revelation (vv. 5–6). Childs points to these verses as an early canonical awareness (*IOTS*, 556–57). The section continues and concludes with a long list of numerical proverbs.

The sayings of King Lemuel are actually passed down from his mother. They concern the proper way for kings to behave.

The book concludes with a powerful acrostic poem on the virtuous woman. This woman reflects her association with Lady Wisdom in Proverbs 8. She is capable both in the home and outside. It is intentional that in the Hebrew Bible the book of Proverbs (and specifically Proverbs 31) is followed first by Ruth and then by the Song of Songs. All three texts present positive feminine characters who are capable without being completely dependent on males.

THEOLOGICAL MESSAGE

Most readers associate the book of Proverbs with the short, pithy statements that are found in the latter two-thirds of the book. With some exceptions, these proverbs do not refer explicitly to God, the history of redemption, or the

The similarities between Proverbs and the Instruction of Amenemopet may be at least in part explained by the international character of wisdom recognized within the Bible itself.

covenant. On a surface reading, they strike one as good, practical advice or observations on life, humanistic observations rather than divine authority. The first proverb is a case in point:

> Wise children bring joy to their father,
>> but foolish children bring grief to their mother. (Prov. 10:1)

It is therefore not surprising to find comments like those of Eissfeldt scattered throughout the literature on Proverbs:

> But the piety here commended is of a general human character, and the specifically Israelite contribution is in the background. The basis for the commendation of wisdom and piety is on the one hand purely secular and rational. . . . (*OTI*, 477)

More recently, it has been noted that, although there is little explicit God-talk in the proverbs (note exceptions like 10:3, 22, 27, 29, etc.), the introductory chapters of the book provide a hermeneutical grid through which the rest of the book should be read, thus placing a profound theological nuance on the individual proverbs (for the full argument, see Longman 2002 as well as Bostrom 1990).

We have already observed (see Literary Structure above) how the book may be divided into two main parts. In the first nine chapters, we read extended discourses that give way in the last part to the pithy proverbs characteristic of the book. Here we will observe that the discourses provide the broader context for the interpretation of the proverbs.

In other words, before encountering the proverbs of chapters 10–31, the reader first hears the teaching of 1–9. The dominant theme of these early chapters is the great value of wisdom and the fearful danger of folly. This teaching comes to a climax in chapter 9, and we will concentrate our discussion there.

The reader encounters two women in Proverbs 9, both beckoning for his attention. These women are Wisdom and Folly. The reader is a part of this extended metaphor and is imagined to be a young man walking along the path of life. As he travels, he hears the two voices, vying for his attention. Both women begin with the same appeal:

> "Let all who are simple come in here!"
>> she says to those who lack judgment. (vv. 4, 16 NIV)

The implied reader is male, especially attentive to the feminine voices he hears from the path. But who are these women? What or whom do they stand for?

By the time we come to Proverbs 9, Wisdom is already an established figure in the book. As early as Proverbs 1:20–33, we encounter a woman on the streets who is calling and beseeching men to come in for an education; and in Proverbs 8, Wisdom reflects on her nature and purpose, as well as her relationship with God.

Personified Folly is not as clearly present in the preceding chapters. There is, however, a close similarity with the "strange" woman, the adulteress against whom the wise father warns his son (2:16–19; 5; 6:20–35; 7).

A key to understanding the nature of Wisdom in Proverbs 9 is the location of her house on the "highest point of the city" (9:3). In the ancient Near East, only one person had the right to dwell on the highest point in the city, the god of that city. In Jerusalem as well, the building on the highest point was the temple on Zion. This observation confirms what we already know about Wisdom from chapter 8; she stands for God's wisdom and ultimately (as a synecdoche) for God himself.

On the other hand, the reader encounters Folly, also personified as a woman and also appealing to the naive young men who are walking by on the path of life. Significantly, her house too is "at the highest point of the city" (9:14). She also stands for the divine, but in this case for all of the deities of the ancient Near East who stand over against Yahweh. Throughout its history, Israel was tempted to worship gods like the Babylonian Marduk or Ishtar, or even more strongly, the Canaanite Baal and Asherah.

The reader is thus confronted with a decision. Both women are calling him to come to them to dine, to share intimacy, and, unpacking the metaphor, to worship them. Will it be Wisdom or Folly? Will it be Yahweh or Baal?

Thus, now we clearly see the alternative before us as we walk along the path of Proverbs that is really the path of life. We may embrace either Yahweh or another god. Which will it be?

This was indeed the situation that confronted the ancient Israelite. He or she had a choice—Yahweh worship or Baalism. Many tried to synthesize the two, but the prophets sternly pointed out that compromise was equivalent to apostasy (1 Kings 18:21). It was either Yahweh alone or nothing. So the practical situation for the Israelites was exactly that of Proverbs 9. They had a choice of two alternatives. Proverbs 1–9, with its climax in the last chapter, powerfully sets out that choice.

Once passing through the prism of Proverbs 1–9, we recognize how deeply theological the individual proverbs that follow really are. In the light of the alternative laid out in Proverbs 9, we see how each individual proverb exceeds the "good advice" that it imparts on a surface reading.

Proverbs 10:1, cited above, illustrates the point. If children bring joy to their parents, then they are wise. In the language of Proverbs 9, they have shown by their behavior that they have embraced wisdom, which means that they have committed themselves to Yahweh. On the other hand, if children bring grief to their parents, then by their behavior they have shown their allegiance to Dame Folly, the poetical representative of a pagan deity.

In this light, the alternative between wisdom and folly is more than "how to get along and advance in the world." It is a matter of life and death. Proverbs

3:18, after all, tells us that those who embrace Wisdom embrace life. Moreover, the horrible truth about Dame Folly is that she is a murderess. She invites people in for a fine dinner, but they never come out: "her guests are deep in the realm of the dead" (9:18).

APPROACHING THE NEW TESTAMENT

Many Christians use the book of Proverbs as an anthology of "mottos." The catchy proverbs provide a series of statements on the right way to behave. On a more sophisticated level, Proverbs is often used as a source book for "biblical counseling."

It cannot be denied that the book provides guidelines for "wise," that is, godly behavior, and much of the recent writing that stresses this perspective is helpful. However, two pitfalls must be avoided: (1) the tendency to absolutize the proverbs; (2) reading the proverbs in an isolated and abstract manner.

Absolutizing the Proverbs

The individual proverbs must be interpreted and applied within the context of the whole book and, indeed, of the whole Bible. They are not divine promises for the here and now, but true observations that time will bear out.

> Those who fear the LORD have a secure fortress,
>   and for their children it will be a refuge. (14:26)

The book of Job is a corrective to the belief that this proverb is true all the time in the present. A mechanical application of this proverb to the here and now was the impetus behind the arguments of Job's "three friends." However, in the light of the biblical teaching about God's justice and the final judgment, this teaching is certainly true. The Lord is a "secure fortress" even for those who die at the hands of evil men and women.

Furthermore, some proverbs are true, but true only in certain situations. The proverbs embody wisdom; only a wise person knows the situation in which a particular proverb applies.

The most dramatic illustration of the context-bound application of proverbs is seen in a comparison of Proverbs 26:4 and 5:

> Do not answer fools according to their folly,
>   or you yourself will be just like them.
> Answer fools according to their folly,
>   or they will be wise in their own eyes.

In other words, it depends on the fool, and the truly wise person will be so sensitive to human nature that he will know when to apply the one and not the other.

Isolating the Proverbs

The other potential pitfall in reading Proverbs is to isolate the individual proverbs from their canonical setting, gleaning the book for little nuggets of good advice. The above analysis of the relationship between Proverbs 1–9 and 10–31 is the first step toward rectifying an exclusively moralistic reading of the book. The next step is to relate the theology of the book of Proverbs to the theology of the New Testament.

One starting point is Jesus' being associated with the figure of Wisdom. For instance, when Paul writes, "The Son is the image of the invisible God, the first-born over all creation" (Col. 1:15), he is using language from Proverbs 8. Similarly, Revelation 3:14, which refers to Jesus as the "ruler of God's creation," evokes the picture of Wisdom's role at creation. At one point, Jesus himself draws the connection. When his behavior angered his opponents, he responded by saying, "Wisdom is proved right by her actions" (Matt. 11:19). The point is not that Jesus identifies himself with Wisdom, so that Proverbs 8 is a kind of prophecy of Christ; on the contrary, Proverbs 8 is a poetic representation of God's attribute of wisdom with no narrowly prophetic intention. To believe Proverbs 8 is prophetic would lead to the Arian heresy, since wisdom is described as created at a point in time by a preexistent God. However, the association between Jesus and Wisdom is appropriate because Jesus embodies the wisdom of God. Christ's wisdom is one of his most frequently foregrounded traits in the New Testament. Jesus Christ is the wisdom of God (1 Cor. 1:30). He is the one "in whom are hidden all the treasures of wisdom and knowledge" (Col. 2:3). Even during his earthly ministry, his wisdom was revealed through his teaching (Mark 1:22). During his youth, he confounded the teachers of the law (Luke 2:41–50), and he "increased in wisdom" (Luke 2:52). His predominant teaching form was the parable (*parabolē*, in Hebrew *māšāl* [also translated "proverb"]), a wisdom form.

Thus, as Christians read the book of Proverbs in the light of the continued revelation of the New Testament, they are confronted with the same question as the ancient Israelites, but with a different nuance. Will we dine with Wisdom or with Folly? The Wisdom who beckons us is none other than Jesus Christ, while the folly that attempts to seduce us is any created thing that we put in the place of the Creator (Rom. 1:22–23).

CHAPTER EIGHTEEN

ECCLESIASTES

Ecclesiastes gives the appearance of having been written with our time in mind. Of course, it was not; all biblical books address the time period in which they were written. However, Ecclesiastes' main voice, calling himself Qohelet, expresses a skepticism that sounds modern. Consequently, many people have turned to this book for help when they have experienced disillusionment with their world and even with their God.

BIBLIOGRAPHY

Commentaries

G. A. **Barton,** *Ecclesiastes* (ICC; T. & T. Clark, 1908); W. P. **Brown,** *Ecclesiastes* (Interp; Westminster John Knox, 2000); J. L. **Crenshaw,** *Ecclesiastes* (OTL; Westminster, 1987); F. **Delitzsch,** *Proverbs, Ecclesiastes, Song of Solomon* (Eerdmans, 1975 [orig. 1872]); M. A. **Eaton,** *Ecclesiastes* (TOTC; InterVarsity Press, 1983); M. V. **Fox,** *Qohelet and His Contradictions* (Sheffield: Almond, 1989); idem, *A Time to Tear Down and a Time to Build Up: A Rereading of Ecclesiastes* (Eerdmans, 1999); D. A. **Garrett,** *Proverbs. Ecclesiastes. Song of Songs* (NAC; Holman, 1993); C. D. **Ginsburg,** *The Song of Songs and Coheleth* (Jersey City: KTAV, 1970 [orig. 1957]); R. **Gordis,** *Koheleth: The Man and His World* (Schocken, 1951; rev. ed. 1987); D. **Kidner,** *A Time to Mourn and a Time to Dance* (InterVarsity Press, 1976); A. **Lauha,** *Kohelet* (BKAT 19; Neukirchener Verlag, 1978); T. **Longman** III, *Ecclesiastes* (NICOT; Eerdmans, 1997); R. E. **Murphy,** *Ecclesiastes* (WBC; Dallas, 1992); I. **Provan,** *Ecclesiastes/Song of Songs* (NIVAC; Zondervan, 2001); R. B. Y. **Scott,** *Proverbs, Ecclesiastes* (AB 18; Doubleday, 1965); C.-L. **Seow,** *Ecclesiastes* (AB; Doubleday, 1999); R. N. **Whybray,** *Ecclesiastes* (NCB; Eerdmans, 1989).

Monographs and Articles

G. **Bartholomew,** *Reading Ecclesiastes: Old Testament Exegesis and Hermeneutical Theory* (Biblical Institute Press, 1998); E. S. **Christianson,** *A Time to Tell: Narra-*

tive Stratagies in Ecclesiastes (Sheffield, 1998); M. **Dahood,** "The Phoenician Background of Qoheleth," *Bib* 7 (1966): 264–82; M. **Fox,** "Frame-Narrative and Composition in the Book of Qohelet," *HUCA* 48 (1977): 83–106; D. C. **Fredericks,** *Qoheleth's Language: Re-evaluating Its Nature and Date* (ANETS 3; Lewiston: Edwin Mellon, 1988); idem, *Coping with Transcience* (Sheffield, 1993); E. W. **Hengstenberg,** *Der Prediger Salomo* (Berlin, 1858); B. **Isaksson,** *Studies in the Language of Qoheleth* (Uppsala, 1987); W. C. **Kaiser** Jr. *Ecclesiastes: Total Life* (Moody, 1979); E. Levine, *The Aramaic Version of Qoholet* (Sepher-Hermon, 1978); T. **Longman** III, *Fictional Akkadian Autobiography* (Eisenbrauns, 1991); idem, "Israelite Genres in Their Ancient Near Eastern Setting," in *The Changing Face of Form Criticism,* ed. M. A. Sweeney and E. Ben Zvi (Eerdmans, 2003), 177–98; D. **Michel,** *Untersuchungen zur Eigenart des Buches Qohelet* (de Gruyter, 1989); A. **Poebel,** *Das Appositionell Bestimmte Pronomen der 1–Pers. Sing. in den Westsemitischen Inschriften* (AS 3; 1931, repr. Eisenbrauns); R. N. **Whybray,** "Qohelet: Preacher of Joy," *JSOT* 23 (1982): 87–92; A. S. **Wright,** "The Riddle of the Sphinx: The Structure of the Book of Qoheleth," *CBQ* 30 (1968): 313–34; idem, "The Riddle of the Sphinx Revisited: Numerical Patterns in the Book of Qoheleth," *CBQ* 42 (1980): 38–51; idem, "Additional Numerical Patterns in Qoheleth," *CBQ* 45 (1983): 32–43; J. S. **Wright,** "The Interpretation of Ecclesiastes," in *Classical Evangelical Essays,* ed. W. C. Kaiser Jr. (Baker, 1972 [orig. 1945]), 133–50.

HISTORICAL BACKGROUND

Date and Authorship

Traditional View. The traditional approach to the question of authorship begins with a close look at the main speaker in the book. He is called Qohelet, which is not his given name, but rather a pseudonym. The verbal root of the name means "to assemble"; thus his name (a qal feminine participle) is literally translated "assembler." Common English translations, "Preacher" or "Teacher," are a result of guessing what type of group Qohelet is gathering to instruct. Neither translation is precise, but "Assembler" sounds awkward in the context.

Traditionalists point to indications that Qohelet is a nickname for none other than Solomon. For one thing, the root of his name ("assemble") is used frequently in 1 Kings 8 when Solomon gathers the people at the dedication of the temple. Furthermore, Qohelet identifies himself as a king and a son of David (1:1–2). These explicit statements, connected with Solomon's well-established reputation as a wisdom teacher, confirm Solomonic authorship and date in the minds of many.

Once this point is made, the book of Ecclesiastes is used to fill out the story of the life of Solomon. The historical books tell us only that Solomon was a wise and godly king who fell into apostasy at the end of his life. As far as the book of Kings is concerned, Solomon never returned to a strong devotion to the Lord.

Indeed, the split between the northern and southern kingdoms (1 Kings 12) is attributed to his sin.

That so much profound and godly wisdom originates with a man who eventually apostatized is too much for some, so an early tradition arose that Ecclesiastes is the writing of a repentant and old Solomon, showing the evils of his apostasy. To make this work, not only must Qohelet be Solomon, but also the voice that addresses Qohelet in the epilogue must be his (12:8–14).

We will call the view that identifies Solomon with Qohelet and dates the book to the tenth century BC the "traditional view." It is not the conservative view, since as we will see, a number of conservative scholars have not agreed with it.

Critical View. With a few exceptions (e.g., Dahood), most critical scholars date the book late in the history of Israel (see most recently Seow, who dates it to the Persian period). As we will see below, there are good reasons for dating Ecclesiastes late. What distinguishes a critical from a conservative late dating, however, is that the former feels no compulsion to follow the claims of the book, while the latter does.

Crenshaw (1987) and Lauha (1978, 3) are typical in dating Ecclesiastes to the late postexilic, but pre-Maccabean period. Crenshaw is more precise: "A date for Qohelet between 225 and 250 remains most likely" (1987, 50).

The main argument used by critics to promote a late date for the book is language and style. For instance, the vocabulary and syntax of Ecclesiastes is compared to late Hebrew and Aramaic, and this argument pushes some to date the book very late. Even Delitzsch, a well-known conservative scholar, has said, "If the book of Koheleth were of old Solomonic origin, then there is no history of the Hebrew language" (1872, 190). Fredericks (1988), however, has devoted a careful study to all the linguistic arguments used to date the book late and has concluded that they are unpersuasive. In any case, so little is known about transmission of the biblical text during its earliest stages that we cannot rule out linguistic updating.

Another approach shows affinities between Qohelet's speech and, for instance, Hellenistic thought. This method too is dubious, since connections can be made with far earlier thought and literary forms (Dahood) and also with much later foreign thought.

All of this is not to dispute the possibility that Ecclesiastes is non-Solomonic and late (see below), but it does question the typical arguments used to support the critical position. In the past it has also been typical for critical scholars to argue that the book contains contradictions, specifically both orthodox and unorthodox statements. They have reasoned that the original speaker in the book was a radically unorthodox skeptic whose thought was later mitigated by a redactor or a series of redactors. The orthodox redactor was responsible, for instance, for the epilogue. A reading of the book that takes into account the two different voices of the book (see Structure below) does not have to resort to this hypothesis.

An Alternative View. Internal considerations are of paramount importance in determining the date and authorship of a book. Tradition is often helpful and never to be ignored, but even the earliest tradition concerning Ecclesiastes' authorship does not go back beyond the time of Christ, and theological considerations may have already distorted the truth. As Etan Levine points out, "Pharisaic Judaism had ascribed the Book of Qohelet to Solomon . . . not *ad majorem gloriam Salomonis*, but to gain its acceptance into the Hebrew Bible" and "assure that the book would be interpreted in accordance with the letter and spirit of Pharisaic Judaism" (1978, 66).

While some within the evangelical tradition treat the Solomonic authorship of Ecclesiastes as a litmus test of orthodoxy, many others have questioned the attribution. Stuart, Hengstenberg, Delitzsch, Young, and Kidner have all raised objections against equating Solomon with Qohelet.

Why, after all, would Solomon choose to use a pseudonym? What need would there be for him to hide his identity? No good reason can be given. On the other hand, no one can deny that the author of the book of Ecclesiastes alludes to Solomon as he describes Qohelet's search for meaning in the first part of the book (1:12–2:26). After this section, the allusions stop, and indeed, Qohelet speaks of the royal office as an outsider (8:2–8). The pseudonym is better explained as a literary device employed by a skeptical wise man who seeks meaning in life "under the sun." He, in effect, pretends he is Solomon as he considers wealth, pleasure, and philanthropy as sources of meaning. After all, "what more can the king's successor do than what has already been done?" (Eccl. 2:12b).

A careful reading of the book will take note of other indications that Qohelet is not Solomon. For instance, Qohelet's statement in 1:16, "I have grown and increased in wisdom more than anyone who has ruled over Jerusalem before me," is strange to imagine in the mouth of Solomon. After all, there was only one other Israelite king, his father David, who ruled in Jerusalem before him. It is inconceivable that he would be thinking of the Jebusite rulers who preceded David (Young, *IOT*, 348).

Young also points out that the use of the past tense in 1:12, "I . . . was king over Israel in Jerusalem," is unlikely for Solomon, since there was never a time when he was older but not ruling as king (348). Also:

> The background of the book does not fit the age of Solomon. It was a time of misery and vanity (1:2–11); the splendour of Solomon's age was gone (1:12–2:26); a time of death had begun for Israel (3:1–15); injustice and violence were present (4:1–3); there was heathen tyranny (5:7, 9–19); death was preferred to life (7:1); "one man ruled over other men to their hurt" (8:9). (Young, *IOT*, 348, based on Hengstenberg).

Thus the internal evidence leads us, at the least, to question the relationship between Solomon and Qohelet. It is much to be doubted that the author intended to equate the two.

The internal evidence leads us, at the least, to question the relationship between Solomon and Qohelet. It is much to be doubted that the author intended to equate the two.

In any case, this issue, though important, is irrelevant to the issue of authorship. Traditionalists not only believe that Solomon is Qohelet but that Qohelet=Solomon wrote the book. This view does not take into account the fact that a fair and natural reading shows that there are two voices within the book: Qohelet and a second wise man, the latter being the narrative voice in control of the book.

As explained more fully below under Structure, the book may be divided into three parts: a prologue (1:1–11), the main body (1:12–12:8—an autobiographical monologue), and an epilogue (12:8–14). The prologue and epilogue are a frame that refers to Qohelet in the third person. In the body of the book, Qohelet speaks in the first person.

Of most interest to the question of authorship is the epilogue. Those who wish to defend the unity of the narrative voice of the book argue that Qohelet=Solomon speaks in the first person when he recounts his past, but shifts to the third person to evaluate that past from a present perspective. This approach is quite awkward and has no precedents. It is much more natural to understand the second voice as that of an unnamed speaker who is evaluating the words of Qohelet for his son. The intrusive use of the third person in 7:27 confirms this view (Fox 1977, 1999, picked up by Longman 1997). As we will see below, both the topic of the book and the interplay between the second speaker and his son betrays a wisdom context, so it is appropriate to refer to this second unnamed speaker as the "second wise man" or the frame-narrator (Fox 1977).

Realizing that Qohelet is not to be identified with the speaker of the epilogue removes the question of Solomonic authorship. The book itself suggests that the second wise man, not Qohelet, is the author of the book. As with many other books of the Old Testament, we do not know the proper name of the author of the book.

LITERARY ANALYSIS

Structure

The book of Ecclesiastes is divided into three parts. It begins with a short prologue introducing some of the themes of Qohelet's thought (1:1–11), continues with a long monologue by Qohelet (1:12–12:8), and concludes with a brief epilogue (12:8–14).

The prologue and epilogue are differentiated from the body of the book by its third-person references to Qohelet. Together they frame Qohelet's speech. The bulk of the book is Qohelet's speech that is made up primarily of autobiographical reflections on the meaning of life.

While the general structure of the book is clear, scholars have experienced frustration as they seek a minute analysis of the book. Attempts to discover an underlying structure to Qohelet's musings (most notably A. S. Wright 1968, 1980,

1983) have not been followed by many other scholars. Close study shows that Qohelet's thought rambles, repeats (1:12–18 and 2:11–16; 4:1–3 and 5:8–9; 4:4–12 and 5:10–6:9), and occasionally contradicts itself. Such a lack of order, far from detracting from the message of the book, actually contributes to it, however.

While Qohelet's thought does not have a detailed outline, some features may be observed in its progress. His speech begins (1:12) with a formula that is well known in the autobiographical tradition of the ancient Near East (Poebel 1931; Longman 1991, 1997). From 1:13–2:26 Qohelet recounts his search for meaning in life "under the sun," adopting the literary persona of Solomon. From 3:1–6:9 the persona is dropped, but the quest for meaning continues. In 6:10–12 there is a kind of transitional summary statement to the second part of Qohelet's speech. This second part is dominated by advice and instruction. The conclusion of the speech in 12:1–7 is a meditation on death, an appropriate conclusion for an autobiography.

Genre

There are no exact parallels to Ecclesiastes in the Bible or in the ancient Near East. Some of the same questions are raised in other Near Eastern texts, and one text from Mesopotamia is even known as "A Babylonian Qohelet" (ANET, 438–40). Another well-noted parallel is between Ecclesiastes 9:7–9 and the Gilgamesh Epic:

> When the gods created mankind,
> Death for mankind they set aside,
> Life in their own hand retaining.
> Thou, Gilgamesh, let full be thy belly,
> Make thou merry by day and by night.
> Of each day make thou a feast of rejoicing,
> Day and night dance thou and play!
> Let thy garments be sparkled fresh,
> Thy head be washed; bathe thou in water.
> Pay heed to the little one that holds on to thy hand.
> Let thy spouse delight in thy bosom!
> For this is the task (of mankind)!

These and other ancient texts from Babylon, Egypt, and Greece show similar thoughts and attitudes to the speech of Qohelet—as opposed to the book of Ecclesiastes (see below).

Of more interest, though, are texts that bear a rough structural similarity to Qohelet's speech. While Qohelet has been studied in relation to royal testaments and Egyptian instruction before, the closest similarities may be drawn with the wisdom autobiographies (Cuthaean Legend of Naram-Sin, Adad-guppi autobiography, and the so-called Sin of Sargon text) of Mesopotamia (Longman

1991, chap. 6; 2003). They both begin with the same type of formulaic introduction and conclude with instruction and advice.

In conclusion, it is best to identify the book as a framed autobiography. This genre identification will be significant as we interpret the message of Ecclesiastes.

THEOLOGICAL MESSAGE

Ecclesiastes is a shocking book. If we compare the teaching of Proverbs with Qohelet's teaching, we can see why. Proverbs, on the one hand, extols wisdom, family life, and long life (3:13–18). Qohelet, on the other hand, says:

> "The fate of the fool will overtake me also.
>   What then do I gain by being wise?"
> I said to myself,
>   "This too is meaningless."
> For the wise, like the fool, will not be long remembered;
>   The days have already come when both have been forgotten.
> Like the fool, the wise too must die! (Eccl. 2:15–16)

> A man may have a hundred children and live many years; yet no matter
>   how long he lives, if he cannot enjoy his prosperity and does not
>   receive proper burial, I say that a stillborn child is better off than he.
>   (6:3)

Moreover, some of his advice sounds quite dubious:

> Do not be overrighteous,
>   neither be overwise—
>   why destroy yourself?
> Do not be overwicked,
>   and do not be a fool—
>   why die before your time?
> It is good to grasp the one
>   and not let go of the other.
>   Whoever fears God will avoid all extremes. (7:16–18)

Then there are the recurrent refrains that buzz in our ears as we read through the book: "Chasing after the wind," "What profit is there?" The most frequent refrain and the most skeptical sounding of all is the refrain that also brackets Qohelet's speech (1:2; 12:8): "Meaningless! Meaningless! Everything is meaningless!"

It is precisely this strong note of skepticism that pervades the book that resulted in early debates concerning the canonicity of Ecclesiastes as well as a convoluted history of interpretation. According to Levine, the history of interpretation is characterized by "censorship, suppression and polemic" (1978, 64). How is the message of the book rightly understood, and is it in harmony with the rest of the canon?

The traditional approach (see above) answers the second question positively by appealing to the last section, the epilogue. The epilogue, according to this view, expresses the conclusions of Solomon, the repentant apostate, as he looks back over his godless wanderings. In the past, when he excluded God from his life (living "under the sun"), life was meaningless. The final word, however, is "fear God and keep his commandments" (12:13).

According to the traditional view, Qohelet's speech contains much that is dubious when compared to the rest of the Bible, but the unorthodox and skeptical teachings are part of the rebellious period of Solomon's life and therefore not normative theology.

Some recent interpreters have disputed what appears to be a plain reading of the text. They deny that there is anything unorthodox or pessimistic in Qohelet's teaching. He is rather a "Preacher of Joy" (Whybray) and a paragon of orthodoxy (Kaiser; Fredericks). To achieve such an interpretation, one must suppress and distort many of the plain statements of the book. This approach, while enjoying a minor resurgence, actually dates back to the Targum of the book, where one can see clearly the exegetical gymnastics required (Levine).

How then is the book to be read? We take our departure from the literary analysis above. Two voices may be heard within the book of Ecclesiastes, Qohelet's and the unnamed wisdom teacher who introduces the book in the prologue and evaluates Qohelet in the epilogue. Qohelet is a doubter and skeptic; the unnamed speaker in the frame is orthodox and is the source of the positive teaching of the book.

The book of Ecclesiastes, therefore, is similar in structure to the book of Job. It also evokes a similar reading strategy. The bodies of both books contain dubious teaching when judged in the light of the rest of the canon (the speeches of the three friends, Elihu, and Job). Not that everything that is said is wrong, but nearly so. The same is true of the book of Ecclesiastes. The body of the book that contains the introspective autobiography of Qohelet contains much that offends traditional Old Testament sensibilities. The positive teaching of both books comes at the end, with Yahweh's speech from the whirlwind in Job and with the second wise man's warnings to his son in Ecclesiastes.

To understand the book of Ecclesiastes, then, it is important to read the epilogue closely. Even the traditional translation of a few phrases in the epilogue is suspect.

Following the suggestive comments of Fox, we interpret 12:8 as the beginning of the frame narrator's last contribution to the book. He summarizes Qohelet's thought, using the latter's own refrain, "Meaningless! Meaningless! Everything is meaningless!" Next, he pays his respects to Qohelet's efforts. He

> The book of Ecclesiastes is similar in structure to the book of Job. It also evokes a similar reading strategy. The positive teaching of both books comes at the end.

acknowledges that he was a wise man who worked hard at his task. It is important, however, to note that while true wisdom is always characterized by righteousness and godliness (Prov. 1–9), the office of wisdom teacher was occasionally occupied by some wicked people during the Old Testament period (most notoriously Jonadab, cf. 2 Sam. 13).

The next few verses are increasingly critical of Qohelet. Fox (1989, 96) translates verses 10–12:

> "Utterly absurd," said Qohelet, "Everything is absurd." Now furthermore, Qohelet was a wise-man. He constantly taught the people knowledge, and weighing and investigating, he composed many sayings. Qohelet sought to find fine words and to write the most honest words of truth. The words of the wise are like goads, and the (words of) masters of collections are like implanted nails that are given by a shepherd. And furthermore, my son, beware of these things. It is pointless to make a lot of books, and much talking wearies the flesh. Finally, when everything has been heard: Fear God and keep his commandments, for that is the whole duty of man. For God will bring every deed into judgment, (judging) even every hidden matter, whether good or bad.

It is faint praise to say that Qohelet "searched to find just the right words," since he himself admits that he seldom succeeded (7:1–29)! It is possible, however, that Fox's suggested translation (also followed in Longman 1997) is not correct and that indeed the frame narrator is evaluating Qohelet's viewpoint as "true." If so, it is best to understand this evaluation as referring, as Qohelet himself puts it, to life "under the sun." That is, though he does not use this theological language, life in a fallen world without recourse to God ("above the sun") is difficult with a sad end in death.

In either interpretation, the metaphors of goads and embedded nails, while usually understood positively, are better taken as negative. Goads and nails are painful! The famous verse 12, quoted by so many students, does not, as thought by many, exclude Qohelet's speech, but certainly includes it.

So if Qohelet's lengthy speech is pessimistic and out of sorts with the rest of the Old Testament, why is it included in the canon? Qohelet's speech (1:12–12:7) is a foil, a teaching device used by the second wise man to instruct his son (vs. 12) concerning the dangers of speculative, doubting wisdom in Israel. Just as in the book of Job, most of the book is given to the unorthodox speeches of the human participants of the book, only to have it torn down and demolished when God speaks out of the whirlwind.

The positive teaching of the book of Ecclesiastes is found in the last two verses of the book:

> Now all has been heard;
>> here is the conclusion of the matter:

Fear God and keep his commandments,
>   for this is the duty of every human being.
For God will bring every deed into judgment,
>   including every hidden thing
>   whether it is good or evil. (12:13–14)

In brief compass, the second wise man and implied author of the book summarizes the message of the Old Testament. He calls his son to a right relationship with God ("fear God"), obedience, and a proper understanding of the future judgment. In these verses, we have "the gospel in a nutshell."

APPROACHING THE NEW TESTAMENT

Ecclesiastes is never quoted in the New Testament, but there is an allusion to the message of the book in Romans 8:18–22:

> I consider that our present sufferings are not worth comparing with the glory that will be revealed in us. The creation waits in eager expectation for the children of God to be revealed. For the creation was subjected to *frustration*, not by its own choice, but by the will of the one who subjected it, in hope that the creation itself will be liberated from its bondage to decay and brought into the freedom and glory of the children of God (italics added).

The word translated "frustration" is the word used in the Septuagint to translate the motto word of Ecclesiastes, "meaninglessness." While Qohelet sounds unorthodox in the light of the rest of the canon, he represents a true assessment of the world apart from the light of God's redeeming love. His perspective on the world and life is restricted; he describes it as life "under the sun." In other words, his hopelessness is the result of covenant curse without recourse to God's redemption.

Qohelet sounds modern because he so vividly captures the despair of a world without God. The difference, though, is that the modern world believes God does not exist; Qohelet believed that God existed but questioned his love and concern (5:1–7). As a result, nothing had meaning for Qohelet—not wealth or wisdom or charity. After all, death brought everything to an end. Qohelet is preoccupied with death throughout the book (2:12–16; 3:18–22; 12:1–7) because he sees nothing beyond that point.

On one level, therefore, Qohelet is exactly right. The world without God ("under the sun") is meaningless. Death ends it all, so Qohelet alternated between "hating life" (2:17) and taking what meager enjoyment God hands out (vv. 24–26).

As we have seen above, the message of the book is not the message of Qohelet's speech; it is rather the simple instruction in the last few verses.

Nonetheless, we may still admit that Qohelet has rightly described the horror of a world under covenant curse and apart from God. What he did not have is hope.

As we turn to the New Testament, we see that Jesus Christ is the one who redeems us from the vanity, the meaninglessness under which Qohelet suffered. Jesus redeemed us from Qohelet's meaningless world by subjecting himself to it. Jesus is the Son of God, but nonetheless he experienced the vanity of the world so that he could free us from it. As he hung on the cross, his own Father deserted him. At this point, he experienced the frustration of the world under curse in a way that Qohelet could not even imagine. "Christ redeemed us from the curse of the law by becoming a curse for us" (Gal. 3:13).

As a result, Christians can experience deep significance precisely in those areas where Qohelet felt most oppressed. Jesus has restored meaning to wisdom, labor, love, and life. After all, by facing death, Jesus conquered the biggest fear facing Qohelet, and he showed that death is not the end of all meaning, but the entrance into the very presence of God.

CHAPTER NINETEEN

SONG OF SONGS

The history of the interpretation of the Song of Songs is a fascinating story (Longman 2001, 20–49). Perhaps no other biblical book has been read so differently from one time period to another. In the Middle Ages, very few would interpret the book in connection with human sexuality. Indeed, to do so was dangerous and could result in excommunication or worse (Pope 1977, 112–16). Today, most Christians find such an approach natural and sensible. However, is it correct to interpret the Song in such a "nontheological" manner? Why is a book that has such obviously erotic overtones in the canon?

BIBLIOGRAPHY

Commentaries

J. **Bekkenkamp** and F. **van Dijk,** "The Canon of the Old Testament and Women's Cultural Traditions," in *A Feminine Companion to the Song of Songs,* ed. A. Brenner (Sheffield: JSOT Press, 1993); G. B. **Caird,** *The Language and Imagery of the Bible* (Westminster, 1980); G. Lloyd **Carr,** *Song of Solomon* (TOTC; InterVarsity Press, 1984); F. **Delitzsch,** *Proverbs, Ecclesiastes, Song of Songs,* trans. J. Martin (Eerdmans, 1975; orig. Engl. trans. 1885); C. D. **Ginsburg,** *The Song of Songs and Coheleth* (Jersey City: KTAV, 1970 [orig. 1857]); S. C. **Glickman,** *A Song for Lovers* (InterVarsity Press, 1976); R. **Gordis,** *The Song of Songs and Lamentations,* rev. ed. (New York, 1974); R. S. **Hess,** *Song of Songs* (BCOTWP; Baker, 2005); S. **Horine,** *Interpretive Images in the Song of Songs: From Wedding Chariots to Bridal Chambers* (Peter Lang, 2001); O. **Keel,** *Song of Songs* (CC; Fortress, 1994); T. **Longman** III, *Song of Songs* (NICOT; Eerdmans, 2001); R. E. **Murphy,** *The Song of Songs* (Hermeneia; Fortress, 1990); M. H. **Pope,** *Song of Songs* (AB 7C; Doubleday, 1977); I. **Provan,** *Ecclesiastes/Song of Songs* (NIVAC; Zondervan, 2001); P. **Roberts,** *"Let Me See Your Form": Seeking Poetic Structure in the Song of Songs* (forthcoming); C. **Seerveld,** *The Greatest Song* (Trinity Pennyasheet Press, 1967); Y. **Sefati,** *Love Songs in*

Sumerian Literature: Critical Edition of the Dumuzi-Inanna Songs (Bar-Ilan University Press, 1998); J. G. **Snaith,** *The Song of Songs* (NCB; Eerdmans, 1993).

Articles and Monographs

A. **Brenner,** *A Feminist Companion to the Song of Songs* (Sheffield: JSOT Press, 1993); D. J. A. **Clines,** "Why Is There a Song of Songs and What Does It Do to You If You Read It?" *Jian Dao* 1 (1994): 1–27; J. S. **Cooper,** "New Cuneiform Parallels to the Song of Songs," *JBL* 90 (1971): 157–62; R. M. **Davidson,** "Theology of Sexuality in the Song of Songs: Return to Eden," *AUSS* 27 (1989): 1–19; M. **Falk,** *Love Lyrics from the Bible* (Sheffield: Almond, 1982); M. V. **Fox,** *The Song of Songs and Ancient Egyptian Love Songs* (Madison: University of Wisconsin Press, 1985); G. **Gerleman,** "Die Bildsprache des Hohenliedes und die altägyptische Kunst," *ASTI* 1 (1962): 24–30; F. **Godet,** *Studies in the Old Testament,* 9th ed. (Hodder and Stoughton, 1894): 241–90, reprinted in *Classical Evangelical Essays,* ed. W. C. Kaiser Jr. (Baker, 1972); M. D. **Goulder,** *The Song of Fourteen Songs* (JSOTS 36; Sheffield: Almond, 1986); M. **Kellner,** *Commentary on the Song of Songs: Levi ben Gershom (Gersonides)* (New Haven: Yale University Press, 1998); A. **LaCocque,** *Romance She Wrote: A Hermeneutical Essay on the Song of Songs* (Harrisburg, Pa.: Trinity Press International, 1998); W. G. **Lambert,** "Divine Love Lyrics from Babylon," *JSS* 4 (1959): 1–15; idem, "The Problem of the Love Lyrics," in *Unity and Diversity: Essays in the History, Literature, and Religion of the Ancient Near East,* ed. H. Goedicke and J. J. M. Roberts (Johns Hopkins University Press, 1975): 98–135; F. **Landy,** *Paradoxes of Paradise: Identity and Difference in the Song of Songs* (Sheffield: Almond, 1983); A. **Mariaselvan,** *The Song of Songs and Ancient Tamil Love Poems: Poetry and Symbolism* (Rome: Editrice Pontificio Istituto Biblico, 1989); C. **Rabin,** "The Song of Songs and Tamil Poetry," *Studies in Religion* 3 (1973): 205–19; G. M. **Schwab,** *The Song of Songs' Cautionary Message concerning Human Love* (New York: Lang, 2002); M. H. **Segal,** "The Song of Songs," *VT* 12 (1973): 470–90; P. **Trible,** *God and the Rhetoric of Sexuality* (Fortress, 1978); J. G. **Wetzstein,** "Sprachliches aus den Zeltlagern der syrische Wüste," *ZDMG* 22 (1868): 69–194; J. B. **White,** *A Study of the Language of Love in the Song of Songs and Ancient Egyptian Poetry* (Scholars, 1978).

LITERARY ANALYSIS

Genre

Due to the history of interpretation of the book, two separate issues must be addressed in a discussion of the genre of the Song of Songs. First, is the book a drama or a series of love poems? A second, but related, question concerns whether the book is an allegory.

Drama. Many contemporary translations of the Song of Songs show the influence of a dramatic interpretation of the book by adding rubrics in the margins that indicate the speakers. The TNIV, for instance, attributes the opening verses (1:1–4) to "She." Other characters are ascribed to the "Friends" and "He." These rubrics were not in the original; they first appear in Codex Sinaiticus in c. AD 400. While the TNIV shows that the rubrics are not original by putting them in italics, they nonetheless influence the interpretation of the book in the direction of drama.

However, upon close study, the dramatic approach is not as clear-cut as the rubrics indicate. As a matter of fact, assuming a dramatic approach, it is difficult to determine even the number of characters required by the text. And even if that issue can be resolved, there is still difficulty in assigning specific speeches to the different characters. There are two main schools of thought among those who advocate a dramatic approach: a two-character and a three-character view.

The former approach identifies two main characters in the story: Solomon and the Shulammite, the lover and the beloved. They are interrupted only by the daughters of Jerusalem who serve as a kind of chorus.

The plot centers on the love between the king and the woman. The woman is usually pictured as a beautiful "rustic maiden" (Delitzsch 1975, 3). She has captured the heart of the urbane and sophisticated king. He is helpless before her.

The story progresses from their initial meeting and expressions of affection to marriage (often associated with 3:6–5:1). The relationship is troubled following the marriage, but at the end (8:5–14) their bond is deep and committed.

Thus the Song has a unified plot that recounts the purifying love shared by Solomon and the Shulammite. It narrates Solomon's move away from the wickedness of polygamy and sophisticated love toward the monogamy and simple love of a country girl.

Defenders of a three-character approach (H. G. A. Ewald; Godet; Ginsburg; Seerveld) detect a love triangle in the Song. Solomon and the Shulammite are still main characters, but no longer is the woman thought to be in love with Solomon. Rather, she is in love with a simple country boy, often referred to as a shepherd. Solomon, the brazen apostate and polygamist, has insensitively and lustfully abducted the Shulammite in order to add her to his harem. She is devoted and pure, however, and retains her ardent love for the shepherd.

In a recent work, Provan has suggested an interesting twist on the three-character approach. He believes that Solomon has forced the young woman into his harem, but she remains in love with the shepherd boy back home. In this way, the Song celebrates real love over coerced legal love.

There are several almost insurmountable difficulties with the dramatic approach to the Song of Songs: (1) It is impossible to definitively assign passages to specific characters. This ambiguity is particularly clear in the debate between the two- and three-character views. It should be a relatively simple matter to recognize the number of characters in a drama. The inability to do so with the Song hurts the credibility of the dramatic approach. (2) Dramas are unattested in the Bible and in the literature of the ancient Near East. (3) The book does not show features commonly associated with a narrative. There is much confusion among advocates of a plot-oriented approach to the book as to the events and acts of the play. The only real consistency is locating the marriage before the first obvious act of intercourse between the man and the woman (4:16–5:2). (4) Positively, love poems from Mesopotamia and Egypt (see below) bear interesting similarities with the Song of Songs.

The dramatic approach fails most obviously because it is unable to demonstrate an obvious plot structure. The fact that advocates of a dramatic approach cannot agree whether there are two or three major characters in the book illustrates the problem. The book does not read like a narrative with an introduction that builds to a climax and then concludes. There are, however, continuities of theme and character, though there is some ambiguity in the latter. As interpreters move further away from the dramatic approach, they move closer to the view that the Song of Songs is a collection of love poems, an erotic anthology.

Love Poems. This genre identification has been aided by the relatively recent parallels drawn between the Song and both ancient and modern love poetry. For instance, John White and Michael Fox have shown numerous parallels between the Song and Egyptian love poetry, including the reference to the beloved as "my sister, my bride." In the last century, J. G. Wetzstein demonstrated parallels between the poems in the Song and songs that were sung during wedding ceremonies in the Syrian villages that he visited. (Examples of both Egyptian and Syrian poetry will be given below.) There is thus a growing consensus that the Song of Songs is a collection of loosely related love poems.

Perhaps the best statement of the view that the Song is a collection of lyric poems about love is that of Maria Falk. In her book *Love Lyrics from the Bible*, she analyzes the Song as a collection of thirty-one poems, not united by narrative wholeness, but rather by thematic connections. She then applies a literary analysis to the book that unpacks images rather than imposing a plot. More recently, Longman (2001) has analyzed the Song as a collection of twenty-three poems.

The Song, after all, is a Song of Songs—that is, there are many poems (songs), but there is also a coherence in theme and character, so that there is a kind of unity.

The weakness of this understanding of the Song, as Falk and Longman both admit, is that it is not possible to demonstrate conclusively that there are exactly twenty-three or thirty-one poems. But neither is it crucial to do so for the interpretation of the book. The Song, after all, is a Song of Songs—that is, there are many poems (songs), but there is also a coherence in theme and character, so that there is a kind of unity, though not a narrative unity. Hess (2005) has recently argued that indeed the coherence of the Song is such that we should not speak of it as a collection but as a single love poem (see also the thorough analysis of Roberts).

On the basis of both internal analysis and the comparative evidence, therefore, the best conclusion is that the Song of Songs is a collection of poetry that extols the love that a man and a woman have for each other. It is on this basis that we will interpret the Song of Songs.

The Issue of an Allegorical Interpretation

The identification of the Song as a collection of love poems, however, does not fully decide the manner of the book's interpretation. Allegory is more a type of interpretive method than a specific genre. Many different genres may be read allegorically.

As a matter of fact, the Song of Songs has been read as an allegory for many centuries (see Pope 1977, 89–229, for a detailed history of interpretation). Allegory was the leading, almost exclusive way of approaching the book in both Christian and Jewish circles until very recently. Jewish scholars interpreted the book as an allegory of the love between Yahweh and Israel, while Christian theologians argued that the book was messianic and praised the love between Christ and the church (Eph. 5:22–33).

The Targum of the Song (seventh century AD) is an example of an allegorical interpretation from a Jewish perspective. The Lover is Yahweh, and the Beloved is the nation of Israel as in most Jewish allegorical interpretations. In the Targum, the Song is also interpreted as a history of redemption. Israel's history is characterized by Israel's love for Yahweh and desire to be in Yahweh's presence. However, this desire is marred by Israel's sin against God. The book is divided into five sections that relate to five different historical periods.

As an example, we will note how the Targum interprets Song of Songs 1:2–4:

> Let him kiss me with the kisses of his mouth—
>   for your love is more delightful than wine.
> Pleasing is the fragrance of your perfumes;
>   your name is like perfume poured out.
>   No wonder the young women love you!
> Take me away with you—let us hurry!
>   Let the king bring me into his chambers.

Read from an allegorical perspective, this passage is interpreted as a reference to the exodus. God takes Israel away from Egypt and into God's own chambers—that is, the Promised Land.

There are other types of Jewish allegories of the Song. For instance, Jewish mystics identified the Lover and the Beloved with the active and passive aspects of the mind (Moses Ibn Tibbon, Immanuel ben Solomon, see Pope 1977, 105; for a specific study of Levi ben Gersonides, see Kellner 1998). The union between the two describes the ecstasy at the mystical union of the two aspects of the intellect.

Early Christian interpretation was also allegorical. The earliest preserved Christian interpretation of the Song is found in some fragments from

Hippolytus (around AD 200). He interprets the above passage (1:2–4) as a reference to Christ, who brings the saints into the church. A further example is Cyril of Alexandria. According to his allegorical approach, in

> My beloved is to me a sachet of myrrh
>   resting between my breasts, (1:13)

the breasts are symbols for the Old and New Testaments, while the sachet of myrrh is Christ, who "rests between both testaments."

In order to evaluate the allegorical approach, it is necessary to ask what motivated it. There is, for instance, use of marriage as an image of the relationship between God and his people elsewhere in the Old Testament. Its most frequent form, however, is negative. That is, when God's people rebel against him and turn to other gods, they are described as committing adultery against him (e.g., Ezek. 16, 23; Hos. 1–3). This recurrent marriage imagery does inform our understanding of the book (see Theological Message below), but it does not require a type of allegorical approach that ignores the physical-human references of the images in the book.

In fact, there is nothing in the book itself that suggests an interpretation that transfers the meaning of the clearly erotic language of the book to a spiritual realm. Why, then, did the church, through most of its history, almost exclusively promote such a reading?

A partial answer is provided by the subtle acceptance by early church and synagogue of certain Hellenistic ways of thinking—"Platonic dualism, stoicism, and Hellenistic-Roman cults" (Davidson 1989, 2)—about the relationship between the body and soul. It is well known that early and medieval Christian thinkers imbibed the philosophical system of Plato and Aristotle. The result was a view of the body and its activities as temporary, sinful, and evil. Harsh treatment of the body (for example, fasting and whipping) was promoted. Sexual abstinence was viewed as a virtue, a viewpoint culminating in the monastic movement. In this intellectual environment, reading the Song as erotic poetry would have been an embarrassment in the face of its obvious delight in physical pleasures.

As can happen in any age, cultural presuppositions biased interpreters against the original meaning of the text, and a spiritual rather than a sexual interpretation of the Song was the result. As Pope points out, Origen did to the Song of Songs what he did to his own body—"he denatured it and transformed it into a spiritual drama free from all carnality" (1977, 115). Pope also reproduces a letter written by Jerome to Paula, one of his disciples, concerning the proper education that she should give her daughter in the Scriptures (119). He advises:

> Let her treasures be not silk or gems but manuscripts of the holy scriptures;
> and in these let her think less of gilding, and Babylonian parchment, and

arabesque patterns, than of correctness and accurate punctuation. Let her begin by learning the Psalter, and then let her gather rules of life out of the Proverbs of Solomon. From the Preacher let her gain the habit of despising the world and its vanities. Let her follow the example set in Job of virtue and of patience. Then let her pass on to the gospels never to be laid aside once they have been taken in hand. Let her also drink in with a willing heart the Acts of the Apostles and the Epistles. As soon as she has enriched the storehouse of her mind with these treasures, let her commit to memory the prophets, the heptateuch, the Books of Kings and of Chronicles, the rolls also of Ezra and Esther. When she has done all these she may safely read the Song of Songs but not before: for, were she to read it at the beginning, she would fail to perceive that, though it is written in fleshly words, it is a marriage song of a spiritual bride. And not understanding this she would suffer from it.

We observe in Origen and Jerome a strong impulse to distance the spiritual from the physical in a way that would influence the interpretation of the Song of Songs in the church for centuries, moving away from a natural to an allegorical approach. Indeed, the impulse is so strong that even today, when the allegorical approach is in disfavor with a large majority of the academic community of all religious stripes, it is still frequently heard from pulpits and is regarded as correct by many lay students of the Bible.

However, in the middle of the nineteenth century the tide began to turn against the allegorical approach. There were many reasons for the shift, but high among them was certainly the discovery of love poems from Mesopotamia and Egypt (Cooper; Lambert; White; Fox; Sefati). These had many similarities with the Song and could only be interpreted as extolling love between men and women. In the following example from Papyrus Harris 500 (translated by White 1978, 176–77), notice how the beloved is called "sister" as in the Song and also the poem's frequent references to nature:

Sa'am plants are in it,
by which one is elevated in their presence.
I am your best sister.
(As for) me, behold I am like the Crown Lands
which I planted
with flowers and with all fragrant [h;wt] plants.
Lovely is the water canal in it,
which your hand digs out
in order to refresh ourselves with the northwind.
A good place for my walking (is) there.
Your hand is in my hand.
My body is at ease.

My heart is joyful because of our journeying together.
Pomegranate-wine is my hearing your voice.
I live because I hear.
If I am seen in every glance,
it is more splendid for me than eating and drinking. (Poem 19)

Toward the end of the nineteenth century J. G. Wetzstein, the German consul to Damascus, reported his study of wedding songs among the Arab inhabitants of Syria. These songs also bore strong resemblances to the poems of the Song of Songs, particularly the *wasf* that extolled the physical beauty of the bride and the groom (cf. 4:1–5:2; 7:1–9). In an appendix to Delitzsch's commentary, Wetzstein gave a preliminary report of his findings that included excerpts from the Arabian poems. In this short example (Delitzsch 1975, 174–76), it is easy to see the similarities with the above-mentioned passages from the Song:

I say: O fair one, thine attractions I am never able to relate.
And only the few will I describe which my eyes permit me to see:
Her head is like the crystal goblet, her hair is like the black night,
Her hair is like the seven nights, the like are not in the whole year;
In waves it moves hither and thither, like the rope of her who draws
    water.
And her sides breathe all manner of fragrance, which kills me. . . .
Her nose is like the date of Irak, the edge of the Indian sword;
Her face is like the full moon, and heart breaking are her cheeks. . . .
Her spittle pure virgin honey, and healing for the bite of the viper.
Comparable to elegant writing, the Seijai waves downwards on her
    chin. . . .
Her breasts like polished marble tablets, as ships bring them to Sidon.
Thereon like apples of the pomegranate two glittering piles of jewels. . . .

These parallels and many more like them overcame the allegorical approach and resulted in the interpretation of the Song of Songs as a collection of love poems that delight in God's good gift of sexuality and intimate love between a man and a woman. As such, much of the book's imagery is recognized as sexual. As one example, there are a number of beautiful and provocative metaphors for the woman's vagina. It is a well or a garden of aromatic spices (Song 4:12–15). In a description of her premarital chastity, her vagina is called a "wall," and, in keeping with a well-attested Near Eastern image, a promiscuous woman is a "door" (8:9–10). Lovemaking between the man and the woman is described in images that delightfully express the pleasure of the senses: sight (7:1), smell (4:13–14), taste (5:1), hearing (5:2), and of course touch (7:8).

As a poem that reflects human experience, it is obvious that the Song is a further example of Wisdom Literature in the Bible. Like Proverbs, it downplays

Israel's covenant relation with God and her unique history or even any kind of direct talk about God. Strikingly, God's name does not appear in the book (Song 8:6 is not an exception). Interpreted within the context of the canon, however, it does provide divine insight and instruction about an important area of human experience: sexuality.

Before going on to the theological message of the book, one other point should be addressed. That is the connection between the book and marriage. Nowhere in the book are the lover or the beloved said to be married. Also, though there are wedding songs, no marriage ceremony is explicit in the book. However, the canonical context of the book makes it clear that this poem describing such intense lovemaking between the two requires that we presume they are married (Childs, *IOTS*, 575). In other words, the Song must be interpreted within the context of the law of God, which prohibits any kind of pre- or extramarital intercourse. Recently, Horine (2001) has argued that much of the imagery also points to a marital context for the relationship between the man and the woman in the Song.

HISTORICAL BACKGROUND

The issue of authorship and date has been reserved until now because its solution depends on a proper literary analysis. Most significant is the conclusion that the Song is really a collection of songs and not a unified narrative. This fact leaves open the possibility (though it does not settle it) that the Song is an anthology of poems by different authors and from different times. In this respect it could be like the book of Psalms.

However, first we must take into account the superscription that opens the book: Solomon's Song of Songs. The title, Song of Songs, is a form of superlative in Hebrew. It designates this song as the apex of all songs, along the lines of the expression "King of kings."

More to the point of authorship, how does Solomon relate to the book? In the Hebrew, Solomon's name is connected to the title by means of the preposition *l*^e. Hebrew prepositions have a wide semantic range and many functions, and thus are often difficult to interpret, especially in a place like Song of Songs 1:1, where there is not a broader context to help narrow down the meaning.

A similar problem is found in the titles of the Psalms. There we saw that the evidence leans heavily in favor of Davidic authorship. Such an interpretation of the meaning of the titles of the Psalms gives us a strong presumptive argument in favor of the view that sees the opening verse of the Song as ascribing authorship to Solomon.

However, there are vigorous arguments brought against an early date for the book. Perhaps the most frequent is the linguistic argument that points to various forms that for one reason or another are considered late. Linguistic arguments, though, are rarely determinative. For one thing, it is hard to be dogmatic about signs of lateness. Until recently, for instance, the use of the relative pronoun $\check{s}^e$ (as opposed to ʾ$^a\check{s}er$) was taken as a sure sign of lateness. On the contrary, as Pope (1977, 33) has pointed out, the short form occurs in early poetry (Judg. 5:7) and cannot be evidence of a late date. Pope also counters the argument for a late date that points to Aramaisms in the text by simply pointing out that Aramaic "is as old as Hebrew" (33).

More troubling, though, is the contrast between the love described in the Song and the picture that the book of Kings gives us of a man with many wives and concubines (1 Kings 11). The historical books also specifically pinpoint Solomon's sexual life as the source of his notorious apostasy (1 Kings 11:1–13). Furthermore, those passages within the book that mention Solomon by name seem to look at him from a distance (3:6–11; 8:10–12). There is also a contrast between 3:6–11, which extols Solomon, and 8:10–12, which rebuffs him.

On the other hand, there are many features of the book that are best explained as originating in the Solomonic period. The interest in flora and fauna in the Song of Songs has been compared with 1 Kings 4:33, where Solomon's interest in such things is described. Detailed arguments in favor of assigning the book to Solomon's age (though not necessarily to Solomon) have been made by M. H. Segal (1973), G. Gerleman (1962), and C. Rabin (1973).

Short of taking the ambiguous superscription as a dogmatic statement of authorship, it is impossible to definitely settle the issue. Perhaps the most likely hypothesis, taking the superscription seriously, is that a few, but not all, of the twenty-three poems of the book are Solomonic. We have a clear instance of partial Solomonic authorship in the book of Proverbs.

Note should be taken of recent attempts to identify the author of the Song with a female voice. These scholars point out that the woman's voice dominates the book (Brenner 1993, 79; Bekkenkamp and van Dijk). It is not just women scholars who argue for this position; they are joined also by F. Landy and A. LaCocque. Indeed, the latter quotes the former as he states his opinion that "the author of the Song was a female poet who intended to 'cock a snook at all Puritans'" (LaCoque 1998, xi, citing Landy 1983, 17). In other words, the Song was written by a woman who was resisting social norms, including the idea that women should be receivers not initiators of love.

Against this rising tide supporting the idea of female authorship of the Song comes D. J. A. Clines, always reading "against the grain." In a nutshell, his opinion is that the woman of the Song is the perfect woman from a male perspective, the ideal dream of most men, and thus a fabrication by men.

The discussion of the gender of the author of the Song reveals more about us as commentators than it does about the Song. It relies on a theory of literature and of genre that believes that women and men are typecast in the way that they write.

THEOLOGICAL MESSAGE

The genre analysis above leads to what might be considered a negative conclusion concerning the theological message of the book. The book's primary aim is not to portray the relationship between God and his people, but rather to extol sexual love between a man and a woman.

However, such a message is as important today as it has ever been. Both society and the church have often perverted human sexuality, so it is important to be reminded that sex within the parameters of marriage is a God-given gift.

The perversion of sexuality comes in two forms. On the one hand, our society makes sex an idol. Sex is a major obsession. It does not matter what kind of sexuality it is: heterosexual, homosexual, adulterous—our society promotes the idea that a life without some type of sexual stimulation is boring at least, perhaps even meaningless. What has happened is that sexuality has been made into an idol. Many have rejected the Creator and have tried to fill the void in their lives with sexual relationships.

On the other hand, the church at times perverts sexuality by making it unclean or taboo. There is still an ongoing bias against the body in many parts of the church that suggests that sexuality is base or wicked even within the context of marriage.

The Song of Songs, however, is a canonical corrective to the perversion of sexuality. It reminds us that sex is good and pleasurable. It is not evil when enjoyed within the parameters of marriage. Thus, most of the Song is a celebration of physical lovemaking. Furthermore, Schwab has reminded us that there is what he calls a cautionary note in the Song. This side of heaven intimate relationships will not be untroubled, and some of the poems (see 5:2–6:3) show that love can bring pain as well as joy.

However, the Song is more than a canonical sex manual as some recent treatments have implied. The book contributes to a biblical-theological study of sexuality. The lovemaking that takes place in the garden (2:3–13; 4:12–5:1; 5:2–6:3; 6:11; 7:10–13; 8:13–14) should remind us of the garden of Eden. Genesis 2:18–25 is the story of the creation of woman and the resultant intimate relationship between the man and her. This intimacy is given sexual significance in verse 25, which states, "The man and his wife were both naked, and they felt no shame."

However, in the next chapter Adam and Eve give in to the temptations of the serpent. As a result, there is a disruption of the perfect relationship between them and God. Furthermore, sin produces alienation between Adam and Eve. This estrangement is given a sexual cast in 3:7: "Then the eyes of both of them were opened, and they realized they were naked; so they sewed fig leaves together and made coverings for themselves."

When we turn to the Song of Songs, we see the man and his wife in the garden naked and feeling anything but shame! As Trible (1978, 144) puts it, "The

> *The book's primary aim is not to portray the relationship between God and his people, but rather to extol sexual love between a man and a woman.*

Song of Songs redeems a love story gone awry." The book pictures the restoration of human love to its pre-fall bliss.

But the story does not end here. While the primary reference is to human sexuality, the book does teach us about our relationship with God. Although God is never mentioned by name in the book, the marriage metaphor is a strong one in the Old Testament. God has a covenant with his people much like the marriage covenant: it promises and requires exclusive allegiance when Israel commits adultery against the Lord. They in effect seek to divorce him (Ezek. 16, 23; Hos. 1–3).

APPROACHING THE NEW TESTAMENT

The New Testament uses the same metaphor positively. Ephesians 5:22–33 teaches that the relationship between a man and his wife is an analog to the relationship between Jesus and the church. The intimacy of marriage pictures the intimacy of God's love for us. It is thus not inappropriate to read the Song of Songs as a poem reflecting on the relationship between God and his people, as long as the primary reference to human sexuality is not repressed.

CHAPTER TWENTY

ISAIAH

For sheer grandeur and majesty probably no book in the Hebrew Bible can be compared with Isaiah. Because the New Testament writers made frequent appeal to the book in presenting their claims about the nature of Jesus and the church, Isaiah assumed a role of particular importance in Christian interpretation. The important place of the book and its length combined also to make it the testing ground—and battleground—for the place of historical criticism. Traditional rabbinic and Christian interpretation had viewed the book as the work of the prophet Isaiah, who lived in Jerusalem in the late eighth and early seventh centuries BC. Critical scholarship, beginning in the late eighteenth century, argued that the book was largely the product of at least two or three different authors widely separated in time and place. For a time there was seemingly less interest in the grandeur and majesty of the book's message than in the battle over its unity and compositional history.

BIBLIOGRAPHY

Commentaries

R. E. **Clements,** *Isaiah 1–39* (NCB; Eerdmans, 1980); B. **Duhm,** *Das Buch Jesaja ubersetz und erklart,* HKAT 3/1 (Göttingen, 1892; 4th edition 1922); J. **Goldingay,** *Isaiah* (NIBCOT; Hendrickson, 2001); G. B. **Gray,** *A Critical and Exegetical Commentary on the Book of Isaiah 1–27* (ICC; T. & T. Clark, 1912); A. S. **Herbert,** *The Book of the Prophet Isaiah,* 2 vols. (CBC; Cambridge: 1975); O. **Kaiser,** *Isaiah 1–39* (OTL; Westminster, 1972); A. **Motyer,** *Isaiah* (Leicester, UK: Inter-Varsity Press, 1999); C. R. **North,** *Isaiah 40–55* (TBC; SCM, 1952); J. N. **Oswalt,** *The Book of Isaiah, Chapters 1–39* (NICOT; Eerdmans, 1986); idem, *The Book of Isaiah, Chapters 40–66* (NICOT; Eerdmans, 1998); idem, *Isaiah* (Zondervan, 2003); J. **Ridderbos,** *Isaiah* (BSC; Zondervan, 1985); J. F. A. **Sawyer,** *Isaiah,* 2 vols. (DSB; Westminster, 1984, 1986); J. **Skinner,** *Isaiah Chapters 1–39* (Cambridge University Press, 1909); J. **Watts,** *Isaiah* (WBC 24–25; Word, 1985, 1987); C. **Westermann,**

Isaiah 40–66 (OTL; Westminster, 1969); R. N. **Whybray,** *Isaiah 40–66* (NCB; Eerdmans, 1980); H. **Wildberger,** *Jesaja,* 3 vols. (Neukirchen: Neukirchener Verlag, 1972–82); E. J. **Young,** *The Book of Isaiah,* 3 vols. (NICOT; Eerdmans, 1965, 1969, 1972).

Monographs and Articles

P. R. **Ackroyd,** "Isaiah 1–12: Presentation of a Prophet," VTSup 29 (1978): 16–48; O. T. **Allis,** *The Unity of Isaiah* (Presbyterian and Reformed, 1950); F. I. **Andersen,** *Style and Authorship* (Tyndale Lectures, Parkland, Australia, 1976: Tyndale Fellowship for Biblical Studies in Australia, 1976); W. A. M. **Beuden,** "The Main Theme of Trito-Isaiah, 'The Servants of YHWH,'" *JSOT* 47 (1990): 67–87; W. H. **Brownlee,** *The Meaning of the Qumran Scrolls for the Bible* (New York: Oxford University Press, 1964); W. **Brueggemann,** "Unity and Dynamic in the Isaiah Tradition," *JSOT* 29 (1984): 89–107; B. S. **Childs,** *Isaiah and the Assyrian Crisis* (SCM, 1967); R. E. **Clements,** "Beyond Tradition History: Deutero-Isaianic Development of First Isaiah's Themes," *JSOT* 31 (1985): 95–113; idem, *Isaiah and the Deliverance of Jerusalem* (JSOTS 13; Sheffield: JSOT, 1980); idem, "The Unity of the Book of Isaiah," *Interp* 36 (1982): 117–29; D. J. A. **Clines,** *I, He, We, and They: A Literary Approach to Isaiah 53* (JSOTS 1; Sheffield: JSOT, 1976); R. B. **Dillard,** "Remnant," in *Baker Encyclopedia of the Bible,* ed. W. Elwell (Baker, 1988), 2:1833–36; S. R. **Driver,** *Isaiah: His Life and Times* (Frances Griffens, 1905); W. **Dumbrell,** "The Purpose of the Book of Isaiah," *TynBul* 36 (1985): 111–28; C. A. **Evans,** "On the Unity and Parallel Structure of Isaiah," *VT* 38 (1988): 129–47; A. **Kaminka,** *Studies in the Bible, Talmud, and Rabbinic Literature* (Hebrew; Tel Aviv: 1935); P. **Machinist,** "Assyria and Its Image in the First Isaiah," *JAOS* 103 (1983): 719–37; R. **Margalioth,** *The Indivisible Isaiah* (New York: Yeshiva University, 1964); R. **Melugin,** "The Servant, God's Call, and the Structure of Isaiah 40–48," *SBL 1991 Seminar Papers,* ed. E. Lovering Jr. (Atlanta: Scholars, 1990), 21–30; E. **Merrill,** "Isaiah 40–55 as Anti-Babylonian Polemic," *GraceTJ* 8 (1987): 3–18; idem, "The Literary Character of Isaiah 40–55," *BibSac* 144 (1987): 24–43, 144–56; D. **Odendaal,** *The Eschatological Expectation of Isaiah 40–66* (Presbyterian and Reformed, 1970); R. H. **Pfeiffer,** *Introduction to the Old Testament* (Harper & Brothers, 1941); S. **Portnoy** and D. **Petersen,** "Biblical Texts and Statistical Analysis: Zechariah and Beyond," *JBL* 103 (1984): 11–21; Y. T. **Radday,** *The Unity of Isaiah in the Light of Statistical Linguistics* (Hildesheim: Gerstenberg, 1973); R. **Rendtorff,** "The Book of Isaiah: A Complex Unity. Synchronic and Diachronic Reading," *SBL 1991 Seminar Papers,* ed. E. Lovering Jr. (Atlanta: Scholars, 1990), 8–20; idem, "Zur Komposition des Buches Jesaja," *VT* 39 (1984): 295–320; C. **Seitz,** ed. *Reading and Preaching the Book of Isaiah* (Fortress, 1988); G. T. **Sheppard,** "The Anti-Assyrian Redaction and the Canonical Context of Isaiah 1–39," *JBL* 104 (1985): 193–216; M. **Sweeney,** *Isaiah 1–4 and the Post-Exilic Understanding of the Isaianic Tradition, BZAW* 171 (Berlin: de

Gruyter, 1988); J. **Vermeylen,** "L'unité du livre d'Isaïe," *The Book of Isaiah—Le livre d'Isaïe,* ed. J. Vermeylen, BETL 81. (Leuven: Peeters, 1989): 11–53; R. N. **Whybray,** *Thanksgiving for a Liberated Prophet* (JSOTS 4; Sheffield: JSOT, 1978); E. J. **Young,** *Isaiah Fifty-three* (Eerdmans, 1952); idem, *Isaiah's Message for Today* (Cincinnati Bible Seminary, 1961); idem, *Studies in Isaiah* (Eerdmans, 1954); idem, *Who Wrote Isaiah?* (Eerdmans, 1958).

HISTORICAL BACKGROUND

Authorship

Writing about the history of research into Isaiah is a daunting task; entire books could be devoted to this subject. While many of the prophetic books have generated little interest and research, nearly every line of Isaiah has been the subject of widely ranging opinion. At the cost of an unavoidable oversimplification, we will try to sketch the movement in this research on a broad scale.

The Traditional Approach. Jewish and Christian interpreters alike regarded Isaiah son of Amoz (1:1), the eighth-century prophet, friend and confidant of Hezekiah, as the author of the entire book. Isaiah lived in Jerusalem at least until the death of Sennacherib (37:37–38). This opinion prevailed until the last two centuries.[1] Interpreters prior to the Enlightenment had no difficulty in accepting the reality of divine intervention into human history in prophetic inspiration; they did not regard detailed prophetic utterance about the future to be impossible or consider such prophecies as evidence that a passage was spurious.

The Critical Approach. Beginning at the end of the eighteenth century with Döderlein (1789) and Eichhorn (1783), scholars began to question the unity of the book of Isaiah and to divide the book at the beginning of chapter 40. Scholars began to distinguish between Isaiah ben Amoz (or "Isaiah of Jerusalem") and Second Isaiah (or Deutero-Isaiah). There were three major lines of argument advanced for attributing Isaiah 40–66 to another author.

1. The historical situation. The first half of the book presumes a setting in Jerusalem in the eighth century during the period when Assyria was dominant

---

[1]Scholars have debated the significance of comments by Rabbi Abraham Ibn Ezra (1092–1167) in his commentary on Isaiah 40:1; 42:10; 49:4. Ibn Ezra alludes to "the secret of the second half of the book," from which many have concluded that he anticipated later critical opinion that the second half of the book should not have been assigned to Isaiah ben Amoz. However, Ibn Ezra's remarks at 54:4–5 show that he considered the book the product of a single author. Some have also suggested that Rabbi Aravanel (1437–1508) similarly anticipated the division of the book, though these assertions appear to rest on a misunderstanding of his words. See Radday (1973, 2, 14) and Margalioth (1964, 18).

in the region. However, in the second half of the book, the audience addressed is already in exile in Babylon (48:20). They anticipate an imminent redemption and return to Zion (40:9–11; 42:1–9; 43:1–7; 44:24–28; 48:12–22; 49:8–23; 51:11; 52:1–12) and divine judgment against their captors (43:14–15; 47:1–15; 48:14; 49:24–26; 51:21–23). They live at a time when Jerusalem and the temple were in ruins, but they anticipate reconstruction (e.g., 45:13; 51:3; 54:11–14; 58:12; 60:10; 61:4). In the days of Isaiah ben Amoz, Babylon had not yet become a world empire, nor had it been the oppressor of Israel such that the Lord would take vengeance on Babylon. Cyrus the king of Persia is within the immediate fore view of the prophet and is mentioned by name (44:28; 45:1, 13). The putative audience of Isaiah 40–66 is different from that presumed in Isaiah 1–39. Isaiah 40–66 does not predict the exile as something future; rather, it is presupposed. It is the release from exile that is predicted. The author, then, lived in the circumstances that his prophecy presupposed (Driver 1905, 237). He wrote toward the end of the exile, predicting the coming conquest of Babylon by Cyrus and the restoration of the Jews to Jerusalem; in this regard he was doing just what Isaiah had done earlier in predicting the failure of the coalition between Rezin and Pekah (Isa. 7) or the defeat of Sennacherib (Isa. 36–39). Both prophets spoke of the future, but it was a more immediate future.

2. Theological differences. Isaiah 1–39 is said to emphasize God's majesty, whereas Isaiah 40–66 emphasizes his universal dominion and infinitude. In the first part of the book, the nation is led by a king descended from David (11:1); in the second, however, leadership belongs to priests and Levites (61:6; 66:21), and there is no mention of the Davidic dynasty (however, see 55:3–4). The messianic king of the first half of the book (9:6–7; 11:1–11) is replaced in Second Isaiah by the Servant of the Lord, a figure not mentioned in the earlier portion. The doctrine of a faithful remnant is a distinctive element of Isaiah 1–39, but is far less prominent in the second half of the book. The first portion of the book mentions concrete historical details as background for many of the oracles, whereas no historical setting is provided in the second half. In the second half, rather than concern with the circumstances surrounding the prophet's utterances, Isaiah himself is not specifically named.

3. Language and style. Judgments about style are precarious at best. The second half of the book is often described as more "lyric, flowing, impassioned, hymnic" than the first. These labels are impressionistic generalizations for which numerous examples can also be found in Isaiah 1–39; as subjective impressions, they cannot have much evidential weight. However, other stylistic features are more amenable to description and measurement. For example, in Isaiah 40–66 the writer often repeats elements (e.g., "awake" in 51:9; "I, even I" in 51:12; "comfort" in 40:1; cf. 43:11, 25; 48:11, 15; 51:17; 52:1, 11; 57:6, 14, 19; 62:10; 65:1). Others emphasize the frequent use of interrogative pronouns, imperatives, wordplay, and rhetorical questions in Isaiah 40–66. Yet many of these items are also found in the first part of the book, even if with somewhat reduced frequency.

Others have pointed to vocabulary for evidence that the two halves of the book are from differing authors. Scholars drew up lists of words and constructions occurring only after chapter 40 (e.g., Driver 1905, 238–40) and argued that they point to the style of a different author.

It was important to explain how two books written by two different authors could have coalesced into a single volume. Pfeiffer (1941, 415) suggested that a scribe had room left on his scroll after copying Isaiah 1–39 and that he filled out the scroll with the writings of an anonymous prophet (Isa. 40–66). Since no superscription or title separated the works, they were soon read as one book.

Once the door was opened to prying beneath the book of Isaiah to find the underlying sources and to separate out the genuine utterances of the historical Isaiah, the theories multiplied. Scholars soon noticed a different perspective and background for the last chapters of Isaiah (56–66) and attributed them to a Third Isaiah, who lived in Palestine after the initial wave of returnees had arrived. There was disagreement over where Trito-Isaiah began, whether at chapter 56 or 58 or earlier. The arguments were difficult since there is so much similarity between Second and Third Isaiah and since Third Isaiah did not show the coherence that characterized Second Isaiah. Nevertheless, Isaiah 56–66 was regarded as reflecting the conditions of the restoration community back in Israel: the walls of Jerusalem were standing (62:6), and the people were frequenting the high places (57:3–7) in hilly terrain uncharacteristic of Babylon. The distinctions continued to multiply. For chapters 40–66 alone, various scholars began to identify a second, third, fourth, fifth, and sixth Isaiah.

The dissection of the book also continued unabated in Isaiah 1–39. Isaiah 36–39, since it is similar to 2 Kings 18:13–20:19, was described as a secondary narrative appendix to Isaiah 1–35. Most modern critics also questioned the genuineness of Isaiah 13–14. These chapters are uttered against Babylon, whereas at the time of First Isaiah, Assyria was the enemy; prophecy of the destruction of Babylon by the Medes (13:17) would be more at home in the sixth century at the time of Second Isaiah instead of in the eighth century.[2] Isaiah 24–27 has an internal cohesion and unity such that it is often called "the Isaiah apocalypse," but since the eighth century is too early a date for such apocalyptic literature according to the critical consensus, these chapters too must come from some other author and a later date. Because chapter 12 resembles a psalm that may have been composed during the exile or after, some assign it to a later date as well. Any element

---

[2]The circularity in this argument is hard to miss. Having already divided Isaiah into two parts (1–39 and 40–66), any characteristics of the second part that are found in the first are declared to have been misplaced or to be later additions. The theory is salvaged by dismissing as spurious any evidence to the contrary.

of Isaiah 1–39 that critical scholars felt did not clearly show relevance to events in the eighth century was excised. In its most extreme form, critical dissection of the book left between 20 and 40 percent of Isaiah 1–39 as genuinely from the hand of Isaiah (Robinson; Duhm; Cheyne; cf. Radday 1973, 9).

The Traditionalist Response. The division of Isaiah at least into two major parts attained the status of one of the assured results of modern critical study of the Bible early in the twentieth century. However, not all were persuaded. Although they were a minority, many scholars from both Jewish (e.g., Kaminka 1935; Margalioth 1964) and Christian (e.g., Allis 1950; Young 1954, 1958) viewpoints continued to defend the unity of the book. They sought to undermine the confidence in the critical consensus by refuting the individual arguments on which it was based, by presenting evidence of common themes and vocabulary that united the book and by calling attention to dependence on Isaiah by other preexilic prophets. For evangelical Christians who held to the infallibility and inerrancy of Scripture, two additional arguments were also important: the attribution of the book to Isaiah ben Amoz (1:1), and the citations in the New Testament that spoke of the entire book as from the hands of Isaiah.

1. Themes and vocabulary. Margalioth argued that there was not a single chapter in Isaiah 1–39 that was not reflected in Isaiah 40–66 and that hundreds of words and phrases peculiar to the book of Isaiah occur in both halves (1964, 35). She argued from fifteen different subject areas in the book, showing that both halves had common designations: (1) for God, (2) for Israel, (3) for introductory formulas for oracles, (4) for pairing Zion and Jerusalem, (5) for the ingathering of the exiles, (6) for messages of consolation and encouragement, (7) for expressions of joy and gladness, (8) for hopes of a universal millennium, (9) for words of admonition and (10) chastisement, (11) in the use of thesis-antithesis pairs, (12) in distinctive words and linguistic forms, (13) for word pairs, (14) for similar constructions, and (15) for parallel groups having similar content. Since so large a number of specific parallels between any other two books of Scripture by different authors cannot be found, she concluded it was more reasonable to maintain the unity of Isaiah. For example, God is called the "Holy One of Israel" twelve times in the first part and thirteen in the second. Israel is described in both halves of the book as "blind" (29:18; 35:5; 42:16, 18, 19; 43:8; 56:10) and "deaf" (29:18; 35:5; 42:18–19; 43:8), recalling the prophet's call and commission (6:9–10). The people of Israel are the "ransomed of the LORD" who will return to Zion (35:10; 51:11 NIV) in both halves. The common prophetic formula, "the word of the LORD came to me," found at least fifty times in Jeremiah and Ezekiel, is not found in Isaiah, but instead both sections use "the LORD will say" (1:11, 18; 33:10; 40:1, 25; 41:21; 66:9) or "the mouth of the LORD has spoken" (1:20; 40:5; 58:14) or "a voice" calls (6:4; 40:3) or other phrases. In both halves the Lord sets up an ensign as a gathering point for the dispersed nation (11:12; 49:22) and commands the preparation of a highway

(11:16; 35:8; 40:3; 62:10). In both halves "the law will go out from Zion" (2:3; 51:4); in both the Spirit of the Lord rests upon the messianic king/servant (11:2–4; 42:1; 61:1). In both halves the wolf, lamb, and lion are peaceable companions (11:6–9; 65:25). Margalioth calls attention to dozens of such examples.

2. Dependence on Isaiah by other prophets. Zephaniah, Nahum, and Jeremiah contain passages quite similar to utterances in Isaiah 40–66. If this dependence could be established beyond question, it would mean that Isaiah 40–66 itself was also preexilic. Zephaniah 2:15 resembles Isaiah 47:8. The announcement of "feet bringing good news" is found in both Nahum 1:15 and Isaiah 52:7. Jeremiah's reference to the stirring sea and roaring waters (31:35) is close to a similar statement in Isaiah (51:15), and Jeremiah refers to Israel as "my servant" (30:10), possibly reflecting the famous servant songs of Isaiah (41:8–9; 42:1, 19; 44:1–2, 21; 45:4; 48:20; 52:13; 53:11).

3. New Testament citations. Isaiah is cited by name about twenty times in the New Testament, and such citations include references to both halves of the book. John cites Isaiah 6:10 and 53:1 in consecutive verses, identifying both as Isaiah (John 12:38–41); Isaiah said these things because "he saw Jesus' glory and spoke about him" (John 12:41). Luke says that the Ethiopian eunuch was reading in "the Book of Isaiah the prophet" when he was approached by Philip (Acts 8:28); the passage the Ethiopian was reading was Isaiah 53:7–8. New Testament citations of Isaiah by name are drawn from twelve different chapters, seven from Isaiah 1–39 and five from Isaiah 40–66. As Allis remarked (1950, 42–43), such evidence carries great weight with every Christian who values the testimony of the New Testament.

> *Isaiah is cited by name about twenty times in the New Testament, and these citations include references to both halves of the book.*

It is, of course, not just the New Testament that regards the book as the product of a single author; no references to the book before the eighteenth century ever clearly raise the issue of additional authors. The earliest extrabiblical evidence regarding attitudes to the authorship of Isaiah is found in Ecclesiasticus, a book from the mid-second century BC. There the author says that at the time of Hezekiah, Isaiah "comforted them that mourn in Zion" by revealing things before they took place (Ecclus. 48:24–25), thereby assigning the second half of Isaiah to the time of the eighth century. The great manuscript of Isaiah from the second century BC recovered at Qumran shows no awareness of a break in the book at chapter 40, but rather begins with 40:1 as the first line at the bottom of a column; this suggests that ancient scribes accepted the unity of the two sections of the book and had no notion that Isaiah 40–66 was a secondary appendix.

4. The superscriptions. The most obvious reason for regarding Isaiah as the author of the book that bears his name is the superscription to the book (1:1). All fifteen books of the "latter prophets" in the Hebrew Bible begin with a similar heading; in each case the heading is most naturally understood as providing the name of the prophet whose utterances are found in the book. In addition to the superscription to the book as a whole, the individual passages attributed to Isaiah reiterate the point (2:1; 7:3; 20:2; 37:2, 5–6; 38:1, 4; 39:5). The oracles against Babylon in Isaiah 13–14, a passage almost routinely assigned to a later exilic redactor in critical scholarship, begin by identifying them as things that "Isaiah son of Amoz saw" (13:1). If lesser prophets were faithfully remembered in the superscriptions to the books that they wrote, how could this greatest prophet of Israel (the author of Isaiah 40–66) have been forgotten and fallen into anonymity?

More Recent Critical Scholarship. Although earlier critical scholarship tended to describe the composition of Isaiah as in part the fortuitous or accidental joining of two independent works (e.g., to fill out the available space at the end of a scroll), most recognized to various degrees the common themes and vocabulary in the two parts of the book. The most common way of explaining such was by assigning the composition of Isaiah 40–66 to the prophet's disciples or a "school" of his followers (8:16–18; 50:4) that preserved his memory and applied his perspective in later generations. These otherwise unknown individuals saw in later events situations to which they could apply Isaiah's earlier preaching.

Arguments for multiple authorship based on language have also come into more careful scrutiny. Earlier generations had been content with lists of vocabulary or constructions unique to each half of the book to establish an argument for different authors. With the advent of computer technology, far more sophisticated linguistic studies were possible. Y. T. Radday (1973) took account of many linguistic discriminators (sentence length, word length, relative frequency of parts of speech, use of transitional markers, vocabulary in discrete semantic domains, vocabulary concentration and richness) that had not characterized earlier studies. Radday's studies confirmed (1) two different parts for the book (Isaiah 1–35 and 40–66, omitting chapters 36–39 from consideration); (2) he found chapters 1–12 and 40–48 to be linguistically quite dissimilar, whereas (3) Isaiah 13–23 were sufficiently similar to Isaiah 1–12 that attributing both to Isaiah was highly probable; (4) Isaiah 49–57 and 58–66 had so many affinities together and so many differences with the rest of the book that they most naturally required a third author. Radday's work both confirmed and challenged traditional critical thinking about the book. Yet Radday's own methods were also subjected to vigorous critique in terms of his linguistic and statistical models (F. I. Andersen 1976; cf. S. Portnoy and D. Petersen 1984, 11).

The development of a critical approach usually called "canon criticism" also focused attention on Isaiah in its canonical form. Rather than insist on divorcing biblical texts from their context as Scripture in order to recover a presumably earlier and more valid context through the tools of historical criticism, canon criticism has emphasized the function of biblical texts within the context of the biblical canon as Scripture. Rejecting the atomism and fragmentation of the text, canon criticism has tended to focus more attention on the received form of the book than on its history of composition. As an approach, it fosters reading biblical books as a unity in their present form. When this approach is applied to

Isaiah, Brevard Childs (*IOTS*, 324, 337) insists that (1) regardless of the provenance of the individual pericopes in the book as a whole, the book itself presents Isaiah 40–66 as the word of an eighth-century prophet speaking to the future; and (2) this literary context for the book cannot be turned into a historical fiction if the reader wants to interpret the book correctly.

The emphases of canon criticism and literary analysis called increased attention to the thematic and theological connections in both halves of Isaiah. Symptomatic of this heightened interest was the formation of a consultation on the unity of Isaiah within the Society of Biblical Literature at annual meetings in the early 1990s. In many respects the arguments of Ackroyd (1978), Rendtorff (1984, 1990), Melugin (1990), Seitz (1988, 105–26), and others had already been anticipated by earlier Jewish and Christian scholars who had argued for the authorial unity of Isaiah. Instead of finding Isaiah the end product of more or less accidental and arbitrary historical developments, scholars increasingly viewed the book as the result of careful, deliberate, and thoughtful theological and literary work. In some respects, the debate about the unity of Isaiah has come full circle, with one crucial difference: rather than a unity resulting from the hand of a single author, the book is now widely viewed as a redactional unity. Instead of viewing Isaiah 40–66 as an independent work accidentally appended to the work of the eighth-century prophet, some scholars now argue that Isaiah 40–66 never existed apart from the first half of the book and that it was composed (through what could yet be a complex redactional process) in light of the earlier material.

An Assessment. In many respects, contemporary critical opinion about Isaiah has recovered from the excesses that characterized scholarship in the late eighteenth and early nineteenth centuries. The consensus among critical scholars has moved in the direction of acknowledging much of what was dear to conservatives: that Isaiah is not the result of a haphazard accident and internally contradictory, but rather the book as a whole shows a unity of themes and motifs. The tenor of much of the debate has shifted from focus on dissecting the text to recover sources and settings to efforts to expound the coherence and unity of the text as it exists. Arguments from conservatives for unity of authorship based on common themes and vocabulary have now in large part been taken over and pressed into service as arguments for a redactional unity in the book.

To be sure, critical and conservative opinion remain divided on the issue of authorship. Although there is a growing consensus about the overall unity of Isaiah, for critical scholarship it is a unity forged through a history of redaction rather than a unity that derives from a single individual author.

Conservative opinion is anchored in its theological conviction (1) about the reality of prophetic revelation—that the Spirit of God did give to ancient writers insight into the future, and (2) about the integrity and trustworthiness of the Scripture as a whole—that its statements in the superscriptions and New Testament citations require acceptance. The sustained polemic of Isaiah 40–66 is that Yahweh has announced the future and is able to bring it to pass (40:21; 41:4, 21–29; 43:12–13; 44:6–8, 24–28; 45:11–13). Already in Isaiah 1–39, the exile and restoration are anticipated in passages almost universally considered genuinely Isaianic. In his call, the prophet anticipates the day when Jerusalem would be destroyed and depopulated (6:11–12), and he names a son in light of the anticipated restoration (7:3—"Shear-Jashub" means "a remnant will return"). The prophet's pervasive use of the remnant motif in Isaiah 1–39 anticipates the threat that will come from Babylon (39:5–8). The prophet made clear his own understanding that aspects of his prophecy were not related to the immediate, but to the distant future (8:16).

Critical opinion is anchored most particularly in the fact that Isaiah 40–66 presumes a historical setting other than that of Isaiah in Jerusalem in the eighth century, as outlined above. Both positions need scrutiny.

On the one hand, if one accepts the reality of a sovereign God and prophetic inspiration, one cannot say, "God could not have revealed himself to Isaiah this way." Such naive confidence in the historical critical method is every bit as much a theological statement as insisting that he did. However, as Oswalt (2003, 2) points out, Isaiah is different than most prophets who "speak about future times, but no other seems to speak to future times as Isaiah does." When critical scholars conclude from the setting of Isaiah 40–66 that the author of these chapters lived fairly late in the Babylonian exile, this is not in principle a different argument from that which conservatives are ready to make, for example, about Deuteronomy 34. Whatever one concludes about the historical relationship between Moses and Deuteronomy, it is clear that Moses did not write the account of his own death (Deut. 34:1–8); the person who wrote this final section of the book lived at a time when a number of prophets had come and gone, but none like Moses (Deut. 34:10–12). This is to say that the setting presumed by this chapter (a time after the death of Moses) precludes Moses' having written it. Although the New Testament cites Deuteronomy and attributes it to Moses (24:1–3 in Mark 10:4; 25:4 in 1 Cor. 9:9), no one would seriously argue that this includes Deuteronomy 34. Recognizing that the setting of Deuteronomy 34 requires an author living later than Moses, the author traditionally assigned to the book, is not materially different from recognizing that the background of Isaiah 40–66 presumes an author living during the exile. Isaiah is not mentioned in the second half of the book. However, the reality of prophetic inspiration is not thereby eliminated: an author living later in the exile foresaw through divine inspiration what God was about to do through Cyrus, just as Isaiah foresaw what God would soon do with Tiglath-Pileser III (see Historical Period below). This later author saw in Isaiah's prophecies of exile and a remnant events that were transpiring in his own day, and he wrote to develop and apply Isaiah's preaching to his fellow exiles. Although the anonymity of this great prophet is a problem, it is no more unusual than the anonymity of the historical books or the book of Hebrews.

A labyrinth of theological, hermeneutical, and exegetical questions surrounds the issue of the composition and authorship of Isaiah. Such complex questions are not often amenable to being settled once and for all by slogans or theological dicta. Rather, only careful study and patience with the efforts of others investigating the same issues can contribute to progress. The question of the authorship of Isaiah probably should not be made a theological shibboleth (Judg. 12:6) or test for orthodoxy (Goldingay provides an excellent example of an evangelical commentary that argues for multi-authorship). In some respects, the end results of the debate are somewhat moot: whether written by Isaiah in the eighth century or others who applied his insights to a later time, Isaiah 40–66 clearly was addressed in large measure to the needs of the exilic community. As noted by E. J. Young (1958, 71), chapters 1–39 provide "a staircase, as it were, which gradually leads one from the Assyrian to the Chaldean period. The two belong together, since the former is the preparation for the latter, and the latter is the completion of the former."

Historical Period

Isaiah ben Amoz was a resident of Jerusalem. He began his prophetic ministry in the year that King Uzziah died (740 BC—6:1) and continued through the reigns of Jotham, Ahaz, and Hezekiah (1:1). Although the superscription to the book does not make the point, he probably continued to live into the reign of Manasseh (696–642 BC); he reports the death of Sennacherib (681) in 37:38. The apocryphal book Assumption of Isaiah preserves the tradition that he was sawn in two during the reign of Manasseh (cf. Heb. 11:37); the Talmud also reports that he was related to the royal house, a cousin of Uzziah (*Meg* 10b). He was married to a prophetess and was the father of at least two sons (7:3; 8:3). The sources used by the author of Chronicles attribute to him a history of Uzziah's reign (2 Chron. 26:22).

He lived during the period of the ascendancy of the Assyrian Empire. When Tiglath-Pileser III (745–727 BC) had expanded Assyrian control into Aram, Isaiah warned Ahaz against participating in an anti-Assyrian coalition led by Aram and Israel (Isa. 7). This coalition then turned against Ahaz to press him into allying Judah with their efforts, and Ahaz looked to Assyria for help. For Tiglath-Pileser III, this show of weakness on Ahaz's part was an invitation to assert Assyrian domination over Judah (2 Chron. 28:16–21). After the death of Tiglath-Pileser, Shalmaneser and Sargon moved against the northern kingdom, destroying Samaria and deporting the population (722 BC). When Sargon died in 705, Sennacherib faced rebellions both among the Syro-Palestinian states and in Babylon. Merodach-baladan of Babylon sent envoys to Hezekiah to enlist his participation in a coalition that would force Sennacherib to fight on two fronts (39:1–8; 2 Kings 20:12–19; 2 Chron. 32:31). Sennacherib was busy for a few years dealing with the revolts in other regions, but he turned his attention to

Judah in 701. Although Jerusalem was miraculously delivered from destruction, Hezekiah was reduced to paying tribute to Sennacherib (Isa. 36–39; 2 Kings 18:13–16). The mission of Merodach-baladan's emissaries to Hezekiah is reported out of its chronological sequence in Isaiah 36–39; the announcement that all the wealth of the royal palace would be carried off to Babylon (39:6) signals the transition from the first half of Isaiah and its concern with the Assyrian crisis to the affairs of the Judean exiles in Babylon (Isa. 40–66).

THEOLOGICAL MESSAGE

Many regard Isaiah as the theologian of the Old Testament. His description of God and the divine attributes and acts in history are both profound and beautiful. Yet Isaiah is not a theologian of the abstract; he applies his apprehension of God's nature and purpose to the practical issues confronting Israel. Several themes predominate his utterances.

God as the Holy One of Israel

When Isaiah received his call to prophetic ministry in the year that King Uzziah died (Isa. 6), he saw the Lord seated, high and exalted, on his throne, surrounded by seraphs calling out "Holy, holy, holy is the LORD Almighty; the whole earth is full of his glory." The prophet's experience in his call set the tone for the remainder of his ministry. Throughout the book, Isaiah's favorite designation for God is "the Holy One of Israel" (1:4; 5:19, 24; 10:17, 20; 12:6; 17:7; 29:19, 23; 30:11–12, 15; 31:1; 37:23; 40:25; 41:14, 16, 20; 43:3, 14–15; 45:11; 47:4; 48:17; 49:7; 54:5; 55:5; 60:9; cf. 2 Kings 19:22). Outside of Isaiah, this phrase occurs only six times in the remainder of the Old Testament.

From the outset of Israel's national election, God's command to his people was "Be holy as I am holy" (Lev. 11:44–45; 19:2; 20:7; cf. 1 Peter 1:16). Isaiah recognized from the first moments of his call that this national mandate had not been realized in the life of Israel; the prophet lived among an unclean people who were calloused and without understanding (6:5, 9), a people whose refusal to heed the prophetic message would bring destruction and deportation (6:11). Yahweh's moral perfection would not be ignored by the nation with impunity.

God as Savior and Redeemer

But God's holiness also meant that he would be faithful to his own promises. It was because God was holy that he would not utterly abandon Israel but would be her savior and redeemer (41:14; 43:3, 14; 47:4; 48:17; 49:7; 54:5). Isaiah's own name ("Yahweh will save" or "Yahweh is salvation") reflects this aspect of God's character. He would deliver the nation from the Syro-Ephraimite coalition (8:1–14), from Assyria (17:10; 11:10–12:3), and from Babylon (45:17; 48:14, 20; 49:25–26). The Lord would vindicate himself before the eyes of the nations by saving his

Isaiah recognized from the first moments of his call that God's national mandate — "Be holy as I am holy" — had not been realized in the life of Israel.

people (52:7–10). Their real father was not Abraham, Isaac, or Jacob, but the Lord himself, and he would have compassion on his children (63:16).

In the Hebrew Bible the term *gô'ēl* ("redeemer") is closely associated with the semantic domains of salvation and deliverance. In particular, the laws regarding the kinsman-redeemer were designed to protect the individual Israelite from losing his property or falling into debt bondage. The kinsman-redeemer would cover the debt of the individual in order to protect his inheritance or freedom (Lev. 25:47–49; Ruth). Just as Yahweh had redeemed Israel from Egypt (Ex. 13:15; Deut. 7:8; 9:26; 13:5; 15:15; 24:18; 2 Sam. 7:23; 1 Chron. 17:21; Mic. 6:4), so also he would redeem them from bondage in Babylon and restore them to the inheritance he had provided in Canaan (e.g., 1:27; 29:22; 35:9; 41:14; 43:1, 14; 44:6, 22–24; 47:4; 48:17, 20; 49:7, 26; 51:10). They had been "sold for nothing" and would be redeemed "without money" (52:3). Israel would be redeemed by her near kinsman, her very own husband (54:5). Instead of a blind and deaf nation, they would become "the Holy People"; instead of being held in bondage, they would become "the Redeemed of the Lord"; instead of rejected, "Sought After"; instead of barren and depopulated, "the City No Longer Deserted" (62:12).

The Remnant Theme

Isaiah's concern to present God both as the Holy One of Israel and as her savior and redeemer leaves a profound tension. How can the divine holiness and the resulting just judgment against sin be reconciled with divine grace and promise? In the Old Testament this theological tension is addressed most often through the remnant theme (Dillard 1988, 1833–36).

The remnant is that group of people who survive some catastrophe brought about by God, ordinarily in judgment for sin. This group becomes the nucleus for the continuation of humankind or the people of God. This surviving remnant inherits the promises of God afresh; the future existence of a larger group will grow from this purified, holy remnant that has undergone and survived divine judgment. The remnant motif distinguishes between (1) the true and false people of God and (2) the present and future people of God. Those who survive divine judgment become a purged, purified, and faithful remnant, the nucleus of a renewed and chosen people.

The remnant theme can emphasize the holiness of God: God is on the verge of destroying his people because of their sin; the very continuation of the nation may be threatened. They will be left "like a shelter in a vineyard, like a hut in a field of melons" (1:8); the stump of a felled tree (6:13); a few olives in a treetop (17:4–6); a pole on a hilltop (30:17). Yet it also speaks equally well of divine grace, election, and mercy: new life will sprout from that stump, a righteous Branch for the Davidic line (4:2–3; 11:1–16). This purified remnant will make Jerusalem the "City of Righteousness, the Faithful City" (1:21–26). Out of destruction a remnant will return, those who truly lean on the Lord (10:20–23); they will take root in the land and be a fruitful people (37:30–32). The names of Isaiah's sons reflect this two-sided dimension of the remnant theme: Maher-Shalal-Hash-Baz ("quick to the plunder, haste to the spoil"—8:1–3) bespeaks the certainty of coming judgment; Shear-Jashub ("a remnant will return"—7:3) speaks of future hope. Isaiah's sons were portents to Israel about the intent of God (8:16–18).

The Servant of the Lord

Few items in the study of the Old Testament have generated as much interest as the so-called Servant Songs, first separated as isolated poems by Duhm in his 1892 commentary.[3] Already in 1948, C. R. North could list over 250 works devoted to these passages; the rate of publication has continued unabated since. The servant of Isaiah 40–66 has been variously identified as a collective group or as an individual. Collective interpretations identify the servant as the nation Israel, as the faithful remnant, or as some other ideal representation of the nation. Individual interpretations have identified the servant as a particular person (Zerubbabel, Jehoiachin, Moses, Uzziah, Ezekiel, the prophet himself, a leper, Cyrus) or as an eschatological figure (the Messiah or Jesus as Messiah). In some respects, this debate is a dead end, for the passages themselves will not be pinned down to a collective or individual interpretation alone; instead, they require both approaches. The key to this dilemma is also found in the remnant motif.

Scholars have often contrasted the theology of Isaiah 1–39 with the remainder of the book by saying that the remnant theme plays no important role in the second half. However, the so-called Servant Songs are directly related to this theme. There can be little question that Isaiah's servant is at least to be identified as Israel; the servant is specifically called "my servant Israel/Jacob" (41:8–9; 44:1–2, 21; 45:4; 48:20; 49:3–6). It is because the faithful remnant arises from a period of judgment that surviving Israel could be called the "Suffering Servant." God had been with them through the fire and through the deep (43:1–2), and now he will make "little Israel" strong again (41:8–14). His servant would be righteous and would bring justice to the nations (42:1–9). God would bring his people from the ends of the earth to be his witnesses, his servants (43:5–13). He will pour out his Spirit on the offspring of the servant of the Lord, and they

---

[3]There is some disagreement over which passages should be designated Servant Songs and where they begin and end. For the most part, interpreters designate 41:1–4; 49:1–6; 50:4–9; 52:13–53:12 as part of this group; many include 61:1–3. With reference to the Servant Songs, see Clines (1976); Whybray (1978); C. R. North, *The Suffering Servant in Deutero-Isaiah, an Historical and Critical Study* (1948); W. Zimmerli and J. Jeremias, *The Servant of God* (1958); J. Rembaum, "The Development of a Jewish Exegetical Tradition Regarding Isaiah 53," *HTR* 75 (1982): 289–311; C. McLain, "A Comparison of Ancient and Medieval Jewish Interpretations of the Suffering Servant in Isaiah," *Calvary Baptist Theological Journal* 6 (1990): 2–31.

will flourish like grass in a meadow (44:1–4). Though the nation had sinned, this surviving remnant-servant would be faithful.

Yet Isaiah's servant also points beyond the nation Israel. Isaiah had already made a distinction between Israel as a nation and Israel as a faithful remnant/servant (49:5–6). Isaiah also individualized this servant: he is born of a woman, and he comes as one who is distinct from the nation, one who will restore the tribes of Jacob and bring back Israel (44:24; 46:3; 49:1).

The remnant community in the restoration period did not attain Isaiah's lofty goal of being a purified nation, purged from its sin and living in obedience to divine command; a holy people, righteous and blameless before God. Isaiah himself spoke of the injustices in the restoration community (Isa. 58–59). Zechariah notes the incongruity: in one of his night visions, he sees a scroll of the law hovering over the restoration community, bringing it under the judgment of a curse. The scroll is followed by a basket containing a figure representing the iniquity of the people; two winged creatures carry that basket back to Babylon, back to the place of judgment and purging (Zech. 5). Ezra too sees the anomaly of sin in the remnant community. At the end of a lengthy prayer of praise and confession of sin (Ezra 9:1–15), he asks God, in the event that the people continue in their sin: "Would you not be angry enough to destroy us, leaving us no remnant or survivor? LORD, the God of Israel, you are righteous! We are left this day as a remnant. Here we are before you in our guilt, though because of it, not one of us can stand in your presence." The restoration prophets see the problem clearly: the period of judgment and refining in the exile had not produced a pure people, an Israel wholly faithful to the commands of God.

Christian readers can readily understand how the New Testament writers were following the lead of Isaiah himself. In their eyes, Jesus had become a remnant of one. He was the embodiment of faithful Israel, the truly righteous and suffering servant. Unlike the remnant of the restoration period, he committed no sin (53:9; 1 Peter 2:22). As the embodiment of the faithful remnant, he would undergo divine judgment for sin (on the cross), endure an exile (three days forsaken by God in the grave), and experience a restoration (resurrection) to life as the foundation of a new Israel, inheriting the promises of God afresh. As the remnant restored to life, he becomes the focus of the hopes for the continued existence of the people of God in a new kingdom, a new Israel of Jew and Gentile alike. As the nucleus of a renewed Israel, Christ summons the "little flock" that will receive the kingdom (Dan. 7:22, 27; Luke 12:32) and appoints judges for the twelve tribes of Israel in the new age (Matt. 19:28; Luke 22:30). The church is viewed as the Israel of that new age (Gal. 6:16), the twelve tribes (James 1:1), "a chosen people, a royal priesthood, a holy nation, God's special possession" (Ex. 19:6; 1 Peter 2:9). A sinful nation, Israel could not suffer vicariously to atone for the sins of the world. The sinfulness of the nation made it unacceptable for this role, just as flaws would disqualify any other offering. Only a truly righteous servant could bear this awful load.

The Spirit of the Lord

In much of the Old Testament, and particularly in the prophetic books, the Spirit of God is the spirit that inspires and enables the prophets (Num. 11:25–29; 1 Sam. 10:6, 10; 19:20–23; 2 Kings 2:15; Neh. 9:30; Ezek. 13:3; Joel 2:28; Zech. 7:12—cf. Luke 1:67; Acts 2:17–18; 19:6; 28:25; 1 Cor. 14:1, 32, 37; Eph. 3:5; 2 Peter 1:21; Rev. 17:13; 19:10; 22:6). This emphasis is not missing in Isaiah: the Spirit of God gives wisdom and understanding (11:2); the Lord's servant, anointed by God's Spirit, responds by proclaiming good news (61:1). In 40:7–8 the prophet may be engaging in a pun on the ambiguity of the Hebrew word *ruaḥ,* a term which means both "spirit" and "wind." Although the grass withers when the wind/breath (*ruaḥ*) of the Lord blows upon it, the word of the Lord (which also comes from his *ruaḥ*) stands forever. The Spirit of the Lord makes possible the announcing of the purposes of God (48:16).

However, in the remainder of Isaiah, the Spirit of God is the Spirit that brought order out of chaos (Gen. 1:2). Where once God's Spirit was active in creation, in Isaiah it is God's Spirit that brings re-creation to desolate land (32:15; 34:16–35:2; 59:21–60:2; 63:10–14). Out of moral chaos the Spirit brings order and justice (28:6; 42:1; 44:3).

God's Rule Over History

The major criterion used in the Old Testament for distinguishing the word of the true prophet from that of the false is the fulfillment of the prophet's utterances (Deut. 18:21–22). The premise of this criterion is that the Lord who reveals his plans to his prophets (Amos 3:7) rules over the course of history to bring his purpose to fruition.

This celebration of God's rule over history has reached its height in Isaiah 40–66. Just as Israel had seen what God had announced and done in the former Assyrian crisis, now they could believe him when he announced that he was about to do a new thing for the nation (42:9; 43:9, 19; 48:3, 6). Because he had spoken with power and authority before past events, God can be believed when he speaks about the future. The idols have never done this, and their inability shows that they are not gods at all (43:8–11). Only the Lord God of Israel has revealed, saved, and proclaimed his actions (v. 12): he announces his intent beforehand, he brings it to pass, and he sees to its proclamation. Isaiah exults in the sovereign rule of God over the course of history (41:21–24; 43:8–13; 44:6–8; 45:20–21; 46:8–10).

Isaiah's description of Israel's God was a radical contrast to the theological thinking of the people of Mesopotamia among whom the exiles lived. In their respective mythologies, the gods of the nations lied, schemed, seduced, deceived, and made war on one another; they were caught up in all the contingencies, vagaries, and uncertainties of human life. They had to effect their individual purposes for and against one another through trickery and brute force; their wills could be realized only by carefully manipulating the balance of power among the gods. The God of Isaiah was sharply different: he faces no contingency or surprise, and he but speaks to effect his will. His purposes cannot be frustrated. His purpose was in part to do good for his people, and they could take confidence that his announced purpose would soon be realized among them.

LITERARY STRUCTURE

Isaiah is one of several Old Testament books that have a similar structure in broad outline. The first part of the book is largely taken up with issues of the immediate present and impending judgment on Israel (Isa. 1–12). This portion is then followed by an extended series of oracles focusing on judgment against foreign nations (chaps. 13–35). The remainder of the book is given to describing future blessing for the people of God (chaps. 40–66). Chapters 36–39 provide a narrative transition from the time of the Assyrian crisis to the concerns of exilic and later times (see Historical Background above). A similar structure is found in Ezekiel, Zephaniah, Joel, and the Septuagint of Jeremiah.

Brownlee (1964, 247–59) suggested that the present form of the book of Isaiah was the result of a deliberate effort to arrange the book as a two-volume work in which chapters 1–33 (volume 1) are parallel to chapters 34–66 (volume 2). His argument was based in part on the presence of a three-line gap between chapters 33 and 34 in the great Isaiah scroll discovered at Qumran and on the suggestion of earlier scholars that chapters 34–35 should be attributed to Deutero-Isaiah. His suggestions about the structure of the book have been followed by R. K. Harrison (1969, 764) and C. A. Evans (1988). Here is a summary of the "bifid" approach to Isaiah:

Table 12
Bifid Approach to Isaiah

Volume 1	Volume 2
1. Ruin and restoration of Judah (1–5)	1. Paradise lost and regained (34–35)
2. Narrative (6–8)	2. Narrative (36–39)
3. Agents of blessing and judgment (9–12)	3. Agents of deliverance and judgment (40–45)
4. Oracles against foreign nations (13–23)	4. Oracles against Babylon (46–48)
5. Judgment and deliverance of God's people (24–27)	5. Redemption through the Lord's servant; glorification of Israel (49–55)
6. Ethical sermons (28–31)	6. Ethical sermons (56–59)
7. Restoration of Judah and Davidic kingdom (32–33)	7. Paradise regained (55–66)

Brownlee (1964) and Evans (1988)[4] both explore these parallels more fully. In section 1, both halves summon creation to listen (1:2; 49:1) and order the nations to hear (1:10; 34:1). God threatens revenge in both (1:24; 34:8; 35:4). He promises to ransom Zion (1:27; 34:8; 35:10) and to destroy transgressors in fire (1:31; 34:10). Certainty of these things is due to the mouth of the Lord that has decreed them (1:20; 34:16). Other parallels are found in 5:24 and 34:3; 5:17 and 34:10; 1:20 and 34:5–6; 1:11–15 and 34:6–7; 4:3 and 35:8.

In section 2, both narratives report the appearance of the prophet before the kings of Judah on issues pertaining to Assyria (7:3–17; 37:5–7, 21–35; 38:1–8; 39:3–8). Both kings hear messages from God by the "aqueduct of the Upper Pool on the road to the launderer's field" (7:3; 36:2). Both chapters 6 and 40 open with scenes set in the divine council and report visions of God's glory (6:3; 40:5). In both, the prophet replies with a question (6:11; 40:6). In Isaiah's call, the people are described as unwilling to hear, see, know, or understand (6:9–10), whereas in chapter 40 they will hear, see, know, and understand (40:5, 21, 26, 28).

In section 3, both volumes depict an ideal king (9:1–7 [MT 8:23–9:6]; 11:1–10; 41:1–43:13) and a second exodus (11:11–16; 41:17–20; 42:15–16; 43:14–44:5). Both ideal king and servant will be a light to the nations (9:1–2 [MT 8:23–9:1]; 42:6), dispel darkness (9:2 [MT 9:1]; 42:7), and establish justice (9:7 [MT 9:6]; 42:1–4) and righteousness (11:4; 42:6, 21). The Lord's Spirit rests on this king and servant (11:2; 42:1), and because of him others will know the Lord (9:9; 45:6). Both volumes speak of a highway prepared for the exodus of the Lord's people (11:11–16; 43:16–21), who are gathered from the ends of the earth (11:11; 41:9; 43:5).

In section 4, oracles against Babylon bracket the oracles against foreign nations in volume 1 (13:1–14:23; 22:1–10), a way of underscoring the importance of Babylon parallel to the second half of the book. In both volumes, the king of Babylon is removed from his throne and forced to sit on the ground (14:9; 47:1; cf. 66:1). Babylon will experience the fury she directed against others (14:6; 47:6, 11) and will suffer the loss of her children (13:16; 14:22; 47:9). Her images will be smashed (21:9; 46:1).

In section 5, the parallels are not as plentiful or as clear. In both volumes, the Lord summons guests to his banquet (25:6; 55:1–2). God will swallow up death and sorrow (25:7–8; 49:19), and sorrow will flee away (25:8; 51:11). Joy is the lot of the righteous (25:9; 51:3; 55:12). The Lord is the one who slays the sea monster (27:1; 51:9). The everlasting covenant, broken by the people (24:5), will be renewed (45:3); God will once again have compassion on his people (27:11; 29:10–15; 54:8–10; 55:7).

---

[4]See Evans (1988) for even more detailed evaluation of Brownlee's thesis.

In section 6, the issue is the removal of the sins of the nation. Judah is guilty of falsehood (28:15; 59:3–4) and of divided allegiance, seeking refuge in foreign nations instead of God (28:15, 17; 30:2–3; 57:13). Her prophets are drunk (28:1, 7; 29:9; 56:12) and blind (29:18; 56:10) and know nothing (29:12; 56:10–11), but this spirit of stupor will be replaced with the Spirit of God (29:10; 59:21). Judgment hangs over them like a breach in the wall (30:13; 58:12).

In section 7, where once the land mourned and Sharon was like a desert (33:9), in the renewal of the world, mourning will end (61:2–3; 66:10) and Sharon will become lush pastureland (65:10). Rivers will flow in Zion (33:21; 66:12). Jerusalem will be restored (33:20; 66:13–14), and there will no longer be sickness or sorrow in Zion (33:24; 65:19–20). God's Spirit will make the renewal and restoration possible (32:15; 61:1; 63:14).

Although not all sections have strong parallels in language and concepts, the parallels in sections 2, 3, and 4 appear strong (Evans 1988, 145).

APPROACHING THE NEW TESTAMENT

It would be difficult to overstate the importance of Isaiah for the Christology of the church. The New Testament writers appealed to Isaiah repeatedly to explain events in their own day. John the Baptist was the voice crying in the wilderness, preparing the way for the coming glory of God (40:3; Matt. 3:3; Luke 3:4–6; John 1:23). Isaiah spoke of the virgin birth of Jesus (7:14; Matt. 1:23; Luke 1:34). The obduracy of Isaiah's own generation explains why Jesus taught in parables and why his message was not received by hearers (6:9–10; 29:13; Matt. 13:13–15; 15:7–9; John 12:39–40; Acts 28:24–27). Jesus was identified with the suffering servant of Isaiah; this identification explained in part his rejection and suffering (53:1; John 12:38; Acts 8:27–33) and his miracles of healing (53:4; Matt. 8:17). Isaiah's utterances provided the rationale for Jesus' mission to the Gentiles (9:1–2; Matt. 4:13–16); when challenged in Nazareth, his hometown, about his preaching and miracles in Galilee of the Gentiles, Jesus identified himself as the servant spoken of in Isaiah and justified his mission in that role (61:1–3; Luke 4:14–21). Jesus' avoidance of notoriety was explained in an appeal to Isaiah (42:1–4; Matt. 12:13–21). For John, the glory of the enthroned Lord that Isaiah had seen in his inaugural vision was the glory of Jesus (6:1–3; John 12:41).

The apostle Paul appeals to Isaiah both to explain the incorporation of the Gentiles into the people of God and to proclaim a remnant for Israel.

The impact of Isaiah on the early church included far more than Christology, however. Paul appeals to the prophet both to explain the incorporation of the Gentiles into the people of God (11:10 in Rom. 15:12; 65:1 in Rom. 10:20) and to proclaim a remnant for Israel (1:9 in Rom. 9:29; 10:22–23 in Rom. 9:27–28). Apart from explicit citations of Isaiah, the New Testament writers make use of a panoply of themes found in the prophet—for example, the renewal of creation in paradise regained (65:17–66:24; Rom. 8:18–25; Rev. 21–22), God's

Messiah and people in arboreal imagery (5:1–7; 6:13; 4:2–3; 11:1–3, 10–11; John 15), warnings against hypocritical practices (58:1–14; Matt. 23), divine armor (59:15–17; Eph. 6), and many others.

All this makes Isaiah, as we have said, more than a book of particular importance in biblical interpretation. It is also a book of grandeur and majesty.

CHAPTER TWENTY-ONE

JEREMIAH

In the Hebrew text, the book of Jeremiah is the largest book of the prophets, longer than the twelve so-called minor prophets combined. The prophet Jeremiah is among the most accessible personalities of the Old Testament: we have a wealth of historical and biographical material bearing on his life, and the prophet openly bares his soul in a number of his prayers.

Jeremiah ministered during the tumultuous years surrounding the decline of Assyria and the rise of the Babylonian Empire. Judah passed quickly through rapid cycles of independence and subjection, first to Egypt and then to Babylon. The prophet's ministry is set primarily against the background of the rule of Josiah's three sons and a grandson, the last four rulers of Judah. The nation's independence was at an end, and Jeremiah would witness the destruction of the city and the temple.

BIBLIOGRAPHY

Commentaries

J. **Bright,** *Jeremiah* (AB 21; Doubleday, 1962); R. P. **Carroll,** *The Book of Jeremiah* (OTL; Westminster, 1986); R. E. **Clements,** *Jeremiah* (Interp; John Knox, 1988); H. **Cunliffe-Jones,** *Jeremiah* (TBC; Macmillan, 1961); R. **Davidson,** *Jeremiah and Lamentations,* 2 vols. (DSB; Westminster, 1983, 1985); A. **Dearman,** *Jeremiah/Lamentations* (NIVAC; Zondervan, 2002); B. **Duhm,** *Jeremia* (Tübingen: Mohr, 1901); T. E. **Fretheim,** *Jeremiah* (SHBC; Smyth and Helwys, 2002); R. K. **Harrison,** *Jeremiah and Lamentations* (TOTC; InterVarsity Press, 1973); W. L. **Holladay,** *Jeremiah,* 2 vols. (Hermeneia; Fortress, 1986, 1989); G. T. **Keown,** P. J. **Scalise,** and T. **Smothers,** *Jeremiah 26–52* (WBC; Word, 1995); T. **Laetsch,** *Jeremiah* (Concordia, 1965); J. R. **Lundbom,** *Jeremiah 1–20* (AB; Doubleday, 1999); idem, *Jeremiah 21–36* (AB; Doubleday, 2004); idem, *Jeremiah 37–52* (AB; Doubleday, 2004); W. **McKane,** *A Critical and Exegetical Commentary on Jeremiah,* 2 vols.

(ICC; T. & T. Clark, 1986, 1996); E. W. **Nicholson,** *Jeremiah,* 2 vols. (CBC; Cambridge, 1973, 1975); W. **Rudolph,** *Jeremia,* 3rd ed. (HAT; Tübingen: J. C. B. Mohr, 1968); J. A. **Thompson,** *The Book of Jeremiah* (NICOT; Eerdmans, 1980).

Monographs and Articles

P. R. **Ackroyd,** "The Book of Jeremiah—Some Recent Studies," *JSOT* 28 (1984): 47–59; G. L. **Archer,** "The Relationship Between the Septuagint Translation and the Masoretic Text in Jeremiah," *TJ* 12 NS (1991): 139–50; S. H. **Blank,** *Jeremiah—Man and Prophet* (Cincinnati: Hebrew Union College, 1961); P.-M., **Bogaert,** ed. *Le livre de Jérémie* (BETL 54; Leuven: Leuven University Press, 1981); J. **Bright,** "The Date of the Prose Sermons of Jeremiah," *JBL* 70 (1951): 15–35; W. **Brueggemann,** "The Book of Jeremiah: Portrait of a Prophet," *Interp* 37 (1983): 130–45; R. P. **Carroll,** *From Chaos to Covenant: Uses of Prophecy in the Book of Jeremiah* (SCM, 1981); R. **Clements,** "Jeremiah, Prophet of Hope," *RvExp* 78 (1981): 345–63; T. **Eskenazi,** "Exile and Dreams of Return," *CurrTM* 17 (1990): 192–200; J. P. **Hyatt,** *Jeremiah, Prophet of Courage and Hope* (Abingdon, 1958); J. G. **Janzen,** *Studies in the Text of Jeremiah* (HSM 6; Cambridge: Harvard University Press, 1973); D. **Jobling,** "The Quest of the Historical Jeremiah: Hermeneutical Implication of Recent Literature," *USQR* 34 (1978): 3–12; J. **Lundbom,** "Baruch, Seraiah, and Expanded Colophons in the Book of Jeremiah," *JSOT* 36 (1986): 89–114; J. G. **McConville,** "Jeremiah: Prophet and Book," *TynBul* 42 (1991): 80–95; idem, *Judgment and Promise: The Message of Jeremiah* (Eisenbrauns, 1993); M. **Menken,** "The References to Jeremiah in the Gospel according to Matthew," *EphTL* 60 (1984): 5–24; S. **Mowinckel,** *Zur Komposition des Buches Jeremia* (Kristiana: Jacob Dybwad, 1914); idem, *Prophecy and Tradition* (Oslo, 1946); E. W. **Nicholson,** *Preaching to the Exiles: A Study of the Prose Tradition in the Book of Jeremiah* (Oxford: Blackwell, 1970); K. **O'Connor,** *The Confessions of Jeremiah: Their Interpretation and Role in Chapters 1–25* (SBLDS 94; Atlanta: Scholars Press, 1988); T. **Overholt,** *The Threat of Falsehood* (SBT, 2nd ser., 16; Allenson, 1970); L. G. **Perdue** and B. W. **Kovacs,** *A Prophet to the Nations: Essays in Jeremiah Studies* (Eisenbrauns, 1984); T. M. **Raitt,** *A Theology of Exile: Judgment and Deliverance in Jeremiah and Ezekiel* (Fortress, 1977); H. W. **Robinson,** *The Cross in the Old Testament* (SCM, 1955); C. R. **Seitz,** "The Prophet Moses and the Canonical Shape of Jeremiah," *ZAW* 101 (1989): 3–27; idem, *Theology in Conflict: Reactions to the Exile in the Book of Jeremiah* (BZAW 176; Berlin: de Gruyter, 1989); H. **Shanks,** "Jeremiah's Scribe and Confidant Speaks from a Hoard of Clay Bullae," *BAR* 5 (1987): 58–65; J. **Skinner,** *Prophecy and Religion* (Cambridge University Press, 1922); M. S. **Smith,** *The Laments of Jeremiah and Their Contexts* (Scholars, 1990); L. **Stulman,** *The Prose Sermons of the Book of Jeremiah* (Atlanta: Scholars, 1986); E. **Tov,** "Some Aspects of the Textual and Literary History of the Book of Jeremiah," in Bogaert (1981), 145–67; *The Septuagint Translation of Jeremiah and Baruch* (HSM 8; Cambridge: Harvard University Press, 1976); J. **Unter-**

man, *From Repentance to Redemption* (Sheffield: JSOT, 1987); M. **Weinfeld,** "Jeremiah and the Spiritual Metamorphosis of Israel," *ZAW* 88 (1976): 17–56; H. **Weippert,** *Die Prosareden des Buches Jeremia* (Berlin: de Gruyter, 1973); M. J. **Williams,** "An Investigation of the Legitimacy of Source Distinctions for the Prose Material in Jeremiah," *JBL* 112 (1993): 193–210; J. **Willis,** "Dialogue Between Prophet and Audience as a Rhetorical Device in the Book of Jeremiah," *JSOT* 33 (1985): 63–82; R. **Winkle,** "The Jeremiah Model for Jesus in the Temple," *AUSS* 24 (1986): 155–72; idem, "Jeremiah's Seventy Years for Babylon: A Re-assessment," *AUSS* 25 (1987): 201–14, 289–99; L. **Wisser,** *Jérémie, Critique de la vie sociale* (Le Monde de la Bible; Geneva: Labor et Fides, 1982).

HISTORICAL BACKGROUND

In this section we will discuss the authorship and historical period of the book, considering (1) the political situation, (2) the prophet himself, and (3) historical-critical approaches.

The Political Situation

Although the Assyrian Empire had dominated the ancient Near East for over two centuries, its demise came very quickly. After the death of Ashurbanipal (c. 631 BC), the last great king of Assyria, the Assyrian Empire contracted and disintegrated in just over twenty years. Nations that had once been great empires in their own right were once again free of the Assyrian yoke; both Babylon and Egypt began to reassert their own imperial ambitions in the wake of Assyria's demise. Nabopolassar and then his great son Nebuchadnezzar spurred the advance of Babylonian armies northwest along the Tigris and Euphrates. In Egypt Psammetichus and his successor Neco pressed northward through ancient Israel and Syria. Both armies were making a bid to control the remnants of the once-great Assyrian Empire. The Medes under Cyaxeres captured Asshur by 614 BC. The Babylonians, then in league with the Medes, besieged Nineveh until it fell in 612. The armies of Egypt under Neco en route to assist what remained of the Assyrian state advanced toward Haran in 609; Josiah of Judah had sought to interdict Neco's progress, and it cost him his life at Megiddo. Eventually, the major battle for influence and control over the remnants of Assyria would be fought in north Syria at Carchemish (605); here Nebuchadnezzar gained a decisive victory. The future of the states of the ancient Near East would lie with the Babylonians until Cyrus and the Persians came to power in 539.

In Judah, Josiah (640–609 BC) had become king when he was eight years old. By the time he was twelve, he began a series of religious reforms that led to the discovery of the law book in the temple when he was eighteen. As Assyria's control and fortunes declined, Judah too was freed from the Assyrian yoke. Josiah sought to reestablish the influence of the dynasty of David over territories that once had been part of a united kingdom. As part of his own territorial ambitions, and possibly even in league with the Babylonians, Josiah sought to block the northward expansion of Egypt by interdicting the armies of Pharaoh Neco at Megiddo. Josiah died in that battle. The citizens of Jerusalem anointed Josiah's second son Jehoahaz as king, but Neco promptly replaced him with his older brother Eliakim, assigning him a regnal name Jehoiakim (609–598 BC). Jehoiakim tried his hand at power politics—alternately feigning subjection to Egypt and Babylon—until his refusal to pay tribute provoked a Babylonian siege of Jerusalem. Jehoiakim died before the siege was concluded, but his own son Jehoiachin was then taken into captivity to Babylon along with the royal establishment, the leading citizens and craftsmen of Judah. Nebuchadnezzar placed Mattaniah, yet another son of Josiah, on the throne and changed his name to Zedekiah (598–586 BC). In 588 the Babylonians again laid siege to Jerusalem, and a year and a half later destroyed the temple and city. Judah now became a province of Babylon under the governorship of Gedaliah, who had been appointed by Nebuchadnezzar.

Jeremiah was an eyewitness and participant in these tumultuous years when Judah was striving to maintain her independence in the flow of the crosscurrents and riptides of the imperial ambition of the surrounding states. The book vividly describes the nationalism, the paranoia, the competing interests of pro-Babylonian and pro-Egyptian groups, the struggle between the "hawks" and the "doves" in Judah. In the midst of it all, Jeremiah was called to proclaim the word of God, first offering God's blessing if the nation would repent, then assuring her of a future restoration when divine judgment could no longer be averted (see Unterman 1987).

The Prophet Himself

Jeremiah's career runs from the time of his call to prophetic ministry during the thirteenth year of Josiah's reign (627/26 BC; Jer. 1:2) through the destruction of Jerusalem and his subsequent departure into Egypt (41:16–44:30). Although Jeremiah probably died in Egypt, it is not possible to establish the date of his death with certainty; the book ends by citing the release of Jehoiachin from prison during the reign of Evil-Merodach (562–560; Jer. 52:31–34), but chapter 52 is largely drawn from the parallel in 2 Kings 25 and was probably appended to the book after the prophet's death (cf. 51:64b).

Although an approximate range of dates for his ministry is secure, Jeremiah's age during his ministry is more difficult to establish. Jeremiah described himself as "too young" (1:6–7) when he received his call. Following a traditional approach, many suggest that he was about the age of twelve in 627 BC (Josiah's thirteenth year). However, if he was actively engaged in prophetic ministry as a young man during the years of Josiah's reform, it is problematic that none of his oracles can be dated with certainty to the period of Josiah's reign, and there is no direct reference to the reforms or the discovery of the Book of the Law. Apart from the reference to Josiah's thirteenth year in the superscription (1:2, see below on 3:6), the earliest dated event in the prophet's career is the temple sermon delivered during the year of Jehoiakim's accession to the throne (609, Jer. 26:1). Furthermore, since Jeremiah's call to celibacy is the sign of Yahweh's irrevocable decision to punish his people (16:1–4), it would presumably have been issued after Jehoiakim burned Jeremiah's first scroll (36:9; Jehoiakim's fifth year, c. 604),[1] by which time the offer of repentance (36:7) appears to have been superseded by the announcement of irrevocable judgment (36:31). If Jeremiah had been born around 640, he would have been in his mid- to upper-thirties at the time of his call to celibacy (see Holladay 1989; 2:25–26). Oracles about a "foe from the north" would also be unclear: Assyria was already in decline by 627, and the Babylonians were yet to attain power in the region.[2]

For these reasons other scholars (e.g., Holladay, Hyatt) have taken a lower chronology for Jeremiah's life, identifying the thirteenth year of Josiah (1:2) as the year of Jeremiah's birth (1:5). On this basis there would be no need to explain the apparent period of silence during Josiah's reform (627–622 BC) since the prophet would only have been about five years old when the law book was discovered. Jeremiah would have begun his career in 609 (26:1) at about the age of eighteen. He would have been called to celibacy in his mid-twenties, an age at which this decision would be the more poignant. Babylon would also have begun its resurgence by this time.

However, several arguments also cast doubt on identifying the thirteenth year of Josiah (627 BC) as the date of Jeremiah's birth and 609 (the date of Josiah's death and Jehoiakim's accession) as the beginning of his preaching. Jeremiah specifically speaks of an oracle received during the lifetime of Josiah (3:6–14). The prophet's allusion to Assyria (2:18) also suggests a time when it was still a military power to be reckoned with, which Assyria no longer was by 609 if Jeremiah did not begin to preach until that date.

The arguments regarding when the prophet began his public ministry are inconclusive. However, the language of Jeremiah 1:2 ("The word of the LORD came to") occurs over a hundred times in the Old Testament, the word always coming to an adult person, and ordinarily to a prophet during the course of his

---

[1]The LXX of 43:9 (=36:9) reads "eighth year" instead of MT "fifth year"; this would push the date of Jehoiakim's burning of the scroll to 601 BC.

[2]For this reason earlier commentators identified the "foe from the north" with a Scythian invasion. Herodotus (Hist. 1.103–6) speaks of a Scythian invasion in western Asia around 625 BC, about the time that Assyrian power began to wane. However, since the description of this foe in Jeremiah does not fit a Scythian raid or incursion very well, and since it is doubtful that these peoples ever reached Israel, this identification has been abandoned in recent research.

ministry. The phrase serves ordinarily to introduce a message that the prophet will presumably deliver to the nation, and as such it would scarcely be applicable to an infant.

The prophet was born into a family of priestly lineage in Anathoth, a scant two or three miles from Jerusalem. Although born of priestly lineage, his own family would eventually oppose him (11:21–23; 12:6), but the reasons for their plot against him are not given.

Jeremiah often withstood the political and religious establishment of his day, and as with many others in the succession of prophets in Israel, he would suffer for it. He was persecuted for his message; whipped and put in stocks by a temple overseer (20:2); accused of treason, sedition, and desertion (chap. 26; 37:11–16); plotted against (18:18; 12:6); imprisoned in a cistern (38:1–13); and held under arrest in the courtyard of the guard (38:14–28). The prophet's own suffering may be in part the background for the intensely personal outcries and prayers commonly called Jeremiah's "confessions" (11:18–12:6; 15:10–21; 17:12–18; 18:18–23; 20:7–18). The prophet gives expression to feeling abandoned by God or prays that God will take vengeance on his enemies, or he questions the goodness and constancy of God in the face of his suffering (see the discussion in Smith 1990).

Historical-Critical Approaches

Part of the difficulty in studying the book of Jeremiah is the seeming disarray of the materials. Oracles from many different periods of his ministry are arranged in sequences for reasons that are difficult to discern, and most are not assigned a specific date whereby one can assess how Jeremiah responded to the various international and social crises he encountered (see the appended list of datable materials in Jeremiah at the end of the chapter). The assignment of undated materials to various periods of Jeremiah's life can only be done on the basis of the "fit" various interpreters find between the oracles or narratives and the particular socio-geo-political situation of Judah at a given time. For this reason there has been wide disagreement over the historical setting for much of the book. The materials are not in a chronological sequence and do not seem to follow a coherent plan—or at least, if there is some inner logic to the arrangement, it has escaped interpreters.

The discussion about Jeremiah in historical-critical scholarship has revolved around the question of the relationship between Jeremiah the man and the book that bears his name. Two broad approaches have characterized the history of scholarship about the book. One approach finds in the book an essentially accurate picture of the man Jeremiah and his words and deeds (Lundbom 1986 is a representative of this view). The other approach finds in the book collections of independent materials gathered and arranged by later editors; proponents of this approach concentrate instead on recovering the history of the book's composition through various redactional stages.

> *The materials are not in a chronological sequence and do not seem to follow a coherent plan — or at least, if there is some inner logic to the arrangement, it has escaped interpreters.*

Scholars following this second approach have seen little connection between the man and the book; Jeremiah as we meet him in the book becomes largely the creation of later editors rather than the historical figure depicted there. During the heyday of the older criticism, Duhm (1901) argued that only the poetic oracles were original with Jeremiah; even among the poetic material, Duhm assigned very few verses to the prophet himself. Mowinckel (1914) followed Duhm's lead but distinguished further three types of material in the book: the prophetic oracles themselves ("A"), biographical accounts ("B"), and prosaic sermons ("C"). The sermons were, as with Duhm, attributed to a "Deuteronomic" source. Mowinckel later (1946, 61–63), spoke of three layers of tradition instead of three distinct literary sources. For example, Jeremiah's temple sermon is reported twice, once as biographical prose (chap. 7) and once as sermonic prose (chap. 26). Many scholars subsequently followed this tripartite division of the material but took varying positions on how historically to relate poetic materials ("A") with the prose sermons ("C"). A considerable discussion has surrounded the question of the extent of Deuteronomic redaction in the book. Some find extensive evidence of Deuteronomistic theology and language in the poetic oracles as well as in the prose passages; by contrast, McConville (1991, 82–83) emphasizes the theological contrast between Jeremiah and the Deuteronomic History in Kings. The more recent commentaries of Carroll (1986) and McKane (1986) exemplify an approach that does not see much connection between the book of Jeremiah and the historical figure by that name.

Other scholars have argued for a close association between the book and the man and credit Jeremiah or his amanuensis, Baruch, with most of the material. Among recent commentaries, Holladay (1986, 1989), Lundbom (1999, 2004, 2004), and Thompson (1979) are representative of this approach. Holladay argues from Deuteronomy 31:9–13 that the book of Deuteronomy was read in a public assembly every seven years. He dates these readings to 622, 615, 608, 601, 594, and 587 and uses these supposed readings to provide a chronological structure for Jeremiah's career. Holladay thus feels that he can locate most of the undated material in the book at precise moments in Jeremiah's life when the prophet would have preached to the assembled pilgrims in Jerusalem.

The contrast between these two methods can be illustrated in many different passages. For example, for scholars emphasizing the close connection between man and book, Jeremiah's "confessions" (above) are received as autobiographical statements by the man Jeremiah; they reveal his personal religious struggles with faith and calling, his doubts about himself and about God. For those seeing little connection between man and book, these same confessions are anonymous contributions from later editors, similar to the anonymous communal laments in the psalms.

Scholars working on Jeremiah have also sought to recover the contents of the original scroll that Jeremiah read before Jehoiakim in his fourth year of reign (605

BC, Jer. 36). After Jehoiakim had cut this scroll into pieces with a scribe's knife and had burned it in a brazier, God commanded Jeremiah to rewrite the scroll. Jeremiah "took another scroll and gave it to the scribe Baruch" and "as Jeremiah dictated, Baruch wrote on it all the words of the scroll that Jehoiakim king of Judah had burned in the fire. And many similar words were added to them" (36:32). But once again, scholars have had widely differing opinions regarding what portions of the book were included in this first edition.[3] There is little question that portions of Jeremiah reflect different emphases in his preaching. Much of Jeremiah's preaching is aimed to produce repentance on the part of his hearers (e.g., the temple sermon, 7:1–5; 26:2–6), whereas in other parts of his preaching, there is only the announcement of certain doom and disasters to come (e.g., 4:5–8, 19–21).

These differences may well reflect different stages in Jeremiah's preaching, such that there was a transition to a time when repentance and averting disaster was no longer possible and there remained only the certain expectation of judgment and exile (Unterman 1987). The prohibitions against the prophet's intercessory prayer (7:16; 11:14; 14:11–15:1) presume such a transition. In the vision of the two baskets of figs (chap. 24), those who go into exile are the good figs; they have accepted God's purpose and will yet be blessed by him. But the bad figs are those who remain in the land and who will be rejected. As McConville notes (1991, 87), the preaching of repentance gives way to an acknowledgment of its failure and the certainty that God will act in some other way. This transition may have come in connection with Nebuchadnezzar's rise to power and his conquests south along the Mediterranean coast in the fourth year of Jehoiakim (605–604 BC, 25:1–38), the year after Jehoiakim had burned the scroll (36:9) and Jeremiah had announced irrevocable judgment (36:27–31). But this prophet of inevitable annihilation is yet a preacher of hope and restoration, a possible third phase in his preaching (e.g., the "Book of Consolation," chaps. 30–33). Yet these distinctions and other efforts to trace a chronological development in Jeremiah's preaching may be too rigid and simplistic; oracles of divine judgment may always have aimed at repentance even when not explicitly mentioned, and the relationship between judgment, repentance, and restoration in the book may be theologically more sophisticated or complex than such a solution allows. McConville (1991, 95) suggests that the materials are indeed the authentic words of Jeremiah ben Hilkiah but are recorded for us in the light of his own later and mature reflection on God's dealings with Judah.

THE TEXT OF JEREMIAH

Jeremiah presents us with the clearest example of the intersection of the concerns of so-called "lower criticism" (textual criticism) and "higher criticism"

---

[3]See Thompson (1980, 56–59) for the history of this research.

(historical-critical, literary-critical approaches). For generations it has been recognized that the Septuagint of the text of Jeremiah does not contain the equivalents for about 2,700 words in the Masoretic text of the book, about one-seventh of the total. Not only is the LXX shorter, but the materials are arranged in a different order; most notably, the oracles against the foreign nations (Jer. 46–51 in the MT) have been relocated to a position after Jeremiah 25:13, and the order in which the various nations are introduced has also been altered. Scholars debated for generations whether this represented an abridgment and editorial recasting of the MT by the LXX translators, or whether the LXX translators had followed a different Hebrew text than that represented by the MT. The debate remained largely unsettled until the discoveries in the caves at Qumran.

From the excavation of cave 4 at Qumran, fragments of three manuscripts of Jeremiah emerged. Of these, two (4QJer[a], 4QJer[c]) represent a text very similar to that in the MT and provide the earliest witnesses for the MT in this book. However, 4QJer[b], although quite fragmentary, agreed in the main with the type of Hebrew text that was used by the translators of the LXX.[4] In particular, it showed the two major features that distinguish the reconstructed *Vorlage* of the LXX from the MT: the shortness and the arrangement of the text.

The differences between the two versions of Jeremiah cannot be explained solely by the ordinary dynamics of textual transmission in which scribes occasionally lose their place and leave out material (haplography), accidentally repeat material (dittography), misread or otherwise make spelling errors, introduce short explanatory notes, and so forth. Here we are looking at issues that involve the compositional history of the book; two distinct editions have been preserved in the MT and LXX, and apparently existed side by side in the library of Qumran. The debate since Qumran has shifted, focusing now on the relationship between these two different text types. If we are able to see the final stages of a process of literary growth in Jeremiah, it is important to ask also whether other books of the Old Testament were not edited and rewritten in a similar way, even though the earlier editions may no longer be preserved.

At first impression, it is natural to assume that the shorter text represents an earlier stage in the textual history of the book; this earlier stage would have been expanded or elaborated by later copyists attempting to clarify, explain, or otherwise assist the reader. In most instances, the additional material in the longer text (the MT) is the result of the typical changes that scribes introduce into their work. Tov (1981) classifies these broadly as (1) editorial, and

---

[4]QJer[b] contained fragments of chapters 9, 10, 43, and 50, and was provisionally published by Janzen (1973). Although in the main it agrees with LXX against the MT, in five instances it agrees with the MT against the LXX, and it also contains several unique readings (Tov 1981, 146–47).

(2) exegetical changes. Editorial changes include such subcategories as (a) text arrangement (e.g., the position of the oracles against foreign nations); (b) the addition of headings to prophecies (2:1–2; 7:1–2; 16:1; 27:1–2), somewhat analogous to the addition of headings to various psalms in the LXX; (c) repetition of sections (e.g., 6:22–24 = 50:41–43; 10:12–16 = 51:15–19); (d) addition of new verses and sections (see below); (e) the addition of details (e.g., 25:20, 25, 26); and (f) modifications of content or reformulations (e.g., 29:25; 35:18; 36:32). Exegetical changes include such subcategories as (a) harmonistic additions that fill out the patronymic of personal names, amplify divine titles, or give to similar verses the same textual form (harmonistic additions are the most frequent and characteristic feature of the MT as over against the LXX); (b) contextual exegesis (adding material to clarify words or phrases [e.g., 27:5, 8; 28:3, 15], especially in the prose sections); and (c) insertion or amplification of formulaic expressions, often at the beginning or end of prophetic utterances (e.g., the phrase "says the LORD" occurs 109 times in the LXX but an additional 65 times in the MT). These changes are most easily understood as later modifications to an earlier text rather than as abridgment of a previously existing longer edition. Although in Jeremiah the LXX differs perhaps more widely from the MT than in any other book of the Old Testament, one should not overstate these differences. Fairly few involve extended passages,[5] and most represent spelling out or clarifying material already present or implicit in the text.

Who was responsible for the later and expanded version of Jeremiah represented by the MT? The majority of scholars view the additional material in the MT as originating with later scribes and interpreters, and seek to investigate the date and social setting under which these later materials were inserted. Most additions have been assigned to the postexilic period. On the other hand, some have suggested that Jeremiah himself or his amanuensis, Baruch, created these two different surviving editions (e.g., Archer 1991). We do know that there were at least two editions of the book: the one destroyed by Jehoiakim and then replaced at God's command (chap. 36). It is certainly possible that the shorter text of the LXX rests on a Hebrew *Vorlage* originally produced by Jeremiah or Baruch during their time in Egypt (41:16–44:30). This edition would have circulated in Egypt, where it became the basis for the LXX translation of the book made there. Later in his life, Jeremiah may have expanded on the book, or Baruch may have incorporated additional material after his mentor's death. Tov (1981, 154) dismisses the skepticism that would deny attributing any of the additional material in the MT to Jeremiah; for example, he argues that the bur-

---

[5]Examples of MT passages, including at least entire verses not represented in the LXX, can be found in 10:6–8; 17:1–4; 46:26 (missing at LXX 26:26); 51:45–58 (missing at LXX 28:45–58); 48:40 (missing at LXX 31:40); 33:14–26; 39:4–13 (LXX chap. 46); 29:16–20 (LXX chap. 36). See Archer (1991, 144–47).

Table 13
Jeremiah 27:1–11 in the MT and LXX

MT	LXX

27:1 Early in the reign of Jehoiakim son of Josiah king of Judah, this word came to Jeremiah from the Lord: 27:2 This is what the Lord said to me: "Make a yoke out of straps and crossbars and put it on your neck. 27:3 Then send word to the kings of Edom, Moab, Ammon, Tyre and Sidon through the envoys who have come to Jerusalem to Zedekiah king of Judah. 27:4 Give them a message for their masters and say, 'This is what The LORD Almighty, the God of Israel, says: "Tell this to your masters: 27:5 With my great power and outstretched arm I made the earth and its people and the animals that are on it, and I give it to anyone I please. 27:6 Now I will hand all your countries over to my servant Nebuchadnezzar king of Babylon; I will make even the wild animals subject to him. 27:7 All nations will serve him and his son and his grandson until the time for his land comes; then many nations and great kings will subjugate him. 27:8 "' "If, however, any nation or kingdom will not serve Nebuchadnezzar king of Babylon or bow its neck under his yoke, I will punish that nation with the sword, famine and plague, declares the Lord, until I destroy it by his hand. 27:9 So do not listen to your prophets, your diviners, your interpreters of dreams, your mediums or your sorcerers who tell you, 'You will not serve the king of Babylon.' 27:10 They prophesy lies to you that will only serve to remove you far from your lands; I will banish you and you will perish. 27:11 But if any nation will bow its neck under the yoke of the king of Babylon and serve him, I will let that nation remain in its own land to till it and to live there, declares the Lord."' "	(Jer. 27 = Jer. 34 in LXX)
	
	27:2 This is what the Lord said : "Make a yoke out of straps and crossbars and put it on your neck. 27:3 Then send word to the kings of Edom, Moab, Ammon, Tyre and Sidon through the envoys who have come to Jerusalem to Zedekiah king of Judah. 27:4 Give them a message for their masters and say, 'This is what the Lord , the God of Israel, says: "Tell this to your masters: 27:5 With my great power and outstretched arm I made the earth,
	
	         and I give it to anyone I please. 27:6 I will hand the countries over to my servant Nebuchadnezzar king of Babylon; even the wild animals subject to him. 27:7
	
	         27:8 "' "If, however, any nation or kingdom will not bow its neck under his yoke, I will punish them with the sword and famine, declares the Lord, until I destroy it by his hand. 27:9 So do not listen to your prophets, your diviners, your interpreters of dreams, your mediums or your sorcerers who say, 'You will not serve the king of Babylon.' 27:10 They prophesy lies to you that will only serve to remove you far from your lands.
	
	27:11 But if any nation will bow its neck under the yoke of the king of Babylon and serve him, I will let that nation remain in its own land to till it and to live there."' "

den of proof is on those who deny 33:14–26 (absent in the LXX) to the prophet in whose name it has been transmitted.

Although the expanded version (MT) of Jeremiah may well contain material that originates with Jeremiah or Baruch, some of the material gives clear indication of originating at a later time from different hands. Two examples will have to suffice. (1) The LXX does not contain the section heading that is found in the MT at 27:1–2 (see comparison of texts in the table below). The heading of this section assigns the following material to the reign of Jehoiakim (27:1), though the oracle that follows in fact concerns Zedekiah (27:3, 12) and events after the reign of Jehoiachin (27:20), that is, events and rulers that came after Jehoiakim. In this instance, the individual who provided a section heading for this part of Jeremiah appears simply to have been mistaken,[6] and since neither Jeremiah nor Baruch would likely make such a mistake, it is more easily understood as the work of someone who added the gloss at a later time. (2) In Jeremiah 25:15–32 the prophet describes how all the nations of the ancient Near East would taste the cup of the wine of God's wrath through the warfare and disaster that the king of Babylon would bring to them. In 25:26b, however, there is a small problem: the king of Babylon is bringing divine judgment not only against all the other nations, but also against "Sheshak," a coded writing for "Babylon."[7] It is somewhat anomalous that the king of Babylon, while bringing judgment through the conquest of all these other nations, should somehow bring judgment on himself the same way. The LXX of Jeremiah does not contain either passage in the MT of the book that mentions "Sheshak" (25:26; 51:41). The insertion of this short note into Jeremiah 25:26 appears to be a later gloss that disturbs the context of the passage, and it too is most readily understood as the work of a later hand than that of the original author(s).

LITERARY ANALYSIS

As mentioned above, part of the challenge represented by Jeremiah is that the materials in the book are not presented in a sequence or structure that is readily discernible, or at least an overall coherent structure for the book has eluded interpreters. There are, however, a number of smaller collections of material in the book that reflect a topical arrangement; Jeremiah is in this regard a "book of books," built up by amassing these smaller topical collections. A number of

---

[6]This was recognized by the copyists in a few Hebrew manuscripts that correct "Jehoiakim" to "Zedekiah."

[7]"Sheshak" is a coded writing using a simple substitutionary code called 'atbash writing. Using the twenty-two characters of the Hebrew alphabet, the first letter of the alphabet is represented by the last letter of the alphabet, the second letter by the next-to-last, and so forth.

these smaller collections are introduced with their own titles: "The word of the LORD that came to Jeremiah concerning the drought" (14:1–15:4); concerning "the royal house of Judah" (21:11–22:30); "concerning the prophets" (23:9–40); "This is the word of the LORD that came to Jeremiah the prophet concerning the nations" (46:1–51:64); "This is the word the LORD spoke through Jeremiah the prophet concerning Babylon and the land of the Babylonians" (50:1–51:64). Other notices appear to call attention to the end of a section: "I will bring on that land all the things I have spoken against it, all that are written in this book and prophesied by Jeremiah against all the nations" (25:13); "The words of Jeremiah end here" (51:64).

Several other collections of material are commonly identified in the book. The largely poetic announcements of judgment against Judah and Jerusalem in chapters 1–25:13 may have originally been one such unit. In 25:1–3 the prophet refers back to the beginning of his ministry reported in chapter 1; furthermore, there are a number of verbal similarities between 25:3–9 and 1:15–19 that suggest that chapter 1 and 25:1–13 form an inclusio beginning and ending a larger section. The reference to "all that are written in this book" (25:13) also suggests the end of an earlier collection of material. Some have identified 1:1–25:13 as containing essentially the poetic oracles from the first scroll written by Jeremiah, the scroll destroyed by Jehoiakim (chap. 36). Within this larger unit there may have been other smaller collections, for example, the passages concerning the prophet's own struggles with his call, his doubts about himself and his questioning of God, often grouped together as "Jeremiah's Confessions" (above).

Chapters 30–33 are often called the Book of Consolation or the Book of Comfort. The two chapters primarily of poetry (30–31) and two chapters of prose (32–33) express hope for the future restoration of Jerusalem. But even this little book of hope is interlaced with the somber expectation of imminent judgment (30:5–7, 12–15, 22–23; 31:15, 18–19; 32:26–35; 33:4–5).

Chapters 46–51 form the collection of Jeremiah's oracles against foreign nations. In the LXX these materials are introduced after 25:13 in the MT (25:14 is not found in the LXX). The order of the oracles against the nations also differs in the two texts: the order in the MT is roughly geographical, moving from south to north and west to east; the order in the LXX appears instead to approximate the order of political importance (Thompson 1980, 31). Almost all of the prophetic books contain utterances directed to foreign states. Moses' call to prophetic office was first to deliver the word of God to a foreign power (3:10–12); like his great predecessor, Jeremiah was "appointed as a prophet to the nations" (1:5, 10).

Two other blocks of material are found between these three larger collections (chaps. 26–29; 34–45). These largely consist of biographical narratives recounting incidents from Jeremiah's life, though these are not in a chronological order.

Other smaller units of material appear to have been gathered around particular themes or catchwords. For example, chapters 4–8 often mention the "foe from the north"; the themes of "youth" and "harlotry" combine in chapters 2–3.

The book also contains a large number of symbolic actions. Like preachers today, Israel's prophets used stories in their sermons. But they also used "props" or "object lessons" to make their points, and these devices are ordinarily called by Old Testament scholars "symbolic actions." Jeremiah hid a linen belt in a rock crevice to show how Judah would become ruined and useless (13:1–11). He bought an earthenware jug from a potter and smashed it at the Potsherd Gate as a symbol of the way in which God would destroy both city and people (chap. 19). He made a yoke and wore it around his neck to proclaim the way that Nebuchadnezzar would bring the nations under his yoke (27:1–15); the false prophet Hananiah broke the yoke as another symbolic action to contradict the preaching of Jeremiah (28:1–4). An enterprising cousin saw that exile was imminent and wanted quick cash from some property; since Jeremiah had been preaching that there would be a restoration for Judah, the cousin urged Jeremiah to "put his money where his mouth was" and act as the kinsman-redeemer for the piece of property. Jeremiah bought the field and used the deed as a symbolic token that "fields and vineyards will again be bought in this land" (32:6–15). A scroll announcing God's judgment on Babylon was sent to the exile community in Babylon with the command that it be thrown into the Euphrates as an illustration of how Babylon will "sink to rise no more" (51:59–64). Once Jeremiah arrived in Egypt with those fleeing Jerusalem after the murder of Gedaliah, he took large stones and buried them at the entrance to a royal palace in Tahpanhes; the stones were a visual proclamation that one day the king of Babylon would set his royal throne also in Egypt, above these very stones (43:8–13). The symbolic actions of Jeremiah and the rest of Israel's prophets were part of their preaching, and they were, therefore, the efficacious word of God.

Some of the prophet's symbolic actions did not involve manipulation of physical objects. These included his renaming Pashhur the priest with a symbolic name (20:3), the command that he remain celibate as a sign to the nation (16:1–3), and his refusal to observe customary mourning rites at a funeral (16:5–9).

Jeremiah not only used physical object lessons, but also saw symbols in other aspects of the physical world. An almond branch (šōqed) reminds Jeremiah that God is a "watcher" (šāqed), watching over his word to bring it to pass (1:11–12); a boiling pot tipped away from the north illustrates for the prophet how disaster will soon spill over the nations from the north (1:13–16). Two fig baskets (chap. 24) illustrate the separate fates of those going into exile and those remaining in the land. A visit to the house of a potter (chap. 18) provides instruction about the sovereignty of God.

Commentators have long recognized a probable relationship between Jeremiah and Hosea.[8] The two prophets made common use of some figures and language. Jeremiah lived a bit north of Jerusalem, just at the southern edge of the northern kingdom, and he may have known of traditions about Hosea in part through geographical proximity to the north. Some have suggested that Jeremiah's own family was descended from a line of priests through Abiathar (1 Kings 2:26–27) reaching back to Eli at Shiloh (Jer. 7:12; 26:6) in the north. It is particularly in Jeremiah 2–3 that Jeremiah's debt to Hosea is prominent. Hosea spoke often of God's "loyalty, faithfulness, love" (ḥesed) to Israel (4:1; 6:4, 6; 12:6). Just as Hosea had typified Israel as an adulterous wife, so too Jeremiah describes Israel as an unfaithful wife turned to pursue her lovers (3:1–5, 20; Hos. 2:14–15 [MT 16–17]). Jeremiah longs that Israel return to the devotion (ḥesed) of her youth as a bride in the wilderness (2:2). But like Gomer, the wife of Hosea, Israel too became promiscuous and a harlot (3:1–20), even though the Lord would remain her husband (3:14; Hos. 2:2, 16 [MT 4, 18]). Jeremiah's instruction to Israel, "Break up your unplowed ground and do not sow among thorns" (4:3), may be a citation of Hosea 10:12. Both prophets were also concerned with "the knowledge of God." Hosea complained that there was no knowledge of God in the land (Hos. 4:1) and that the people were destroyed for the lack of that knowledge (Hos. 4:6). Through Jeremiah, God complained that those who dealt with the law did not know him (2:8) and declared, "My people are fools; they do not know me" (4:22). Both prophets foresaw a day when Israel would "know" the Lord (31:34; Hos. 2:20 [MT 22]). Both prophets indicted the nation for lists of offenses that violate the Decalogue (7:9; Hos. 4:2). These are a few of the items that appear to indicate possible familiarity with Hosea on the part of Jeremiah.

THEOLOGICAL MESSAGE

Jeremiah never gathered his teaching under the traditional headings and categories of systematic theology. His "theology" was formed in the dynamic relationship the prophet had, on the one hand, with the God for whom he served as a messenger and, on the other hand, with the citizens of Jerusalem as they encountered the changing geopolitical and religious conditions of Jerusalem shortly before the city was destroyed. Although the pronouncements and implications of Jeremiah's preaching reach in all but innumerable directions, several distinct themes provide a window into Jeremiah's teaching.

Jeremiah's God

In an earlier period of critical scholarship, the prophets were often described as the creative innovators of Israel's theology. But this idea would be quite foreign

---

[8]See Thompson (1980, 81–85) for a full discussion.

to Jeremiah. Jeremiah does not introduce any "new ideas" about God—quite to the contrary, he proclaims Yahweh to the nation in much the same way as other prophets did before him. Jeremiah implores the nation to "ask for the ancient paths, ask where the good way is, and walk in it" (6:16). The prophet thought of himself as one who called the nation to fidelity in her ancient covenant with God. Yahweh was the living God, the source of life-giving waters (2:13).

For Jeremiah, Yahweh was absolutely sovereign over the world. He was the creator of the universe, but he could also withhold his hand from the creation and allow it to dissolve again into primeval chaos as he executed judgment upon the world (4:23–26; 18:1–11). The Lord held absolute sway over his creation and all that was within it. Although Yahweh was uniquely the God of Israel (2:3–4; 10:16; 17:13), he held dominion over all nations. Jeremiah was sent, not to Israel alone, but to be "a prophet to the nations" (1:5), to be "over nations and kingdoms to uproot and tear down, to destroy and overthrow, to build and to plant" (1:10). Jeremiah's extended oracles against foreign nations are a testimony to the prophet's confidence in Yahweh's universal rule.

By placing a tremendous emphasis on the sins and wickedness of Israel, the prophet also drew attention to the holiness of God. God was just, and he would punish the stubborn, rebellious, and unrepentant nation as their sins required. But alongside the holiness and justice of God, Jeremiah found God to be patient, compassionate, merciful, and longsuffering (3:12; 13:14; 15:15). Even though God's compassion would be strained to its limits and his wrath would be poured out on Jerusalem, yet he would again show his people compassion and favor (12:15; 30:18; 31:20; 33:26; 42:12).

The People and the Covenant

For Jeremiah, Israel was God's elect nation, those whom he had chosen (33:24). The prophet uses many images to portray this unique national status: Israel was the Lord's "firstfruits" (2:3), his "choice vine" (2:21), his beloved bride (2:2; 3:14), his "flock" (13:17), his "vineyard" (12:10), his own inheritance (12:7–9); the Lord was father to a wayward son, husband to a faithless wife (3:19–20).

Israel was a nation in covenant with God. The prophet called the nation back to the days of the Mosaic Age, that pristine time when Israel was Yahweh's devoted bride (2:2). The nation must live in faithful obedience as required at Sinai; they must love God with all their heart and soul and flee from idols—if they are to possess the land (chap. 11). The blessings and the curses from Mount Ebal and Mount Gerizim remain relevant to the generation of Jeremiah's day (11:26–32; 22:9; cf. Deut. 27–28). God's ancient covenant with Israel represented the nation's claim on his mercy and favor (14:21), but Israel must keep *torah* (5:4–5; 8:7).

Yet Judah in Jeremiah's day was not the devoted bride. From the time of the conquest onward, she had become the harlot (3:1–20). She followed the Baals,

The prophet called the nation back to the days of the Mosaic Age. Israel must live in faithful obedience as required at Sinai.

pursued her lovers, and became a she-camel in heat, a wild donkey sniffing the wind in her lust (3:23–24). She refused correction (2:30; 5:3; 17:23; 32:33; 35:13), so the curses of the covenant sanctions would come upon the nation (Deut. 28:49–68).

In his sermons Jeremiah warns against a false confidence in God's covenant with Israel. The Lord's choice of Zion did not mean that the city was inviolable if the nation did not heed his commands. In his famous temple sermon (chaps. 7, 26), Jeremiah indicts the nation for disobedience to the Decalogue: the temple would be no refuge for those who steal, murder, commit adultery, give false testimony, and commit idolatry; the temple is not a safe haven when it has been made a den of robbers (7:9–11).

Nor should there be false confidence in God's covenant with David. Here in Jeremiah, as in other books of the Old Testament, we meet this paradox of the relationship between God's promises to David and his insistence on obedience. On the one hand, God's covenant with David is conditioned on obedience (17:24–25; 21:12; 22:1–5; 38:20). On the other, it cannot be broken irrevocably, for God will make a new covenant with David and his descendants (23:5; 30:9; 33:15–17, 21–22), a covenant as sure as the day and night (33:23–26).

God's Word in Jeremiah

Jeremiah was the royal messenger of a heavenly king. The prophet was quite conscious of his standing in the succession of prophets deriving from Moses (see below). In this regard, he knew that God's word was in his mouth as Moses had promised the prophets that would follow him (1:9; Deut. 18:18); Jeremiah's utterances had the validity and power of the words of God delivered by Moses from Mount Sinai (Deut. 18:14–22). God's word for Jeremiah was powerful and self-authenticating (1:12; 4:28). It could not be restrained; the prophet himself could not hold it inside: "If I say, 'I will not mention his word or speak anymore in his name,' his word is in my heart like a fire, a fire shut up in my bones. I am weary of holding it in; indeed, I cannot" (20:9). It was overwhelming for Jeremiah: "My heart is broken within me; all my bones tremble. I am like a drunken man, like one overcome by wine, because of the LORD and his holy words" (23:9; cf. Acts 2:13). God's word was the hammer that smashed rock, the consuming fire in the straw (23:29). Even when Jeremiah was tried for treason and under threat of death, his defense could only be that the Lord had sent him to speak in his name (26:12, 16).

Yet in spite of this certainty and authority on the part of Jeremiah, the people still would not listen; instead, they rebuked and reproached him (6:10, 19; 8:9; 17:15; 20:8; 38:4). They chose instead the comforting and reassuring words of the false prophets (14:13; 28:1–3). But the false prophets had not stood in the divine council to hear the word of the Lord, and they ran as messengers without having been sent, proclaiming the delusions of their own minds (23:16–22).

Jeremiah and Moses

Beyond the question of the larger influence of Deuteronomy on the book of Jeremiah, many have also noted the way the man Jeremiah also appears in the book as a kind of "second Moses" (cf. Seitz 1989). Moses set the model for the prophets who came after him. Just as God had put his words into the mouth of Moses so that what he spoke was in truth the very word of God, so God put his words into the mouth of his prophet Jeremiah (1:9; Deut. 18:18). Moses had been called at the outset as a prophet sent to a Gentile nation (Ex. 3:10), a fact mirrored in Jeremiah's own call (1:4, 10). Both Moses and Jeremiah protested, pleading their inability to speak (1:6; Ex. 4:10).

Moses was also a prophetic intercessor: his duty was not simply to represent God to the people but also to represent the people before God. Moses interceded for the nation after the rebellion at Kadesh (Num. 14:17–19; Deut. 9:23–29), offered his own life at Sinai (Ex. 32:31–32; Deut. 9:15–21; Ps. 106:19–23), and pleaded for Miriam (Num. 12:9–15). Jeremiah would again follow the example set by Moses (21:1–2; 37:3; 42:2–4), but with an ironic twist: Jeremiah, who had presumably interceded with God over many years in behalf of the nation, was now commanded to intercede no longer; God's irrevocable judgment was about to break out against the nation, and he would hear their prayers no more (7:16; 11:14; 14:11–15:1). Moses had saved the nation from destruction through his intercessory prayer, but now Jeremiah was commanded to no longer exercise this responsibility. Moses had once led the nation out of Egypt, and now in the end Jeremiah returns there (43:1–7). Thus we have come full circle in the history of the nation: as at the time before the entrance into the land, there is no longer a state, a king, a priest, a temple, or even a population. Because of their faithfulness, Ebed-Melek (38:7–12; 39:16–18) and Baruch (45:1–5), like Caleb and Joshua before them, are contrasted to the generations of which they are a part (Seitz 1989, 17–18).

Hope for the Future

When Jeremiah purchased the field belonging to his cousin (32:6–15), his deeds spoke as loudly as his preaching of his confidence that the Jews would yet return to Jerusalem, and "fields and vineyards will again be bought in this land." He comforted those in captivity, telling them that though the exile would be long instead of short, the Lord still had a message of grace: "I know the plans I have for you . . . plans to prosper you and not to harm you, plans to give you hope and a future" (29:11). Although the well-known passage in 31:31–34 is not found in the Septuagint of Jeremiah, many concur that Jeremiah's proclamation of a new covenant, while perhaps not embodying the exact words of the prophet, reflects the prophet's own teaching. In place of law written on stone, God would yet write his law on hearts.

Jeremiah also expressed messianic hopes for the future. God would raise up "for David a righteous Branch" (23:5–6; 33:15–16). Jeremiah is probably drawing on imagery from Isaiah in describing the Messiah as "Branch" (Isa. 4:2; 11:1, 10); Zechariah would follow Jeremiah's lead (Zech. 3:8; 6:12). Jeremiah appears to be making a wordplay on the name of King Zedekiah. When Nebuchadnezzar placed Mattaniah on the throne, he changed his name to Zedekiah, which means "Yahweh is righteous." To know that Yahweh is righteous was to know him in judgment. But Jeremiah speaks of a day when Israel's king will be known by the name "The LORD Our Righteous Savior" (23:6; cf. 33:16). To know that Yahweh is "our righteousness" is to know him in grace. God's purpose for Jeremiah was not only to "uproot, tear down, destroy, and overthrow," but also to "build and plant" (1:10).

APPROACHING THE NEW TESTAMENT

The book of Jeremiah made a strong impression on the writers of the New Testament. There are about forty direct quotations of the book in the New Testament, most in Revelation in connection with the destruction of Babylon (e.g., 50:8 in Rev. 18:4; 50:32 in Rev. 18:8; 51:49–50 in Rev. 18:24).

Jeremiah was a man who knew great sorrow of heart as he saw the divine judgment about to overtake Jerusalem; in tradition, he has become known as "the weeping prophet." One cannot but wonder if Luke does not have the image of Jeremiah in mind when he writes that Jesus wept over the city of Jerusalem, lamenting that the city would not experience peace, but rather a siege and destruction.

Jesus, like Micah and Jeremiah before him, made pointed announcements about the pending destruction of Jerusalem and the temple (7:1–15; 26:1–15; Mic. 3:9–12); but at Jesus' trial for sedition, the crowd did not cry out, "This man should not be sentenced to death!" (26:16). The crowds in Matthew's account of Jesus' entry to the temple clearly regarded Jesus as a prophet (Matt. 21:11–12, 46). Jesus' cleansing of the temple draws its rationale from Jeremiah (7:11; Matt. 21:13).

Winkle (1986) has noted a number of strong parallels between Matthew 23:29–24:2 and Jeremiah's temple sermons (chaps. 7 and 26): (1) God had sent the prophets to Jerusalem (7:25; 26:4–6), but the people refused to listen; Jesus also sent prophets to the nation (Matt. 23:34; cf. Matt. 5:12; 10:16). (2) Jeremiah warns about shedding innocent blood in the temple precincts (7:6), and after his temple sermon, his own death becomes the issue (26:15). The Old Testament records the explicit murder of only two prophets: Zechariah (2 Chron. 24:18–22) and Uriah (Jer. 26:20–23). In Matthew 23:29–37, Jesus also teaches about the murder of the prophets and the shedding of innocent blood, and it is his own blood that will be shed in the city. (3) Jeremiah had warned that the temple could be abandoned just as God had abandoned Shiloh (7:12, 14; 26:6). As he himself left the temple precincts for the last time, Jesus also warned the people that their "house" (temple/city/country) would be left desolate (Matt. 23:39–24:1). But in Matthew's gospel, the God who abandons the temple is none other than Jesus himself (Winkle 1986, 171); he goes out, never to return.

It was perhaps the fact that both Jeremiah and Jesus made pronouncements against the temple and city or the fact that there was a resemblance between the "Man of Sorrows" and the broken-hearted prophet Jeremiah that prompted the populace to associate Jesus with Jeremiah (Matt. 16:13–14). There was a conspiracy against Jeremiah, and he compared himself to a lamb on the way to slaughter; this became reality for Jesus (11:19; Isa. 53:7; Acts 8:32).

Stephen would later repeat Jeremiah's denunciation of Israel as uncircumcised in heart and ear (6:19; 9:26; Acts 7:51) in an address that cost him his life.

Paul regarded the lessons from Jeremiah's visit to the house of a potter as instruction about God's sovereignty in his calling of the Gentiles (Jer. 18; Rom. 9:20–24).

Table 14
Dated Material in Jeremiah

The following references in Jeremiah have fairly clear chronological notices. The dating of the other material is more difficult.*

Josiah	year 13	627 B.C.	1:1–19:	Jeremiah's call
Jehoahaz	year 1	609	22:10–12:	Jehoahaz's exile
Jehoiakim	year 1 (?)	608(?)	26:1–24:	destruction of temple
	years 1–3 (?)	608–605(?)	22:13–19:	abuse of power
	year 4	605/4	25:1–30:	cup of wrath
	year 4	605/4	46:1–49:33:	oracles against Egypt and other nations
	years 4–5	605–603	36:1–32:	burning of scroll
	year 4	605/4	45:1–5:	Lord to spare life of Baruch, Jeremiah's scribe
	year ?	?	35:1–19:	blessing for Recabites
Jehoiachin	year 1	598	22:24–30:	judgment and exile
Zedekiah	year 1	597	24:1–10:	good and bad figs
	year 1 (?)	597(?)	49:34–39:	oracle against Elam
	year 1	597	29:1–19:	letter to exiles
	year 4	594	51:59–64:	scroll thrown into Euphrates
	year 9 (?)	589	34:1–22:	Jerusalem's fall prophesied; freeing slaves
	year 10 (?)	588	37:1–38:28:	Zedekiah told to surrender to Nebuchadnezzar
	year 10 (?)	588	37:1–38:28:	Jeremiah in cistern; siege of the city
	year 10	588	32:1–44:	Jeremiah's purchase of a field
	year 10	588	33:1–26:	assurances of restoration
	year 11	586	39:1–40:7:	fall of Jerusalem; release of Jeremiah
	year 11	586	52:1–30:	fall of Jerusalem; tally of the exiles
Gedaliah as governor		586	40:8–41:16:	appointed and assassinated
Johanan as leader of remnant		586	42:1–22:	advice to stay in the land
		585	43:1–13:	flight to Egypt
		585	44:1–30:	last speech to exiles in Egypt
		560	52:31–34:	released by Jehoiachin Evil-Merodach

*The MT assigns 27:1–32 to the reign of Jehoiakim, but this is clearly an error. The oracle belongs in the reign of Zedekiah (28:1; 27:3, 12). The LXX at this point does not contain a date formula, and the notice in the MT appears to be an erroneous insertion by a later editor.

CHAPTER TWENTY-TWO

LAMENTATIONS

The physical, psychological, and spiritual devastation of Jerusalem in 587 BC was horrific. The extent of the destruction is described in 2 Kings 25:1–21—city walls torn down, palace and great houses burned, but perhaps most debilitating of all, the temple set on fire and its precious metals carted away as plunder. In addition, the Babylonian officials led all but the poorest inhabitants off into exile. While this did not empty the land (Barstad 1996), it was a devastating blow (read also Jer. 39–44 for a window into the exile and the situation in Palestine in the first few years after the destruction of Jerusalem).

The narrative account of the exile captures the event well, but it is the poetic book of Lamentations that records the utter despair felt at this momentous time. This book expresses the emotion following the discovery that the power behind the carnage was ultimately not the Babylonian war machine—it was God himself.

BIBLIOGRAPHY

Commentaries

R. **Davidson,** *Jeremiah* (vol. 2) *and Lamentations* (DSB; Westminster, 1985); A. **Dearman,** *Jeremiah/Lamentations* (NIVAC; Zondervan, 2002); F. W. **Dobbs-Allsopp,** *Lamentations* (Interp; Westminster John Knox, 2002); E. **Gerstenberger,** *Psalms, Part 2, and Lamentations* (FOTL; Eerdmans, 2002); R. K. **Harrison,** *Jeremiah and Lamentations* (TOTC; InterVarsity Press, 1973); D. R. **Hillers,** *Lamentations* (AB; Doubleday, 1972, rev. ed. 1992); R. **Martin-Achard** and S. P. **Re'emi,** *Amos and Lamentations* (ITC; Eerdmans, 1984); I. **Provan,** *Lamentations* (NCB; Eerdmans, 1992).

Articles and Monographs

B. **Albrektson,** *Studies in the Text and Theology of Lamentations* (Lund: Gleerup, 1963); H. M. **Barstad,** *The Myth of the Empty Land* (Oslo: Aschehoug AS, 1996); D. L. **Bock,** ed., *Show Them No Mercy: 4 Views on God and Canaanite Genocide* (Zondervan, 2003); J. **Bright,** *A History of Israel,* 2nd ed. (Westminster, 1972); M. E. **Cohen,** *The Canonical Lamentations of Ancient Mesopotamia,* 2 vols. (DCL Press, 1988); F. W. **Dobbs-Allsopp,** *Weep O Daughter of Zion: A Study of the City-Lament Genre in the Hebrew Bible* (PBI, 1993); P. W. **Ferris** Jr., *The Communal Lament in the Bible and the Ancient Near East* (Scholars, 1992); W. R. **Garr,** "The Qinah: A Study of Poetic Meter, Syntax, and Style," *ZAW* 95 (1983): 54–75; R. **Gordis,** "The Conclusion of the Book of Lamentations (5:22)," *JBL* 93 (1974): 289–93; N. K. **Gottwald,** *Studies in the Book of Lamentations* (SCM, 1954); D. **Grossberg,** *Centripetal and Centrifugal Structures in Biblical Poetry* (Scholars, 1989); H. **Gunkel,** "Klagelieder Jeremiae," in H. Gunkel and L. Zscharnack (eds.), *Die Religion in Geschichte und Gegenwart,* vol. 3, 2nd ed. (Tubingen, 1929, cols. 1049–52); W. C. **Gwaltney** Jr., "The Biblical Book of Lamentations in the Context of Near Eastern Lament Literature," *Scripture in Context II,* ed. W. W. Hallo, J. C. Moyer, and L. G. Perdue (Eisenbrauns, 1983); W. C. **Kaiser** Jr., *A Biblical Approach to Personal Suffering* (Moody, 1982); S. N. **Kramer,** "Lamentation Over the Destruction of Sumer and Ur," in ANET; idem, "Lamentation over the Destruction of Ur," in ANET; idem, "Sumerian Literature and the Bible," AnBib 12 (Studia Biblica et Orientalia 3 [1959]: 198–225; idem, "Lamentation Over the Destruction of Nippur: A Preliminary Report," *Eretz Israel* 9 (1969): 85–115; J. **Krašovek,** "The Structure of Hope in the Book of Lamentations," *VT* 57 (1992): 223–33; R. **Kutscher,** *Oh, Angry Sea (a-ab-ba hu-luh-ha): The History of the Sumerian Congregational Lament* (New Haven: Yale University Press, 1975); W. F. **Lanahan,** "The Speaking Voice in the Book of Lamentations," *JBL* 93 (1974): 41–49; T. **Longman** III, "Form Criticism, Recent Developments in Genre Theory, and the Evangelical," *WTJ* 48 (1985): 46–67; T. **Longman** III and D. **Reid,** *God Is a Warrior* (Zondervan, 1995); T. F. **McDaniel,** "Alleged Sumerian Influence on Lamentations," *VT* 18 (1968): 198–209; A. **Mintz,** "The Rhetoric of Lamentations and the Representation of Catastrophe," *Prooftexts* 2 (1982): 1–17; M. S. **Moore,** "Human Suffering in Lamentations," *RB* 90 (1983): 534–55; I. **Provan,** V. P. **Long,** and T. **Longman** III, *A Biblical History of Israel* (Westminster John Knox, 2003); W. H. **Shea,** "The *Qinah* Structure of the Book of Lamentations," *Bib* 60 (1979): 103–7.

HISTORICAL BACKGROUND

Author and Date

Like so many other biblical books, Lamentations is an anonymous work. Also as with many other biblical books, tradition has ascribed the name of the missing author—for this book, Jeremiah.

This tradition is certainly not impossible, but neither is it certain. However, it is not worth argument, since the text does not insist on it and its interpretation does not depend on it (Provan 1992, 7–11).

The Hebrew textual tradition does not even hint at a connection between Jeremiah and Lamentations, since the book is found in the third part of the canon, the Writings (*Ketubim*) and not with Jeremiah in the second, the Prophets (*Nebi'im*). The order varies somewhat within the writings, but it is usually listed with the other Megilloth, books that are associated with specific Jewish festivals, in this case the Ninth of Ab.

The Greek Old Testament, however, makes the connection between Lamentations and Jeremiah obvious in two ways: (1) it places Lamentations immediately after Jeremiah and before Ezekiel, and (2) it adds the following words to the beginning of the book: "And it came to pass that Jeremiah sat weeping and composed this lament over Jerusalem and said—" (Hillers 1972, 11). The Targum, the Peshitta, the Babylonian Talmud, and the Vulgate all follow the Greek tradition.

Those who depart from Jeremiac authorship of the book are occasionally open to accepting multiple authorship. H. von der Hardt, who was the first to depart from the tradition in 1712, argued, humorously enough, that the five chapters were written by Daniel, Shadrach, Meshach, Abednego, and King Jehoiachin respectively (see Kaiser 1982, 24). Although based in part on the fact that the five chapters may be read as five separate elegies (see comments on acrostic structure below), multiple authorship is an unnecessary hypothesis.

Apart from the specific identity of the author, vast agreement attends the issue of the relative date of the book (Provan's skepticism [1992, 7–19] is an exception). Because of the vivid description and the sincere emotion expressed in the book, few would date the composition more than seventy-five years after the destruction of Jerusalem. Most date Lamentations much earlier, but one school of thought argues that the genre is associated with the rebuilding of temples (see below), the rebuilding of the temple on Zion occurring around 520–515 BC.

Historical Period

The book was written in reaction to the destruction of Jerusalem at the hands of the Babylonians in 587 BC. Thus it is a composition of the exilic period (for a description of this period see Provan, Long, and Longman 2003, 278–86).

According to the perspective of the biblical historians and prophets, the exile was the climax of a long struggle that pitted the people of Israel and Judah against their God. God had warned them long before through Moses that their presence in the land depended on their obedience to the covenant relationship that he established with them on Sinai (Deut. 28:15–68). Nonetheless, he remained faithful to them through long years of rebellion and sin, sending prophet after prophet to call them back to a sincere and vital relationship with him.

The final spiral began with the death of Josiah in 609. Josiah and his supporters had tried to turn the tide of religious apostasy by instituting reforms into the society and cult (2 Kings 22:1–23:30). His reign experienced momentary relief from foreign domination, but when he was killed on the battlefield, Judah became a pawn in the power play between the great superpowers of the day: Egypt and Babylon.

Josiah's son Jehoahaz became king in his place. Although he was likely a younger son (Bright, 324), he succeeded his father with the expectation that he would continue his father's anti-Egyptian, pro-Babylonian policy. Because of this political stance, when Neco, the Egyptian pharaoh, was repulsed by Babylon, he tried to solidify his power base in the Levant by deporting Jehoahaz and placing his brother Eliakim, whom he renamed Jehoiakim, on the throne. Jehoiakim was a vassal of Egypt and is notable for his conflicts with Jeremiah (Jer. 1:3; 24:1; 27:1, 20; 37:1; 52:2).

In 605 BC Nebuchadnezzar, the Babylonian general, crushed the Egyptians at Carchemish and then chased the Egyptians back to their homeland. Now all of Syria and Palestine was ripe for the picking. After a momentary delay caused by the death of Nabopolassar, king of Babylon, the now King Nebuchadnezzar returned to Judah in 604 and made Jehoiakim his vassal (2 Kings 24:1). However, as soon as the opportunity presented itself, Jehoiakim turned to Egypt again, and this led to the Babylonian incursion of 598.

Jehoiakim was not there to meet Nebuchadnezzar, having died in the meantime. The biblical text gives no indication of the cause of his death (though the speculation is that he was assassinated), but it led to the coronation of his son Jehoiachin, who had the unenviable task of awaiting the onslaught of the Babylonian army. Jehoiachin, only eighteen at the time, did not last long before he surrendered. He was carried off to Babylon, and an ostensibly pro-Babylonian member of the royal family, Mattaniah (renamed Zedekiah), was placed on the throne.

Zedekiah made the fatal mistake of rebelling against Babylon (2 Kings 24:20b), and this led to the final destruction of Jerusalem in the year 587/6. Lamentations was written in reaction to the physical devastation of the city and expresses the psychological and spiritual anguish over God's abandonment of his people and his hostility toward them.

Lamentations expresses the psychological and spiritual anguish over God's abandonment of his people and his hostility toward them.

LITERARY ANALYSIS

Genre

Hermann Gunkel initiated the modern discussion of the genre of Lamentations by concluding that it was a *Mischgattung*, a combination of several different types of literature. He argued that chapters 1, 2, and 4 were funeral songs; chapter 3, an individual lament; and chapter 5, a communal lament.

Recent studies have tended to view the book more holistically, a position typified by Grossberg's (1989) extensive studies of the literary features that not only create variety within the poem but also unify it. Ferris is typical in his conclusion that Lamentations is to be classified as a communal lament similar to those found within the Psalter. He defines a communal lament as

> a composition whose verbal content indicates that it was composed to be used by and/or on behalf of a community to express both complaint, and sorrow and grief over some perceived calamity, physical or cultural, which had befallen or was about to befall them and to appeal to God for deliverance. (Ferris 1992, 10)

The tone, content, and structure of the work all support its identification as a corporate lament. Indeed, the various titles given to the book indicate an awareness of its proper genre. In antiquity, the book was referred to by its opening word: 'êkâ ("how"). The rabbis referred to the book as *qînôt*; the Greek Old Testament entitled the book *Threni*, and the Vulgate referred to it as *Lamenta*, all meaning lamentations and leading to the title given to the book in English translations.

Debate has surrounded the question of whether the poem is consistently corporate, especially in the light of 3:1–21. This unit begins "I am the one who has seen affliction . . ." and is often understood as the expression of a single individual. Much effort has been spent in an attempt to identify the speaker. A sample of suggestions include Jehoiachin, a defeated soldier (Lanahan 1974, 45), and Jeremiah himself. More likely is the interpretation that the speaker is personified Jerusalem, but even if it is an individual, that individual gives utterance to the suffering and pain of the whole community. Thus, although there is variety of expression, the book as a whole is still correctly identified as a corporate lament.

Ferris (1992) rightly associates the book of Lamentations with the communal laments in the Psalter. He identifies about twenty examples in the Psalms, some of which could be debated, but especially relevant are the five which give expression to the despair of the people after defeat in battle (Pss. 44, 60, 74, 79, 80).

The content of the book of Lamentations makes it clear that it is defeat in battle that evokes the poem's composition. It is interesting that although there is little doubt of its association with the devastation of 587 BC, the precise historical event is not explicitly named. This lack of historical specificity is in keeping with the nature of the type of poetry found also in the Psalter (see Introduction; Historical Background in chap. 16). Nonetheless, the setting of Lamentations is wartime defeat.

Ferris insightfully speaks of yet another setting in life, perhaps to be described as textual or conceptual,[1] in Solomon's prayer at the time of temple dedication in 1 Kings 8. Among a number of national calamities that he names, calamities that occasion corporate prayer, he specifically mentions defeat in bat-

---

[1] See Longman (1985) for the idea of multiple settings in life.

tle (8:33–34). Solomon envisions Israel turning to God when they experience military defeat. The book of Lamentations is just such a prayer.

Other scholars have argued that the setting may be more closely specified than simply following a defeat in battle. By analogy with Mesopotamian laments, they believe that the book was composed on the occasion of the reconstruction of the temple. However, the analogy between the biblical book and the Mesopotamian genre has been disputed, and it is to that discussion that we now turn.

Mesopotamian Laments

The lament genre is not unique to Israel. Most significant in the book of Lamentations are the six city laments, written in the *emesal*[2] dialect of Sumerian, five of six of which were composed within the century following the defeat of the Ur III Empire (2004 BC):

1. The Lamentation over the Destruction of Sumer and Ur (ANET, 455–63)
2. The Lamentation over the Destruction of Ur (ANET, 611–19)
3. The Lamentation over the Destruction of Eridu
4. The Lamentation over the Destruction of Nippur
5. The Lamentation over the Destruction of Uruk
6. The Lamentation over Ekimar

These six literary compositions bemoan the military defeat of cities, attributing the actions of the attacking armies to a divine cause and sharing many other themes with the biblical book of Lamentations (Gwaltney 1983, 205–11). S. N. Kramer (1959 and 1969) popularized the comparison, advocating the view that the biblical book was influenced by the Sumerian precursors. His view, shared in part by C. J. Gadd, H.-J. Kraus, and others, came under attack by McDaniel (1968), who drew attention to the large time and culture gap between the Sumerian and the biblical texts.

Gwaltney (1983), whose view is accepted by Hillers, has attempted to defend Kramer's old view by citing the continuation of the lament genre in Mesopotamia in the form of the *balag* and *eršemma* lamentations, written in Akkadian from the Old Babylonian period on into the first millennium (see Kutscher 1975). To Gwaltney, this removed the objection of cultural and chronological distance and permitted him to highlight the common themes and structures of the Mesopotamian and biblical genres.

Ferris has analyzed Gwaltney's arguments and assessed the strength of his proposal that the Sumero-Akkadian lament tradition influenced the book of Lamentations. His conclusion is that Gwaltney tended to overstate the

---

[2]This dialect of Sumerian is usually found in the mouths of women or certain types of priests (*gala*).

connections and that the best solution to the similarities and differences may be found in a common cultural and literary tradition (Ferris 1992, 174–75, quoting Mowinckel).

The loose connection between the Sumero-Akkadian genre and the biblical one renders doubtful the hypothesis that the book of Lamentations was written at the time of the rededication of the temple. Much more likely is the view that it was composed closer to the time of the destruction, when the pain and suffering of the event were still quite fresh.

Structure

On the one hand, the book neatly divides into five units correlated with the five chapters of the book. On the other hand, the structure of the book is a complex multilevel matter, the description of which will be treated only in a preliminary way in this book. We may begin with a reminder of Grossberg's conclusions that the book demonstrates literary forces that contribute to a unified reading (centripetal) as well as those that draw our attention to the individual parts (centrifugal). Or, in the words of Gottwald: "Like a great cathedral, its unity is broken in innumerable pleasing ways, never distracting but always contributing to the total impression" (1954, 23). Primary among the latter is the use of the acrostic pattern in the book.

The first four chapters are individual, complete acrostics, though they differ in their detail. Chapters 1 and 2 are three-line acrostics, that is, the first letter of the three-line stanza begins with the relevant letter. Chapter 3 also contains three-line stanzas, but in this case all three of the lines begin with the relevant letter (similar to the stanzas of Psalm 119). Lamentations 4 has two-line stanzas, more in keeping with the style of chapters 1 and 2.[3] Most interesting of all is chapter 5, which is not an acrostic at all, but nonetheless alludes to the acrostic structure by having twenty-two lines.

The purpose of such an acrostic is not at all clear. Guesses have ranged from its being a mnemonic device to its giving a sense of completeness to the subject of the poem, in Lamentations this being a kind of "A to Z" of suffering (Ferris 1992, 102–3, citing de Wette). From a literary point of view, what is notable is that although the author subjected himself to what is really a rather rigid poetic self-discipline, this does not minimize the spontaneity of the poem's emotional expression.

And it is the emotional expression of the book that allows for one of the most interesting entrees into the structure of the book. W. Kaiser helpfully charts the way the book reaches a high point of hope in the middle of the third chapter,

---

[3]Note that in chapters 2, 3, and 4 the letters 'ayin and pe are reversed from their usual order. There is some evidence that perhaps this was simply the correct order of the day (Hillers 1992, 29).

only to descend to the pits of despair again (as he graphically portrays it in figure 3 [1982, 24]).

The third chapter contains the most explicit statement of hope in the midst of the destruction. However, the poet does not reach resolution in a state of calm but descends once again into the fray. He concludes the remaining two chapters with the plaintive cry of 5:19–22:

> You, LORD, reign forever;
> your throne endures from generation to generation.
> Why do you always forget us?
> Why do you forsake us so long?
> Restore us to yourself, LORD, that we may return;
> renew our days as of old
> unless you have utterly rejected us
> and are angry with us beyond measure.

By the end of the poem we have the hope, not the fact, of reconciliation. Gordis (1974, 292–93) argues that the last poetic line should be rendered:

> even though you had despised us greatly
> and were very angry with us.

While this may make the plea for restoration more confident, it too nonetheless ends the book looking to the future for an uncertain divine intervention.

Figure 3
Literary Structure of Lamentations

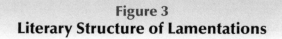

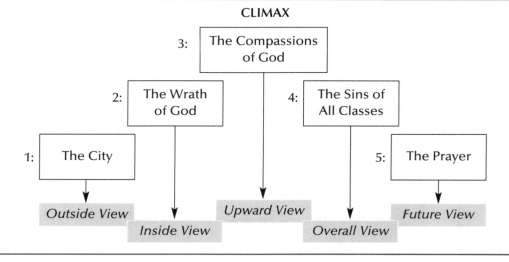

Style

The poetic style of Lamentations has many facets. We can treat only three representative characteristics in this brief chapter (see also on acrostic form above): *qinah,* persona, and "the ministry of language."

Qinah. Earlier, we discounted the presence of meter in Hebrew poetry. A special kind of meter has been associated with Lamentations and other lament literature, which receives the label *qinah.* The main characteristic of this meter is that the second colon of the parallel line is consistently shorter than the first. It is usually described as a 3:2 meter, as opposed to the more balanced 3:3 form. The unbalanced meter has often been described as a kind of "limping" rhythm, supposedly appropriate for the mourners who are dragging themselves along in a funeral procession. Garr (1983) has studied the syntax of this poetic form and concluded that the first colon does not deviate from the regular word order of prose, while the second takes its cue from the first.

There is little doubt that the poetry of dirge and lament often has this characteristic of a long first line and shorter second line, but it is doubtful that we are dealing with meter here, as opposed to some kind of consistent rhythm. Also, the fact that this form is also found with non-lament poetry (Hillers 1992, 18) weakens the close connection drawn between the *qinah* and the lament.

Persona. As Mintz (1982, 1–2) points out, language is often inadequate to express profound suffering. However, one important strategy to overcome this weakness "was to transfer to the collective the attributes of individual experience and to view the nation as a whole in the aspect of a single individual; simply put: personification. The nation is represented as an abandoned woman or, in a more complex instance, as a persecuted man." The former occurs right from the start of the poem:

> How deserted lies the city,
>   once so full of people!
> How like a widow is she,
>   who once was great among the nations!
> She who was queen among the provinces
>   has now become a slave.
>
> Bitterly she weeps at night,
>   tears are on her cheeks.
> Among all her lovers
>   there is none to comfort her.
> All her friends have betrayed her;
>   they have become her enemies. (1:1–3)

The latter waits until chapter 3. As mentioned above, there have been innumerable attempts to identify this male figure with a specific individual. This search is fruitless and unnecessary—the unnamed sufferer stands for the collective whole:

> I am the one who has seen affliction
>> by the rod of the LORD's wrath.
> He has driven me away and made me walk
>> in darkness rather than light;
> indeed, he has turned his hand against me
>> again and again, all day long. (3:1–2)

Both of these literary figures make graphic and vivid the suffering of the survivors of Judah as they face the years following the destruction of Jerusalem.

In a seminal study, Lanahan (1974) has furthered our understanding of the use of persona in Lamentations by identifying five personae including the two we have already described. The five speak in the following locations in the book:

1. City of Jerusalem (as a woman; 1:9c, 11c–22; 2:20–22)
2. An objective reporter (1:1–11b [excepting 9c], 15, 17; 2:1–19)
3. A first person male sufferer (chap. 3; Lanahan calls him "a soldier")
4. The bourgeois (chap. 4)
5. Choral voices of Jerusalem (chap. 5)

The effect of this use of personification is captured by Ferris: "By means of various personae, the covenant people appear to talk the issues over among themselves as they recount their former glory in light of their current grief" (1992, 136).

"The Ministry of Language." The phrase comes from Mintz (1982, 7) and refers to use of language in Lamentations that goes beyond description of the destruction. The purpose of the author of Lamentations is to function not merely as an analyst but also as a healer. Language is inadequate, but through the use of "inadequate metaphors" the poet can communicate with God just how incredibly shocking and devastating the ruin of Jerusalem is, and thus he can appeal to God to intervene.

THEOLOGICAL MESSAGE

In a sense, the book of Lamentations grapples with the question of corporate suffering in much the same way that the book of Job struggles with the issue of individual suffering. As may be implied from what was said above, the theological purpose of Lamentations is to acknowledge God's judgment against Jerusalem and move God to intercede for and restore his people (see the conclusion to the book).

Over the past few decades, a lively debate has sprung up concerning the theological traditions that propel the book. Gottwald (1954) began the discussion when he proposed that the theological message of the book may be found in the contrast between the Deuteronomic version of faith and historical reality as represented in the destruction of Jerusalem. Deuteronomy promises blessings, security, and prosperity to the people of God, but the people experience God's presence as an enemy (Lam. 2:4).

Albrektson (1963), however, is certainly correct when he states that Gottwald's is a facile understanding of Deuteronomic theology. Nowhere does Deuteronomy promise Israel unconditional blessing. When Israel sins, they will be cursed, and Lamentations recognizes that God's movement against them is the result of their sin (Krašovek 1992, 223). In the place of Deuteronomic theology, Albrektson simply places Zion theology. When impregnable Zion fell, so did the people's faith.

In fact, many theological traditions are at play in the book of Lamentations and all in continuity with their use in other parts of the Bible. Two interrelated traditions that are especially noteworthy but infrequently mentioned in articulations of the theological message of the book are the covenant and the Divine Warrior themes (Longman and Reid 1995; Gundry 2003).

Covenant may be a broader term for what Gottwald refers to as Deuteronomic traditions, but the point is that the destruction of Jerusalem does not occur in spite of the Deuteronomic covenant but because of it:

> If you do not obey the LORD your God and do not carefully follow all his commands and decrees I am giving you today, . . . the LORD will bring a nation against you from far away, from the ends of the earth, like an eagle swooping down, a nation whose language you will not understand, a fierce-looking nation without respect for the old or pity for the young. (Deut. 28:15, 49–50)

Behind this judgment, which is due to the sin of the people, is God himself. It is not the Babylonians, but God himself who will destroy them, specifically, God the Warrior. Normally, of course, God fought on behalf of his obedient people, but at times of judgment he fought against them, as we see in Lamentations 2:4–5 (cf. Josh. 7; 1 Sam. 4):

> Like an enemy he has strung his bow;
>   his right hand is ready.
> Like a foe he has slain
>   all who were pleasing to the eye;
> he has poured out his wrath like fire
>   on the tent of Daughter Zion.
>
> The Lord is like an enemy;
>   he has swallowed up Israel.
> He has swallowed up all her palaces

and destroyed her strongholds.
He has multiplied mourning and lamentation
for Daughter Judah.

But the theological message of Lamentations is not purely negative. There is also hope, but it is of minimal significance in the book. In the heart of the book (3:22–33) the poet expresses his assurance that God does not abandon those who turn to him for help. Although Israel has sinned in the past (1: 8, 14, 18; 2:14; 4:13), they appeal to God for help, expecting that he will forgive and restore. His compassion is greater than his anger (3:31–33; Krašovek 1992).

APPROACHING THE NEW TESTAMENT

Lamentations pinpoints God as the enemy. He has waged war against his people because of their sin. The note of hope expressed in the book finds partial fulfillment in the restoration to the land following the decree of Cyrus. However, although the people return to the land, they do not have political independence. Although the temple is rebuilt, it does not reflect its former glory. The people are left expecting more.

The prophets of the exilic and postexilic periods look into the future and have a vision of a future intrusion of God the Warrior into history to fight on behalf of his people (Dan. 7 and Zech. 14). The New Testament identifies Jesus Christ as the Divine Warrior who defeats the forces of evil on the cross (Col. 2:13–15) and as the one who will come again in the future for the final battle against all human and spiritual enemies of God (Rev. 19:11ff.). Jesus Christ is the Divine Warrior who fights on behalf of his people against the most powerful enemy of all, Satan.

Although we earlier made a comparison between the book of Job and Lamentations, there is one major difference. In Job, the individual's suffering was not caused by his own sin. By contrast, the corporate suffering of Lamentations was the direct result of the guilt that the nation had incurred through the centuries. However, as Job's suffering anticipated the suffering of the truly innocent sufferer, so the suffering of Israel at the time of the exile also anticipates Christ's hanging on the cross. In this case, however, the sin is not his; it is ours. The church has recognized the analogy, witness the practice of the Roman Catholic Church to read the book during the last part of Passion Week (Gottwald 1954, 112).

Although the temple is rebuilt, it does not reflect its former glory. The people are left expecting more.

CHAPTER TWENTY-THREE

EZEKIEL

Ezekiel was the son of a priest. Since he was called to prophetic office when he was thirty years old, during the fifth year of the exile of Jehoiachin, king of Judah (592 BC, 1:1–2),[1] the prophet must have been born around 623–622. His ministry continued for at least twenty-two years, through the time of the last dated oracle in the book in Jehoiachin's twenty-seventh year of exile (571, 29:17). His membership in a priestly family reveals itself throughout the book in Ezekiel's concern with the temple and its rituals.

An eligible man ordinarily began his service in the temple when he reached thirty years of age (Num 4:3). However, Ezekiel was unable to fulfill his calling as a priest while living in exile far from Jerusalem. Instead, in the year that Ezekiel would have begun his priestly vocation, God called him to serve as a prophet. In his inaugural vision, Ezekiel saw God riding in his war chariot—it was an ominous portent, for God would soon abandon Jerusalem (10:1–2, 18–22). Rather than defend the city, God would decree, plan, and superintend its destruction.

The exiles among whom Ezekiel lived had come from the upper classes of Judean society. They were a privileged group that had not often heeded prophetic warnings in the past (2:3–8). They hoped for a short time of exile and a speedy return to their positions of wealth and privilege. They were hostile to Ezekiel's message and dismissed his words as entertaining prattle (20:49; 33:30–32). But God would soon vindicate himself and his prophet (33:33). The exile would not be brief, and the city would not be spared.

---

[1] The book begins with a double date formula (1:1–2) that appears to synchronize the fifth year of Jehoiachin's exile with an unspecified thirtieth year. The most probable conclusion is that this thirtieth year refers to the prophet's age. Numerous other suggestions have been made throughout the history of interpretation; see the discussions in the commentaries.

BIBLIOGRAPHY

Commentaries

L. C. **Allen,** *Ezekiel 20–48* (Word, 1990); J. **Blenkinsopp,** *Ezekiel* (Interp: Westminster John Knox, 1990); D. **Block,** *Ezekiel 1–24* (NICOT; Eerdmans, 1997); idem, *Ezekiel 25–28* (NICOT; Eerdmans, 1998); W. H. **Brownlee,** *Ezekiel 1–19* (WBC 28; Word, 1986); P. C. **Craigie,** *Ezekiel* (DSB; Westminster, 1983); I. **Duguid,** *Ezekiel* (NIVAC; Zondervan, 1999); W. **Eichrodt,** *Ezekiel* (OTL; Westminster, 1970); P. **Fairbairn,** *An Exposition of Ezekiel* (T. & T. Clark, 1851; repr. Grand Rapids: Sovereign Grace, 1971); D. E. **Gowan,** *Ezekiel* (KPG; John Knox, 1985); M. **Greenberg,** *Ezekiel 1–20* (AB 22; Doubleday, 1983); R. M. **Hals,** *Ezekiel* (FOTL; Eerdmans, 1989); J. B. **Taylor,** *Ezekiel* (TOTC; InterVarsity Press, 1969); J. W. **Wevers,** *Ezekiel* (NCB; Eerdmans, 1969); W. **Zimmerli,** *Ezekiel*, 2 vols. (Hermeneia; Fortress, 1979, 1983).

Monographs and Articles

R. **Abba,** "Priests and Levites in Ezekiel," *VT* 8 (1978): 1–9; P. **Ackroyd,** *Exile and Restoration* (OTL; Westminster, 1968); M. C. **Astour,** "Ezekiel's Prophecy of Gog and the Cuthaean Legend of Naram-Sin," *JBL* 95 (1976): 567–79; E. C. **Broome,** "Ezekiel's Abnormal Personality," *JBL* 65 (1946): 277–92; W. H. **Brownlee,** "'Son of Man Set Your Face,' Ezekiel the Refugee Prophet," *HUCA* 54 (1983): 83–110; K. W. **Carley,** *Ezekiel Among the Prophets* (SBT, 2nd series, 31; Allenson, 1974); R. B. **Dillard,** Notes on Ezekiel in *The Reformation Study Bible* (Thomas Nelson, 1995); G. R. **Driver,** "Ezekiel: Linguistic and Textual Problems," *Bib* 35 (1954): 145–59; 299–312; J. **Finegan,** "The Chronology of Ezekiel," *JBL* 69 (1950): 61–66; M. **Fishbane,** "Sin and Judgment in the Prophecies of Ezekiel," *Interp* 38 (1984): 131–50; M. V. **Fox,** "The Rhetoric of Ezekiel's Vision of the Valley of the Bones," *HUCA* 51 (1980): 1–15; D. N. **Freedman,** "The Book of Ezekiel," *Interp* 8 (1954): 446–71; B. **Gosse,** "Le recueil d'oracles contre les nations d'Ezéchiel XXV–XXXII dans la rédaction du livre d'Ezéchiel," *RB* 93–94 (1986): 535–62; M. **Greenberg,** "The Design and Themes of Ezekiel's Program of Restoration," *Interp* 38 (1984): 181–208; idem, "Ezekiel 17: A Holistic Interpretation," *JAOS* 3 (1983): 149–54; idem, "The Vision of Jerusalem in Ezekiel 8–11: A Holistic Interpretation," in *The Divine Helmsman,* ed. J. Crenshaw (New York: KTAV, 1980), 143–64; B. **Halperin,** *Seeking Ezekiel: Text and Psychology* (Penn State University Press, 1993); M. **Haran,** "The Law Code of Ezekiel XL–XLVIII and Its Relation to the Priestly School," *HUCA* 50 (1979): 45–71; G. **Hölscher,** *Hesekiel, der Dichter und das Buch* (BZAW 39; Giessen: Töpelmann, 1924); W. A. **Irwin,** *The Problem of Ezekiel* (University of Chicago Press, 1943); T. **Kruger,** *Geschichtskonzepte im Ezechielbuch* (BZAW 180; Berlin: de Gruyter, 1988); W. S. **LaSor,** D. A. **Hubbard,** and F. W. **Bush,** *Old Testament Survey* (Eerdmans, 1982); W. E. **Lemke,** "Life in the Present and Hope for the Future," *Interp* 38

(1984): 165–80; J. D. **Levenson,** *Theology of the Program of Restoration of Ezekiel 40–48* (HSM 10; Missoula: Scholars, 1976); J. **Lust,** "Ezekiel 36–40 in the Oldest Greek Manuscript," *CBQ* 43 (1981): 517–33; J. G. **McConville,** "Priests and Levites in Ezekiel: A Crux in the Interpretation of Israel's History," *TynBul* 34 (1983): 3–31; C. A. **Newsom,** "A Maker of Metaphors—Ezekiel's Oracles Against Tyre," *Interp* 38 (1984): 151–64; S. **Niditch,** "Ezekiel 40–48 in a Visionary Context," *CBQ* 48 (1986): 208–24; J. **Pons,** "Polémique a Tel-Aviv en 591 av. J. C.," *ETRel* 61 (1986): 165–75; W. R. **Roehrs,** "The Dumb Prophet," *CTM* 29 (1958): 176–86; H. H. **Rowley,** "The Book of Ezekiel in Modern Study," *BJRL* 36 (1953): 146–90; C. **Sherlock,** "Ezekiel's Dumbness," *ExpTim* 94 (1983): 296–98; S. **Talmon** and M. **Fishbane,** "The Structuring of Biblical Books: Studies in the Book of Ezekiel," *ASTI* 10 (1976): 129–53; C. C. **Torrey,** *Pseudo-Ezekiel and the Original Prophecy* (Yale University Press, 1930; reissued by KTAV, 1970); E. **Tov,** "Recensional Differences Between the MT and LXX of Ezekiel," *EphTL* 62 (1986): 89–101; K. **Van Nuys,** "Evaluating the Pathological in Prophetic Experience (Particularly in Ezekiel)," *JBR* 21 (1953): 244–51; R. R. **Wilson,** "Prophecy in Crisis: The Call of Ezekiel," *Interp* 38 (1984): 117–30; A. **York,** "Ezekiel I: Inaugural and Restoration Visions," *VT* 27 (1977): 82–98.

HISTORICAL BACKGROUND

Ezekiel was born just a year or so before the law book was discovered in the temple as part of Josiah's reforms (621 BC, 2 Kings 22–23), and as the son of a priest he no doubt witnessed the consequences of Josiah's piety in the royal support of the temple and the worship of Yahweh in Judah. The prophet would have been a boy through the period when Assyria's power continued to decline. He no doubt hoped as a young man that the failing fortunes of Assyria might mean freedom from foreign domination for Judah. He would have known about the ominous recrudescence of Babylon and Egypt as they too escaped the yoke of Assyria. When he was barely a teenager, he would have heard the news of Josiah's death at Megiddo while seeking to block the advance of Pharaoh Neco (609 BC—2 Kings 23:29; 2 Chron. 35:20–25). Ezekiel had probably heard the preaching of Jeremiah and may have known the ministries of Habakkuk and Zephaniah. He witnessed the period of political instability and vacillation following Josiah's death when Judah's fortunes shifted with her allegiance to Egypt and then to Babylon in turn.

After Josiah's death, Pharaoh Neco deposed his successor, Jehoahaz, after a reign of only three months and installed Jehoiakim as an Egyptian puppet. When Egypt was defeated at Carchemish in 604, Jehoiakim shifted his allegiance to Nebuchadnezzar, only later to rebel against Babylon and align himself with Egypt once again. Jehoiakim died and left his son Jehoiachin to face the fury of a Babylonian reprisal. Jehoiachin was dethroned and taken into cap-

Table 15
Chronological Notes in Ezekiel

Our chronology for the latter half of the first millennium BC is quite firm due to chronological records both from the Bible and from extrabiblical documents in a variety of languages from the ancient Near East. Astronomical observations recorded by ancient scribes enable us to correlate the ancient and modern calendars with a high degree of confidence. Although it is conceivable that some of the dates below will in the future be adjusted in the light of further discovery, the changes will not be great.

All of the dates in Ezekiel are in terms of the year of Jehoiachin's exile, with the exception of 1:1, which refers to the year of Ezekiel's life.

Reference	Yr/Mon/Day	Julian calendar	Event
1:1	30/4/5	July 31, 593	Call narrative
1:2	5/4(?)/5	July 31, 593	Call narrative
8:1	6/6/5	Sept. 17, 592	Vision of events in Jerusalem
20:1	7/5/10	Aug. 14, 591	Elders come to inquire
24:1	9/10/10	Jan. 15, 588	Siege of Jerusalem begins
26:1	11/-/1	Between Apr. 587 and Apr. 586	Oracle against Tyre
29:1	10/10/12	Jan. 7, 587	Oracle against Egypt
29:17	27/1/1	Apr. 26, 571	Egypt instead of Tyre
30:20	11/1/7	Apr. 29, 587	Oracle against Pharaoh
31:1	11/3/1	June 21, 587	Oracle against Pharaoh
32:1	12/12/1	Mar. 3, 585	Oracle against Pharaoh
32:17	12/-/15	Between Apr., 586 and Apr., 585	Oracle against Egypt
33:21	12/10/5	Jan. 8, 585	Escapee from Jerusalem arrives
40:1	25/1/10	Apr. 28, 573	Vision of restored Jerusalem

tivity in 597 with the royal household and the leading citizens of Judah, including Ezekiel. Nebuchadnezzar placed Zedekiah on the throne in his place, and although Zedekiah would preside over Judah until the destruction of Jerusalem in 587/6, the exiles continued to regard Jehoiachin as the legitimate king. No other prophetic book contains as many dated oracles as Ezekiel, and these dates are given in terms of the years of Jehoiachin's exile.

Ezekiel lived with his wife (24:15–27) in a community of Judean exiles along a large irrigation canal ("Kebar River," 1:1) near Nippur in southern Mesopotamia. From this vantage deep in the heart of Nebuchadnezzar's kingdom, Ezekiel proclaimed the word of God concerning the rise of the Babylonian Empire to its zenith and the corresponding falling fortunes of his own nation and surrounding peoples. It was only after the destruction of Jerusalem that the prophet turned to preaching dominated by the themes of hope, restoration, mercy, and grace for Israel (Ezek. 33–48).

MAJOR ISSUES IN THE HISTORY OF RESEARCH

In the early generations of critical scholarship, Ezekiel was treated with what Rowley (1953, 163) called a certain "critical gentleness." At the turn of the century and in the early years of the twentieth century, critical scholarship remained impressed with the strong stamp of the single personality that pervades the book. G. B. Gray in 1913 wrote, "No other book of the OT is distinguished by such decisive marks of unity of authorship and integrity as this."[2] S. R. Driver in 1905 said, "No critical question arises in connexion with the authorship of the book, the whole from beginning to end bearing unmistakably the stamp of a single mind."[3] J. Skinner wrote, "Not only does it bear the stamp of a single mind in its phraseology, its imagery and its mode of thought, but it is arranged on a plan so perspicuous and so comprehensive that the evidence of literary design in the composition becomes altogether irresistible."[4]

The following years would witness the demise of this consensus. Critical scholarship was troubled by the tensions it observed within the book. How could Ezekiel be a prophet with a strong sense of social justice and also be a priest concerned with the meticulous details of temple and cult? Traditional critical scholarship had commonly pitted moral and social concerns against the legalistic and cultic interests of the priests. How could a prophetic contemporary of Jeremiah produce literature so different from that of that sober prophet? The book of Ezekiel is full of complex visions and allegories; the prophet seemed to move in a single step to the very dawn of apocalyptic. But such a single step challenged the common unilinear developmental notions for literary genres in critical scholarship. How could this prophet living in Babylon have such detailed knowledge of events in Jerusalem? Ezekiel's conduct was also cause for concern—his *aphasia*, his lying motionless for prolonged periods, the mysterious visions: were these the common experience of prophets, or were they symptomatic of some form of mental illness?

It is difficult to group and summarize all the variables, but these issues have stimulated many to question the authenticity of the book or various portions of it. Scholars have pared away what they regarded as secondary accretions in order to uncover the historical Ezekiel. Depending on which of the supposed tensions and inconsistencies the individual scholar chose to eliminate, very different pic-

[2]*A Critical Introduction to the Old Testament* (London, 1913).
[3]*An Introduction to the Literature of the Old Testament*, 11th ed. (Scribner, 1905), 279.
[4]*A Dictionary of the Bible*, ed. J. Hastings and J. Selbie (1898), 817.

tures of the prophet emerged. Scholars not only dissected the book but also provided historical reconstructions of the settings in which the secondary material may have arisen. The following constitute the major issues.

The Authenticity of the Date of the Book

This issue was raised in its most extreme form by C. C. Torrey. The book of Ezekiel itself presents all of Ezekiel's ministry as set among the exiles. However, Torrey argued that the book did not reflect actual conditions among the exiles but was instead a pseudepigraph from the third century BC. For Torrey, the prophecy was a literary creation and Ezekiel was not a historical individual. Chapters 40–48 were said to reflect an anti-Samaritan bias against the Gerizim temple. The description of the sins described in Jerusalem in chapters 8–10 suggested that a group of prophecies originally from the days of Manasseh were used by a third-century editor and assigned to the period of the exile.

The Authenticity of Individual Passages

There are many doublets in the book, and numerous passages have been identified as glosses. Some have argued that chapters 40–48 were not original; others add chapters 38–39 and portions of chapters 27, 36, or other passages to this list. Hölscher and Irwin took the approach to its extreme. Hölscher (1924) argued that Ezekiel was a poet, so he disallowed all but a very few prose passages as original. He left the original prophet with about one-seventh of the book after identifying only 21 passages as genuine, comprising 170 verses out of 1,273 in the book; the remainder he attributed to a fifth-century editor. Irwin (1943) similarly dismembered the book and left the prophet only 251 verses of the entire book.

More recently, Greenberg has provided a holistic approach to Ezekiel, concentrating on the book as it now is rather than on the "slippery ground of assumptions and conventions on which so much biblical scholarship has come to grief" (1983, 19). Other recent scholarship, though generally more restrained than that represented by Hölscher or Irwin, largely continues its preoccupation with the literary growth of the text. Rather than presenting the issue as one of authenticity versus inauthenticity, more recent scholarship has tended to approach Ezekiel by using a tradition-historical method. This method makes allowance for deliberate elaboration, successive adaptation, and updating within the text of the book, but it concentrates on the organic connection of such later elaboration with earlier stages of the text's growth and on the process of redaction that resulted in the final text. Fresh appreciation of the literary and structuring devices within the book has integrated into the book much material earlier judged inauthentic in critical scholarship.

Zimmerli's commentary (1979, 1983) has been quite influential and more or less represents the current critical consensus. Zimmerli (1979, 71–74) identifies four passages as later insertions that intrude by breaking the flow of the surrounding context: (1) 3:16b–21; (2) chapter 18; (3) the oracles against the nations, chapters 25–32; and (4) 29:17–21. He also regards the oracles against Egypt (chaps. 29–32) and Tyre (26:1–28:19) as originally independent collections having their own redactional history. He considers the program of restoration (chaps. 40–48) as an addition in the final stage of redaction.

Authenticity of the Prophet's Location

The book itself places Ezekiel's ministry entirely among the exiles in Babylon, but chapters 8–11 assume that the prophet is present in Jerusalem to observe the death of Pelatiah, to see the idolatry in the temple, and to observe the departure of the glory of God from the temple. How can one reconcile the presence of Ezekiel in Babylon with his detailed knowledge of affairs in Jerusalem?

Some have suggested that the prophet began his career in Jerusalem and only later moved to Babylon, or that he made a number of trips back and forth between the two cities. W. O. E. Oesterly and H. W. Robinson placed the prophet's call in the reign of Jehoiakim and held that the prophet was deported to Babylon with the exiles, and then continued to minister there.[5] Bertholet followed essentially the same course but dated the initial call slightly later in the time of Zedekiah; he distinguished the initial call to service in Palestine from a second call (the watchman motif, chaps. 3 and 33) in Babylon.[6] Others argued that the prophet was in Jerusalem all the time. This position was most recently championed by Brownlee (1986), who argued that the prophet lived in Gilgal and that this geographical name was confused by later scribes as the gôlâh, the Hebrew term meaning "exile."

There is no question that many of Ezekiel's oracles are addressed to people living in Jerusalem. However, this is far from adequate evidence to require that they were delivered there. The large collections of oracles against foreign nations in the canonical prophets did not require that the prophet travel to those places to deliver them. We need to make a distinction common in literary theory between the putative (or "implied") audience and the actual audience to understand this clearly. Nahum provides another good example: though his ministry and preaching are ostensibly oriented to Assyria (putative audience), the book itself is intended for an audience in Israel (actual audience). When Ezekiel proclaimed oracles about events in Jerusalem, the actual audience to whom he spoke was his fellow exiles in Babylon. As Block (1997, 5) states, "Ezekiel's primary audience was the community of Jews in Babylon." Furthermore, there is ample evidence for frequent contact between the exiles and their countrymen in Israel. Letters to and from the exiles speak eloquently of this. If Shemaiah's oracles and

---

[5]*Introduction to the Old Testament*, 2d ed. (Meridian, 1958), 328–29.

[6]A. Bertholet and K. Galling, *Hesekiel* (HAT 13; Tubingen: Mohr, 1936).

letters could reach Jerusalem and receive public attention and awareness (Jer. 29:24–32), so could Ezekiel's. One must also explain why an editor would go out of his way to transfer Ezekiel's ministry to Babylon if it had been exercised in whole or part in Palestine (Rowley 1953, 174); cogent explanations for this have eluded proponents. Ezekiel often describes his visionary experiences in terms of transport by the Spirit (3:12, 14; 8:3; 11:1, 24; 40:1–3; 43:5). Once again the chariot of God would bear a prophet away (2 Kings 2; cf. 2:11–12, 16; 5:26)—as with Paul, we do not know whether in or out of the body (2 Cor. 12:1–2).

The Prophet's Mental Health

Anyone reading the book cannot but be impressed with the power and intensity of the prophet's experience. By modern Western standards the prophet's behavior is often judged as pathological. He lies motionless for protracted periods (4:4–7); is dumb, or mute (3:24–27; 24:25–27; 33:22); does not mourn at the death of his wife (24:15–27); has visionary transports (8:1–4); reports extraordinary stories and visions (1–3; 8–11; 15–18; 21; 23–24; 37–48); and engages in almost bizarre conduct (4:12; 5:1–4; 12:3–5).

Psychoanalysis is difficult at best when dealing with a living patient who is a product of one's own culture, but this has not dissuaded people from making a variety of efforts to assign a clinical diagnosis to Ezekiel's behavior from a vantage culturally far removed and twenty-five hundred years later. The common language of daily life used by the prophet to describe his experiences in the book gives way to the textbook vocabulary of psychoanalysts, and Ezekiel is identified as psychic, schizophrenic, epileptic, catatonic, psychotic, or paranoid or is given other such labels, depending on the particular school of psychoanalysis in vogue at the time. Perhaps the most notorious example of this sort of approach to the prophet was the Freudian analysis offered by Broome (1946, 291–92), who concluded that Ezekiel was "a true psychotic" characterized by "a narcissistic-masochistic conflict, with attendant phantasies of castration and unconscious sexual regression," "schizophrenic withdrawal," and "delusions of persecution and grandeur." A more recent advocate of this type of reading is Halperin (1993) who thinks that Ezekiel's attitude and behavior resulted from abuse that he received as a child and that it manifested itself primarily as anger directed toward women. However, although similar behavior to that of Ezekiel is reported in other prophetic books (e.g., Jer. 16:2; 27:2; 28:10; 32:8–15), scholars have not felt compelled to regard such behavior as symptomatic of mental pathology.

The book of Ezekiel is different from other prophetic books primarily in the frequency with which such actions are encountered. While modern preachers tend to illustrate their sermons with stories, Israel's prophets more often used props and presented their sermons in symbolic actions. Their behavior was the culturally expected and symptomatic behavior of those possessed by God's

When Ezekiel proclaimed oracles about events in Jerusalem, the actual audience to whom he spoke was his fellow exiles in Babylon.

Spirit. The prophet so identified with the fate of his people as vicariously to take their suffering on himself and to dramatize their fate in his own agony. Rather than find his behavior peculiar or appalling, we ought to see in it the depths of his commitment to God and to his people and to appreciate the way in which the prophet was bearing the shame that so often accompanied proclaiming God's word. Ezekiel became "a prophetic symbol of his people even in his bodily life, as it were submerged in their dying, overwhelmed by the destructive power of the divine wrath which he himself proclaimed, anticipating the punishment of his fellow countrymen by willingly bearing their guilt" (Eichrodt 1970, 33).

The Text of Ezekiel Is Also Problematic

The LXX is 4 or 5 percent shorter than the MT, and this raises the question of whether, as in the case of Jeremiah, we may not be looking at two different editions of the book (Tov 1986; Lust 1981). The MT when compared with the LXX shows a significant number of short additions or glosses, a different arrangement of the text in chapter 7, and a substantial addition to chapter 36. The differences are probably better explained as reflecting different literary traditions or redactional stages than as the result of the common sorts of problems that accidentally or occasionally develop in copied texts. Even so, Block (1997, 41–42), concludes, along with recent scholarship, that the MT is to be preferred overall, even though in individual instances the LXX is a great help to recover what is likely the most authentic text.

LITERARY ANALYSIS

The book of Ezekiel shows the same literary macrostructure as several other prophetic books. Isaiah, Zephaniah, and the LXX of Jeremiah all (1) begin with a series of oracles oriented largely to judgment during the historical moment in which the prophet himself lived, then (2) turn to an extended section of oracles against foreign nations, and (3) conclude with prophecies of blessing more oriented to a distant future. In Ezekiel, chapters 1–24 concern the prophet's call and his warnings concerning the impending destruction of Jerusalem. The call narrative was one way in which a prophet established his credentials; it provided evidence that he had been admitted to the heavenly council (Jer. 23:18). The following is an outline of Ezekiel:

    I. Judgment on Judah and Jerusalem (1–24)
        A. The prophet's call (1–3)
        B. Symbolic actions about the destruction of Jerusalem (4–5)
        C. Oracle against the mountains of Israel (6)
        D. The end (7)
        E. A vision of judgment in Jerusalem (8–11)

The utterances of woe for Jerusalem continue until the time that Ezekiel's wife dies; the death of his wife anticipated the news reaching the exiles that Jerusalem had been destroyed (24:15–27).

The oracles of woe against Jerusalem then give way to a series of oracles against surrounding nations, though primarily against Tyre and Egypt (chaps. 25–32). The prophet addressed short oracles to Israel's immediate neighbors (Ammon, Moab, Edom, and Philistia) because of their gloating over the fall of Jerusalem and their aid to the city's enemies (25). Tyre, like Jerusalem, had revolted against Nebuchadnezzar. The Babylonians would besiege the city for thirteen years. The prophet envisages the eventual destruction of Tyre and castigates the city for its complicity in the fall of Jerusalem (26–28). He describes this great port city set on an island as a merchant vessel sinking into the sea (27). Two oracles are directed against the king of Tyre (28). These contain a number of allusions to Canaanite mythology. One depicts the king's hubris by describing him as a select cherub guarding the gate to Eden (28:11–19).

The oracles against Egypt (29–32) describe that nation's baneful influence over Israel throughout its history, whether as enemy or ally. Egypt will fall, just as Jerusalem had (29:19). Pharaoh and his army will join the rulers and armies of past empires in the netherworld (32).

After prophesying against foreign nations, the prophet turns to describing a blessed future for Israel (33–48). The final portion of the book begins by reiterating the prophet's call as a watchman (33:1–20; cf. 3:16–27) and his preaching of individual moral responsibility (33:10–20; cf. chap. 18), and by ending the period of dumbness that had followed his wife's death (24:25–27; 33:22). With Jerusalem destroyed, Ezekiel's focus will now be on the future city and people of God.

The length and nature of Ezekiel's dumbness is among the most debated features of the book. It is not clear when his dumbness began. The call narrative suggests that Ezekiel would not be totally mute, but rather would speak only when God had given him a message to proclaim (3:26–27). The prophet delivered many oracles to the exiles during the six years between his call and the destruction of Jerusalem; the chronological notes for his oracles and the very existence of chapters 1–24 attest to this. Whenever it began, this partial muteness lasted until word reached the exiles that the city of Jerusalem had been destroyed (24:27; 29:21; 33:22); then God opened the prophet's mouth and the tenor of his messages turned to blessing and hope.

Modern readers of the Bible most often think of the prophets primarily in terms of their delivering the word of God to others. However, the traffic was not just in one direction. The prophets regularly represented God's people before him and interceded in their behalf (Gen. 18:23–33; 20:7; Ex. 32:11–14; Num. 12:10–13; Isa. 37:21; Jer. 10:23–11:14; 14:11–15:1). What sacrifice was for a priest, prayer was for a prophet. At the very least, Ezekiel's dumbness conveyed the idea that he would not be interceding with God in the nation's behalf. God's decree that Jerusalem be destroyed was now irrevocable, and intercession was pointless. The only words from the prophet's mouth would be announcements of impending doom until that divine decree had come to pass.

The third portion of the book, those chapters oriented to Ezekiel's pronouncements about the future of Jerusalem and Israel, has long been the subject of intense interest. When reading visions and allegories in the prophets, readers need to be aware of the symbolic nature of such literature. A fair amount of mischief has been done to Ezekiel by interpreters committed to reading visions and allegories in a highly literalistic way. Moses himself warned against trying to do this with these genres of text (Num. 12:6–8).

Many popular preachers wax eloquent whenever there is military unrest in the Middle East; they tend to go straight from the pages of the newspaper to select passages in Ezekiel. This is particularly true of popular speculation about Ezekiel 38–39. In this passage Gog, the chief prince of Meshech and Tubal (Ezek. 38:2), is often identified as the leader of cities known from current geography. Simply on the basis of phonetic similarity, Meshech is said to be Moscow, and Tubal is identified with the Russian city Tobolsk, both localities geographically far removed from the region Ezekiel is describing. Furthermore, since the word *chief* in the phrase "chief prince" is the Hebrew word *rô 'š,* some have insisted that the phrase means "prince of Russia." Even if one reached the improbable conclusion that this term should have been translated as a geographical name instead of as "chief," it would scarcely refer to modern Russia. The word "Russia," insofar as can be determined, was brought into the region north of Kiev in the Middle Ages by the Vikings and therefore would not have been in use over a millennium earlier in Ezekiel's time as a designation for modern Russia. The terms Meshech and Tubal are known from Assyrian documents dated in the twelfth to eighth centuries BC; they are also mentioned by Herodotus (7:72) and Josephus (*Ant* 1:124). In these ancient sources Meshech and Tubal designated tribes that lived in central and eastern Anatolia. One king of the Mushku (Meshech) in the late eighth century was known to the Assyrians as Mitas, the Midas known in the classical historians for his legendary wealth. Since Ezekiel's terms have recognizable equivalents in use during his own time and geographically proximate to the biblical world, speculation about some sort of Russian invasion of other lands in the Middle East receives no warrant from this passage.

In describing the threats to Israel's existence, the Bible commonly refers to foes coming from the north (Isa. 41:25; Jer. 1:13–15; 4:6; 6:22; 10:22; 13:20; 15:12; 25:9, 26; 46:10, 20, 24; 50:3, 9, 41, 49; Ezek. 26:7; 38:6, 15; 39:2; Dan. 11; Zech. 2:6; 6:6–8; cf. Isa. 5:26–29; 13:1–13; Nah. 2:2–10; 3:1–3; Hab. 1:5–11). References to these northern foes in the preexilic period are ordinarily references to Israel's traditional historical enemies (Assyria, Babylon, Persia); however, in the exilic and postexilic writings, the foes from the north take on a more

> *Some mischief has been done to Ezekiel by interpreters committed to reading visions and allegories in a highly literalistic way. Moses himself warned against trying to do this.*

transhistoric and apocalyptic coloring. In his description of this eschatological conflict with Gog and his hordes, Ezekiel has chosen to mention tribes on the fringes of kingdoms to the north as an embodiment of the foes from the north that already figured in Israel's eschatology. Rather than fuel concrete speculation about future events, modern readers should probably understand that Ezekiel himself intends to use these nations as symbolic references to all powers arrayed against God's people. Although Ezekiel does contain many oracles against foreign nations (Ezek. 29–32), Babylon itself, where he and the exiles were held in captivity, is nowhere the subject of an oracle of judgment in this book. Some suggest, therefore, that Magog, Meshech, and Tubal are simply being used as surrogates for what is really an oracle against Babylon.

Similar misreading widely attends Ezekiel's vision of the restoration community (Ezek. 40–48). Almost all scholars recognize that the return to Jerusalem following Cyrus's decree (539 BC) fell short of the glorious restoration depicted in Ezekiel's vision. A temple was built, but it was not as spectacular as what the prophet described. Nor were all the tribes resettled in a new geographic distribution (47:13–48:29). The character of the terrain around the Dead Sea did not change (47:1–12).

Since no such temple as Ezekiel 40–43 describes has ever actually been built, many who urge a literal reading of the Bible insist that Ezekiel is providing the blueprint and specifications (cf. Ezek. 43:10–11) for a future temple that the citizens of modern Israel will build in Jerusalem. However, some elements of the prophet's vision seem to go beyond a reasonable literal understanding (Ezek. 47:1–12). Since the entire passage (Ezek. 40–48) is a vision, it is better to respect the essentially symbolic character of that genre and to understand the entire vision as a symbolic portrayal of the way in which God would bless his people in the future. The temple preeminently represented the presence of God in the midst of his people. Under the form of vision and symbol (Ezek. 40:2; cf. Num. 12:6), the prophet describes a time when God's presence in Israel would transcend anything in Israel's historical experience, a time when Israel would enjoy order, peace, and just rule. For Christian readers, that transcending experience of God's presence that brought with it peace and justice would occur when God incarnate would walk the streets of Jerusalem and build his church as a new temple. The presence of Immanuel would mark the day that "the LORD is there" (48:35).

It is interesting to note in passing that there are numerous points of detail on which Ezekiel's ordinances and prescriptions for the new temple (44–46) differ from the legislation in the Pentateuch. (See the commentaries for a discussion.)

Ezekiel clearly looked for a new exodus, a return from exile, a new covenant, and a new heart and spirit for the restoration community (36). The revival of the nation would be like the resurrection of the dead (37).

The book of Ezekiel is intensely personal. We cannot but enter into the prophet's own experience of awe, fear, distress, revulsion, agony, and other emotions when reading it. One reason this is so is that Ezekiel is the only prophetic book written entirely in the first person. We encounter Ezekiel's experience, not through a third-person narrator, but as he described it from his own mouth.

The prophet is addressed by God throughout the book as "son of man" (as, for instance, in Ezek. 2:1, 3, 6, 8; 4:1, 16; 5:1; 14:3, 13; 15:2; 16:2; 23:2, 36). This phrase means "person, human being" and emphasizes the humanity and frailty of the prophet, especially as it contrasts with the glory and power of the God whom Ezekiel saw in his visions.[7]

A wide variety of literary forms are used in the book (Zimmerli 1979, 21–40). There are funeral laments (19; 27; 28:11–19; 32:2–16); fables and allegories (15, 16, 17, 23); visions (1:1–3:15; 8–11; 37:1–14; 40–48); symbolic actions (4:1–5:17; 12:1–20; 21:11–29; 24:1–27; 33:21–22; 37:15–28); historico-theological narrative (20); legal sayings (14:1–11; 18; 22:1–16); ritual and priestly regulations (43:18–27; 44:17–31; 45:18–46:12); disputation oracles (33:1–20; 3:17–21); and many shorter forms, such as quotations, oaths, sayings, and proverbs. The prophet enlisted a panoply of literary genres to present his case effectively.

Modern preachers most often use stories to illustrate their sermons; Ezekiel and the prophets more commonly used props as part of symbolic actions. Their symbolic enactments shared in the same efficacy that characterized their other pronouncements. The prophet enacted the siege of Jerusalem by using an iron pan, sketching the events on a clay tablet (4:1–8), and eating siege rations (4:9–17). He shaved his beard, divided and discarded the hair in ways that foresaw the fate of the citizens of Jerusalem (5). He packed his belongings and dug through a wall to depict the exile of the population (12:1–20). A kind of "sword dance" became an object lesson about the sword the king of Babylon was bringing against Jerusalem; the king's strategy was portrayed in a map drawn in the sand (21:8–23). Everything—from a scorched cooking pot to the death of his own wife—could serve as an object lesson about the coming fate of the nation (24).

THEOLOGICAL MESSAGE

The book of Ezekiel is of such length and richness that any effort to summarize its themes is inevitably reductionistic. Nevertheless, much of the material in the book can be grouped under several headings.

---

[7]This use of the phrase "son of man" should be distinguished from its use more than seventy-five times in the Gospels as the favorite self-designation of Jesus (e.g., Matt. 8:20; 9:6; 10:23; 11:19; 12:8, 32, 40; 13:37, 41). In Jesus' use of the phrase, the emphasis appears to be to associate him with the "son of man" known from Daniel 7:13–14, and there is ambiguity that speaks to both his human and divine natures.

The Holiness and Transcendence of God

In the book of Ezekiel, God is beyond the creation and beyond the prophet. Revelation to Ezekiel was often mediated by an angelic guide (8, 40–48). The prophet sees angelic messengers and warriors doing God's bidding (9–10). When the prophet does receive a vision of God, it is "the appearance of the likeness of the glory of the LORD" (1:28) that he sees, a way of speaking that carefully avoids even the hint of actually seeing or describing God.

Because God is holy, he will not brook the sin of Israel. Sin was an affront to the holiness of God. Chapters 4–24 are devoted largely to oracles announcing that God will no longer ignore the sin of the nation. Israel had been a rebellious people (2:3–8; 3:9, 26–27; 12:2–3, 9, 25; 17:12; 24:3; 44:6), and the idolatry of the nation could no longer be ignored. The exile would produce a purged people, a purified remnant ready to live in obedience to a holy God (6:8; 9:8; 11:12–13; 12:16; 14:22–23).

The Grace and Mercy of God

The fact that God would judge Judah and Jerusalem would not frustrate his purpose in electing Israel. God would show mercy to a remnant; these would survive the exile, inherit his promises afresh, and enjoy restoration to their land. God would again be in their midst (48:35; cf. 11:20; 14:11; 36:23, 27–28). The nation would again live under a Davidic prince (37:24–25; 45:7) who would rule righteously (34:24). God would give to his people a new heart and a new spirit (36:24–28). The God who had abandoned his temple (10) would return to it in glory again (43).

The Sovereignty of God

God rules over the affairs and destiny not only of Israel but also of all other nations (Ezek. 25–32). He was not tied to a place, to a small room in the back of the temple in Jerusalem. The nations did his bidding. The words that God spoke through his prophet would be performed. The book is pervasively concerned with demonstrating the trustworthiness of the prophet's words. The phrase "they/you will know that I am the LORD" or its equivalent occurs with great frequency (2:5; 5:13; 6:7, 10, 13–14; 7:4, 9, 27; 11:10, 12; 12:15–16, 20; 13:9, 14, 21, 23; 14:8, 23; 15:7; 16:62; 17:21, 24; 20:12, 20, 26, 38, 42, 44; 21:5, and in many other verses); it is often called the "recognition formula."[8] God would vindicate himself and his prophet by fulfilling the words spoken by Ezekiel. When the Lord brought to pass what Ezekiel had announced beforehand, Israel and the nations would know that Yahweh was God (cf. Isa. 43:12). The destruction of Jerusalem did not result from an inability or lack of power in God—to

---

[8]Compare its use also in other prophetic books (Isa. 49:23; 60:16; Jer. 44:29; Joel 2:27; 3:17; Zech. 2:9, 11; 4:9; 6:15; Mal. 2:4).

the contrary, it was his own hand at work. The same power that was seen in the destruction of the city could also be trusted for its promised restoration. God rules not only over nations but also over time.

Individual Responsibility

The exile had come about in part as a result of the cumulative guilt of generations of Israelites who had lived in rebellion against God and his law. While guilt always has this corporate dimension, Ezekiel, more than any prophet before him, emphasized the individual consequences of both obedience and transgression (18:1–32; 33:10–20). The people had been using a proverb that in effect claimed that God was unjust (18:2) in punishing their generation for the sins of the fathers; by doing this, they were shrugging off any need to face their own sinfulness. But God would not allow them to sidestep the issue of their own sin and guilt. The sins of the exiles' generation also contributed to the destruction of Jerusalem. The writer of Chronicles would later rewrite the history to Israel in part to demonstrate the validity of this approach to punishment.

> *God rules over the affairs and destiny not only of Israel but also of all other nations. He was not tied to a place in the back of the temple in Jerusalem.*

APPROACHING THE NEW TESTAMENT

Just as it tends to reductionism to summarize the teaching of the book itself, it is also difficult to summarize the many ways in which the New Testament further develops and reflects on themes from Ezekiel. There are at least sixty-five direct or indirect quotations of Ezekiel in the New Testament, forty-eight of them in Revelation (LaSor, Hubbard, and Bush, 478). In the New Testament period, Jerusalem and its temple had once again been destroyed. With the birth of the infant church, a new restoration was under way with a new Israel. Jesus was their faithful Shepherd King (Ezek. 34), and he was building his temple in their midst out of living stones. The early church would see in Ezekiel's prophecies the same reasons that led to the destruction of Jerusalem in their own day; the church would view itself as the heir of the promises of restoration. Ezekiel's vision of the restoration informed John's portrayal of the new heavens and earth, when a new city of God would descend from heaven and God's dwelling would be irrevocably and forever with his people (Ezek. 48:35; Rev. 21:3).

Apart from these broad historical parallels between Israel at the time of Ezekiel and the situation of the church and Israel in the first century AD, numerous other themes and motifs found in Ezekiel are developed in other ways in the New Testament. Space allows sketching only a few representative ways of approaching these individual passages.

Ezekiel had a vision of a river trickling from south of the altar and turning into a great torrent that brought life everywhere it went and turned the Dead Sea into fresh water (47:1–12). Jesus identified himself as the source of this life-giving water when he spoke with a woman at a well in Samaria (John 4:10–14).

Later he would tell a crowd in Jerusalem on one of the holy days: "Whoever believes in me, as Scripture has said, rivers of living water will flow from within them"; John remarks that "by this he meant the Spirit" (John 7:38–39). He was what the temple was all about, and he was bringing a transforming presence into the world. Ezekiel had seen orchards bearing twelve harvests a year; when Jesus left Samaria with the disciples, he taught them that an unending harvest had already begun (John 4:35–36). The great bronze Sea that sat south of the altar in Solomon's temple was replaced by this life-giving river in Ezekiel's vision; in the New Jerusalem, there is no sea, but a river of life flows from the throne of God (Rev. 21:1; 22:1).

Ezekiel condemned the false prophets for their self-interest. When the going got rough and there was risk for them, they were nowhere to be found. They did not "stand in the gap" in the walls when they had been breached. In describing the false prophets this way, Ezekiel is contrasting them to Moses, who did stand in the gap before an angry God in behalf of a guilty Israel (Ps. 106:23). Later, when God had announced his determination to destroy the city, no one could be found to "stand before me in the gap on behalf of the land so I would not have to destroy it" (Ezek. 22:30). Jesus is that prophet greater than Moses; at his own risk he went into that breach between an angry God and sinful human beings so that those who believe would not be destroyed.

Ezekiel's vision of the restoration included a glorious temple. He foresaw a time when the presence of God in the midst of his people was so overwhelming that under the form of a vision he could only describe it in terms of size and splendor. John writes that when Jesus came and templed in our midst, we saw "his glory, the glory of the one and only Son, who came from the Father, full of grace and truth" (John 1:14); Jesus was "the radiance of God's glory and the exact representation of his being" (Heb. 1:3). There is no historical evidence that the visible cloud of God's glory ever came to the second temple as it had to the tabernacle and Solomon's temple; God's glory came to the second temple when Jesus entered Jerusalem.

CHAPTER TWENTY-FOUR

DANIEL

Daniel is a book of polarities. It may be described, for instance, as one of the simplest or as one of the most complex books of the Bible. The stories of the first six chapters are the staple of Sunday school classes and vacation Bible schools. On the other hand, scholars endlessly debate the complex visions that make up the second half of the book. Other contrasts include the use of two languages, Aramaic and Hebrew, in the book; the predominant use of two genres, story and apocalyptic; and contrasting attitudes toward such things as Gentile rulers.

Daniel is a fascinating book and a difficult one. It is the source of numerous debates, particularly over historicity and the interpretation of prophecy. As we will see, while the book is a powerful witness to God's power over evil, some aspects of it remain a mystery to us.

BIBLIOGRAPHY

Commentaries

J. G. **Baldwin,** *Daniel: An Introduction and Commentary* (TOTC; InterVarsity Press, 1978); J. J. **Collins,** *Daniel with an Introduction to Apocalyptic Literature* (FOTL 20; Eerdmans, 1984); idem, *Daniel* (Hermeneia; Fortress, 1993); J. E. **Goldingay,** *Daniel* (WBC 30; Word, 1989); L. P. **Hartman** and A. A. **DiLella,** *The Book of Daniel* (AB 23; Doubleday, 1978); A. **Lacocque,** *The Book of Daniel* (John Knox, 1979); T. **Longman** III, *Daniel* (NIVAC; Zondervan, 1999); E. **Lucas,** *Daniel* (Apollos; InterVarsity Press, 2002); J. A. **Montgomery,** *A Critical and Exegetical Commentary on the Book of Daniel* (ICC; T. & T. Clark, 1927); N. W. **Porteous,** *Daniel: A Commentary* (OTL; Westminster, 1965); A. **Preminger** and E. L. **Greenstein,** *The Hebrew Bible in Literary Criticism* (Ungar, 1986); W. S. **Towner,** *Daniel* (Interp; John Knox, 1984); E. J. **Young,** *The Prophecy of Daniel* (Eerdmans, 1949).

Articles and Monographs

J. **Barr,** "Jewish Apocalyptic in Recent Scholarly Study," *BJRL* 58 (1975/76): 9–35; P.-A. **Beaulieu,** *The Reign of Nabonidus 556–539 B.C.* (YNER 10; Yale University Press, 1989); J. **Berquist,** *Judaism in Persia's Shadow* (Fortress, 1995); J. H. **Charlesworth,** *The Old Testament Pseudepigrapha: Apocalyptic Literature and Testaments,* vol. 1 (Doubleday, 1983); J. J. **Collins,** "The Court-Tales in Daniel and the Development of Apocalyptic," *JBL* 94 (1975): 218–34; idem, *The Apocalyptic Vision of the Book of Daniel* (HSM 16; Missoula: Scholars, 1977); idem, *Semeia* 14: *Apocalypse: The Morphology of a Genre* (Missoula: Scholars, 1979); idem, "Apocalyptic Genre and Mythic Allusions in Daniel," *JSOT* 21 (1981): 83–100; J. **Day,** "The Daniel of Ugarit and Ezekiel and the Hero of the Book of Daniel," *VT* 30 (1980): 174–84; idem, *God's Conflict with the Dragon and the Sea* (Cambridge University Press, 1985); R. B. **Dillard,** "Harmonization: A Help and a Hindrance," in *Inerrancy and Hermeneutic,* ed. H. Conn (Baker, 1988), 151–64; H. H. P. **Dressler,** "The Identification of the Ugaritic *Dnil* with the Daniel of Ezekiel," *VT* 29 (1979): 152–61; D. N. **Fewell,** *Circle of Sovereignty: A Story of Stories in Daniel 1–6* (Sheffield: Almond, 1988); J. G. **Gammie,** "The Classification, Stages of Growth, and Changing Intentions in the Book of Daniel," *JBL* 95 (1976): 191–204; H. L. **Ginsberg,** "The Composition of the Book of Daniel," *VT* 4 (1954): 246–75; L. L. **Grabbe,** "Another Look at the Gestalt of 'Darius the Mede,'" *CBQ* 50 (1988): 198–213; A. K. **Grayson,** *Babylonian Historical-Literary Texts* (University of Toronto Press, 1975); S. **Gundry,** *Show Them No Mercy: Four Views on God and the Canaanite Genocide* (Zondervan, 2003); R. J. M. **Gurney,** "The Seventy Weeks of Daniel 9:24–27," *EvQ* 53 (1981): 29–36; P. D. **Hanson,** *The Dawn of Apocalyptic* (Fortress, 1975); G. F. **Hasel,** "The Book of Daniel: Evidences Relating to Persons and Chronology," *AUSS* 19 (1981): 37–49; J. H. **Hayes** and J. M. **Miller,** *Israelite and Judean History* (Westminster, 1977); W. L. **Humphreys,** "A Life-Style for Diaspora: A Study of the Tales of Esther and Daniel," *JBL* 92 (1973): 211–23; S. P. **Jeasonne,** *The Old Greek Translation of Daniel 7–12* (CBQMS 19; Washington, D.C.: Catholic Biblical Association, 1988); J. **Kugel,** *The Idea of Biblical Poetry* (Yale University Press, 1981); T. **Longman** III, *Fictional Akkadian Autobiography* (Eisenbrauns, 1991); idem, *Literary Approaches to Biblical Interpretation* (FCI 3; Zondervan, 1987); A. B. **Mickelsen,** *Daniel and Revelation: Riddles or Realities?* (Thomas Nelson, 1984); idem, *God as a Warrior* (Zondervan, 1995); R. H. **Pfeiffer,** *Introduction to the Old Testament* (Harper & Brothers, 1941); P. A. **Porter,** *Metaphors and Monsters: A Further Literary Critical Study of Daniel 7 and 8* (CBQMS 20; Lund: CWK Gleerup, 1983); C. **Rowland,** *The Open Heaven* (Crossroads, 1982); H. H. **Rowley,** *Darius the Mede and the Four World Empires in the Book of Daniel* (Cardiff: University of Wales Press Board, 1935); W. H. **Shea,** "Darius the Mede: An Update," *AUSS* 20 (1982): 229–47; (J. **Trever,** "The Book of Daniel and the Origin of the Qumran Community," *BA* 48 (1985): 89–102; E. **von Voigtlander,** "A Survey of Neo-Babylonian History," Ph.D. dissertation, University of Michigan, 1963; J. H. **Walton,** "The Four Kingdoms of Daniel," *JETS* 29 (1986): 25–36; J. C. **Whitcomb,** *Darius the Mede: A Study in Historical Identification* (Eerdmans, 1959); R. D. **Wilson,** *Studies in the Book of Daniel,* 2 vols. (Baker, 1972 [orig. 1917, 1938]); R. R. **Wilson,** "From Prophecy to Apocalyptic: Reflections on the Shape of Israelite Religion," *Semeia* 21 (1981): 79–95; D. J. **Wiseman,** *Chronicles of the Chaldean Kings* (British Museum Publications, Ltd., 1956); D. J. **Wiseman** et al., *Notes on Some Problems in the Book of Daniel* (London: Tyndale, 1965); E. J. **Young,** *The Messianic Prophecies of Daniel* (Delft: van Keulen, 1952).

HISTORICAL BACKGROUND

Author and Date

Up until the twentieth century, the predominant opinion of both Jewish and Christian scholars was that the book of Daniel was written by Daniel, a statesman and prophet who flourished during the sixth century BC. The fact that Daniel speaks in the first person in the second half of the book (e.g., Dan. 7:2, 4, 6, 28; 8:1, 15; 9:2; 10:2) provides the internal evidence for Daniel's authorship. It is further supported by the angelic command to Daniel to "seal the words of the scroll" in Daniel 12:4.

At the least, the internal evidence leads us to believe that Daniel was the source of the vision reports of Daniel 7–12. These vision reports are often framed by third-person introductions (e.g., Dan. 7:1), and this leaves open the possibility that the final editing was done by someone other than Daniel. In this connection it is also significant to note that the first six chapters of Daniel are all written in the third person. The New Testament cites the book of Daniel frequently, but names Daniel as the author only in Matthew 24:15–16, mentioning the prophecy of the "abomination that causes desolation" found in Daniel 9:2; 11:31; 12:11 (all first-person passages).

Thus, the internal evidence requires only that the first-person visions of the second half of the book be accepted as directly from Daniel. However, these are precisely the portions of the book that are most contested due to their extraordinary predictions of later history.

Since the turn of the century, scholarship has increasingly challenged the traditional understanding of the origin of the book of Daniel. Porphyry (AD 233–304) is an often-cited precursor to this critical view that is today the predominant view of the book. Most scholars now believe that the book of Daniel is a work that was in actuality composed in the second century BC and is thus a pseudonymous work that employs "prophecy after the fact" (*vaticinium ex eventu*). This includes some evangelical scholars (Goldingay; Lucas, citing fictional Akkadian autobiographies) who argue (wrongly, see Longman 1991) that such writings were known in the ancient Near East and did not intend to deceive their audience.

Many are confident that the final redaction of the book can be dated almost to the year. According to Eissfeldt (*OTI*, 520), "It can be clearly proved that the book derives from the period between the return of Antiochus IV from his second campaign against Egypt (167) and his death in April 163." Eissfeldt arrives at this date by a close reading of the end of Daniel 11. He argues that 11:29–39 is a "prophecy after the fact" because it accurately describes the second campaign of Antiochus in 167. However, he feels that Daniel's attempt at real prophecy in 11:40–45 fails to describe Antiochus's death rightly: "He will pitch his royal tents between the seas at the beautiful holy mountain. Yet he will come to his end, and no one will help him" (Dan. 11:45). However, we know from Polybius that Antiochus died in Syria, not in Palestine.

Baldwin (1978, 199–203; see also Longman 1999) represents a conservative reaction to the well-entrenched critical view by appealing to a well-known phenomenon in prophecy—telescoping, a metaphor to describe prophecy's "compressed" nature. That is, a prophet relates events that, when fulfilled, will actually take place at different periods of time. A commonly accepted example is found in the message of John the Baptist (Matt. 3:1–12). In the same context of his prophecies of the coming of the Messiah, John also describes Christ's ministry as one of violent judgment: "His winnowing fork is in his hand, and he will clear his threshing floor, gathering his wheat into the barn and burning up the chaff with unquenchable fire" (v. 12). Unknown even to John (Matt. 11:1–19), his prophecy telescoped the first and second comings of Christ.

Baldwin applies this concept to her understanding of Daniel 11:29–45 and suggests that the whole section applies to Antiochus IV, but not exclusively. It also is relevant to other future oppressive rulers, hinting that the ultimate fulfillment of the passage is the Antichrist, who will embody evil at the end of the age.

At the bottom of the disagreement between conservative and critical scholars are the completely different approaches to the text. These fundamental attitudes dramatically affect treatment of historical issues as well. In regard to prophecy, Towner in his comments on Daniel 8 (1984, 115) expresses an opinion that appears to be operative in much critical thinking about Daniel:

> We need to assume that the vision as a whole is a prophecy after the fact. Why? Because human beings are unable accurately to predict future events centuries in advance and to say that Daniel could do so, even on the basis of a symbolic revelation vouchsafed to him by God and interpreted by an angel, is to fly in the face of the certainties of human nature. So what we have here is in fact not a road map of the future laid down in the sixth century B.C. but an interpretation of the events of the author's own time, 167–164 B.C.

Towner bases his distrust of Daniel's prophecy in the "certainties of human nature." This presupposition is unacceptable, not because he is wrong about human nature, but because he discounts the power of God to speak predictively and, indeed, without error through sinful human agency.

While critical thought dates the prophecies to the second century BC, it is becoming increasingly popular to date the stories of the first six chapters to an earlier period, usually sometime during the third century BC. The predominant signal for this dating is the positive attitude toward monarchs like Nebuchadnezzar in Daniel 4. It is rightly pointed out that such a positive attitude toward a Gentile ruler would not have been appropriate for the time period of the persecutions of Antiochus IV. For a suggested three-stage development of the book of Daniel, see Gammie (1976).

In summary, there are two reasons for moving away from a sixth-century date for the book. The first is the opinion that such exact prophecy is not possible. We have found this to be an unacceptable presupposition. Second, however, there are the supposed historical errors. These are difficult and will be dealt with below. There we will see that reasonable, though not certain, harmonizations are possible.

This chapter will proceed on the basis of the view that Daniel, a sixth-century figure, was the subject and author of the book that bears his name. This view does not rule out the possibility that some later unnamed disciples framed his speeches or even added some or all of the third-person stories. However, it does exclude the idea that the predictive prophecies were given "after the fact."

We know little about Daniel except what we learn from his book. He is mentioned as a model of righteousness along with Noah and Job (see the debate between Dressler and Day) in Ezekiel 14:14, 20. His name probably is best translated "God is my Judge," and this fits in with the character of God described in the book.

Historicity

The book opens with this statement: "In the third year of the reign of Jehoiakim king of Judah, Nebuchadnezzar king of Babylon came to Jerusalem and besieged it" (Dan. 1:1). The precise dating and the specific and well-known names of kings and places all signal that the author intends to impart historical information to the reader. This initial impression is carried through the whole book and is supported (but not proved) by other passages in the Old Testament (Ezek. 14:14, 20; 28:3) and the New Testament (Matt. 24:15–16). That particularly the first six chapters bear some resemblances to folk stories does not mitigate their historical intention (Longman 1987, 63–74).

Critical scholars often use the label "fictional" to refer to the book of Daniel (see Genre below), but most recognize its historical intention (Towner 1984), while also claiming that it is inaccurate in its historical statements. Its claims for a sixth-century BC date are frequently rejected because of its supposed historical errors.

Two facts must be stated at the outset. First, there is no doubt that Daniel claims to be a product of the sixth century BC and looks forward to the future (including the Maccabean period) with prophetic predictions. Second, it is impossible to prove or disprove definitively a sixth-century date for the book and its contents. The best that can be done is to show that the contents of the book and a sixth-century date are reconcilable. The lack of positive evidence is the result of a dearth of detailed knowledge of the period in question and the nature of harmonization (Dillard 1988).

In light of the lack of information from the Persian period, it is necessary to restrain critical judgment. Over a century ago it was believed that Babylonian history had no place for Belshazzar on the throne of Babylon. It was learned from the ancient documents that Babylon fell while a king named Nabonidus was on the throne. Many scholars felt that the book of Daniel must have been in error or confused when it referred to King Belshazzar (Dan. 5:1–2; 7:1; 8:1). However, further study led to the discovery that Nabonidus had a son, Bel-šar-uṣur (Hebrew transliteration=Belshazzar, "God, protect the king"), who ruled in Babylon. Nabonidus, it appears, left Babylon early in his reign to live in Teima, an oasis in northwest Arabia approximately one thousand miles from Babylon. His motives for moving were both religious and political (Beaulieu 1989; von Voigtlander 1963, 183–207), but what is important for the book of Daniel is that his son ruled in Babylon during his absence. This strange state of affairs explains why Daniel interacts with Belshazzar, not Nabonidus, at the end of the Babylonian period and likely explains Belshazzar's cryptic promise that he would reward Daniel by making him the third highest ruler in the kingdom (5:16).

While this historical difficulty has reached a satisfactory resolution, there are still a number of other historical problems surrounding the book of Daniel. Not all of them can be dealt with here in any detail. R. D. Wilson devoted two large volumes to these questions (1917, 1938). His analysis, while dated and overly dogmatic, still retains value today. We will content ourselves with looking at two of the stickier problems of the book. We will attempt to show that, while a final solution cannot be reached, the problems are not insuperable. It must be borne in mind, though, that our answers are hypotheses and not certain fact.

Daniel 1:1. "In the third year of the reign of Jehoiakim king of Judah, Nebuchadnezzar king of Babylon came to Jerusalem and besieged it." This chronological statement is said to be in contradiction with Jeremiah 25:1, which synchronizes the first year of Nebuchadnezzar with the fourth year of Jehoiakim. It is further claimed that the Babylonians did not come to Jerusalem until the fifth year of Jehoiakim (Jer. 36:9). A surface reading of the Babylonian Chronicle appears to support this opinion. According to Hartman and DiLella (1978, 48), the second-century author of Daniel was confused and misled by his understanding of 2 Chronicles 36:6–7 in connection with 2 Kings 24:1.

This argument is countered by the fact that there were two systems of dating current in the ancient Near Eastern world, both of which can be found in the Old Testament (Wiseman et al. 1965, 16–18). The passages may be harmonized by assuming that Jeremiah utilized the Judean method of chronological reckoning, which counts the first year of a king's reign as the first year, and that Daniel used the Babylonian system, which counts the first year as an "accession year." Hasel helpfully diagrammed the results (1981, 47–49):

Table 16
Chronology of Kings in Jeremiah and Daniel

Accession-year method:	Accession yr	1st yr	2nd yr	3rd yr	Daniel 1:1
Nonaccession-year method:	1st yr	2nd yr	3rd yr	4th yr	Jeremiah 25:1, 9; 46:2

It has been persuasively argued that the Babylonian Chronicle fails to mention the siege of Jerusalem because it is preoccupied with "the major defeat of the Egyptians" and "a successful incursion into Judah by the Babylonian army group which returned from the Egyptian border could be included in the claim that at that time Nebuchadnezzar conquered 'all Hatti'" (Wiseman et al. 1965, 18).

Darius the Mede. After the fall of Babylon, Belshazzar was executed and Darius the Mede became king (Dan. 5:30; 9:1). He was sixty-two years old (5:31) and a "Mede by descent" (9:1). He was the king who reluctantly sent Daniel to the lion's den (chap. 6) and appointed 120 satraps over his kingdom (6:1).

Unfortunately, while Darius the Mede is an important character in the book of Daniel, he is unknown by that name outside of the book. Furthermore, one would expect that the great Persian conqueror Cyrus would be the only one given the title "king of Babylon." In addition, the earliest extrabiblical evidence for the satrapy system is not until the reign of a later Darius (Hystaspes) who appointed only approximately twenty satraps over the entire Persian Empire.

Rowley set forth the classic critical argument against the historicity of Darius the Mede in 1935. He argued that Darius the Mede is the product of fuzzy historical memory. The account was written centuries after the conquest of Babylon. Darius the Mede never existed and is the "conflation of confused traditions" (1935, 54). The first confusion centers on Darius Hystaspes who reconquered Babylon in 520 BC when it rebelled upon the death of Cambyses. Rowley, however, believes the confusion goes well beyond this simple mix-up (54–60). The writer of Daniel not only transposed Darius Hystaspes back to 539, but merged his identity with Cyrus, who was about sixty-two at the time of the fall of Babylon. In addition, some account must be taken of the biblical claim that Darius was a Mede, since neither Cyrus nor Darius Hystaspes were

Medes. According to Rowley, the confusion arose because of passages like Jeremiah 51:11, 28, which look forward to the destruction of Babylon at the hands of the Medes. One last confusion resulted in Darius the Mede's patronymic, Ahasuerus (Xerxes). In reality, Ahasuerus was the son of Darius Hystaspes, not his father.

In summary, Rowley says that the Bible's use of the name Darius the Mede is the result of confusion based on a lack of any real knowledge of the Persian period. The author, in the opinion of Rowley and others, must have lived much later and have lost touch with historical reality.

This difficult historical problem has not gone unaddressed by more conservative scholars. A number of possible scenarios have been brought forward in the attempt to rescue Darius the Mede from historical skepticism. Working with hints in the biblical text and a few extrabiblical references, the case has been made for the historical trustworthiness of the text of Daniel.

None of these attempted harmonizations have convinced all scholars, even those who are conservative. This multiplicity of approaches should not be taken as utter capitulation to skepticism any more than the variety of critical approaches renders the conservative position more likely (though it has been argued so on both sides). The Bible, while set in history, is not a history textbook concerned to answer all our modern questions. This reticence on the part of the biblical narrative, along with a lack of extrabiblical documentation, means that we are dealing with historical probabilities, not certainties. There is, accordingly, more than one way to harmonize Darius the Mede with known history. The three most promising harmonizations are those by Whitcomb, Wiseman, and Shea.

Whitcomb. By the time Whitcomb of Grace Theological Seminary wrote his book *Darius the Mede* (1959), conservative scholars had long thought that Darius was a throne name, that is, a name given to an individual along with his new political status. A notable example of this phenomenon is found in 1 Chronicles 5:26, where Tiglath-Pileser is also referred to as Pul. With this in mind, it is possible to consider connecting Darius with someone with another name in the extrabiblical materials.

After surveying the evidence, Whitcomb concluded that Darius the Mede is actually Gubaru, known from the Akkadian texts as governor of Babylon. His unique contribution is in differentiating Gubaru from Ugbaru in the cuneiform documents and insisting that he was not the general who took Babylon for Cyrus in 539 BC (1959, 21–22). He points out that according to the Nabonidus Chronicle, Ugbaru died a few days after the victory over Babylon (but see Shea below). The confusion between Gubaru and Ugbaru arose because in one of the original translations both names were transliterated Gobryas (like the figure known in the writings of the Greek historians). In the past these two had been combined, rendering the identification of Gubaru as Darius difficult.

Whitcomb's thinking still faces a number of objections. For instance, why does the book of Daniel refer to Cyrus's governor of Babylon as "king"? R. D. Wilson had already answered this objection decades before by showing that the Hebrew word *king* could be used for a governor of Babylon; and in any case, from the perspective of the Babylonians, Darius was kinglike. Furthermore, Whitcomb as well as others point to Daniel 9:1, which says that Darius "was made king over the realm of the Chaldeans," not "he became king" (KJV). He argues that this language subtly infers the existence of an even greater authority, namely Cyrus. This is much too subtle for many critics of this view, both critical (Grabbe 1988, 205) and conservative (Wiseman 1956, 11–12) alike.

Wiseman. D. J. Wiseman was the noted British Assyriologist who, with his publication of works on the Babylonian historical texts (1956), became one of the foremost authorities on the neo-Babylonian period. Wiseman, like many others, had difficulty with the idea that another besides the great conqueror Cyrus was given the title of king. As a result he identifies Darius the Mede with Cyrus the Great (1965, 12–16). He understands the name Cyrus to be the name taken by Cyrus as ruler of Babylon. Historical sources attest the practice of a king ruling two nations under two different names. Accordingly, he translates Daniel 6:28: "Daniel prospered in the reign of Darius, even the reign of Cyrus the Persian." By so translating, he is treating the *waw* as explicative not conjunctive. Wiseman points specifically to 1 Chronicles 5:26 as an analogy.

Shea. Perhaps the most attractive of all proposed harmonizations is that by Shea. He presented his view in a series of articles beginning in 1971 and concluding in 1982.[1] His starting point is an analysis of royal titles in the period of time under question. From his study he reports that there is a shift in the titulature from the late Babylonian to early Persian period. In the neo-Babylonian period, the kings referred to themselves as "king of Babylon." In the late Persian period, the preferred title was "king of the Lands." In the intervening early Persian period, the common title was "king of Babylon, king of the Lands." However, Shea points out:

> There is but one significant exception to this pattern and that is the title employed for Cyrus during his accession year and first year of rule over Babylonia. In contrast to the Neo-Babylonian kings who ruled over Babylonia before him, it is clear from the contract tablet evidence that Cyrus *did not* take up the title "king of Babylon" during his accession year and most of his first year of rule there. Only late in his first year was "king of Babylon" added to "king of the Lands" in titularies of tablets dated to Cyrus so as to make up the full titulary of the early Persian period. (1982, 236)

---

[1]The articles were published in various issues of the journal *Andrews University Seminary Studies*, ranging from vol. 9, no. 1 (1971) through vol. 20, no. 3 (1982).

As an explanation, Shea proposed that during a fourteen-month period Cyrus ruled through a vassal who was styled "king of Babylon." This vassal he identified with Darius the Mede.

But as we have seen, the texts know of no person named Darius the Mede at this time. Thus Shea, like the interpreters before him, sought to identify Darius with someone known from the extrabiblical texts. After careful study, he concluded that Darius the Mede is the Gubaru of the Nabonidus Chronicle. This is the Gu/Ugbaru who as a general in the Persian army defeated Babylon, not the governor of the same name with whom Whitcomb associated Darius. In answer to Whitcomb's objection that Ugbaru the general died a few days after the conquest of Babylon, Shea suggests a "consecutive" and not a "retrospective" reading of the Chronicle at the relevant passage (1982, 240–43). The significant implication is that Gubaru the general died, not a few days after the conquest of Babylon, but a year and a few days after. This period allows for the necessary time for Darius to serve as vassal king of Babylon.

While these three attempts to harmonize the book of Daniel with history have been quietly ignored by most nonconservative scholars, Grabbe (1988) has taken them to task. Against Whitcomb, he argues that Gubaru the governor (whom Whitcomb differentiates from the general) did not come to office until Cyrus's fourth year, much too late to fit the biblical picture of Darius. Wiseman's thesis gets a cold shoulder from Grabbe, not because it is possible to prove it false, but because it is motivated solely by the wish to prove Daniel historical, an "exercise in apologetics" as he puts it (1988, 207). Wiseman probably would not disagree with Grabbe's accusation but would simply say that the burden of proof should be on the person who argues against the veracity of an ancient historical document.

Grabbe has most respect for Shea's thesis. He agrees that the cuneiform evidence points to an unusual situation in Cyrus's first year. This is the year in which Shea would place the vassal kingship of Darius. However, other scholars, including Grabbe, would argue that the unusual titulature is the result of a co-regency with Cambyses during Cyrus's first year of rule in Babylon. Shea's original position was to argue that the year-long co-regency should be set within the last year of Cyrus's rule as is typical in father-son co-regencies. Grabbe argues that the co-regency must be during the first year of rule over Babylon because there are two tablets that correlate Cambyses as "king of Babylon" with "the first year of Cyrus." Nonetheless, in response to Grabbe, it must be allowed that the Babylonian dating system is used here where the first year is the accession year and the second year is counted as the first year. Then we are back to Shea's second suggestion that the Cambyses-Cyrus co-regency is dated to the latter's second year. As Shea argued, the second year is better than the first because "Cambyses's participation in the Babylonian New Year's festival is placed at the beginning of Cyrus's 2nd regnal year" and this "is tantamount to designating him as king" (1982, 240). Thus it appears that Shea anticipated Grabbe's objection.

To conclude briefly, the matter of Darius the Mede is one of the unsolved mysteries of biblical history. Three attempted harmonizations have been offered. Whitcomb's is admittedly improbable, perhaps even impossible. Wiseman's is possible, but there is little evidence supporting it. Shea's is the most likely, but there are still difficulties. Conservative scholars have erred in presenting their attempted solutions too dogmatically. It must be admitted that there are theological motives at work here. It is only to be hoped that more evidence will be forthcoming.

> *The matter of Darius the Mede is one of the unsolved mysteries of biblical history. It is only to be hoped that more evidence will be forthcoming.*

The Broader Background

The book is set in the context of world events from approximately 605 BC to the mid-530s—that is, from the year that Nebuchadnezzar carried Daniel and his three friends into exile to Babylon (1:1) until the third year of Cyrus (10:1). Events within the book are dated to the reigns of Nebuchadnezzar (chaps. 1–4), Belshazzar (5–7), Darius the Mede (5:30–6:28; 9), and Cyrus (10–12). Daniel was a public person who interacted with the leading political figures of his day. It is instructive to study the book in the light of political-military history.

When Israel became a nation under Moses, God entered a covenant relationship with his people. The covenant itself is recorded in Exodus 19–24, and its renewal forty years later is found in the book of Deuteronomy. At that time, God warned Israel that, though it would be blessed if obedient, curse would be the result of disobedience. Indeed, God would curse Israel with destruction and exile (Deut. 28).

The books of Kings demonstrate the repeated disobedience of Israel and its leaders. The northern kingdom had been overtaken by the Assyrians as early as 722. Judah had been spared, but had lived under the threat of Assyrian domination for decades. This threat, however, did not stir Judah on to repentance and obedience. Its sins continued and, under Manasseh, reached a horrible climax. Even the reforms of Josiah could not turn away the coming destruction (2 Kings 23:26–27), and when he died in 609, the end was in sight.

Josiah's successor, Jehoahaz, ruled for only three months. The Egyptians were controlling Judahite politics at this time, and they replaced Jehoahaz with another son of Josiah, Jehoiakim. Jehoiakim was thus an Egyptian vassal, but as mentioned in Daniel 1:1 and as recorded in 2 Kings 24, Nebuchadnezzar was able to push Egyptian control out of Palestine and exert his influence.

Nebuchadnezzar was the second ruler of what is now called the neo-Babylonian period. His father, Nabopolassar, had successfully reasserted Babylonian independence from Assyria, establishing Babylon as a fast-growing empire. His revolt, which began in 626, climaxed in 612 with the destruction of Nineveh. A remnant of Assyrian power had survived under a king named Ashur-uballit III, but even with Egyptian help, it dissolved before the army led by the crown prince Nebuchadnezzar. In 605 Nabopolassar died. Nebuchadnezzar was in Syria leading the army. He rode quickly to Babylon to secure his power.

Jehoiakim, however, was pro-Egyptian, and after three years he revolted against Babylon. He likely had hoped that Egypt would come to his aid, but that was not to happen (2 Kings 24:7). Before Babylon could respond, Jehoiakim died and was succeeded by his son Jehoiachin, who was only eighteen years old. Jehoiachin ruled three months before Jerusalem fell to the Babylonian army. (Daniel was by this time in Babylon.) This conquest resulted in more booty and people being taken to Babylon. Nonetheless, Judah continued to exist under a Babylonian-appointed but native king (Zedekiah) for eleven years. However, in 587 Zedekiah too revolted. This time Babylon completely crushed Judah and exiled most of its inhabitants.

The book of Daniel begins in the early part of Nebuchadnezzar's reign. The next king cited in the book is Belshazzar, mentioned above as co-regent to Nabonidus, the last king of the neo-Babylonian period. There were three Babylonian kings who reigned between Nebuchadnezzar and Nabonidus but are not mentioned in the book of Daniel. These are Nebuchadnezzar's son, Amel-Marduk (562–560)—also known as Evil-Merodach (2 Kings 25:27–30 NIV); Nebuchadnezzar's son-in-law, Neriglissar (560–556); and Neriglissar's young son, Labashi-Marduk (556).

Much of the book of Daniel finds its setting during the reign of Nabonidus, who is not mentioned in the text because he had left his royal duties in Babylon to his son and co-regent Belshazzar (see above). Nabonidus's move angered many in Babylon, particularly the powerful Marduk priesthood. They were upset that the king favored the cult of the moon god Sin. Nabonidus's devotion to Sin may in part explain his move away from Babylon and certainly gives reason why he neglected the New Year festival in Babylon.

While internal tensions were fomenting in Babylon, a new star was rising in the east. Cyrus, a Persian vassal, rebelled against his Median overlord Astyages and deposed him by the year 550. From this base, he expanded his kingdom by defeating Lydia and taking Upper Mesopotamia and Syria from the control of Babylon. He even apparently expanded his kingdom to the east into what is today Afghanistan.

It was not until 539, however, that Babylon became the object of his attention. By that time, the former great empire was a fig to be plucked. No buffer zone was left, and its own inhabitants were dissatisfied with Nabonidus. Before Cyrus's general Gobryas reached Babylon, the army had collapsed in a battle at a location called Opis on the Tigris River. Gobryas apparently took Babylon without a struggle, and Cyrus himself entered the city a few weeks later to be greeted by enthusiastic crowds. The head of gold was replaced by the chest and arms of silver (Dan. 2:31–32).

Cyrus set up a vassal kingship in Babylon, appointing Darius the Mede as ruler (see discussion above). His vassalship lasted only a short time, and then Cyrus exerted his rule directly. The latest dating in the book of Daniel is the third year of Cyrus's reign (10:1). It seems that Daniel's ministry was coming to a close around this time.

However, Daniel's vision extended into the near and far future, and it is instructive to examine the history of the Near East in general outline at least up to the second century BC. Since Daniel's prophecy focuses on the succession of dominant kingdoms, that will be our concentration here rather than reporting on events in Palestine.

Cyrus built an empire that would last for approximately two centuries. His son Cambyses enlarged the empire to include even Egypt. After Cambyses's suicide, many vassals revolted. Although Darius Hystaspes was a brilliant ruler and administrator, the empire had stopped its rapid expansion. While his son and successor, Xerxes, had temporary successes in Greece, he was decisively defeated in an important naval battle near Salamis (479).

Persian power did not disappear overnight though, and for the next century and a half its fortunes waxed and waned. However, by the time Darius III became ruler in 336, Greek rule came to Alexander, whose father Philip had built up Greek power from his Macedonian base. The bear was about to face the leopard for supremacy in the Aegean world (Dan. 7:5–6).

Alexander's brief life left a deep mark on the history of the world and earned him the epithet "the Great." In 333 he encountered the Persian army under the leadership of Darius III in the battle of Issus in Asia Minor. The Persians were no match for Alexander's army, and Darius fled. Alexander continued his march and took all of Asia Minor. He then turned south and proceeded to take the Levant, including the provinces of Judah and Samaria. Egypt did not resist and was included in his empire.

At this point Alexander turned toward the heart of the Persian Empire, encountering a Persian army under Darius III, this time at Gaugamela. Once again, the Greek forces overran the Persians, and Darius himself was assassinated soon after the battle.

The Persian Empire was Alexander's, and he continued his campaign east until he reached the Indus in 327. At the age of 30 Alexander had established an empire of unprecedented proportions.

However, Alexander did not live to enjoy the fruits of his conquests. He died in Babylon in 323 at the age of thirty-three. He had not consolidated his empire so that there would be a clear-cut transition of power, and as a result, his four most powerful generals grabbed as much as they could for themselves. The resulting four kingdoms were Thrace, Macedonia, Ptolemaia, and Seleucia. The "four wings" and the "four heads" of Daniel 7:6 may refer to this fourfold split of the kingdom. The Ptolemies and the Seleucid rulers fought for centuries over

Palestine. After a period of intense struggle, the Ptolemies were able to control Palestine for a period (301–200). Finally, at the battle of Paneion in 200 BC, Antiochus III defeated the Ptolemaic general Scopus and inherited Palestine.

Critical scholars date the book of Daniel to this period. More specifically, they date the book to the period of Antiochus IV Epiphanes (see above). He is usually identified as the "master of intrigue" of Daniel 8:23–25 and is the object of the prophecy found in Daniel 11:21–45.

The beginning of Seleucid rule was favorable for Judah. Antiochus allowed them to be ruled by "ancestral laws," which in this case meant the Torah (Hayes and Miller 1977, 577). However, he seriously offended Jewish cultural and religious sensibilities. For instance, at the beginning of his reign, Antiochus IV, as a result of a bribe, manipulated the high priesthood by inserting Jason in that office, replacing the legitimate occupant Onias.

This cavalier attitude toward the native culture was just the beginning. Allied with the powerful Tobiad family, Antiochus IV aggressively promoted Hellenistic culture in the city. The gymnasium, not the temple, was to be the social and even religious heart of the city. Even Jason turned out to be too traditional for the Tobiads and Antiochus, and Jason was finally replaced as high priest by one Menelaus, who was an ardent Hellenist.

In 170 BC, though, Jason returned with an army of a thousand men while Antiochus was concluding a successful war against the Ptolemies in Egypt. When he returned in 169, Antiochus devastated Jerusalem and the temple. He then systematically tried to purge native religious customs out of Judah. The worst was that in 167 he put an altar dedicated to Zeus in the temple—an act that was known in Daniel 11:31 as the "abomination that causes desolation."

The book of Daniel, born of the exile and the political oppression of the Babylonian conquerors, was especially meaningful to those who lived during the time of the Seleucid oppression and persecution. However, the forward vision of the book of Daniel does not halt with Antiochus, but looks beyond the Seleucids to the Romans (the beast with the large iron teeth) and even further to the time when God would directly intervene and bring all oppressive human governments to an end, a day when the people of God will receive the power of the kingdoms of the earth (Dan. 7:23–25). That day, obviously, is still to come.

LITERARY ANALYSIS

Genre

Two genres characterize the book of Daniel: court narrative and apocalyptic prophecy. Intriguingly, the two genres divide the book, but this division does not coincide with the use of Hebrew and Aramaic that also divides the book. The court narratives make up the first half of the book (1–6), while the apocalyptic portion is the last part (7–12). Daniel 2, while it is a court narrative, has affinities with apocalyptic in Nebuchadnezzar's dream that is highly symbolic and reveals a four-kingdom scheme similar to that found in Daniel 7.

Court Narrative. The first half of the book of Daniel contains six separate stories that focus on Daniel and/or his three comrades—Hananiah, Mishael, and Azariah. Numerous attempts to define precisely the type of story found here have been made. Collins lists them as "Märchen, Legend, Court Tale, Aretalogical Narrative, and Midrash" (1984, 42). However, all five of these genre labels imply a lack of historical intent.

Court Tale (Collins's own category) does, however, rightly locate the setting of all the stories in Daniel 1–6. The six stories focus on the interaction between the heroes of the book and the members of the foreign court. Collins (1975) and Humphreys (1973) provide a further subdivision between "Tales of Court Contest" and "Tales of Court Conflict" that is very helpful. Daniel 5 exemplifies the former. The king confronts a problem of interpretation. The writing on the wall is clearly oracular, but it is undecipherable. He calls in the wise men of his kingdom. They fail. Daniel enters, reads the inscription, and is rewarded. Daniel 3 is a "tale of court conflict." Daniel is not present in this chapter, but his three friends are threatened because they refuse to bow down to Nebuchadnezzar's golden image. Their enemies in the Babylonian court inform on them, and they are thrown into the fiery furnace. God delivers them, and they are promoted to even higher levels of honor.

Identifying the genre of the first six chapters of Daniel in this way allows us to see the connections with other biblical texts such as sections of the Joseph narrative and Esther (Humphreys 1973), as well as extrabiblical texts such as Ahikar, Tobit, and 3 Ezra 3 (Collins 1984, 42).

We can also recognize a common function in these stories. They have a clearly didactic function. They are teaching the people of God how to act in the presence of oppressors. Towner has correctly summed up the moral teaching of these chapters in this way: "Those who trust and obey God will be vindicated, and they will make it big, even in Babylon" (1984, 21). This message is later relevant to the Jews who are persecuted by Antiochus Epiphanes, and again to Christians who are persecuted in the New Testament era.

The identification of the genre of these texts as court narrative leaves open the question of the historical intention of the writer. Towner (1984, 22) typifies the conclusions of most writers on the book of Daniel today when he calls it "fictional." He explains that "clearly the writer's forte is narrative art, not historical detail!" However, as Collins points out, the issue of "inaccuracy is compatible with the genre of history writing" (1984, 41). In other words, the issue of historicity is not solved by the genre identification and vice versa. Collins himself decides in favor of nonhistorical reading because of the "folkloristic" pattern of the stories and the "marvelous" elements. The issue of historicity is discussed above, where the conclusion is that if one accepts a biblical worldview that

Two genres— court narrative and apocalyptic prophecy— divide the book, but this division does not coincide with the use of Hebrew and Aramaic that also divides the book.

includes the supernatural and the possibility of predictive prophecy, then there is nothing to prevent a straightforward historical reading of the text.

Apocalyptic Prophecy. Although it is the shorter half, Daniel as a whole is often characterized as an apocalyptic prophecy. After all, it is the only nondisputed apocalypse in the Old Testament. A number of other Old Testament passages are often called apocalyptic (and rightly so)—for instance, Isaiah 24–27 and Zechariah (or at least chapters 9–14)—but this identification is debated by many. The difficulty arises from the lack of agreement concerning the definition of the genre.

The typical approach to the genre is to isolate a trait or complex of traits that must be present in a text to identify it as an apocalypse. For instance, the genre is often closely identified with a certain type of eschatology, one that looks beyond the historical process to the "end times" when God will intervene and bring victory to the oppressed (Hanson 1975). In a similar vein, Rowland (1982) has argued that apocalyptic is better defined, not as a specific type of eschatology, but as a specific type of revelation, one that opens up heavenly realities to the seer. Another approach to the definition of apocalyptic has been taken in a very informative article by Collins in 1979. Rather than relying on a single trait, Collins lists a series of traits found in those writings that we identify as apocalyptic. In his definition the essential characteristics reduce to three: a narrative frame, a mediated revelation, and content that is eschatological and heavenly. Not long after that, J. Carmignac also compiled a list of traits by which scholars have recognized an apocalypse.[2]

Although apocalyptic has been treated as a separate category since the work of F. Lücke in the early nineteenth century, no definite consensus has been reached as to what constitutes the genre. The point is to differentiate apocalyptic from prophecy, of which it is a particular type. We implicitly recognize a difference between texts like Daniel 7–12 and the book of Enoch on the one hand, and Nahum and Jeremiah on the other—but how do we define the differences?

Difficulties have resulted from defining the difference between apocalyptic and prophecy too sharply and too simply. Genres, after all, are not rigid categories built into the nature of things, but rather, they are fluid literary characterizations that have overlapping boundaries. By recognizing the fluid relationship between Hebrew prose and poetry, Kugel (1981) broke through the impasse that obstructed the definition of the latter. The relationship between prophecy and apocalyptic is best described in the same way.

In other words, there are a number of traits that are often (though not in every case) found in apocalyptic texts that are less occasionally found in prophetic texts. These traits include the following:

---

[2]J. Carmignac, "Qu'est-ce que l'Apocalyptique? Son emploi a Qumran," *RevQ* 37 (1979): 3–33.

Narrow eschatology. Apocalyptic texts look beyond the near future to the end of time. Daniel, for instance, looks beyond the period of Persian, Greek, and Roman oppression to the time when God will intervene and bring all oppression to an end once and for all. The New Testament understood the book of Daniel to refer to the second coming of Christ. Revelation 1:7 alludes to Daniel 7:13: the Son of Man who rides the cloud into the presence of the Ancient of Days is Jesus returning at the end of history to deliver his people from oppression.

Mediated revelation. The prophet is one who brings the word of God to the people. For example, God spoke to Jeremiah, who was then commissioned to speak to the people of Judah. When the people responded, the prophet would then go back to God for further instructions (Jer. 12). A different dynamic is at work in apocalyptic. God speaks to Daniel through a mediator—usually an angel (Dan. 12:5–13). He is not commissioned to speak to the people, but rather to "close up and seal the words of the scroll until the time of the end" (v. 4).

A second type of mediation occurs by means of an "otherworldly journey" (Collins 1979). That is, an interpreting angel conducts the apocalyptic seer on a journey by which he reveals heavenly and eschatological realities to the seer. An example of this is 1 Enoch.

Unusual imagery. In Daniel as well as other books identified as apocalyptic literature, there is a heightened use of imagery. While imagery is found in classical prophecy as well as in all poetry, the imagery of apocalyptic borders on the bizarre. Evil is pictured in the most grotesque terms. In Daniel, evil kingdoms are represented by hybrid beasts. Such a mixing of species would have been particularly abhorrent to the Israelites, with their keen sense of creation order and distinctions.

As Collins (1981) has pointed out, the imagery is not created out of whole cloth. Rather, its basis is often found in pagan mythology. The four beasts arise out of the sea. As is well known, the sea is the symbol of chaos and anticreation forces in the mythology of the Near East (Day 1985). Yam (the Sea) fights Baal in Canaanite religious texts, while Tiamat (the Sea) battles Marduk to the death in the Mesopotamian myth Enuma Elish. On the side of the forces of good, the Son of Man rides the cloud into the presence of the Ancient of Days, reminiscent of Baal's frequent epithet "Rider on the Clouds."

Setting of oppression. Apocalyptic literature is the product of an oppressed society or an oppressed class within society. Daniel reflects the period of the Babylonian exile and the following domination by the Persians. It prophetically anticipates the threat of Hellenism, particularly the ruthless behavior of Antiochus Epiphanes. The book of Revelation, the prime New Testament example of apocalyptic, was composed by John, who was exiled on the island of Patmos (Rev. 1:9).

Oppression explains in large measure the grotesque pictures of evil and the anguished cries for salvation that we encounter in apocalyptic literature. Hope is in the distant future. The major function of apocalyptic literature in general and of Daniel in particular is to comfort the oppressed. An (overly) neat distinction between prophets and apocalypticists is this: a prophet afflicts the comforted; the apocalyptic seer comforts the afflicted.

One of the most commonly recurring themes in apocalyptic literature is the picture of God as a warrior. Apocalyptic prophets anticipate the violent intervention of God to result in their deliverance and the judgment of their oppressors.

Deterministic view of history and attendant optimism. One of the functions of a classical prophet is to warn the people of God of the coming judgment of God. Accordingly, the prophet calls the people to repentance. Daniel, on the other hand, proclaims the judgment as certain. His prophecy functions to inform the faithful few (the wise [Dan. 12]).

Many have thus characterized Daniel as pessimistic: judgment cannot be avoided. However, from the perspective of the author and his faithful audience, the opposite is true. God is coming to deliver them. The deliverance may be a hope to be realized in the distant future, but it is nonetheless a sure one.

Pseudonymity and prophecy after the fact. Apocalyptic texts are frequently written under an assumed name (Enoch, Zephaniah, Ezra [Charlesworth 1983, 3–772]). However, while many apocalyptic texts are pseudonymous, not all are. Most scholars are agreed, for instance, that John wrote Revelation. The case for Daniel is hotly debated (see above).

Under the cover of pseudonymity, the apocalyptic writer attempts to gain credibility for his prophecy by beginning with a number of prophecies of events that had already taken place. In 2 Slavonic Apocalypse of Enoch, for example, Enoch predicts the flood, but of course the book was written millennia after Enoch and the flood.

Implications and Origins. The latter half of the book of Daniel clearly exhibits most of the traits that we associate with apocalyptic literature. It prophesies the end of time through an angelic mediator with strange, sometimes bizarre imagery. The purpose of the visions is not to elicit repentance but rather to encourage the faithful in a time of distress.

What are some of the implications for reading the book of Daniel? In the first place, we become sensitive to the imagery of the book. Because it was written during a time of oppression, its imagery serves a double function. It both reveals and conceals. While Babylon is in control (Dan. 7:1), it is much safer to use metaphors and privately circulate the belief that Babylon will be destroyed than to say it in simple prose. The heavy use of imagery will also discourage a literalistic reading of the so-called apocalyptic timetables (e.g., Dan. 9:25–27). To compute the time of the end from Daniel's seventy weeks is to misuse the text, for "apocalyptic time measurements (highly symbolic) simply provide a framework for important truths for Daniel and his people" (Mickelsen 1984, 196).

The peculiar nature of apocalyptic metaphor will also lead us to investigate possible allusions to Near Eastern mythology. Porter (1983, 15), for instance, persuasively argues that the animal imagery in Daniel 7 and 8 is "ultimately traceable to Mesopotamian mantic wisdom traditions."

A genre identification always leads to a literary context for study. Serious students of the book of Daniel will research intertestamental apocalyptic, but especially other biblical examples such as Isaiah 24–27 and the book of Zechariah. Genre identification also highlights the clear interrelationship between the book of Daniel in the Old Testament and the book of Revelation in the New.

The origins of biblical apocalyptic are within the prophetic tradition. There are also traces of wisdom influence. In the past, it has been fashionable to speak of a Persian influence on later biblical books, particularly the apocalypse of Daniel. However, recent studies have shown that apocalyptic is not evidence for a late date for Daniel, since there are apocalyptic-like texts as early as 1200 BC in the ancient Near East (Longman 1991). Yet the closest Near Eastern analog to the apocalyptic section of the book of Daniel is the Dynastic Prophecy dated to the Seleucid period (Grayson 1975).

Language

Besides employing two genres, Daniel also used two languages. Daniel 1:1–2:4a and 8:1–12:13 are in Hebrew, while 2:4b–7:28 is in Aramaic. This extensive use of two languages is unique in a single book.

This arrangement raises some problems that do not admit of easy answers. For instance, why does the Aramaic begin in chapter 2? It is introduced by the phrase "the astrologers answered the king in Aramaic," so some think that the Aramaic begins here because the narrator wants to give the dialogue in the language in which it was spoken. While it is true that Imperial Aramaic was the language of the neo-Babylonian court, why is the dialogue of chapter 1 not reported in Aramaic? Again, why is the narrative in Aramaic? Lastly, why is chapter 7, which is a vision report, not given in Hebrew like the other visions?

Few doubt that the Aramaic of Daniel was original because "there is not the slightest indication that any part of these chapters is 'translation Aramaic' of a Hebrew original" (Hartman and DiLella 1978, 11). However, it is not at all obvious why the book has two languages. Some scholars believe that chapters 2–7 were originally separate from the rest of the book. Ginsberg (1954) has argued that the whole book was in Aramaic and then the first and last chapters were translated into Hebrew "in order to ensure that the book would receive canonical recognition" (Hartman and DiLella 1978, 14). Perhaps chapter 7 was retained in Aramaic because its message was similar to that of chapter 2.

It is impossible to resolve these issues conclusively. Furthermore, it makes little difference in our understanding of the final text. Of most interest is the way that the language overlaps the various genres and leads us to read the book as a final, if not an original, unity.

Style

At least in the modern period, scholars have not given Daniel high marks on style: "There is everywhere incongruity, the very opposite of the Greek laws of harmony" (Ernest Renan, *L'Antechrist*, 1896).
Pfeiffer says:

> The author of Daniel is far more notable for his religious zeal than for his literary art. . . . Daniel's style is crude, the plots are elementary, and the happy endings are produced less subtly and more artificially by an abrupt intervention of the *deus ex machina*.[3]

Besides the mixture of genre and language, other characteristics distance Daniel from what is today considered the apex of literary achievement in the Old Testament—texts such as the Joseph and David narratives. For example, the characterization is not profound by modern standards. Daniel and his three friends are rather two-dimensional compared with Abraham, Moses, and Samuel—indeed, compared with virtually any other person in the Old Testament. The narrative does not share any doubts or sins on their part. They are the ideal righteous men.

The characterization also leaves the reader with questions about the religious status of the Gentile rulers. Nebuchadnezzar proclaims the Lord the God of the universe more than once. Is he becoming a Yahweh worshiper? Is he simply affirming the Lord as one among many gods? Does he apostatize soon after his affirmations? The text is not interested in answering these questions.

That the text is giving us an idealized picture of Daniel does not mean that it is an unhistorical report. Daniel was an exceptionally righteous individual. Idealization is a function of selection, not distortion or deception. But the fact that the text does not report flaws or sins does not mean that the historical Daniel was without them. The book's treatment of Daniel reminds one of the Chronicler's treatment of Solomon. We know from the Deuteronomic account that Solomon committed apostasy. One would never learn that from the Chronicler. The latter had different purposes.

Indeed, it is in accordance with the purpose of the book of Daniel that we look for a reason why Daniel is idealized. The book presents him as a model for behavior during periods of oppression and persecution. He is a historical embodiment of righteousness.

Thus there is no denying that the book of Daniel has simple, fairly episodic plots with idealized characterization in the first half of the book. Nor can we deny that the second part is difficult to understand because of the bizarre imagery and abrupt Hebrew prose. Nonetheless, it is wrong to write it off as

The book presents Daniel as a model for behavior during periods of oppression and persecution. He is a historical embodiment of righteousness.

---

[3]Renan's and Pfeiffer's quotations are found in Preminger and Greenstein 1986, 291–98.

simplistic or crude. The simple plots, idealized characters, and vivid imagery exert a powerful pull on the imagination not only of children but also of adults, who find in Daniel a source of consolation for the present and of hope for the future.

UNITY OF DANIEL

The book of Daniel exhibits such variety of genre and language that the issue of the original unity of the book has been debated for a long time. On the one side, most modern commentators believe that the different attitudes toward pagan kings in the first and second halves of the book demonstrate that the first part was written in an earlier period than the second half (Gammie; Collins). On the other side, conservative scholars have defended the unity of the book because of their concern to attribute the authorship of the whole book to the prophet Daniel (Young). Moreover, occasionally nonconservative scholars are persuaded of the unity of the book (Rowley).

It is important to first clarify what is meant by unity. Contemporary biblical scholarship has increasingly focused its attention on the final form of the text regardless of its origin. Even if Daniel was originally composite, it is now a unity and should be interpreted in the light of its canonical shape. Nonetheless, it is still of interest to ask the question about the original unity of the text, particularly in the light of the claims of the text itself. Thus the question of the unity of the text is intertwined with the issues of date and authorship dealt with above. The internal claims of the book of Daniel are only that Daniel was the recipient of the visions in the second half of the book and that he is the object of the stories in the first half. Tradition goes further and assigns the whole book to his authorship. We gave reasons above supporting the traditional view of authorship and date.

Even granting single authorship, does this necessarily mean that the author wrote the book at one sitting or even in one period of time? If with tradition we attribute the whole book of Daniel to a single author, this unity does not entail a single time period for its composition. Daniel could have written the book in parts throughout his life. This long period of time could conceivably account for the variety within the book, but even this variety could have arisen in the process of writing the book at one period of time, say, at the end of his life.

It should readily be admitted that it is impossible to solve the issue of unity to everyone's satisfaction. While the language and the genre are varied, the theme of the book is consistent throughout (see Theological Message). The use of more than one genre in a book by a single author is not a real obstacle to unity. Indeed, the differences of genre and language do not jibe with each other. Generically, the book is composed of stories in 1–6 and visions in 7–12, but the book is in Hebrew in 1:1–2:3 and 8:1 to the end of 12, and in Aramaic in 2:4 to the end of 7. A clear chiasm also links the opening vision chapter (7) with the stories:

Table 17 Chiastic Structure in Daniel		
2 a	3 b	4 c
Four-kingdom vision	Tales of deliverance	Gentile kings
7 a'	6 b'	5 c'

A further issue connected with the unity of the canonical book of Daniel is the existence of three stories that are found in the Septuagint and, while not included in the Protestant canon, are found in the Apocrypha. The first is the Prayer of Azariah and the Song of the Three Young Men. This addition is connected with Daniel 3 and the fiery-furnace ordeal. While in the fire, Azariah prays, then afterward, all three sing a psalm. The second story, Susanna, recounts the wisdom of Daniel as he exposes two elders who try to molest Susanna sexually and, upon their failure, accuse her of sexual sin. Bel and the Dragon is the third apocryphal story. Once again, the story highlights Daniel's wisdom as he exposes the deceitfulness of the priests of Babylon, who fool the people into believing that their gods actually eat the food placed before them.

All three of these books are entertaining and even serve a useful didactic purpose, though they are very likely not preserving historical tradition. These three stories lack the kind of thematic unity of the canonical Daniel, as was noticed by H. H. Watts, who said, "In the Bel and the Dragon stories and in The History of Susannah, Daniel appears not as a seer and a defier of pagan authority [as he does in the canonical book] but in the role of a clever secular man who by his own wit sets matters to rights" (quoted in Preminger and Greenstein 1986, 294).

THEOLOGICAL MESSAGE

At first thought, the task of summarizing the theological message of the book of Daniel is daunting. After all, the two halves of the book seem so different and the apocalyptic visions so complex. Nonetheless, while the book is theologically rich and incapable of exhaustive description, there is a clear message that rings through every chapter of the book. In spite of present circumstances, *God is sovereign. He overrules and eventually will overcome human evil.* This theme is found in both parts of the book.

The initial six stories (chaps. 1–6) are admittedly set in a more friendly environment than the second part. The text's attitude toward the Gentile rulers is, for the most part, favorable. However, many of the stories contain either a real or threatened danger to God's people represented by Daniel and his three friends, and in any case, the exile looms over the characters throughout.

In the first half of the book, we see God intervening in the historical circumstances of the characters, delivering them from danger and even using their distress to further their own careers and power. Daniel 6 is a case in point. It is not Darius, but rather his jealous satraps who plot to endanger the hero's life. They trap the king in a situation where he must impose the death penalty on Daniel. Daniel is thrown to the lions, while the king spends the night in anguish. The next morning Darius rushes to the den and discovers that Daniel has survived. God has intervened by sending an angel to "shut the mouths of the lions" (6:22).

God can overrule evil and bring justice. The evil plotters themselves receive the death penalty that they tried to impose on Daniel (6:24), and the king praises Daniel's God (6:26–27).

In summary, the stories are a tract directed to the people of God on how to act in times of oppression. The stories are similar to the Joseph narrative and the book of Esther, two books that have been correctly compared to Wisdom Literature. All three clearly embody and illustrate principles that the sages teach in Proverbs. Daniel is the prototypical wise man who knows how to handle himself before potentially hostile kings. All biblical narrative has a didactic edge to it (Longman 1987, 70), but Daniel especially so.

The second half of the book of Daniel also addresses the people of God as they live under oppression and even persecution. However, here God's deliverance is more a future hope than a historical reality. Even in the first half of the book, Daniel and his three friends realize that their salvation and vindication may not take place immediately. In a deeply profound statement, Shadrach, Meshach, and Abednego express their deep trust in God, though they might even die in the fiery furnace: "King Nebuchadnezzar, we do not need to defend ourselves before you in this matter. If the God we serve is able to deliver us, then he will deliver us from the blazing furnace and from Your Majesty's hand. But even if he does not, we want you to know, Your Majesty, that we will not serve your gods or worship the image of gold you have set up." (3:16–18). They recognize that they might be burned alive, but nonetheless they trust that God will care for them. They are to be obedient.

Daniel powerfully paints evil's potency in the second half of the book. The imagery of the seventh chapter is illustrative. The vision opens (7:2) with a description of a churned up sea. By this time, the sea was an evocative image of evil and chaos. As mountains represented order and the divine, so the sea symbolized confusion and disorder, wickedness and evil (Psalm 46).

A monster of grotesque description rises out of the sea. It is a hybrid, having characteristics of a lion, an eagle, and a man. Whether the symbolism of the beasts has its origins in Mesopotamian mantic wisdom (Porter 1983), Canaanite mythology (Collins 1981), or historical symbolism is unimportant here, though probably all three are operative. That the symbolism with its mixed kinds offended Israelite sensibilities as manifested in the creation order and dietary laws is inescapable. The four beasts above all else represent powerful and grotesque evil.

While there is no doubt that Daniel intends these beasts to stand for the evil strength of pagan states that exploit the people of God (7:17), debate has raged for centuries regarding the exact identity of the kingdoms. The traditional identification (Young 1949) suggests:

First Beast: Babylon
Second Beast: Medo-Persia
Third Beast: Greece
Fourth Beast: Rome

This schema seems best, since a low view of predictive prophecy is usually operative with the main alternative that identifies the four kingdoms as Babylon, Media, Persia, and Greece (Rowley 1935), though some evangelical scholars have suggested that Greece is indeed the beast with the iron teeth (Gurney; Walton).

In either case, however, there is no doubt about the power and grotesqueness of human evil, especially on the level of the state. Indeed, the people of God felt the pain of oppression from each of these imperial states. But furthermore, the image of Daniel 7 (as well as the other apocalyptic visions of Daniel) tells us that these evil kingdoms feed on one another. None of them last long. From history, we know that Babylon fell to Persia (with a Median contingent), Persia fell to Greece, Greece to Rome.

Daniel does not leave us in the dark about the source of this horrendous evil. Time and time again Daniel points to human pride that reaches gigantic proportions. For instance, we read about Nebuchadnezzar boastfully claiming: "Is not this the great Babylon I have built as the royal residence, by my mighty power and for the glory of my majesty?" (Dan. 4:30). In the vision of Daniel 11 we read about a king who will come in the future who "will exalt and magnify himself above every god and will say unheard-of things against the God of gods. . . . He will show no regard for the gods of his ancestors or for the one desired by women, nor will he regard any god, but will exalt himself above them all" (11:36–37). Pride propels the evil actors of the book of Daniel.

Daniel does more than graphically picture evil; he also describes its antithesis. In Daniel 7:9, an abrupt transition takes place. We change scenes from the chaotic sea to the divine throne room:

As I looked,
thrones were set in place,
    and the Ancient of Days took his seat.
His clothing was as white as snow;
    the hair of his head was white like wool.

His throne was flaming with fire,
> and its wheels were all ablaze.
A river of fire was flowing,
> coming out from before him.
Thousands upon thousands attended him;
> ten thousand times ten thousand stood before him.
The court was seated,
> and the books were opened. (7:9–10)

The first thing to notice in this picture of the Ancient of Days—and the soon-to-be-introduced Son of Man—is that these are not animal images. God is here pictured in human form, as a venerable, wise, and powerful judge. This human imagery contrasts and highlights the bestial imagery used for the realm of human evil. And indeed, that is precisely what this chapter as well as other parts of Daniel are doing—presenting a stark contrast between two kingdoms, the kingdom of man and the kingdom of God. On one side stand human beings who in their pride reject God and attempt to amass power to themselves. On the other side stand the Ancient of Days, the Son of Man and angels, and men and women who are in conflict with the powers of evil.

The book of Daniel teaches that this warfare between the evil kingdom of man and the good kingdom of God (which includes righteous men and women) takes place on both the heavenly and earthly spheres (10:12–14). While Daniel lived and prophesied, the people of God were oppressed and downtrodden, but the message of Daniel's prophecy is that the kingdom of God will be victorious. This victory will be both certain and complete. Speaking of the boastful single horn that culminates the first half of the vision (7:8), the angel interprets:

> But the court will sit, and his power will be taken away and completely destroyed forever. Then the sovereignty, power and greatness of all the kingdoms under heaven will be handed over to the holy people of the Most High. His kingdom will be an everlasting kingdom, and all rulers will worship and obey him. (7:26–27)

In summary, the message of Daniel fits into the message of the whole Old Testament—indeed, the whole Bible. God is at war with evil and without a doubt will overcome evil. This message brought comfort to the faithful in Israel in Daniel's day and does so today as well.

Unfortunately, though, Christian interest in the book of Daniel has too often become obsessed with the puzzle of the time schemes in the book. Do the seventy "sevens" (9:25–27) or the 1,335 days (12:11–12) give us a chronological blueprint? Does the book of Daniel tell us when the end time will come?

The obviously highly figurative context in which these numbers occur as well as the New Testament warnings that no man knows the time of the end (Mark 13:32–36; Acts 1:6–7) should keep us from becoming dogmatic in our

The book of Daniel teaches that the warfare between the evil kingdom of man and the good kingdom of God takes place on both the heavenly and earthly spheres.

interpretation of these numbers. Mickelsen (1984, 186) put it best when he said, "Apocalyptic time measurements (highly symbolic) simply provide a framework for important truths for Daniel and his people, and they are not meant to convey exact time periods."

APPROACHING THE NEW TESTAMENT

Does the book, then, have any relevance for the Christian? The story that God will once and for all defeat evil is completed in the New Testament. Jesus battles with Satan and evil during his earthly ministry and, ironically, defeats the powers of evil on the cross (Col. 1:13–15).

However, this victory is anticipatory and will culminate in the second coming of Christ. The book of Revelation, which deals with this future victory, frequently alludes to the book of Daniel, drawing a close connection between them. For instance, the image of ultimate evil in the book of Revelation is the beast that arises out of the sea (Rev. 13), reminiscent of the four beasts that arise out of the sea in Daniel 7. Even more striking is the picture of Jesus Christ as the Divine Warrior who comes to finally end and completely defeat the powers of evil (Rev. 19:11–21). Right at the beginning of the book (Rev. 1:7), he is described by a quotation from Daniel 7:13 as the one who rides the cloud war chariot. The characteristics of the Ancient of Days are also ascribed to him (Rev. 1:12–16).

The book of Revelation confirms that in the book of Daniel we have prophetically anticipated the coming of Christ, who will remove all evil from the world and save his people from their oppressors. Just as this message comforted faithful Israelites at the time of the book of Daniel, it also comforts us, who live in an imperfect, at times horrifying, world.

CHAPTER TWENTY-FIVE

HOSEA

Familiarity with the book of Hosea is usually limited to the first three chapters. In those chapters, Hosea confronts his readers with the striking analogy between his failed marriage and Israel's relationship with God. While we are left with some profound issues of interpretation in these chapters, Hosea's message of God's judgment and love toward Israel is generally clear and indisputably striking.

In contrast, the remaining chapters (4–14) are among the most difficult in the entire Bible. Andersen and Freedman's comment (1980, 66) that Hosea "competes with Job for the distinction of containing more unintelligible passages than any other book of the Hebrew Bible" certainly is true for this section of the book.

These difficulties have kept many from delving into this part of the canon. We do not deny the persistent problems, but to avoid studying Hosea because of them is regrettable, for some of the most moving language about God and his relationship to his people may be found in this book.

BIBLIOGRAPHY

Commentaries

F. I. **Andersen** and D. N. **Freedman,** *Hosea* (AB; Doubleday, 1980); G. I. **Davies,** *Hosea* (NCB; Eerdmans, 1992); D. A. **Garrett,** *Hosea. Joel* (NAC; Broadman, 1997); D. A. **Hubbard,** *Hosea* (TOTC; InterVarsity Press, 1989); K. **Marti,** *Das Dodekapropheton* (Tübingen, 1904); J. L. **Mays,** *Hosea* (OTL; Westminster, 1969); T. E. **McComiskey,** "Hosea," in *The Minor Prophets: An Exegetical and Expository Commentary*, ed. T. E. McComiskey (Baker, 1992), 1–237; G. A. **Smith,** *Hosea/Joel/Micah* (NIVAC; Zondervan, 2001); D. K. **Stuart,** *Hosea-Jonah* (WBC; Word, 1987); H. W. **Wolff,** *Hosea* (Hermeneia; Fortress, 1965).

Articles and Monographs

W. **Brueggemann,** *Tradition for Crisis: A Study in Hosea* (John Knox, 1968); M. J. **Buss,** "Tragedy and Comedy in the Latter Prophets," *Semeia* 32 (1984): 71–82; D. R. **Daniels,** *Hosea and Salvation History* (De Gruyter, 1990); J. **Day,** "Pre-Deuteronomic Allusions to the Covenant in Hosea and Psalm LXXVIII," *VT* 36 (1986): 1–12; G. I. **Emmerson,** *Hosea: An Israelite Prophet in Judean Perspective* (JSOT, 1984); F. C. **Fensham,** "The Marriage Metaphor in Hosea for the Covenant Relationship Between the Lord and His People (Hos. 1:2–9)," *JNWSL* 12 (1984): 71–78; P. A. **Forseth,** "Hosea, Gomer, and Elective Grace," *Reformed Journal* 35 (1985): 15–18; G. **Hall,** "The Origin of the Marriage Metaphor," *HS* 23 (1982): 169–71; J. G. **Janzen,** "Metaphor and Reality in Hosea 11," *Semeia* 24 (1982): 7–44; W. C. **Kaiser** Jr., "Inner Biblical Exegesis as a Model for Bridging the 'Then' and the 'Now' Gap: Hos. 12:1–6," *JETS* 28 (1985): 33–46; P. A. **Kruger,** "Prophetic Imagery: On Metaphors and Similes in the Book of Hosea," *JNWSL* 14 (1988): 143–51; J. L. **Mays,** "Response to Janzen: Metaphor and Reality in Hosea 11," *Semeia* 24 (1982): 45–51; S. **McKenzie,** "The Jacob Tradition in Hosea XII 4–5," *VT* 36 (1986): 311–22; R. C. **Ortlund** Jr., *Whoredom: God's Unfaithful Wife in Biblical Theology* (Eerdmans, 1996); B. **Peckham,** "The Composition of Hosea," *HAR* 11 (1987): 331–52; I. **Provan,** V. P. **Long,** and T. **Longman** III, *A Biblical History of Israel* (Westminster John Knox, 2003); H. H. **Rowley,** *Men of God* (London, 1963), 65–73; Y. **Sherwood,** *The Prostitute and the Prophet: Hosea's Marriage in Literary-Theological Perspective* (JSOTS 212; Sheffield Academic Press, 1996; N. **Stienstra,** *YHWH Is the Husband of His People: Analysis of a Marriage Metaphor with Special Reference to Translation* (Pharos, 1993); A. **Stock,** *The Way in the Wilderness* (Liturgical Press, 1968); R. J. **Weems,** "Gomer: Victim of Violence or Victim of Metaphor?" *Semeia* 47 (1989): 87–104; H. W. **Wolff,** *Old Testament: A Guide to Its Writings* (Augsburg Press, 1974); D. B. **Wyrtzen,** "The Theological Center of the Book of Hosea," *BibSac* 141 (1984): 315–29; G. A. **Yee,** *Composition and Tradition in the Book of Hosea: A Redaction Critical Investigation* (Scholars, 1987).

HISTORICAL BACKGROUND

Date and Authorship

At first sight the date and authorship of Hosea seem straightforward. The superscription names the author as "Hosea son of Beeri" and gives the date with a typical formula naming the kings who ruled during his ministry: "the reigns of Uzziah, Jotham, Ahaz and Hezekiah, kings of Judah" and "the reign of Jeroboam son of Jehoash king of Israel" (1:1).

Problems arise once we convert these statements into our own chronological system. While it is true that the superscription places Hosea's life and work solidly in the eighth century BC, there are some apparent tensions and issues when we try to be more precise.

For example, disagreements exist about the end of the reign of Jeroboam II (Hubbard 1989, 22–23) due to some confusion over how to handle the length of Pekah's reign (i.e., how much of his reign was over the entirety of the northern kingdom and how much of it was a co-regency). In any case, the suggested dates for the end of Jeroboam II's reign range from 753 to 746 BC.

The reigns of the kings who are listed from the southern kingdom of Judah are more secure. The beginning of Uzziah's rule is 791 (Jeroboam II assumed the throne of the north around 793) and Hezekiah died in 687/6. Of course, Hosea could not have served as a prophet for nearly a hundred years, so it is assumed; and it is indirectly supported by internal considerations that he began his work late in Jeroboam's reign and completed his work early in Hezekiah's (which began in 715).

Thus, the superscription may be interpreted as informing the reader that Hosea was active in the period between c. 750 and 715 BC. He was thus one of the earliest (along with Amos and Micah) of the minor prophets. Isaiah completes the list of eighth-century prophets.

Issues and Alternative Viewpoints

Before presenting the historical background that informs a reading of the book of Hosea, we need to consider some objections to the biblical picture of its composition.

Indications of a composite authorship begin, according to some, with the superscription itself. Hosea, as we will see, is clearly a prophet of the North, and his prophecy is in the main directed toward the North. This observation raises the question of the long list of southern kings by which the book is dated and the fact that the southern list does not match the northern list in terms of its end point. Furthermore, there are occasional, and, it is argued, added references to Judah throughout the final redaction of Hosea. Emmerson (1984, 56–116) lists and discusses a number of direct references to Judah (1:7; 2:2 [1:11]; 4:15; 5:5, 10, 12, 13, 14; 6:4, 11; 8:14; 10:11; 12:1, 3 [11:12; 12:2]) and a single mention of the Davidic king (3:5).[1] These convince many critical scholars that the book had a later Judean redaction: "Its origins lie in the northern kingdom, its transmission belongs for the greater part of its history to Judah" (Emmerson 1984, 1).

Salvation oracles directed to Judah are especially the focus of critical attention. Gone are the days when all of Hosea's salvation oracles were considered inauthentic (so Marti 1904) simply on the basis of the prejudice that prophets

---

[1]The numbers in brackets correspond to the versification in the TNIV. Emmerson uses verse numbering based on Hebrew texts. For further on this, see the translators' footnotes in Hosea in the TNIV.

did not speak words of hope. However, it is thought that as Hosea's prophecies circulated in the South, those who followed him there began applying his message to their own situation, and thus the prophecy grew over time.

While it is up to close studies of the text (such as commentaries on the book) to argue this on the level of individual passages, it must be said that such critical conclusions restrict the future vision of the prophet (judgment and hope) as well as his concern for the whole people of God (North and South). Recent critical scholarship has been more open to Hosean authorship of larger parts of the book. In the words of Andersen and Freedman, "We believe that the book is essentially the work of a single person, and that the text is basically sound" (1980, 59; similarly Wolff 1965). Garrett's recent commentary supports the view of Hosea as an authorial unity and does not allow for later redactions.

Nonetheless, it is not impossible that later faithful followers of the prophet's tradition saw the analogy between the situation in the South some decades after the prophet's death and made the connection by inserting Judean concerns into the text. This may account for the occasionally awkward occurrences of Judah in the text.[2] Such additions would be part of the process of composition of the biblical book and do not in any way impugn the canonical authority of these texts (roughly similar to the updatings found in the Pentateuch).

> *It is possible that later faithful followers of the prophet's tradition saw the analogy between the situation in the South and made the connection by inserting Judean concerns into the text.*

Historical Period

Hosea's prophetic ministry probably began late in the reigns of Jeroboam II in the North and Uzziah in the South and ended early in Hezekiah's rule of the South (see Provan, Long, and Longman 2003, 266–77).

The beginning of his ministry accordingly took place during a period of expansion and prosperity in both North and South. Assyria was preoccupied with its northern and eastern borders (the Urartians were pressing its borders), and the Arameans were also in a weakened position (Davies 1992, 26); thus, Israel did not feel the pressure that normally was exerted on its northern borders (2 Kings 14:25). As may be seen also in the prophecy of Amos, which originates from this period, the increased prosperity of the land led not to increased faithfulness to Yahweh but rather to godlessness and abuse of power and privilege (Amos 3–6).

Hosea's focus is on the North, and here, after Jeroboam II, the political situation rapidly unwinds. Hubbard (1989, 24–25) succinctly summarizes the history by referring to "the dynastic instability that plagued Israel after Jeroboam's

---

[2]For instance, the mention of Judah in 12:2 draws attention to itself in the manner of its parallelism with Jacob in the second part of the verse as well as the context in which it appears. Thus with Emmerson (1984, 64) we say, "By the substitution of the name Judah for Israel the prophetic word of judgment has been applied to a new situation."

death and saw six kings toppled in thirty years, three of whom ruled two years or less and four of whom were assassinated (2 Kings 15; Hos. 7:7; 8:4; 10:3; 13:9–11), while the fifth was deposed (2 Kings 17:4–5)." The post–Jeroboam II period also saw a renewed, powerful, and aggressive Assyria, first led by Tiglath-Pileser III (745–727 BC), then by Shalmaneser V, who eventually began the conflict that led to the total defeat and annexation of the North to the Assyrian Empire in 722.

But before this final defeat took place, an important conflict took place between the northern and southern kingdoms that also influenced the book of Hosea. As has been mentioned, it was not long after Jeroboam II that Tiglath-Pileser III began to make incursions to the west. The first was in 738 BC, when he took Hamath. This shattered the tranquility of Syria-Palestine because the kings of Israel and Syria knew that the imperial interests of Assyria would not stop with Hamath. However, Rezin of Syria and Menahem of Israel tried to stave off aggression by paying tribute (2 Kings 15:19–20).

It would be four years before Tiglath-Pileser III would again return to the west, and in the meantime Pekah, apparently an anti-Assyrian usurper, assassinated Pekahiah, Menahem's son (2 Kings 15:23–25). He and Rezin of Syria then determined to throw off Assyrian vassalage. It is disputed, but likely, that they expected Egyptian help, but they definitely desired the aid of Judah, then ruled by Ahaz.

When Ahaz refused to join an anti-Assyrian coalition, Pekah and Rezin went to war against him to force him to do so (c. 735 BC). This war is commonly referred to as the Syro-Ephraimite War (2 Kings 16:1–9; 2 Chron. 28:5–7; Isa. 7:1–8:22; Mic. 7:7–20), and with the threat to his borders, Ahaz called on Tiglath-Pileser III to save him from his northern neighbors. The Assyrian king's attack on the North (c. 733) resulted in the exile of a portion of its population and the appointment of the pro-Assyrian Hoshea as king of the North. Although not as severe, the impact of this war also led to increased foreign interference in Judean politics as well, since the help of Tiglath-Pileser III did not come free (2 Kings 16:7–8).

A number of Hosea's oracles may be associated with these historical events,[3] but we will mention only a few (for fuller discussion, see Hubbard 1989, 25; and Davies 1992, 28–29). The opening of the book, for instance, contains a prophecy that the Lord will "soon punish the house of Jehu for the massacre at Jezreel" (1:4). This oracle may be dated to the time of Jeroboam II, anticipating the end of the house of Jehu, when Zechariah, Jeroboam's son and last of the dynasty,

---

[3]We should, however, note a disparity between those scholars who are optimistic about associating the oracles with historical events (see Wolff 1974) and those who are not (Andersen and Freedman 1980, 35).

was assassinated by Shallum (2 Kings 15:8–12). Davies (1992, 28) also suggests that 2:2–5, 8–13; 4:1–19; 12:2–10 belong to this early period characterized by economic success and religious impiety.

These and many other oracles show that Hosea's work is best understood in the light of the historical events that took place during the second half of the eighth century BC.

Hosea, the Man

The prophetic superscription introduces Hosea, who is not known outside of his book, by a typical patronymic; he is the "son of Beeri" (1:1).

The only personal information we gain from the book comes from the first three chapters; however, it is subject to great debate. No doubt surrounds the subject matter or the message of the chapters. The prophetic oracles reflect an early and striking use of the analogy between human marriage and God's relationship with his people (see Theological Message). Israel's rebellion against its divine partner is reflected in the infidelity of Hosea's wife. The children of this troubled marriage are given symbolic names indicative of the breaking of the covenant relationship between Yahweh and Israel (1:4, 6, 9).

The problems reside in the relationship between the analogy with history and the details of the marriage relationship as they are described in chapters 1–3. As has often been pointed out, even by those who choose another final conclusion, the text reads like a typical historical narrative. The tension arises because a straightforward reading of the text leads to the conclusion that God ordered Hosea to marry a whore. The problem begins with the divine command "Go, marry a promiscuous woman" (1:2).

The tension is felt by critical and conservative scholars alike. Some attempt a solution. For centuries it has been believed that, though there are no explicit signals in the text itself, the text must be read as a symbolic event and/or as a vision rather than as a historical event (Gressmann 1921; Young, *IOT*, 253). Stuart (1987, 11) also disdains the historical view and argues that Gomer is a harlot in the way that all the Israelites were, that is, she was an idolater. However, one wonders how that saves God's good character. Although he is not commanding the prophet to marry a woman who broke the seventh commandment, he is to marry one who broke the first two. Most ingenious is the solution of Wolff, who argues that Gomer was not a street prostitute, or even a temple prostitute. Rather, she simply took part in the bridal rituals of the Canaanites that involved a single act of cultic intercourse (Wolff 1974, xxii; see also Fensham 1984).

We cannot provide a definitive answer to this problem. Stuart is definitely right in saying that these chapters do not intend to provide us with a biography of Hosea (1987, 11). Nonetheless, it needs to be reemphasized that a straightforward reading of the text leads most naturally to the conclusion that Hosea was ordered by God to marry a promiscuous woman in order to symbolize God's relationship with Israel. It is methodologically dangerous to depart from this reading based on what we consider to be moral problems with the command, and indeed, this latter may be questioned. Nowhere does God command anyone but priests to avoid marriage with a prostitute (so Hill and Walton, citing Lev. 21:7, 14).[4]

In the midst of all the problems, we should not lose sight of the clear teaching of the section. Hosea's marriage with Gomer (whether historical, symbolic, allegorical, or visionary) is used by God to indicate both his disgust with and his love for his covenant people (see Theological Message).

LITERARY ANALYSIS

Genre and Forms of Speech

The book of Hosea is a prophecy, and as such is a collection of prophetic oracles. The superscription signals this genre classification when it describes the work as "the word of the LORD" (1:1).

Most of the book is poetic, with only two major sections of prose oracles (1:2–2:1 and 3:1–5). Typically, the poetic oracles are thought to have an oral origin, but this is uncertain. In any case, unless the original oral utterance of the prophet is wrongly given authoritative value over the literary form (correctly disputed by Yee 1987, 27–50), the issue makes no significant impact on the question of the interpretation of the book.

As in many areas, the prophetic oracles of Hosea 1–3 are much easier to delineate and describe than those found in Hosea 4–14 (see Structure). For instance, it is clear that Hosea 1:2–9 is a judgment speech (more specifically, a prophetic memoir used as a judgment speech) and 1:10–2:1 is a salvation speech.

In the case of Hosea 4–14, it is usually easy to distinguish salvation language from judgment by the tone, but it is much more difficult to distinguish individual oracles from one another. The book of Hosea lacks a number of the typical introductory phrases (such as "thus says the LORD") and closing phrases that are found in other prophecies. It is also difficult to be more specific in distinguishing particular types of, say, judgment oracles, though Wolff (1965, xxiii–xxiv) has correctly emphasized the pervasive legal language found in Hosea's speech.

---

[4]Andrew E. Hill and John H. Walton, *A Survey of the Old Testament*, 2nd ed. (Grand Rapids: Zondervan, 2000), 468. Space does not allow us to engage a number of issues related to Hosea's marriage, for example, the relationship between the women in chapters 1 and 3 or whether chapter 2 continues the story or is a metaphorical use of the historical marriage. For fuller accounts and discussions, see Rowley, Stuart, McComiskey, and Andersen and Freedman.

It is also noteworthy to recognize and distinguish first-person speech about God (divine speech) and third-person speech about him (prophetic speech), though Davies rightly points out that the confusion and subtle shifts between the two may point to Hosea's close identification with God (1992, 34–35).

Structure

Hosea's structure is difficult. While the first three chapters may easily be divided into sections on which the majority of commentators agree, the last eleven chapters may be delineated only in broad outline. We must admit that any general outline of the book misses some of the rapid and subtle transitions of the prophecy and must be taken only as a beginning guide through the book.

Everyone agrees that there is a major break between Hosea 1–3 and 4–14. The marriage analogy dominates through the first part, but the large second part of the book uses a multitude of images.

A further division between chapters 11 and 12 may also be argued, resulting in two cycles of judgment and hope in chapters 4–14, which parallel the twofold transition from judgment (1:2–9; 2:2–13) to hope (1:10–2:1; 2:14–3:5, which may be further broken down into two separate salvation oracles: 2:14–23; 3:1–5). Other scholars have recognized this threefold division of Hosea, notably Wolff (1974, xxix–xxxii) and Yee (1987, 51).

Superscription (1:1)
  I. Hosea's troubled marriage reflects God's relationship with Israel (1:2–3:5)
    A. Hosea, Gomer, and their children (1:2–2:1)
      1. Prophetic sign-act of judgment (1:2–9)
      2. The relationship restored (1:10–2:1)
    B. The Lord's marriage to Israel (2:2–23)
      1. The relationship broken (2:2–13)
      2. The relationship restored (2:14–23)
    C. Hosea's restored marriage relationship (3:1–5)
  II. First prophetic cycle (4:1–11:11)
    A. God accuses Israel of unfaithfulness (4:1–19)
    B. God punishes Israel (5:1–15)
    C. Hosea's call to repentance ignored (6:1–7:16)
    D. God punishes Israel for rejecting him (8:1–10:15)
    E. God's love for Israel overwhelms his anger (11:1–11)
  III. Second prophetic cycle (11:12–14:8)
    A. Israel sins against God (11:12–12:14)
    B. God is angry with his people (13:1–16)
    C. Israel repents and is blessed (14:1–8)
Wisdom colophon (14:9)

LITERARY STYLE

As mentioned above, the book is primarily poetic, though prose is found in two major places (1:1–2:1 and 3:1–5).[5] The single most striking feature of the poetic/literary nature of the book is its use of metaphor and simile.

These images may be divided in the main into two types, based on their referent: God or Israel. A second line of demarcation arises as to whether God's attitude toward Israel is positive or negative. For instance, God is a jealous husband (2:2–13), a frustrated shepherd (4:16), a destructive moth or undesired rot (5:12), a ferocious lion (5:14, cf. also 13:7–8), and a trapper (7:12). On the other hand, he is also a forgiving husband (3:1–5), a healing physician (6:1–2), the revivifying rains (6:3), a loving parent (11:3–4), a protecting lion (11:10–11), a life-giving dew (14:5), and a fertile pine tree (14:8).

The book most notably and frequently describes Israel, in particular the northern kingdom but on occasion including the southern kingdom, as an unfaithful wife (1:2–9; 3:1–5; 9:1). Other more local images describe Israel as the rapidly disappearing morning mist (6:5), hot ovens (7:4–7), a silly dove (7:11), a faulty bow (7:16), and a wild donkey (8:9). God's coming judgment upon Israel is likened to harvesting the whirlwind (8:7), the washing away of debris (10:7), and the yoking of a recalcitrant heifer (10:11).

Other literary devices support these images, perhaps the most important of which is the use of wordplay. Hosea's children are called "Jezreel," because God will punish the house of Jehu for the sin that took place in the valley of Jezreel; Lo-Ruhamah ("no compassion"), because God will no longer have compassion on Israel; and Lo-Ammi ("not my people"), because he disowns Israel as his people. Also notable is the wordplay that takes place between Ephraim (*'eprayîm*), wild ass (*pr'*), and fruitfulness (*pry*).

THEOLOGICAL MESSAGE

Hosea is a profound book that is difficult to summarize. The prophet presents us with a plethora of metaphors concerning God and his relationship to his people, only some of which we will touch upon here.

The Covenant

As with all the prophets, the covenant, particularly the Mosaic covenant, underlies and motivates much of Hosea's message (see Brueggemann 1968).

---

[5]This statement simplifies the argument somewhat, since there are some who argue that Hosea's poetry at times contains a number of prose elements. Andersen and Freeman (1980, 60–66), for instance, do a statistical analysis of these elements in the book and conclude that the book is not clearly categorized as either poetry or prose.

Thus we agree with Stuart (1987, 6–7) when he writes, "Understanding the message of the book of Hosea depends upon understanding the Sinai covenant. The book contains a series of blessings and curses announced for Israel by God through Hosea. Each blessing or curse is based upon a corresponding type in the Mosaic law."

Stuart draws innumerable connections between Hosea's judgment speeches and specific covenant curses. One example of many is his analysis of Hosea 4:10–11a (his translation):

> They will eat but not be satisfied;
>> they will practice prostitution but not break forth,
>> because they have abandoned Yahweh, to revere prostitution.

He rightly categorizes this judgment speech as derived from covenant curses of "hunger and infertility" and cites Deuteronomy 28:17–18 and 32:24–28 in support.

Occasionally Hosea will be explicit about the role of the covenant in his message. The Israelites will experience judgment because they have broken the covenant (6:7; 8:1).

Hosea's Marriage

We noted above the symbolic-theological use of Hosea's marriage. Hosea was commanded to marry a woman whose unfaithfulness represented Israel's infidelity to God. Hosea was one of the first to so draw a connection; the relationship between human marriage and the divine-human covenant was a close one that continued to be used throughout Scripture (see Approaching the New Testament below). Ortlund has recognized that this theme of sexual infidelity is found earlier in the Pentateuch in passages like Exodus 34:11–16 and Deuteronomy 31:16. After all, there are only two relationships that are appropriately exclusive: marriage and covenant. Rivals could not be tolerated in either relationship. Thus Gomer's sexual promiscuity paralleled the Israelites' religious promiscuity.

Although Hosea explores the relationship between a marriage gone bad and idolatry primarily in the first three chapters of the book, it is not absent from the rest (see particularly 6:10; 7:4; 9:1).

In a recent book, Y. Sherwood (1996) has provided a postmodern feminist reading of the marriage of Hosea and Gomer. She fittingly critiques those views that try to explain away the relationship as visionary or metaphorical only. However, as a feminist she questions what she considers Hosea and Yahweh's abusive treatment of this woman and her children. In addition, she reads between the lines to recover a compassionate Gomer. Of course, in this reading she departs from the perspective of the text itself. (For an excellent critique, which includes appreciation for positive contributions, see Garrett 1997, 124–33.)

Judgment and Salvation

From the foundation of covenant, which is symbolized by marriage, flows God's judgment of a disobedient Israel and also the hope of God's future salvation (see Structure above).

Israel's disobedience manifested itself in many ways, but underlying it all was their apostasy. They left the worship of the true God and substituted idols in his place (see 4:1–13; 5:11; 8:6; 13:2). In particular, it is the leaders of Israel who have led the people astray: the priests (4:6; 5:1; 6:9; 10:5), the prophets (4:5), and the political rulers (5:1, 10; 7:3–7; 9:15). But it is thus that God's "people are destroyed from lack of knowledge" (4:6). Their lack of trust in God was also manifested in their readiness to enter into foreign alliances to solve their foreign policy woes rather than trust in the sovereign God who promised to protect them (5:13; 7:8–10; 8:9).

Thus, God threatens to punish them severely. We have listed above under Literary Style the many metaphors Hosea uses to describe that coming judgment. One further metaphor comes from the historical traditions of Israel.[6] Hosea likens the coming judgment to a return to the wilderness. They will once again wander away from God (2:14). In historical retrospect, the immediate fulfillment of his prophetic word came first when the northern tribes were defeated by Assyrian forces in 722 BC and then in 586 when Babylon completely subdued Judah, destroyed the temple, and placed most of the survivors in exile.

Nonetheless, Hosea's message of judgment gives way to a note of hope for the future. In perhaps one of the most profound passages of the book, Hosea describes God's inner turmoil concerning his people:

> How can I give you up, Ephraim?
>   How can I hand you over, Israel?
> How can I treat you like Admah?
>   How can I make you like Zeboyim?
> My heart is changed within me;
>   all my compassion is aroused.
> I will not carry out my fierce anger,
>   nor will I devastate Ephraim again.
> For I am God, and not a human being—
>   the Holy One among you.
>   I will not come against their cities. (11:8–9)

God will not leave his people under judgment and in exile forever. He will cause Israel to experience a second exodus (2:14–15). In the end, he will heal

> *Israel's disobedience manifested itself in many ways, but underlying it all was their apostasy. They left the worship of the true God and substituted idols in his place.*

---

[6]Space does not permit a full treatment of Hosea's use of Israel's historical traditions, but see especially Daniels 1990.

Israel of the wounds caused by their disobedience and reestablish them in the land (14:1–9).

APPROACHING THE NEW TESTAMENT

There are a few, but highly significant quotations from Hosea in the New Testament. Paul (Rom. 9:25) and Peter (1 Peter 2:10; cf. Hos. 1:6, 9; 2:1, 22) both cite the negative to positive use of the prophet's children's names to support their contention that the Gentiles are now a part of the people of God. Hosea's sarcastic call to personified Death (perhaps reflecting the Canaanite god Mot): "Where, O death, are your plagues? Where, O grave, is your destruction?" (13:14) is cited by Paul when he celebrates Christ's victory over death (1 Cor. 15:55). Lastly, and most difficult, is the quotation of Hosea 11:1 ("When Israel was a child, I loved him, and out of Egypt I called my son.") in Matthew 2:15 as a prophecy of the return of Jesus from his short sojourn in Egypt.

This latter, however, must be understood in the light of the New Testament belief that Jesus was the righteous Son of God who, unlike the Israelites, was obedient to his heavenly Father. Thus much of the gospel, particularly the gospel of Matthew, is a reflection of the book of Exodus (see Stock).

A last theme we will mention that extends from Hosea, through other prophets (Jeremiah and Ezekiel in particular) and into the New Testament is the idea that the divine-human covenant is mirrored by human marriage (see Stienstra 1993). Ephesians 5:22–33 is the most explicit development of this theme from a Christian perspective.

CHAPTER TWENTY-SIX

JOEL

The book of Joel is attributed in its superscription (1:1) to an otherwise unknown Joel, son of Pethuel. Although another dozen persons mentioned in the Old Testament are named Joel, the prophet cannot with confidence be associated with any of these other individuals. The fact that no other information is included in the superscription may imply that Joel was well known to his contemporaries and that further identification was unnecessary. The prophet presumably lived in the environs of Jerusalem which provide the setting for the book. Because of his familiarity with the temple and concern with worship there, some have identified him as a cultic or temple prophet (Kapelrud; Ahlström).

BIBLIOGRAPHY

Commentaries

L. L. **Allen,** *The Books of Joel, Obadiah, Jonah, and Micah* (NICOT; Eerdmans, 1976); J. A. **Bewer,** *The Book of Joel* (ICC; T. & T. Clark, 1911); M. **Biè,** *Das Buch Joel* (Berlin: Evang. Verlagsanstalt, 1960); P. **Craigie,** *Twelve Prophets,* vol. 1 (DSB; Westminster, 1984); R. B. **Dillard,** "Joel," in *The Minor Prophets: An Exegetical and Expository Commentary,* ed. T. E. Comiskey (Baker, 1992); T. **Finely,** *Joel, Amos, Obadiah* (WEC; Moody, 1990); D. **Garrett,** *Hosea. Joel* (NAC: Broadman, 1997); D. R. **Jones,** *Isaiah 56–66 and Joel* (TBC; SCM, 1972); C. A. **Keller,** *Joël, Abdias, Jonas* (CAT 11a; Neuchâtel: Delachaux et Niestlé, 1965); M. G. **Kline,** *Images of the Spirit* (Baker, 1980); S. **Romerowski,** *Les livres de Joël et d'Abdias* (CEB; Vaux-sur-Seine: Édifac, 1989); W. **Rudolph,** *Joel, Amos, Obadia, Jona* (KAT 13/2; Gütersloh: Mohn, 1971); D. **Stuart,** *Hosea–Jonah* (WBC 31; Word, 1987); J. D. W. **Watts,** *The Books of Joel, Obadiah, Nahum, Habbakuk and Zephaniah* (CBC; London: Cambridge University Press, 1975); A. **Weiser,** *Die Propheten Hosea, Joel, Amos, Obadja, Jona, Micha* (ATD 24; Göttingen: Vandenhoeck und Ruprecht, 1979); H. W. **Wolff,** *Dodekapropheten: Joel* (BKAT 14/5; Neukirchen: Neukirchen

Verlag, 1963); idem, *Joel and Amos,* trans. W. Janzen et al. (Hermeneia; Fortress, 1977).

Monographs and Articles

G. W. **Ahlström,** *Joel and the Temple Cult of Jerusalem* (VTSup 21; Leiden: Brill, 1971); S. **Baron,** *The Desert Locust* (Scribner, 1971); W. **Baumgartner,** "Joel 1 and 2," in *Karl Budde zum siebzigsten Geburtstag,* ed. Karl Marti (*BZAW* 34; Giessen, 1920): 10–19; J. **Bourke,** "Le Jour de Yahve dans Joel," *RB* (1959): 5–31, 191–212; B. **Duhm,** *The Twelve Prophets* (Adam and Charles Black, 1912); C. A. **Evans,** "The Prophetic Setting of the Pentecost Sermon," *ZNW* 74 (1983); Y. **Freund,** "Multitudes, Multitudes in the Valley of Decision," *Beth Mikra* 65 (1975): 271–77; G. B. **Gray,** "The Parallel Passages of Joel and Their Bearing on the Question of Date," *Expositor* 8 (1893): 208–25; A. S. **Kapelrud,** *Joel Studies* (Uppsala: Almqvust och Wiksell, 1948); L. **Keimer,** "Pendeloques en forme d'insectes faisant partie de colliers égyptiens," *Annales de Service des Antiquités de l'Egypte* 32 (1932): 129–50; 33 (1933): 97–130; 37 (1937): 143–64; A. **Kerrigan,** "The Sensus Plenior of Joel III:1–5 in Act.II:14–36," *Sacra Pagina* 2 (1959): 295–313; E. **Kutsch,** "Heuschreckenplage und Tag Jahwes in Joel 1 und 2," *TZ* 18 (1962): 81–94; J. M. **Myers,** "Some Considerations Bearing on the Date of Joel," *ZAW* 74 (1962): 177–95; G. **Ogden,** "Joel 4 and Prophetic Response to National Laments," *JSOT* 26 (1983): 97–106; W. S. **Prinsloo,** *The Theology of the Book of Joel* (*BZAW* 163; Berlin: Walter de Gruyter, 1985); B. **Reicke,** "Joel und seine Zeit," *ATANT* (Fs. Walter Eichrodt): 59 (1970): 133–41; W. **Rudolph,** "Wann wirke Joel?" *BZAW* 105 (1967): 193–98; O. R. **Sellers,** "Stages of Locust in Joel," *AJSL* 52 (1935–36): 81–85; F. R. **Stephenson,** "The Date of the Book of Joel," *VT* 19 (1969): 224–29; J. A. **Thompson,** "The Date of Joel," in *A Light Unto My Path,* Fs. J. M. Myers; ed. A. Bream et al. (Philadelphia: Temple University Press, 1974); idem, "Joel's Locusts in the Light of Near Eastern Parallels," *JNES* 14 (1955): 52–55; idem, "The Use of Repetition in the Prophecy of Joel," *On Language, Culture, and Religion,* Fs. E. A. Nida; ed. M. Black (Hague: Mouton, 1974): 101–10; M. **Treves,** "The Date of Joel," *VT* 7 (1957): 149–56; J. D. **Whiting,** "Jerusalem's Locust Plague," *National Geographic* 28, 6 (1915): 511–50.

HISTORICAL BACKGROUND

We may outline Joel as follows:

> Superscription (1:1)
>   I. The locust plague: the immediate disaster (1:2–20)
>   A. Effect and extent of the disaster (1:2–12)
>   1. Elders and citizens (1:2–4)
>   2. Drunkards (1:5–7)

Since we know little about the prophet himself, we are forced to examine the internal evidence of the book to determine the sociological, religious, political, and cultural milieu in which he lived in the hopes that it may provide additional information about the date and intent of the book.

1. Most would agree that the book was written sometime after the outbreak of a locust plague (chap. 1). However, such outbreaks were probably reasonably common; even if we had some source reporting the history of such outbreaks, we would probably not be able to date the one reported in the book.

2. The book presumes the existence and routine operation of the temple (1:9, 13–16; 2:15–17); for this reason a date between 586 and 516 BC can be eliminated with confidence.

3. A number of other nations are mentioned, primarily as enemies on whom the Lord will take vengeance (Phoenicians, Philistines, Egypt, Edom, the Greeks, and Sabeans—chap. 3 [MT 4]). However, these are largely traditional enemies of Israel; it is probably not possible to assign the date of the book to a period in which these particular foes were known to be active. Greek trade in

the Levant is known from Assyriological sources as early as the eighth century (3:6 [MT 4:6]). Although the Sabeans dominated trade routes to the east in the fifth century (3:8 [MT 4:8]), they were also active in trade in the Solomonic period (1 Kings 10; 2 Chron. 9).

What is striking in this regard is less the names that are mentioned than those that are not. One cannot but notice the absence of any reference to the Assyrians or Babylonians, those powers whose military conquests had the greatest impact on Israel and Judah. Although it is, of course, an argument from silence, this suggests that the book was prior to the hegemony of Assyria along the Mediterranean coast (mid-eighth century) or after the fall of Babylon (late sixth century).

> *What is striking in the book is less the names that are mentioned than those that are not. One cannot but notice the absence of any reference to the Assyrians or Babylonians.*

4. The book presumes a situation in which the leadership of the community is in the hands of elders and priests (1:2, 13; 2:16); there is no mention of kings or royal officials. Although once again it is an argument from silence, this suggests a period either without a monarchy (postexilic period) or in which the monarchy has a limited role (such as the minority of Joash in the late ninth century—1 Kings 11–12; 2 Chron. 23–24).

5. Also as an argument from silence, there is no mention of the northern kingdom. The designation of Judah as "Israel" (2:27; 3:2, 16 [MT 4:2, 16]) most naturally presumes a time when the northern tribes had been carried into exile (722 BC), since designating Judah as "Israel" is more common in postexilic books.

6. There are numerous agreements in phraseology and concepts between Joel and other prophetic books. This can be explained in several ways: (1) Joel may have made extensive use of earlier prophetic literature; (2) his prophecy may have had a decided impact on those who followed and cited his work; (3) Joel often employed a common stock of prophetic idioms and was not really dependent on other compositions; or (4) each citation must be evaluated on its own merits to determine whether Joel used or was used by others. Most have concluded that Joel was dependent on the earlier texts (see Gray 1893).

7. The theological concepts in the book may also provide evidence for the date of its composition. God did not reveal himself to Israel all at once, but instead gradually unfolded the nature of his relationship to Israel over a period of time through the prophets. In many instances one can trace the way in which particular themes, motifs, or images were successively used and modified through time so that the development of a particular concept can be arrayed in a chronological order. Joel's portrayal of the nations assembled for battle against the Lord (3:9–17 [MT 4:9–17]) is found primarily in late materials (Ezek. 38–39; Zech. 12:1–5; 14:1–7; cf. Isa. 66:18). The description of a fountain flowing from the temple (3:18 [MT 4:18]) is also found in Ezekiel 47:1–12 and Zechariah 14:3–8. Although these examples are drawn from the later stages in the growth of biblical literature, it is at least possible that they depended on ear-

lier materials; once again it is difficult to make confident assertions regarding the date of Joel from this evidence.

8. Earlier scholarship often regarded the references to the wall of the city (2:7, 9) as implying that the date of the book was after the completion of the city wall by Nehemiah. This line of argument is now largely abandoned. Although extensive damage was done to the walls of Jerusalem (Jer. 52:14; 2 Kings 25:10; 2 Chron. 36:19), the statements that at the time of Nehemiah the *breaches* in the wall were repaired (Neh. 2:13; 3:8; 4:1) indicates that the entire wall was not leveled during the destruction of the city in 586 BC; furthermore, had the walls been leveled in their entirety, Nehemiah and his workers could scarcely have completed the repairs in fifty-two days (Neh. 6:15). Ahlström (1971, 114–15) compares the references to the wall in 2:7, 9 to the reference to the temple in Jeremiah 41:5: though the temple had been destroyed, individuals could still bring offerings "to the house of the LORD"; sufficient structure remained after the destruction that the temple could still be identified, and mentioning it did not imply in this context that it had already been rebuilt. Garrett (1997) recently has disputed this view by claiming that an army is said to scale the wall. If it had breeches in it, why would they have to scale it? However, even a fallen wall provides something of a barrier that would need to be overcome. And in any case, as he himself points out, this invasion is likely visionary.

9. References to the dispersion of the Jews into surrounding lands (3:1–2 [MT 4:1–2]) may also suggest a postexilic date, though such scattering was by no means limited to the actions of the Babylonians (Zech. 1:18–21 [MT 2:1–4]). Population relocation was a routine policy of the Assyrians; the annals of Sennacherib report that he had already subjected Judah to a major deportation, so that references to a Diaspora need not refer to the Babylonian captivity alone.

10. Arguments from style and date of language are largely inconclusive. While many linguistic features of Joel are held in common with late biblical books, we lack sufficient data to determine whether these features were innovations later in the development of Hebrew or simply coincidences. Arguments from language can have a corroborative role for other arguments, but we lack a sufficient corpus to use them with confidence. Many linguistic features that have been identified as late have been disputed by Kapelrud (1948, 86–87, 111–12) and Ahlström (1971, 1–22).

11. The position of Joel in the Hebrew canon between the eighth-century prophecies of Hosea and Amos has been taken by many as indicative of date; however, in the LXX Joel was found after Micah. Its position between Hosea and Amos is probably the result of the similarities between Amos 1:2; 9:13 and Joel 3:16, 18 [MT 4:16, 18] and the fact that both Amos and Joel mention Tyre, the Philistines, and Edom (Allen 1976, 21).

12. Although once again an argument from silence, it is worth noting the absence of any polemic against syncretized worship or the worship of foreign

deities, indictments so characteristic of preexilic prophecy. Even if idolatry had been briefly suppressed at the time of Joash, one would at least expect some references to it in Joel's preaching, especially since the book is taken up with issues of rainfall and fertility, areas of concern in fertility cults and the particular areas of Baal's expertise as a storm deity. Kapelrud (1948) did attempt to read Joel's concern with fertility against the backdrop of Canaanite fertility religion, but by and large his efforts have not proved convincing.

This survey of the major lines of evidence cited for establishing the date of Joel is inconclusive, though it is fair to say that it also tilts toward a date in the postexilic period. In the history of scholarship a wide variety of dates have been proposed for the book. Here is a representative list of some of the dates proposed by various scholars; see the more detailed discussion in Prinsloo (1985, 5–8) and Allen (1976, 19–24):

- Ninth century, time of Joash: K. A. Credner, G. C. Aalders, E. J. Young, M. Bič̈y
- Late seventh century: A. S. Kapelrud, C. A. Keller, K. Koch; D. Garrett
- Early sixth century: W. Rudolph
- Late sixth century to mid-fifth: W. F. Albright, J. M. Myers, B. Reicke, G. W. Ahlström, L. L. Allen
- Late fifth century to mid-fourth: A. Weiser, H. W. Wolff, J. A. Bewer, F. R. Stephenson
- Early third century: M. Treves
- As late as second century: B. Duhm

Stuart (1987, 226) associates the impetus for the book with invasions of Judah by the Assyrians or Babylonians in 701, 598, or 588 BC.

In spite of Delitzsch's judgment that the "bringing down of Joel into a postexilic age by Duhm, Merx, Stade, and others, is one of the most rotten fruits of criticism,"[1] the position argued by Ahlström, Myers, and Allen appears to represent the best handling of the evidence.

LITERARY ANALYSIS

The fact that the book of Joel so resists attempts to date it may in part reflect another important characteristic of the book. Several features suggest that the book of Joel as a whole is either a liturgical text intended for repeated use on occasions of national lament or at least a historical example of one such lament.

Several features suggest that the book of Joel as a whole is either a liturgical text intended for repeated use on occasions of national lament or at least a historical example of one such lament.

---

[1]*Old Testament History of Redemption,* trans. S. Curtiss (Scribner and Welford, 1881), 113.

Some psalms appear to have been composed for such occasions, and a few narratives also provide examples of the practice. In times of natural disaster or military threat, (1) the people were often summoned to a fast at a sanctuary (Joel 1:13–14; 2:15–17; cf. 2 Chron. 20:3–4; 1 Kings 21:9–12; Isa. 22:12; 32:11–14; Ezra 8:21; Jer. 36:8–10; 49:3–6; Jonah 3:7–8), where (2) they would present their complaint to God in prayer and remind him of his past mercies (Joel 1:2–12, 15–20; 2:1–11; cf. 2 Chron. 20:5–13; Pss. 12:1–4; 60:1–5; 85:1–7) and (3) receive an answer of weal or woe from God (Joel 2:12–3:21 [MT 4:21]; cf. 2 Chron. 20:14–17; Pss. 12:5–6; 60:6–12; 85:8–13). (See R. B. Dillard, *2 Chronicles* [WBC 15; Word, 1987], 154–55; Ogden 1983, 97–106.)

If the book of Joel was intended to serve as part of a liturgy at the temple, the difficulty in dating the book is all the more easily understood. Repeated liturgical use would call for a composition that could be used on many different occasions, whether natural or military disaster threatened. Specific historical references would narrow the range of events to which the text could be applied or for which it could be used liturgically. Note also how the text is "dehistoricized" in reference to the confession of sin: although the text calls for repentance (1:13–14; 2:13–14), no particular sin is mentioned as causing the plight of the people. The less specific a liturgical text is, the wider the range of its applicability. This feature of the book may help explain not only why it is so difficult to date, but also how it achieves the kind of timelessness that makes it such powerful literature in our own day.

Up until the early part of this century, the unity of the book of Joel remained essentially unchallenged. However, early in the twentieth century B. Duhm (1912) advanced the argument that the book consisted of the work of at least two different individuals. A preexilic prophet delivered oracles concerning a local locust outbreak; his utterances constitute the bulk of 1:1–2:27. A later apocalypticist assigned to the Maccabean period incorporated this earlier prophet's work into his own utterances regarding the Day of the Lord. Duhm attributed 2:28–3:21 [MT 3:1–4:21]; 1:15; 2:1–2, 10–11 to this later figure. Other scholars followed Duhm's lead, but with minor modifications.

More recent scholarship (Allen, Chary, Dillard, Garrett, Kapelrud, Keller, Myers, Romerowski, Rudolph, Stuart, Thompson, Weiser, Wolff) has tended to view the book as the composition of a single author, though possibly including smaller redactional additions. The most influential argument in favor of the essential unity of the book derives from appreciating the literary structure of the book as a lament. Those passages identified as interpolations from a later writer into chapters 1–2 are viewed as integrally related to their context.

The relationship between the descriptions of the locust plague in chapter 1 and 2:1–11 is one of the major debates in the history of the exegesis of Joel. There are a number of representative positions with intermediate variations, each having advocates both ancient and modern. We will sketch the representative approaches under three categories.

1. Some interpreters regard chapter 2 as containing simply another description either (1) of the same locust plague or (2) of the outbreak of a historical locust plague in the season following that described in chapter 1. This approach in effect denies the metaphorical character of chapter 2 and argues instead that actual locusts are described as God's army (2:25). No one seriously disputes that locusts are described in 2:1–11 and that the phenomena described there (darkness, noise, invincibility, being driven by the wind into the sea, stench, etc.) reflect the realities of a locust plague. Moreover, the statement (2:25) that the Lord would repay Judah for the years devoured by the locusts may imply more than one outbreak.

2. Others regard the description in chapter 2 as either (1) metaphorical for an anticipated invasion by a foreign army, one of Israel's traditional foes, or (2) allegorical for all of Israel's traditional enemies. On this approach, a recent locust outbreak (chap. 1) becomes the harbinger of an even greater invasion by a historical foe. A recent commentator who identified the foe in 2:1–11 with the Assyrians or Babylonians was Douglas Stuart (1987, 206, 232–34, 250). Stuart also considers the description of the locust plague in chapter 1 to be metaphorical for a historical enemy. The invaders are described as an army on the march; the consequence of their invasion is that the Gentiles rule over Jerusalem (2:17). It is Gentile armies that are judged in 3:4–14, 19 [MT 4:4–14]), and Judah is promised that she will no longer be humiliated before the Gentiles (2:19, 26–27). All recognize some contact between Joel and Exodus 10; the locust plague in Exodus occurred in connection with a victory over the most powerful nation of that period, and victory over some other powerful nation should be expected in connection with Joel. Israel's traditional foes were primarily armies from the north (2:20). Other elements from the exodus events are reused by other prophets in reference to Assyria and Babylon (Stuart 1987, 234). Other traditional foes of Israel are also described as insects (Isa. 7:18). But some aspects of the text do not fit an actual army very well: the darkening of the sky (2:2), or leaping over the mountains (2:5). It would also be curious to find the locusts likened to an army if an army is what is actually intended; that is, the metaphor is in some sense neutralized by the simile (see the counterargument by Garrett [1997, 298–301], who takes a position similar to Stuart).

3. The approach favored by the majority of modern commentaries regards the second description of the locust invasion as an extended metaphor based on the locust outbreak described in chapter 1; the prophet uses the recent plague as a harbinger of the impending Day of the Lord, the day of judgment when the Lord himself would come at the head of his own heavenly army in Holy War against evil. The threat in this case would not be coming from some particular historical foe, but rather from the Lord's own army (2:11). This approach is favored by the extensive use of language in 2:1–11 that is most often reserved to

describe theophanies. It also preserves the metaphorical character of the language: God's army is often likened to human armies. Allen (1976, 64) describes the earlier motifs of the locust plague as "taken up and transposed into a higher key, a more strident setting and a faster pace" in 2:1–11, such that they cannot be reduced to another description of an encounter between Judah and a mass of insects. Moreover, in the concluding section of the book, the Lord promises Judah not only relief from the effects of the recent locust outbreak but also freedom from the eschatological day of judgment. All in Israel who call on the name of the Lord will be saved (2:32 [MT 3:5]), and the Lord will be a refuge for his people (3 [MT 4]:16), whereas the nations will then face the divine army (3 [MT 4]:1–3, 9–15). The fact that the prophet devotes so much space to his description of the removal of an apocalyptic threat suggests that his second description of a locust army was where this threat was originally introduced.

Each of these approaches and their variations yield reasonably plausible scenarios for understanding the relation of the two accounts, but the approach described last best reflects the flow of the argument in the book as a whole. Yet it must also be asked whether the ambiguity regarding the relationship of chapters 1 and 2 felt by modern readers of Joel is the fortuitous product of our not knowing the circumstances of its original composition, or whether such ambiguity is the deliberate product of the author. If Joel is indeed a liturgical text, the very ambiguity within the book would facilitate its use and application in contexts other than that which originally prompted the book, and in this sense it could be a deliberate ambiguity.

THEOLOGICAL MESSAGE

Joel preached the sovereignty, holiness, and compassion of God. The holy God would not ignore sin among his own elect people. The prophet saw in the outbreak of a locust plague the hand of God chastening and driving Israel to repentance. This locust outbreak was a warning that if Israel was not repentant, a yet more devastating army would come against the nation. Israel had so often anticipated and hoped for divine intrusion against her historical enemies. But Joel reverses that motif in a somewhat satirical parody (Kline 1980, 119–20): Israel had anticipated the protective presence of winged cherubim, the glorious retinue of the Divine Warrior; the Lord would bring winged warriors all right, but they would come to bring judgment on Israel as a cloud of locusts (2:1–11).

Israel had often anticipated and hoped for divine intrusion against her historical enemies. But Joel reverses that motif in a somewhat satirical parody.

But God's sovereignty was not confined to Israel. He rules over the affairs of all nations, and the angelic armies would yet come to vindicate God's name among the nations (chap. 3 [MT 4]). Joel portrays not simply the victory of Israel over a particular historical foe, as was often the case in oracles against foreign nations in other prophetic books, but a decisive universal and eschatological cosmic battle against evil on the Day of the Lord.

This terrible Day of Judgment on the nations would also be a day when God would show compassion and mercy to those among his people who were repentant and who called on the name of the Lord (2:32 [MT 3:5]).

APPROACHING THE NEW TESTAMENT

The church too needs to hear God's message to Israel through Joel—it remains true that God chastens those he loves (Prov. 3:11–12; Heb. 12:5–11) and that he will yet vindicate his name among the nations.

Joel is most familiar to Christians because of the extensive use made of 2:28–32 [MT 3:1–5] in the New Testament.

In the Old Testament the Spirit of God is preeminently the spirit that empowers and enables prophecy. Moses said, "I wish that all the LORD's people were prophets and that the LORD would put his Spirit on them" (Num. 11:29). Joel foresees a day when God would answer Moses' prayer and the Spirit of prophecy would be poured out on all his people (2:28–29). Peter saw the fulfillment of Joel's prophecy in the events of the Day of Pentecost (Acts 2:14–21) with its accompanying fire theophany (Joel 2:30 [MT 3:3]). The fire of the divine presence would not be a threat to the new Israel, the church, but rather would empower their speech.

In ancient Israel the sociological pecking order placed the older free Jewish male at the top. Most of Israel's prophets belonged to this group. An ancient prayer uttered at daybreak by the Jewish male reflects this structure; in the prayer a man thanks God that he was not born "a slave, a Gentile, or a woman." Joel's prayer envisages a change, for in the Israel Joel foresees, prophetic endowment will not be for men alone, but also for women ("daughters . . . men and women"), not for the older alone, but also for the young ("your sons and daughters . . . young men"), and not for the free alone, but also for the enslaved ("servants, both men and women"). Joel's reference to "all people" in 2:28 [MT 3:1] was to the citizens of Judah, but inasmuch as the new Israel, the church, consists of Jew and Gentile, even this barrier would fall. Paul may well have this passage in mind when he says that in Christ "there is neither Jew nor Gentile, neither slave nor free, neither male nor female, for you are all one in Christ Jesus" (Gal. 3:28). In Romans 10:12–13 Paul cites Joel 2:32 [MT 3:5] in his argument that "there is no difference between Jew and Gentile"; the "all who call" must include both. Although in Joel this section is addressed to Israel alone, Paul interprets it as applying to the true Israel rather than simply Israel according to the flesh (Rom. 9:6–15). Those who call on the Lord are those whom he has called (Rom. 9:24; cf. Joel 2:32b [MT 3:5b]), both Jew and Gentile.

The same Spirit that empowered the prophets of old would also empower the church, for it too would receive power to bear witness for God after the Spirit came upon it (Acts 1:8). Protestant theology commonly speaks of the "priesthood of all believers"; perhaps we should speak too of the "prophethood of all believers."

The New Testament often speaks of "calling" on the Lord or the name of the Lord (Acts 4:9–12; 9:14, 21; 22:16; 1 Cor. 1:2; 2 Tim. 2:22). In this regard, they recall Peter's appeal to Joel 2:32 [MT 3:5] in his sermon on Pentecost (Acts 2:21). Peter leaves no doubt that "calling on the name of the Lord" meant calling on the name of Jesus, the only name by which we must be saved (Acts 4:12).

CHAPTER TWENTY-SEVEN

AMOS

Amos is not a large book, only nine chapters consisting of 146 verses and 2,042 words. However, in spite of its small size, it has been the object of intense study. In his volume *Understanding the Book of Amos,* G. Hasel (1991, 26) noted that in the three decades from the 1960s through the 1980s, sixty different commentaries on Amos appeared. Hasel also discovered more than eight hundred publications on this small book written in the period between 1969 and 1990. A bibliographical survey of resources for studying the book was published by A. van der Wal (1986). Not surprisingly, studies have continued up to the present day, but perhaps not with the same intensity.

BIBLIOGRAPHY

Commentaries

S. **Amsler,** *Amos* (Neuchâtel: Delachaux & Niestlé, 1982); F. I. **Andersen** and D. N. **Freedman,** *Amos* (AB; Doubleday, 1989); A. G. **Auld,** *Amos* (Sheffield: JSOT, 1986); P. C. **Craigie,** *Twelve Prophets,* 2 vols. (DSB; Westminster, 1985); T. J. **Finley,** *Joel, Amos, Obadiah* (WEC; Moody, 1990); W. R. **Harper,** *Amos and Hosea* (ICC; T. & T. Clark, 1905); D. A. **Hubbard,** *Joel and Amos* (TOTC; InterVarsity Press, 1989); J. **Jeremias,** *The Book of Amos* (OTL; Westminster John Knox, 1998); J. **Limburg,** *Hosea–Micah* (Interp; John Knox, 1988); R. **Martin-Achard** and S. Paul **Re'emi,** *Amos and Lamentations* (ITC; Eerdmans, 1984); J. L. **Mays,** *Amos* (OTL; Westminster, 1979); J. A. **Motyer,** *Amos: The Day of the Lion* (BST; InterVarsity Press, 1974); J. **Niehaus,** *"Amos"* in *The Minor Prophets: An Exegetical and Expository Commentary,* ed. T. E. McComiskey (Baker, 1992); S. M. **Paul,** *Amos: A Commentary on the Book of Amos* (Hermeneia; Fortress, 1991); W. **Rudolph,** *Joel, Amos, Obadja, Jona* (*KAT*; Gütersloh: Gütersloher Verlagshaus Gerd Mohn, 1971); B. K. **Smith,** *"Amos,"* in *Amos, Obadiah, Jonah* (NAC; Broadman, 1995), 23–170; G. A. **Smith,** *The Book of the Twelve Prophets,* 2 vols. (Armstrong, 1928); G. V.

Smith, *Amos: A Commentary* (Zondervan, 1988); idem, *Hosea/Amos/Micah* (NIVAC; Zondervan, 2001); R. **Soggin,** *The Prophet Amos: A Translation and Commentary* (SCM, 1987); D. **Stuart,** *Hosea–Jonah* (WBC 31; Word, 1987); B. **Vawter,** *Amos, Hosea, Micah, with an Excursus on Old Testament Priesthood* (OTM; Wilmington: Michael Glazier, 1981); J. D. W. **Watts,** *Vision and Prophecy in Amos* (Leiden: Brill, 1958); H. W. **Wolff,** *Joel and Amos* (Hermeneia; Fortress, 1977).

Monographs and Articles

B. **Alger,** "The Theology and Social Ethics of Amos," *Scripture* 17 (1965): 109–16, 318–28; L. C. **Allen,** "Amos, Prophet of Solidarity," *Vox Evangelica* 6 (1969): 42–53; S. **Amsler,** "Amos, prophéte de la onziéme heure," *TZ* 21 (1965): 318–28; J. G. **Bailey,** "Amos, Preacher of Social Reform," *The Bible Today* 19 (1981): 306–13; H. M. **Barstad,** *The Religious Polemics of Amos* (Leiden: Brill, 1984); J. **Barton,** *Amos's Oracles Against the Nations: A Study of Amos 1:3–2:5* (Cambridge University Press, 1980); J. **Bright,** "A New View of Amos," *Interp* 25 (1971): 355–58; R. **Coote,** *Amos Among the Prophets: Composition and Theology* (Philadelphia: Fortress, 1981); P. **Craigie,** "Amos the *nôqēd* in the Light of Ugaritic," *Studies in Religion* 11 (1982): 29–33; idem, "The Tablets from Ugarit and Their Importance for Biblical Studies," *BAR* 9 (1983): 62–73; J. **Dearman,** *Property Rights in the Eighth-Century Prophets: The Conflict and Its Background* (Atlanta: Scholars, 1988); J. **de Waard,** "The Chiastic Structure of Amos v 1–17," *VT* 27 (1977): 170–77; idem, "Translation Techniques Used by the Greek Translators of Amos," *Bib* 59 (1978): 339–50; J. **de Waard** and W. A. **Smalley,** *A Translator's Handbook on the Book of Amos* (United Bible Societies, 1979); R. B. **Dillard,** "Remnant," *Baker Encyclopedia of the Bible* (Baker, 1988): 2:1833–36; W. J. **Doorly,** *Prophet of Justice: Understanding the Book of Amos* (New York: Paulist, 1989); L. **Epstein,** *Social Justice in the Ancient Near East and the People of the Bible* (SCM, 1986); D. N. **Freedman,** "Confrontations in the Book of Amos," *Princeton Sem Bul* 11 (1990): 240–52; D. A. **Garrett,** "The Structure of Amos as a Testimony to Its Integrity," *JETS* 27 (1984): 275–76; H. **Gese,** "Komposition bei Amos," VTSup 32 (1981): 74–95; J. B. **Geyer,** "Mythology and Culture in the Oracles Against the Nations," *VT* 36 (1986): 129–45; Y. **Gitay,** "A Study of Amos's Art of Speech: A Rhetorical Analysis of Amos 3:1–15," *CBQ* 42 (1980): 293–309; B. **Gosse,** "Le recueil d'oracles contre les nations du livre d'Amos et l' 'Histoire deuteronomique,'" *VT* 38 (1988): 22–40; G. **Hasel,** "The Alleged 'No' of Amos and Amos' Eschatology," *AUSS* 29 (1991): 3–18; idem, *Understanding the Book of Amos* (Baker, 1991); J. H. **Hayes,** *Amos, His Time and His Preaching: The Eighth-Century Prophet* (Abingdon, 1988); H. **Huffmon,** "The Covenant Lawsuit in the Prophets," *JBL* 78 (1959): 285–95; idem, "The Social Role of Amos' Message," in *The Quest for the Kingdom of God: Studies in Honor of G. E. Mendenhall,* ed. H. B. Huffmon et al. (Eisenbrauns, 1983); A. **Kapelrud,** "God as Destroyer in the

Preaching of Amos," *JBL* 71 (1952): 33–38; K. **Koch,** *Untersucht mit den Methoden einer strukturalen Formgeschichte* (Neukirchen-Vluyn: Verlag Butzon & Burcker Kevelaer, 1976); B. **Lang,** "The Social Organization of Peasant Poverty in Biblical Israel," in *Anthropological Approaches to the Old Testament,* ed. B. Lang (Fortress, 1985): 83–99; J. **Limburg,** "Sevenfold Structures in the Book of Amos," *JBL* 106 (1987): 217–22; T. E. **McComiskey,** "The Hymnic Elements of the Prophecy of Amos: A Study of Form-Critical Methodology," in *A Tribute to Gleason Archer,* ed. W. Kaiser and R. Youngblood (Moody, 1986), 105–28; R. **Melugin,** "The Formation of Amos: An Analysis of Exegetical Method," in *SBL 1978 Seminar Papers* (Missoula: Scholars, 1978), 369–91; D. L. **Petersen,** *The Social Roles of Israel's Prophets* (Sheffield: JSOT, 1981); M. E. **Polley,** *Amos and the Davidic Empire: A Socio-Historical Approach* (New York: Oxford University Press, 1989); I. **Provan,** V. P. **Long,** and T. **Longman** III, *A Biblical History of Israel* (Westminster John Knox, 2003); D. **Reid** and T. **Longman** III, *God Is a Warrior* (Zondervan, 1995); S. N. **Rosenbaum,** *Amos of Israel: A New Interpretation* (Macon: Mercer University Press, 1990); H. J. **Routtenberg,** *Amos of Tekoa: A Study in Interpretation* (Vantage, 1971); L. **Ryken,** "Amos," in *A Complete Literary Guide to the Bible,* ed. L. Ryken and T. Longman III (Zondervan, 1993), 337–47; W. **Schottroff,** "The Prophet Amos: A Socio-Historical Assessment of His Ministry," in *God of the Lowly: Socio-Historical Interpretations of the Bible,* ed. W. Schottroff et al. (Orbis, 1984), 27–46; F. H. **Seilhamer,** "The Role of the Covenant in the Mission and Message of Amos," *A Light unto My Path: Old Testament Studies in Honor of Jacob M. Myers,* ed. H. Bream et al. (Temple University Press, 1974), 435–51; L. A. **Sinclair,** "The Courtroom Motif in the Book of Amos," *JBL* 85 (1966): 351–53; W. A. **Smalley,** "Recursion Patterns and the Sectioning of Amos," *The Bible Translator 30* (1979): 118–27; A. S. **Super,** "Figures of Comparison in the Book of Amos," *Semitics* 1 (1970): 67–80; S. **Terrien,** "Amos and Wisdom," in *Israel's Prophetic Heritage: Essays in Honor of James Muilenburg,* ed. B. Anderson and W. Harrelson (Harper & Brothers, 1962), 108–15; B. A. **Thorogood,** *A Guide to the Book of Amos, with Thema Discussions on Judgement, Social Justice, Priest and Prophet* (London: SPCK, 1971); N. J. **Tromp,** "Amos V 1–17: Towards a Stylistic and Rhetorical Analysis," *OTSWA* 3 (1984): 65–85; A. **van der Wal,** *Amos: A Classified Bibliography,* 3rd ed. (Amsterdam: Free University Press, 1986); idem, "The Structure of Amos," *JSOT* 26 (1983): 107–13; B. **Vawter,** "Were the Prophets *nabî's?*" *Bib* 66 (1985): 206–19; L. **Walker,** "The Language of Amos," *SWJT* 9 (1966): 37–48; M. **Waltzer,** "Prophecy and Social Criticism," *The Drew Gateway* 55 (1984–84): 13–27; J. **Ward,** "The Eclipse of the Prophet in Contemporary Prophetic Studies," *USQR* 42 (1988): 97–104; D. L. **Williams,** "The Theology of Amos," *RvExp* 63 (1966): 393–403; H. G. M. **Williamson,** "The Prophet and the Plumb-line," in *In Quest of the Past,* ed. A. van der Woude (OTS 26; Leiden: Brill, 1990): 101–21.

AUTHORSHIP AND HISTORICAL BACKGROUND

The book tells us a lot about the man Amos. He lived in the first half of the eighth century during the reigns of Jeroboam II (793–753 BC) in Israel and Uzziah (791–740) in Judah (1:1). Estimates for how long Amos acted as a prophet vary from a single occasion consisting of a "twenty-minute harangue" (Rosenbaum 1990, 76, 100), a single day, or a few days to much longer periods; the book does not provide the information needed to make this decision. The superscription may suggest a relatively short period before a great earthquake (1:1; cf. Zech. 14:5).

His preaching is set in the northern kingdom against the backdrop of the great success that attended the reigns of Jeroboam and Uzziah. It was a period of unprecedented prosperity for the post-schism kingdoms (Provan, Long, and Longman 2003, 268–70). Under these two kings the territory of Israel and Judah had expanded to encompass almost all the land held during the empire of David and Solomon, just as Jonah had prophesied in reference to Jeroboam (2 Kings 14:25). As a consequence of the military successes and territorial expansion (2 Kings 14:25–28; 15: 2 Chron. 26:6–8), great wealth accrued to the two kingdoms. A powerful and profligate wealthy class had developed in Samaria; it was the abuse of wealth, power, and privilege by the wealthy in Samaria that formed the focus of so much of Amos's preaching. But this period of material and military success was to be only a brief and glorious sunset for the Israelite kingdoms: the Assyrians were already building their empire to the north, and both kingdoms would soon fall under its sway. Amos's preaching occurs under the ominous shadow of a threatened invasion (3:11; 5:3, 27; 6:7–14; 7:9, 17; 9:4).

Although he preached in the northern kingdom, Amos was himself from Tekoa, a town in Judah five miles south of Bethlehem. Traditionally, he has been thought to have come from the lower social classes of ancient Israel. He was a shepherd who tended flocks (1:1). During the hot summer months, the shepherds moved flocks to lower elevations, where Amos also worked as a "dresser" or "piercer" of sycamore fig trees (7:14), possibly in exchange for grazing rights (Hasel 1991, 53).[1]

In some respects, it is the task of scholarship to leave no stone unturned. Although the text's assertions about Amos appear at first glance to be coherent and straightforward, scholarly scrutiny has prompted questions about almost

---

[1]The sycamore fig should not be confused with the sycamore tree of North America. In ancient Israel the sycamore fig grew mainly in the plains (1 Kings 10:27; 1 Chron. 27:28; 2 Chron. 1:15; 9:27). It was used for food; however, it was not as highly prized as the common fig, and it was therefore primarily the food of the poor. The fruit was gashed to encourage ripening; this gashing increased the production of ethylene gas, which hastened the maturing of the fruit, according to O. Borowski, *Agriculture in Iron Age Israel* (Eisenbrauns, 1987).

every statement pertaining to the book and the prophet. These questions include issues regarding Amos's social status, his relationship to other prophets and to the cult, the location of the Tekoa that was his home, and how much of the book actually reflects the writing or preaching of the prophet himself.

The Prophet's Social Status

At first glance, Amos appears to be a man of humble status. A shepherd and migrant orchard worker, he was counted among the poor and exploited classes in the society, a member of those lower strata of society in behalf of whom he spoke. However, since the 1950s many scholars have argued the exact opposite: that Amos was instead from the upper echelons of Israelite society. Amos's designation as a "shepherd" (1:1) is not the common term for that profession (*rô'ēh*), but rather a different term (*nôqēd*). A cognate for this term in Ugaritic suggests that Amos may have been a large-scale breeder or a broker of herds (Craigie 1982, 1983). Others appeal to an Akkadian cognate (*nâqidu*), which designates a mid-level managerial official on the staff of a Mesopotamian temple, and suggest that Amos supervised or managed the flocks belonging to the temple in Jerusalem. Although the existence of such herds and flocks is clear for Mesopotamian temples, there is no clear indication in the Bible that the Jerusalem temple invested its resources in livestock and landed estates.

Amos was not a simple farmer or peasant, but rather a member of those wealthier social classes against which he delivered his indictments.

Whether a wealthy individual or a manager in the employ of the temple, Amos was not a simple farmer or peasant, but rather a member of those wealthier social classes against which he delivered his indictments. For some, his further designation as a dresser of sycamore figs is dismissed in light of the fact that Amos 7:10–17 is widely regarded as a secondary insertion into the book (for example, Auld 1986, 40)[2] or by further philological arguments that reinterpret the phrase "dresser of sycamore trees" (7:14; the TNIV simply says that he "took care of sycamore-fig trees") to mean something like "tax collector" or "government commissioner" (Rosenbaum 1990, 48–49).

In the final analysis, however, it is unclear whether Amos was among the wealthier members of Israelite society. Arguments from Ugaritic or Akkadian cognates require a jump of culture, time, and geography and may not actually reflect the use of the term *nôqēd* in Hebrew. Amos does speak of himself as "tending the flock" (7:15), as in fact a shepherd instead of a wealthy livestock broker. Philological arguments that assign some other meaning to the phrase "dresser of sycamore trees" are unconvincing, nor is simply excising 7:10–17

[2]Critical scholars commonly find 7:10–17 as a secondary insertion since it is the only third person narrative in the book. Hayes (1988), for example, detaches the passage from its immediate context and appends it as a separate section at the end of his commentary. Others regard it as a secondary insertion but consider it well placed in its context (Andersen and Freedman 1989; Hubbard 1989; Stuart 1987; see Hasel 1991, 41–42).

an approach that is methodologically satisfying. The traditional understanding yet has much to commend it.

Which Tekoa?

The only village designated by the name Tekoa in the Bible is the Judean village south of Bethlehem, and this is the site traditionally identified as the home of Amos. However, in light of the fact that Amos's ministry is set in the northern kingdom and the fact that the sycamore-fig tree does not grow in the vicinity of Judean Tekoa, a number of scholars (most recently Rosenbaum 1990) have suggested that Amos must have been from another village with the same name somewhere in the northern kingdom, perhaps in the area around Galilee. The arguments for this position are not very compelling and are easily answered (see Hasel 1991, 49–55).

Amos and Other Prophets

The statement "I was neither a prophet, nor the disciple of a prophet" (7:14) is one of the most familiar quotations from the Bible, and it is among the most debated verses in the prophetic books. The Hebrew text itself reads more literally "I not prophet; I not son of prophet [or, 'disciple of prophet']." If these two clauses are translated with past tense verbs, "I was not a prophet, nor the son of a prophet," Amos is reflecting on the fact that he had no prior experience in the office or calling of a prophet until God took him from tending the flocks (7:15) and commissioned him to become a prophet.

However, if the clauses are translated with present tense verbs ("I am not a prophet and not the son of a prophet"), Amos is dissociating himself from others who might be identified as prophets and himself never claimed to be a prophet (*nabî'*), at least not in the sense that the northern priest Amaziah would associate with the term. This position challenges the reader to ask why Amos would have avoided the use of the term in reference to himself (1) when it would later become the standard designation for the office and (2) when in the immediate context (7:12), Amaziah the priest calls him by the title "seer" (*hôzeh*), a title he does not appear to reject. Many have suggested that the issue here is simply chronology: that *nabî'* had yet to become the standard term for designating a prophet. Others suggest that some pejorative meaning had become attached to the term at the time of Amos and that the prophet was seeking to avoid the label. Petersen (1981) distinguishes the two terms by arguing that *hôzeh* was the term used in the southern kingdom, Judah, and that *nābî'* was used in the northern kingdom; on this basis Amos would have accepted the designation "seer" (appropriate to someone from Judah) while rejecting designation as a "prophet" from Israel. Yet it is not clear that there is some dissonance in the use of these two terms in the immediate context; it is equally plausible that the use of both *hôzeh* and *nabî'* in 7:12, 15 suggests that the prophet himself saw them as essentially synonymous. In any event, the immediate context suggests that translating with past tenses is the correct approach: Amos had been a herder and tree dresser, but now God had constituted him a prophet, something he had not been before. Amos's actions are those of a prophet: he has visions and he preaches. There is little reason to suggest he was avoiding the term. Both Amaziah and Amos describe his activity by the verb "prophesy" (*hitnabbe'*, 7:12, 13, 15), a verbal root derived from the noun "prophet" (*nābî'*), further suggesting that both Amos himself and Amaziah considered Amos a "prophet" (contrast Vawter 1985).

The Prophet's Relationship to the Book

Traditional and precritical views of the book identified its first-person oracles as written by the prophet himself; even 7:10–17, a third-person narrative, was associated with the prophet or with someone who was an eyewitness in his own generation. Critical study broke this connection between the prophet and the book to varying degrees. The study of Amos has mirrored the development of various critical methods. Hasel (1991, 20–27) identifies three major stages in this history of critical study.

The first phase, concurrent with the rise and predominance of pentateuchal source criticism, had as its objective to separate the authentic words of Amos from those of later additions. This was the search for the historical Amos, not unlike the then-current search for the historical Jesus in Gospels criticism. Scholars sought to isolate the *ipsissima verba* (the "very words") of the prophet from the inauthentic and nongenuine material in the book. The commentaries by G. A. Smith (1928) and W. R. Harper (1905) were representative of this approach. Amos was associated with the development of a new phase of Israel's religious understanding, the innovation of a genuine ethical monotheism that would become the basis for the preaching of Israel's classical prophets.

The development of form criticism and tradition-historical criticism inaugurated a second phase in critical study of Amos. As these methods were applied to Amos, the interest was not only the authentic kernel of Amos's original utterances in the book, but instead moved in two directions: (1) investigation of the social setting and structure of his originally oral pronouncements (i.e., getting behind even the written text), and (2) paying attention to the stages of growth in the written text itself through successive layers of redaction. Awareness of the relationship between Amos and the traditions of ancient Israel did provide a happy corrective to the earlier critical scholarship: Amos was found to be not an innovator of some new phase in Israel's religion, but rather to have been deeply immersed in Israel's historical traditions.

Efforts to investigate the redactional history of Amos approach the book almost as if it were a piece of baklava pastry from which the various thin layers could be peeled and evaluated. As is commonly the case with redactional studies of other Old Testament books, scholars reached a wide variety of conclusions on the number and extent of the various editorial layers in Amos. Wolff and Coote are representative of the approach: Wolff (1977, 106–14) identified six stages of development; Coote (1981, 1–10) found three levels. Redaction-critical approaches have in common that they view the book as the result of a gradual process of growth. Some originally authentic oracles of Amos were supplemented with other materials from disciples of the prophet and yet later editors.

A number of passages in Amos are widely regarded as secondary. The narrative in 7:10–17 is often regarded as a later addition both because it is the only third-person narrative in the book and because it seems intrusive in the series of visions (7:1–8:3; see above). This biographical narrative interrupts the two visions where Amos is successful at intercession (7:1–3, 4–6) and the two visions where judgment is presented as irrevocable (7:7–9; 8:1–3) by coming between numbers three and four. Numerous theories have been offered to explain why the redactor would have inserted this material at this point (Freedman 1990; Williamson 1990).

Among the oracles against foreign nations (chaps. 1–2), the oracles against Tyre (1:9–10), Edom (1:11–12), and Judah (2:4–5) are often viewed as secondary because of minor deviations compared with the forms of oracles against the other nations mentioned. These three do not have the closing formula "Yahweh said," and they have a more abbreviated announcement of judgment.

A number of "hymn fragments" have been identified in the book (1:2; 4:13; 5:8–9; 8:8; 9:5–6), and these are often regarded as insertions from an editor in the Jerusalem cult. Others argue instead that these "fragments" are too deeply embedded in the rhetorical argument of their respective passages to be regarded as later insertions (McComiskey 1986).

The salvation promise in 9:11–15 is often considered a product of the postexilic period, reflecting the pro-Judah or pro-Jerusalem stance of a later editor (a summary of the debate is found in Hasel 1991, 12–15). Scholars are troubled, as Wellhausen put it, by the sudden switch to "roses and lavender instead of blood and iron."[3] However, many scholars also consider this final oracle as authentic (Hasel 1991, 15).

Other short passages are also commonly viewed as secondary additions; for example, the statement about prophecy in 3:7 is often credited to Deuteronomistic sources in the sixth century BC, and the aphorism in 5:13 is attributed to a later editor.

Many scholars have increasingly questioned whether the tools of critical scholarship permit such fine dissecting of biblical books, especially in a book as small as Amos, and especially when such differing results themselves cast doubt on the usefulness of the method.

---

[3]Wellhausen, *Die kleinen Propheten: Übersetzt und erklärt* (1892, 4th unchanged edition, 1963), 96, cited in Hasel 1991, 12.

In a third phase in the study of Amos, scholars approach the book with greater interest in its literary structure and rhetorical development. More recent approaches are less fixated on diachronic questions (how the book came to be) and more interested in synchronic issues (the meaning of the book as it exists). Individuals taking this approach tend to view the book as essentially the product of one individual, either Amos himself or an editor who had been a colleague of the prophet and who unified and integrated the materials into a coherent whole. The commentaries by Andersen and Freedman (1989), Paul (1991), Niehaus (1992), G. V. Smith (1988; 2001), and Stuart (1987) are representative of this methodological shift. A comparison of the two commentaries on Amos in the Hermeneia series (Wolff 1977; Paul 1991) shows quite clearly the dramatic shift in approach.

LITERARY STRUCTURE

The book of Amos falls into three sections: the oracles against the nations (chaps. 1–2), a series of judgment speeches against Israel (chaps. 3–6), and a group of vision reports culminating with an oracle of salvation (chaps. 7–9).

The Oracles Against the Nations (chaps. 1–2)

Amos delivers prophetic indictments against eight nations as he zeroes in to at last deliver his indictment against Israel.[4] These indictments circle Israel in a kind of "geographical chiasmus" (Niehaus 1992, 323): Syria to the northeast, Philistia to the southwest, Tyre to the northwest, and then Edom, Ammon, and Moab to the southeast, Judah to the south, and finally coming home to Israel itself. The Gentile nations are indicted primarily for war crimes. Each of the separate oracles uses the numerical scheme "X and X+1" ("for three sins, even for four") common to Wisdom Literature. Geyer (1986) notes that Amos's oracles against the nations lack the mythological motifs that characterize the major collections of oracles against the nations in Isaiah, Jeremiah, and Ezekiel. Unlike those other collections, these oracles in Amos are largely a rhetorical device leading up to his condemnation of Israel. His listeners would readily have agreed with the denunciation of atrocities committed by neighboring states, only to be surprised at the condemnation of social injustice on the home front. Ryken (1993, 342) sees in these oracles an increasing sense of urgency that culminates in the oracle against Israel. The arrangement of the oracles is itself clever and subversive; oracles that construct a circle of despised enemy peoples turn out to be a trap sprung on an unsuspecting Israel.

---

[4]For a discussion of oracles against the nations in general, see chapter 28, "Obadiah."

Scholars have long debated the basis for the moral authority of Amos's indictments (see Barton 1980). Is the appeal to some universally recognized international law? Or to some form of natural law? Or does Amos base his indictment on some specific application of Israel's own covenant law? The use of literary devices characteristic of Wisdom Literature does suggest an appeal to universally recognized precepts embedded in the moral order. The ancient treaty literature of the Hittites contained specific provisions regarding the conduct of war and the treatment of prisoners, attesting to the broad acceptance of the moral premises that underlie Amos's words.

Judgment Speeches Against Israel (chaps. 3–6)

In chapters 3–6 Amos uses a wide variety of literary forms. The prophetic lawsuit speech is prominent. Here the prophet serves as the lawsuit messenger to present God's case against Israel (Niehaus 1992, 318–19). In the prophetic lawsuits of the Bible, as in their extrabiblical counterparts (Huffmon 1959), the suzerain or lord in a treaty relationship sends a messenger to remind the disobedient vassal or client of his obligations under the terms of their covenant and of his failure to keep those terms. The setting is judicial: (1) the plaintiff-judge is introduced; (2) the past relations of the contracting parties are reviewed, specifically the recent history of disobedience on the part of the vassal; (3) witnesses are summoned; (4) indictments are delivered; (5) rhetorical cross-examination is common; (6) repentance is offered—i.e., possibilities for repair of the covenant-treaty are announced; and (7) the threatened punishment is specified.

Many of these elements occur, for example, in Amos 3:1–15. The plaintiff and defendant are introduced (3:1a); a short history of the past relationship and the breech in the relationship are pronounced (3:1b–2); the cross-examination is characterized by the use of rhetorical questions (3:3–6); and the status of the prophet-lawsuit messenger is confirmed (3:7–8). Witnesses are summoned from the surrounding nations (3:9) to hear the announced judgment (3:10–15).

In addition to the elements of the prophetic lawsuit, Amos also uses judgment speeches (4:1–13; 5:1–17) and woe oracles (5:18–27; 6:1–14). Scholarly research has in the past concentrated on the presumed editorial layering and chronological relationship of these speech forms in 3:1–6:14. More recent approaches have tended to observe a deliberate inner coherence and unity in the structure of these materials, somewhat vitiating the need to posit chronological redactions (Hubbard 1989, 119; see Gitay 1980; de Waard 1977; Tromp 1984).

The Vision Reports (chaps. 7–9)

The prophet gives an autobiographical account of five visions he received. The first four of these (7:1–3, 4–6, 7–9; 8:1–3) are similar to one another, but also distinct from the fifth (9:1–10). In the first four God "showed" (7:1, 4, 7;

8:1) the prophet objects or events, and there is dialogue between God and the prophet. In the last vision the object seen is the Lord himself, and there is no dialogue between God and the prophet; no particular action is seen, and the prophet remains a silent listener to the words of God.

The first four visions are also clearly related to one another and have their own structure as a group. The first two visions portray events (locust plague and drought); the second two, objects (plumb line and fruit basket). In the first two, Amos intercedes with God and successfully pleads that he withhold the disaster; in the second two, the portent of the vision cannot be evaded. The first two visions represented the greatest threats to an agrarian society (locusts and drought) and needed no further explanation, but the second two visions required elaboration. The plumb line represented God's standards, his law; it was the measure of rectitude that contrasted with Israel's disobedience. A city with walls out of plumb could not expect to continue standing. In the last vision, the basket of summer fruit, Amos engages in a wordplay similar to visions in Jeremiah (1:11–14): the summer (*qayiṣ*) fruit invoked a message about the end (*qēṣ*) of Israel; the nation had become ripe for judgment. The two groups of paired visions may reflect different chronological moments in the ministry of Amos: his earlier preaching, during which averting judgment was still possible (visions one and two), and his later preaching when his message had been rejected (7:10–17) and judgment was inevitable.

The book ends with an abrupt shift to an oracle of salvation. The out-of-plumb nation once ruined (7:7–9) is rebuilt (9:11–12); the overripe people (8:1–3) will once again enjoy restoration to a fruitful land. Israel becomes Eden restored (9:13–15); agricultural plenty is a common motif in the prophets for describing the blessings of the eschatological future (e.g., Ezek. 47; Joel 3:17–21 [MT 4:17–21]; Zech. 3:10). Although many have associated this oracle with a later redactor (see above), the prophet here appears to hold out hopes for the reinstitution of a united monarchy involving both North and South, united under David's shelter (9:11; "tent" NIV).

Amos makes use of a wide range of literary devices in presenting his oracles: metaphors, simile, epithets, proverbs, short narratives, sarcasm, direct vituperation, vision, taunt, dialogue, irony, satire, parody—"a virtual anthology of prophetic forms" (Ryken 1993, 342). Extensive agrarian imagery may reflect his own background as a shepherd and orchard worker (1:3; 2:13; 4:9; 5:11, 16–17; 7:1–2, 14–15; 8:1–2; 9:9–15). The prophet appears to have enjoyed structured repetition (as in the oracles against the nations or the vision reports) and the use of rhetorical questions (3:3–6) and repeated phrases (3:4, 8). He makes frequent use of "summary quotations," a device in which he cites the words of his opponents (2:12; 4:1; 6:2, 13; 7:11, 16; 8:5–6, 14; 9:10). He uses a few puns (5:5; 6:1, 6, 7; 8:1–2) and often calls for the attention of his hearers with a repeated summons (3:1; 4:1; 5:1; cf. 8:4).

THEOLOGICAL THEMES

Much of Amos's preaching can be gathered under several distinct themes.

Divine Sovereignty and Judgment

It goes almost without saying that Amos shares with the other canonical prophets his belief in the sovereignty of Israel's God over the historical process. Amos announces God's rejection of the religious and social practices of the northern kingdom and his determination to punish that nation for its disobedience. Hubbard (1989, 108–9) sees this process of sovereign rule and judgment operative at four different levels. First, at the *personal, divine* level, it is Yahweh himself who takes the initiative in judgment (e.g., 1:4; 3:2, 14; 9:4); disobedience has been directed toward him, and his is the obligation to punish. Second, at the level of *creation*. The cosmos itself rises up in judgment against wickedness; created reality convulses at the presence of the Divine Warrior coming to execute judgment on the nation (2:13; 8:8; 9:1, 5; cf. 1:1). Third, at the level of *moral causality*, evil directed toward others produces evil in return (3:10–11; 5:11); rejection of God's word through the prophet brings the moral consequence of a famine of the word of God (8:11–12). The punishment fits the crime. Fourth, at the level of *political history*, God's sovereign rule extends over the nations of the world. They are not only subject to his judgment (chaps. 1–2), but they also do his bidding in bringing judgment on Israel. They come to invade the land (3:11), devastate Israel's armies (5:3) and populace (6:9–10), seize territory and destroy cities (3:14; 6:14), and exile leaders (4:2–3; 5:27). God displays his sovereign power in all areas of the cosmos. There would be no escaping his judgment—not in the depths of the sea or on the heights of the mountains, in the grave or in the heavens (9:2–4).

> *Amos's message of divine judgment is directed at two particular areas: idolatry and social injustice.*

Idolatry and Social Injustice

Amos's message of divine judgment is directed at two particular areas: idolatry and social injustice. Idolatry was commonplace in the Israel of Amos's day (2:8; 5:5, 26; 7:9–13; 8:14). The worship of Yahweh had itself become corrupt, a religion content with external and perfunctory fulfillment of sacrificial duty (4:4–5; 5:21–26) and Sabbath commands (8:5), all the while missing the "weightier matters of the law." For others the commandments of God were openly defied (2:7–8).

The material prosperity that had accompanied political and military successes under Jeroboam II had created a powerful and wealthy upper class in Israel (3:12, 15; 6:4–6). New levels of leisure time and disposable wealth had brought open vice (2:7–8); alcohol abuse had now become a problem even for women (4:1; cf. 2:8). For the wealthy justice could be purchased (5:12), while those less fortunate were reduced to chattel (2:6–7; 8:6); the poor and needy were crushed by the powerful (2:7; 4:1; 5:11; 8:4). God had revealed himself as the protector of the poor, the widow, and the orphan; he would undertake the defense of the downtrodden. The abuse of power and wealth would bring disaster to the northern kingdom. Ill-gotten gains would become plunder for others, and those who had enslaved their fellow Israelites would become slaves in distant lands (9:4). Father and son who had engaged the same prostitute (2:7–8) would witness wives turned into prostitutes and children dying by the sword (7:17). Those who crushed the poor (2:7; 4:1) would be crushed in turn (2:13). A just God demands justice among his covenant people (5:15), obedience rather than sacrifice (5:18–24).

The Covenant and the Remnant

Amos was not the radical religious innovator depicted in earlier biblical criticism. His status as a covenant-lawsuit messenger presupposes the existence of that covenant. The book itself is replete with many allusions to pentateuchal language (see the chart in Niehaus 1992, 322) and also shows familiarity with covenantal ideology. For example, Amos makes explicit use of earlier pentateuchal materials in 2:8 (Ex. 22:26; Deut. 24:12–13); 2:12 (Num. 6:2–21); 4:4 (Deut. 14:28); 4:11 (Gen. 19). Amos saw himself as part of the succession of prophets to follow Moses (3:7; Deut. 18:14–22). The divine judgments proclaimed against Israel are drawn from the lists of curses in Deuteronomy 28 and Leviticus 26. Amos was not calling upon Israel to adopt some new religious novelty, but rather, like Jeremiah, he urged a nation at crossroads to choose the "ancient paths" and to "walk in the good way" (Jer. 6:16).

Israel's status as an elect people, a redeemed nation in covenant relationship with Yahweh, is important in the book (3:1–2). The Lord had irrevocably committed himself to the descendants of Abraham, but he also required that they be a holy nation. Failure to live in accord with the dictates of the covenant brought divine wrath and punishment. An unavoidable tension arose in Israel between God's gracious commitment to his people and the nation's failure to keep his commandments. This tension is addressed in the prophets primarily through the remnant motif (Dillard 1988; Hasel 1991b): God's holiness required that he respond in judgment on the sins of the nation, but his commitment to Israel meant that there would always be a remnant, those who had undergone divine judgment and survived to become the nucleus for the continuation of the people of God. These survivors, the remnant, would inherit afresh God's promises to his people. For Amos, the contemplated divine judgment threatened the continued existence of Ephraim and Manasseh (5:15; 6:6). The nation would be like grain in a sieve: not a kernel would reach the ground, and all the sinners among the people would die (9:9–10). But God would yet again plant and bless his people in their land (9:11–15).

The Day of the Lord

Israel had ordinarily viewed the day of the Lord as the day of national vindication, the time in which the Divine Warrior would move in judgment against the enemies of Israel (Reid and Longman 1995, 61–71, 124–28, 171–73). But Amos sets this concept in reverse: the day of the Lord would mean judgment for Israel, and the Divine Warrior would bring enemy armies against his own people in judgment for their sin (Amos 5:18–20). Israel was just like the other nations and would fare no better on the day of his wrath. There has been considerable debate about Amos's eschatology (Hasel 1991, 5–8). Some identify the day of the Lord in Amos as a noneschatological concept, others regard Amos as countering the popular eschatology of the people, and still others regard Amos as making an eschatological pronouncement. The answer to this question depends in part on how one understands the term *eschatology*. If one intends a universal, end-time, cataclysmic event, Amos's use of the "day of the Lord" is probably not eschatological; but if one understands Amos's use of the concept as reference to a definite, future divine intrusion in judgment (though not the absolute end of history), Amos's use is indeed eschatological.

God's Word

Amos shares with the other prophets his confidence in the power and efficacy of the divine word as revealed through the prophets (3:1; 4:1; 5:1; 7:14–16; 8:12). When the Lord speaks from his dwelling, the earth responds and convulses (1:2). The roar of a lion brought a response—but Israel believed they could ignore the divine word revealed by his servants the prophets (3:3–8).

APPROACHING THE NEW TESTAMENT

The New Testament shares Amos's concern with issues of social justice and the abuse of the poor. In the church there should be no differentiation in the treatment of the rich and the poor (1 Cor. 11:22; James 2:1–10). True religion requires caring for those in need, not oppressing them (James 1:27; 5:1–6). Those who are poor are the particular objects of God's care (James 2:5). Among the Gospels, it is Luke who shows particular interest in demonstrating Jesus' concern for those in need (Luke 4:18; 6:20; 7:22; 11:41; 14:13, 21; 18:22; 19:8; 21:2–3; cf. Acts 9:36; 10:4, 31; 24:17).

Amos is specifically cited in several New Testament passages. Paul's exhortation to "hate evil and love good" may have been drawn from Amos (5:15; Rom 12:9). Stephen cites the prophet to recall Israel's national idolatry during the wilderness wandering (5:25; Acts 7:42). Perhaps of greatest interest is the citation of Amos 9:11–12 in Acts 15:16–17. Although the source for the actual text cited in Acts is difficult to establish, at the council of Jerusalem James appears to argue that the incorporation of the Gentiles into the church fulfills God's promise to reunify Israel. Rebuilding David's fallen tent, repairing its breeches (the breakup of the united kingdom), does not apply to the physical nation of Israel alone; it includes the ingathering of the nations.

CHAPTER TWENTY-EIGHT

OBADIAH

The old adage that "good things come in small packages" is apt for this shortest book of the Old Testament. Conversely, many have also come to agree with Jerome's comment regarding the book: *"quanto brevius est, tanto difficilius"* ("It is as difficult as it is brief").

BIBLIOGRAPHY

Commentaries

L. C. **Allen,** *The Books of Joel, Obadiah, Jonah, and Micah* (NICOT; Eerdmans, 1976); D. W. **Baker,** T. D. **Alexander,** and B. K. **Waltke,** *Obadiah, Jonah, and Micah* (TOTC; Leicester: Inter-Varsity, 1988); R. J. **Coggins** and S. P. **Re'emi,** *Nahum, Obadiah, Esther: Israel Among the Nations* (ITC; Eerdmans, 1985); J. H. **Eaton,** *Obadiah, Nahum, Habakkuk, Zephaniah* (TBC; SCM, 1961); T. J. **Finley,** *Joel, Amos, Obadiah* (WEC; Moody, 1990); C. A. **Keller,** *Joël, Abdias, Jonas* (CAT 11a; Neuchatel: Delachaux et Niestlé, 1965); J. **Limburg,** *Hosea-Micah* (Interp; Louisville: Knox, 1988); J. **Niehaus,** "Obadiah," in *The Minor Prophets: An Exegetical and Expository Commentary,* ed. T. E. McComiskey (Baker, 1992), 495–541; P. **Raabe,** *Obadiah* (AB; Doubleday, 1996); W. **Rudolph,** *Joel, Amos, Obadia, Jona* (*KAT* 13/2; Gütersloh: Mohn, 1971); B. K. **Smith,** *Amos, Obadiah, Jonah* (NAC; Broadman, 1995); J. M. P. **Smith,** W. H. **Ward,** and J. A. **Bewer,** *Micah, Zephaniah, Nahum, Habakkuk, Obadiah and Joel* (ICC; T. & T. Clark, 1911); D. **Stuart,** *Hosea–Jonah* (WBC 31; Word, 1987); J. A. **Thompson,** "Obadiah," *IB* 6 (1956): 855–67; J. D. W. **Watts,** *The Books of Joel, Obadiah, Nahum, Habakkuk and Zephaniah* (CBC; London: Cambridge University Press, 1975); A. **Weiser,** *Die Propheten Hosea, Joel, Amos, Obadja, Jona, Micha* (ATD 24; Göttingen: Vandenhoeck und Ruprecht, 1979); H. W. **Wolff,** *Dodekapropheten* (BKAT 14/5; Neukirchen: Neukirchen Verlag, 1963); idem, *Obadiah and Jonah* (Augsburg, 1986).

Monographs and Articles

M. **Biè**, "Zur Problematik des Buches Obadja," *Congress Volume,* Copenhagen, 1953 (VTSup 1; 1953): 11–25; D. J. **Clark**, "Obadiah Reconsidered," *Bible Translator* 42 (1991): 326–36; J. R. **Lillie**, "Obadiah—a Celebration of God's Kingdom," *CurrTM* 6 (1979): 18–22; G. S. **Ogden**, "Prophetic Oracles Against Foreign Nations and Psalms of Communal Lament: The Relationship of Jeremiah 49:7–22 and Obadiah," *JSOT* 24 (1982): 89–97; D. **Reid** and T. **Longman** III, *God Is a Warrior* (Zondervan, 1995); R. B. **Robinson**, "Levels of Naturalization in Obadiah," *JSOT* 40 (1988): 83–97; S. D. **Snyman,** "Cohesion in the Book of Obadiah," *ZAW* 101 (1989): 59–71; P. **Weimar,** "Obadja: eine redaktionskritische Analyse," *BN* 27 (1985): 35–99; H. W. **Wolff,** "Obadja: ein Kultprophet als Interpret," *EvTh* 37 (1977): 273–84.

HISTORICAL BACKGROUND

Authorship and Historical Period

The superscriptions to the prophetic books often contain some information about the time in which the prophet lived, an indication of his home town, and the name of his father. None of the above is provided for Obadiah, and even his exact name is a matter of debate. The Hebrew vocalization of Obadiah means "worshiper of Yahweh" in the Septuagint (*Abdiou*) and Vulgate (*Abdias*); however, his name is read with different vowels and takes the meaning "servant of Yahweh." Stuart (1987, 406) suggests that these were bi-forms of the same name, analogous to English pairs like Bert and Burt or Beth and Betty. At least a dozen individuals are called by the name Obadiah in the Old Testament. Another very common name, Obed, is a hypocorism (a shortened form, a "nickname") of the name Obadiah. But our prophet cannot be identified with any of these other individuals.[1] The very lack of information about the prophet may suggest that he was well known among his contemporaries. Some scholars contend that oracles against foreign nations were delivered at sanctuaries, and for this reason some have suggested that Obadiah was himself a cultic prophet attached to the temple staff in Jerusalem, and furthermore, that this book may have been associated with a particular festival or cultic event. These conclusions

---

[1] A tradition in the Babylonian Talmud (*Sanh.* 39b), also known by Jerome, identifies the prophet Obadiah with a man by that name at the royal court of King Ahab (1 Kings 18:3–16); he was a palace administrator who allied himself with Elijah and protected the lives of many prophets. This is without doubt an incorrect identification: the book appears to date from the sixth century, whereas the other Obadiah lived in the ninth. The identification reflects the penchant of some scholars to associate particular sites or persons with other known events and individuals.

are highly speculative, however. Allen (1976, 136) notes that the historical specificity in the book militates against its having been a liturgical composition, since such compositions tend to be more general in tone.

As with the books of Nahum, Habakkuk, and Joel—books that also provide minimal information about the prophet known from the title—the reader must examine the internal evidence within the book to determine a date and historical setting for it. However, this data has not always led to a unified conclusion in the history of scholarship.

Most scholars have concurred in the judgment that Obadiah should be dated in the sixth century BC, either reasonably early in the Judean exile (Raabe 1996) or later in that century. The prima facie evidence for this date is Obadiah's apparent denunciations against Edom for its raids into Judah at the time of Jerusalem's fall (vv. 11–16), an event remembered in other biblical passages (Ps. 137:7; Lam. 4:21–22). The apocryphal book 1 Esdras (4:45) blames Edomites for burning the temple in Jerusalem, but the historical basis for this claim cannot be confirmed.

A few scholars have argued for a yet later date. J. A. Bewer (1911) and others regard the prophecies of Edom's destruction as *vaticinium ex eventu* (prophecy after the event); they argue that such prophecies must have been issued sometime later than the destruction of Edom by the Nabateans late in the fifth century. However, verses 2–9 are a prophetic threat and not a description of past events.

C. F. Keil, E. J. Young, and a few other scholars have also opted for an earlier date in the mid-ninth century BC by associating the book with events during the reign of Jehoram (2 Kings 8:20–22; 2 Chron. 21:8–10). A date this early is attractive primarily if one also believes that the present canonical order of the twelve minor prophets was intended to be chronological. Although the books are in a chronological sequence where that chronology is demonstrable, the positioning of the chronologically less certain books appears due to thematic associations and shared vocabulary; the order in the Septuagint is different from that in the Hebrew text.

The book of Obadiah is an oracle against Edom. This land was also known as Seir (Gen. 32:3; 36:20–21, 30; Num. 24:18). It was located to the south and east of the Dead Sea, from the Wadi Zered to the Gulf of Aqabah. It was a fairly narrow strip of marginally arable land. Two major north-south routes passed through the region: (1) the so-called King's Highway running through the arable regions where water was more readily available, but which also required crossing deep east-west canyons; and (2) the route further east at the outer edge of the arable zone, but which did not require crossing such steep canyons. These trade routes were the main arteries east of the Jordan. The goods and commodities of Europe, Asia, and Africa were carried along these roads; revenues from taxes levied on caravans provided the foundation for Edom's income.

The Bible records a long history of frequent contact between Israel and Edom, primarily in military conflict. The Edomites are described as the descendants of Esau (Gen. 36:1, 9), the brother of Jacob/Israel. After the exodus, Edom denied Israel right of passage through her land (Num. 20:14–21; Judg. 11:17–18). Balaam predicted that Edom would be conquered (Num. 24:18). The kings of the united monarchy—Saul, David, and Solomon—fought the Edomites and eventually subdued that land for a time (1 Sam. 14:47; 2 Sam. 8:13–14; 1 Kings 9:26–28; 11:14–22). During the ninth century, Edom allied itself with Moab and Ammon in a raid against Judah at the time of Jehoshaphat (2 Chron. 20). A few years later Edom was more successful in its rebellion against Jehoram and managed to achieve freedom from Israelite domination for about forty years (2 Kings 8:20–22; 2 Chron. 21:8–10). In the early eighth century King Amaziah of Judah conquered Edom once again and inflicted heavy casualties after the battle itself had been won (2 Kings 14:7; 2 Chron. 25:11–12). By the middle of the eighth century, during the reign of Ahaz, Edom was itself able to launch raids into Judah and to take captives (2 Chron. 28:17); at that time she escaped Israel's yoke and would not be subjugated again.

During the period of Assyrian and Babylonian domination, Edom was reduced to vassal status to these great powers. At one point Edom was involved in plans for a rebellion against Babylon (Jer. 27). After the fall of Jerusalem, Edom took advantage of the moment and either cooperated with the Babylonians or launched independent raids into Judah and Jerusalem that served as the stimulus for the book of Obadiah (see above).

Archaeological evidence suggests growing Arab influence and infiltration in the area of Edom during the period of the Persian Empire (late sixth to fourth centuries; Neh. 2:19; 4:7; 6:1). By late in the fourth century BC, the Arab kingdom of Nabatea was centered around Petra. Pressure from the Nabateans displaced many Edomites into the Negev of Judah. This region then came to be called Idumea, preserving the ancient name of Edom.

> *All of the prophetic books except Hosea and Haggai contain oracles against foreign nations.*

LITERARY ANALYSIS

From the inception of the prophetic order, the prophets addressed not only Israel but also foreign nations. Moses' call was to address the pharaoh of Egypt (Ex. 3:10). Jeremiah was "appointed as a prophet to the nations" (Jer. 1:5), appointed "over nations and kingdoms" (Jer. 1:10). All of the prophetic books except Hosea and Haggai contain oracles against foreign nations. Extensive collections of such oracles are found in Isaiah 13–23; Jeremiah 46–51; Ezekiel 25–32, 35; and Amos 1–2.

What would be a single oracle against a foreign nation in one of the other prophetic books has in Obadiah become an independent book. There are other oracles against Edom in Isaiah 34:5–15; Jeremiah 49:7–22; Ezekiel 25:12–14;

35; Amos 1:11–12; and Malachi 1:2–5. Edom is the subject of more separate oracles against foreign nations and more brief or passing hostile references in the prophetical books than any other nation (Stuart 1987, 404; cf. Joel 3:19 [MT 4:19]; Isa. 11:14; Jer. 25:21; Lam. 4:21). In particular, Obadiah 1–9 has many close verbal and thematic links to Jeremiah 49:7–16, such that some literary dependence is all but certain (see the detailed discussion in Raabe 1996, 22–31). The direction of this dependence, however, is not clear; Obadiah could have preceded or followed Jeremiah. The two oracles have the same introduction (Obad. 1; Jer. 49:7); both oracles report Edom's lack of wisdom (Obad. 8; Jer. 49:7). Obadiah 1b–4 resembles Jeremiah 49:14–16; Obadiah 5, Jeremiah 49:9; Obadiah 6, Jeremiah 49:10a. Ogden (1982) regards both as examples of responses to a lament liturgy in the temple.

As with most of the prophetic books, even one this short, critical scholarship has discovered reasons to question the unity and literary integrity of Obadiah. As Stuart (1987, 403) notes, scholarly debate on a portion of Scripture often increases in inverse proportion to the data available to decide the question. Efforts to assign stages to the composition of the book follow two major approaches with numerous variations. The first (Bewer, Keller, and others) attributes verses 1–14, 15b to Obadiah and the remainder (vv. 15a, 16–21) to a later individual or several individuals. The primary reason for this division is that the first part of the book deals with a concrete historical situation; it reflects on the fall of Jerusalem and the pending divine judgment against Edom. The remainder, however, is more characteristic of apocalyptic: it announces the day of the Lord and addresses divine judgment and vindication of Israel against the nations more broadly than against Edom alone. The second approach (Weiser, Rudolph, and others) denies only verses 19–21 to Obadiah and regards verses 15a, 16–18 as a genuine but independent oracle from the prophet. Verses 15a, 16–18 are concerned with the same historical situation as verses 1–14, 15b. In the first part the nations punish Edom, whereas in the second, the nations are victims alongside Edom. In the first part Edom is addressed; in the second, Israel.

In contrast to these approaches, which find a compositional history in this short book, others have defended its essential unity (Thompson, Allen, Stuart). As with all oracles against foreign nations, although a particular foreign power is addressed as the putative audience, the real audience is in Israel or Judah; the transition from addressing Edom to addressing Judah should come as no surprise. Thompson, Allen, and L. H. Brockington have called attention to parallels with the book of Joel: Joel saw in immediate events (the locust plague) a dire portent of an even greater pending and apocalyptic appearance of the day of the Lord against the nations. This is the same theological progression that is found in Obadiah. Just as Edom had annexed the territory of Judah, this act will be reversed: Edom will be stubble for a fire ignited in Israel, and her own mountains will be occupied (vv. 18–19); the Lord will amass the nations for battle against Edom (v. 1b), and Mount Zion will produce those who "govern the mountains of Esau" (v. 21). The shift from the immediate historical moment to a more apocalyptic outlook is not a valid criterion for isolating separate editorial layers. Although the second half of the book concerns Israel and the nations more broadly, Edom is still to the fore (vv. 19, 21).

Structural analysis of this little book has also yielded a wide variety of results. Various scholars have identified two, three, four, five, or six sections and have outlined the book in different ways; see the history of this discussion in Allen (1976, 140–42) or Snyman (1989, 59–71). The prophet presents himself as an envoy from the heavenly court, sent by his Lord to summon the nations for battle against Edom (v. 1). The Lord announces his sentence against Edom (vv. 2–9) and expounds the basis for his divine judgment (vv. 10–14). Edom's experience of the day of the Lord is but a harbinger of a yet greater day of divine wrath against his enemies and vindication for his people (vv. 15–21).

THEOLOGICAL MESSAGE

The little book of Obadiah shares the theological underpinnings of other oracles against foreign nations. All of these oracles have at least three items in common:

1. They express the universal rule of Yahweh. The God of Israel is not the god of a single nation. He is the Lord of all nations and places. The power of his word is not confined in some way within the borders of Israel; his word effects his will at any time or place to which it is addressed. He orders the history of nations and reveals his will to his prophets.

2. They express the outworking in Israel of the Abrahamic covenant: "I will bless those who bless you, and whoever curses you I will curse" (Gen. 12:3). The long history of warfare between Jacob and Esau, between Israel and Edom, means for Edom: "As you have done, it will be done to you; your deeds will return upon your own head" (Obad. 15b).

3. They reflect the involvement of Israel's prophets in Holy War as the messengers of the Divine Warrior (Reid and Longman 1995, 55–60). In the historical books, and most frequently in the periods before the appearance of the classical canonical prophets, Israel's prophets were actively involved in the nation's warfare, expressing God's will as to whether to go to battle and giving instructions even about the conduct of the battle. The oracles against foreign nations are extensions of prophetic involvement in warfare; instead of the nitty-gritty details of particular historical battles, the prophets address the Divine Warrior's intent to nations both near and far. It is Holy War transferred to a more verbal plane. The customary speech before the battle becomes an oracle

against a foreign power when the armies are not actually arrayed on the field for combat.

A sense of outrage permeates this little book, outrage directed toward Edom. The precise context of the book may be elusive, but a wealth of intertextual associations provoke reading the book in the light of a larger literary context. For the Israelite reader, Obadiah would have evoked a whole series of associative allusions beyond the context of the book itself. The repeated use of the name Esau (vv. 6, 8, 9, 18, 21) and the description of Jacob as his brother (vv. 10, 12) move us beyond the realm of international politics and into the world of family relationships. These two nations—Israel and Edom—are inextricably bound together from their birth in the tents of Isaac and Rebekah. Obadiah pronounces that Edom will be *despised* among the nations, the same word used to describe how Esau *despised* his birthright (v. 2; Gen. 25:34). Esau's "blessing" is that he will serve his younger brother Jacob/Israel (Gen. 25:23; 27:27–40), the child who received the promises given to Abraham; Esau's role in the divine economy was fixed from that moment for all time (Robinson 1988, 92). Throughout its history, Edom had attempted to throw off the yoke of its younger brother (Gen. 27:40), but even Esau had never attacked his brother Jacob (Gen. 33). With the dynamic of the divine promises to Abraham and the blood relationship between Jacob and Esau as the literary backdrop for Obadiah, no wonder the sense of outrage at Esau's treachery. Edom's attack on Israel was more than simply a matter of international politics and opportunism: it was the betrayal of a brother and a strike against God's plan for Edom established so many centuries ago when they came from Rebekah's womb. This plan established in the distant past would yet be realized in the eschatological future: Edom will yet serve his brother as God had purposed (Robinson 1988, 94–95).

> *For his contemporaries who had suffered great tragedy, Obadiah holds out confidence in the triumph of divine justice and God's ultimate purposes.*

In addition to this emphasis on God's sovereignty and his power to effect his will, Obadiah also shows a pronounced interest in divine justice. For his contemporaries who had suffered great tragedy, Obadiah holds out confidence in the triumph of divine justice and God's ultimate purposes. The *lex talionis*, the law of compensatory judgment, is pronounced: "As you have done, it will be done to you; your deeds will return upon your own head" (v. 15b). Edom had cut down the survivors in Judah, but she will be left without survivors (vv. 14, 18). Edom had occupied Judah's territory (vv. 13, 16), but ultimately Esau would be governed from Mount Zion (v. 21).

Though short, Obadiah shares a number of theological themes with the other prophetic books. As Raabe (1996, 3) states, "this short book summarizes many of the great prophetic themes, such as divine judgment against Israel's enemies, the day of Yahweh, the *lex talionis* as the standard of judgment, the cup-of-wrath metaphor, Zion theology, Israel's possession of the land, and the kingship of Yahweh."

APPROACHING THE NEW TESTAMENT

The ancient rivalry and ongoing conflict between Jacob and Esau, Israel and Edom has its echoes in the New Testament. We see it when Herod the Great, an Idumean and descendant of Edom, seeks to destroy Jesus at his birth (Matt. 2:16). An Idumean/Edomite sought to destroy that child who embodied all that Israel was meant to be.

Paul, too, recalls this ancient saga. He defends God's own sovereign right of election. Rebekah's two children had one and the same father, and the sons were twins. But God had determined that "the older will serve the younger" (Gen. 25:23; Rom. 9:12), just as Malachi had said, "I have loved Jacob, but Esau I have hated" (Mal. 1:2–3).

CHAPTER TWENTY-NINE

JONAH

Jonah contains one of the most memorable stories in the Bible. Many people know the account of the prophet who was swallowed by a great fish. This story has evoked wonder in many and ridicule from others. Unfortunately, the debate that surrounds the historicity of this story has obscured its literary beauty and theological significance.

No one can deny that Jonah is a book unlike any other prophetic book in the canon. Most prophecies center around the preaching of the prophet. Jonah, on the other hand, is a prose narrative. The prophet's preaching is reluctant and contained in a single verse (3:4), which does not even mention God's name. While unique and at times perplexing, the book of Jonah contains a theological message that is relevant for today.

BIBLIOGRAPHY

Commentaries

L. C. **Allen,** *The Books of Joel, Obadiah, Jonah and Micah* (NICOT; Eerdmans, 1976); D. W. **Baker,** T. D. **Alexander,** and B. K. **Waltke,** *Obadiah, Jonah, Micah* (TOTC; InterVarsity Press, 1988); J. **Baldwin,** "Jonah," in *The Minor Prophets: An Exegetical and Expository Commentary,* ed. T. E. McComiskey (Baker, 1992), 543–90; P. C. **Craigie,** *Twelve Prophets* (DSB; Westminster, 1985); J. **Limburg,** *Jonah* (OTL; Westminster, 1993); F. S. **Page,** *Amos, Obadiah, Jonah* (NAC; Broadman, 1995); W. **Rudolph,** *Joel, Amos, Obadja, Jona* (*KAT*; 1971); J. M. **Sasson,** *Jonah* (AB; Doubleday, 1990); D. **Stuart,** *Hosea–Jonah* (WBC; Word, 1987); H. W. **Wolff,** *Obadiah and Jonah: A Commentary,* trans. M. Kohl (Augsburg, 1986).

Articles and Monographs

G. Ch. **Aalders,** *The Problem of the Book of Jonah* (London: Tyndale, 1948; repr. 1976); T. D. **Alexander,** "Jonah and Genre," *TynBul* 36 (1985): 35–59; A. **Berlin,** *Poetics and Interpretation of Biblical Narrative* (Almond, 1983); D. E. **Hart-Davies,** "The Book of Jonah in the Light of Assyrian Archaeology," *Journal of the*

Transactions of the Victoria Institute 69 (1937): 230–47; J. D. **Magonet**, *Form and Meaning: Studies in the Literary Techniques in the Book of Jonah* (Bern: Herbert Lang, 1976); R. D. **Wilson,** "The Authenticity of Jonah," *PTR* 16 (1918): 280–98; H. W. **Wolff,** *Studien zum Jonahbuch* (1964, 2nd ed. 1975).

HISTORICAL BACKGROUND

The book contains no indication of author or date of composition (contra Young, *IOT,* 261). Jonah, the main character of the book, was a real prophet who lived during the reign of Jeroboam II (786–746). He was from Gath-Hepher (el-Meshded), northeast of Nazareth. According to 2 Kings, he prophesied the expansion of the northern kingdom, which took place during Jeroboam's reign.

Some conservative scholars insist that the book must be a type of historical narration. After all, we know from Kings that Jonah was a real prophet. Furthermore, the book is closely related in form to the so-called historical books of the Old Testament. Third, advocates of this position argue that Jesus' reference to Jonah and Nineveh (Matt. 12:39–40; Luke 11:29–30) shows that he believed the book was a historical report.

Objections have been raised against a straightforward historical reading of the book, however. The most common has been the infamous debate surrounding Jonah's three days in the fish's belly. Skeptics have found the story preposterous; others have suggested that it is an indication that the book as a whole is not a simple historical report. Conservative apologists (see Page 1995) respond by citing occasions in modern times when sailors have survived (though often in a poor state of repair) a stay in the innards of a large fish (Aalders 1976, 5–6). Such a line of argumentation leaves careful readers unsatisfied, since the biblical account implies a miraculous intervention by God.

The book of Jonah displays other characteristics that may further signal that the author did not intend his readers to understand his account to be historical. There is, for instance, a level of vagueness in the world of the story. Jonah is the only character with a name. Even the "king of Nineveh" is unnamed, his title being unusual since Nineveh was the name of the capital city, not of the empire itself.

The book is a literary tour de force. It is brilliant in its use of structure, irony, and rhetorical ornamentation (see next section). This clear literary artifice is taken by some as a signal that the story should be described as some kind of fiction rather than as a historical report. Besides the fish incident, there are other elements that are interpreted as fanciful exaggerations. The two most notable are the "repentance of the animals" (3:7–8) and the description of the size of Nineveh (3:3–5).

Persuaded by these arguments, a number of scholars (notably Allen 1976) reject the historical interpretation and substitute an alternative in its place. While an allegorical approach was popular in the past, today the main alternative is a parabolic interpretation. Limburg, for instance, concludes, "The book of Jonah may be described as a fictional story developed around a historical figure for didactic purposes" (1993, 24). One must be careful not to oversimplify by categorizing all people who argue for a parabolic interpretation as deniers of the miraculous. Clearly, some are driven to a nonhistorical reading of the book because they do not believe the fish incident is possible. But others, such as Allen, are convinced that the inspired author intended his book to be read as a parable, not as a historical report.

When all the arguments are in, two points emerge. The first is that it is impossible to be dogmatic either way. There are plausible, but not provable, arguments to counter the points against a historical reading (see Alexander 1985 for the best defense of a historical reading; also Page 1995). For instance, those who identify the genre of Jonah as historical report can point to a text in Herodotus that mentions animals engaged in mourning rites and can appeal to Judith 4:10. They can say that when the narrator describes the size of Nineveh what is meant is the administrative district and not the city itself. On the other hand, there are plausible, but not provable, answers to the arguments in favor of a historical reading. The most compelling argument in favor of a historical reading is that Jesus' reference to Jonah and Nineveh indicates that he believed the book was historical. However, while this is possible, it is not certain. After all, Jesus could refer to the event in his preaching even if it were a parable. In a similar way, a preacher today exhorts the congregation to be like the Good Samaritan even though few believe that the Good Samaritan was a historical person.

The second point is that the question is irrelevant to the interpretation of the book. This is not to say that the issue is unimportant. If the book intends to be historical but makes a historical error, that is theologically significant. But the question of the intention of historicity is totally without effect on the interpretation of the book's theological message or even the exegesis of individual passages.

LITERARY ANALYSIS

Genre

Since the text's genre is so closely tied to the issue of historicity, we found it necessary to discuss this issue in the preceding section. In the final analysis, it is impossible to definitively decide the issue. From our chronological distance, the generic signals at times point to a historical reading of the text, but at other times they open the possibility of a parabolic interpretation. This is an area where room for disagreement must be allowed to exist.

Style

Even if Jonah is intended to be read as a historical account, there is no doubt that the prose is highly stylized. The author bolstered his message with close attention to literary style.

This concern for rhetoric may be seen in the strategic repetition of certain key terms (*Leitwörter*) that provide a thread through the book or a single episode of the book (Magonet 1976). One of those *Leitwört* is the verb "rise up" (*qûm*). In 1:2 God commands Jonah, "Arise, go to Nineveh" (KJV, RSV; TNIV, NIV, NRSV collapse to simply "Go"). The next verse begins in a way that would lead the reader to expect a typical command-fulfillment pattern "and Jonah rose up . . ." (again omitted from the TNIV). But instead of completing this sentence with the expected "to go to Nineveh," the author-narrator inserts "to flee to Tarshish" (KJV). A further ironic play on this verb is met in 1:6. God pursues Jonah as he flees to Tarshish by stirring up a storm that threatens the safety of the ship. The pagan sailors who are working feverishly to save the ship are dumbfounded to learn that Jonah is asleep in the hold. We still have God's initial command to Jonah to "rise up" ringing in our minds when we hear the captain of the ship tell Jonah, "Arise, call upon your god!" (RSV). An initial resolution to the story comes in 3:2–3 after Jonah spends a few nights in the belly of the "great fish." God commissions the prophet a second time by repeating his command "Arise, go to Nineveh." This time Jonah obeys: he "arose and went" (RSV).

This short analysis is just one example of a common characteristic of the literary style of Jonah. Similar studies could be made of the words "great" (*gâdôl:* 1:2, 4, 12, 17; 3:2, 3; 4:11), "to provide" (*mânâ:* 1:17; 4:6, 7, 8); "go down" (*yârad:* 1:3 [2 times], 6; 2:6).

Structure

The book may be divided into two major acts with two scenes apiece. The acts are divided by the repetition of God's commission to the prophet in 1:1–2 and 3:1–2. The first act takes place at sea for the most part. Its two scenes are (1) on board ship and (2) in the belly of the fish. The second two chapters (3 and 4) constitute the second act, each chapter making up a single scene. In the initial scene of the second act, Jonah preaches and Nineveh repents. The setting of the last scene shifts to east of Nineveh, where Jonah struggles with God's ways of judgment and salvation.

Jonah's Psalm

The only serious issue surrounding the literary unity of the book of Jonah arises with the psalm in the second chapter (2:2–9). Some scholars have expressed the opinion that the psalm fits poorly into the context and presents a picture of Jonah that is out of character with the rest of the book.

On a surface reading of the story, for instance, we might expect a different type of psalm. Jonah has just been swallowed by the fish; we expect him to offer a lament psalm in the midst of his trouble. We are surprised by what is clearly a thanksgiving psalm. Particularly in 2:2, 6, and 9, he talks as if he is already saved.

Such questions arise, though, due to a faulty assessment of Jonah's situation. The fish was not an instrument of God's judgment, but rather of his salvation, since it saved Jonah from death by drowning.

More perplexing, however, is the fact that Jonah affirms his loyalty to God in a most profound way in the psalm, but then, in the following chapter, he is the reluctant prophet once again. Indeed, in the last chapter he is antagonistic toward God as well.

In answer to this issue, it is only necessary to say that Jonah is not a flat, but a complex character. That is, in his spiritual ups and downs he acts like a real person. This roundness of character (Berlin 1983, 23–42) is one of the reasons that Jonah is such a fascinating and rich book.

THEOLOGICAL MESSAGE

As we have seen, Jonah is an unusual book in many ways. One of the most striking characteristics of the book in its Old Testament setting is its attitude toward those outside of the covenant community. It is certainly not unprecedented that God shows concern for Gentiles. Indeed, the all-important promise to Abraham includes the idea that "all the people of the earth will be blessed through you" (Gen. 12:3; 21:8–21; 2 Kings 5) Even so, the inclusion of the Gentiles is not a frequent Old Testament theme.

The book of Jonah focuses in two ways on God's compassion for those outside of Israel. In the first place, the book contrasts spiritually sensitive pagans with the reluctant Israelite prophet. In chapter 1, the pagan sailors shake before God's wrathful storm, while Jonah sleeps in the hold of the ship. They are concerned that God not hold them accountable for Jonah's death when they cast him overboard. In the last half of the book, Jonah preaches to the people of Nineveh (3:4), but he mentions neither God's name nor the possibility of repentance. Nonetheless, the people repent (3:5), and the king, who only hears of Jonah's message secondhand, calls for city-wide repentance (3:7–9). In the second place, the book ends on a note that focuses on God's feelings toward Nineveh as he rhetorically asks Jonah, "Should I not have concern for the great city Nineveh?"

While expressing God's compassion toward non-Israelites, the book also delivers a stern rebuke to Israel. Jonah represents the Israelites in the book; indeed, he is the only Israelite in the book. As a prophet, he should be the apex of spirituality. The prophets were the servants of the Lord. This servant, however, did everything he could to avoid fulfilling the divine command. When he finally went to Nineveh, he did so quite reluctantly. Then when the people of Nineveh repented and God spared them punishment, Jonah sank into a deep depression and anger toward God. Jonah is out of touch with God. How much more Israel!

One of the most striking characteristics of the book in its Old Testament setting is its attitude toward those outside of the covenant community.

One issue over which there has been some discussion is the cause of Jonah's depression. Some believe that Jonah was reluctant to preach to Nineveh because he was afraid that he would be perceived as a false prophet (Rendtorff, *OTI*, 226). That is, God wanted him to go to Nineveh and warn the people of coming doom, but since God is a longsuffering God (4:2), he might relent of his judgment and the prophecy would then not come true.

As Childs points out against this line of reasoning (*IOTS*, 420–21), the prophet's purpose was to call a wayward people back to repentance. His message of doom was contingent, in one sense, upon the reaction of the people.

It is better to understand Jonah's reluctance and resultant depression as stemming from God's compassion, not just toward a Gentile nation, but a vicious and cruel imperial power that constantly threatened his homeland. Jonah felt Israel deserved better than to have its God forgive its enemies. The psalmist constantly calls upon God to destroy his enemies. Here, God forgives them.

We learn, then, that God is the God of the universe and not just of Israel. This message is highlighted in another way as well that can be followed by examining another *Leitwört*, "to appoint," or "to provide" (*mânâ*). Throughout the story Jonah tries to escape God, but God utilizes his creation to bring him back. God provides a great fish (1:17), a vine (4:6), a worm (4:7), and a scorching east wind (4:8) to show Jonah that there is no way he can escape God. He is the God of Israel, the God of Nineveh, the God of the entire creation.

APPROACHING THE NEW TESTAMENT

The New Testament, of course, proclaims that Gentiles can come to God and be part of the covenant people. Jesus Christ was sent to the world, not just to Israel (John 1:6–14).

Jesus himself compared and contrasted his ministry with the ministry of Jonah (Matt. 12:38–45; Luke 11:24–32). He was asked for a miraculous sign, and in response he said that he would be three days and three nights in the earth. He compared this with Jonah's stay in the belly of the fish, referring to the time between his crucifixion and his resurrection (Luke 24:46). He is "greater than Jonah," however, because while Jonah reluctantly preached to save a city against his will, Jesus freely gave up his life to save many.

CHAPTER THIRTY

MICAH

According to Luther, "the prophets have a queer way of talking, like people who instead of proceeding in an orderly manner, ramble off from one thing to the next so that you cannot make head or tail of them or see what they are getting at" (quoted in Smith 1984, 8). No prophet illustrates this statement better than Micah. It is easy to get lost in the mix of his judgment and salvation speeches. The structure is hard to fathom.

On the other hand, Micah, the sixth of the minor prophets,[1] compares with Isaiah in terms of rhetorical eloquence and power. Also, embedded in Micah are some of the most well-known texts in the Old Testament, texts that describe the elevation of the mountain of God (4:1–5); foretell of a ruler who will come out of Bethlehem (5:2); and list justice, mercy, and humility as the traits God desires to see in his people (6:6–8).

BIBLIOGRAPHY

Commentaries

L. C. **Allen,** *The Books of Obadiah, Jonah, and Micah* (Eerdmans, 1976); F. I. **Andersen** and D. N. **Freedman,** *Micah* (AB; Doubleday, 2000); D. W. **Baker,** T. D. **Alexander,** and B. K. **Waltke,** *Obadiah, Jonah, Micah* (TOTC; InterVarsity Press, 1988); E. **Ben Zvi,** *Micah* (FOTL; Eerdmans, 2000); D. **Hillers,** *Micah* (Hermeneia; Fortress, 1984); T. **Longman** III, "Micah," in *Evangelical Old Testament Commentary,* ed. W. A. Elwell (Baker, 1989), 659–764; J. L. **Mays,** *Micah* (OTL; Westminster, 1976); G. V. **Smith,** *Hosea/Amos/Micah* (NIVAC; Zondervan, 2001); R. L. **Smith,** *Micah–Malachi* (WBC; Word, 1984); B. W. **Waltke,** "Micah," in *The Minor Prophets: An Exegetical and Expository Commentary,* ed. T. E. McComiskey (Baker, 1992), 591–764.

---

[1]That is, Micah is sixth in the Masoretic tradition. The Greek Old Testament places Micah third after Amos and Hosea, two of his older contemporaries.

Articles and Monographs

S. **Dawes,** "Walking Humbly: Micah 6:8 Revisited," *SJT* 41 (1988): 331–39; K. **Jeppesen,** "New Aspects of Micah Research," *JSOT* 8 (1978): 3–32; idem, "How the Book of Micah Lost Its Integrity: Outline of the History of the Criticism of the Book of Micah with Emphasis on the 19th Century," *ST* 33 (1979): 101–31; J. **Jeremias,** "Die Bedeutung der Gerichtswörte Michas in der Exilszeit," *ZAW* 83 (1971): 330–53; A. S. **Kapelrud,** "Eschatology in the Book of Micah," *VT* 11 (1961): 392–405; I. **Provan,** V. P. **Long,** and T. **Longman** III, *A Biblical History of Israel* (Westminster John Knox, 2003); B. **Renaud,** *Structure et attaches littéraires de Michee IV–V* (Paris, 1964); idem, *La Formation du Livre de Michee* (Paris, 1977); L. P. **Smith,** "The Book of Micah," *Interp* 6 (1952): 210–27; B. **Stade,** "Bemerkungen über das Buch Micha," *ZAW* 1 (1881): 161–72; A. S. **Van der Woude,** "Micah and the Pseudo-Prophets," *VT* 19 (1969): 244–60.

HISTORICAL BACKGROUND

Authorship and Date

The first verse of the book is a typical prophetic superscription, which, among other things, names the prophet along with his hometown (Micah of Moresheth) and dates his ministry by listing contemporaneous kings. The name Micah is common in the Old Testament (a longer form of the name is Micaiah) and means "Who is like Yahweh?"

Moresheth was a village approximately twenty-five miles southwest of Jerusalem. The village was located on the edge of the rolling hills of the Shephelah, near the coastal plain. Scholars are not certain why Micah's parentage is not mentioned, but it may be because his family was not prominent. He is identified by means of his hometown because his ministry took place at a different city (probably Jerusalem).

Micah is mentioned in only one other place in the Old Testament (Jer. 26:17–19). When Jehoiakim came to the throne in Judah, the priests and the false prophets tried to put Jeremiah to death. Some elders interceded for him and cited the ministry of Micah as a justification for Jeremiah's prophecy of judgment. As opposed to Jehoiakim, who wanted Jeremiah dead for his prophecy of judgment, Hezekiah repented.[2]

Typically, critical scholars have raised the issue of authenticity. Was Micah responsible for the oracles he is associated with? A common critical position is that the genuine oracles of Micah are restricted to the first three chapters (see History of Research below). If one grants the possibility of predictive prophecy,

---

[2]Indeed, according to A. F. Kirkpatrick, "Hezekiah's reformation was due to the preaching of Micah" (quoted by Allen 1976, 240).

however, there are no persuasive reasons for denying Micah the authorship of any part of the book.

The first verse is our source of information on the date of Micah's ministry. Three kings of Judah are listed to provide the period of time during which Micah preached judgment and salvation among the people: Jotham (750–732 BC), Ahaz (732–716), and Hezekiah (715–686). Micah's work may have begun toward the end of Jotham's reign and ended at the beginning of Hezekiah's, so we cannot be certain about the exact length of his ministry. In any case, he overlapped with Isaiah (Smith 1952, 211).

The reference to the coming judgment of Samaria (1:6) indicates that Micah's preaching began well before 722 BC, the year in which Samaria fell to the forces of Assyria. Another oracle that may be fairly certainly dated is the lament in 1:8–16. The cities mentioned in this section coincide with the probable route of Sennacherib's army as he approached Jerusalem in 701. The reference in Jeremiah 26:18 cites Micah 3:12 as an oracle delivered during the reign of Hezekiah.

Historical Period

A brief overview of the history of Israel and Judah (for more detail, see Provan, Long, and Longman 2003, 271–77) that relates to the prophecy of Micah begins with the downfall of Samaria at the hands of the Assyrian army under the leadership of Shalmaneser V (722 BC). During the reign of Sargon II, Israel did not rebel, but upon this strong king's death and the accession of his son Sennacherib, Hezekiah joined a coalition led by a Babylonian rebel, Merodach-baladan (2 Kings 18ff.). In reaction, Sennacherib threatened the independence of Jerusalem (701), but through the ministry of Isaiah and Micah, Hezekiah repented of his sins and God spared the city. Nevertheless, it was not long after Hezekiah's death that the rulers of Judah turned against the Lord. Manasseh, his son, for instance, brought much grief to Judah. Micah's prophecy looks forward to the destruction of Judah at the hands of the Babylonians, which took place in 586 BC, and even further ahead to the restoration from captivity (539).

History of Research

As mentioned above, it is almost a commonplace in critical circles to say that authentic Micah oracles are restricted to the first three chapters. Jeppesen (1978) has written a helpful summary of the research that led to this conclusion, which he questions.

The turning point in the history of the interpretation of Micah comes with an article by Bernhard Stade in 1881. However, before recounting that article, Jeppesen sets the scene for his work by recounting the encroachment of Enlightenment presuppositions in the study of the prophets, which included the denial of supernatural prophecy. The first prophet whose unity came under suspicion was Isaiah at the end of the eighteenth century.

The early decades of the nineteenth century were a time of transition and turmoil concerning the date and authenticity of Micah. But no consensus was reached. One of the matters of dispute concerned the relationship between the prophetic superscription (1:1) and the connection drawn between the prophet and Hezekiah in Jeremiah 26. Most scholars felt that all of the prophet's ministry should be dated to this king's time period and none before. This conclusion concerns the authentic material. Glosses from later periods were also present. Jeppesen (1978, 114–15) notes that it is during this period of time that H. G. A. Ewald convinced the academic guild that chapters 6–7 presupposed a different, later setting than chapters 1–5.

It was Stade (1881) who first formulated the theory that rapidly became the consensus in the field, namely, that Micah's authentic oracles are limited to the first three chapters and that the final form of the book we have today dates from the postexilic period. He agreed with Ewald about chapters 6–7 and dated it to the period of Deutero-Isaiah. Since the time of Stade, it has been a critical commonplace to consider Micah a composite work whose final date is in the postexilic period.

Recent efforts have been expended toward the discovery of the redactional history of the book's development. These scholars have concluded that the book came into being over a long period of time and that it was not completed until the postexilic period. However, while agreeing in principle, they have come up with rather divergent pictures of the composition of the book (see especially Jeremias, Mays, and Renaud; consult Childs, *IOTS*, 431–34, for a critique[3]).

LITERARY ANALYSIS

Much debate surrounds the structure of the book of Micah. Opinions vary radically. *Some argue that the book has no overall structure but is simply a loose collection of prophetic oracles. Others identify extremely complex and sophisticated structures.* A few points are certain:

1. Micah did not speak these oracles at one time. The book is best taken as an anthology of his prophetic messages over the years of his ministry.

2. Chronology is not the key to the structure of the book, though early in the book Micah does predict the capture of Samaria and Sennacherib's invasion, while at the conclusion of this book, he looks forward to the Babylonian captivity and the restoration.

3. The prophecy is roughly structured on the basis of alternating messages of threat and hope. God through his prophet disputes with his people in two rounds. The first is found in chapters 1–5. There is a harsh message of judg-

---

[3]Childs himself argues that Micah's message was shaped by the same circle of tridents who worked with the Isaianic materials (434–36).

ment (1:2–3:9 [2:12–13 may be an exception]), but also a note of salvation (4–5 [5:10–15 may be an exception]). The second round (6–7) also begins with judgment (6:1–7:7), but concludes on a profound note of hope (7:8–20).

Outline

Superscription (1:1)
I. First round of judgment and salvation (1:2–5:15)
   A. God's judgment of apostasy and social sin in Samaria and Judah (1:2–3:12)
   B. God's word of hope to Israel (4:1–2:15)
II. Second round of judgment and salvation (6:1–7:20)
   A. God's dispute with Israel (6:1–8)
   B. God's reproach for Israel's social sins (6:9–16)
   C. The prophet laments Israel's condition (7:1–7)
   D. Psalms of hope and praise (7:8–20)

Style

Micah's powerful literary style has been overlooked for two reasons. First, the Hebrew is difficult, and the structure is not immediately clear to contemporary readers. Second, Micah has been overshadowed by his better-known contemporary, Isaiah.

Nonetheless, the prophet Micah was a master with words and images. Perhaps nowhere in the book is this better illustrated than in Micah 1:10–16. Historically, this is a prophetic description of the route taken by Sennacherib's army as it marched toward Jerusalem. Specific towns and cities are mentioned, and Micah uses interesting wordplays to narrate what will happen. The wordplays relate the cities' names to their fate. For the most part, English translations cannot convey the connection, but James Moffatt's paraphrase gives the reader an idea of what is going on (quoted by Smith 1952, 213):

Tell it not in Tellington!
Wail not in Wailing!
Dust Manor will eat dirt,
Dressy Town flee naked.
Safefold will not save,
Wallchester's walls are down,
A bitter dose drinks Bitterton.
(Towards Jerusalem, City of Peace,
The Lord sends war.)
Harness the war-steeds,
O men of Barstead!
(Zion's beginning of sinning,

Equal to Israel's crimes.)
To Welfare a last farewell!
For Trapping trapped Israel's kings.

THEOLOGICAL MESSAGE

The theology of Micah is largely concerned with divine judgment against sin. Yahweh commissioned Micah to bring this message of judgment against his people. Israel and Judah had both departed from the way of the Lord and angered him by their sin. The sin is cultic (1:5–7) as well as social (2:1–2). Israel's civil (3:1–3) and religious leaders (2:6–11 [prophets]; 3:11 [priests]) have rejected the ways of God. They have a false security in the Lord.

This assertion may be illustrated by the attitudes of the false prophets against whom Micah frequently speaks. They taught that Israel was secure, and thus they did not speak the word of God. Van der Woude (1969) made the case that Micah often quoted his prophetic opponents as, for instance, in Micah 3:11:

> Her leaders judge for a bribe,
>   her priests teach for a price,
>   and her prophets tell fortunes for money.
> Yet they lean upon the LORD and say,
>   "Is not the LORD among us?
>   No disaster will come upon us."

The Lord, accordingly, presses his case against his people, who have broken covenant with him. He reveals himself as a warrior against his people (1:3–4). The Lord desires that his people love him and act justly. He calls them back to himself.

Perhaps one of the most moving passages in the book, and certainly the most well known today, is 6:6–8, taken in Jewish tradition as a summary of the law:

> With what shall I come before the LORD
>   and bow down before the exalted God?
> Shall I come before him with burnt offerings,
>   with calves a year old?
> Will the LORD be pleased with thousands of rams,
>   with ten thousand rivers of oil?
> Shall I offer my firstborn for my transgression,
>   the fruit of my body for the sin of my soul?
> He has shown all you people what is good.
>   And what does the LORD require of you?
> To act justly and to love mercy
>   and to walk humbly with your God.

While some have tried to read this as a polemic against all priestly religion, Dawes (1988) has rightly pointed out that it is simply to correct an unhealthy emphasis on external religion among some Israelites (see also Amos 5:21–27; Hos. 6:6; Isa. 1:10–17).

While judgment against sin is the dominant note of the book, hope is not lacking. As early as 2:12–13, Yahweh speaks in comforting tones of salvation after judgment. The final picture of God (7:18–20) shows him to be unprecedented in grace and true to his covenant promise to Abraham. The promises to David are not dead, but will be fulfilled in the future (5:1–2).

APPROACHING THE NEW TESTAMENT

While Micah directed his oracles of judgment and hope toward Israel and Judah of his day, he used words that transcended the immediate historical crisis and, by doing so, took his readers into the more distant future (see Kapelrud 1961 for an analysis of the eschatology of Micah from a moderate critical point of view).

The New Testament authors recognized this. The gospel of Matthew cites Micah 5:2 in references to Jesus' birth in Bethlehem (see Matt. 2:5–6). In its Mican context, the oracle looks forward to a future David-like ruler. That is the significance of the Bethlehem birthplace.

Micah 4:1–5 evokes the picture of the exalted mountain of God and a time when the peoples of the world will flock to the worship of God. There will be peace and no war. This oracle is introduced by the rubric "in the last days." As redemptive history unfolds, it appears that this prophecy finds several anticipatory fulfillments before its ultimate fulfillment in the eschaton. In Waltke's words:

> In this vision Micah presents the final, consummating vision with Mount Zion established forever as the cultic and moral center of all nations. In the succeeding oracles he presents the steps by which it will be fulfilled.
>
> The first stage in the fulfillment of this prophecy occurred with the return from Babylon and the rebuilding of the second temple. Its next, and much greater stage, was realized when Christ ascended into the heavenly sanctuary and the earthly type was done away. The third stage, the climactic moment, will be consummated in the new heavens and new earth when kings of the earth bring their splendor into the new Jerusalem that comes down out of heaven (Rev. 21:1, 10, 22–27). (Baker, Alexander, and Waltke 1988)

Micah used words that transcended the immediate historical crisis and, by doing so, took his readers into the more distant future.

CHAPTER THIRTY-ONE

NAHUM

The prophet Nahum, whose name means "compassion," delivered a stern message of judgment against Assyria in the seventh century BC. The tone of the book is harsh, and the message, directed toward a particular nation at a specific time, appears to many to be irrelevant. This assessment, though faulty, has kept many Christians from studying the book. No one denies the book's aesthetic value, and if understood within its historical and theological context, it has tremendous significance for us today.

BIBLIOGRAPHY

Commentaries

E. **Achtemeier,** *Nahum–Malachi* (Interp; John Knox, 1986); D. W. **Baker,** *Nahum, Habakkuk and Zephaniah* (TOTC; InterVarsity Press, 1988); M. H. **Floyd,** *Minor Prophets, Part 2* (FOTL; Eerdmans, 2000); C. A. **Keller,** *Nahoum* (Neuchâtel: Delachaux et Niestlé, 1971); T. **Longman** III, "Nahum," in *Commentary on the Minor Prophets*, ed. T. E. McComiskey (Baker, 1993); W. A. **Maier,** *The Book of Nahum: A Commentary* (Concordia, 1959; repr. Baker, 1980); R. **Patterson,** *Nahum, Habakkuk, Zephaniah* (WEC; Moody, 1991); J. M. **Roberts,** *Nahum, Habakkuk, and Zephaniah* (OTL; Westminster John Knox, 1991); W. **Rudolph,** *Micha, Nahum, Habakuk, Zephanja* (Guterslow: Verlagshaus Gerd Mohn, 1975); J. M. P. **Smith,** *A Critical and Exegetical Commentary on the Book of Nahum* (ICC; T. & T. Clark, 1912); R. L. **Smith,** *Micah–Malachi* (WBC; Word, 1984); K. **Spronk,** *Nahum* (HCOT; Kok Pharos, 1997); A. S. **Van der Woude,** *Jona, Nahum* (Nijkerk, 1978).

Articles and Monographs

K. J. **Cathcart,** *Nahum in the Light of Northwest Semitic Philology* (Rome: Pontifical Biblical Institute, 1973); idem, "The Divine Warrior and the War of Yahweh in

Nahum," in *Biblical Studies in Contemporary Thought*, ed. M. Ward; Somerville, Mass., 1975), 68–76; J. S. **Cochrane,** "Literary Features of Nahum," Th.M. thesis (Dallas Theological Seminary, 1954); T. F. **Glasson,** "Final Question in Nahum and Jonah," *ExpTim* 81 (1969): 54–55; A. **Haldar,** *Studies in the Book of Nahum* (Uppsala, 1947); F. **Horst,** "Die Visionsschiderungen der alttestamentlichen Propheten," *EvTh* 20 (1960): 193–205; W. **Janzen,** *Mourning Cry and Woe Oracle* (*BZAW* 125; Berlin: De Gruyter, 1972); J. **Jeremias,** *Kultprophetie und Gerichtsverkundigung in den spaten Konigszeit Israels* (WMANT 35; Neukirchen-Vluyn, 1970); T. **Longman** III, "The Divine Warrior: The New Testament Use of an Old Testament Motif," *WTJ* 44 (1982): 290–307; idem, "Psalm 98: A Divine Warrior Victory Song," *JETS* 27 (1985): 267–74; idem, "The Form and Message of Nahum: Preaching from a Prophet of Doom," *Reformed Theological Journal* 1 (1985): 13–24; T. **Longman** III and D. **Reid,** *God Is a Warrior* (Zondervan, 1995); R. **Lowth,** *Lectures on the Sacred Poetry of the Hebrews* (1753; repr. London: T. Tegg and Son, 1835); J. A. **Naudé,** "*Maúûâ'* in the Old Testament with a Special Reference to the Prophets," *OTSWA* 12 (1969): 91–100; H. **Schulz,** *Das Buch Nahum* (*BZAW* 129; Berlin-New York, 1973); M. **Sister,** "Die Typen der prophetischen Visionen in der Bible," *MGWJ* 78 (1934): 399–430; M. A. **Sweeney,** "Concerning the Structure and Generic Character of the Book of Nahum," *ZAW* 104 (1992): 364–77; A. S. **Van de Woude,** "The Book of Nahum: A Letter Written in Exile," *OTSWA* 20 (1977); J. **Van Doorslaer,** "No Amon," *CBQ* 11 (1949): 280–95; E. **von Voigtlander,** "A Survey of Neo-Babylonian History," Ph.D. diss. (University of Michigan, 1963); D. **Wiseman,** *Chronicles of the Chaldean Kings (626–556 B.C.)* (British Museum Publications, 1956); S. **Zawadzki,** *The Fall of Assyria and Median-Babylonian Relations in Light of the Nabopolassar Chronicle* (Delft: Eburon, 1988).

HISTORICAL BACKGROUND

Authorship

The superscription of the book informs us that the author's name was Nahum. We know little more about him except that he comes from a town called Elkosh. Unfortunately, we have no firm evidence on this town's location. Four hypotheses have been proposed in the history of interpretation: (1) Eastern medieval tradition located Elkosh in the vicinity of Nineveh (at a site called Al-Kush) and argued that Nahum was the descendant of an exiled northern Israelite family. (2) Others (Jerome in antiquity and Van der Woude more recently) place Elkosh in Galilee at a site called El-Kauzeh. (3) A second site in the northern kingdom has also been proposed. This is Capernaum on the northern shore of the Sea of Galilee. A possible etymology of Capernaum is "Nahum's city." (4) A still further proposed location is in Judah. In a tradition beginning with Pseudo-Epiphanius and continued today by R. K. Harrison (*IOT*, 26), Elkosh is believed to be in the area around Begebar, the modern Beit Jibrin.

These four sites cover all the possibilities, including Assyria, the area of the former northern kingdom, and Judah. Unfortunately, to say more is to move into the realm of utter speculation and does little to help us understand the book.

Historical Period

Nahum is deeply integrated into its historical milieu. Accordingly, it is especially important to understand the historical background to the book in order for its message to make sense to the modern reader.

The prophecy places itself in the seventh century BC. This date is established by the mention of the destruction of Thebes, which occurred in 664 BC (3:8), and the major focus of the prophecy, the destruction of Nineveh, which took place in 612. If the prophetic nature of the book is taken seriously, then Nahum must be dated at least a couple of years before the destruction of the city. It is difficult to be more precise. Some scholars (Maier 1959, 35–36) argue that the reference to Thebes is so vivid that the prophecy must be dated closer to the early date than to the fulfillment of the prophecy. This line of argumentation is weak, however, in the light of the prophet's poetic power. Nahum's masterful use of imagery shows that he has the ability to make even the most ancient event "come alive." However, more plausible is the argument that Nahum wrote before the Assyrian Empire significantly weakened (a process that noticeably began around the year 630 BC). This position is based on Nahum 1:12, which describes Assyria as "intact" and large. One should not be inflexible on the precise date, but the most likely time for the prophecy is between 652 (the time of the civil war [see below]) and 626, the year that Babylon began its long war to throw off Assyrian hegemony.

The focus of the prophecy is the judgment of Assyria, so it is important to learn the history of Assyria in the period under discussion. The latter half of the eighth and into the seventh centuries was a period of Assyrian power and expansion. Under such able leaders as Tiglath-Pileser III (745–727), Shalmaneser V (726–722), Sargon II (721–705), Sennacherib (704–681), and Esarhaddon (680–669), the Assyrian Empire had reached unprecedented heights of imperial control. Assyrian power and culture climaxed in the early years of Ashurbanipal (668–627?). Although his father, Esarhaddon, had made an incursion into Egypt, it is perhaps correct to say that Assyria hit its imperial high level mark when Ashurbanipal captured Thebes, the ancient capital of Egypt (664).

Significant problems arose as early as 652, however. Babylon had been a political vassal of Assyria for years, but it had always been a problem. Esarhaddon had devised a plan that he thought would solve the Babylonian problem and also the potentially dangerous rivalry that might arise between his offspring after his death. The history of the ancient Near East is full of stories of brothers fighting against brothers for control of the throne. Esarhaddon directed that upon his death one of his sons (Ashurbanipal) would take the throne of Assyria, and the other son, Šamaš-šum-ukin, would ascend to the throne of Babylon. Of course, Šamaš-šum-ukin was subordinate to Ashurbanipal, just as Babylon was to Assyria. Nevertheless, this arrangement worked well for over a decade. But in the year 652 Šamaš-šum-ukin led a revolt of Chaldeans against his brother. While Ashurbanipal eventually won the war, it was at a heavy cost. Assyrian energy waned, and thus began a long, slow spiral to destruction.

The last few years of Ashurbanipal and the years immediately after his death are poorly documented and therefore poorly known, but from Babylonian records (Wiseman) we know that a Chaldean leader named Nabopolassar rallied his people in a revolt against Assyria that waged back and forth for many years. The climax of the war came in the year 612 with the destruction of Nineveh.

There is some ambiguity in the Babylonian and later descriptions of the fall of Nineveh (Zawadzki 1988), but it appears to have been the Medes who actually destroyed the city. Indeed, the Babylonians were very careful in their records to distance themselves from the general looting of the city and especially the temples of this great city. However, it is clear that the Medes were either uninterested or unable to keep the city for a permanent possession, and it fell to their allies, the Babylonians, to possess it.

The history of the ancient Near East is full of stories of brothers fighting against brothers for control of the throne.

LITERARY ANALYSIS

Style

Nahum's poetic style is strikingly good. Its beauty contrasts with the harshness of its message. Bishop Lowth stated this well when he wrote:

> None of the minor prophets, however, seem to equal Nahum in boldness, ardour, and sublimity. His prophecy too forms a regular and perfect poem: the exordium is not merely magnificent, it is truly majestic; the preparation for the destruction of Nineveh, and the description of its downfall and desolation, are expressed in the most vivid colours, and are bold and luminous in the highest degrees. (1753, 234)

Both in his imagery and in his use of compact parallelism Nahum showed himself a master poet.

Genre

The superscription that begins the book has three terms that describe the kind of writing the reader is about to encounter in this prophecy. They are "book," "vision," and "oracle" and will be discussed in that order.

The reference to "book" (*seper*) indicates that Nahum's prophecy is somewhat different from others. Most of the prophets were preachers, and their prophecies are later collections of their oral utterances. Nahum, it appears, wrote a book. A number of the poetic devices of the book—for instance, the partial acrostic in Nahum 1 (Longman 1993)—appeal to the eye and not the ear. The written character of the prophecy may also explain why Nahum is such a well-structured prophecy (see next section), unlike many others that are more like sermonic anthologies (e.g., Micah).

The book is further specified as containing a "vision" (h^a zôn). While the whole prophecy is not a vision, there are two striking passages that contain an event vision: 2:3–10 and 3:2–3 (Horst, Sister).

In some sense, though, the most important indication of genre is the term "oracle" (*maúûâ'*). This term used to be translated "burden," but modern interpreters have determined that the correct meaning is "oracle" (Naudé 1969). Indeed, "oracle" may be too broad a translation since the word occurs predominantly in contexts where the prophet inveighs against a foreign nation. Thus *maúûâ'* appears to be the ancient name for what in English we call the "war oracle" or "oracle against a foreign nation."

With this in mind, it is hard to appreciate the arguments of Sweeney (1992) and Floyd (2000, 10–18), who contend that Nahum is not an eschatological vision that looks forward to the destruction of Nineveh or anticipates later intrusions of the Divine Warrior (as reflected in the poem celebrating the Divine Warrior at the beginning of the book—1:2–8). Floyd argues that since this opening poem is not in and of itself eschatological, it does not thereby render the whole book future-oriented. However, what we have in the poem is the statement of a principle: the Divine Warrior will intrude to save his people and judge his enemies. Then it applies this principle to the near-future demise of Nineveh. When later readers read the book in the light of the rest of the canon, they can then discern its eschatological relevance.

STRUCTURE

Superscription (1:1)
    I. Hymn to God the Divine Warrior (1:2–8)
    II. The Divine Warrior judges and saves his people (1:9–2:2)
    III. The vision of Nineveh's demise (2:3–10)
    IV. The lion taunt (2:11–13)
    V. Woe-oracle against Nineveh (3:1–3)
    VI. The sorceress-harlot taunt (3:4–7)
    VII. Historical taunt comparing Thebes and Nineveh (3:8–10)
    VIII. Further insults against Nineveh (3:11–15c)
    IX. Locust taunt (3:15d–17)
    X. Concluding dirge (3:18–19)

A close analysis of the book reveals its tight structure. The book opens with a fairly typical prophetic superscription (1:1) that gives the prophet's name, the name of the city, and his topic: "a prophecy concerning Nineveh." The prophecy itself begins with a magnificent Divine Warrior victory hymn (1:2–8) similar to many found in the Psalter (Pss. 24 and 98, for instance). This hymn is historically nonspecific and extols God as judge of the wicked and protector of his people. The next section (1:9–2:2) flows naturally from this two-pronged victory song. Unique to the prophets, Nahum intertwines salvation oracles directed to Judah (1:12–13, 15; 2:2) with judgment oracles against Nineveh (1:9–11, 14; 2:1). The dramatic suspense in this section is heightened by the delayed identification of the recipients of salvation and judgment. Judah is not explicitly mentioned until 1:15, and Nineveh is not mentioned in this section.

The prophecy continues with one or two visions found in the book (2:3–10). This is an event vision, and it is as if Nahum were actually present at the final destruction of Nineveh. With the idea of the end of that powerful and oppressive city in mind, Nahum taunts Nineveh. Nahum 2:11–3:7 has a kind of concentric structure (Schulz 1973). Both 2:11–13 and 3:4–7 are metaphorical taunts with the same structure (note the concluding judgment formulae in 2:13 and 3:5). The first ridicules Assyria as the desolate lion, and the second as a sorceress-whore. In the middle, Nahum inserts a woe-oracle with appended event vision (3:1–3). The origin of this form is in the funeral lament. Nahum is saying, in effect, that Nineveh is as good as dead.

> *Part of the book has a kind of concentric structure, with metaphorical taunts directed toward Nineveh. Nahum is saying, in effect, that Nineveh is as good as dead.*

The taunts continue virtually to the end of the book. First, Nahum sarcastically compares Nineveh with Thebes in what might be called a "historical taunt." Then the prophecy continues with a series of short taunts that appear to be based on treaty curses (3:12–13). The prophecy ends with a dirge that sarcastically laments the end of Nineveh (3:18–19). Only one other book ends with a rhetorical question, and that is Jonah, the prophecy of salvation toward Nineveh. A conscious contrast is surely intended to be highlighted (Glasson 1969).

THEOLOGICAL MESSAGE

Nahum 1:7–8 summarizes the main message of the prophet Nahum:

> The LORD is good,
>   a refuge in times of trouble.
> He cares for those who trust in him,
>   but with an overwhelming flood
> he will make an end of Nineveh;
>   he will pursue his foes into darkness.

In the book of Nahum, God appears as a warrior ready to do battle on behalf of his people. To the Judeans who first read this book in the seventh century BC, this prophecy was a long-awaited message of hope. They had been living in the shadow of Assyrian oppression for many years; now God was going to act against their wicked foe. The message of the judgment of the Assyrians—and, specifically, the destruction of Nineveh—communicated compassion toward the people of God.

God fulfilled the promise of this prophecy, and Nineveh was destroyed by the Medes and Babylonians in 612 BC. However, the people of Judah themselves continued to try the patience of God with their sinful rebellion. As a result, they soon found that they were in serious trouble as Babylon turned its attention on Palestine. In 586 the great king of Babylon Nebuchadnezzar subjugated Judah.

APPROACHING THE NEW TESTAMENT

Many have seen absolutely no relevance to the book of Nahum for the church today. The prophecy is so specific and so bloody that it appears to have nothing to do with Jesus Christ.

We have observed the movement of the book of Nahum from a general to a particular historical situation. The abiding significance of Nahum may be most readily seen by returning to 1:2–8, the great song of praise to God the Divine Warrior, who both delivers his people and judges his enemies.

The picture of God as the Divine Warrior in the Old Testament anticipates the coming of Jesus Christ, who is also frequently imaged as a warrior in the New Testament (Longman 1982; 1985a, b; Longman and Reid 1995). However, the object of divine warfare is different from what it was in the Old Testament. In the Old Testament Yahweh warred against the flesh-and-blood enemies of Israel (Canaanites, Philistines, Assyrians, and so forth) and finally against disobedient Israel itself (Lam. 2:6). In Paul, on the other hand, Christ's death, resurrection, and ascension are seen as the culmination of his warfare against Satan and his cohorts (Col. 2:14–15; Eph. 4:7–10). The Old Testament picture of God as warrior and Christ's warfare against Satan anticipate the consummation of this theme in the book of Revelation (see, for instance, Rev. 19:11–21), when evil comes to an end as Jesus leads his army in the final battle against Satan and his demonic and human army. Thus, although Nineveh no longer exists, the abiding significance of the book of Nahum is found in the warring Christ of the New Testament.

CHAPTER THIRTY-TWO

HABAKKUK

Little is known about the prophet Habakkuk. His name occurs only in the superscriptions to the book and the psalm it contains (1:1; 3:1). Some think the name is derived from a Hebrew verb meaning "embrace"; others think it is from an Akkadian term for a garden plant.

Many have concluded that Habakkuk was a cult prophet (see the discussion in Floyd 2000, 84–86, where he concludes that although there may be liturgical elements in the book, this does not make it a liturgy as such). The book does make use of the lament genre, a form of literature associated with the temple, and the musical terms in the psalm in chapter 3 also suggest liturgical use. Levitical musicians did have a prophetic function (1 Chron. 25:1–6). The description of a theophany (chap. 3) is perhaps also most natural in a cultic setting. However, the phrase "cult prophet" is not itself unambiguous. The precise relationship of the prophets with the temple is one of the most debated elements in Old Testament study. If by "cult prophet" one intends a cultic official whose maintenance was drawn from temple revenues and who performed his prophetic duty as a part of temple liturgy, there is insufficient data to warrant identifying Habakkuk in this way, and such an identification is questionable for the other prophets mentioned in the Bible. Some prophets were also priests (e.g., Ezekiel, Zechariah), but they are not prophets by virtue of their priestly office. The prophetic office was not hereditary. However, if one intends to indicate no more than a prophet whose ministry routinely brought him into the environs of the temple, this appellation could apply to Habakkuk and a great number of others. Childs (*IOTS*, 452) argues that although much of the material in Habakkuk may have originated in a liturgical setting, the autobiographical elements in the book (2:1; 3:2, 16–19) show instead that it should not be attributed to the influence of the cult in its present form.

The fact that little is known about the prophet helps to explain why a variety of legends have attached to him. One manuscript of Bel and the Dragon (an apocryphal addition to Daniel) identifies Habakkuk as a Levite, a tradition reflecting his association with the temple. Other rabbinical sources identify him with the son of the Shunamite woman, an identification prompted by the occurrence of the term "embrace" in 2 Kings 4:16. Others identified him with the watchman mentioned in Isaiah 21:6, no doubt prompted by the prophet's use of this image in 2:1. None of these traditions provide trustworthy information about the prophet.

The Talmud (Makkot 23b) records the remark of one rabbi that "Moses gave Israel 613 commandments, David reduced them to 10, Isaiah to 2, but Habakkuk to one: *the righteous shall live by his faith*" (see 2:4).

BIBLIOGRAPHY

Commentaries

F. I. **Andersen,** *Habakkuk* (AB; Doubleday, 2001); D. W. **Baker,** *Nahum, Habakkuk, and Zephaniah* (TOTC; InterVarsity Press, 1988); F. F. **Bruce,** "Habakkuk," in *Commentary on the Minor Prophets*, ed. T. E. McComiskey (Baker, 1993); J. **Bruckner,** *Jonah, Nahum, Habakkuk, Zephaniah* (NIVAC; Zondervan, 2004); J. H. **Eaton,** *Obadiah, Nahum, Habakkuk, and Zephaniah* (TBC; SCM, 1961); K. **Elliger,** *Das Buch der zwölf kleinen Propheten* (ATD 25; Göttingen: Vandenhoeck und Ruprecht, 1950); M. H. **Floyd,** *Minor Prophets, Part 2* (FOTL; Eerdmans, 2000); D. E. **Gowan,** *The Triumph of Faith in Habakkuk* (John Knox, 1976); C. A. **Keller,** *Nahoum, Habacuc, Sophonie* (CAT 11b; Neuchâtel: Delachaux et Niestlé, 1971); R. **Patterson,** *Nahum, Habakkuk, Zephaniah* (WEC; Moody, 1991); J. M. **Roberts,** *Nahum, Habakkuk, and Zephaniah* (OTL; Westminster John Knox, 1991); O. P. **Robertson,** *The Books of Nahum, Habakkuk, and Zephaniah* (NICOT; Eerdmans, 1990); W. **Rudolph,** *Micha–Nahum–Habakuk–Zephanja* (*KAT* 13:3; Gütersloh: Mohn, 1975); R. L. **Smith,** *Micah–Malachi* (WBC 32; Word, 1984); R. F. von **Ungern-Sternberg** and H. **Lamparter,** *Der Tag des Gerichtes Gottes. Die Propheten Habakuk, Zephanja, Jona, Nahum* (Botschaft des Alten Testaments; Stuttgart: Calwer Verlag, 1960); J. D. W. **Watts,** *Joel, Obadiah, Jonah, Micah, Nahum, Habakkuk, Zephaniah* (CBC; Cambridge University Press, 1975).

Monographs and Articles

W. F. **Albright,** "The Psalm of Habakkuk," in *Studies in Old Testament Prophecy Dedicated to T. H. Robinson*, ed. H. H. Rowley (T. & T. Clark, 1950), 1–18; W. M. **Brownlee,** "The Composition of Habakkuk," in *Homages à Andre Dupont-Sommer* (Paris: Librairie d'Amerique et d'Orient Adrien-Maisonneuve, 1971), 255–75; idem, *The Text of Habakkuk in the Ancient Commentary from Qumran* (Philadelphia: JBL Monograph Series, 1959); idem, *The Midrash Pesher of Habakkuk* (Missoula: Scholars, 1979); S. **Coleman,** "The Dialogue of Habakkuk in Rabbinic Doctrine," *Abr Naharain* 5 (1964–65): 57–85; A. H. J. **Gunneweg,** "Habakkuk and the Problem of the Suffering Just," in *Proceedings of the Ninth World Congress of Jewish Studies* (Jerusalem: World Union of Jewish Studies, 1986), A:85–90; T. **Hiebert,** *God of My Victory: The Ancient Hymn in Habakkuk 3* (Scholars, 1986); J. G. **Janzen,** "Eschatological Symbol and Existence in Habakkuk," *CBQ* 44 (1982): 394–414; P. **Jöcken,** *Das Buch Habakuk: Darstellung der Geschichte seiner kritischen Erforschung mit einer eigenen Beurteilung* (BBB 48; Bonn: Hanstein, 1977); C. A. **Keller,** "Die Eigenart des Propheten Habakuks," *ZAW* 85 (1973): 156–67; B. **Margulis,** "The Psalm of Habakkuk: A Reconstruction and Interpretation," *ZAW* 82 (1970): 409–42; E. **Nielsen,** "The Righteous and the Wicked in Habaqquq," *ST* 6 (1953): 54–78; K. G. **O'Connell,** "Habakkuk, Spokesman to God," *CurrTM* 6 (1979): 227–31; E. **Otto,** "Die Theologie des Buches Habakuk," *VT* 35 (1985) 274–95; R. D. **Patterson,** "The Psalm of Habakkuk," *GraceTJ* 8 (1987): 163–94; B. **Peckham,** "The Vision of Habakkuk," *CBQ* 48 (1986): 617–36; W. **Rast,** "Habakkuk and Justification by Faith," *CurrTM* 10 (1983): 169–75; J. A. **Sanders,** "Habakkuk in Qumran, Paul and the Old Testament," *JR* 38 (1959): 232–44; H. H. **Walker** and N. W. **Lund,** "The Literary Structure of the Book of Habakkuk," *JBL* 53 (1934): 355–70; G. J. **Zemek,** "Interpretive Challenges Relating to Habakkuk 2:4b," *GraceTJ* 1 (1980): 43–69.

HISTORICAL BACKGROUND

Habakkuk was written at the time when God was "raising up the Babylonians" (1:6), that is, at a point late in the seventh or early in the sixth century BC. Assyria had begun a rapid decline around 625 BC, approximately the time that Nabopolassar, the father of Nebuchadnezzar, took the throne of Babylon. Nebuchadnezzar became king of Babylon after his father's death and during the events surrounding the battle of Carchemish (604); the Babylonian armies then overwhelmed the city-state remnants of the once-great Assyrian Empire and turned their attention to the states of Syria-Palestine. In 598 Nebuchadnezzar carried Jehoiachin king of Judah into exile along with much of the royal family and the leading citizens of Jerusalem (2 Kings 24:8–17; 2 Chron. 36:9–10). The mention of the rise of the Babylonians (1:6) suggests a date between 625 and 604, whereas the mention of the numerous conquests of the Babylonian armies (2:5, 8–10) suggests a somewhat later date. Andersen (2001, 27) proposes a date between 605 and 575 BC. Habakkuk was probably a contemporary of Jeremiah, Zephaniah, Nahum, and possibly Joel.

Although the internal evidence of the book appears to establish a secure range of dates, critical scholarship has not always been content with this data. Scholars have assigned the book to dates ranging from the early seventh to the early second centuries BC; Jöcken (1977) provides an in-depth survey of this research.[1] The issue of date is largely tied up with the question of the identity of the wicked mentioned in 1:4 and 1:13. In 1:4 the wicked appear to be the evil inhabitants of Judah and Jerusalem; however, some scholars identified them as the Assyrians, the oppressor of Israel defeated by the Chaldeans. Yet it is unlikely that wicked Assyrians would be described in terms of their "paralyzing the law" (1:4), an idiom more appropriate for internal corruption within Judah. In 1:13 the wicked appear to be the Babylonians.

Other scholars have questioned whether an earlier edition of the book ended with the psalm in chapter 3. The psalm is introduced with a separate superscription (3:1), a fact that suggests it may have had an independent existence apart from the larger composition it now concludes. Furthermore, the commentary on Habakkuk found in 1948 in Cave One at Qumran ends with chapter 2 and does not include the psalm. However, this fact may reflect that the Qumran sectarians found the material in chapters 1–2 more useful for their purposes, so that no commentary was written on chapter 3. The psalm is found in all complete manuscripts of the LXX and was also found in the Wadi Murabba'at scroll from the beginning of the second century AD (Brownlee 1959, 92).

LITERARY ANALYSIS

We may outline Habakkuk as follows:
Superscription (1:1)
    I. Initial exchange (1:2–11)
      A. The prophet's complaint (1:2–4)
      B. God's response (1:5–11)
    II. Second exchange (1:12–2:5)
      A. The prophet's complaint (1:12–17)
      B. God's response (2:1–5)
    III. Woe oracles against the oppressor (2:6–20)
      A. The plunderer plundered (2:6–8)
      B. The conqueror shamed (2:9–11)
      C. The builder undone (2:12–14)

---

[1] A radically late date for the book, assigning it to the time of Alexander or the Seleucids, depends on emending *kasdim* (Chaldeans) to *kitttim* (Greeks). Bernhard Duhm and Stephen Happel suggested this emendation early in the twentieth century, though their conclusions were rejected by most scholars. Ironically, the Qumran sectarians in their commentary on Habakkuk were later discovered to have made the same change; for the members of the Qumran sect, however, *kittim* was a code word for the Romans. The very presence of Habakkuk among the Qumran scriptures makes such a late date unlikely.

The first part of the book (1:2–2:5) consists of a dialogue between God and the prophet. In 1:2–4 and 1:12–17, the prophet presents his complaints before God in the form of a lament, somewhat resembling lament psalms (Pss. 6; 12; 28; 31; 55; 60; 85). Such laments in the psalms are commonly followed by a divine response of assurance that the Lord will hear the writer's complaint, save and sustain him, and judge his or Israel's enemies (Pss. 6:8–10 [MT 9–11]; 12:5–8 [MT 6–9]; 28:6–9; 31:22–23 [MT 23–24]; 55:22–23 [MT 23–24]; 60:8–10 [MT 10–12]; 85:8–13 [MT 9–14]).

Habakkuk initially complained about the wickedness, injustice, and violence rampant in Judah (1:2–4). The prophet is asking the age-old question, "Why do the wicked prosper?" The Lord's answer was not what the prophet expected: God will judge the wickedness in Judah by raising up the Babylonians who will advance on Judah with destruction and death (1:5–11). Not much comfort here! The divine response does not solve the prophet's question, but rather moves it to an even higher level. God is going to bring judgment on the wicked, but he will do it with an instrument even more wicked than the evil in Judah. Those who are even more wicked will then prosper the more.

This prompts the prophet's second complaint (1:12–17). How can God in his holiness tolerate the treacherous? How can he allow the wicked to swallow up those more righteous than themselves (v. 13)? Are they to continue to prosper, filling their nets and living in luxury (vv. 16–17)? The prophet waits patiently as a watchman to see how the Lord will answer (2:1). God tells the prophet to write down the revelation he is about to receive, so that it will be a witness when it is fulfilled (2:2–3). God will yet judge the unrighteous. The hubris of Babylon will not escape his judgment (2:4–5). Human opinion about righteousness and wrong lacks the capacity to evaluate God's actions in history; those who are truly righteous must live in faithful confidence that God will keep his promises (2:4b). Just as Abraham had believed God and had been credited with righteousness (Gen. 15:6), the prophet too must continue to have confidence in God.

The fact that God would yet judge also the Chaldeans is confirmed in the series of five woe oracles that follow (2:6–20). Wickedness will not always prosper. The earth will yet be filled with the knowledge of the glory of the Lord (v. 14) and will stand in silence before him (v. 20). Even when things appear to go from bad to worse, God still rules and will vindicate himself.

> *The prophet is asking the age-old question, "Why do the wicked prosper?" The Lord's answer was not what the prophet expected.*

The prophet's response to his vision is a hymn, a victory song describing the appearance of the Divine Warrior in his war chariot. At his coming, the heavens and earth convulse (3:3–7). The Lord shows his dominion over the chaotic waters as he had done at creation; he comes with his weapons to judge the nations as he had done at the exodus (3:8–15). Habakkuk takes confidence from the deeds of God in the past and believes, "waiting patiently for the day of calamity to come on the nation invading us" (3:16).

The psalm in chapter 3 appears to be written in an archaic form of Hebrew. Some have concluded that the prophet was consciously archaizing as he recited the deeds of God in the past. Others see this psalm as possibly composed of fragments from a larger and ancient epic poem no longer extant (Patterson 1987).

This structure is widely accepted in the most recent commentaries (see Andersen 2001, 3–8), but Floyd (2000, 81–84; Roberts 1991; and Bruckner 2004 are close to this) disputes it and argues that each chapter is a separate part of an outline of the book. Thus, chapter 1 concerns a complaint about a previously spoken prophecy, chapter 2 is the "report of an oracular inquiry," and chapter 3 articulates the prophecy in a poetic format.

THEOLOGICAL MESSAGE

Habakkuk addressed Judah and Jerusalem during the last act of that kingdom's role on the stage of history. The kingdom was rife with internal corruption, and the rising power of Babylon would soon issue in the destruction of temple and city. Yet in the face of these twin evils, God seemed to the prophet to be inactive and unconcerned.

Many have compared Habakkuk's complaints about the prospering of evil and the suffering of the righteous to the book of Job. The prophet learned, as had Job, that in spite of all appearances to the contrary, and no matter how difficult conditions might become, he must continue to believe, continue to trust the promises of God, and have confidence that the Lord of all the earth would do right (3:16–19). Habakkuk was learning to live by faith (2:4). In the face of calamity, the prophet was learning to sing the praise of his redeemer and Lord.

APPROACHING THE NEW TESTAMENT

Hundreds of years after Habakkuk, wickedness and injustice were again flourishing as they had so often before. Once again the temple of God was threatened—but this time it was the temple represented by the presence of the Christ. People taunted Christ, once again asking, "Where is God?" (Matt. 27:41–43). God did not come to deliver him, and to all appearances evil had triumphed again. Yet he trusted in God (Matt. 27:43; Heb. 10:38a), and God vindicated him by raising him from the dead (Rom. 1:4). The resurrection of Jesus is God's own proclamation that he is not far, and that evil will not triumph.

Paul goes on to admonish the infant church that Jesus has called his followers to a life of faith. Paul appeals to Habakkuk (2:4) in his argument that righteousness—from first to last, for Abraham, Job, Habakkuk, and for all—is by faith (Rom. 1:17). Although we live in a present evil age (Gal. 1:4), "the righteous will live by faith" (Gal. 3:11). Faith is "being sure of what we hope for and certain of what we do not see" (Heb. 11:1). The ancients were commended for their believing God when the circumstances all conspired to say that such faith would not be rewarded (Heb. 11:2–40). We too are called to that same life of faith, for God will yet come as Divine Warrior and will vindicate his name (Rev. 19:11–16).

CHAPTER THIRTY-THREE

ZEPHANIAH

Zephaniah is the only prophet introduced with a lineal genealogy of such depth. His ancestry is traced back four generations to a person named Hezekiah (1:1). Although this Hezekiah is not specifically designated as the famous king by that name, there can be little question that this is the reason for the length of the genealogy.[1] His membership in the royal family probably also gave him access to the royal court, a position from which he could observe and then decry the sins of Judah's leaders (1:8, 11–13; 3:3–4).

The superscription sets Zephaniah's ministry during the reign of Josiah; thus, Zephaniah was probably a contemporary of both Habakkuk and Jeremiah. The prophet would have grown up in the years of apostasy and Assyrian oppression during the reigns of Manasseh and Amon.

BIBLIOGRAPHY

Commentaries

D. W. **Baker,** *Nahum, Habakkuk, and Zephaniah* (TOTC; InterVarsity Press, 1988); A. **Berlin,** *Zephaniah* (AB: Doubleday, 1994); J. H. **Eaton,** *Obadiah, Nahum, Habakkuk, and Zephaniah* (TBC; SCM, 1961); K. **Elliger,** *Das Buch der zwölf kleinen Propheten* (ATD 25; Göttingen: Vandenhoeck und Ruprecht, 1950); M. H. **Floyd,** *Minor Prophets, Part 2* (FOTL; Eerdmans, 2000); C. A. **Keller,** *Nahoum, Habacuc, Sophonie* (CAT 11b; Neuchâtel: Delachaux et Niestlé, 1971); O. P. **Robertson,** *The Books of Nahum, Habakkuk, and Zephaniah* (NICOT; Eerdmans, 1990); W. **Rudolph,** *Micha–Nahum–Habakuk–Zephanja* (KAT 13:3; Gütersloh:

---

[1]Bentzen (*Introduction to the Old Testament* [Copenhagen: G. E. C. God, 1948–49], 2:153) argued that since Cush is the biblical name for northern Nubia, Zephaniah's father Cushi was probably an Ethiopian or Nubian black temple slave, and therefore the longer genealogy was to legitimize his standing in Israel. The simple occurrence of this personal name is a slim basis to support the remaining inferences.

Mohn, 1975); L. **Sabottka,** *Zephanja* (Rome: Biblical Institute Press, 1972); R. L. **Smith,** *Micah–Malachi* (WBC 32; Word, 1984); R. F. von **Ungern-Sternberg** and H. **Lamparter,** *Der Tag des Gerichtes Gottes. Die Propheten Habakuk, Zephanja, Jona, Nahum* (Botschaft des Alten Testaments; Stuttgart: Calwer Verlag, 1960); J. D. W. **Watts,** *Joel, Obadiah, Jonah, Micah, Nahum, Habakkuk, Zephaniah* (CBC; Cambridge University Press, 1975).

Monographs and Articles

G. W. **Anderson,** "The Idea of the Remnant in the Book of Zephaniah," *ASTI* 11 (1977/78): 11–14; I. J. **Ball,** "The Rhetorical Shape of Zephaniah," in *Perspectives on Language and Text*, ed. E. Conrad and E. Newing (Eisenbrauns, 1987); H. **Cazelles,** "Sophonie, Jérémie et les Scythes en Palestine," *RB* 74 (1964): 24–44; R. **Dillard,** "Remnant," *Baker Encyclopedia of the Bible* (Baker, 1988), 2:1833–36; G. **Gerleman,** *Zephanja: textkritisch und literarisch untersucht* (Lund: Gleerup, 1942); P. R. **House,** *Zephaniah: A Prophetic Drama* (Sheffield: Almond, 1988); J. P. **Hyatt,** "The Date and Background of Zephaniah," *JBL* 7 (1949): 25–29; A. S. **Kapelrud,** *The Message of the Prophet Zephaniah* (Oslo: Universitetsforlaget, 1975); G. **Langohr,** "Le livre de Sophonie et la critique d'authenticité," *EphTL* 52 (1976): 1–27; B. **Renaud,** "Le livre de Sophonie: le jour de YHWH theme structurant de la synthese redactionnelle," *RSciRel* 60 (1986): 1–33; T. T. **Rice,** *The Scythians* (London: Thames and Hudson, 1957); L. P. **Smith** and E. R. **Lacheman,** "The Authorship of the Book of Zephaniah," *JNES* 9 (1950): 137–42; D. L. **Williams,** "The Date of Zephaniah," *JBL* 82 (1963): 77–88; E. M. **Yamauchi,** *Foes from the Northern Frontier* (Baker, 1982).

HISTORICAL BACKGROUND

Two issues surrounding the interpretation of Zephaniah are indissolubly intertwined in assessing the historical background of the book: (1) Was Zephaniah's ministry set before or after the reform of Josiah associated with the discovery of the law book in 621 BC? (2) The prophet expects an imminent invasion, but from which foreign power?

The Time of Zephaniah's Ministry

The book does not contain any clear allusions to the reform activities associated with the discovery of the law book (2 Kings 22–23). This fact alongside the abuses and the low state of popular religion described in the book (1:4–6, 8–9, 12; 3:1–4, 7) has suggested to the majority of commentators that Zephaniah's ministry took place before 621 BC. However, the mention of the "remnant of Baal" (1:4) may indicate that Baalism was already being suppressed and that the reform activities were already underway. Nor is it altogether clear that Josiah's reform did not begin until 621. The book of Kings describes the reform as proceeding in concentric circles from the discovery of the law book in the temple, through the city of Jerusalem, and into the territory of outlying tribes. Chronicles, on the other hand, describes the reform in chronological sequence, so that many of the items associated in Kings with events after Josiah's eighteenth year (621 BC—2 Kings 22:3; 2 Chron. 34:8) actually began instead in his twelfth year (627 BC—2 Chron. 34:2–7), when Josiah, at age twenty, was no longer a minor. It is also possible that we need to maintain a distinction between the official reforming activities of the king and the abuses among the wealthy and the general populace, such that the sins decried in the book cannot be used with confidence to determine whether Zephaniah was active before or after Josiah's reform. While the reform would almost certainly have affected the character of popular religious expression, it is unrealistic to think that it eliminated all commercial and religious transgression. In the final analysis, it is probably not possible to determine a more precise setting for Zephaniah's ministry.

Who Are the Invaders?

The prophet does appear to expect an imminent foreign invasion that will bring the destruction of Jerusalem (1:4, 10–13; 2:1; 3:1–4). Scholars have been divided regarding what enemy the prophet anticipates.

1. Many scholars (e.g., Smith 1984, 123) argue that the enemy anticipated is Assyria. Judah had been an Assyrian satellite through much of the seventh century; annexation by Assyria and the accompanying deportation of the population, both being the fate of the northern kingdom, were constant threats for Judah as well. However, in about the middle of the reign of Ashurbanipal (669–627 BC), Assyria lapsed into a rapid decline. By the year 627, Assyrian power had been broken, and Assyria represented little threat to Judah. The mention of Nineveh (2:13–15) as a candidate for divine judgment does not mean that Assyria was still a threat to Judah (cf. Kapelrud 1975, 122); to the contrary, the prophet appears to reflect on the fact that Assyrian power was already diminished (2:15). Even if one could establish a date for Zephaniah's ministry before Josiah's reforms, Assyria is not likely to have been a serious threat to Judah.

2. The Scythians were a group of nomadic tribes inhabiting the southern steppes of Russia, largely an area north of the Black Sea. Herodotus (1:105) mentions that the Scythians conducted a raid against the Philistine city of Ashkelon and against Egypt during the reign of Psammetichus I (664–610 BC). This raid would have come between 633 and 610 (Yamauchi 1982, 84). Scholars have long debated whether this raid formed the backdrop for Zephaniah's anticipation of a foreign attack and for Jeremiah's prophecies about a foe from the north (Jer. 4–6, 8–9). Many have been skeptical about the reliability of Herodotus's report, though archaeological evidence increasingly lends credence to the reality of a Scythian incursion (Yamauchi 1982, 87–99). However, the Scythian raid reported by Herodotus was apparently brief and may have been confined to sites

along the international coastal highway Via Maris, such that it had little direct impact on Judah. A distinctive type of arrowhead associated with the Scythians has been found in significant numbers in the excavations of sixth- and seventh-century cities such as Samaria, Lachish, and Amman (Yamauchi 1982, 87). These arrowheads suggest the presence either of Scythian raiding parties or of Scythian mercenary units in the later Babylonian invasions. However, one must also take into account the extensive trade in military hardware and the spread of military technology in the ancient Near East; a technology that may have originated with the Scythians may not have been used by them alone.

3. Zephaniah is anticipating a disaster on "the day of the Lord" that will affect the surrounding nations (2:4–12) and even Assyria itself (2:13–15). He appears to expect the destruction of Jerusalem and the deportation of the population, so that he looks forward to the survival and gathering of a remnant (3:10–20). Such a far-reaching disaster seems beyond a Scythian raid; if Assyria is one of the targets, the threat would scarcely originate in Assyria. The only remaining candidate for the source of the threat Zephaniah anticipates would be Babylon. The writer of Kings reports that the coming invasion by Babylon was already anticipated at the time of Josiah (2 Kings 22:15–20). However, Babylon was only beginning its resurgence to power at the time of Josiah's death (609 BC), and Babylonian incursions into Syria-Palestine would not begin until after the battle of Carchemish (604). Unless one is willing to accept some prophetic insight or prescience on the part of the prophet, one must reject assigning the book to the time of Josiah (1:1)[2] or consider those passages reflecting the Babylonian exile and the restoration as later additions to the text.

LITERARY ANALYSIS

We may outline Zephaniah as follows:
   Superscription (1:1)
      I. Oracles against Judah (1:2–2:3)
         A. Universal judgment (1:2–3)
         B. The Lord's sacrifice (1:4–9)
         C. Judgment of Jerusalem (1:10–13)
         D. The Day of the Lord (1:14–2:3)
      II. Oracles against the nations (2:4–3:8)
         A. Philistia (2:4–7)
         B. Moab and Ammon (2:8–11)
         C. Cush (2:12)
         D. Assyria (2:13–15)

---

[2]Hyatt (1949) and Williams (1963) recognized that the anticipated foe in Zephaniah was Babylon, and for this reason they assigned the book to the time of Jehoiakim (609–598 BC).

     E. Jerusalem (3:1–7)
     F. Universal judgment (3:8)
  III. Oracles of salvation (3:9–20)
     A. Universal worship (3:9–10)
     B. Blessing and restoration for Judah (3:11–20)

Traditional critical scholarship has been concerned to separate the original, authentic words of the prophet from later additions and glosses. The criteria by which later materials are isolated have varied with the individual scholars, and therefore the results of such a method have not been consistent. The oracles of salvation in 3:14–20 have been widely considered later additions; others also excise 2:7–9a, 10–11, 15; 3:1–4, and other passages or snippets. Langohr (1976) surveys the history of this research and provides a recent example of the approach. The major reasons for isolating some material as secondary are the postexilic perspective of 3:4–20, language and concepts similar to Ezekiel and the latter part of Isaiah, and eschatological expectation resembling apocalyptic (Childs, *IOTS*, 458). Childs (461) considers these secondary additions as examples of the canonical process, whereby succeeding generations in Israel reinterpreted the words of Zephaniah in light of the historical circumstances of their own time.

Many have recognized the similarity of structure in Zephaniah to that of other prophetic books — broadly speaking, Isaiah, Ezekiel, the Septuagint of Jeremiah, and Zephaniah.

Other approaches have noted the logical, orderly flow of thought in the book and tend to emphasize that Zephaniah is a carefully constructed unity. The prophet announces universal judgment (1:2–3; 3:8) and then details its effects on Judah (1:4–2:3; 3:1–7) and the nations (2:4–15); this is followed by an announcement of universal blessing and its effects on Judah and the nations (3:9–20). Ball (1987) views the book as a unity resulting from a rhetorical expansion of 2:1–7 and emphasizes the integrity of the work. House (1988) observes the alternation between first-person divine speech and third-person speeches from the prophet; he then identifies the book as a prophetic drama and divides it into scenes and acts. Although not convincing in the final analysis, House's application of a literary approach to the book highlights many interesting rhetorical features.

Many have recognized the similarity of structure in Zephaniah to that of other prophetic books. Broadly speaking, Isaiah, Ezekiel, the Septuagint of Jeremiah, and Zephaniah all (1) begin with a set of oracles pertaining to the immediate historical situation of Judah, then (2) turn to oracles against foreign nations, and (3) end with oracles of future eschatological blessing.

THEOLOGICAL MESSAGE

Themes of judgment, grace, and mercy predominate in the book. Divine judgment is portrayed primarily through the imagery of the day of the Lord; divine grace, primarily through the motif of the remnant and the restoration.

1. The day of the Lord is a frequent theme in the prophets; Zephaniah appears to be aware of the earlier use of similar concepts in Amos (Amos 5:18–20; 8:3–13) and Isaiah (Isa. 2:6–22). This day is the day when God vindicates his own honor and appears with destructive judgment against sin, whether among Gentile nations (2:4–15) or in Israel itself (1:14–2:3). Creation dissolves: the cosmos convulses and returns to the darkness of primeval chaos (1:2–3, 15–18; 3:6–8); the universe reverts to its lifeless and unformed state (1:3). Yahweh comes as a warrior (1:14–16) on that great day of holy war against evil. His presence is signaled by a blazing theophany (3:8). For Zephaniah this great day was an imminent historical expectation. However, this historical act of divine intrusion also foreshadowed an eschatological judgment when sin would be abolished from the earth (1:3).

2. Alongside this frightening anticipation of divine fury, there is the countervailing theme of God's faithfulness and mercy to the remnant (3:12–13). The remnant motif is found in many books of the Bible. When a group undergoes some catastrophe ordinarily brought about as punishment for sin, those who survive to become the nucleus for the continuation of the human race or the people of God are called the remnant (see Dillard 1988). The future existence of the people of God focuses in this purified, holy remnant that inherits afresh the promises of God. The prophet holds open the possibility of surviving the day of the Lord (2:3). The divine fury Zephaniah anticipates will purge the nation so that a sinless remnant will emerge (3:13); that remnant will be gathered from the nations, restored to the land and to divine favor (2:7; 3:19–20). God's purposes in choosing Israel will not be frustrated by the imminent outbreak of judgment, but will be realized in an elect remnant. The almighty God will not brook hubris (1:12–13; 2:10, 15), but the meek and humble will be preserved (3:12).

3. The God of Israel is the universal God. He does not have sovereignty only over a stretch of land in the eastern Mediterranean; rather, he rules over all nations, holding them to account in light of his holiness and how they have dealt with his people (2:4–15). He created the earth, and his judgments extend throughout it (1:2–3). He who rules over the universe has always had a gracious intent toward all nations (Gen. 12:3; 22:18). He who assembled the nations to hear his judgment (Zeph. 3:8) will also assemble them to receive his grace (v. 9); all will call on the name of the Lord.

APPROACHING THE NEW TESTAMENT

Christian readers recognize in Zephaniah many images and motifs that are also used in the New Testament. Zephaniah anticipated an imminent historical threat and outbreak of divine judgment. This historical outbreak of the day of the Lord in the Babylonian conquest and exile was but a foretaste of that great and terrible day on an eschatological and cosmic scale. Paul writes often of the day of the Lord, the day of Christ (Rom. 2:16; 1 Cor. 1:8; Phil. 1:6, 10; 2:16; 2 Tim. 4:8) and looks for that final theophany and final vindication of God in history. John describes the Warrior God coming with his armies to execute judgment (Rev. 19:11–16). Zephaniah had announced a terrible sacrifice that God himself would offer (1:7), and John makes use of the same image when he describes the day of the Lord (Rev. 19:17–18; cf. Ezek. 39:18–20).

Along with other prophets, Zephaniah looked to a day when all nations would acknowledge and worship the God of Israel (3:9–10). For the church, the new Israel composed of Jew and Gentile alike (Gal. 3:8–9, 14, 26–29), this is present reality. The church too lives with the knowledge and hope that the world will yet acknowledge the rule of its true King (Phil. 2:9–11).

CHAPTER THIRTY-FOUR

HAGGAI

We know fairly little about the prophet Haggai beyond what can be deduced from the book itself. We do know that he was preaching in Jerusalem at the same time as Zechariah; see the chronological chart in the chapter on Zechariah. The fact that he is simply identified as "the prophet" and is mentioned without any patronymic suggests that he was well known to his contemporaries (Ezra 5:1; 6:14). Zechariah ordinarily gets far more attention as one of the longest of the so-called minor prophets, whereas Haggai is among the shortest books in the Old Testament.

Haggai's name is derived from the Hebrew word *hag*, meaning "feast, festival," a fact that suggests he may have been born on one of the religious holidays of Israel's liturgical calendar. Compare the Latin *Festus* or the Greek *Hilary*. The names Haggi (Gen. 46:16; Num. 26:15) and Haggith (2 Sam. 3:4) are similar. Compare too a name like Shabbethai (Ezra 10:15, possibly "born on the Sabbath").

According to Jerome's commentary on Haggai, this prophet was also a priest, as was his contemporary Zechariah, but this tradition cannot be verified. Some of the psalm titles in the Septuagint and the Peshitta attribute various psalms to Haggai.

BIBLIOGRAPHY

Commentaries

S. **Amsler,** *Agee, Zacharie, Malachie* (CAT 11c; Paris: Delachaux et Niestlê, 1981); J. G. **Baldwin,** *Haggai, Zechariah, Malachi* (TOTC; London: Tyndale, 1972); M. J. **Boda,** *Haggai, Zechariah* (NIVAC; Zondervan, 2004); M. H. **Floyd,** *Minor Prophets, Part 2* (Eerdmans, 2000), 251–300; D. R. **Jones,** *Haggai, Zechariah, and Malachi* (TBC; SCM, 1964); C. L. **Meyers** and E. M. **Meyers,** *Haggai; Zechariah 1–8* (AB; Doubleday, 1987); J. A. **Motyer,** "Haggai," in *The Minor Prophets: An Exegetical and Expository Commentary,* ed. T. E. McComiskey (Baker, 1998), 963–1002; D. **Petersen,** *Haggai and Zechariah 1–8* (OTL; Westminster, 1984);

W. **Rudolph,** *Haggai—Sacharja 1–8/9–14—Maleachi* (*KAT* 13/4; Gutersloh: G. Mohn, 1976); R. L. **Smith,** *Micah–Malachi* (WBC 32; Word, 1984); P. **Verhoef,** *The Books of Haggai and Malachi* (NICOT; Eerdmans, 1987).

Monographs and Articles

P. R. **Ackroyd,** *Exile and Restoration* (OTL; Westminster, 1968); idem, "The Book of Haggai and Zechariah 1–8," *JJS* 3 (1952): 151–56; idem, "Studies in the Book of Haggai," *JJS* 3 (1952): 163–76; J. **Berquist,** *Judaism in Persia's Shadow: A Social and Cultural Approach* (Fortress, 1995); W. **Beuken,** *Haggai—Sacharja 1–8. Studien zur Überlieferungsgeschichte der frühnachexilischen Prophetie* (SSN 10; Assen: van Gorcum, 1967); M. J. **Boda,** "Haggai: Master Rhetorian," *TynBul* 51 (2000): 295–304; T. **Chary,** "Le culte chez les prophetes Aggee et Zacharie," *Les prophetes et le culte a partir de l'exil* (Paris: Gabalda, 1955), 119–59; A. **Gelston,** "The Foundation of the Second Temple," *VT* 16 (1966): 232–35; P. **Hanson,** *The Dawn of Apocalyptic* (Fortress, 1975), 246–62; R. A. **Mason,** "The Purpose of the 'Editorial Framework' of the Book of Haggai," *VT* 27 (1977): 415–21; F. S. **North,** "Critical Analysis of the Book of Haggai," *ZAW* 68 (1956): 25–46; D. **Petersen,** "Zerubbabel and Jerusalem Temple Restoration," *CBQ* 36 (1974): 366–72; I. **Provan,** V. P. **Long,** and T. **Longman** III, *A Biblical History of Israel* (Westminster John Knox, 2003); P. **Verhoef,** "Notes on the Dates in the Book of Haggai," in *Text and Context,* ed. W. Classen (JSOTS 48; Sheffield: JSOT, 1988), 259–67; W. J. **Wessels,** "Haggai from a Historian's Point of View," *OTE* 1, 2 (1988): 47–61; H. **Wolf,** "'The Desire of All Nations' in Haggai 2:7: Messianic or Not?" *JETS* 9 (1976): 97–102; H. W. **Wolff,** *Haggai* (BS 1; Neukirchen: Buchhandlung des Erziehungsvereins, 1951); J. S. **Wright,** *The Building of the Second Temple* (London: Tyndale, 1958).

HISTORICAL BACKGROUND

See the discussion of historical background in the chapter on Zechariah (also Berquist 1995; and Provan, Long, and Longman 2003, 285–303).

One might have anticipated a mass exodus of Jews from their captivity in Babylon once Cyrus issued his decree (539 BC; 2 Chron. 36:23; Ezra 1:2–4) authorizing their return. After all, who would not want to "go home" from a period of captivity and deportation? But this was not to be the case. The exiles had followed the advice of Jeremiah to "build houses and settle down; plant gardens and eat what they produce. Marry and have sons and daughters" (Jer. 29:5–6), and they had prospered as Babylon prospered (v. 7). Almost fifty years had passed since the destruction of Jerusalem. Most of the generation that had been carried into exile had died; the generation born during the exile only knew Babylon as home. So rather than joining a mass return to Jerusalem, most of those in Babylon chose to keep the financial security and comfort they had built up during the exile.

Almost fifty thousand of the exiles chose to make the return trip (Ezra 2:64; Neh. 7:66). When they arrived, they faced a number of difficulties: (1) Land had lain fallow, and ancestral homes were in disrepair; there was much work to be done. (2) The lower classes of Judeans who had been left in the land (Jer. 52:15–16) had taken over the holdings of those who were deported (Ezek. 11:3, 15). A complex legal situation arose, requiring reconciliation of the rights of the returnees with those of the population that had remained. Tensions developed between the returnees and those who had remained, tensions that would still be felt a century later (Neh. 5:6–8). (3) The rebuilding of Jerusalem and the temple also faced external opposition from neighboring peoples and Persian officials appointed in the area (Ezra 4:1–5; 5:3–5). After the initial restoration of the altar in the temple courtyard and efforts to lay the foundation for the building itself (Ezra 3:2–10), little work appears to have been done. (4) Initial efforts to begin construction on the temple were also met with discouraging remarks and onerous comparisons with the grandeur of the first temple on the part of those who had been alive to see it (Ezra 3:12–13; Hag. 2:3; Zech. 4:10).

With these and other issues pressing, it is no surprise that the returnees felt comparatively little urgency about rebuilding the temple but instead poured their energies into reconstructing their homes and restoring agricultural production (Hag. 1:3–11). Years passed until finally, in 520 BC, God raised up two prophets, Haggai and Zechariah, who urged the people to get their priorities straight and to build the temple. The people responded to the preaching of both prophets, and the temple was completed in 516 (Ezra 6:15).

Although the prophecy of Ezekiel has a larger number of dates than this short book, of all the prophetic books, Haggai has the greatest "density" of dated material. Each of the four oracles that make up the book is introduced with a notation concerning the date on which it was announced (Hag. 1:1; 2:1, 10, 20; cf. 1:15). All are set in less than a four-month period in the second year of Darius I (522–486 BC). Cyrus had died in battle in 530; he was succeeded by Cambyses (530–522). When Cambyses came to the throne, he assassinated his brother Bardiya in order to consolidate his hold on the kingdom and eliminate a potential rival. Cambyses appears to have taken his own life, and Darius arose from the royal entourage to secure the succession for himself. At the time of Darius's accession to the throne, rebellions broke out in various parts of the Persian Empire. The major rebellion was led by a figure who claimed to be Bardiya; Darius crushed this pseudo-Bardiya by the end of September 522. It is not clear how soon Darius was able to quell the uprisings elsewhere in the empire. Many scholars have interpreted various utterances by Haggai and Zechariah as reflecting this turmoil in the Persian Empire early in Darius's rule (e.g., Hag. 2:6–7; Zech. 1:11–15; 2:7–9). It may be that instability in the Persian Empire stimulated hopes for freedom from foreign domination and the restoration of Davidic rule (Hag. 2:20–23). The restoration community lived with the hopes of a glorious future as proclaimed by Isaiah (e.g., 40:9–10; 41:11–16; 43:1–7; 44:1–5, 21–23); Cyrus was to inaugurate the new era (Isa. 44:28–45:4, 13).

Beyond the four months of his public ministry known from the book, we know nothing of the fate of Haggai. If he had himself originally been one of the citizens of Jerusalem taken into captivity by Nebuchadnezzar, as some deduce from 2:3, he would have been an elderly man by the time of his ministry. Once the work on the reconstruction of the temple had begun, his prophetic call had been discharged, and he may have died shortly after that.

LITERARY STRUCTURE AND THEOLOGY

The book of Haggai consists of four oracles dated to the second year of Darius I (Hystaspes). Archaeological records containing astronomical observations have made it possible to convert these ancient dates to dates in our modern calendar with great precision.

Most of the other prophetic books consist of collections of prophetic sermons and oracles. Haggai, on the other hand, consists of direct address oracles set in a prose narrative framework (1:1, 3, 12, 15; 2:1, 10, 20) such that the book appears as more of a report on Haggai's utterances and the effect they had on the hearers (Verhoef 1988, 9). Since Haggai is referred to in the third person in the framework, many scholars have concluded that he was not himself the author of the book but that an editor set the prophet's utterances into their narrative context. Rudolph (1976) identified this editor with a friend or disciple of Haggai who was seeking to enhance Haggai's role in the rebuilding of the temple over against that of Zechariah. Ackroyd and Beuken (1967) both regarded this editor as having lived a century or two later and as having been under the influence of the Chronicler. However, similarities between Haggai and Chronicles should probably be attributed to the fact that the books of Haggai and Zechariah were already in existence and influenced the compiler of Chronicles, rather than the reverse. Others have maintained that Haggai was himself the author of the book, choosing the third-person narratives in the framework in order to enhance the objectivity and historical reality of the report or to authenticate his oracles as the word of God. Meyers and Meyers (1987) argue that Haggai (and Zechariah 1–8) in final form should be dated before the actual dedication of the temple, arguing that such a momentous event would certainly have been mentioned if it had taken place. They also argue that the rededication of the temple would have enhanced Haggai's reputation. While Boda (2004) believes that this is true of Haggai, he disputes it for Zechariah 1–8.

The first oracle (1:1–11; August 29, 520 BC) consists of a brief disputation and a judgment speech. It was delivered on the first day of the month (according to the ancient calendar), quite possibly at a public gathering to observe the festival of the New Moon (Num. 28:11; 10:10; Ps. 81:3 [MT 4]; Ezra 3:5). The presence of the leaders and the people in the area of the temple ruins would have provided the perfect setting for the prophet's inaugural oracle. It had been quite easy to rationalize postponing the work on the temple (1:2). In spite of the energy devoted to their own well-being in the construction of homes and cultivation of crops, the returnees had been met by crop failure, inflation, and drought; their labor seemed futile. Haggai asserts that these failures were due to their neglect of the temple. Note the displeasure with which God addresses the nation: he calls them "these people" instead of "my people" (1:2). Poor harvests (Deut. 28:38–40), insufficient food (v. 48), drought (vv. 23–24), and frustrated labor (v. 20) are all curses for covenant disobedience.

Whereas Israel's response to the preaching of the prophets had often been indifference, mocking, or hostility, here instead the people recognize the rightness of what the prophet has said and respond with enthusiastic obedience (1:12–15). The work was begun twenty-three days later (1:15; September 21, 520 BC).

Haggai's second oracle (2:1–9; October 17, 520) came less than a month after the work on the temple had begun. The seventh month was Tishri (also called Ethamin), the month during which the Feast of Tabernacles was observed, beginning on the fifteenth day of the month and lasting for seven days (Lev. 23:33–43; Num. 29:12–39; Deut. 16:13–15; Ezek. 45:23–25). The twenty-first day of the month, then, would have been the last day of that festal observance (Verhoef 1988, 263). The reference to "this house" (2:3) also confirms that this oracle was delivered during a public assembly in the temple precincts. The comparison with Solomon's temple (2:3) was all the more appropriate on this occasion since the dedication of the former temple took place also in connection with the Feast of Tabernacles (2 Chron. 7:8–10; 1 Kings 8:2). Now that the work crews were three weeks into the project, it was apparent that this second temple would be much less grand than the first. Most of those who remembered the former temple would by then have been in their seventies. The prophet provides a message of encouragement to all and assures them that the glory of this second temple would exceed that of the former (2:6–9).

Haggai's third and fourth oracles (2:10–19, 20–23) were both delivered on the same day (December 18, 520 BC), three months after the work on the temple had begun (1:15). The third oracle has two parts: (1) a question about Torah (2:10–14; see the remarks on Zech. 7:1–3) cast in the form of the dialogue between Yahweh and the prophet, and (2) a message of encouragement (2:15–19). The point of the ruling on the legal question was that holiness was not contagious—just working on the temple would not make the people holy—but ritual uncleanness or defilement was contagious, and the temple itself could be defiled by the uncleanness of the people. The only hope the nation had for divine approval and acceptance was the grace of God. The temple would not be a magical talisman. Perhaps in the three months since the work had begun, the people

> *The prophet provides a message of encouragement to all and assures them that the glory of this second temple would exceed that of the former.*

had become a bit discouraged, and the prophet encourages them in their work with assurances of divine blessing. December was the middle of the growing season, and the prophet assures the people that time away from farm work to work on the temple would not mean poor harvests, but to the contrary, a great harvest was ahead (cf. 1:5–11).

Haggai's fourth oracle (2:20–23) was addressed to Zerubbabel, the governor of Judah and a descendant in the line of David through Jehoiachin. In the book of Jeremiah, God had earlier described Jehoiachin as a signet ring on his hand (Jer. 22:24–25), a ring that would be pulled off and discarded. In Haggai God uses the same imagery, but reverses it, this time describing a descendant of Jehoiachin as a valued signet ring on the hand of God. Although Haggai, Zechariah, and their contemporaries may have hoped for the overthrow of foreign domination and the restoration of Davidic rule in their own day, Zerubbabel would not be this Davidic king, but rather would point forward to an eschatological day when God would shake the heavens and the earth (2:6–7, 21).

APPROACHING THE NEW TESTAMENT

In the Old Testament, God's acceptance of a sanctuary or a sacrifice was often signified by the appearance of fire, more particularly the pillar of fire and cloud that the rabbis came to call the "Shekinah glory" (Ex. 40:34–38; Judg. 6:21; 1 Kings 8:10–11; 18:38; 1 Chron. 21:26; 2 Chron. 5:13–14; 7:1–3). The same word "glory" could also refer to wealth and riches. In line with the expectation and hope of Isaiah (Isa. 66), the restoration community looked for a time when the wealth of the nations would flow into Jerusalem. Haggai appears to be making use of this ambiguity in the term "glory" by using it in both senses in 2:3, 7–9 (Wolf 1976). Yet, although the Persians would underwrite the construction and ritual of the second temple (Ezra 1:6–7; 6:7–10; 7:15–18), this fell far short of prophetic descriptions of Gentile wealth pouring into the city. In spite of Ezekiel's depiction of the glory of God returning to the city (Ezek. 43:1–7), there is no hint or suggestion that the pillar of fire and cloud ever appeared above the second temple. So too, although the Jews of Judah would enjoy a measure of autonomy under Persian rule, the power of foreign nations was not broken (2:22), and Judeans would continue to serve a variety of foreign masters.

A new era had been inaugurated with the decree of Cyrus, the reconstruction of the temple, and the administration of the Davidic prince Zerubbabel. But it was only a provisional step anticipatory of events yet to come. The visible presence of God would finally appear at the second temple, when Jesus "tabernacled in our midst and we beheld his glory" (John 1:14, author's translation), for he was "the radiance of God's glory and the exact representation of his being" (Heb. 1:3). The wealth of nations comes to Jerusalem in the gifts of Gentile wise men (Matt. 2:1–12) and in a new temple made of living stones, Jew and Gentile alike (1 Cor. 3:16–17; 1 Peter 2:4–10). A new kingdom—one not of this world, one that transcends and rules all others—is introduced by another son of David; he rules now and is putting all things under his feet.

These things too are but a step toward the consummation, when all things will be new and the dwelling of God will be with men in a city rich beyond description, where all tears are wiped away (Rev. 21).

The election of Zerubbabel was tied to more than the inauguration of a Davidic prince; it also prefigured a cataclysmic change in the cosmos (2:6–7, 21–22). The writer of Hebrews views this eschatological age as already inaugurated in the person of Christ (Heb. 12:26–29; cf. Ex. 19:18; Matt. 27:51).

CHAPTER THIRTY-FIVE

ZECHARIAH

Zechariah is the longest of the minor prophets. It is also perhaps the most difficult. Jerome called it the "most obscure" book of the Hebrew Bible, an opinion often cited and widely shared by subsequent readers. The difficulties of the book have spawned many opinions about the date and authorship of various portions as well as the interpretation of the individual pericopes. Yet it is also a very important book to Christian readers: Zechariah 9–14 is the most frequently cited portion of the Old Testament in the Passion narratives (Lamarche 1961, 8–9), and apart from Ezekiel, this book has exercised more influence than any other on the author of Revelation.

Zechariah was apparently a popular name: more than twenty-five individuals in the Bible are known by it. The prophet is identified as the son of Berekiah the son of Iddo (1:1), probably the same person known in a telescoped form as Zechariah son of Iddo (Ezra 5:1; 6:14; Neh. 12:16). If this identification is correct, Zechariah was a member of one of the families of priests who returned from the captivity; this would also serve to explain his familiarity with and interest in matters pertaining to the temple (e.g., 1:16; 3–4; 6:9–15; 8:9, 20–23; 14:16–21).

BIBLIOGRAPHY

Commentaries

S. **Amsler,** *Aggée, Zacharie, Malachie* (CAT 11c; Paris: Delachaux et Niestlé, 1981); J. G. **Baldwin,** *Haggai, Zechariah, Malachi* (TOTC; Tyndale, 1972); M. J. **Boda,** *Haggai, Zechariah* (NIVAC; Zondervan, 2004); M. H. **Floyd,** *The Minor Prophets, Part 2* (FOTL; Eerdmans, 2000); G. **Gaide,** *Jérusalem, voici ton Roi. Commentaire de Zacharie 9–14* (Paris: L'editions Cerf, 1968); D. R. **Jones,** *Haggai, Zechariah, and Malachi* (TBC; SCM, 1964); P. **Lamarche,** *Zacharie ix–xiv: Structure, Litteraire, et Messianisme* (Paris: J. Gabalda, 1961); T. E. **McComiskey,** "Zechariah," in *The Minor Prophets: An Exegetical and Expository Commentary,* ed. T. E. McComiskey (Baker, 1998), 1002–244; C. L. **Meyers** and E. M. **Meyers,** *Haggai;*

Zechariah 1–8 (AB; Doubleday, 1987); idem, *Zechariah 9–14* (AB; Doubleday, 1993); D. **Petersen,** *Haggai and Zechariah 1–8* (OTL; Westminster, 1984); idem, *Zechariah 9–14 and Malachi* (OTL; Westminster John Knox, 1995); A. **Petitjean,** *Les oracles du Proto-Zacharie* (Paris: J. Gabalda, 1969); W. **Rudolph,** *Haggai— Sacharja 1–8/9–14—Maleachi* (*KAT* 13/4; Gütersloh: G. Mohn, 1976); R. L. **Smith,** *Micah–Malachi* (WBC 32; Word, 1984).

Monographs and Articles

P. R. **Ackroyd,** *Exile and Restoration* (OTL; Westminster, 1968); S. **Amsler,** "Zacharie et l'origine d'apocalyptique," VTSup 22 (1972): 227–31; J. **Berquist,** *Judaism in Persia's Shadow: A Social and Cultural Approach* (Fortress, 1995); W. **Beuken,** *Haggai—Sacharja 1–8. Studien zur Überlieferungsgeschichte der früh- nachexilischen Prophetie* (SSN 10; Assen: van Gorcum, 1967); M. **Biè,** *Das Buch Sacharja* (Berlin: Evangelische Verlagsanstalt, 1962); M. J. **Boda,** "From Fasts to Feasts: The Literary Function of Zechariah 7–8," *CBQ* 65 (2003): 39–407; idem, "Reading Between the Lines: Zechariah 11:4–16 in Its Literary Contexts," in *Bring- ing out the Treasure: Inner Biblical Allusion and Zechariah 9–14,* ed. M. J. Boda and M. H. Floyd (Sheffield, 2003), 277–91; F. F. **Bruce,** "The Book of Zechariah and the Passion Narrative," *BJRL* 43 (1961): 336–53; H. **Gese,** "Anfang und Ende der Apokalyptik, dargestellt am Sacharjabuch," *ZTK* 70 (1973): 20–49; B. **Halpern,** "The Ritual Background of Zechariah's Temple Song," *CBQ* 40 (1978): 167–90; P. **Hanson,** "In Defiance of Death: Zechariah's Symbolic Universe," *Love and Death in the Ancient Near East,* ed. J. Marks and R. Good (Guilford, Conn.: Four Quarters, 1987): 173–79; idem, *The Dawn of Apocalyptic* (Fortress, 1975); A. E. **Hill,** "Dating Second Zechariah: A Linguistic Reexamination," *HAR* 6 (1982): 105–34; C. **Jere- mias,** *Die Nachtgeschichte des Sacharja* (Göttingen: Vandenhoeck und Ruprecht, 1977); A. R. **Johnson,** *Sacral Kingship in Ancient Israel* (Cardiff: University of Wales Press, 1955); J. **Kremer,** *Die Hirtenallegorie im Buch Zacharias* (Munich: Aschen- dorff, c. 1930); E. **Lipiñski,** "Recherches sur le livre de Zacharie," *VT* 20 (1970): 25– 55; R. A. **Mason,** "The Relation of Zech. 9–14 to Proto-Zechariah," *ZAW* 88 (1976): 227–39; D. **Petersen,** "Zechariah's Visions: A Theological Perspective," *VT* 34 (1984): 195–206; S. **Portnoy** and D. **Petersen,** "Biblical Texts and Statistical Analysis: Zechariah and Beyond," *JBL* 103 (1984): 11–21; I. **Provan,** V. P. **Long,** and T. **Longman** III, *A Biblical History of Israel* (Westminster John Knox, 2003); Y. **Radday** and D. **Wickmann,** "The Unity of Zechariah Examined in the Light of Statistical Linguistics," *ZAW* 87 (1975): 30–55; P. L. **Redditt,** "Nehemiah's First Mission and the Date of Zechariah 91–14," *CBQ* 56 (1994): 676–86.

HISTORICAL BACKGROUND

Zechariah is set against the background of the first generation of returnees from the Babylonian exile (Berquist 1995; Provan, Long, and Longman 2003, 285–303).

His night visions are dated to the second year of Darius (520/519 BC). Although Cyrus, the king of Persia, had authorized the Jews to return to Jerusalem and rebuild the temple of God in 539, the returnees found themselves facing external opposition (Ezra 3:8–4:5, 24; 5:1–6:22) and a variety of personal and practical difficulties (Hag. 1:5–11; 2:15–19; Zech. 8:9–13). Work on the house of God was delayed until God raised up two prophets, Haggai and Zechariah, to spur the people to tend to the construction of the temple (Ezra 5:1–2). The work on the temple was resumed, and the construction was completed in 516 (Ezra 6:13–15). Since Haggai and Zechariah were preaching to the same audience under the same historical circumstances, it is not surprising to find common themes in their pronouncements (cf. Hag. 1:5–11 and 2:15–19 with Zech. 8:9–13; Hag. 2:20–23 with Zech. 4:6–10).

Essentially, the first eight chapters of Zechariah are taken up with issues of more immediate concern to the restoration community. The night visions raise the question of retribution against Gentile nations (1:7–21 [MT 2:4]; 6:1–8), the security of Jerusalem (2:1–12 [MT 5–17]), the construction and completion of the temple (4:1–14), and the problem of sin in a supposedly purified remnant (3:1–10; 5:1–11). A delegation comes to the city from Jews in the Diaspora to seek clarification on whether fasts commemorating various stages of the destruction of the city should continue to be observed (chaps. 7–8). These chapters reflect the historical background of the community early in the restoration period. The final six chapters, however, seem less oriented to issues of immediate concern; instead, they include eschatological and apocalyptic imagery largely pertaining to a more distant future. For this reason and several others, critical scholarship has reached a consensus that chapters 9–14 are from a different author and period.

Table 18
Dates Correlating Haggai and Zechariah

Reference	Y/M/D of Darius	Date	Content
Hag. 1:1	2/6/1	Aug. 29, 520	Temple to be built
Hag. 1:15	2/6/24	Sept. 21, 520	Work on temple resumed
Hag. 2:1	2/7/21	Oct. 17, 520	Glory of the temple
Zech. 1:1	2/8/-	Oct./Nov. 520	Zechariah's authority
Hag. 2:10, 20	2/9/24	Dec. 18, 520	Blessing for future; Zerubbabel as God's signet
Zech. 1:7	2/11/24	Feb. 15, 519	First night vision
Zech. 7:1	4/9/4	Dec. 7, 518	An issue about fasting
Ezra 6:15	6/12/3	Mar. 12, 515	Temple completed

LITERARY ANALYSIS

The prevailing consensus in critical biblical scholarship that Zechariah 1–8 and 9–14 are from two different periods and authors derives from many lines of evidence. (1) As mentioned above, the two sections focus on different temporal horizons: 1–8 is concerned with issues of immediate interest to the restoration community, whereas 9–14 reflect more apocalyptic and eschatological imagery. (2) In terms of literary form, 1–8 is composed essentially of Zechariah's night visions and the sermons on fasting that followed an inquiry about the practice (7–8); whereas 9–14 consists of two larger sections (9–11; 12–14), each designated an "oracle" (*maúûâ'*, 9:1; 12:1; cf. Mal. 1:1; translated generically as "prophecy" in TNIV). (3) Some vocabulary and syntactic constructions that occur in one half do not occur in the other; this evidence is often construed as pointing to a different author. Radday and Wickmann (1975) evaluated this traditional argument afresh with a far more sophisticated statistical model than had been used heretofore; they also had the advantage of computers to compile the data. Their findings were that there is insufficient linguistic evidence to suggest a different author in 9–11 from the author of 1–8; however, the statistical data also suggested that it was highly improbable that 12–14 was from the same person as 1–11. Portnoy and Petersen (1984) criticized the statistical methods used by Radday and Wickmann and argued that errors in their statistical model invalidate their conclusions; Portnoy and Petersen proposed a different statistical model, which confirmed the traditional critical consensus of a distinction in authorship not only between 1–8 and 9–14, but also between 9–11 and 12–14.

(4) The internal evidence for the date of 9–14 does not agree with the setting of 1–8 in the early restoration period. For example, references to a king in Gaza (9:5) or to Assyria and Egypt as enemies (10:11) favor a setting in the preexilic period, a date too early; whereas the reference to the Greeks (9:13) is ordinarily understood as pointing to a period after Alexander's conquests, at least two centuries later than the setting of chapters 1–8. (5) The somewhat opaque 11:4–17 is often applied to different scenarios in the Maccabean period. The good shepherd has been identified as Onias III (2 Macc. 4:1), and the three shepherds who are cut off (11:8) are identified with Simon, Lysimachus, and Menelaus, the sons of Tobias. (6) In chapters 1–8 specific historical persons play the major roles (Zechariah, Joshua, Zerubbabel, the participants in 6:10–11; 7:2), whereas in 9–14 no personal names occur. (7) In 1–8 dates are important; 9–14 are undated. (8) In 1–8 Joshua the high priest and Zerubbabel, a Davidic descendant, are the leaders of the community; 9–14 use instead the metaphor of shepherds applied to an undefined referent. These are the major lines of evidence ordinarily advanced in critical scholarship in this form or a variation for dissociating Zechariah 9–14 from 1–8.

Although more specific interaction with these lines of argument is required, a brief response is in order: With reference to 1, 2, 6, 7, and 8 above, these premises have in common that they are based on observed differences in the two halves of the book; the differences are felt to be sufficiently numerous and important as to warrant the suggestion of a different author and historical setting. Yet it must be asked whether or not other suggestions would also account for these differences. If a modern author carefully arranges his material into various groups by subject or literary form, we ordinarily consider this to be evidence of an orderly mind at work and do not feel compelled to suggest the material must be from different individuals. In the same way, if an ancient author separates material by literary form (vision, oracle), subject (immediate issues vs. distant), or other criteria (e.g., dated versus undated), this would seem from our Western vantage the actions of a rational, orderly person. These items scarcely in themselves provide an argument for multiple authorship unless one implicitly adheres to a rather foolish notion that any one author will write only one kind of literature.

With reference to item 3 above, several caveats must be kept in mind. (1) As a generality from observing the discourse grammar of human language, one should expect changes in sentence length, vocabulary, syntactic construction, and so forth, as the subject of one's writings also changes. A current example might be helpful: there is no doubt a great difference in vocabulary, sentence length, and syntactic construction in the editorial writings of a William F. Buckley when compared with his novels; the linguistic data do not reflect a different author in this case, but rather are tied to the different genres in which he writes and the different subject matter in view. The reader could note similar differences between his or her own past academic writings in high school or college as compared to letters home or devotional writing. Certainly one should not be surprised to see major differences of these types in contrasting essentially prose (1–8) and poetic (9–14) literature. Portnoy and Petersen (1984, 12) note the problem that the heterogeneity in the book of Zechariah represents for authorship questions. (2) At the time of this writing, biblical scholarship is still in its infancy with reference to the use of sophisticated statistical models to assess authorship questions. The disagreement on method between Radday and Wickmann on the one hand, and Portnoy and Petersen on the other, is symptomatic of an area beset with theoretical difficulties; conclusions from such studies cannot be used with much confidence other than as corroborative evidence for hypotheses developed from other arguments. (3) The book of Zechariah is too meager a body of literature for applying statistical means with any confidence (Portnoy and Petersen 1984, 12).

We know fairly little about the prophet Zechariah. It is certainly within reason that he lived well beyond the events narrated in Zechariah 1–8, and a significant passage of time may also underlie the two halves of the book. While

Zechariah 1–8 shows a few features of apocalyptic literature, chapters 9–14 contain these elements with greater frequency; this is commonly viewed as a more "advanced" apocalypticism, and hence, as significantly later. However, one wonders about the validity of a rather simplistic linear view of the development of apocalyptic. It is quite plausible that if chapters 9–14 come from a later stage in the prophet's life, sufficient time would have passed for the underlying social situation to have changed from the optimism of work underway in 1–8 to the longing for direct divine intrusion that characterizes the later chapters. It is doubtful that such a passage of time is even necessary, however, for both attitudes to coexist in a single individual or society.

With reference to item 4 above, it is gratuitous to assume that the mention of the Greeks (9:13) requires a date after Alexander's conquests. The inscriptions of Sargon II and Sennacherib show that Greek traders and mercenary soldiers were active in the Near East at least as early as the eighth century BC (cf. Ezek. 27:13; Joel 3:6 [MT 4:6]). With reference to item 5 above, there is also considerable disagreement. Kremer (1930, 83–87) identified no fewer than thirty proposed identifications for the three shepherds (cf. Harrison, *IOT*, 953).

In summary, it seems fair to say that while an impressive body of evidence can be marshaled to show that Zechariah 9–14 is not from the same time or author as Zechariah 1–8, the evidence does not require that conclusion (for recent arguments placing the date of chapters 9–14 closer to that of chapters 1–8 ([in the early Persian period], see Hill; Boda; Redditt). To the contrary, most of the arguments advanced in favor of multiple authorship are quite amenable to reading the book as a unity. Furthermore, a number of themes are held in common in the two halves of the book (Smith 1984, 242, 248; Childs, *IOTS* 482–83): (1) the importance assigned to Jerusalem (1:12–16; 2:1–13 [MT 2:5–17]; 9:8–10; 12:1–13; 14:1–21); (2) the cleansing of the community (3:1–9; 5:1–11; 10:9; 12:10; 13:1–2; 14:20–21); (3) the place of the Gentiles in the kingdom of God (2:11 [MT 2:15]; 8:20–23; 9:7, 10; 14:16–19); (4) dependence on the works of the former prophets (1:4; Isa. 58 in 7:4–10; Amos 1:9–10 and 5:27–62 in 9:1–8; Jer. 25:34–38 in 11:1–3; Ezek. 47:1–10 in 14:1–4); (5) the restoration of paradisiacal fertility (8:12; 14:8); (6) renewal of the covenant (8:8; 13:9); (7) the regathering of the exiles (2:6 [MT 2:10]; 8:7; 10:9–10); (8) the outpouring of the Spirit (4:6; 12:10); and (9) the Messiah (3:8; 4:6; 9:9–10).

Most of the arguments advanced in favor of multiple authorship are quite amenable to reading the book as a unity.

As described above, the consensus among critical scholars has been that chapters 9–14 are from a different author or authors than chapters 1–8. However, beyond this assertion there is little unanimity. A bewildering variety of dates and settings have been proposed for the second half of the book, ranging from the eighth century BC to the Maccabean period. The references to Ephraim as an independent political entity (9:10, 13) and the mention of Assyria and Egypt as enemies (10:10; 14:19) have suggested to some a date before the fall of Samaria. In the seventeenth century a Cambridge scholar, Joseph Mead, had already suggested that since Matthew 27:9 appears to attribute Zechariah 11:13 to Jeremiah, chapters 9–11 were the work of Jeremiah.

Others suggest that the reference to Greece in 9:13 presumes a unified Greek empire and that 9:1–8 describes the rapid advance of the Greek armies under Alexander. The warfare and unrest of this period provide the background for chapters 9–14 and explain the rise of messianic hope.

A date in the Maccabean period was championed by scholars who saw the actions and fate of Maccabean rulers depicted in the shepherd imagery of 11:4–17 and 13:7–9 and the reference to a murder in 12:10. This identification was also argued from the idea that the more "advanced" apocalypticism of the second half of the book favored a setting in the second century BC.

In addition to questions about the date of the second half of the book, scholars also questioned its unity. Some scholars proposed different settings for 9–11 and 12–14, while others considered 9–14 a patchwork or mosaic to which numerous sources contributed.

Others have sought to locate the second half of the book in the cult of ancient Israel or in the sociological setting of the postexilic period. Johnson (1955, 58–59) associated Zechariah 9–14 with a New Year festival hypothesized for ancient Israel. However, even the existence of this festival in ancient Israel is questionable; the festival and rituals associated with it are inferences from the surrounding cultures and the indirect evidence of a few biblical texts. Hanson (1975) viewed Zechariah 9–14 as polemical literature produced by followers of Second Isaiah and disenfranchised Levites who were opposing the hierocratic, priestly influence and government in the early postexilic period. According to Hanson, the ruling priestly parties were content with things as they were, a sort of theology for the status quo. A coalition of Levites and prophets (visionaries, apocalypticists) sought to overturn the status quo by insisting that the present structures of society would be overcome and supplanted through divine intrusion. Others have judged Hanson's polarization of theological parties in the early postexilic period misleading and reductionistic.

Viewed as a whole, once having made the decision to separate Zechariah 9–14 from the earlier chapters, there is scarcely a more vexing problem in Old Testament studies than providing the historical and sociological background for the latter half of the book.

THEOLOGICAL MESSAGE

Let us look first at the outline of Zechariah and then examine the two halves of the book in closer detail.

> I. Zechariah's claim to authority (1:1–6)
> II. The night visions (1:7–6:8)

Zechariah 1–8

A number of the prophetic books include an account of the prophet's call; like Moses before them (Ex. 3), the prophets are given access to the divine presence in an inaugural vision (Isa. 6; Jer. 1; Ezek. 1–2; cf. Judg. 6; 1 Kings 22). These call narratives constitute part of the prophet's claim to authority. Although Zechariah does not begin with a call vision, the prophet clearly considered himself one who stood in the line of Moses' successors, who had spoken with power and authority to Israel (1:1–6), and these introductory verses take the place of a call narrative. The prophet warns the nation to heed his words, for his words shared in the efficacy of the words of the prophets who had preceded him (1:4–6). The restoration community should reflect on the past and not make the same mistakes as their forefathers.

Zechariah's eight night visions appear to be arranged in a rather loose chiastic structure. Visions 1 and 8 (1:7–17; 6:1–8) both portray four multicolored groups of horses and concern the fate of Gentile nations. The parallels between two pairs of visions—2 and 3 (1:18–21 [MT 2:1–4]; 2:1–12 [MT 2:5–17]) and 6 and 7 (5:1–4, 5–11)—are less apparent: both concern obstacles facing the restoration community, on the one hand opposition from the Gentile nations (visions 2 and 3), and on the other, sin within the covenant community (visions 6 and 7). Both pairs deal with God's judgment (1:21 [MT 2:4]; 5:4) and an exile (2:6 [MT 2:10]; 5:10–11). The central pair (visions 4 and 5 [3:1–10; 4:1–14]) is set within the temple precincts and concerns the civil and cultic leaders of the restoration community (Joshua, Zerubbabel); these visions both mention the seven eyes of the Lord (3:9; 4:10). Taken together, the visions form a concentric pattern moving from the Gentile world at large (1, 8), to concern with the city (2, 3, 6, 7), to the temple environs (4, 5).

The first night vision (1:7–17) addresses the problem of unrealized eschatology: the Jews had experienced the day of the Lord and had known the fury of a holy God, but the Gentile nations appear "at rest and in peace" (1:11). The angel of the Lord, here in the role of the captain of the Lord's army, intercedes with God for the end of his anger and the vindication of his people. The prophet hears words of reassurance and comfort that God has not forgotten his people; in words somewhat reminiscent of Isaiah 40:2, the nations are indicted for their excessive zeal when used as God's instruments to punish Israel. The nations would yet experience the day of the Lord, and Zion would again be the particular object of his favor.

In the second night vision (1:18–21 [MT 2:1–4]), the major interpretive issue has been the identity of the four horns and the four craftsmen. Many interpreters associate the four horns with the fourfold image or the four beasts in the book of Daniel (Dan. 2, 7); others see the number four here as representative of universal opposition, more or less like the use in the "four winds of heaven" (2:6 [MT 2:10]; 6:5). While the details may be difficult, the point of this night vision is reasonably clear: whatever opposition has been directed against God's people will be smashed.

A city without walls was vulnerable; conquerors commonly pulled down the walls of ancient cities in order to keep them defenseless. The returnees from the exile were no doubt concerned with their vulnerability and small numbers. In the third of the night visions (2:1–13 [MT 5–17]), the prophet sees the Lord as a wall of fire around the city, a city overflowing with prosperity. The imagery is that of the entire city being taken within the pillar of fire, the Shekinah glory; no longer is the presence of God confined to the Most Holy Place within the temple, but the entire city has become the dwelling place of God. This theme appears again in Zechariah 14:20–21 and is used as well in Revelation 21:3, 22–27.

Several biblical texts portray a personification of evil as having access to the presence of God (Job 1–2; 1 Kings 22:21–23). In the fourth night vision (3:1–10) Zechariah sees a judicial scene: the angel of the Lord is seated as judge, and a prosecutor ("Satan" means "accuser") is there to bring charges against the high priest, who stands in his filthy garments. The occasion for this vision is much debated. Several features in the passage make the most probable setting the Day of Atonement: the passage is concerned with an occasion when the high priest would stand in God's presence; in Israel's cult this would most naturally be the occasion of his entry into the Most Holy Place on the Day of Atonement. The passage is also concerned with the garments of the high priest, a particular focus also on the Day of Atonement (Lev. 16:4), and with the removal of sin from the land, which was the particular object of the liturgy of that day (3:9). Others suggest instead a setting in a ceremony of priestly investiture or some other liturgical occasion. In many ways this vision too anticipates themes later developed in the New Testament, so much so that it could almost be designated "the gospel according to Zechariah." When God cleanses the high priest and provides for him a righteousness not of his own making (3:4), he effectively removes the basis for any charge the accuser might level. Centuries later, Paul would say, "If God is for us, who can be against us? . . . Who will bring any charge against those whom God has chosen? It is God who justifies" (Rom. 8:31–33). The priestly labors could not remove sin (Heb. 10:1–4, 11–13), but God would remove the sin of the land in a single day (3:9). In the context of the historical events of Zechariah's own day, the high priest represented the nation; his cleansing by God affirms that the returnees of that generation would be able to build an acceptable temple for God.

In the fifth night vision (4:1–14), the prophet sees a lampstand consisting of a single basin with seven lamps around its rim, each having spouts for seven wicks, so that there would be a total of forty-nine flames. The oil for the lamp comes from olive trees and clusters of fruit in the background. Pipes deliver the oil from the trees directly to the lamp. The priests used to tend the lampstands in the temple twice a day, once in the morning and again in the evening, trimming the wicks and refilling the lamps with oil. Here was a lampstand, however, which did not need human tending. The point of the vision was also clear: the work on the temple was God's work (4:6), and he would see to its completion (4:9). Although some found the temple they were building to be disappointing (Hag. 2:2–3; Ezra 3:12–13), God rejoiced in the work (4:10). The translation of the TNIV at 4:10 somewhat obscures this point; the verse would have been better translated as "Who despises the day of small things? The eyes of the LORD, which range throughout the earth, rejoice when they see the plumb line in the hand of Zerubbabel." Zerubbabel and Joshua were those through whom God would accomplish this task (4:12–14). John would later modify this imagery somewhat and use it for a different purpose (Rev. 11:4).

The sixth and seventh night visions (5:1–11) are in effect two acts from a single play. The flying scroll appears to summarize the Ten Commandments: the first four commandments were offenses against God and are represented by swearing falsely in God's name (5:4; Ex. 20:7); the last six commandments were offenses against others and are represented by stealing (5:4; Ex. 20:15). The exile had been intended to purge Israel and to produce a purified people. However, the law (the scroll) identifies sin in the restoration community, sin that would still be judged. Then the prophet sees a basket containing a figure representing sin. This sin would be taken back to Babylonia (Shinar, 5:11), back to the place of judgment. In visions 2 and 3, obstacles to realizing the goal of the restoration community had come from external opposition, but in visions 6 and 7, the obstacles are within the community.

The eighth night vision (6:1–8) reuses the imagery of horses of various colors found in the first vision (1:7–17). While some of the details are difficult, the point of the vision is clear: God would avenge himself by punishing the nations.

The remainder of the material in the first half of the book is not in the form of visions, but rather, of reports or historical events. In 6:9–15, some exiles visit Jerusalem, bringing gifts for the temple from Jews still living in exile. The gold is used to make a crown for the high priest. Many commentators have found this problematic: a crown would more naturally sit on the head of a royal figure like Zerubbabel, a descendant of David who was eligible for kingship. Although some translations of the Bible actually substitute Zerubbabel's name for Joshua's (6:11), no ancient text attests to this change. Although the messianic title "Branch" (6:12) belongs to someone in the Davidic line (Isa. 4:2; Jer. 23:5; 33:15), Joshua has already been associated with that title in Zechariah 3:8. Christian interpreters have traditionally seen in this passage the blending of the offices of priest and king in the Messiah.

During the period of the exile, four fasts had been observed, commemorating various events surrounding the destruction of Jerusalem. Now that the exile was over and the temple was being completed, the Jews began to ask whether they should continue to observe fasts pertaining to the destruction of the city. A delegation came to Jerusalem to ask the priests there for a ruling (7:1–3; cf. Hag. 2:11; Mal. 2:7). Zechariah uses their inquiry as an occasion for several sermons about hypocritical fasting and religion preoccupied with details of the law instead of obedience from the heart (7:4–8:23). Although Israel was preoccupied with maintaining separation from the Gentiles in much of the postexilic period (Ezra 9–10; Neh. 13:23–30), Zechariah foresees a day when Gentiles would worship the Lord on an equal footing with the Jews (8:20–23; 14:16–21).

Zechariah 9–14

Some recent scholarship has emphasized the unity of Zechariah 9–14, and further, its unity or proximity in time with the earlier chapters (Biè 1962; Lamarche 1961; Jones 1964; Baldwin 1972). Lamarche has argued that the entirety of chapters 9–14 is an intricate chiasmus from a single author built around recurring themes: the salvation and judgment of both Israel and the nations by war (9:1–8; 9:11–10:1; 10:3b–11:3; 12:1–9; 14:1–15), the day of the Lord introduced with the appearance of a messianic king (9:9–10; 11:4–17; 12:10–13:1; 13:7–9), and the suppression of idolatry (10:2–3a; 13:2–6).

Whether one accepts a division in authorship between the two halves of the book or not, the book as it stands presents itself as a literary unity. An interpreter must pay attention to the way in which each half influences the interpretation of the other. Within the prophetic expectation of Israel, the restoration fulfilled many of the promises of God to Israel; the place of the restoration community within the purpose and plan of God is largely the concern of chapters 1–8. The return was a new exodus, a new redemption—but it would not be the final redemption. Notwithstanding all that the return from the exile represented, a yet fuller redemption was still ahead in the future; this complete redemption is largely the concern of chapters 9–14. Although the return from captivity involved many themes from the prophetic hopes of Israel (see Literary Analysis above), the return was only an inaugural and provisional stage in the ulti-

> Although Israel was preoccupied with maintaining separation from the Gentiles, Zechariah foresees a day when Gentiles would worship the Lord on an equal footing with the Jews.

mate redemption God would provide. The restoration from captivity was but a token and taste of the great redemption to come.

APPROACHING THE NEW TESTAMENT

Christian readers of this prophet cannot but notice that the coming age of full redemption is inaugurated by a messianic king who makes a humble appearance, bringing righteousness and salvation to Jerusalem while riding on a donkey (9:9; Matt. 21:5). He is the shepherd king, but a smitten shepherd (13:7; Matt. 26:31), betrayed and pierced (11:12–13; 12:10; Matt. 26:15; 27:9–10; John 19:34, 37). But it is this King who will subdue the nations (12:8–9) and establish his kingdom among men (14:3–9).

CHAPTER THIRTY-SIX

MALACHI

The book of Malachi is the twelfth of the Minor Prophets and brings the second part (the *Nebi'im*) of the three-part Hebrew canon to an end. In English translations of the Bible, which follow the Greek tradition, Malachi concludes the canon of the Old Testament. Its position among the twelve is likely due to the fact that Malachi was the last to minister. While the collocation is not intentional, it is notable that the book concludes the Old Testament by looking forward to the coming of the prophet Elijah, while one of the early voices of the New Testament period is that of John the Baptist, whom Jesus identifies with Elijah (Matt. 11:14).

BIBLIOGRAPHY

Commentaries

E. **Achtemeier,** *Nahum–Malachi* (Interp; John Knox, 1986); J. G. **Baldwin,** *Haggai, Zechariah, Malachi* (TOTC; InterVarsity Press, 1972); P. C. **Craigie,** *Twelve Prophets* (DSB; Westminster, 1985); C. D. **Isbell,** *Malachi* (Zondervan, 1980); W. C. **Kaiser,** *Malachi: God's Unchanging Love* (Baker, 1984); H. G. **Mitchell,** J. M. P. **Smith,** and J. A. **Bewer,** *Haggai, Zechariah, Malachi, and Jonah* (ICC; T. & T. Clark, 1912); G. S. **Ogden** and R. R. **Deutsch,** *Joel and Malachi: A Promise of Hope, a Call to Obedience* (ITC; Eerdmans, 1987); R. L. **Smith,** *Micah–Malachi* (WBC; Word, 1984); P. A. **Verhoef,** *The Books of Haggai and Malachi* (NICOT; Eerdmans, 1987).

Articles and Monographs

D. C. **Allison** Jr., "'Elijah Must Come First,'" *JBL* 103 (1984): 256–58; J. G. **Baldwin,** "Malachi 1:11 and the Worship of the Nations in the Old Testament," *TynBul* 23 (1972): 117–24; J. L. **Berquist,** "The Social Setting of Malachi," *BTB* 19 (1989): 121–26; C. L. **Blomberg,** *CTR* 2 (1987): 99–117; E. R. **Clendenen,** "The Structure of Malachi: A Textlinguistic Study," *CTR* 2 (1987): 3–17; W. J. **Dumbrell,** "Malachi and the Ezra-Nehemiah Reforms," *RTR* 35 (1976): 42–52; J. A. **Fischer,**

"Notes on the Literary Form and Message of Malachi," *CBQ* 34 (1972): 315–20; M. **Fishbane,** "Form and Reformulation of the Biblical Priestly Blessing," *JAOS* 103 (1983): 115–21; J. A. **Fitzmyer,** "More About Elijah Coming First," *JBL* 104 (1985): 295–96; B. **Glazier-McDonald,** *Malachi: The Divine Messenger* (SBLDS 98; Atlanta: Scholars, 1987); D. E. **Johnson,** "Fire in God's House: Imagery from Malachi 3 in Peter's Theology of Suffering (1 Pet. 4:12–19)," *JETS* 29 (1986): 285–94; G. L. **Klein,** "An Introduction to Malachi," *CTR* 2 (1987): 19–37; B. V. **Malchow,** "The Messenger of the Covenant in Malachi 3:1," *JBL* 103 (1984): 252–55; S. L. **McKenzie** and H. N. **Wallace,** "Covenant Themes in Malachi," *CBQ* 45 (1983): 549–63; E. M. **Meyers,** "Priestly Language in the Book of Malachi," *HAR* 10 (1986): 225–37; J. **Proctor,** "Fire in God's House: Influence of Malachi 3 in the NT," *JETS* 36 (1993): 9–14; C. C. **Torrey,** "The Prophecy of Malachi," *JBL* 17 (1898): 1–17.

HISTORICAL BACKGROUND

Author

The first verse reads simply: "A prophecy: The word of the LORD to Israel through Malachi." The form of the verse is a prophetic superscription, but its terseness has led to questions. Unlike other superscriptions, it gives no information concerning the prophet's ancestry or home town; he is not called "a prophet" or given any other title. While most other prophetic superscriptions provide one or more of these points of information, Malachi's simple naming of the prophet is not unprecedented.

Some scholars do argue that Malachi is not a proper name but simply a noun that is translated "my messenger," which should be identified with the "messenger" mentioned in 3:1.[1] However, that messenger is one who is coming in the future (so Childs, *IOTS*, 493) and should not be identified with the author of the book.

To see the impetus behind the view that Malachi is really an anonymous book, we need to revert to the book of Zechariah for a moment. After the night visions, there are two sections that begin with the term "oracle" (*maúûâ'*; cf. 9:1 and 12:1; TNIV translates with the generic "prophecy"). Since these sections contain predictive prophecy that extends beyond the time period of the historical prophet Zechariah, scholars who do not admit the possibility of predictive prophecy argue that these sections should be taken as anonymous prophecies that have simply been appended to the end of that book. The term "oracle" (*maúûâ'*) also begins Malachi, but it was treated separately only to make a twelfth book, because the number twelve gave the collection a sense of closure and completeness.

---

[1]Indeed, Torrey (1898, 1) feels he can simply "assume" this view.

This argument has no force for those who affirm supernatural revelation and predictive prophecy (see, for instance, Baldwin 1972, 221).

The most natural reading of the superscription regards Malachi as the proper name of a prophet who is mentioned no other place and about whom we know very little.[2] His name may contain an abbreviated reference to the divine name (in analogy with Abi in the Hebrew text of 2 Kings 18:2; cf. Abiyyah in the Hebrew text of 2 Chron. 29:1), thus "Yah is my messenger," but it more likely does mean "my [Yahweh's] messenger."

Date and Historical Setting

With little exception, scholars agree with Glazier-McDonald (1987, 14) that Malachi is a "child of the Persian period." The evidence is overwhelming. The temple has been rebuilt,[3] but already disillusionment has set in. Furthermore, *peḥâ*, the word used for "governor" in 1:8, is a technical term from the Persian period.

Although we can place the book in the Persian period, it is difficult to be much more precise. However, since disillusionment about the temple has already set in, it is probable that a few decades have passed since its completion. Furthermore, since Ezra and Nehemiah are not mentioned in the book, it is usually assumed that Malachi preceded them. Thus most scholars conclude that the book was written between 475 and 450 BC.

The time period was especially gray for Israel. The immediate postexilic period (begun in 539 BC with the decree of Cyrus) was a time of great optimism. Access was granted to Palestine; the process of rebuilding had begun. In particular, the temple, the symbol of God's presence in the city, was rebuilt.

Nonetheless, Judah remained a relatively insignificant province of the Persian Empire. God did not appear to give success to his people. Thus discouragement set in, with concomitant moral lapses. Kaiser has pointed out that many of the problems that Malachi faced are similar to the ethical issues of Nehemiah. He lists five (1984, 16):

1. Mixed marriages (Mal. 2:11–15; cf. Neh. 13:23–27)
2. Failure to tithe (Mal. 3:8–10; cf. Neh. 13:10–14)
3. No concern to keep the Sabbath (Mal. 2:8–9; 4:4; cf. Neh. 13:15–22)
4. Corrupt priests (Mal. 1:6–2:9; cf. Neh. 13:7–9)
5. Social problems (Mal. 3:5; cf. Neh. 5:1–13)

---

[2] It is true that there is some early evidence for misunderstanding Malachi for something other than a proper name. The Septuagint translates it as "his angel," apparently mistaking the final *yod* for a *waw*. However, the Septuagint traditionally also gave the name of the book as Malachi, intending to refer to a proper name. In the words of Klein (1987, 22), "the testimony of the LXX is not as decisive in favor of anonymity as some think."

[3] It was finished in 516/515 BC.

LITERARY ANALYSIS

Genre and Structure

The superscription (1:1) uses native genre labels that indicate that the book is a prophecy ("oracle" and "word of the LORD"). The book's contents support this genre identification, since the author inveighs against cultic and societal evils as well as predicting a future day of judgment that leads to the redemption of the faithful.

A close reading reveals the unique shape of Malachi's prophecy. As many scholars have seen (Clendenen is a rare exception), the book has at its heart a series of disputations in which the Lord through his prophet describes his character, challenges the abuses of his wayward people, and maps out his judgment.

After the superscription, Malachi disputes the people six times.

1. The first (1:2–5) illustrates the common pattern. The Lord begins by asserting a truth about his nature to the people: "I have loved you." The people are then provoked to question the Lord, "How have you loved us?" The Lord then responds to the challenge by describing the destruction of the Edomites, the offspring of Esau. Edom had been a particularly annoying adversary to Israel (see chap. 28, "Obadiah"), and their destruction was most welcome and to be interpreted as a sign of God's love for Israel.

Five more, and lengthier, disputations follow, having roughly the same pattern:

2. Dispute about the contempt the priests show God (1:6–2:9)
    a. Introduction: God is father and master, deserving of honor.
    b. Question: "How have we shown contempt for your name?"
    c. Answer "By offering defiled food on my altar."
3. Dispute about Israel's covenant breaking (2:10–16)
    a. Introduction: God is the father and creator of all.
    b. Question: "Why do we profane the covenant of our ancestors by being unfaithful to one another?"
    c. Answer: By divorcing the "wife of your youth."
4. Dispute about God's justice (2:17–3:5)
    a. Introduction: The Lord is weary of the words of his people.
    b. Question: "How have we wearied him?"
    c. Answer: By accusing God of honoring or ignoring evil.
5. Dispute concerning repentance (3:6–12)
    a. Introduction: God does not change, but you must.
    b. Question: "How are we to return?"
    c. Answer: By not robbing God of the tithe.
6. Dispute about harsh words against the Lord (3:13–4:3 [MT 3:13–21])
    a. Introduction: The Lord accuses the people of harsh words.
    b. Question: "What have we said against you?"
    c. Answer: You have said, "It is futile to serve God."

After this analysis, three verses remain, which form a kind of double appendix: (1) 4:4 [MT 3:23] is a call to observe the Lord; (2) 4:5–6 [MT 3:24–25] announces the future arrival of the prophet Elijah on the eve of the day of the Lord. It is on this note that the book of Malachi, the last book (according to the Greek-English tradition), ends.

For the most part, the book's unity is uncontested—with one significant exception: the so-called appendices. R. L. Smith (1984, 340–41) argues that these verses have no formal connection with what precedes and that the content differs in two ways. First, the messenger has a different name and function than in 3:1. Second, the future day of the Lord goes by a different name in the appendix than earlier.

Close examination, however, shows that harmonization is possible, even easy. In both cases, the appendix simply describes in more detail the concepts introduced in a general way earlier (Clendenen 1987, 17 n.26). No serious reservations can be marshaled against the unity of the book of Malachi as a whole.

Style

> *The most commonly used Hebrew Bible puts the book of Malachi in poetic format, while the most commonly used English versions of the Bible consider the book to be in prose.*

The most striking and creative aspect of Malachi's style is its disputational form (discussed above).

Debate has centered on whether Malachi is a prosaic or poetic composition (compare W. Kaiser with B. Glazier-MacDonald). The most commonly used Hebrew Bible (BHS) puts it in poetic format, while the most commonly used English versions of the Bible consider the book to be in prose. That such a discussion even takes place is testimony to the difficulty of defining what constitutes poetry in biblical Hebrew and also to the close connection between these two modes of discourse (see Introduction; Literary Analysis in chap. 1).

Very early, Malachi's writing was considered an example of the degeneracy of Hebrew literary style at the end of the Old Testament period (De Wette, Duhm, quoted by Torrey 1898, 14–15). This is unfair. Malachi's writing is creative in its form, clear in its message, and compelling in its argumentation.

THEOLOGICAL MESSAGE

At the heart of Malachi's message to Israel stands the covenant. Three covenants are mentioned explicitly: the covenant with Levi (2:8),[4] the covenant of the fathers, and the covenant of marriage (2:10–16). Malachi announces to Israel that God's love toward them is founded on the covenant (1:2–5) and his judgments are based on their violation of these covenant relationships. Indeed, the

---

[4]See McKenzie and Wallace (1983) for the difficulty in pinpointing the origins of the covenant, though in the context of Malachi there is no mistaking that this covenant established the privileges and responsibility of the priesthood.

covenant of Levi is evoked in order to point out that the priests were not living up to their responsibilities before the Lord. Fishbane (1983) insightfully described how the disputation against the priests (1:6–2:9) uses the language of the priestly blessing in Numbers 6:22–27 in order to curse the priests for their sins. It is difficult to determine whether the covenant with the fathers is a reference to the patriarchal or the Sinaitic covenant, but in any case it lends power to the accusation that the people have broken covenant with the Lord. Malachi cites the marriage covenant because the Israelites were apparently divorcing their native-born wives in order to take up with foreign wives who worshiped idols. This act too indicated the direction of the Israelites' hearts during the period of Malachi's ministry.

Thus Malachi speaks to show that God, while still showing signs that he loved Israel (1:2–5), doubted that Israel loved him. As the exile proved earlier, covenant violation led to the judgment of exile, so Malachi warns Israel using the disputational style noted above. As Fischer pointed out, each of the six sections of the disputation taught something positive and fundamental about God. Specifically, he analyzed the introductory statement to the disputations and came up with the following theological statements about God and his relationship with his people:

1. God loves his people (1:2)
2. God is Israel's father and master (1:6)
3. God is Israel's father and creator (2:10)
4. God is the god of justice (2:17)
5. God does not change (3:6)
6. God is honest (3:13)

But Malachi did not just warn Israel to repent in the present because of past sins; he also presented a vision of hope for their future. Malachi, as mentioned above, ministered in a time of disillusionment. Previous prophets presented a picture of restored Israel as a time of glory and power (see Klein 1987, 29–30, for an analysis of the impact of Isaiah 40ff. on the postexilic generation). But now a significant amount of time had passed, and they still lived under foreign overlordship.

Thus, among other things, Malachi intended to rekindle this future hope of something more glorious. Yes, a day was coming, a day that would see God intervene in the affairs of men and women, bringing victory to those who obey God's laws and judgment to those who do not (3:1–5; 4:1–6).

APPROACHING THE NEW TESTAMENT

The gospel of Mark opens with a quotation that collates Malachi 3:1 with Isaiah 40:3:

> I will send my messenger ahead of you,
>   who will prepare your way—
> a voice of one calling in the wilderness,
>   "Prepare the way for the Lord,
>   make straight paths for him." (Mark 1:2–3)

In the so-called appendix to the book of Malachi, this messenger is further identified with Elijah, who will precede the Lord on the day of victory and judgment. In the New Testament the messenger who prepares the way is John the Baptist, who brings the kind of stern message of coming destruction as described in Malachi 3:1–5. He precedes and introduces Jesus' earthly ministry, and it is Jesus himself who identifies John as Elijah, whose heralding role is anticipated in Malachi (Matt. 11:7–15; see also Luke 7:18–35). Blomberg (see detailed discussion in 1987, 104) notes the high Christology here, since Jesus implicitly identifies himself with the coming Lord of the Malachi passage. In short, the eschatological hopes of the book of Malachi find their fulfillment in the pages of the Gospels.

SCRIPTURE INDEX

NAME INDEX

SUBJECT INDEX